Skill Formation in Central and Eastern Europe

NEUE DENKANSÄTZE IN DEN BILDUNGS- UND SOZIALWISSENSCHAFTEN
NEW APPROACHES IN EDUCATIONAL AND SOCIAL SCIENCES

Herausgegeben von / Edited by Gerd-Bodo von Carlsburg, Natalija Mažeikienė und / and Airi Liimets

BAND 40

*Zu Qualitätssicherung und Peer Review der vorliegenden Publikation*

Die Qualität der in dieser Reihe erscheinenden Arbeiten wird vor der Publikation durch die Herausgeber der Reihe geprüft.

*Notes on the quality assurance and peer review of this publication*

Prior to publication, the quality of the work published in this series is reviewed by editors of the series.

Vidmantas Tūtlys / Jörg Markowitsch /
Jonathan Winterton / Samo Pavlin (eds.)

# Skill Formation in Central and Eastern Europe

## A search for Patterns and Directions of Development

PETER LANG

**Bibliographic Information published by the Deutsche Nationalbibliothek**
The Deutsche Nationalbibliothek lists this publication in the Deutsche Nationalbibliografie; detailed bibliographic data is available in the internet at http://dnb.d-nb.de.

**Library of Congress Cataloging-in-Publication Data**
A CIP catalog record for this book has been applied for at the Library of Congress.



ISSN 1434-8748
ISBN 978-3-631-81092-7 (Print)
E-ISBN 978-3-631-88107-1 (E-PDF)
E-ISBN 978-3-631-88108-8 (EPUB)
DOI 10.3726/b19799



Peter Lang – Berlin · Bruxelles · Lausanne · New York · Oxford



www.peterlang.com

*Dedication*

*Учітесь, читайте, І чужому научайтесь, Й свого не цурайтесь.*
*(Тарас Григорович Шевченко, 1814–1861)*

*Study, read and learn Thoroughly the foreign things— But do not shun your own (Taras Hryhorovych Shevchenko, 1814–1861)*

# Table of contents

# List of figures

# List of tables

# Preface

The idea of this book emerged from various comparative educational research projects and European fora of researchers and experts of vocational and higher education, skill formation, qualifications and human resource development in recent decades. Although the accession of eleven countries of Central and Eastern Europe (CEE) to the European Union (EU) after 2004 stimulated interest in skill formation, there has been no systematic research of recent developments of skill formation processes and institutions in this part of Europe. Existing typologies and models of skill formation predominantly characterise well established skill formation systems of post-industrial Western economies. Liberal market economies like the UK are contrasted with coordinated market economies like Germany in the literature on Varieties of Capitalism (Hall & Soskice 2009). Associated with these economies are market-based skill formation systems in the UK and Ireland, collective skill formation systems in the German speaking countries and neo-corporatist state-led skill formation systems in the rest of Continental Europe (Brockmann, Clarke & Winch 2011).

Categorising and characterising the skill formation systems and regimes of the post-communist countries is a challenge in many respects. Although Central and Eastern European countries are often labelled post-communist, or post-socialist, in reference to their common history in the second half of the 20th century, this 'historical' categorisation is not very helpful, because of the rich variety of socio-economic, institutional and cultural transformations of these countries after the fall of the Berlin wall. The variety of societal and institutional development pathways produced a diversity of skill formation systems in this region. There is no holistic understanding of skill formation systems and models of Central and Eastern Europe, especially with respect to the implications of different educational reforms and other political, legal and institutional transformations. Development of skill formation in this region should be regarded as an historical process with uniqueness and contingency of change, irreversibility, givenness and unpredictability as well as its dynamic and processual character.

These knowledge gaps were instrumental in developing the idea of this book in Spring 2019 and in November of that year the editors, Vidmantas Tūtlys, Jonathan Winterton, Jörg Markowitsch and Samo Pavlin, met in Vienna to discuss the concept in more detail. Vienna, the hospitality of 3s and conviviality of Jörg Markowitsch provided a stimulating environment for the conception of this book. We agreed to invite leading researchers and experts in vocational education, higher education and skill formation from the Baltic states, Poland, Czech Republic, Slovakia, Hungary, Romania, Bulgaria, Slovenia, Croatia and Ukraine to contribute chapters on the skill formation systems and institutions in their respective countries. These chapters aimed to describe, analyse and explain trajectories of development of skill formation from the communist period to the present, with some prognosis for the future. The findings of these chapters are compared and discussed in five concluding chapters focused on important cross-cutting topics: development of social dialogue over skill formation, specificities of qualifications policy and development of qualifications systems, implications of European integration and EU policies for governance and institutional reform of skill formation, features and implications of policy borrowing and policy learning from the Anglo-Saxon and German speaking countries, respectively.

The contributors of this book explore and analyse institutional and processual development of skill formation in the geopolitical region of Europe which emerged after the collapse of communism and the fall of the Berlin wall in the end of the 20th century. The institutional development of skill formation in CEE after the fall of the Berlin wall has been shaped and defined by global, regional and national socio-economic and political changes. The authors of the country chapters refer to such critical junctures as transition from the communist/socialist state to market economy and liberal democracy, the Russian economic crisis in 1999, EU accession of CEE countries from 2004, the global financial crisis of 2008–2009 and the COVID-19 pandemic. Now we are witnessing a new major critical juncture with potentially profound implications for the social, economic and political development of CEE – the military aggression of the Russian Federation on Ukraine launched on 24 February 2022. This critical juncture is highlighted here, because none of the chapters of the book mentions the war because they were concluded before the invasion. There are already signs that this war marks the end of the historical period of democratic transformation in the CEE countries since the collapse of communism, the period on which this book focuses. The importance of this new critical juncture requires further reflection on the possible implications for skill formation institutions and processes in Ukraine and the whole region of CEE.

Although there is still much uncertainty about the consequences of this war for the future of Ukraine and the world at the time of writing, existing evidence enables some cautious observations. The resistance of this country to aggression and the heroic mobilisation of society demonstrate that the Ukrainian nation and civil society are stronger than ever before. Attempts to suppress or destroy Ukraine by the invading regime are expected ultimately to fail, thus rendering impossible the country's annexation and the overthrow of democratic rule sought by the aggressor. The education system and skill formation institutions of Ukraine described in the chapter by Melnyk have contributed to developing this resilience of the Ukrainian nation and society. By extrapolation, tentative conclusions can be proposed about the implications of these events for the development of skill formation in Ukraine and other CEE countries.

In relation to the implications for skill formation in Ukraine, we posit several assumptions. Dealing with the consequences of war in the short-term perspective will create skills shortages and growing demand in areas like waste (especially dangerous waste) disposal, de-mining and land reclamation. Increased demand for social, rehabilitation, medical and psychological services to the suffering population, could accelerate restructuring of obsolete post-Soviet institutions of social infrastructure. Reconstruction of the economy and infrastructure after the war, including possible de-industrialisation of territories in the Eastern part of the country can be anticipated, along with restructuring of sectors like engineering and military-industrial complexes and transformation of agro-industrial complexes. Rehabilitation of the natural environment and natural landscapes in the context of such restructuring will require major mobilisation of human capital that could alter patterns of population migration and enhance return migration, in some sectors. Such trends could trigger the development of continuing training and competence development processes in key sectors of economy. The need to strengthen digitalisation of society, ensuring sustainable access to reliable information, as well as developing cybersecurity will require investment in skill formation in the ICT (information and communication technologies) sector and in the development of digital skills of civil society. Reconstruction of the skill formation system will be necessary because of the destruction of infrastructure, and the loss of teachers and trainers to the conflict. The processes of reconstruction could facilitate the development of a more open and balanced skill formation system with active engagement of civil society, SMEs, trade unions and NGOs, in contrast with the domination of big enterprises and government before the war. Another possible implication of the war could be strengthening and intensifying efforts to Europeanize skill formation processes and institutions to accelerate efforts towards EU integration. Of course, the war itself has disrupted the reform of the skill formation system and relaunching the process will depend on the success of the restitution of institutions and actors, which could be a key priority for EU and international actors supporting reconstruction. A major challenge for pedagogical processes is the integration of Ukrainian war refugees in the education and skill formation systems of receiving countries and their successful reintegration in the education system or labour market of Ukraine after the war.

What could be the implications of the war for skill formation processes and institutions in other CEE countries? Firstly, the education systems and skill formation institutions in countries close to Ukraine (Poland, Romania, Moldova, Czech Republic, Lithuania, Slovakia) now are facing the challenge of integrating large numbers of war refugees, which includes not only the provision of shelter, but also at least temporary integration into the labour market and economy. This could have positive implications for developing the capacities of skill formation institutions to integrate refugees and migrants in these countries. Secondly, the war will probably strengthen the efforts of these and other EU countries to gain energy independence from Russia or at least reduce dependence on supplies of energy from this country. In addition to profound implications for the energy sector, this should prompt demand for new skills and qualifications associated with green energy and renewables, as well as exploitation of alternative technologies with diversification of transport and storage of hydrocarbon energy sources or switching to hydrogen from hydrocarbon fuels. Thirdly, the ongoing aggression changes the attitudes of societies and governments to military defence, leading not only to increased public funding and investment in military hardware, but also to expansion of the armed forces through conscription and fostering voluntary military service and activities of the paramilitary organizations and structures. Such 'Israel-like' reorientation of public defence policies can have profound implications for skill formation policies and processes, starting from the stronger integration of the military sector qualifications in the national system of qualifications and increased attention to policy measures for integration of former/retired military personnel in civilian labour markets (Tūtlys, Liesionienė & Winterton 2018, 2019). Increased attention to developing civil safety and security capacities, as well as developing civil engagement and resilience to totalitarian ideologies might strengthen the provision of these skills and competencies in public education systems, including VET and HE. Whatever the wider implications of this military aggression, it is evident that skill formation institutions must be an integral part of human efforts to prevent their recurrence.

We are convinced that this book offers valuable new information and analysis for all those interested in comparative education and labour market research. It provides a new reference for the international research community and has the potential to stimulate national debates in CEE countries. It is aimed equally at researchers, students, policy makers and practitioners.

## References

Brockmann, M., Clarke, L. and Winch, C. (2011). *Knowledge, Skills and Competence in the European Labour Market. What's in a Vocational Qualification?* London: Routledge.

Hall, P. A. and Soskice, D. (2009). 'An Introduction to Varieties of Capitalism'. In B. Hancké (ed.), *Debating Varieties of Capitalism*, pp. 21–74. Oxford: Oxford University Press.

Tūtlys, V., Winterton, J. and Liesionienė, O. (2018). 'Integrating retired military officers into the civilian labour market: A competence-based approach', *European Journal of Training and Development*, 42,5/6, 319–341.

Tūtlys, V., Winterton, J. and Liesionienė, O. (2019). 'Institutional aspects of competence-based integration of retired military officers into the civilian labour market', *Personnel Review*, 48, 1, 21–39.

# Acknowledgements

This book was only possible through substantial collaborative effort and reflects the work of many people in addition to our own contributions as editors and co-authors. We thank all the contributors to this book: Radostina Angelova, Sandra Bohlinger, Branko Bembič, Nikola Buković, Ilze Buligina, Horacy Dębowski, Dominik Dvořák, Christiane Eberhardt, Klara Skubic Ermenc, Éva Farkas, Petr Gal, Kaloyan Ganev, Genutė Gedvilienė, Dagmar Jelínková, Lina Kaminskienė, Andrea Laczik, Krista Loogma, Teo Matković, Sergii Melnyk, Andreas Saniter, Ralitsa Simeonova-Ganeva, Biruta Sloka, Eglė Stasiūnaitienė, Wojciech Stechły, Jana Straková, Juraj Vantuch, Zoica Elena Vladut and Emma Wallis.

Some contributors presented the findings of their chapters in two symposia organized at the online ECER conference on the 7th and 10th of September 2021. We thank the organizers of the conference and VETNET network for this possibility to present and discuss selected draft chapters of the book. We are grateful to Emma Wallis for her careful and attentive work in editing the English text.

We should like to express our special gratitude to the Peter Lang team, and in particular Ms. Utte Winkelkötter, for their highly professional advice, patience, cooperation and trust in us when working on this book in these challenging times. Special thanks must also go to the academic institutions and organizations providing financial, intellectual and moral support to the project of this book: Institute of Educational Research at Vytautas Magnus University (Lithuania); Leeds University Business School (UK); 3s Research & Consulting (Austria); and the Ljubljana University Faculty of Social Sciences (Slovenia).

Jörg Markowitsch
Samo Pavlin
Vidmantas Tūtlys
Jonathan Winterton

# Abbreviations

| | |
|---|---|
| ACPART | National Agency for Qualifications in Higher Education and Partnership with Economic and Social Environment of Romania |
| AE | Adult Education |
| AHEI | Act on Higher Education Institutions (CR) |
| AI | Artificial Intelligence |
| ASHE | *Agencija za znanost i visoko obrazovanje (CR)*<br>The Agency for Science and Higher Education |
| ANQ | National Authority of Qualifications of Romania |
| ASOO AVETAE | *Agencija za strukovno obrazovanje i obrazovanje odraslih (CR)*<br>The Agency for Vocational Education and Training and Adult Learning |
| AQHEPESE | Authority of Qualifications in Higher Education and Partnership with the Economic and Social Environment (Romania) |
| BA | Bachelor Degree |
| BBS | *Betriebsberufschulen (DE)*<br>Company vocational schools |
| BIBB | *Bundesinstitut für Berufsbildung (DE)*<br>Federal Institute for Vocational Education and Training |
| CCE | Croatian Chamber of Economy |
| CCTC | Croatian Chamber for Trades and Crafts |
| CEE | Central and Eastern Europe |
| CME | Coordinated Market Economy |
| CMEA | Council for Mutual Economic Assistance |
| COSA | Council of Occupational Standards and Qualifications |
| CPI | *Centre Republike Slovenije za poklicno izobraževanje (SI)*<br>The Institute of the Republic of Slovenia for Vocational Education and Training |
| CROQF | Croatian Qualification Framework |
| CVET | Continuing Vocational Education and Training |

| | |
|---|---|
| CVT | Continuing Vocational Training |
| DACUM | Developing a Curriculum |
| DoC | Diversity of Capitalism |
| DQR | *Deutscher Qualifikationsrahmen (DE)*<br>German Qualification Framework |
| EBRD | European Bank for Reconstruction and Development |
| ECTS | European Credit Transfer and Accumulation System |
| ECVET | European Credit system for Vocational Education and Training |
| EEC | European Economic Community |
| EHEA | European Higher Education Area |
| ELLS | Estonian Lifelong Learning Strategy |
| ENCA | European Association for Quality Assurance in Higher Education |
| EQA | Estonian Qualifications Authority Foundation |
| EQF | European Qualifications Framework for Lifelong Learning |
| ERDF | European Regional Development Fund |
| ESC | Economic and Social Council |
| ESCO | Classification of European Skills, Competences, Qualifications and Occupations |
| ESF | European Social Fund |
| ESFA | Education and Skills Funding Agency |
| ESG | Standards and Guidelines for Quality Assurance in the European Higher Education Area |
| EstQF | Estonian Qualification Framework |
| E&T | Education and Training |
| ETF | European Training Foundation |
| EQAVET | European Quality Assurance in Vocational Education and Training |
| EU | European Union |
| FDI | Foreign Direct Investment |
| GDP | Gross Domestic Product |

| | |
|---|---|
| GDR | German Democratic Republic |
| GE | General Education |
| GFC | Global Financial Crisis |
| GIZ | *Deutsche Gesellschaft für Internationale Zusammenarbeit (GIZ) GmbH (DE)*<br>German Corporation for International Cooperation |
| HCCI | Hungarian Chamber of Commerce and Industry |
| HDZ | *Hrvatska demokratska zajednica (CR)*<br>Croatian Democratic Union |
| HE | Higher Education |
| HEI | Higher Education Institution |
| HRD | Human Resource Development |
| HRK | Croatian Kuna |
| IALS | International Adult Literacy Study |
| ICFTU | International Confederation of Free Trade Unions |
| ICT | Information and Communication Technologies |
| ILO | International Labor Organization |
| IMF | International Monetary Fund |
| IQR | Integrated Qualifications Register |
| IQS | Integrated Qualifications System Act |
| ISCED | International Standard Classification of Education |
| ITB | Industrial Training Board |
| ITUC | International Trade Unions Confederation |
| IVET | Initial Vocational Education and Training |
| JMO | *jedinstveni model obrazovanje (CR)*<br>Joint Model of Education |
| LCSPD | Local Committees for Social Partnership Development |
| LFS | Labour Force Survey |
| LLL | Lifelong Learning |
| LME | Liberal Market Economy |
| LO | Learning Outcomes |
| LTQF | Lithuanian Qualification Framework |

| | |
|---|---|
| LQF | Latvian Qualification Framework |
| MA | Master Degree (Master of Arts) |
| MCI | Management Charter Initiative |
| MES | Ministry of Education and Science |
| MoE | Ministry of Education |
| MoL | Ministry of Labour |
| MOSTA | Mokslo ir studijų stebėsenos ir analizės centras (LT)<br>Centre for Monitoring and Analysis of Science and Studies |
| MSZMP | *Magyar Szocialista Munkáspárt (HU)*<br>Hungarian Socialist Workers' Party |
| NAS | National Academy of Science |
| NATB | National Adult Training Board |
| NATO | North Atlantic Treaty Organisation |
| NCAEA | National Council for Academic Evaluation and Accreditation |
| NCATDUC | National Council for Attestation of Titles, Diplomas and University Certificates |
| NCC | National Curriculum Council |
| NCHPD | National Council for Human Potential Development |
| NCPHEE | National Committee for Professional Higher Education Excellence |
| NCSHETD | National Council for Science, Higher Education and Technological Development |
| NCTC | National Council for Tripartite Cooperation |
| NCTVETD | National Centre for Technical and Vocational Education and Training Development of the Republic of Romania |
| NCVQ | National Council for Vocational Qualifications |
| NEET | Not in Education, Employment, or Training |
| NGO | Non-Governmental Organization |
| NPM | New Public Management |
| NRP | National Reform Programme |
| NSK | *Národní soustava kvalifikací (CZ)*<br>National Qualifications Framework of the Czech Republic |

| | |
|---|---|
| NSO | National System of Occupations |
| NTOs | National Training Organizations |
| NQA | National Qualifications Agency |
| NQF | National Qualification Framework |
| NQS | National Qualifications System |
| NVQ | National Vocational Qualification |
| NVQR | National Vocational Qualifications Register |
| OECD | Organisation for Economic Co-operation and Development |
| OPHRD | Operational Programme of Human Resource Development |
| OSKA | Estonian Labor Demand Monitoring and Forecasting System |
| PHARE | Poland and Hungary Aid for Economic Restructuring |
| PIAAC | Programme for the International Assessment of Adult Competencies |
| PISA | Programme for International Student Assessment |
| PR | Public Relations |
| PTE | Professional Tertiary Education |
| RCSPD | Regional Committees for Social Partnership Development |
| R&D | Research and Development |
| SAM | *scoala de arte si meserii (RO)*<br>School of Arts and Crafts |
| SDP | *socijaldemokratska partija Hrvatske (HR)*<br>Social Democratic Party of Croatia |
| SFS | Skill Formation System |
| SKKR | Slovenský kvalifikačný rámec (SK)<br>Slovak National Qualification Framework |
| SNO | Slovak National Observatory of Vocational Education and Training |
| SOŠ | *stredná odborná škola (CZ)*<br>lyceum, secondary technical school |

| | |
|---|---|
| SOU | *stredné odborné učilište (CZ)*<br>vocational secondary schools |
| SSC | Sector Skills Council |
| STEM | Science, Technology, Engineering, and Mathematics |
| SQF | Sectoral Qualification Framework<br>Slovenian Qualification Framework |
| SQS | Sectoral Qualifications System |
| SURS | *Statistični Urad Republika Slovenija (SI)*<br>Statistical Office of the Republic of Slovenia |
| SVQs | Scottish Vocational Qualifications |
| SWOT | Strengths, Weaknesses, Opportunities and Threats |
| TACIS | Technical Assistance to the Commonwealth of Independent States |
| TFP | Total Factor Productivity |
| TNC | Transnational Companies |
| TTSC | Teacher Training Support Centre |
| TVET | Technical Vocational Education and Training |
| UK | United Kingdom |
| UNESCO | United Nations Educational, Scientific and Cultural Organization |
| USSR | Soviet Union (Union of the Soviet Socialistic Republics) |
| VER | Vocational Examination Requirements |
| VET | Vocational Education and Training |
| VoC | Variety of Capitalism |
| VOE | Vocational Oriented Education<br>*usmjereno obrazovanje (CR)* |
| VOŠ | *vyššá odborná škola*<br>post-secondary professional school |
| WB | World Bank |
| WBL | Work-Based Learning |
| WW2 | Second World War |

Vidmantas Tūtlys, Jonathan Winterton, Jörg Markowitsch and Samo Pavlin

# 1. Skill formation in the post-communist CEE countries

**Abstract:** This chapter presents the rationale, aim, objectives and research questions of this collection, as well as provides theoretical framework of the study. This book seeks to explore and compare the development of skill formation systems in post-communist European countries offering a comparative analysis that highlights similarities and differences in the evolution of methodological approaches and political-institutional development in vocational education and training (VET), higher education (HE) , adult education and lifelong learning in these countries. This study fills the gap of systematic and comprehensive research on skill formation in post-communist CEE countries and facilitates holistic and systemic understanding of skill formation processes, policies and reforms in this region. Historical development of skill formation in the post-communist CEE countries is defined by several critical junctures, such as post-communist transition to market economy and democratic society, EU-accession and global economic crisis. These critical junctures enabled existing variety of the national skill systems in the region with the specific links between education systems and social stratification, trends of stratification of education, and standardization of education systems by introducing uniformly regulated curricula and qualifications. The chapter concludes with the overview of the main concepts discussed in this book and presentation of the suggested conceptual model of skills formation and deployment.

**Keywords:** Central and Eastern Europe, critical juncture, institutional development, national skill system, skill formation

## Rationale for this book

There has been an abundance of research on the different political-economic, institutional, educational and social aspects of skill formation models in developed Western economies. For example, literature on the varieties of capitalism (VoC) contrasted models of skill formation in the Anglophone liberal and Continental coordinated market economies (Hall and Soskice 2009). Research into the political economy of skill formation has been focused on analysing institutional skill formation systems and regimes in the developed economies of EU15 member states, typically distinguishing market-based skill formation systems of the UK and Ireland; collective skill formation systems of the

German speaking countries; and neo-corporatist state-led skill formation systems found in France, Italy, Spain, Portugal and Greece (Brockmann, Clarke and Winch 2011). The categorisation of skill formation systems and regimes of the post-communist countries of Central and Eastern Europe (CEE) is not yet established, although it is widely agreed that there are diverse skill formation systems in this region (Le Deist and Tūtlys 2012; Martinaitis 2010). In most cases research on skill formation systems (including those of CEE) is strongly focused on the influence of different macroeconomic factors and processes related to skill and human capital, such as labour market demand and supply, investment in education and human capital, models of work organisation, welfare provision and public spending on social programmes, systems of industrial relations and patterns of collective bargaining. Such analysis is often strongly economically determined and involves overly schematic analysis and understanding of skill formation by largely overlooking the influence of important factors and processes related to education policy and the institutional development of education systems and processes. Moreover, little is known of the relation between particularities of various post-communist educational reforms and the development of skill formation approaches in this region. In brief, the research problem is a lack of holistic approaches to analysing mechanisms and processes of skill formation in the post-communist countries.

The research presented in this book explores and compares the development of skill formation systems in post-communist European countries. It also offers a comparative analysis that highlights similarities and differences in the evolution of methodological approaches and political-institutional development in vocational education and training (VET), higher education (HE) , adult education and lifelong learning in these countries.

Our approach leads to the following research questions:

1. What similarities and differences are discernible in the pathways of vocational and further education (initial VET, HE, adult education and lifelong learning) in post-communist CEE countries?
2. To what extent are specific institutional educational pathways and policy patterns in this region responses to trends of socio-economic development?

There are two defining aspects of this research: its geographical scope (CEE countries) and the particularities of skill formation processes and institutions. In defining the geographical scope of the research, we establish criteria for selection of countries. A key criterion is the shared historical fate of these countries after the Second World War, when they became 'socialist' or 'communist' countries behind the Iron Curtain, which determined their institutional, socio-economic and cultural development for many years, even after the Berlin wall fell in 1989 and the Soviet Union collapsed in 1991. This historical peculiarity brought the legacy of the communist system of skill formation and the institutional setting as a departure point for 'post-communist' transformation. Those countries that were formerly and formally part of the Soviet Union (Baltic countries, Ukraine) involved more deep and profound institutional and socio-economic transformations than those that were Warsaw Pact countries. The duration countries were under the communist system is also important, so the legacy of the communist era is more profound in Ukraine or Belarus, which were part of the Soviet Union for more than 70 years, than in the Baltic States, which were occupied for 50 years. The core source of specificity for the transition lies in the influence of the communist period on society and institutions. The differences in development following the collapse of the Soviet Union also played an important role in the transformation of skill formation institutions. Access to the EU in 2004 and later years was an important critical juncture, determining different pathways of development between those CEE countries that became EU members and those that did not. In this respect, the study captures all the 'historical-geographical' regions of the post-communist area: (1) former socialist countries, which got into the 'socialist camp' after the Second World War, were liberated from it in 1989–1990 and became EU member states in 2004 and later years; (2) a former socialist country that followed the same course but has not yet joined the EU (Serbia); (3) countries which belonged to the USSR since 1940, regained their freedom in 1990–1991 and became EU member states in 2004 (Baltic States); and (4) one country that was a part of the USSR since its establishment in 1922, regained its independence in 1991, and is a potential EU candidate country (Ukraine). This choice of countries facilitates exploring the role of the intensity and duration of socialist influence for the institutional development of skill formation and deployment.

The methodological approach is deliberately multi-disciplinary. The book aims to fill the gap of systematic and comprehensive research on skill formation in post-communist CEE countries that will facilitate holistic and systemic understanding of skill formation processes, policies and reforms in this region. Our aim is to provide a handbook that will be of value not only to researchers, but also for stakeholders and policy makers.

## Common features and specificities of historical development of skill formation in the post-communist countries

Skill formation systems are dynamic and, following Thelen (2004), in this book we are taking an historical institutional perspective exploring the emergence, development and adaptation of skill formation institutions. Busemeyer and Trampusch (2011: 4) argued that VET systems are not only dynamic, but 'vulnerable and, in part, even fragile institutional arrangements that need the continuous political support of relevant stakeholders.' The countries of CEE have in common three features: communist past, economic transition towards a market economy and candidature or accession to the European Union. West (2013) provided a useful starting point in exploring recent developments in VET in CEE, attempting to identify the impact of these three features, which inevitably vary in importance between individual countries. Each is briefly considered below.

Drawing on a study by Grant (1969), who was sympathetic to state socialist education, West (2013: 10–11) characterised education in the communist era as driven by ideological socialisation designed to instil notions of equality and promote positive attitudes towards manual labour. The integration of education and labour was achieved through work-based education and, excepting the former Yugoslavia, highly centralised state planning in which the Party ensured the alignment of VET with the human capital needs of state enterprises. Martinaitis (2010: 10) noted that under communism, the CEE countries shared a common characteristic of very heavy investment in specific skills, and broadly similar skill formation systems. The level of participation in VET programmes was over 70 per cent and for the most part such training was terminal and linked to local state-owned enterprises (Sondergaard and Murthi 2012: 64).

The integration of the CEE in the global economy after the collapse of communism was a leap of abrupt change compressed in time (Hardy 2014) and influenced some lock-in effects, such as becoming predominantly low-skilled economy competing in providing raw materials and components for more advanced European economies. The events of 1989–1992 necessitated the establishment of new institutions for VET, especially in countries that did not exist as independent states beforehand (the Baltic States, Czech Republic and Slovakia, Slovenia and the other states of former Yugoslavia). The loss of *Comecon* markets caused an immediate economic rupture with a drop in GDP, privatisation and restructuring of enterprises, job losses leading to unemployment, growing inequalities and increased emigration to EU countries. The initial stage of post-communist transformation was marked by significant institutional changes and interventions: from reductionism and primitivism of economic relations in the

Baltic countries (shift to barter exchange, domination of raw materials exports, etc.), processes of technological involution, to the development of deliberate economic structures and reciprocal relationships, as well as execution of industrial policies in the Visegrád countries and Slovenia aimed at protecting strategic sectors from collapse (Norkus 2008).

Economic growth in post-communist CEE countries was accompanied with deepening social inequalities, increased research and development (R&D) costs, deterioration of economic structure, liberalisation and privatisation, bringing about a deep economic crisis (Tiits, Kattel, Kalvet and Tamm 2008). With competition primarily on cost, rather than knowledge intensity, demand for formal education and training fell, as did market demand to reform public education and R&D systems. The loss of skilled manufacturing during the transition was partially compensated by new demand for skilled labour from outsourcing by Western companies (Tiits et al. 2008). Transformation of the former communist elite into a new economic elite during privatisation also significantly influenced skill formation, because these elites usually lacked entrepreneurial ideas and rarely understood the need to invest in human capital (Norkus 2008). During the first decade of transformation (1990s–2000s) the development of welfare systems was not a policy priority, which was focused on establishing market economy institutions (Josifidis, Supic and Glavaski 2018).

Accompanying demographic changes included a declining population of upper secondary age from 1994 (Poland from 2000). West (2013: 21) noted that in the widespread policy and administrative changes, 'there was no cogent and coherent educational programme in any country.' With the collapse of the Soviet Union in 1991, in many, but not all CEE countries, the share of upper secondary students enrolled in VET programmes fell substantially as the quality and relevance of VET appeared to deteriorate 'at the same time that firms [were] increasing their demands for higher level technical skills' (Sondergaard and Murthi 2012: 65). The evidence provided in the World Bank study showed the fall from 1989 to 2007 to be greatest in the Baltic States, Poland and Hungary, and least in the Czech Republic, Slovakia, Bulgaria, Croatia and Serbia, with Romania and Slovenia between these two groups (ibid: 66). Moreover, except for the Czech Republic, Slovakia and Slovenia, fewer employees participated in continuing VET than in the EU27 overall in 2005 (ibid: 72). There was a significant growth in higher education, especially business and law rather than technical areas. The 'mismatch between the sectors in which programmes were offered, and the restructured economy' (West 2013: 33) coupled with subsequent orientation towards new capitalist markets, demanded a refocusing of VET.

The involvement of the EU in CEE countries formally started with the Strasbourg Summit of December 1989, which established the European Bank for Reconstruction and Development (EBRD) to assist in the transition towards market economies, offered CEE countries access to existing training programmes, and agreed to establish an agency to provide support for training and development. The European Training Foundation (ETF) became operational in 1994 and was established to mirror the work of Cedefop in the candidate countries. The Copenhagen Summit in June 1993 agreed in principle to admit CEE countries into the EU, specifying conditions to be met. By the Gothenburg Summit in June 2001, a timetable was established for the integration of eight CEE member states in May 2004 (plus the two Mediterranean island states). The *Phare* programme provided aid to support reforms in line with the Copenhagen criteria and projects typically involved transfer of apparent good practice from EU15 countries, including actions in support of the *Copenhagen Process* to increase cooperation in VET, such as modernisation of curricula and developing national qualifications frameworks.

The European Credit Transfer System (ECTS) was developed in 1988 to align higher education systems and provide opportunities for study abroad. When it was expanded in 1999 to establish the Bologna Process in all EU15 countries, the same opportunities were extended to the Accession countries that became formal EU member states in 2004 and later. The Bologna Process represented not only a mechanism to promote student mobility throughout Europe, but also a tool to promote system change in higher education in CEE countries in line with Europeanization. Since then, Kogan, Noelke and Gebel (2011: 349) concluded education has become 'the most important factor structuring the transition from school to work in all CEE countries.'

Integration to the EU and implementation of the EU's *acquis communautaire* required institutional harmonisation in CEE countries to strengthen neoliberal reforms in the case of neo-corporatist regimes (Slovenia) and embedded neoliberalism (Visegrád countries), or to introduce welfare state policies and institutions in neoliberal regimes (Baltic states). The involvement of the EU in the development of VET in CEE countries, Ante (2015) argued, involved too much promotion of market models rather than a more balanced 'market-regulating' integration supporting the European Social Model (Leibfried 2005; Scharpf 1999, 2008). Critics viewed EU initiatives as mechanisms designed to move European economies towards a more liberal market approach to skills formation, undermining the gold standard of the German VET system, increasingly under pressure because of the costs involved (Baethge and Wolter 2015; Culpepper and Finegold 1999). Trampusch (2009), for example, argued that EU education and training policies are market-making policies, viewing the Copenhagen process, and especially the two instruments ECVET and EQF, as designed to promote the marketization of VET. The EQF and similar National Qualifications Frameworks (NQFs) are from this perspective seen to 'break integrated occupations down into their component skill modules' (Powell and Trampusch 2011: 286). Central to this argument is the contrast between the holistic *Beruf* concept at the heart of the German system (Gehmlich 2009) and British market-based approaches flagged up earlier by Finegold and Soskice (1988), that led to National Vocational Qualifications (NVQs).

However, like the limitations of the first version of the Varieties of Capitalism (VoC) approach (Hall and Soskice 2001), VET models are more diverse than a simple binary classification into liberal market and dual systems. Busemeyer and Trampusch (2011: 12) distinguished skill formation systems according to the degree of firm involvement in, and public (state) commitment to, VET. Treating each dimension as a dichotomy between high and low, they identify four types of skill formation systems in which the liberal model (US, IR) is low on both dimensions and the collective system (DE) high on both. Between these polar extremes, they identify the 'statist' model (SE, FR) with high public commitment and low firm involvement and the 'segmentalist' model with low public commitment and high firm involvement (Japan). Lynch (1994: 7), rather erroneously, characterised the UK pre-1980 as based on 'apprenticeship training' in the same category as Germany and put the UK post-1980 alongside Sweden and Norway as a 'government-led/school-based' system. Lynch did, however, raise the issue of the dominant venue of training, which has continued to be the workplace in both the UK and German systems, albeit with very different degrees of state support and employer commitment. An alternative typology (Winterton 2000; 2007) combined the focus (rather than locus) of skill formation (school or workplace) with the regulation of training (state or market), producing four types: the dominant European state-regulated school-based model (including France and Sweden); the market-led work focused liberal voluntarist model (typified by the UK and Ireland); the state-regulated work focused dual system (including Germany and Austria); and the market-led school-based model (Italy and Greece). Greinert (2004) reached a similar conclusion in contrasting the British liberal market model, the French state-regulated bureaucratic model and the German corporatist dual model. These more nuanced differentiations may be relevant in exploring the trajectories of skill formation in the CEE countries over the past three decades.

That there was such a collapse in VET in CEE where this had been the foundation of skill formation is hugely significant, but so are the apparent differences in experience of the individual CEE countries. Martinaitis (2010) found different trajectories of skill formation between the Baltic States, Poland and Hungary, which moved away from industry specific skills to more general skills, and Slovakia, Slovenia and the Czech Republic, which maintained an emphasis on specific skills but reformed the skill formation institutions to meet the needs of a market economy. Martinaitis argued that skill formation systems designed to develop specific skills depended upon stability of employment and government as well as strong employer organisations, whereas those focused on general skills were more likely to be in countries where employment and government was more volatile and employer organisations less developed. In this respect, it is important to acknowledge that the link between employers and VET systems in the CEE countries was ruptured by privatisation and restructuring (Kogan, 2008: 21). The binary distinction between general and specific skills, central to Becker's (1964) work on human capital and returns to education is of course an oversimplification. Streeck (2011: 342) distinguished skills in terms of their portability (general/specific), their breadth (broad/narrow), and their level (high/low), creating eight categories of skills rather than the usual dichotomy. Streeck's distinction is very relevant to the emergence of skill formation systems in the CEE countries and the refinement will be adopted in our analyses.

In the initial stages of post-communist transition, governments of many CEE countries were focused on adopting social policies to prevent counter-mobilisation of those who lost during the transformation crisis, but these measures were temporary and did not lead to the development of a welfare state, especially in conditions of industrial downsizing and divestment (Meardi 2007). Immature political parties coupled with limited experience of democratic representation of interest groups and policy making, created significant obstacles for developing national strategies for skill formation in CEE countries. Those circumstances contributed to emerging skills inequalities in post-communist CEE countries because training opportunities were focused on the higher educated populace and because of lower training participation due to lack of employer investment (Green 2013). Feldman (2006) argued that transition countries that inherited centralised economies would develop into coordinated economies whereas those that inherited more decentralised arrangements would be more likely to adopt principles of market economies. The cases of Slovenia and the Baltic States appear to conform with those predictions, whereas the Czech Republic and Slovakia are not consistent with that hypothesis.

Anioł (2015) concluded in relation to Poland that the neoliberalism modernisation narrative has been more evident than the conservative or social democratic alternatives, although the conservative narrative has been effectively mobilised by those seeking to resist the influence of the EU. That predominance of neoliberalism narratives as well as the specific nature of institutional reforms, Anioł attributed largely to external forces, notably the IMF and the US. Contrasting Poland and Romania between 1989 and 2015, Tarlea (2019) argues that where liberal parties have dominated government (as in Romania), there has been more success in steering the economy towards higher level skills than where nationalist parties are dominant (as in Poland). The strategies of governments in such countries were focused on incentivising learners to invest in skills relevant for economic upgrading and creating higher education qualifications relevant for companies (Tarlea 2019). Overall, governments played the key role in establishing and running institutions and regulatory frameworks of skill formation in many CEE countries because social partners and stakeholders lacked the capacity.

During the post-communist transition many skill systems in CEE countries were at risk of becoming unsustainable through an imbalance between skill formation and deployment, resulting in a high level of over-qualification, underemployment and low trust of employers in skill formation institutions. Some political parties (especially from the economic right) acted as mediators between the institutions and enterprises, designing policies to increase supply of higher skills. Kureková (2012) distinguished the crucial role of industrial policy in attracting and fostering development in the automotive sector in the Visegrád countries, which combines economic support to automotive enterprises and education and training providers to satisfy demand for specialised skills. Kureková (2011) also noted that while earnings differentials between all CEE countries and the West were enough to cause substantial worker mobility, this was more evident in the Baltic countries, Slovakia and Poland than in the Czech Republic, Hungary or Slovenia. Kureková argued that unprecedented structural changes required a major reallocation of labour within CEE economies and that migration became an important mechanism for labour market adjustment. The relative propensity for migration described by Kureková corresponds in most cases with the skill formation characteristics outlined by Martinaitis (2010), with the countries that have general skill formation systems associated with higher rates of migration than those with specialist skill formation systems. The sole exception to this pattern is Slovakia, which has a relatively high migration propensity despite retaining the specialist skill formation system. Among the factors that could explain the apparent anomaly of Slovakia are the relatively low employment rate and high unemployment rate, as well as the ease of migration to the neighbouring Czech Republic, where half of all foreign workers were of Slovakian origin in 2007 (Kureková 2011: 206).

Development of social dialogue over skill formation and deployment in the CEE countries was also quite different from Western Europe. First, there is obviously a weaker influence of labour enabling employers to impose their will in employment relations and in formal negotiations on skill formation at national level through tripartite bodies (Duman and Kureková 2012; Myant 2014). Post-communist reforms and transformations in most of the post-2004 EU member states created space for free collective bargaining by relaxing rules of industrial relations but maintaining labour standards, such as minimum wages and regulated working hours (Myant 2014). The pressure of international capital over policy making in the field of labour relations (pushing their preferences for lower labour costs and deregulated labour markets) has been much stronger and more effective in the post-communist CEE countries than Western European countries (Meardi 2014). Such pressure had a negative impact on skill formation by discouraging national and corporate investments in human capital development.

Duman and Kureková (2012) commented on a mismatch between the actual low capacities of the social partners and undeveloped industrial relations in the field of skill formation, compared with their formal legal empowerment in skill formation under different reforms. National tripartite social partnership structures in many cases have remained advisory and not acquired a more significant role in policy making. Tripartite institutions have been regarded by stakeholders and society as bureaucratic bodies rather than institutions of civic society defending public interests in skill formation. Neoliberal policies adopted by the Baltic states entrenched the lack of social dialogue and representation of employees' interests, making these countries ill-prepared for implementing skills development measures oriented to a high-skills economy and limiting national capacity to design and implement independent socio-economic and institutional models of skills formation (Sommers, Woolfson and Juska 2014). Spasova and Tomini (2013) also claim that top-down implementation of tripartite councils with involvement of ministries hindered development of social dialogue in Bulgaria. By contrast, governments in the Visegrád countries implemented developmental policies in strategic sectors by enabling formation of effective sectoral networks involving producers, suppliers and training providers to solve problems with recruitment, turnover and skills shortages, encouraging companies to invest in training and participate in the national policies (Kureková 2012).

## Critical junctures of institutional transformations of skill formation in the CEE countries

The historical character and complexity of post-communist transformations of skill formation necessitates a holistic methodological research approach such as historical institutionalism. A central concept of historical institutionalism is critical juncture, defined as an abrupt change of institutional development, in which uncertainty creates conditions for political agency to set institutional development on a certain path (Capoccia 2015). Critical juncture analysis is appropriate in situations where 'a common exogenous shock' affects a set of countries causing them to 'diverge' as a result of the combination of a common shock and different antecedent conditions (Capoccia 2015). This is exactly the case with the post-communist transformation of skill formation in the CEE countries.

The methodological steps of analysis of critical junctures proposed by Capoccia (2015) enables us to identify institutional changes in skill formation systems in post-communist CEE countries. The following common critical junctures are evident: collapse of the former socialist systems of skill formation and their subsequent reforms; access to the EU in 2004 and later years and the global economic crisis of 2008–2009. The case of Ukraine is different in relation to access to the EU, because this country still seeks to become a candidate for EU membership, but we can distinguish other specific critical junctures involving institutional changes, notably the democratic movements of 2004 (Orange Revolution) and the Ukrainian Revolution of 2014, which paved the way for EU accession and pro-European reforms in various fields (Plokhy 2016).

## Collapse of the former communist systems of skill formation and their subsequent transformations/reforms

After the collapse of communism, socialist skill formation systems were rejected as unfit for a market economy and democratic society (Norkus 2008; Poviliūnas 2000). That rejection involved an ideological dimension of skill formation (eliminating communist ideology from curricula), as well as a processual dimension (rejecting centrally planned, segregationist provision). The legacy and vestiges of the inherited communist skill formation institutions framed the conditions for the design of new systems. The emerging market economy shaped demand for new skills but simultaneously transition to a market economy brought social tensions with a sharp increase in structural unemployment, poverty and social exclusion, which became the object of skill formation measures. The slow and weak institutionalization and capacity building of social partners left the transitional reforms of skill formation to be driven by governments and often supported by international organizations providing institutional and financial support as well as expertise.

The common goal of all post-communist transition reforms was to implement a functioning market economy and democratic society and the specific pathways were strongly related to attitudes of policy makers and stakeholders to the communist institutional legacy. We distinguish two predominant attitudes. First, a wish radically to abandon the communist legacy as soon as possible, which was typical for Baltic countries that experienced strong impact of Sovietization as member republics of the USSR. They saw a market economy offering the possibility of rapid socioeconomic transformation, establishing a new societal identity, and returning to the community of economically developed Western nations. One of the implications for the neoliberal orientation of transitional reforms was the pressure for radical implementation using 'shock therapy'. The alternative approach was a more pragmatic adjustment, using some elements of socialist institutional legacy in developing new institutions, which was typical for Visegrád countries. The legacy of industrial development and higher capacities of trade unions in these countries had a determining effect on government policy.

Structural antecedents of skill formation and employment (education and training providers inherited from the socialist period, readiness of teaching staff for the reforms, weaknesses of social partners, etc.) brought different iterations and drawbacks in reform in all CEE countries but did not reverse their overall direction. The legacy of relatively developed and accessible education systems and systems of social protection from the communist era (Piketty 2019) helped ensure better access to skills and qualifications for those disadvantaged in the transitional reforms (e.g. in establishing special training centres for unemployed, evening courses for adults, etc.).

Transitional reforms of skill formation led to new institutional settings oriented to the needs of an emerging market economy and democratic society, such as legal regulation of skill formation, governance structures, systems of VET and higher education providers, formal institutionalization of social dialogue over skill formation. These reforms changed the status and power of providers and other stakeholders involved in skill formation, especially social partners, by making them co-responsible for skill formation processes. At the same time, mismatches and imbalances appeared between power and autonomy of stakeholders created by legislation and their insufficient capacities to deploy this autonomy (Kureková 2012). The reforms also enabled curricula changes oriented towards learning outcomes and competence, which also contributed to the irreversibility and durability of reforms.

The abrupt and radical character of post-communist change and strong influence of the dominant Western models of skill formation limited alternative choices of institutional arrangements of skill formation. The neoliberal market-based model typical of Anglophone countries, and, to lesser extent, the collective skill formation systems typical of Germanic countries, were seen as models for imitation. Using the collective skill formation model for these reforms was challenging, given weak institutionalization and insufficient capacities of stakeholders in skill formation, whereas the market-based model was appealing for its attachment to the market economy, as well as its widespread adoption in the world.

## Access to the EU in 2004 and later years

With access to the EU the 'young' skill formation systems of CEE countries had to comply with requirements of the *acquis communautaire*, especially with those requirements related to comparability of skills and qualifications and mobility of workers and learners within the EU. Comprehensive transitional reforms of skill formation systems in most CEE countries reached stabilisation with significant external support provided by the EU (structural funds, know-how and expertise provided by the European Training Foundation, Cedefop, European Council and other European bodies).

These reforms were strongly focused on learning outcomes/competence orientation of curricula (Bologna and Copenhagen processes), systemic provision and governance of qualifications, and development of social partnership-based decision-making mechanisms (Kogan, Gebel and Noelke 2012; Kozma 2014). The institutional change at this period was driven by governments of CEE countries and EU institutions involved in the accession process. The influence of structural antecedents (existing institutional settings of skill formation, skills needs, previous policies and strategies, aims and preferences of governments and stakeholders, etc.) diverged between CEE countries. These antecedents and national specificities were more important and more strongly protected by countries inheriting sustained industrial economies and following a developmental approach (Visegrád countries, Slovenia), and less important in countries strongly following a 'catch-up' approach to radical reforms of economic development and skill formation (Baltic states).

Workforce migration was another important contextual factor affecting skill formation in post-communist CEE countries because access to EU labour markets with free movement of labour facilitated migration from many CEE countries, especially Poland, Baltic states, Romania and Bulgaria to EU15 member states. This migration operated as a safety valve against social unrest caused by unemployment, as well as helping postpone social and labour policies to improve working conditions and social cohesion likely to be unpopular with employers (Aleksandravičius 2010; Meardi 2014). Emigration also had a negative effect on employers' readiness to invest in skill formation, which partly explains the passiveness of employers in relation to vocational training in CEE countries with high rates of emigration, such as Lithuania and Poland.

Nevertheless, access to EU labour markets and programmes increased the capacities of skill formation institutions (VET providers, higher education establishments, adult education providers, etc.) because of the financial support and know-how that could be accessed. Institutional preconditions for systemic development of skill formation processes were established based on qualifications systems. The process increased the autonomy of providers in reform of curriculum design, qualifications and credentials and enabled more intensive involvement of social partners and stakeholders (especially employers) in associated decision making.

Participation of stakeholder institutions in implementing EU strategies increased openness and comparability of skills and qualifications through implementing EU instruments (Copenhagen process and ECVET, Bologna process, ECTS and EQF). It also facilitated comparability and common trends of development of skill formation processes enhanced by policy learning and EU cooperation (Tūtlys, Kaminskienė and Winterton 2016). EU integration also strengthened the neoliberal and developmental orientations of skill formation policies justified by new pressures on competitiveness in a common market with free circulation of goods, capital and labour (Piketty 2019).

The most influential decisions in shaping the outcomes of skill formation reforms during and after EU accession were designed to improve labour market relevance, strengthen competitiveness of human capital and democratise governance of skill formation by involving social partners. Experience of policy learning and cooperating with partners in European projects on skill formation helped establish networks and communities of practice contributing to the reform of skill formation.

## Global financial crisis of 2008–2009 and its aftermath

The global financial crisis increased structural unemployment, skills mismatches and emigration in many CEE countries, especially those that followed neoliberal catch-up policies and faced challenges over relevance of skill formation to actual labour market needs. The crisis had a more severe impact on unemployment and lower positive impact on education in the more neoliberal CEE countries with higher levels of inequality, such as the Baltic countries, whereas countries with lower levels of inequality and higher state involvement in social protection policy succeeded better in reducing unemployment during and after the crisis (Robert, Saar and Kazjulja 2019). Policy responses to the crisis increased governments' attention to human capital development policies directed at fostering competitiveness and recovery, typically in Visegrád countries and Slovenia. Employer interest in skill formation increased because of skills shortages.

Institutional changes in skill formation during and after the crisis were mainly driven by the agency of governments and employers. Some countries implemented industrial policies designed to protect strategic sectors, including supporting skill formation (Visegrád countries). Other countries aimed to optimise the national skill formation systems, developing work-based learning and apprenticeship or establishing simulated work-based learning environments (sectoral practical training centres in Lithuania). These policies were actively supported by employers. Regional initiatives of policy learning and development emerged, such as 'Baltic Alliance for Apprenticeships' uniting policy makers, providers and social partners in the Baltic States via common projects to develop work-based learning.

One institutional outcome of the crisis was an increased role for governments and governmental agencies in the governance and reform of skill formation systems. In Hungary this led to increased centralisation of skill formation (Lazcik and Farkas 2018). The crisis also encouraged the spread of developmental approaches to skill formation and investment in infrastructure and capacity development of providers and social partners. After the crisis, employers were more actively engaged in human capital development.

The economic crisis and subsequent institutional and political crisis of the EU brought governments and employers to the forefront of decision making in various fields and implementing developmental policies in skill formation strengthened their strategic cooperation. Both left and right political powers prioritised policies to grow employment, reduce emigration and optimise output of skill formation institutions. Skill formation also became a tool in policies to protect the socio-cultural and ethnic composition of societies against risks posed by the migration, especially in smaller CEE countries like Estonia and Latvia.

Skill formation policies implemented after the crisis affirm more strategic engagement of governments in the reforms designed to improve competitiveness and reduce skill mismatches, which in some countries further strengthened neoliberal approaches (Lithuania). In other countries that engagement supported developmental approaches to modern welfare state regimes, where improved access to skill formation aligned with flexible employment relations and competitiveness based on innovation and quality (Estonia and Slovenia). Possible alternatives include promotion of local and sectoral social dialogue by empowering social partners, especially trade unions. However, such a scenario is hampered by the strong tradition of voluntarism in the governance of skill formation processes at the local and sectoral levels, as well as weak capacities of social partners at these levels (Klatt, Filip and Grzebyk 2015).

## National skill systems

The implications of post-communist transition for the structure and functioning of national systems of education can be highlighted by the links between education systems and social stratification, trends of stratification of education, and standardization of education systems by introducing uniformly regulated curricula and qualifications. The legacy of socialist education systems, with high stratification and tripartite structure of the upper secondary education enhanced rapid educational expansion at the tertiary level with the emergence of post-secondary and vocationally oriented higher education pathways (Kogan, Gebel and Noelke 2012). But acknowledging the common legacy of socialist education systems should not result in disregarding the differences among the CEE countries. Factors to be scrutinized are: different starting points regarding the political system (countries which formed part of the Soviet Union, the Warsaw Pact or former Yugoslavia); different economic structures and skills systems at the time of collapse; different transition periods (e.g. comparing the repeated recessions in Romania with the special situation of German reunification); and differences in recent political decisions. Furthermore, despite different critical junctures between Eastern and Western Europe, there are remarkable parallels in the evolution of education systems in both regions in the last three decades. In this respect global education trends are also important to be considered. We will return to this issue after a brief description of the transformation of the education systems of the CEE countries covered in this book.

### Secondary education

Soviet ideology was based on equality of opportunity regardless of sex, race or social background, which proscribed stratification at too early an age and supported permeability of educational tracks to revise previous educational choices. Consequently, separation into different types of school was abolished in favour of comprehensive schools integrating primary and lower secondary education with provision of alternative routes to higher education (e.g. evening schools). However, after compulsory education individual preferences had little influence on available educational options which were defined by planning agencies and their efforts to fuel agricultural and industrial modernisation and economic growth (Noelke and Müller 2012: 16). Therefore, upper secondary education was highly stratified, while lower secondary education was comprehensive. At upper secondary level all socialist CEE countries developed the same tripartite structure consisting of general secondary, lower vocational and upper vocational education pathways.

For the education systems of CEE countries, the transition to capitalism resulted in decentralisation (e.g. responsibilities were shifted to municipalities) and liberalisation of the education market (e.g. private suppliers at tertiary level stepped in). Freeing individual education choices entailed academic drift at upper-secondary level at the expense of lower vocational education and a massive increase of enrolments in higher education. Individuals' choices to postpone labour market entry due to the tightened youth labour market and their expectation of higher returns to tertiary education (Noelke and Müller 2012: 19) coincided with political interest to foster higher education. At the same time, lower vocational schools not only lost their links with industry (enterprises stopped providing training to VET students), but also essential funding to update equipment and curricula. The basic tripartite structure of upper secondary education remained, despite major shifts in enrolment from VET to general education and from lower VET to upper VET. Another major consequence of the transition to capitalism was that in many cases, the upper limit of compulsory schooling was reduced to 15 or 16, students were given greater choice in secondary programmes, new examinations were prepared to certify completion of secondary programmes (Benavot 2006) and in some cases, such as East Germany, Czech Republic and Hungary, early tracking at the lower secondary level re-emerged, although this practice had been discredited under socialism (Noelke and Müller 2012).

## Vocational education and training

At different times during the Soviet period the question of where to train was answered differently. However, there was never any question of practical work being only for less academic children and VET was considered as important from the very first day of school (O'Dell 1988: 191). Hence, vocational education, notably the 'labour-training' syllabus was considered an integral component of education at all educational levels, consisting of (a) practical skills, (b) socialisation for work and (c) vocational guidance. Learning practical skills meant all children learnt the basics of woodwork and metalwork or engaged in full-time work on production or on the farm for one month in the ninth year of secondary school. This practice gave all children some taste of what working life was like as well as moral and practical effects (O'Dell 1988: 193). Socialisation for work meant that all students were trained in Soviet attitudes towards work. Vocational guidance was not understood as exploring students' interests but guiding students into occupations most needed according to central planning. These components of labour lessons were reinforced in general subjects, for instance, history lessons dealt with working conditions whilst the reading syllabus included poems more 'extolling the joy of work than odes to the beauties of nature' (O'Dell 1988: 193, see also Soltys 1997). Hence, during the 'heyday' of the communist era around the 1960s we find highly 'vocationalized' education systems in the CEE countries which is not only traceably by the ideological approach to education and the curriculum, but also by increased enrolment in vocational education at secondary level. For the period from 1950 to 1975, Benavot (1983) found Eastern Europe the only world region with increasing enrolments in vocational education, having started already from a very high level. Between 1950 and 1975 the proportion of full-time secondary students in vocational programmes declined globally from 24 per cent to 16 per cent, in Western Europe from 33 per cent to 20 per cent, whereas in Eastern Europe it rose from 50 per cent to 66 per cent (Benavot 1983).

Immediately after the collapse of communism, VET pathways of skill formation lost their popularity in many post-communist CEE countries as VET providers had no industrial partners, which led to disarray in training provision and growing skills mismatches (West 2013). Transition reforms significantly shifted the emphasis onto educational choice and promoting educational pathways away from vocationally and professionally oriented education pathways in the socialist system to more general and higher education following reforms (Laczik and Farkas 2018). Lower vocational education with its specific job-related programmes (typically lasting 2–3 years) lost a tremendous share of students, while the decline of the broader technician programmes (typically lasting four years) was more moderate.

VET was treated rather differently in skill formation systems of CEE countries after the collapse of the Soviet Union, but there were also difference in place already before that. In the neoliberal skill formation systems of the Baltic countries, along with Bulgaria and Romania, the leading role of VET was the social and labour market integration of disadvantaged sections of the population, resulting in increased popularity of tertiary higher education pathways and less interest in lower vocational schools that were viewed as dead-ends (Kogan, Gebel and Noelke 2012). The current set-up of upper-secondary education in Baltic education systems is 'general or non-vocational' and this has hardly changed since the early 1990s. The Baltic countries have some of the lowest rates of enrolment in vocational/technical tracks in Europe (around one third of an age cohort) and practically no work-based learning is offered. VET is considered as vocationally oriented school education which mainly takes place in classrooms with some learning in school workshops. While the ratio between VET and general education has remained stable over the last two decades, all three Baltic countries have seen a net decrease in student population at upper-secondary level due to shrinking youth cohorts. Contrary to upper-secondary level, higher education saw a period of strong expansion in the 1990s in which the number of higher education institutions and students grew constantly (and youth cohorts were still rather stable), but there was a strong decline between 2006 and 2016. Expansion of higher education and vocational drift at higher levels occurred in all three Baltic countries. An increasing share of adult learners in VET is also apparent, although this is still low compared with EU averages (Cedefop 2020). While key figures regarding initial VET suggest stability, content and structure changed substantially in all three states since independence, practically constructing a new VET system and requiring extensive legislation and reform including new ways of education planning, curriculum renewal, and quality-assurance measures (Bünning 2008).

In countries of embedded neoliberalism and neo-corporatism, the Visegrád countries and Slovenia, VET became the source of strategic human resource development (Kogan, Gebel and Noelke 2012; Kureková 2012). They enjoyed steady economic growth for several decades and did not experience extreme economic downturn after the crises as the Baltic States did. Compared to other post-communist countries, some market-oriented reforms were already in place before the transition. At the time of the fall of the Soviet Union, Czechoslovakia and Hungary were the wealthiest CEE countries with a GDP per capita twice that of the poorest CEE countries Romania and Bulgaria. These countries have also been very successful since then in attracting foreign direct investment and the industrial sector (e.g. car manufacturing) has been an engine of growth.

In contrast to the Baltic States, the Visegrád countries all have strong school-based VET systems which have shown steady erosion within the last three decades. In Poland the share of students in vocational education decreased from 78 per cent to 58 per cent between 1990 and 2017; in Hungary it decreased almost to the same extent from 76 per cent to 58 per cent between 1990 and 2018; in the Czech Republic and Slovakia the decline was less, but still remarkable from around 80 per cent to 70 per cent (between 1995 and 2015) (Cedefop 2020). In all Visegrád countries VET programmes not providing access to higher education have dramatically decreased, while at the same time hybrid VET programmes offering dual qualifications (professional diplomas and as higher education entrance qualification) have become an important supplier for a strongly increasing higher education sector (Cedefop 2020). Klatt, Filip and Grzebyk (2015) commented on the low status of VET in Poland, exacerbated by growing dissatisfaction of employers with the practical skill level of graduates, low interest of industry to contribute to VET provision, which is in decline, and further loss of esteem of VET compared with general and higher education. Dębowski and Stęchły (2015) observe a 'de-vocationalization' of the Polish education system during the entire transition period. Only recently, and probably due to increasing skill shortages (the inevitable result of steady economic growth and a shrinking workforce), VET has become a new national policy priority in Poland as reflected in various national and regional strategic documents. A recent study also shows the attitudes of employers have changed and they are now more willing to support the VET system (Dębowski and Reegård 2018).

Other Visegrád countries like Hungary applied different protective interventions to save VET establishments from collapsing together with the former socialist enterprises during the transition (Laczik and Farkas 2018). Such approaches assisted the subsequent modernisation and reforms of VET provision by focusing on the needs of the market economy and modernisation of institutional frameworks, as well as governance of VET through decentralisation and investments in VET providers using EU money. In the aftermath of the global economic crisis of 2008/09 governments of CEE countries increasingly saw VET as an instrument for economic development (especially in Hungary, Czech Republic, Slovakia, and, to some extent in Lithuania). In Hungary it led to more centralised and state-led regulation of VET provision and funding mechanisms, as well as strong state promotion of work-based learning and apprenticeship pathways (Laczik and Farkas 2018).

Like other CEE countries, Romania and Bulgaria experienced a decline in youth population over the years, but an even more pronounced one. Romania and Bulgaria both lost more than a third of their youth population (15–29 years old) between 1995 and 2015 (Cedefop 2020) and the birth rate in Romania decreased between 1990 and 2012 by 43 per cent (Iancu, Hurmuzache, Brad, Sirbu, Iosim and Pirvulescu 2015). Consequently, participation in secondary education has been decreasing and many smaller schools have been merged with bigger ones.

The share of VET students at upper-secondary level in Bulgaria and Romania is clearly above the EU average and most students opt for VET at this level. In Bulgaria, the share of VET has remained rather stable in the last two decades. In Romania, the share of VET at levels 3 and 4 was stable between 1995 and 2005, declined significantly until 2011 and increased since, which can be attributed to restructuring of VET programmes and new policy emphasis on VET as in other CEE countries, e.g. Poland or Hungary, after the crisis (Cedefop 2020).

A similar trend can be observed for Slovenia. While the share of VET students at upper-secondary level steadily dropped from 72 per cent in 1998 to 59 per cent in 2012, the demand for VET seems on the rise again after the crisis (Cedefop 2020). In Croatia, lower vocational programmes leading directly to employment were more affected by overall academic drift in the CEE countries than those providing access to higher education (Ivancic 2008).

## Higher education

Higher education has been viewed by policy makers and stakeholders in post-communist countries as offering a strategic opportunity in the new socio-economic conditions and a driving force for transition to market economies and democratic societies. Intellectuals and representatives of higher education institutions in many CEE countries were at the forefront of the democratic movements that helped dismantle communist systems. This provided important credit and societal support for post-communist reforms of higher education, as well as almost univocal understanding of the priority of higher education for the transition. Catch-up ideology and approaches significantly fostered such ideas, so higher education dominated in skills supply during the post-communist transition in many CEE countries, especially in the Baltic countries, where newly emerging providers of education and skills (enterprises, NGOs, social partner organizations) were weak and very few. This partly explains the domination of the formal provision of skills, slow development of lifelong learning and increasing skills mismatches.

The early reforms of post-communist higher education faced interesting challenges in the choice of ideological orientation of the mission of higher education and two predominant ideological orientations can be identified.

Firstly, the mission of universities to develop and foster a mature and open civil society with actively engaged citizens as well as to facilitate national cultures, sustainable economic development and social peace. In this view the economic mission of the university as a source of human capital development (although being important) was secondary. This ideological choice strongly referred to holistic models of studies as *artes liberales* and the Humboldt model, which do not prioritise acquisition of specific high skills but overall personal development. Such models of higher education were appreciated for their potential to educate a new social elite aligned with the aspirations of freedom, democracy and socio-economic welfare (Šliogeris 2012). Though widely supported by the intelligentsia, there was often scepticism from business leaders and more pragmatic visions generally prevailed.

Secondly, the mission of universities to develop high skills and human capital appropriate for the transition to market economy and economic competitiveness. This ideological orientation facilitated pragmatic and professional orientation of studies addressing labour market needs. One of the widespread manifestations of this orientation was the rising popularity of business studies and creation of business schools. This orientation also fostered binary higher education systems with colleges or universities of applied sciences alongside classical academic universities. Economic industrial development in CEE countries in the first decade of the 21st century and the aftermath of the economic crisis together with technological trends (digitalisation) and catch-up innovation policies further stimulated this approach to higher education reforms.

## Continuing vocational education and lifelong learning

The clear separation between initial and continuing vocational training was a legacy of the Soviet system (West 2013). In modernising VET systems, many post-communist CEE countries tackled this legacy by opening lifelong learning pathways in VET and establishing an integrated system (Kogan, Gebel and Noelke 2012; West 2013). The low participation in lifelong learning in CEE countries is explicable by the rarity of firm-sponsored training (Markowitsch, Käpplinger and Hefler 2013). Here, the legacy of the past and the influence of the economy is most pronounced. There is a strong contrast between the relatively favourable conditions of the Visegrád countries and Slovenia; the transitional recession in the period 1991–1993 in the Baltic countries which suffered heavily due to the breakdown of trade relations with the Soviet Union; and the situation of Bulgaria and Romania which had the lowest GDP per capita of all CEE countries in 1990, and were hit by a second recession at the end of the 1990s due to delayed restructuring. All this is reflected in the participation in lifelong learning which has been lowest in Bulgaria and Romania, followed by the Visegrád and is highest in Slovenia. However, besides economic conditions, there is also a clear momentum of the respective skills and welfare state regimes. Markowitsch, Käpplinger and Hefler (2013) point out that differences in training activity between neo-liberal or neo-conservative welfare states in Eastern Europe and familial welfare states of Southern Europe are not as pronounced as their respective levels of economic development might predict.

By analysing inequality in access to non-formal learning, Roosmaa and Saar (2010) conclude that comparative theoretical frameworks, developed for mostly large, socio-economically advanced Western EU countries are not applicable to the CEE countries. Their analysis clearly shows large differences in the impact of institutional framework on inequality in non-formal learning participation in Western countries. However, the analysis fails to demonstrate a distinct institutional-specific association in the eight newer, post-socialist EU member countries. On the contrary, post-communist countries underscore that certain types of adult learning systems are embedded in institutional frameworks that go beyond national labour markets and welfare systems (Saar, Ure and Desjardins 2013)

## Western trends and eastern peculiarities

The dissolution of the Soviet Union and fall of the Iron Curtain was undoubtedly a unique event in modern history and for social scientists it is an exceptional opportunity to study the social transformations and the trajectories of countries from the collapse, through the transition period to the present day. The distinctiveness of the CEE countries, their commonalities and differences, are so significant that there is a risk of overlooking global trends. Increased enrolment in higher education including vocationally oriented higher education in CEE countries since the early 1990s is unexceptional if compared to universal massification of higher education. Some observations made above therefore warrant further discussion against the background of more general trends. For instance, the ongoing trends towards extended schooling, towards postponing educational choices, towards making VET and general education more equal and towards more comprehensive forms of upper-secondary education (with differences within) can be seen both in former communist countries and Western Europe (Markowitsch and Hefler 2019). This obviously resulted in upper-secondary VET with a predominately preparatory profile, instead of preparing for a single occupation, more like academic tracks, with the further implication that occupational competence and specific vocational qualifications are predominantly acquired later (Markowitsch and Hefler 2019).

The decline of shorter, more practical VET programmes at upper-secondary level at the expense of academic or hybrid programmes witnessed in all CEE countries with previously strong school-based VET is no surprise. Similar developments, though less pronounced, can be found in Western countries with VET systems as different as France, Italy, the UK, Austria and the Netherlands (Cedefop 2020). In countries with predominantly work-based VET (Denmark and Germany), VET came under substantial pressure due to academisation. In countries with both school-based and substantial work-based tracks (Austria and the Netherlands) the apprenticeship tracks lost terrain to school-based tracks (except Norway) (Cedefop 2020).

Given these similarities, it is crucial to explore more closely the opportunities and limitations associated with the specific circumstances of CEE countries. For instance, rapid growth of higher education in Poland would probably have been impossible without numerous private institutions entering the market, whereas in other European countries the increase was achieved with less marketization. Also, it is worth scrutinizing the extent to which approaches were discredited because they appeared to be bringing back communist principles. For instance, the discussions on equity and equality on education, the focus on civic education as part of VET, the idea to foster VET from the early days on, or the likely scenario of a vocationally oriented lifelong learning (Cedefop 2020), may remind us of aspects of the educational approach discussed above.

## Understanding skill formation

This section provides an overview of the main concepts discussed in this book and presents our suggested conceptual model of skills formation and deployment.

Skill formation is typically viewed on the axis between education and the world of work and can be observed from different actors' perspectives. On the *micro level* it includes learners, workers, superiors; on the *mezzo level* various education institutions, employers' and employees' organizations; and on the *system level* state institutions, employers' and employees' associations or other (supra) national agencies. Some countries generate occupational skills more via work-based skill formation systems (e.g. Germany), school-based education (e.g. France) or a combination of both (e.g. Austria), whilst in some countries it is to a great extent organized outside formal settings (e.g. Russian Federation). Skill formation can be viewed in the context of welfare regimes, labour market regulation and legislation, and inequalities in participation in adult education. Relations between various actors in skill formation appear in the context of ideological orientation (liberalism, neoliberalism, developmental state); institutional settings (market economy, democratic civil societies, decentralised governance); institutional processes of skill formation (generalisation and subsequent vocationalization of education, work-based learning practices, etc.). Skill formation also has a historical legacy in terms of institutional infrastructure (e.g. impact of inherited developed education systems with high levels of educational attainment); relationships between institutions and stakeholders (e.g. institutional weakness of social dialogue in the field of skill formation); as well as in such subjective fields as readiness of societies to accept institutional changes in skill formation by using new institutions, or complicated development of social trust in those new settings.

Heckman and Corbin (2016: 344) viewed skills as a major source of well-being, enabling action in a wide array of life domains, with cognitive, socio-emotional, and health skills developed in early life experiences. The opportunity to deploy a wide range of skills at work has been shown to have a major determining role in worker well-being (Kornhauser 1965; O'Brien 1982). Skills are both a source of, and a result of, the 'dichotomy and interlinkage between work-related tacit knowledge and explicit knowledge' (Pavlin et al. 2013: 96). Before elaborating a conceptual framework of skill formation, we provide selected definitions of skills, processes and concepts related to skill formation such as learning, knowledge creation spirals and skill match.

## Defining skills

Skill as a technical concept is both complex and contested. The complexity is reflected in components that include psycho-motor skills and measurable attributes like dexterity (Proctor and Dutta 1995). Its contested nature is related to the social construction of skill labels attached to work and occupations (Attewell 1990), which often reflects feminised labour markets (Cockburn 1983). There is little consistency or consensus in definitions, which are often specific to given contexts (Winterton, 2009). The OECD Programme for the International Assessment of Adult Competencies (OECD, 2011), for example, proposed a rather arbitrary terminological distinction between the terms competence, competencies, learning outcomes and skills: while the Programme name refers to competence, the major survey was labelled the Survey of Adult Skills.

Skill is used as a shorthand for any combination of abilities that take time to acquire, which differs little from an overarching definition of competence as the ability to demonstrate those abilities in a work context. In some definitions of competence, skill is used synonymously with functional competence, and contrasted with the other two dimensions: cognitive competence (knowledge) and social competence (attitudes and behaviours) (Le Deist and Winterton 2005). In this book, unless specified otherwise, we are using skill in the wider sense that it is most often used in policy and practice to encompass all learning outcomes, competencies and capabilities, especially those that can be employed at work.

## Key processes and concepts related to skill formation

### Contextual theories

One of the prevailing approaches for contextualisation of skill formation is related to human capital theories. Adam Smith and Karl Marx employed concepts that equate with the concept of human capital (Winterton and Cafferkey 2019) although Schultz (1961) and Becker (1962) are usually credited with the term, which they used in attempting to demonstrate returns to education. Thurow (1975) challenged their view that education leads to productivity and salary gains, arguing that productivity depends more on the specific job than acquired competencies. Using signal theory, Spence (1974) reduced the role of education to an indication of a jobseeker to employers: rather than preparing students for work, education indicates their potential to develop competence. Credential theory (Collins 1979) argues that the main role of education systems lies in regulating access to the labour market. These are not mutually exclusive and merely emphasise different ways in which education and training have positive labour market outcomes.

### Learning

Human learning is often defined as a process that causes long-term changes based on external stimuli and learning can occur at individual, group or organizational level. Moreover, situation learning (Bandura 1969) based on observation and participation in various social situations, can be distinguished from information-process learning (Anderson 1995), typical in formal education. Not all educational institutions are good learning facilitators, while some work organizations are. Lundvall and Rasmussen (2016: 451–452), for example, clustered different systems of work organization, describing how discretionary learning and lean firms are characterised by high levels of learning and problem-solving in work where the main variation is in relation to levels of autonomy.

### Knowledge creation processes

Recent literature offers several conceptual models describing the formulation of knowledge and skill formation. Lundvall's (2000) knowledge cycle refers to knowledge creation, dissemination and utilisation. While knowledge, traditionally created in research laboratories and universities, was disseminated in educational institutions and utilized at work, increasing numbers of jobs now involve creating, disseminating and using knowledge. Boisot's (2002) model explains how knowledge flows from abstract to concrete and practical and from diffuse to structured form. This model is related to education institutions where professionals master how to structure different types of knowledge into concepts and products. Particularly at higher competence levels, there is a proceduralisation of knowledge, whereby knowledge is converted to skills (Winterton, Le Deist and Stringfellow 2006: 26). The model of the knowledge spiral by Nonaka and Takeuchi (1995) is built upon the interaction of situation (socialisation) and information-process (internalisation). The first form of learning is related to social interactions with co-workers, friends and customers, while the second to reading manuals and attending meetings. These authors described two forms of creation of explicit knowledge: externalisation, the process of documenting knowledge, and combination, by manipulating various data in physical or electronic form.

## Skill match

A key employability issue is the extent to which an individual's skills developed in education and training sufficiently match the requirements of professional destinations. One can identify horizontally (field of study) and vertically (level of study) mismatched individuals. The matching problem inherently relates to several theoretical concerns such as labour market segmentation, mobility, professionalization and seniority. Education matching differs from skill matching. Scholars typically distinguish between formal and real overqualification related to the extent of skill (under)utilisation. The first category reflects formal certified knowledge, while the second reflects skills required at work.

McGuinness et al. (2018) describe how overeducation and undereducation is measured via various approaches: the subjective method (typically based on worker self-assessment); realised matches (derived from micro datasets containing information on educational attainment and occupation); and job evaluation (based on the assessments of professional job analysts); skill obsolescence (measured through retrospective subjective questioning of workers); or utilisation of macroeconomic indicators (based on differences in employment rates across skill groups). For several reasons, skills match is controversial in the context of skill formation and deployment. Firstly, occupational bodies, employers' organizations and some educational institutions are involved in determining professional standards. Secondly, labour market outcomes, such as status, earnings depend not only on skill surplus or shortage, but in some cases more on policy, partisan policies, technological changes and other processes. However, skill mismatch persists as a challenge. In every country, training and education institutions are struggling to keep up with changing labour market needs, while individuals face skill obsolescence and demand deficiency, but transition countries are likely to have specific problems.

## Other perspectives on skill formation

There are several other processes which are typically related to surveying skill acquisition and decline. These are: unlearning or loss of knowledge referring to situations where employees lose skills they have once acquired; linking skills to performance management, which can be viewed in the context of a particular workplace, occupational group or sector; quality of jobs that include themes such as precarisation of work or labour market exclusion; digitalisation of work that is often but not necessarily related to job creation and destruction including emergence of new occupations and industries; and various general perspectives related to changes of educational and training institutions such as for example recognition of skills.

## Conceptual model

Various models have been proposed in relation to skill formation: some remain on the conceptual level while others have been tested empirically. Heckman and Corbin (2016: 345), for example, presented a model explaining how skills are formed from the perspective of capability theory. This model assumes that potential capabilities depend upon several factors: health and cognitive skills; personality; motivation and aspiration skills; financial resources; information; peers; and endowments.

Another model proposed by Saar and Räis (2017) based on Desjardins (2014) described how three groups of factors (individual, workplace and job characteristics) are reflected in job related adult education and training. This model stresses that skill formation in the workplace occurs in the context of broader structural and institutional characteristics: public policy, skill formation system, labour market regulation and wider-socioeconomic norms and practices. Another model has been proposed by Pavlin (2007) based on the sociology of professional groups and explores how different forms of learning at work and externalisation of knowledge generates occupational identity, ethics and regulation. In this model vocational education is viewed as a result of occupational or professional practice.

We acknowledge two models proposed by the OECD (2011: 54–55) in the PIAAC survey. The first model describes skill acquisition and decline, and includes personal and background characteristics (age, gender, socio-economic status, cultural capital etc.) that affect (a) education, training and informal learning (initial and post-initial learning activities), (b) work characteristics (labour market participation and job characteristics) and (c) private life (skill use, voluntary work and political efficacy). In this model work characteristics contribute either to skill obsolescence or skill acquisition. The second model explains how economic and social outcomes are generated. This model explains how labour market outcomes (employment, earnings, job security, career and satisfaction) are conditioned by the match between acquired and required skills as well as other outcomes such as health and political and civic engagement. Key processes in the model – match between acquired and required education and training, acquired and required work experiences, and acquired and required skills – are determined by labour market institutions.

In this book we propose a straightforward model comprising three levels of skill formation and deployment: a micro level representing individual actors – learners, employees, superiors; a mezzo level representing institutions and stakeholders; and a macro level, representing institutions of skill formation and deployment. The model envisages skill formation and deployment as determined by the interaction of: (i) participation/engagement of individuals in the skill formation and deployment; (ii) design and implementation of institutional settings and policies of skill formation and deployment. These interactions are influenced by environmental changes. The model represents two main vectors of institutional change: (1) a bottom-up vector driven by individual behaviours and processes of skill formation at the micro level, which in turn influence development at the mezzo and macro levels; and (2) a top-down vector driven by national policies and strategies of skill formation, influencing institutional development at the mezzo level, as well as changes at the micro level. Extant research generally assumes the top-down vector played a determining role during post-communist institutional transformations, although recently bottom-up changes are recognized. This assumption will be addressed by the analysis in the CEE countries and we will return to it in the concluding chapters of the book.

## References

Aleksandravičius, E. (2010). *Išblukęs žodynas*. Vilnius: Versus Aureus.

Anderson, J. R. (1995). *Learning and Memory: An Integrated Approach*. New York: John Wiley.

Anioł, W. (2015). 'On three modernization narratives in Poland after 1989', *International Journal of Social Economics*, 42 (9), 777–790.

Ante, C. (2015). *The Europeanisation of Vocational Education and Training. A Political Economy of Skills Perspective.* Doctoral dissertation, University, Hertie School of Governance, Berlin.

Attewell, P. (1990). 'What is skill?' *Work and Occupations*, 17 (4), 422–448.

Baethge, B., and Wolter, A. (2015). 'The German skill formation model in transition: From dual system of VET to higher education?' *Journal of Labour Market Research*, 48, 97–112.

Bandura, A. (1969). *Principles of Behavior Modification.* New York, NY: Holt, Rinehart and Winston.

Becker, G. S. (1962). 'Investment in human capital: A theoretical analysis', *Journal of Political Economy*, 70 (5), 9–49.

Becker, G. S. (1964). *Human Capital: A Theoretical and Empirical Analysis, with Special Reference to Education.* Chicago, IL: University of Chicago Press.

Benavot, A. (1983). 'The rise and decline of vocational education', *Sociology of Education,* 56 (2), 63–76.

Benavot, A. (2006). *The Diversification of Secondary Education: School Curricula in Comparative Perspective. IBE Working Papers on Curriculum Issues N° 6.* Geneva: UNESCO.

Boisot, M. (2002). 'The creation and sharing of knowledge'. In C. Choo and N. Bontis (eds.), *The Strategic Management of Intellectual Capital and Organizational Management*, pp. 65–77. Oxford: Oxford University Press.

Bosh, G. (2017). 'Different national skill systems'. In C. Warhurst, K. Mayhew, D. Finegold and J. Buchanan (eds.), *The Oxford Handbook of Skills and Training*, pp. 487–509. Oxford: Oxford University Press.

Brockmann, M., Clarke, L., and Winch, C. (2011). *Knowledge, Skills and Competence in the European Labour Market. What's in a Vocational Qualification?* London: Routledge.

Bünning, F. (2008). *The Transformation of Vocational Education and Training (VET) in the Baltic States-Survey of Reforms and Developments.* Dordrecht: Springer Science & Business Media.

Busemeyer, M. R., and Trampush, C. (2011). 'The comparative political economy of collective skill formation'. In M. R. Busemeyer and C. Trampush (eds.), *The Political Economy of Collective Skill Formation*, pp. 3–38. Oxford: Oxford University Press.

Capoccia, G. (2015). 'Critical junctures and institutional change'. In J. Mahoney and K. Thelen (eds.), *Advances in Comparative-Historical Analysis*, pp. 147–179. Cambridge: Cambridge University Press.

Cedefop. (2020). *Vocational Education and Training in Europe 1995–2035. Scenarios for European VET in the 21st Century.* Luxembourg: Publications Office of the European Union.

Cockburn, C. (1983). *Brothers: Male Dominance and Technological Change.* London: Pluto Press.

Collins, R. (1979). *The Credential Society: An Historical Sociology of Education and Stratification.* New York, NY: Academic Press.

Culpepper, P., and Finegold, D. (eds.) (1999). *The German Skills Machine: Sustaining Comparative Advantage in a Global Economy.* Oxford: Berghahn Books.

Dębowski, H., and Stęchły, W. (2015). 'Implementing ECVET Principles. Reforming Poland's Vocational Education and Training Through Learning Outcomes Based Curricula and Assessment', *Warsaw Forum of Economic Sociology*, 6 (12), 57–88.

Dębowski, H., and Reegård, K. (2018). 'Exit, voice or loyalty? VET stakeholders' responses to large scale skills emigration from and immigration into Poland', *ECER – European Conference on Educational Research*, Bolzano, 7 September.

Desjardins, R. (2014). Participation in Adult Education Opportunities: Evidence from PIAAC and Policy Trends in Selected Countries. Background paper for the Education for All Global Monitoring Report 2015.

Dorothee, B., and Greskovits, B. (2007). 'Neoliberalism, embedded neoliberalism and neocorporatism: Towards transnational capitalism in Central-Eastern Europe', *West European Politics*, 30 (3), 443–466.

Duman, A., and Kureková, L. (2012). 'The role of state in development of socio-economic models in Hungary and Slovakia: the case of industrial policy', *Journal of European Public Policy*, 19 (8), 1207–1228.

Feldmann, M. (2006). 'Emerging varieties of capitalism in transition countries: Industrial relations and wage bargaining in Estonia and Slovenia', *Comparative Political Studies*, 39 (7), 829–854.

Ferry, M. (2014). 'Cohesion policy transfer and institutional change in Central and Eastern Europe', *Regions Magazine*, 296 (1), 23–25.

Finegold, D., and Soskice, D. (1988). 'The failure of training in Britain: Analysis and Prescription', *Oxford Review of Economic Policy*, 4 (3), 21–52.

Gehmlich, V. (2009). '"Kompetenz" and "Beruf" in the context of the proposed German Qualifications Framework for Lifelong Learning', *Journal of European Industrial Training*, 33 (8/9), 736–754.

Grant, N. (1969). *Society, Schools and Progress in Eastern Europe.* Oxford: Pergamon.

Green, F. (2013). *Skills and Skilled Work.* Oxford: Oxford University Press.

Greinert, W.-D. (2004). 'European Vocational Training "Systems"- Some thoughts on the theoretical context of their historical development', *Vocational Training*, 32, 18–25.

Hall, P. A., and Soskice, D. (eds.) (2001) *Varieties of Capitalism. The Institutional Foundations of Comparative Advantage*. Oxford: Oxford University Press.

Hardy, J. (2014). 'Transformation and crisis in Central and Eastern Europe: A combined and uneven development perspective', *Capital & Class*, 38 (1), 143–155.

Heckman, J. J., and Corbin, C. O. (2016). 'Capabilities and skills', *Journal of Human Development and Capabilities*, 17 (3), 342–359.

Iancu, T., Hurmuzache, T. C., Brad, I., Sirbu, C. C., Iosim, I., and Pirvulescu, L. (2015). 'Study on the development of education in Romania', *Procedia-Social and Behavioral Sciences*, 182, 560–565.

Ivancic, A. (2008). 'Slovenia'. In I. Kogan, M. Gebel, and C. Noelke (eds.), *Europe Enlarged – A Handbook of Education, Labour and Welfare Regimes in Central and Eastern Europe*, pp. 353–378. Bristol: Policy Press.

Josifidis, K., Supic, N., and Glavaski, O. (2018). 'Institutional changes and income inequality: Some aspects of economic change and evolution of values in CEE countries', *Eastern European Economics*, 56 (6), 522–540.

Klatt, M., Filip, P., and Grzebyk, M. (2015). 'Understanding youth transition system in Poland through the analysis of partnerships between vocational upper secondary schools and industry', *Journal of Youth Studies*, 18 (9), 1186–1203.

Kogan, I. (2008). 'Education systems of Central and Eastern European countries'. In I. Kogan, M. Gebel, and C. Noelke (eds.), *Europe Enlarged: A Handbook of Education, Labour and Welfare Regimes in Central and Eastern Europe*, pp. 7–34. Bristol: The Policy Press.

Kogan, I., Gebel, M., and Noelke, C. (eds.) (2008). *Europe Enlarged. A Handbook of Education, Labour and Welfare Regimes in Central and Eastern Europe.* Bristol: Polity Press.

Kogan, I., Gebel, M., and Noelke, C. (2012). 'Educational systems and inequalities in educational attainment in Central and Eastern European countries', *Studies of Transition States and Societies*, 4, 69–83.

Kogan, I., Noelke, C., and Gebel, M. (2011). 'Comparative analysis of social transformation, education systems, and school-to-work transitions in Central and Eastern Europe'. In I. Kogan, C. Noelke, and M. Gebel (eds.), *Making the*

*Transition. Education and Labor Market Entry in Central and Eastern Europe*, pp. 320–351. Stanford, CA: Stanford University Press.

Kogan, I., and Unt, M. (2008). 'The role of vocational specificity of educational credentials for labour market entry in Estonia and Slovenia', *International Sociology*, 23 (3), 389–416.

Kornhauser, A. (1965). *Mental Health of the Industrial Worker: A Detroit Study*. New York, NY: John Wiley.

Kozma, T. (2014). 'The Bologna process in Central and Eastern Europe: A comparative view'. In T. Kozma, M. Rébay, A. Óhidy and É. Szolár (eds.), *The Bologna Process in Central and Eastern Europe*, pp. 13–32. Wiesbaden: Springer Fachmedien.

Kureková, L. (2011). *From Job Search to Skill Search: Political Economy of Labor Migration in Central and Eastern Europe.* Doctoral dissertation, Central European University, Budapest.

Kureková, L. (2012). 'Success against all Odds? Determinants of sectoral rise and decline in Central Europe', *East European Politics and Societies*, 26 (3), 643–664.

Laczik, A., and Farkas, É. (2018). 'Past and present developments in vocational learning in Eastern Europe: The case of hungary'. In S. McGrath, M. Mulder, J. Papier and R. Suart (eds.), *Handbook of Vocational Education and Training*, pp. 1089–1106. Cham: Springer.

Le Deist, F. D., and Tūtlys, V. (2012). 'Limits to mobility: Competence and qualifications in Europe', *European Journal of Training and Development*, 36 (2/3), 262–285.

Le Deist, F. D., and Winterton, J. (2005). 'What is competence?' *Human Resource Development International*, 8 (1), 27–46.

Leibfried, S. (2005). 'Social policy. Left to the judges and the markets?' In H. Wallace, W. Wallace and M. Pollack (eds.), *Policy Making in the European Union*, pp. 243–278. Oxford: Oxford University Press.

Lundvall, B.-Å. (2000). 'The learning economy: Some implications for the knowledge base of health and education systems.' In OECD *Knowledge Management in the Learning Society*, pp. 125–141. Paris: Organisation for Economic Cooperation and Development.

Lundvall, B.-Å., and Rasmussen, P. (2016). 'Challenges for adult skill formation in the globalising learning economy – a European perspective' *International Journal of Lifelong Education*, 35 (4), 448–464.

Lynch, L. (1994) 'Introduction.' In L. Lynch (ed.), *Training and the Private Sector: International Comparisons*, pp. 1–24. Chicago, IL: University of Chicago Press.

Markowitsch, J., and Hefler. G. (2019). 'Future Developments in Vocational Education and Training in Europe. Report on reskilling and upskilling through formal and vocational education training', *JRC Working Papers Series on Labour, Education and Technology*, 07.

Markowitsch, J., Käpplinger, B., and Hefler, G. (2013). 'Firm-provided training in Europe and the limits of national skills strategies', *European Journal of Education*, 48 (2), 281–291.

Martinaitis, Z. (2010). *The Political Economy of Skills Formation: Explaining Differences in Central and Eastern Europe*. Doctoral dissertation, Vilnius University.

McGuinness, S., Pouliakas, K., and Redmond, P. (2018). 'Skills mismatch: Concepts, measurement and policy approaches', *Journal of Economic Surveys* 32 (4), 985–1015.

Meardi, G. (2007). 'Restructuring in an enlarged Europe: Challenges and experiences', *Transfer: European Review of Labour and Research*, 13 (2), 253–266.

Meardi, G. (2014). 'The state and employment relations'. In A. Wilkinson, G. Wood and R. Deeg (eds.), *The Oxford Handbook of Employment Relations*, pp. 617–636. Oxford: Oxford University Press.

Myant, M. (2014). 'Economies undergoing long transition. Employment relations in Central and Eastern Europe'. In A. Wilkinson, G. Woods and R. Deeg (eds.), *The Oxford Handbook of Employment Relations*, pp. 359–384. Oxford: Oxford University Press.

Noelke, C., and Müller, W. (2012). 'Social Transformation and Eduaction Systems in Central and Eastern Europe'. In I. Kogan, C. Noelke and M. Gebel (eds.), *Making the Transition – Education and Labor Market Entry in Central and Eastern Europe*, pp. 1–28. Stanford: Stanford University Press.

Nonaka, I., and Takeuchi, H. (1995). *The Knowledge-Creating Company: How Japanese Companies Create the Dynamics of Innovation*. Oxford: Oxford University Press.

Norkus, Z. (2008). *Kokia demokratija, koks kapitalizmas? Pokomunistinė transformacija Lietuvoje lyginamosios istorinės sociologijos požiūriu*. Vilnius: Vilniaus Universiteto leidykla.

O'Brien, G. E. (1982). 'The relative contribution of perceived skill utilisation and other perceived job attributes to the prediction of job satisfaction', *Human Relations*, 35 (3), 219–237.

O'Dell, F. (1988). 'Recent Soviet vocationalization policies'. In J. Lauglo and K. Lillis (eds.), *Vocationalizing Eduaction. An International Perspective*, pp. 293–294. Oxford: Pergamon Press.

OECD (2011). *PIAAC Conceptual Framework of the Background Questionnaire Main Survey*. Paris: Organisation for Economic Cooperation and Development.

Pavlin, S. (2007). *Vloga znanja pri profesionalizaciji poklicev*. (*Znanstvena knjižnica*, 59). Ljubljana: Fakulteta za družbene vede.

Pavlin, S., Svetlik, I., and Evetts, J. (2013). 'Revisiting the role of formal and practical knowledge from a sociology of the professions perspective – The case of Slovenia', *Current Sociology*, 58 (1), 94–118.

Piketty, T. (2019). *Capital et Idéologie*. Paris: Seuil.

Plokhy, S. (2016). *The Gates of Europe. A History of Ukraine*. London: Penguin Books.

Poviliūnas, A. (2000). 'Švietimas- reformos sėkmės ir nesėkmės'. In A. Dobryninas, V. Gaidys, B. Gruževskis, A. Poviliūnas, V. Skapcevičius, M. P. Šaulauskas and S. Žukas (eds.), *Socialiniai pokyčiai: Lietuva 1990–1998*, pp. 120–146. Vilnius: Garnelis.

Powell, J., and Trampusch, C. (2011). 'Europeanization and the varying responses in collective skill systems'. In M. Busemeyer and C. Trampusch (eds.), *The Comparative Political Economy of Collective Skill Formation*, pp. 284–313. Oxford: Oxford University Press.

Proctor, R. W., and Dutta, A. (1995). *Skill Acquisition and Human Performance*. Thousand Oaks, CA: Sage.

Robert, P., Saar, E., and Kazjulja, M. (2019). 'Individual and institutional influences on EU labour market returns to education: A comparison of the effect of the 2008 economic crisis on eight EU countries', *European Societies*, 22 (2), 1–31.

Roosmaa, E. L., and Saar, E. (2010). 'Participating in non-formal learning: Patterns of inequality in EU-15 and the new EU-8 member countries', *Journal of Education and Work*, 23 (3), 179–206.

Saar, E., and Räis, M. L. (2017). 'Participation in job-related training in European countries: The impact of skill supply and demand characteristics', *Journal of Education and Work*, 30 (5), 531–551.

Saar, E., Ure, O. B., and Desjardins, R. (2013).'The Role of Diverse Institutions in Framing Adult Learning Systems, *European Journal of Education Research, Development and Policy*, 48 (2), 213–232.

Saniter, A., and Tūtlys, V. (2015). 'Comparison of historical development pathways of initial vocational education and training in Lithuania and Germany: How does history matter for policy learning?' In E. Berner and P. Gonon (eds.), *History of Vocational Education and Training in Europe. Cases, Concepts and Challenges*, pp. 511–530. Bern: Peter Lang.

Scharpf, F. (1999). *Governing in Europe: Effective and Democratic?* Oxford: Oxford University Press.

Scharpf, F. (2008). 'Negative und positive integration'. In M. Höpner and A. Schäfer (eds.), *Die Politische Ökonomie der Europäischen Integration*, pp. 49–87. Frankfurt: Campus.

Schultz, T. W. (1961). 'Investment in human capital', *American Economic Review*, 1 (2), 1–17.

Šliogeris, A. (2012). 'Apie vieną kitą grėsmę Lietuvai'. In V. Daujotytė, V. Mikelėnas, A. Šliogeris, A. Vasiliauskas and V. Žulkus (eds.), *Nerimas. Svarbiausių humanitarinių ir socialinių grėsmių bei jų pasekmių Lietuvai įžvalgos*, pp. 73–90. Vilnius: Tyto Alba.

Soltys, D. (1997). *Education for Decline: Soviet Vocational and Technical Schooling from Khrushchev to Gorbachev*. Toronto: University of Toronto Press.

Sommers, J., Woolfson, C. and Juska, A. (2014). 'Austerity as a global prescription and lessons from the neoliberal Baltic experiment', *The Economic and Labour Relations Review*, 25 (3), 397–416.

Sondergaard, L., and Murthi, M. (2012). *Skills, Not Just Diplomas. Managing Education for Results in Eastern Europe and Central Asia.* Washington, DC: World Bank.

Spasova, S., and Tomini, L. (2013). 'Building social dialogue institutions in Bulgaria: Between EU conditionality and domestic social actors', *Debatte: Journal of Contemporary Central and Eastern Europe*, 21 (1), 3–24.

Spence, A. M. (1974). *Market Signalling: Informational Transfer in Hiring and Related Screening Processes.* Cambridge: Harvard University Press.

Streeck, W. (2011). 'Skills and politics: General and specific.' In M. R. Busemeyer and C. Trampusch (eds.), *The Comparative Political Economy of Collective Skill Formation*, pp. 317–352. Oxford: Oxford University Press.

Tarlea, S. (2019). 'Low- and high-skills in Central and Eastern Europe: What role for the government?' *East European Politics and Societies*, 33 (1), 157–175.

Thelen, K. (2004). *How Institutions Evolve: The Political Economy of Skills in Germany, Britain, the United States, and Japan*. Cambridge: Cambridge University Press.

Thelen, K., and Conran, J. (2016). 'Institutional change'. In O. Fioretos, T. G. Falleti and A. Sheingate (eds.), *Oxford Handbook of Historical Institutionalism*, pp. 51–70. Oxford: Oxford University Press.

Thurow, L. V. (1975). *Generating Inequality*. New York, NY: Basic Books.

Tiits, M., Kattel, R., Kalvet, T., and Tamm, D. (2008). 'Catching up, forging ahead or falling behind? Central and Eastern European development in 1990–2005', *Innovation: The European Journal of Social Science Research*, 21 (1), 65–85.

Trampusch, C. (2009). 'Europeanization and institutional change in vocational education and training in Austria and Germany', *Governance: An International Journal of Policy, Administration, and Institutions*, 22 (3), 369–395.

Tūtlys, V., Kaminskienė, L., and Winterton, J. (2016). 'Policy borrowing and policy learning in initial VET reforms of Lithuania after 1990'. In S. Bohlinger, T. K. A. Dang and M. Klatt (eds.), *Education Policy: Mapping the Landscape and Scope*, pp. 377–402. Frankfurt: Peter Lang.

West, J. (2013). *Vocational Education and Training in Eastern Europe: Transition and Influence*. London: Centre for Learning and Life Chances in Knowledge Economies and Societies.

Winterton, J. (2000). 'Social dialogue over vocational training in market-led systems', *International Journal of Training and Development*, 4 (1), 26–41.

Winterton, J. (2007). 'Building social dialogue over training and learning: European and national developments', *European Journal of Industrial Relations*, 13 (3), 281–300.

Winterton, J. (2009). 'Competence across Europe: Highest common factor or lowest common denominator?' *Journal of European Industrial Training*, 33 (8/9), 681–700.

Winterton, J., and Cafferkey, K. (2019). 'Revisiting human capital theory: Progress and prospects.' In K. Townsend, K. Cafferkey, A. McDermott and T. Dundon (eds.), *Elgar Introduction to Theories of Human Resources and Employment Relations*, pp. 281–234. Cheltenham: Edward Elgar.

Winterton, J., Le Deist, F. D., and Stringfellow, E. (2006). *Typology of Knowledge, Skills and Competences. Clarification of the Concept and Prototype*. Cedefop Reference series 64, Luxembourg: Office for Official Publications of the European Communities.

Vidmantas Tūtlys, Genutė Gedvilienė, Lina Kaminskienė and Eglė Stasiūnaitienė

# 2. Lithuania: between neoliberalism and statism

**Abstract:** This chapter seeks to explore the main particularities of the institutional settings of skill formation in the post-communist transition of Lithuania and why and how these particularities influence the present processes and institutions by looking more deeply into the typical features of the institutional changes and their implications for socio-economic development. Institutional changes in skill formation in VET, HE and lifelong learning are explored by applying historical institutionalism approach and disclosing reasons, logic and implications of skill formation processes and institutions. There are also considered changes in the labour market and employment, educational access and distribution of learners, migration and social inequalities, using official statistical data. The analysis of social dialogue in relation to skill formation pays particular attention to its institutionalization, since the establishment of formal institutions occurred after the reconstitution of an independent state. The inadequacy of social dialogue is apparent in different iterations of the institutional development of the skill formation system. The development of the national system of qualifications is reviewed by focusing on the drivers and constraints on its implementation. The chapter concludes by outlining the main possibilities for future development of the skill formation system in Lithuania.

**Keywords:** Lithuania, migration, post-communist transition, qualifications, skill formation, vocational education and training

## Introduction

The institutional development of skill formation and deployment in Lithuania has not been widely researched. Existing literature sheds some light on the institutional settings and system of skill formation, but in a rather fragmented way. Martinaitis (2010) analysed the emergence of skill formation systems in eight Central and Eastern European (CEE) countries from the perspective of political economy. Laužackas (2005) explored the institutional reform of initial vocational education and training (VET) including curriculum design, the organization of training, and VET teachers' training. Tūtlys and Kaminskienė (2008) researched the institutionalization of social partnership in the award and accreditation of vocational qualifications in Lithuania. Others (Laužackas, Tūtlys & Spūdytė 2009; Le Deist & Tūtlys 2011; Nazelskis & Tūtlys 2013; Tūtlys & Spūdytė 2011) explored the institutional development of the national system of qualifications, including the design and implementation of the Lithuanian Qualifications Framework. Saniter and Tūtlys (2016) compared historical pathways of the development of initial VET in Lithuania and Germany, exploring the implications for policy learning. Institutional issues and challenges of competence-based reforms of the design of qualifications have been discussed (Spöttl & Tūtlys 2017; Tūtlys & Aarna 2017) as have the implications of policy learning in the initial Lithuanian VET reforms after 1990 (Tūtlys, Kaminskienė & Winterton 2016). Leišytė, Rose and Schimmelpfennig (2018) provided a comprehensive overview of the structural transformation of Lithuanian higher education (HE) since 1990, while Leišytė, Želvys and Zenkienė (2015) explored the implementation of the Bologna process.

Skill formation in Lithuania is predominantly described as neoliberal, characterised with radical and abrupt market-oriented reforms. This chapter seeks to explore the main particularities of the institutional settings of skill formation in the post-communist transition and why and how these particularities influence the present processes and institutions by looking more deeply into the typical features of the institutional changes and their implications for socio-economic development. In analysing institutional changes in skill formation in VET, HE and lifelong learning, we apply the approach of historical institutionalism, which focuses on reasons, logic and implications, taking a panoramic view of these processes. The overview is focused on changes in the labour market and employment, educational access and distribution of learners, migration and social inequalities, using official statistical data. The analysis of social dialogue in relation to skill formation focuses on its institutionalization, since the establishment of formal institutions occurred after the reconstitution of an independent state. The inadequacy of social dialogue is apparent in different iterations of the institutional development of the skill formation system. The development of the national system of qualifications is reviewed by focusing on the drivers and constraints on its implementation. The chapter concludes by outlining the main possibilities for future development of the skill formation system in Lithuania.

## Institutional change and development of skill formation in Lithuania

Post-communist transformation in Lithuania involved the reconstruction of state institutions (Norkus 2014) this being typical of Baltic states that had to establish new institutions of governance, legislation, political regulation and civic participation in various fields, including education and skill formation.

Starting the transition with privatisation, followed by macroeconomic stabilisation (e.g. introduction of national currency), exacerbated the deterioration of the macro-economic situation and held back the modernisation of the economy and human capital (Norkus 2014).

The application of a shock therapy approach to socio-economic reforms by focusing on their speedy implementation was typical for all Baltic states, where it was deemed necessary to abandon the Soviet legacy and adopt Western models for socio-economic development. As a result, the priority of policy making was directed to neoliberal reforms in many fields of society, including education and skill formation.

The abrupt character of the post-soviet reform of skill formation in Lithuania in 1990 and the accompanying radical institutional change was not conducive to the incremental development of original institutions of skill formation. The formal education system inherited from the Soviet period presented multiple challenges. The existence of a vast network of providers, the disinterest of young people in further education, and poor communication between educational institutions and stakeholders in an emerging market economy necessitated new solutions and measures (Dienys & Pusvaškis 1998).

Reforms to the system of skill formation in Lithuania were based on several key ideological approaches. A pivot towards market neoliberalism was typical of the socioeconomic and institutional transformations in many post-soviet CEE countries, but transformation in the Baltic countries was marked with a particular orientation towards catching up with developed Western economies (Gylys 2008). Another typical approach was bureaucratic and 'statist welfarism' based on the technocratic orientation of skill formation to maintain the inherited and formally reconstructed model of social welfare with the state playing a leading role. Finally, the concept of individualism, and 'forced' voluntarism gained momentum because social capital in society, and social dialogue over human capital formation were both underdeveloped.

## Institutional change and development of skill formation during the early post-communist transition 1990–2004

The establishment of institutions, legal regulation and diverging pathways of skill provision had a crucial role in the institutional change and development of initial VET, HE and lifelong learning in the early post-communist transition (Figure 2.1).

The institutional status-quo of VET provision in the initial period of post-communist transition was challenged both by the collapse of the Soviet dual VET

| | | | | | |
|---|---|---|---|---|---|
| **Initial VET** | **1990:** implementation of training programmes of 4 levels, transformation of technikums into higher vocational schools | **1993:** decentralisation of VET curriculum design, updating of curricula by VET schools | **1994:** initiation of EU support programme PHARE for restructuring and updating initial VET provision | **1997:** emergence of strategic policy of VET, acceptance of the VET law, initiation of competence-based VET standards, establishment of tripartite bodies | **2002:** delegation of assessment of competencies and award of qualifications to chambers of commerce, industry and crafts |
| **Higher education** | **1990-1991:** reform of HE degrees and qualifications, introduction of 3 cycles of HE degrees | **1996-1999:** implementation of HE reform supported by EU PHARE program: planning, management, quality assurance of studies | **2000-2001:** establishment of binary HE system by transforming higher VET schools into colleges | **2002 and later:** rapidly increasing enrolments in HE, domination of HE pathway in terms of enrolment over VET | |
| **Lifelong learning** | **1992:** establishment of the Lithuanian Association of Adult Education | **1993-1994:** establishment and development of employment training system with support from the EU PHARE programme | **1994-2004:** development of NGOs working in the field of adult education | | |
| **SOCIOECONOMIC DEVELOPMENT** | **1990-1999:** Institutionalization of state and society: establishment of state institutions, transition to market economy, privatization, economic crises and instability, decentralization of governance. | **2000-2004:** Economic stabilization, institutionalization of social partners and social dialogue, institutional restructuring in preparing for EU accession. | | | |

**Figure 2.1.** Institutional change and development of skill formation during early post-communist transition 1990–2004: critical junctures.

model, which had been based on close links between state enterprises and VET schools, and by the ambitions of the newly emerged state to create a demand-led VET system. In the Soviet period work-based training in state enterprises was an integral and important part of VET (VET students spent a significant part of their training in work-based learning at state enterprises), with big industrial factories often having their own training centres. This legacy was one of the reasons why the national education strategy of 1992 assumed that transformation towards a market economy would not be disruptive and private enterprises would work with reformed public VET schools by assuming responsibility for practical training (Laužackas 2005). Such expectations of policy makers were not realised, however, because of economic restructuring, the collapse of large Soviet style enterprises that constituted the core platform of vocational training, and the emergence of small and medium-sized business with totally different skills needs and capacities. Involving enterprises in new partnerships with VET schools was challenging due to the economic priority of survival in market conditions. The development of VET was also undermined by the persistence of negative perceptions of Soviet initial VET, which was designed to produce a low-skilled and loyal workforce (Laužackas 2005; Profesinio Mokymo Reformos Programos Koordinavimo Centras 1999).

Institutional changes in the field of VET during the initial transition period were driven by the Government's decentralisation of governance and introduction of autonomy for VET providers. The first steps in VET reform included abolishing the centralised enrolment of students, delegating curriculum design, developing training materials and organizing assessment to VET schools. In 1990 the structure and levels of qualifications were revised in line with labour market needs by introducing training programmes providing qualifications at four levels. Revision of initial VET provision under the EU support programme PHARE launched in 1994 established national registers of training and study programmes. Later smaller VET schools were consolidated into larger VET centres and a new legal framework for VET was established with the 1997 Law. In this period there was a strong tendency for local policy makers and VET providers to adopt or 'borrow' policy from elsewhere, leading to fragmentation in policies and methodical approaches. Different EU programmes and projects provided a basic source of 'know-how' for the reform of VET (Laužackas 2005; Profesinio Mokymo Reformos Programos Koordinavimo Centras 1999). Delegating autonomy to VET schools and teachers in curriculum design facilitated developing expertise of VET teachers, which was nurtured by participation in EU projects (Dienys and Pusvaškis 1998). Strategic documents from this period (*White Book on Vocational Education and Training* 1999) prioritised curriculum reform with the adoption of competence-based vocational education and training standards. This process, started in 1997, was coordinated by the newly established Centre for Methodology on Vocational Education and Training under the umbrella of the Ministry of Education and Science.

A school-based model of VET with fragmented movement towards the market model dominated in this period. Public VET schools and training centres provided theoretical training in the classroom and practical training in specially equipped workshops, with the final stage of training involving short internships in enterprises. The curriculum was oriented to completion of the whole training programme without interruption, facilitating acquisition of general vocational knowledge and transferable skills, with less emphasis being placed on specific vocational skills for workplaces. Increased employer dissatisfaction with the skills of VET graduate led to the growth of informal work-based training in enterprises. Another institutional particularity of VET provision which emerged during the initial stage of transformation was the creation of separate networks of initial and continuing VET providers. Initial school-based VET was regulated by the Ministry of Education and Science, whilst vocational training of the unemployed and job seekers was provided by labour market training centres and regulated by the Ministry of Social Affairs and Labour. There was significant overlapping of functions of these networks with obvious budgetary implications.

The initial period of post-communist VET reforms laid the foundations for government domination in institutional and procedural change, because of the need to address both the weak capacity and low levels of involvement of the social partners, especially trade unions. Indeed, development of social dialogue over VET was driven mostly by government even though national and sectoral tripartite bodies were established in 1997–1998 (Council of Vocational Education and Training, regional councils of VET, expert groups of the branches of economy involved in the design of the VET standards). In 2003, the assessment of competencies was delegated to the Chambers of Commerce, Industry and Crafts. However, the effectiveness of these structures was significantly undermined by low capacity and involvement of companies and trade unions at local and sectoral levels (Laužackas 2005; Tūtlys, Kaminskienė & Winterton 2016).

The institutional transformation of HE after the collapse of communism was driven by several factors. Firstly, there was a strong presence of academics drawn from 'revolutionary' social movements that had promoted societal change on the eve of the collapse of Soviet Union. These people formed a critical element within the first elected governance structures of the new independent state in 1990 which created space for political deliberation about change in higher education (Leišytė 2018). Secondly, there is a tradition of radical, though episodic, initiatives of institutional change in HE, such as the re-establishment of Vytautas Magnus University (originally established in 1919 after the creation of the first independent state of Lithuania and closed under Soviet rule in 1950) in 1989 with the support of *émigrées* from the USA, who brought ideas from the American academic system and an *artes liberales* model of higher education studies (Leišytė 2018). The government of the re-established state prioritised HE reform, issuing key legal acts early in 1991 (Law on Education and Law on Higher Education and Science) creating legal preconditions for future institutional reform and entrenching principles of autonomy of universities and academic staff. The reform of HE has also been strongly influenced by the hidden agendas of HE providers. For example, at the initial stage of post-communist transition many HE institutions assumed the formal status of universities without launching any qualitative restructuring of teaching or research (Pilietinės visuomenės institutas 2007).

One of the key goals of HE reform was the decentralisation and liberalisation of provision via improving access, and quality in terms of alignment with labour market needs and improvements in teaching standards. The slow growth of private universities was a result of strong opposition and lobbying from public universities (Leišytė 2018). An important institutional change in the early 2000s was the transformation of former higher vocational schools (established in 1990 by transforming former soviet *technikums*) into colleges or universities of applied sciences. The goal of this reform was to improve access to specialised HE to support regional economic development. Universities expected these new institutions to develop human capital for the regions, while universities would remain national providers of high skills and academic knowledge in the bigger cities (Kaminskas 2019). However, such expectations were never realised and today the strongest colleges also operate in the bigger cities, whereas regional colleges face serious problems with student enrolment (Kaminskas 2019).

The expansion of HE has perhaps been the most notable and durable feature of the initial period of post-communist transformation in HE and has led to increasing student enrolments and the domination of the HE pathway in learner choices. This trend had negative consequences: HE quality has declined, and graduate over-qualification has been a problematic symptom of the orientation of students towards formal degrees and diploma rather than to knowledge and skills ('diploma disease'). One of the most widespread criticisms of the HE system at the beginning of the 21st century has been its emphasis on quantitative rather than qualitative parameters (Pilietinės visuomenės institutas 2007). Other criticisms related to the imbalance between HE and VET enrolments driven by the poor image of VET. These concerns became important factors driving the establishment of the binary HE system mentioned above and the introduction of universities of applied sciences in 2001.

The state, and academic oligarchy played a leading role in HE reforms in the 1990s and 2000s (Leišytė 2018). This was an important factor for the development of the autonomy of universities with respect to the organization of studies and research, but also contributed to distancing universities from the needs of society and business, and a stagnation in quality (Pilietinės visuomenės institutas 2007). As with VET, the state had to assume key responsibilities for HE governance and institutional development because of the low level of involvement of social stakeholders and the absence of social dialogue. The state assumed key responsibilities in monitoring and control of HE quality through bureaucratic and procedural control (Dobbins and Leišytė 2014), which provoked tensions and power struggles between the Government and academic elite. In 1995 the Centre for Quality Assessment in Higher Education was established by the Ministry of Education and Science as an independent public agency responsible for the external quality assurance policy in HE, and for enabling conditions for free movement of students.

Institutional development of *adult education* after the restitution of the independent state left adult education to private providers and social partners who viewed adult education as market oriented and consumerist. Formal bureaucratic institutional changes were based on the Soviet institutional legacy, but many institutions of adult vocational training established in the Soviet era were closed. After privatisation, labour market training centres for the unemployed were established, coordinated by the Labour Market Training Authority established in 1992 (Profesinio Mokymo Reformos Programos Koordinavimo Centras 1999). Adult education was peripheral to the attention of policy makers, who focussed on HE and general education as strategic to the formation of human capital. The absence of government interest in adult education resulted in its development being left to voluntarist initiatives of NGOs like the Lithuanian Association of Adult Education established in 1992. The weak representation of adult education in national policy making during this period led to comparatively slow institutionalization of processes such as the professionalization of adult education providers, the development of qualifications for adult educators and the institutionalization of their training (Gedvilienė et al. 2018).

## Institutional change and development of skill formation after accession to EU 2004–2019

The accession of Lithuania to the EU in 2004 was marked by a shift towards lifelong learning within initial VET and adult education, as well as the systemisation and integration of skill formation pathways through reforms of qualifications and curricula which were launched at this time (Figure 2.2).

| | | | | | |
|---|---|---|---|---|---|
| **Initial VET** | **2007:** new law on VET-apprenticeships, national system of qualifications, opening VET providers for external stakeholders | **2007-2008:** revision and updating of of VET standards | **2012:** launching of competence-based curriculum reform with national modular VET curricula | **2013-2015:** introduction of sectoral practical training centres | **2017:** new law on VET - implementation of dual VET, VET schools as public legal entities, centralized planning of VET enrolments |
| **Higher education** | **2006-2009:** neoliberal reform of HE funding, introduction of voucher system and study loans; market orientation of HE | **2011-2014:** implementation of Bologna reform of HE curricula by introducing learning outcomes and ECTS | **2016-2019:** partially implemented optimization of network of HE providers by "merging" universities | | |
| **Lifelong learning and national system of qualifications** | **2006-2008:** implementation of projects for design of the national system of qualifications and NQF | **2010-2012:** approval of the Lithuanian Qualifications Framework by the Government and referencing to the EQF | **2013-2021:** design and implementation of occupational standards | **2018:** law on informal and continuing adult education | |
| **SOCIOECONOMIC DEVELOPMENT** | **2004-2008:** accession to the EU and post-accession reforms, EU structural funds and policy learning | **2009-2013:** impact of global economic crises - rising unemployment and emigration | **2013-2016:** economic recovery, strengthening Euro-integration (introduction of Euro in 2015) | **2016-2019:** neoliberal-developmental socioeconomic reforms, introduction of new liberal labour code | |

**Figure 2.2.** Institutional change and development of skill formation after the accession to EU 2004–2019: critical junctures.

The influence of the EU strengthened the legitimacy of VET among policy makers and social partners, because this played a major role in EU socio-economic strategies as well as in the national skill formation strategies of leading EU economies, such as Germany, France, the Netherlands and Austria. The orientation of VET reforms to EU agendas (Lisbon Strategy and Copenhagen Process) made the VET system more open and initiated systemic strategic reform in developing the national system of qualifications. The lack of entrenched interests and institutional strategies among VET providers, social partners and government created *tabula rasa* conditions for implementing VET reforms under the Copenhagen Process. However, the implementation of strategic instruments and measures created by these reforms (NQFs, competence-based qualifications and their systems, ECVET, quality assurance instruments) required strong and sustainable institutional capacities that were largely missing in the VET system, and it was hoped that this problem would be solved by 'EU support' (Profesinio Mokymo Reformos Programos Koordinavimo Centras 1999).

EU integration strengthened the role and importance of government and its agencies in VET policy making via EU projects, such as development of the national system of qualifications, the implementation of ECVET, and the institutional integration of initial VET and labour market training. The implementation of these projects also provided impetus and resources for the 'activation' of social partners in VET policies, enhancing the delegation of responsibilities to stakeholders and strengthening their potential, a trend that became more visible after the economic crisis. However, the institutionalization of social dialogue in VET was predominantly top-down. For example, in 2013 tripartite sectoral professional committees were established with responsibility for approving standards and referencing qualifications to the Lithuanian Qualifications Framework. These new institutions were expected to combine central state regulation with delegated responsibility to sectoral stakeholders to meet sector needs. Management of the design of competence-based occupational standards at sector level was also delegated to national employers' organizations. However, serious gaps in capacity resulted from the fact that these new formal institutional structures were established more quickly than the attitudes, knowledge and commitment of key actors within the system changed (Saniter & Tūtlys 2016).

The lasting institutional legacy of EU integration for VET reform includes strong government support for reform, the utilisation of EU support for capacity building within VET providers and stakeholders, and the strategic character of underpinning instruments and measures. For example, VET reforms implemented after EU accession were strongly directed to developing lifelong learning pathways and making VET an integral part of the national system of qualifications. The weakness was evident in 'bottom-up' engagement of stakeholders and initiatives of VET providers. EU structural support also provided mainly short-term incentives for enterprises to provide continuing vocational training of employees, but the potential to sustain these initiatives after EU funding is doubtful.

The global economic crisis of 2007–2008 significantly increased unemployment (Statistics Lithuania 2010). One of the most significant external factors influencing subsequent institutional development of VET provision was significantly increased emigration and commensurate growing skills shortage. The demographic crisis, skills shortages and challenges relating to future competitiveness increased interest in VET provision and the new 2017 Law on VET enabled enterprises to become real stakeholders within VET centres and strengthened the institutionalization of dual apprenticeship as an alternative pathway.

EU accession coincided with the liberalisation and market orientation of HE, and structural reform led by right-wing political powers in 2006 were similarly directed towards liberalisation. It was argued that reform was necessary to prevent a downward spiral of under-funding, inefficient use of resources, decreasing quality of studies, and mismatch between supply and demand (Pilietinės visuomenės institutas 2007). The right-wing political parties in power in this period believed the solution to these problems lay with implementing neoliberal market-oriented reforms through the introduction of changes to the HE funding regime in 2009, revoking universally state funded undergraduate studies and introducing the principle of 'money follows the student' (voucher system) to enhance competition between universities.

Accession to the EU also brought the financial support of EU structural funds alongside access to know-how and policy learning, which led to more strategic monitoring and further development of the HE system. The Research and Higher Education Monitoring and Analysis Centre (MOSTA) was established in 2006. It enabled systemic accumulation and analysis of the data on HE and provided an important lever for the Ministry of Education and Science in implementing HE reforms. For example, in implementing the agenda of optimisation of HE institutions in 2016–2020 the Ministry used this lever to 'press' HE institutions towards mergers. The implementation of the EU agenda (Bologna Process) in HE was strongly driven by eagerness to strengthen the legitimacy and status of universities both nationally and more broadly in the EU, in the context both of increasing competition and decreasing enrolment of students (Leisytė, Želvys & Zenkienė 2014).

The implementation of the Bologna reform in HE with the introduction of ECTS, meant study programmes were adjusted in line with learning outcomes and Dublin descriptors, and instruments of quality assurance and institutional accreditation were introduced to improve the status and image of HE establishments. The implementation of this reform was led by the leading (biggest) universities (for example, the implementation of the ESF funded project on the introduction of the ECTS credits and related transformation of the

HE curricula was led by Vilnius University), and coordinated by the Centre for Quality Assurance of Higher Education. Such reforms did not lead to significant change because compliance was mostly formal and symbolic and decoupled from implementation in study programmes (Leisyte, Želvys & Zenkienė 2014). EU membership and the accompanying implementation of EU priorities with respect to HE reform did little to change the status and power relationships of policy makers and stakeholders, or the political-ideological orientation of institutional development in HE. For example, academic universities imposed their agenda in implementing degrees and qualifications, and maintained their monopoly over master degree studies (Leisyte, Želvys & Zenkienė 2014).

In 2016 new developmentally oriented institutional reform within HE focused on capacity building and quality improvement within institutions, but top-down reform was focused mainly on optimising the network of public HE providers and largely ignored the quality of curricula and study processes. This reform faced significant resistance from universities, which impeded its implementation.

European integration enhanced the development of more open types of *adult educational provision*; integrating different types of education and providing more flexible education services. ESF funded projects in continuing vocational training in enterprises proved important in the aftermath of the economic crisis, as this provided the impetus for enterprises to initiate continuing training projects, which strengthened their power in defining training needs and contents. The needs of employees as learners received little consideration because of the weakness of the trade unions.

With little national regulation of adult education, agreements between stakeholders and providers resulted in the fragmentation of provision. The Law on Non-formal Adult Education and Continuing Training came into force on 1 January 2015, establishing a mixed institutional model for provision, combining regulation with an attempt to involve stakeholders through multipartite collegial advisory bodies.

European integration also increased the salience of the recognition of informal and non-formal learning, but this was limited to conceptual papers and declarations. The formalisation of this issue was slow and inconsistent due to the absence of political strategy and underdeveloped infrastructure. Formalisation was shaped in a fragmented way mainly by the implementation of international and ESF funded projects.

Between 2004 and 2012 it was anticipated that the initial evaluation of experientially acquired competencies would be delegated to public VET providers and funded by the EU. There were also plans for a system to formalise experientially acquired competencies in HE institutions. The Action Plan for the Development of Non-formal Adult Education for 2014–2016 stated that the system of validation of acquired competencies had been established in HE institutions and 33 HE institutions were prepared to provide the service of validation. The Ministry of Education and Science took overall responsibility for governance of the system of assessment and recognition. The institutional model developed for the assessment and recognition of informal and non-formal learning combined decentralised implementation via autonomous assessment bodies with centralised regulation via the national accreditation of those bodies. However, this approach, combined with the fragmented nature of social partner involvement, resulted in there being little awareness of the potential value of a validation system, and little motivation among individuals to gain recognition for non-formal experiences. Additionally, there was little interest among employers formally to certify employee competencies acquired via experiential routes. Despite the important impact of EU policies for designing the open system of validation, in Lithuania, this is far from inclusive, as limited access is available to applicants from other countries, including immigrants and refugees. The internationalisation of this system is one of priorities for future institutional development, which is also driven by economic interests, such as attracting skilled workers from the third countries.

## The implications of skill formation institutions for economic growth and social development

Existing statistical data permit limited inferences on the impact of skill formation and deployment on economic growth and social cohesion in Lithuania However, there are interesting parallels between institutional developments of skill formation and deployment and the indicators of socio-economic development. Labour market indicators show declining employment and growing unemployment up to 2010 resulting from profound economic restructuring, the Russian economic crisis of 1990–2000 and the global crisis that began in 2007.

One of the most significant aspects of labour market restructuring during the first decade of post-Soviet transition was the shift in employment from the public to the private sector, with the private sector accounting for 68.2 per cent of jobs in 1999, rising from just 10 per cent in 1990 (Statistics Lithuania 2019). Decreasing employment and increasing unemployment in the first and second decades of transformation influenced the prioritisation of continuing VET policies to facilitate labour market re-integration of the unemployed, while initial VET facilitated youth employment in the regions. The growth in private sector employment was not accompanied with an improvement in employment quality

**Table 2.1.** Employed and employment rate by education 1997–2017

| Years | Employed by education, thousands | | | | |
|---|---|---|---|---|---|
| | Basic without VET | Basic with VET | Secondary without VET | Secondary with VET | Higher education |
| 1997 | 149.1 | 62.7 | 375.8 | 194.3 | 314.3 |
| 1999 | 131.8 | 83.2 | 334.0 | 269.7 | 323.4 |
| 2004 | 123.1 | 53.8 | 288.2 | 389.5 | 312.8 |
| Years | Employment rate by education, % | | | | |
| | Low: primary, general lower secondary | | Medium: VET, lower and upper secondary | | High: advanced VET (colleges) and higher education (universities) |
| 2005 | 25.7 | | 67.2 | | 86.2 |
| 2010 | 14.0 | | 57.5 | | 85.3 |
| 2017 | 20.9 | | 68.8 | | 90.0 |

*Note.* Statistics Lithuania, http://www.stat.gov.lt.

or the development of skill formation policies at enterprise level. However, some recent research shows that liberalisation and technological advancement led to a decline in the ratio of high to low-skilled workforce in the manufacturing sector in the first decade of the 21st century. This is explained with reference to the low level of FDI during and after the post-communist transition (Christenko et al. 2020).

Statistical data on employment by education level evidence changes in demand both for skills and credentials (Table 2.1).

Prior to EU accession, demand for low-skilled labour decreased except for the period 1997–1999. From the turn of the century, there was a significant increase in demand for workers with secondary education and VET and HE qualifications, as a result both of economic recovery and stabilisation, and the development of the service sector and industries requiring intermediate skills fostered by the trend towards international subcontracting. The growing demand for workers with VET qualifications evidences the development of medium and low value-added sectors in this period, as well as the increasing potential of VET providers to satisfy labour demand in quantitative terms. After EU accession, labour demand did not change significantly, but there was a growing supply of employees with HE qualifications, which increased over-qualification and created competition between HE and VET graduates in the labour market.

**Table 2.2.** Unemployed by education and unemployment rate by education 1997–2017

| **Years** | **Unemployed by education, thousands** | | | | |
|---|---|---|---|---|---|
| | **Basic without VET** | **Basic with VET** | **Secondary without VET** | **Secondary with VET** | **Higher education** |
| 1997 | 41.9 | 16.9 | 74.6 | 39.7 | 16.9 |
| 1999 | 34.9 | 22.9 | 65.1 | 59.9 | 20.7 |
| 2004 | 23.9 | 7.6 | 49.4 | 48.6 | 19.6 |
| Years | Unemployment rate by education, % | | | | |
| | Low: primary, general lower secondary | | Medium: VET, lower and upper secondary | | High: advanced VET (colleges) and higher education (universities) |
| 2005 | 14.4 | | 9.5 | | 4.0 |
| 2010 | 39.3 | | 21.8 | | 7.6 |
| 2017 | 20.4 | | 9.3 | | 2.9 |

*Note.* Statistics Lithuania, http://www.stat.gov.lt.

Increasing unemployment amongst workers with VET qualifications in the period before EU accession demonstrates the growing skill mismatches of VET graduates in this period, which is explained by the comparatively late launch of competence-based curricula reform (1997–1998) and the low level of cooperation between enterprises and public VET providers (Table 2.2).

Changes in the distribution of learners in VET and HE establishments was also influenced by institutional changes in skill formation and deployment (Table 2.3).

Firstly, the increasing number of enrolments were significantly higher for HE (especially the universities) than for VET. The comparatively poor image of VET since 1990, coupled with massive HE expansion accounts for this. Demographic change, alongside the above-mentioned HE funding reform implemented in 2009, which reduced the role of entrance requirements to HE studies by focusing on students' fees, alleviated this problem. Furthermore, emigration provided an alternative pathway for both over-qualified and unemployed youth, whilst also increasing the attractiveness of VET programmes because they facilitated greater employability in destination countries.

The aftermath of the economic crisis was accompanied by relatively low rates of investment in skill formation by individuals, stakeholders and the state. Furthermore, levels of participation among men and rural dwellers were significantly lower than among women and urbanites (Table 2.4).

**Table 2.3.** Distribution of learners in VET and HE establishments 1990–2020

| Years | Students in VET, thous. | Admitted students in VET, thous. | VET graduates thous. | Students in higher vocational schools and colleges thous. | Admitted students in higher vocational schools and colleges, thous. | Graduates of colleges, thous. | Students in universities, thous. | Admitted students in universities, thous. | Graduates of universities, thous. |
|---|---|---|---|---|---|---|---|---|---|
| 1990 | 47.4 | 21.2 | 23.2 | 46.4 | 11.5 | 14.95 | 67.3 | 9.8 | 9.47 |
| 1995 | 49.2 | 19.4 | 12.3 | 24.2 | 8.8 | 6.76 | 54.0 | 19.2 | 12.37 |
| 1999 | 52 | 15.5 | 14.6 | 38.4 | 10.3 | 6.97 | 84.3 | 23.7 | 14.89 |
| 2004 | 46.3 | 21.0 | 12.6 | 52.2 | 23.9 | 8.8 | 138.5 | 42.7 | 24.01 |
| 2010 | 49.5 | 22.2 | 13.9 | 53.3 | 15.96 | 12.67 | 133.56 | 33.39 | 32.33 |
| 2015 | 46.5 | 23.7 | 15.3 | 39.77 | 13.26 | 8.89 | 93.52 | 27.06 | 22.58 |
| 2017 | 42.1 | 19.9 | 16.1 | 35.43 | 11.99 | 8.31 | 82.34 | 22.7 | 19.32 |
| 2019–2020 | 27.8 | 12.9 | 12.1 | 32.93 | 10.66 | 7.438 | 73.01 | 21.43 | 17.36 |

*Note*. Statistics Lithuania, http://www.stat.gov.lt.

**Table 2.4.** Lifelong learning rate (of the population aged 25–64) 2013–2020

| ; | | Lifelong learning rate (of the population aged 25–64) \| per cent | | | | | |
|---|---|---|---|---|---|---|---|
| | | **2013** | **2014** | **2015** | **2016** | **2017** | **2020** |
| Males and females | Urban and rural areas | 5.9 | 5.1 | 5.8 | 6.0 | 5.9 | 7.2 |
| | Urban areas | 7.1 | 6.4 | 7.1 | 7.0 | 7.1 | 8.2 |
| | Rural areas | 3.1 | 2.4 | 3.0 | 3.7 | 3.4 | 4.9 |
| Males | Urban and rural areas | 5.2 | 4.6 | 5.1 | 5.1 | 4.4 | 5.6 |
| | Urban areas | 6.7 | 6.1 | 6.6 | 6.3 | 5.6 | 6.9 |
| | Rural areas | 2.3 | 1.9 | 2.2 | 2.9 | 2.3 | 3.1 |
| Females | Urban and rural areas | 6.5 | 5.6 | 6.5 | 6.8 | 7.3 | 8.7 |
| | Urban areas | 7.5 | 6.6 | 7.5 | 7.6 | 8.4 | 9.5 |
| | Rural areas | 3.9 | 3.0 | 4.0 | 4.7 | 4.6 | 7.0 |

*Note*. Statistics Lithuania, http://www.stat.gov.lt.

**Table 2.5.** Investment of companies in the continuing vocational training 2010–2015.

| Year | 2010 | 2015 |
|---|---|---|
| Working time spent in vocational training courses \| h | 34.0 | 19.0 |
| Employed persons participating in vocational training courses \| per cent | 18.6 | 25.6 |
| Enterprises organising continuing vocational training \| per cent | 51.9 | 61.6 |
| Expenditure of enterprises on vocational training courses \| EUR | 252.0 | 261.0 |

*Note.* Statistics Lithuania, http://www.stat.gov.lt.

This reflected unequal socio-economic development in the regions (polarisation between bigger cities and rural areas), necessitating policy solutions relating to the provision and accessibility of lifelong learning opportunities.

Official statistics show an increase in employee participation in continuing VET, alongside an increase in enterprises providing and spending more on continuing training (Table 2.5) following the economic crisis.

At the same time, the time employees spent in training during working hours decreased, probably because of changes in ESF funding mechanisms in 2013–2015.

## Skill formation and migration

Migration adds an additional layer of complexity to analyses of the socio-economic implications of institutional development of skill formation in Lithuania, not least because it is difficult to establish the direction of causality between skill formation and emigration. Official statistics show that emigration from Lithuania has been constant since the mid-2000s (Figure 2.3), although numbers have fluctuated, decreasing at the peak of economic growth in 2006 and dramatically increasing in the years immediately after the economic crisis.

The impact of emigration on the social and economic development of Lithuania has caused increasing concern, provoking discussion about the loss of human capital ('brain drain') and attempts to encourage repatriation (Barcevičius & Gineikytė 2015; Barcevičius & Žvalionytė 2012). The main factors driving emigration since 2000 have been structural unemployment, skills mismatches, low wages, and over-qualification. Many experts and social partners argue that emigration acted as a safety valve in periods of economic crisis, but this positive impact of emigration has been far outweighed by the negative influence of emigration in terms of the loss of human capital and a lessening of social pressure for improvements in welfare and labour relations. In this way emigration

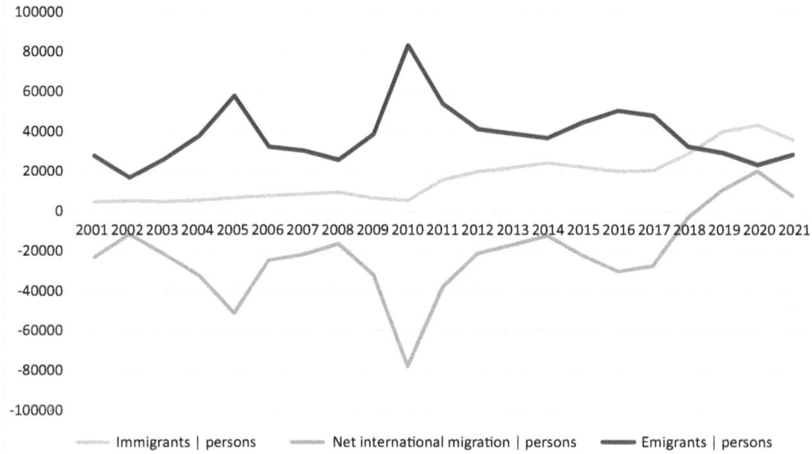


| | | | |
|---|---|---|---|
| 2001 | 4694 | -23147 | 27841 |
| 2002 | 5110 | -11609 | 16719 |
| 2003 | 4728 | -21555 | 26283 |
| 2004 | 5553 | -32138 | 37691 |
| 2005 | 6789 | -51096 | 57885 |
| 2006 | 7745 | -24645 | 32390 |
| 2007 | 8609 | -21774 | 30383 |
| 2008 | 9297 | -16453 | 25750 |
| 2009 | 6487 | -32013 | 38500 |
| 2010 | 5213 | -77944 | 83157 |
| 2011 | 15685 | -38178 | 53863 |
| 2012 | 19843 | -21257 | 41100 |
| 2013 | 22011 | -16807 | 38818 |
| 2014 | 24294 | -12327 | 36621 |
| 2015 | 22130 | -22403 | 44533 |
| 2016 | 20162 | -30171 | 50333 |
| 2017 | 20368 | -27557 | 47925 |
| 2018 | 28914 | -3292 | 32206 |
| 2019 | 40067 | 10794 | 29273 |
| 2020 | 43096 | 19993 | 23103 |
| 2021 | 35889 | 7544 | 28345 |

**Figure 2.3.** Emigration and immigration flows in Lithuania in the period 2003–2020. Source: Statistics Lithuania, http://www.stat.gov.lt.

indirectly sustained the neoliberal pathway of development with the domination of employers and fragmentation of social dialogue over skill and employment. Inadequate industrial development policy at national and sectoral levels encouraged enterprises to compete on price and reduce specialisation. It also reduced the scope for technological and organizational innovation, reduced demand for high skills and made many sectors less attractive for young people.

Emigration was the primary reason for skills shortages both soon after EU accession and during recovery from the global economic crisis. Skills shortages were especially evident in construction in 2001–2007, and in transport, industrial production and engineering during the recovery. International subcontracting in such sectors as engineering increased the proportion of jobs requiring vocational skills and qualifications, at the same time as highly skilled human capital was being lost because of the brain drain. The response of large industrial enterprises to skills shortages focussed on the recruitment of workers from 'third' countries (particularly Ukraine and other former Soviet republics) and on retention strategies built upon improving wages and working conditions.

In some sectors skills shortages in the aftermath of crisis were solved via the recruitment of skilled workers displaced by enterprises that had closed (construction sector). Skills shortages caused by emigration provided an impetus to employers (especially from the industrial sectors and construction) to engage in skill formation through the public education sector, and by initiatives like dual apprenticeship and work-based learning. Employers' organizations started to promote collective skill formation, strengthening social dialogue and supporting sector collective agreements.

Emigration peaked in 2016, when 50,033 left Lithuania, declining to 29,273 in 2019, with net migration ultimately changing from negative (-30,171 in 2016) to positive (10,794 in 2019) (Statistics Lithuania, http://www.stat.gov.lt). The repatriation of Lithuanians was driven both by the improving internal economic situation and by major political changes abroad, notably the 2016 Brexit vote, the 2014 revolution in Ukraine and the uprising, and subsequent repression in Belarus. Such developments necessitated adjustments to the system of skill formation, to make it more accessible and increase its impact on the quality and attractiveness of jobs. Yet a slacker labour market also reduced pressure on employers to attract and retain workers, and to invest in their skills.

## Social dialogue over skill formation and deployment

The introduction of institutional changes in social dialogue, and the implications of this for the reform of skill formation and deployment in Lithuania exemplifies the challenges facing post-communist transition countries. A major challenge relates to the implementation of ambitious reforms regarding skill formation under conditions of under-developed social dialogue and weak social partner institutions (especially trade unions). Such a situation leaves government as the main initiator and executor of reform, with the involvement of social partners in social dialogue over skills and qualifications being imbalanced due to unequal levels of power and influence. Because trade unions lack representative power and capacity, their capability to defend employee interests in relation to skills and qualifications has been minimal, leading to their piecemeal involvement in reforms. As a result, government and education and training providers have assumed more responsibility for defending the interests of employees and apprentices which further increases the power of centralised institutions.

The evolution of social dialogue in Lithuania has been marked with abrupt institutional changes and shifts between different patterns of skill formation. The post-communist transition necessitated constructing a new institutional model of social dialogue. In the Soviet centrally-planned economy real social dialogue based on representing the interests of different stakeholders was impossible because all 'social partners' were strictly subjugated to the totalitarian regime and had no independent power. Furthermore, trade unions lost credibility after the collapse of the Soviet system because of their role as partners of the regime, and became objects of 'de-Sovietization' policies, which often meant they were excluded from decision making over socio-economic development (Gruževskis & Blažienė 2005).

In the initial stage of post-communist transition, decentralisation and the introduction of market economy principles was driven by government without the active involvement of social partners who lacked social legitimacy (Lafoucriere & Magnusson 2005, 16). Low levels of trade union representation and coverage of collective agreements meant employers were able to determine the agenda of tripartite agreements in various fields, including skill formation (Gruževskis & Blažienė 2005). Such imbalance in social dialogue and the domination of neoliberal approaches was considered a normal feature of a 'young' market economy focused on capital accumulation (Pilietinės visuomenės institutas 2007).

Formal social dialogue over skill formation necessitated independent employers' organizations and trade unions. While employers' organizations emerged as completely new institutions, some independent trade unions developed out of former Soviet era unions. The government abolished all previous centralised mechanisms of trade union recruitment, which were regarded as limiting freedom of choice. However, these changes significantly reduced the membership and institutional power of trade unions (Lazutka 2013), particularly in the context of socio-economic crisis. This period also saw the establishment of new employer organizations, such as Chambers of Commerce, Industry and Crafts. Many of these developments resulted from the adoption (often rather uncritically) of models from other countries, notably Germany and the Nordic countries.

One of the most significant institutional changes of the first decade of the independent state was the establishment of tripartite social partnership structures at national level. Such tripartite structures were also established in the field of initial VET both at regional and national levels. However, these bodies were mainly advisory and did not acquire a more significant policy-making role.

The beginning of the 2000s was marked by strengthening, consolidating and restructuring social partner organizations. The establishment and development of national level organizations like the Confederation of Industrialists of Lithuania (established 1989–1993) and the Confederation of Trade Unions (established in 2002) reinforced important changes in the system of skill formation, especially in initial VET and HE. Initial VET standards were designed with the involvement of social partners, as was the development of the system of assessment of competences in initial VET and the introduction of higher vocational studies in the HE system.

The development of national skill formation and lifelong learning policies in the period after EU accession was characterised by ambitious policy initiatives which required the expertise of stakeholders, especially employers, trade unions and professional organizations. New tripartite institutions of social dialogue were established by the skill formation reforms after the economic crisis, including national level sectoral professional committees. At the same time, the implementation of these policy measures faced challenges due to a demographic and labour force crisis caused by emigration, and the absence of civil society structures.

The economic crisis of 2008–2009 and its aftermath strengthened the orientation of skill formation policies to economic development needs, which implied a stronger implementation role for employers. Employers' organizations and enterprises played an active role in developing qualifications with VET providers and representatives of HE institutions, while the trade unions were largely absent from these processes (Tūtlys & Spöttl 2017).

An important turn in the development of social dialogue in the aftermath of the crisis was the introduction of the new Labour Code in 2017, which aimed to make employment conditions more flexible to raise competitiveness and attract investors. This Labour Code also introduced new forms of employment contracts, including apprenticeship contracts, project work contracts and temporary employment contracts. Apprenticeship contracts increased from 156 in 2017–2018 to over 300 in 2018–2019 (Ministry of Social Affairs and Labour 2019). The new Law on Employment sought to encourage graduates, job seekers and employees to invest in their own human capital by introducing wage differentials based on qualification, as well as supportive measures, such as introducing voluntary (unpaid) work with practical training and state financial support, work-based learning through apprenticeship contracts with enterprises, and the recognition of previously acquired skills and competencies. Employers still considered these measures to be inadequate to motivate them to engage more in skill formation in the conditions of highly fluid labour markets and intensive migration of skilled workers, while trade unions criticised the introduction of new forms of employment contracts without legal protections because of their potential for misuse by employers.

## Skill formation and development of the national system of qualifications

The reform of the national system of qualifications between 2006 and 2008 started as an attempt to modernise and update the skill formation system to ensure the competitiveness of human capital and solve socio-economic challenges such as structural unemployment, skill mismatches and (later) emigration. The hopes and expectations of different stakeholders involved in the development of the national system of qualifications were directed at systemising a fragmented skill formation process (Tūtlys & Spūdytė 2011). One contradiction in these reforms was caused by the co-existence of 'wild capitalism' in economic relations with robust state regulation in skill formation (Tūtlys & Aarna 2017). Another contradiction came from the far reaching idealistic ambitions of the architects of reform and actual institutional capacity to implement change. The reform of qualifications was highly ambitious, tackling the goals of communication (making systems clearer and transparent), reforming the system by enhancing the quality of provision and filling gaps that emerged during the post-communist transition (e.g. absence of provision of 'level 5' qualifications and professional qualifications at higher levels), as well as transforming existing qualifications by introducing a new competence-based approach and strengthening the sectoral dimension in the design of qualifications (Tūtlys & Aarna 2017; Tūtlys & Spöttl 2017; Tūtlys & Spūdytė 2011). The Qualifications Framework introduced in 2010 has not solved the key problems of a lack of transparency in qualifications, overlapping of the content of degrees and qualifications offered by the universities and the universities of applied sciences, or the absence of the LTQF/EQF level 5 qualifications demanded by different sectors. However, the implementation of LTQF and occupational standards since 2013 brought about more active involvement of employers and their organizations in this process and facilitated the development of sectoral approaches to qualifications. For example, stakeholders in the construction sector succeeded in developing their own sectoral qualifications framework with internal mechanisms for the recognition of qualifications (introduction of so called 'card of builder-constructor'). Tensions between sectoral stakeholders and national institutions, however, prevented national recognition of the construction sector qualifications framework, and the energy production and distribution, and ICT sectors have faced similar difficulties.

The design and development of sector-oriented occupational standards via the application of work-process analysis increased employer interest and awareness in the development of qualifications (Tūtlys & Spöttl 2017). However, employer involvement in the development of occupational standards has been variable. In some sectors the main motivation was to create a strategic reference instrument for planning, preparation and development of human capital in the sector (ICT, construction, engineering industry). In other sectors employers' organizations and stakeholders were more actively involved as providers of information on the requirements of work-processes and skills needs (Tūtlys & Spöttl 2017). The limited involvement of trade unions and professional organizations in the design and implementation of qualifications is worrying. It creates challenges in awarding professional qualifications referenced to the 6–8 levels of the NQF, where strong involvement of professional organizations is essential. Currently academic degrees serve as proxies and replacements for these qualifications. Yet, government and universities lack expertise and understanding of the economic sectors needed to push the institutionalization of awarding these professional qualifications, while few sectoral employers' organizations have clear strategic interests in this field (with the notable exceptions of ICT, engineering and construction).

## Future issues in skill formation and deployment

Future scenarios for institutional development and their likelihood of realisation are highly dependent on how such issues are framed within public debates. Therefore, this chapter will refrain from proposing hypothetical futures based on scientific political-economic insights and theories, and will instead describe three main scenarios for skill formation in Lithuania, which can be identified within current debates involving policy makers, stakeholders and educational institutions.

## Neoliberal breakthrough scenario

The primary imperative for skill formation and deployment in the *neoliberal breakthrough scenario* is economic competitiveness, which would be achieved through several mechanisms:

1. A specialised focus on developing the most competitive sectors of economy, generating highest added value by becoming flagships of this process (today the examples of such sectors are high-tech sectors, such as biotechnology, laser technologies and fintech). This approach dovetails with the concept of clusters in economic development, and consequently, in skill formation and deployment.
2. Aligning skill formation and development with the specific needs of leading sectors and enterprises.
3. Concentrating skill formation and development processes within the private sector, giving this sector responsibility for key decisions in the processes of skill formation and deployment. This scenario also implies giving business more capacity to shape the personal values that facilitate learning among young people.

In this scenario, VET provision is viewed as predominantly work-based with apprenticeships in enterprises becoming the dominant pathway. Public VET providers are privatized, and priority is given to flexible, modular and competence-based curricula. HE is also viewed as a strategic source of human capital development and networks of partnership between universities and business based on shared interests in R&D (involvement of HE establishments in clusters, 'valleys', etc.) are encouraged. The role of the state becomes limited to coordinating initiatives relating to skill formation put forward by different stakeholders, monitoring labour market skills needs, and ensuring the effective distribution and provision of public funding. This scenario is supported and promoted by representatives of leading business enterprises and sectors, as well as by right-wing politicians. It is regarded by its proponents as the only sound alternative for future development of skill formation given the socio-demographic challenges (depopulation, ageing society, migration) facing Lithuania, and the requirements of technological development (digitalisation, the Fourth Industrial Revolution).

## Decline of skill formation system serving global value chains

This pessimistic scenario is presented by the proponents of the neoliberal approach as the likely consequence if policy makers and stakeholders fail to implement further neo-liberal reform, leading to the decay and erosion of existing institutions and processes of skill formation. The school-based VET system and HE would both be eroded by demographic decline, low economic performance, low quality, the dissatisfaction of learners, students and society, inefficient management, and so on. It would result in growing skills mismatches and over-qualification. Slow economic development and economic decline is defined by the low-skill equilibrium resulting in a low- and middle-income trap. In this scenario demographic trends and continued emigration would create an existential threat the sustainability of the nation and national identity.

### Holistic skill formation scenario oriented to development of new welfare state

This scenario has been attracting increasing attention from policy makers, education and training providers and civil society. It promotes the idea of a new welfare state as a viable alternative to the current neoliberal approach to socio-economic development. A holistic approach to skill formation is prioritised, taking into consideration not only economic, but also social, environmental and cultural issues and the challenges facing society. This scenario favours a collective approach to skill formation based on sustainable social dialogue and the creation of more coherent, accessible and equitable skill formation institutions and processes. This scenario builds upon the preconditions of a comparatively high level of education and skills within the current population and the presence of a developed network of the public education and training centres, universities and adult education providers. Sustaining and improving public institutions of skill formation is regarded as a key mechanism for implementing this scenario, alongside the re-conceptualisation of skill formation as a public good, with the potential to generate cohesive and sustainable regional development, and the personal development of all citizens. The main mechanism to attain this vision, which is shared by centre and left-wing politicians and policy makers, trade unions, some civil society actors, education and training providers, and many academic stakeholders, is via social dialogue over skills in the sectors and the implementation of national instruments and measures of skill formation and qualifications.

## References

Barcevičius, E., & Gineikytė, V. (2015). 'Aukštos kvalifikacijos migrantų sugrįžimas: ar užsienyje įgytos žinios ir įgūdžiai padeda įsitvirtinti Lietuvos darbo rinkoje?', *Politologija*, 2, 14–59.

Barcevičius, E., & Žvalionytė, D. (eds.) (2012). *Užburtas ratas? Lietuvos gyventojų grįžtamoji ir pakartotinė migracija*. Vilnius: Vaga.

Cedefop (2016). *Apprenticeship Review: Lithuania. Signposting the Apprenticeship Path in Lithuania*. Luxembourg: Publications Office of the European Union.

Christenko, A., Martinaitis, Ž., & Kruminas, P. (2020). 'From socialism to capitalism: (un)skill-biased change in Lithuania manufacturing subsectors during the transition', (in-review).

Dienys, V., & Pusvaškis, R. (1998). 'Change of vocational training in Lithuania during first step of the educational reform', *Profesinis rengimas: tyrimai ir realijos*, 1, 118–125.

Dobbins, M., & Leisyte, L. (2014). 'Analysing the transformation of higher education governance in Bulgaria and Lithuania', *Public Management Review*, 16 (7), 987–1010.

Gedvilienė, G., Tūtlys, V., Lukošūnienė, V., & Zuzevičiūtė, V. (2018). 'Development of the profession and qualifications of adult educators in Lithuania in the context of reforms of adult education', *International Review of Education*, 64 (4), 465–487.

Gruževskis, B., & Blažienė, I. (2005). 'EES implementation promoting the development of social dialogue in Lithuania'. In C. Lafucriere & L. Magnusson (eds.), *The Enlargement of Social Europe: The Role of Social Partners in the European Social Strategy*, pp. 61–98. Brussels: ETUI-REHS.

Gylys, P. (2008). *Ekonomika, antiekonomika ir globalizacija*. Vilnius: Vilniaus universiteto leidykla.

Kaminskas, V. (2019). 'Aukštasis mokslas – nuo demokratijos link biurokratijos', <https://www.delfi.lt/news/ringas/lit/vytautas-kaminskas-aukstasis-mokslas-nuo-demokratijos-link-biurokratijos.d?id=82462351>, accessed 10 February 2020.

Kaminskienė, L. (2011). *Referencing Lithuanian Qualifications System to the European Qualifications Framework for Lifelong Learning. Research Report*. Vilnius: Qualifications and Vocational Education and Training Development Centre.

Lafucriere, C., & Magnusson, L. (eds.) (2005). *The Enlargement of Social Europe: The Role of Social Partners in the European Social Strategy Part II*. Brussels: ETUI-REHS.

Laužackas, R. (2005). *Profesinio rengimo metodologija*. Kaunas: Vytauto Didžiojo Universiteto Leidykla.

Laužackas, R., Tūtlys, V., & Spūdytė, I. (2009). 'Evolution of competence concept in Lithuania: from VET reform to development of National Qualifications System', *Journal of European Industrial Training*, 33 (8/9), 800–16.

Lazutka, R. (2013). *Socialinės partnerystės plėtojimas. Tyrimo ataskaita.* Vilnius: Lietuvos Respublikos Vyriausybė.

Le Deist, F., & Tūtlys, V. (2012). 'Limits to mobility: Competence and qualifications in Europe', *European Journal of Training and Development*, 36 (2/3), 262–285.

Leisyte, L. (2018). 'Higher education systems and institutions, Lithuania.' In P. Teixeira & J. Shin (eds.), *Encyclopedia of International Higher Education Systems and Institutions* [E-Book, continuously updated edition]. Dordrecht: Springer.

Leišytė, L., Rose, A. L., & Schimmelpfennig, E. (2018). 'Lithuanian higher education: Between path dependence and change.' In J. Huisman, A. Smolentseva & I. Froumin (eds.), *25 Years of Transformations of Higher Education Systems in Post-Soviet Countries. Palgrave Studies in Global Higher Education*, pp. 27–42. Cham: Palgrave Macmillan.

Leišytė, L., Želvys, R., & Zenkienė, L. (2015). 'Re-contextualization of the Bologna process in Lithuania', *European Journal of Higher Education*, 5 (1), 49–67.

Martinaitis, Ž. (2010). *The Political Economy of Skills Formation: Explaining Differences in Central and Eastern Europe. Doctoral dissertation.* Vilnius: Vilnius University.

Nazelskis, E., & Tūtlys, V. (2013a). 'Involvement of enterprises and sectors of economy in the designing and implementation of the National Qualifications Framework: Experience of Lithuania'. In *EuroMed: The 6th Annual EuroMed Conference Confronting Contemporary Business Challenges through Management Innovation*, pp. 1634–1668. Bradford: EuroMed Press.

Nazelskis, E., & Tūtlys, V. (2013b). 'Profesinių standartų reikšmė Lietuvos ūkio subjektų žmogiškojo potencialo didinimui', *Organizacijų vadyba: sisteminiai tyrimai*, 68, 73–86.

Norkus, Z. (2014). *Du nepriklausomybės dvidešimtmečiai.* Vilnius: Aukso žuvys.

Pilietinės visuomenės institutas (2007). *Lietuvos tauta: būklė ir raidos perspektyvos.* Vilnius: Versus aureus.

Profesinio Mokymo Reformos Programos Koordinavimo Centras (1999). *Baltoji knyga- profesinis rengimas (iki aukštojo universitetinio lygmens).* Vilnius: Lietuvos Respublikos Švietimo ir mokslo ministerija.

Saniter, A., & Tūtlys, V. (2016). 'Comparison of historical development pathways of initial vocational education and training in Lithuania and Germany: How does history matter for policy learning'. In E. Berner and Ph. Gonon (eds.), *History of Vocational Education and Training in Europe. Cases, Concepts and Challenges*, pp. 511–530. Bern: Peter Lang.

Spöttl, G., & Tūtlys, V. (2017). 'From the Analysis of Work-Processes to Designing Competence-Based Occupational Standards and Vocational Curricula', *European Journal of Training and Development*, 41 (1), 50–66.

Statistics Lithuania (2010). *Statistical Yearbook of Lithuania, 2010.* Vilnius: Statistics Lithuania.

Statistics Lithuania (2015). 'Net international migration, Crude emigration rate, Crude immigration rate, Emigrants, Crude net international migration rate, Immigrants', <http://osp.stat.gov.lt/en/statistiniu-rodikliu-analize?portletFormName=visualization&hash=687e2dfa-2c1b-445b-a7ac-a82292c71913>, accessed 28 December 2019.

Tūtlys, V., & Aarna, O. (2017). 'Competence-based approach in the education reforms of Lithuania and Estonia'. In M. Mulder (ed.), *Competence-based Vocational and Professional Education. Bridging the Worlds of Work and Education*, pp. 381–406. Cham: Springer International Publishing.

Tūtlys, V., & Kaminskienė, L. (2008). 'Social partnership in the accreditation of qualifications in the Lithuanian VET system', *European Journal of Vocational Training*, 45 (3), 32–49.

Tūtlys, V., Kaminskienė, L., & Winterton, J. (2016). 'Policy borrowing and policy learning in initial VET reforms of Lithuania after 1990'. In S. Bohlinger, T. K. A. Dang and M. Klatt (eds.), *Education Policy: Mapping the Landscape and Scope*, pp. 377–402. Frankfurt: Peter Lang.

Tūtlys, V., & Spūdytė, I. (2011). 'Implementing a national qualifications framework in Lithuania', *Journal of Education and Work*, 24 (3/4), 429–448.

Ilze Buligina, Biruta Sloka

# 3. Latvia: towards systemic approach to skill formation

**Abstract:** The VET reform in Latvia has been implemented in closed collaboration with social partners and sector associations, thus ensuring the needed quality in skills' formation. This chapter analyses VET policy developments and practical solutions for skills formation in Latvia in the period from the regained independence in 1990s to the aftermath of the global economic crisis. Key attention is being paid to the role of the conceptual and legislative frameworks to support the VET reforms, the continuous support and contribution from international donor organisations and EU funds, as well as the proposed innovative approaches by stakeholders' consortia in Latvia leading to an increasingly competitive VET system nowadays. The implemented national qualifications framework and sector qualifications' frameworks are defined as the backbone for the skill formation according to the labour market needs. The shift to competence-based approach and modularisation of VET programs has contributed to flexibility in VET provision, with parallel digitalisation and continuous professional development of teachers and trainers. The initial piloting and subsequent mainstreaming of work-based learning has been another major shift towards improved labour force training by the VET system. Development of skill formation and lifelong learning approaches in Latvia have been strongly related to the implementation of the EU VET policy strategies, including Riga Conclusions and the Osnabruck Declaration and the Council Recommendation on vocational education and training for sustainable competitiveness, social fairness and resilience.

**Keywords:** Labour market needs, Latvia, skill formation, vocational education and training, work-based learning

## Introduction

Education reforms in Latvia began after the country regained independence in 1991. However, vocational education and training (VET) reform became a policy priority from 2010. After Latvia joined the European Union in 2004, substantial funding from the European Regional Development Fund (ERDF) and the European Social Fund (ESF) became available. Policy discourse on rational planning and the deployment of EU funding became part of the policy agenda, and also served as a basis for future VET reforms. A modern VET system was increasingly seen as a precondition for the development of a workforce with intermediate level skills. However, the challenges of the global economic crisis, including existing and emerging demographic changes (such as low birth rates, and emigration) caused significant shifts in the initial planning of reform, accelerating the need to optimise the network of VET institutions.

Reform necessitated unpopular decisions related to the closure of many VET institutions. At the same time the revision and optimisation of the VET network facilitated the introduction of new approaches, ensuring the longer term development of a network of a limited number of highly developed VET institutions, with modern infrastructure and equipment. In parallel with the optimisation processes, a comprehensive reform of VET content was initiated based on a conceptual policy document (Cabinet of Ministers 2009). The reform gained pace during the planning period 2014–2020 with an ESF funded project on systemic approaches to VET standards and qualifications, which involved adopting a competence-based (learning outcomes) approach and the modularisation of VET programmes to ensure the possibility for continuous upskilling and requalification of the various target groups. Those target groups were identified through combining a lifelong learning perspective with the need to meet labour market skills demands.

An important precondition for the modernisation of VET was the development of the National Qualifications Framework (Latvian Qualifications Framework 2012), with Sector Qualifications Frameworks developed in parallel. Together with the establishment of Sector Expert Councils for all main areas of economic activity these developments enabled VET programmes to become increasingly aligned with labour market needs. The preconditions for more targeted approaches to work-based learning (WBL) and apprenticeship schemes in VET were thereby created. Work-based learning is a high priority for VET in Latvia and has contributed both to the development of skills relevant to the labour market and to the increased employment of VET graduates. The process was started by a WBL pilot project in 2013 with subsequent adoption of a legal framework in 2016.

A network of well-equipped VET Competence centres (VET institutions meeting excellence criteria set by the Government) made it possible to pilot and implement new modular VET programmes compliant with sector qualifications frameworks. Initial and continuing VET programmes are being offered in accordance with national level short and medium-term labour market forecasts, and in response to local and regional needs. The VET Competence centres are becoming important regional players in the promotion of regional development, excellence, innovation and sustainability. Their advisory bodies – the Conventions – comprise representatives from local government, local employers, respective VET Competence centre administration, the relevant ministry and other stakeholders.

Increased attention is paid to early career guidance and counselling to support the future employment choices of young people and to up-skilling and reskilling the existing labour force, using available resources efficiently. Mechanisms for the assessment and validation of prior learning have been established to meet the challenges of lifelong learning, including horizontal and vertical mobility, in a context of rapid changes in the study and work environments.

Two major developments in skills formation in Latvia merit highlighting. First, the amendments to the VET Law (draft 2021) provided a solid legal framework both for comprehensive VET reform after 2010 and the new Education Development Guidelines 2021–2027 (draft). Second, with Latvia joining the OECD in 2016, new possibilities became available for the analysis and improvement of education systems, including VET. The OECD project in Latvia within the OECD Programme 'Building Effective National Skill Strategies' greatly contributed to the development of Latvia's Education Development Guidelines 2021–2027, which proposed solutions to address the educational challenges of the 21st century via the development of a competitive labour force with modern skills.

To contextualise VET developments during the last decade following the economic crises, some key milestones in education policy (including VET) since the regaining of national independence will be presented, taking into consideration the influence of EU policies on VET processes in Latvia. The chapter reviews VET developments and skill formation strategies in the political-economic context in Latvia in the aftermath of economic crises. The research is based on a review of the literature, critical analysis of policy documents and analysis of the available statistical data.

## Research of skill formation and VET in Latvia

Researchers in Latvia have paid significant attention to VET in relation to its role in developing a competitive labour force, studying this issue from multiple perspectives. Several doctoral theses have been defended and research papers published regarding human resource development and VET policy issues in Latvia. These studies have been related to broader societal contexts and the role of public administrations and education systems in skill formation, as well as having a focus on conceptual and methodological approaches to skill provision oriented to labour market needs.

In the context of economic and social growth and in regard to challenges the new countries are facing, the importance of the analysis of qualitative and quantitative aspects in the education systems has been stressed (Kalve 2008). The education processes need to be viewed in diverse cultural, economic and social contexts (Tauriņa 2011), where education and training paradigms are crucial for the development of educations systems, including VET (Zaļaiskalne 2013). There is increased awareness within public administrations of the role of VET in developing a competitive labour force (Buligina 2015).

Knowledge creation, preservation, application and management have been found to be crucial in skills development (Zeibarte 2011). Regarding governance, the roles of, and relationships between, national and local governments with regard to societal needs, including education has been stressed (Vilka 2004). The relationship between the training providers and society is also relevant for skills development in a broader perspective (Vasiļevska 2014).

The need for investment in human capital has been acknowledged in Latvia (Romele 2014) and the importance of human resource development has been analysed in relation to tools for evaluating the process (Peiseniece 2010). Innovation in education and training to meet labour market needs is particularly important, both for the training process itself and in relation to organizational issues (Lapiņa 2007). Attention has been paid to the problem of inconsistent co-operation among stakeholders in relation to quality assurance systems (Rusakova 2011), and the role of education managers at all levels to ensure effective functioning of education institutions (Upenieks 2008).

Relationships between employers and employees, and labour market regulation are key to the optimal use of human capital, labour market flexibility and entrepreneurship development in Latvia (Brence 2010). In small enterprises, the role of knowledge management has also been emphasised (Kantāne 2013).

The role of education advisors in providing career guidance and counselling addresses short and long-term goals in relation to labour market and societal developments (Jaunzeme 2011). Learner-centred approaches are of growing importance for effective education and training systems (Kalvāns 2012). Education processes based on learning outcomes provide links to skills oriented to the labour-market (Kinta 2013), which has implications for the management process in relation to requisite professional competence (Kulberga 2013).

The management of VET institutions and overall performance and quality issues in Latvia have also been compared with other countries (Fernández-González et al. 2019; Luka 2018).

## Key developments in education policy after regaining national independence

It should be noted that in Latvia VET reform was implemented as part of broader education reforms in the post-Soviet period. The education reforms in Latvia were implemented in alignment with European education policy processes, which had an impact on Latvian education policy both before and after Latvia's accession to the EU.

After regaining independence in 1991 there was no clear strategy in place regarding the reform of the education system, including VET. As to the network of VET institutions, VET secondary schools essentially preserved their status, the former *tehnikums* (VET institutions providing higher level skills) were either renamed as VET secondary schools or became colleges offering the so-called 1st level higher education programmes (often alongside VET secondary education programmes). Some VET institutions were closed or merged with larger schools.

The initial education reforms in Latvia were implemented in close collaboration with several international actors and were based on major projects by foreign investors. This reflected that the newly re-established state lacked sufficient financial and human resources to implement a transition involving a paradigm shift in education and training. The reform process in its initial stage was greatly facilitated by World Bank (1999–2005) and European Union supported PHARE (1995–2000) projects, contributing to the development of the Education Law (Saeima 1998) and the VET Law (Saeima 1999). A survey commissioned by the PHARE project to OECD (OECD 2001) regarding skill formation in Latvia served as a basis for conceptual approaches in drafting the VET Law – incorporating comparatively modern developments, e.g. determining five qualification levels already at that time. According to the OECD review of Latvia's education policies and programmes, reform of education, training and human resource development was an integral part of transition to a democratic society and market economy (OECD 2001). A market economy in turn demanded a labour force with different skills and competencies from those needed in the former Soviet type planned economy.

Thus, the possibilities provided by the PHARE project greatly contributed to the initial transformation of the VET system in Latvia and assisted in setting key objectives within the VET Law of 1999 with 15 different amendments, the most recent being in 2017. The VET Law corresponds with other laws including the Law of Education and the Law of Higher Education Establishments. The VET Law determined conditions for acquiring general knowledge and skills and qualifications, stipulating the levels of vocational education, defining the responsibility of the relevant bodies involved in the provision of VET and their right to award vocational qualifications, as well as providing norms to ensure the international comparability of vocational qualifications acquired in Latvia (OECD 2001).

However, the capacity of the existing network of VET institutions still lagged behind the policy aims of the new VET Law. It took more than a decade to establish a system with a balanced network of VET institutions capable of offering modern high-quality VET programmes. The dynamics of the institutional developments for better programmes and skills provision is described in subsequent parts of this chapter. Nevertheless, with the adoption of the new VET Law, from 1999 initial VET began to operate in a clearly defined way. Systemic approaches to curriculum development were initiated, establishing national standards in basic and secondary vocational education, as well as first level higher vocational education. The Register of vocational standards was established in 1998 and amended in 2017, and the development of new standards was achieved in co-operation with the social partners. This approach is different from the standards reflected in the Classification of Professions prepared by the Ministry of Welfare and accepted on 10 October 1998 (now no longer in force as new regulations reflects amendments of VET Law). Since then, the social partners have played an increasingly important role in the development of vocational education and skill formation relevant to labour market needs. The years 2000 and 2001 represent a stabilisation period for VET in Latvia.

Teachers at vocational education institutions – both teachers of general subjects and teachers of vocational subjects – were viewed as an important driving force in the reform, so attention was paid to their initial and continuing education and training. 'Regulations on the required education and professional qualification of teachers' (Cabinet of Ministers 2000) determined the educational and professional requirements for VET teachers and reflected the level at which they were teaching. In-service training for teachers was offered on a regular basis by the Teacher Training Support Centre (TTSC). In 2001, 81 in-service training programmes were funded from the national budget.

The reform processes continued and were intimately linked to the process of joining the EU. The Education Development Concept for 2002–2005 was adopted, as was the Programme for the development of Vocational Education for 2003–2005, which had more specific goals. The overarching aim of the Education Development Concept was to carry out the necessary changes in the education system to facilitate the building of a knowledge-based, democratic and socially integrated society that would increase economic competitiveness and simultaneously preserve and develop Latvian cultural values. Other strategic documents were adopted promoting lifelong learning and human resource development. Such documents detailed mechanisms designed to improve VET opportunities and outcomes, for example, the annual National employment plans.

The EU PHARE programme also had a significant role in preparing Latvian institutions for the opportunities presented by the European Structural Funds, which became accessible from 2004. The PHARE project provided a preparatory programme: 'Special preparatory programme for implementation of the European Structural Funds' attended by several hundred employees of national and local government and social partner organisations.

With support from the European Training Foundation (ETF) the Latvian National Observatory was established to support VET developments. The Observatory undertook research on VET and the labour market in Latvia from 1994 to 2004. After Latvia joined the EU, it became part of the ReferNet network (coordinated by Cedefop) which had similar functions to the earlier Observatory. According to the Observatory Report on Latvia for 2001, the main objective of VET was to create opportunities for the population to acquire skills and knowledge to meet labour market requirements and improve competitiveness in changing socio-economic conditions. The report also referred to the Government's priorities in vocational education development, such as establishing a centralised examination system in vocational education; improving the administrative system for training; strengthening central support institutions for training; establishing regional vocational training support institutions; modernising vocational education curricula; improving the accreditation of vocational education curricula and institutions providing training; and organizing professional up-grading for teaching staff at vocational education institutions (AIC 2021).

Another important programme with respect to VET development was the second phase of the EU Leonardo da Vinci programme which was opened to Latvia in 2000. Through this programme transnational VET collaboration projects were established and VET mobility was encouraged, which contributed to the skills development of the partners involved. These projects not only facilitated new experiences for participants but also made it possible to compare Latvia to other countries.

The implementation of the Strategic Programme for the Development of Education 1998–2003 (IZM 1998) led to a further shift in Latvian education policy with the development and adoption of the Guidelines for Lifelong Learning 2007–2013 (Cabinet of Ministers 2007), which were agreed among the key stakeholders at national level. These Guidelines changed the overall ethos of educational development to one of lifelong learning. To create a unified lifelong learning system, a coherent system of regulatory enactments and the efficient management of resources (including financial resources), observing the principles of shared responsibility and the interaction of sectoral policies, was formulated. The Ministry of Education and Science coordinated lifelong learning policy and the activities of various ministries, institutions and regions.

## Systemic reforms of VET and skill formation after 2010 and their implications

A new period of reform commenced a decade ago, with the aforementioned optimisation of the network of VET institutions, comprehensive VET content reform, stronger involvement of social partners to ensure VET quality and labour market compliance, and the introduction of work-based learning and apprenticeship.

The existing out-dated VET institutions network and infrastructure, the capacity of the teaching staff, historically weak links with the labour market regarding skills development and the overall low prestige of VET were the main challenges for the modernisation of the VET system, with a clear strategy being needed to address these. From 2010 a systemic approach was adopted to optimise the VET institutional network, which recognized the need for fundamental transformation and improvement in the quality of infrastructure, programme content and provision, and teaching and training staff. The optimisation of the VET network was also prompted by the global economic crises which had a major impact on the Latvian economy. The scarcity of resources necessitated reducing the number of VET institutions. Increasing unemployment resulted in large scale emigration which was accompanied by other demographic changes, notably decreasing birth rates. Those processes resulted in depopulation, especially in rural areas. Funding half-empty VET institutions became impossible financially and was unjustifiable from the point of view of efficient use of resources. Today in Latvia there are 23 highly developed public VET providers, 19 of which bear the name VET Competence Centres (denoting compliance to criteria determined by the Cabinet of Ministers). However, it took more than two decades to arrive at this position.

There were other important challenges, including out-dated infrastructure, insufficient linkage between the education and training offer and labour market demand, and a lack of institutional mechanisms to ensure this linkage (Ministry of Education and Science 2020).

A major impetus for the improvement of out-dated VET infrastructure was the availability of EU funding from 2004 with Latvia's accession to the bloc. Prior to this, only some pre-accession funds were available, which were insufficient for systemic transformation. The national budget was also insufficient to address the wide spectrum of emerging challenges in the country which accompanied re-established independence. External financial assistance was therefore crucial for meaningful reforms.

At the same time, Latvia was in step with European education policy developments, via participation in various EU programmes, which created the pre-conditions for accession and ensured the smooth integration into EU processes, including those relating to VET.

There was a strong focus on investing in VET infrastructure and equipment during the first EUR structural funds planning period (2004–2006), which grew rapidly in the planning period of 2007–2013. With the global economic crisis and radical demographic changes, the issue of the network of VET institutions had to be addressed urgently.

Changes in the number of vocational education institutions from 1990 to 2019 is shown in Figure 3.1.

Figure 3.1 shows that the number of VET institutions decreased on average by 3.6 institutions annually. A significant reduction of VET entrants, students and graduates was already evident from the 1997/1998 school year, and the trend has continued through to the 2019/2020 school year, as shown in Figure 3.2.

Enrolments have reduced annually on average by 1,118 students each school year, entrants reduced annually on average by 404 students each school year, and graduates fell annually on average by 278 students each school year (Central Statistical Bureau data).

The national level policy documents 'On the Concept Increasing the Attractiveness of Vocational Education and Participation of Social Partners in Ensuring the Quality of Vocational Education' (Cabinet of Ministers 2009) initiated the systemic reform of VET curricula. To facilitate its implementation, on 23 April 2015 the Latvian Parliament, *Saeima*, passed the 'Amendments to the Law on Vocational Education' (Saeima 2015) which established the legal framework for some of the reforms proposed in the aforementioned Concept.

These amendments to the Law also included the introduction of the Latvian Qualifications Framework (LQF), which was later referenced against the European Qualifications Framework. The full regulation on the LQF entered into force simultaneously with corresponding amendments to the Education Law, which was adopted by the *Saeima* on 18 June 2015. These amendments to Education Law strengthened the normative basis, determining that the LQF is an essential part of the education system.

Amendments to the VET Law in 2015 introduced regulations on Sector Expert Councils, work-based learning, Conventions of VET institutions,

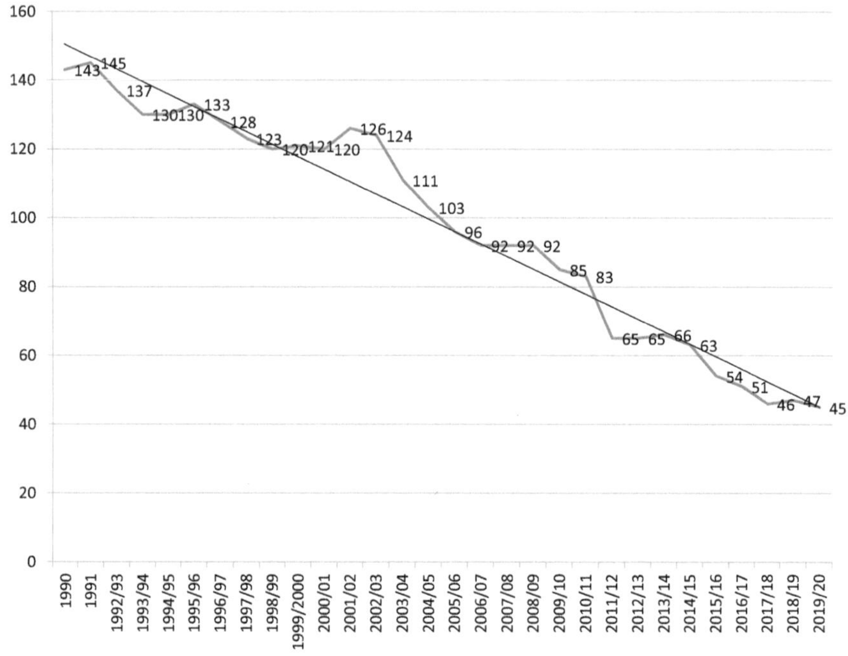


**Figure 3.1.** Number of vocational education institutions in the Republic of Latvia 1990–2019 and linear trend. Source: author's calculation and construction based on Central Statistical Bureau data, www.csb.gov.lv.

and occupational standards developed separately from the occupational classification. All these developments have been fundamental for aligning skill formation with the labour market. Subsequently, the Law of 22 June 2017 'Amendments to the Law on Vocational Education' (Saeima 2017) introduced modules and modular programmes in vocational education, further strengthening the lifelong learning paradigm.

Within the comprehensive VET curriculum reform launched after 2010, the transition to a learning outcomes approach was implemented. This made it possible to estimate the balance between the occupation-specific skills, general subject knowledge and transversal skills and competences included in initial VET programmes or qualifications. The transformation process has been developed in close cooperation with sectoral experts, regularly evaluating and updating the content of vocational education in line with the regular updating of sectoral qualifications.

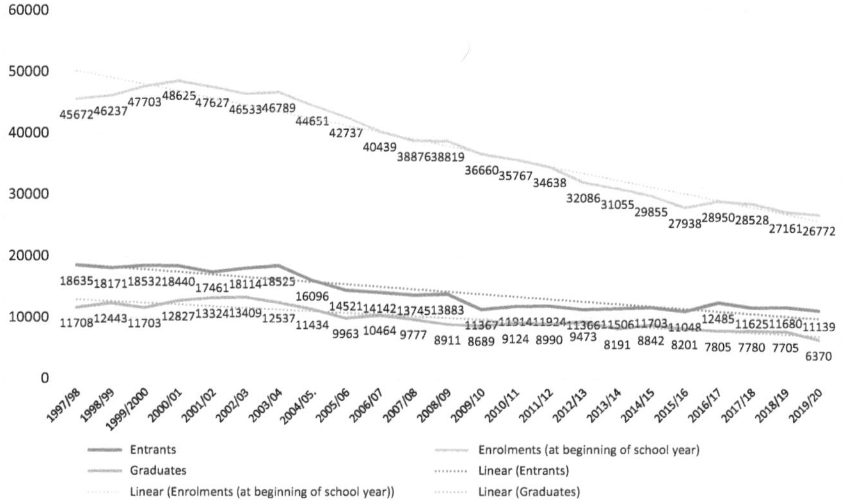


**Figure 3.2.** Number of vocational education entrants, enrolments and graduates in the Republic of Latvia 1997/1998–2019/2020 and respective linear trends. Source: author's calculation and construction based on Central Statistical Bureau data, www.csb.gov.lv.

Among other outputs, this reform has also established continued cooperation between the social partners and sectoral organizations (Ministry of Education and Science 2020) ensuring the alignment of VET content and quality with sectoral needs. It also involved a comprehensive review of the regulatory framework, introducing a single qualification award system, strengthening industry sector responsibility for the award of qualifications, and improving the ability of industry to forecast future skills needs.

These were the major steps to embed the alignment of skill formation with the labour market and the concept of lifelong learning. At present VET qualifications can be obtained via initial and continuing VET programmes. After finishing an initial VET programme, graduates are free to enter the labour market or continue their studies at higher education level (on equal standing with graduates from general education). At the same time, during a person's professional career, possibilities for upgrading and re-skilling are in place through continuing VET or professional development programmes. Also, the validation of non-formal and informal learning is well developed within VET in Latvia, which has offered a full spectrum of possibilities for skills and competence recognition since 2011.

A remaining challenge, however, is to increase the provision of NQF (EQF) level 5 programmes, since highly-skilled medium level specialists (with NQF level 5 qualifications and skills) are in high demand, especially in STEM specialties. At present only colleges are entitled to offer NQF level 5 programmes, however provision is not always sufficient and does not always correspond to labour market demands. Thus, policy discussions have been initiated to enable VET Competence Centres with adequate capacity to offer NQF level 5 programmes to satisfy demand for skilled labour of this type (Cabinet of Ministers 2007).

Reform has contributed to a gradual improvement in the prestige of VET in Latvia, and even though there is not yet parity of esteem for the VET pathway, this is changing. Employment rates of VET graduates are increasing according to the new graduates monitoring results published on 8 April 2021 (Ministry of Education and Science 2021). At the same time, due to the predominance of humanities and social sciences over STEM subjects in higher education, graduate employment is often a challenge. In parallel with the growing prestige of VET due to the improved quality of the offer, labour market demand is also gradually increasing demand for the VET pathway. Amendments to VET were proposed and approved by the Cabinet of Ministers in early 2021, and at the time of writing are being considered by the *Saeima*. The draft Amendments promote more flexible education and opportunities to improve skills throughout life, allowing learners to receive a state-recognized document for acquiring parts of a programme, not simply for the entire programme (qualification).

The new approach represents a substantial change, with learning outcomes being evaluated on the basis of identified achievements rather than deficits, as was the case with the earlier system (Ministry of Education and Science 2020). This fundamental paradigm shift allows individuals to apply the skills they have acquired, to have those skills certified, and to continue education (or building a qualification) at a later stage, without a need to re-learn competencies already developed. The VET system should therefore become increasingly flexible and focus on individual needs and abilities, whilst simultaneously responding faster to labour market needs. The development is closely related to the concept of micro-credentials, now widely discussed in EU policy forums.

Based on draft amendments to the VET Law, the full introduction of modular vocational education programmes is expected to significantly reduce the time needed to respond to labour market demands. Flexible modularised VET curricula are being introduced in vocational basic education, pre-secondary vocational education, vocational secondary education, vocational continuing education and professional development programmes. For this reason, the terms 'related profession' and 'specialization' have been introduced and defined, creating a common understanding of similar professional qualifications that can be acquired in the context of lifelong learning.

Through ECVET, formal, non-formal and informal learning outcomes are accredited, and associated qualifications are recognized in ways that ensure comparability between different VET institutions and different countries, via an accumulation mechanism for qualifications reflected in the Law on the Regulated Professions and the Recognition of Professional Qualifications (Saeima 2001). Lifelong learning opportunities have been expanded by combining formal and non-formal learning, giving every adult the opportunity to improve their general and professional skills, as well as to be up-skilled or change their profession. All these developments have been initiated and tested as part of the VET content reform started in 2010, so the new draft Amendments to the VET Law provide a firm legal framework for a finalised reform package. All VET institutions are in the final stage of transforming their operations to a modular approach based on learning outcomes, facilitating lifelong learning in the VET offer.

Another novel aspect of the Draft Amendments of VET Law is the monitoring of data on VET graduates, and the insuring of students against accidents throughout training which is already reflected in the Regulation of Cabinet of Ministers of Republic of Latvia Nr. 436 issued on 22 June 2021 on Education Development Principles for 2021–2027 (Cabinet of Ministers 2021).

## Work-based learning as a solution to skill mismatches

The development of work-based learning (WBL) in Latvia deserves special attention within an analysis of the evolution of skill formation because it offers insights into the development of new institutional settings, policy learning mechanisms and social dialogue on skill formation. WBL as an apprenticeship type scheme has been a key priority of VET reform in Latvia since 2013. Alongside traditional practical placements, WBL is considered essential for ensuring skill formation is aligned with labour market needs. After studying the experience from other countries (including Germany, the Netherlands, Slovenia and Switzerland), the Ministry of Education and Science initiated social dialogue over piloting WBL. Discussions involving the ministries of education, welfare, economy, justice and finance, the Employers' Confederation of Latvia, the Free Trade Unions Association, and other stakeholders resulted in agreement to adopt this new development before the respective legal framework was adopted. A 2year pilot project began in 2013 to test the proposed approaches. Continuous dialogue and consultation involving stakeholders settled on a 'bottom-up' approach for adopting and implementing WBL. In 2013, WBL did not seem feasible for a country with a school-based VET system and limited awareness, understanding and support from the employers' side for such an approach. As a result of the piloting and the social dialogue, Latvia succeeded in creating a tailor-made approach, with school-based VET and WBL operating in parallel with VET programmes. The approach developed by a team of experts allowed WBL programmes to be introduced without changes to the existing legal framework regarding standard requirements and the proportion of different curricular elements. The task was made more challenging by the fact that the VET diploma in Latvia affords access to higher education, and a certain number of hours must be devoted to general education subjects. Detailed and prolonged discussion involving various stakeholders in relation to the conceptual approaches was facilitated by the EU Erasmus+ funded project 'National Authorities for Apprenticeships: Implementing Work Based Learning in Latvia, Lithuania and Estonia (WBL-Balt)', 2014-3566/001-001, coordinated by the Ministry of Education and Science of Latvia and involving the respective ministries in Lithuania and Estonia (in the context of the Baltic Alliance for Apprenticeships). The solution was found by transforming the practical part of the curriculum, raising the possibility of acquiring theoretical background for practical training as part of the WBL process.

To implement WBL a tripartite agreement was concluded among the key stakeholders – the student, the VET institution and the company. However, the main responsibility for implementing the programme rests with the VET institution, supporting the student and the company for technical and administrative issues, since the gatekeeper to WBL still is the school, not the company. The VET institution prepares an individual plan for each WBL student. It is a legal requirement, however, for the company WBL tutor to have pedagogical competence. The respective sector expert council can be consulted for the quality of the enterprise for WBL implementation. It is compulsory for the company to ensure remuneration for the student, either in the form of an allowance (not subject to income tax) or a salary based on a work contract.

It took time for employers to accept the new WBL approach, with the need to train students and pay a salary or allowance for sub-optimal performance during the training process. However, ESF financial support to companies described later in this chapter facilitated the engagement of an increasing number of employers and raised awareness of the possible benefits accruing from WBL (Ministry of Education and Science 2020). Some companies saw WBL as an opportunity to improve their social visibility, however, recently many companies are experiencing an acute labour shortage and so need little encouragement to accept WBL students. In light of this, government and the trade unions need to ensure all relevant regulations regarding the rights of learners and employees, are observed, especially those relating to young workers.

Increased time spent in the workplace is seen as an important aspect of developing skills relevant to the labour market, yet the share of students in WBL remains relatively low at around 7 per cent of the total number of students. (Ministry of Education and Science 2020). The number is slowly but steadily increasing, but the success of the initiative has been limited by the additional workload, especially for the teachers, and the lack of student motivation. The Ministry of Education and Science is encouraging WBL for STEM sectors because to date most interest, both from students and VET institutions, has related to the service sector (Ministry of Education and Science 2020).

The Latvian led Baltic collaboration in relation to the development of WBL presents a very interesting and original case of organized mutual policy learning in the CEE, which is recognized as useful by EU and international bodies, as well as other European countries both within and beyond the EU.

Amendments to the VET Law were adopted by the *Saeima* on 23 April 2015, which determined WBL as one form of implementing VET. Following the Amendments to the VET Law, on 15 July 2016 Regulation No 484 by the Cabinet of Ministers was adopted "Procedure on the organisation and implementation of work-based learning" (Cabinet of Ministers 2016c). The procedure stipulates the tasks, rights and responsibilities of VET institutions, employers and social partners in implementing WBL, as well as the responsibilities of sector expert councils in coordinating and enhancing the co-operation of companies with education institutions to ensure VET alignment with labour market needs. After extensive social dialogue, the ministries of education, welfare, economy, justice and finances, the Employers' Confederation of Latvia, the Free Trade Unions Association, as well as other stakeholders, agreed on this new development, allowing the associated legal framework to be adopted in 2016.

Two other Regulations by the Cabinet of Ministers regarding the implementation of WBL were adopted in 2016: on 'Establishment and operation of sector expert councils and the coordination of their activities' (Cabinet of Ministers 2016a); and 'Increasing the number of learners of VET institutions involved in work-based learning or training placements at enterprises' of the Operational programme 'Growth and Employment' (Cabinet of Ministers 2016b), which envisaged substantial financial resources from ESF for achieving the set goals.

A special role in further WBL developments in Latvia involved the EU Erasmus+ programme project 'Testing New Approaches to Training VET and Workplace Tutors for Work Based Learning – TTT4WBL', 582951-EPP-1-2016-2-LV-EPPKA3-PI-POLICY, which led to agreement on a Baltic WBL tutor competence profile and similar approaches in the training of WBL tutors in the three Baltic countries.

Erasmus+ programme projects facilitating policy innovation and experimentation, and extending social dialogue were particularly important both for raising overall awareness of WBL, and the participation of stakeholders, so to a great extent these projects determined the success of the WBL initiative in Latvia.

A breakthrough in WBL was reached by way of the ESF project 'To increase the number of learners of VET institutions involved in work-based learning or training placements at enterprises' implemented by the Employers' Confederation of Latvia. Within the framework of the project, by 2 December 2020, 37 educational institutions had applied (adjusted) 346 vocational education programmes for WBL, 487 companies were involved in WBL, 2030 companies had become involved in providing practical training, 2,242 students were involved in the WBL and 7,521 students were in traineeship in an enterprise, according to the project data management system. By the end of 2023, within this project, support will be provided for engaging 3,150 students in WBL learning and 11,025 students in traineeship in an enterprise (Ministry of Education and Science 2020).

At the same time, innovative WBL projects for improved skills formation are being piloted with the support of finance from other EU programmes. For example, the Erasmus+ project 'Individual Approach and Individual Learning Plan in WBL: Training for WBL Tutors (ILP4WBL)', aims to develop skills of VET teachers and WBL tutors in designing individual learning plans for students, and also in motivating and guiding individual learners taking into account their abilities, aptitudes, personality traits and career plans.

Mainstreamed only up to NQF (EQF) level 4, WBL in skills formation for higher level qualifications is yet to be rolled out, although NQF level 5 programmes for VET teachers are being piloted using resources provided by the state budget. EU resources are also being used for piloting WBL at EQF level 5 in some sectors such as the timber processing industry by the project 'Skills for the Baltic Wood industry – European Quality in Vocational Education and Training', (Skilled-up 2018) – co-ordinated by the German–Baltic Chamber of Commerce (Latvia, Lithuania, Estonia and Germany), which is preparing a modular programme in the wood industry at EQF level 5 consisting of 10 modules.

For the new planning period of 2021–2027, WBL continues to be a priority in VET policy, and is being strengthened in technologically oriented programmes through the closer collaboration of local and regional stakeholders to promote sustainable regional development.

Currently the key focus in VET policy is on improving access to continuous personal and professional development through lifelong learning, a priority clearly linked to skills strategies as part of the Education Development Guidelines of 2021–2027, and a key recommendation of OECD Skills Strategy Implementation Guidance for Latvia. To implement the Guidelines, VET institutions with their modernised infrastructure and enhanced human resources, are building capacity to become relevant regional players in providing lifelong learning.

## Implementation of the qualifications frameworks

The National Qualifications Framework created the preconditions for developing Sector Qualifications Frameworks. Respective normative acts (Cabinet of Ministers 2016) set the general framework for developing the standards and qualification requirements in compliance with the Sectoral Qualifications Framework (SQF) as part of the Sector Qualifications System (SQS) in Latvia.

In the period December 2010 to November 2015 the State Education Development Agency (VIAA) together with four partners – the Latvian Employers' Confederation (LDDK), the Latvian Free Trade Union Confederation (LBAS), the National Centre for Education (VISC) and the Education Quality State Service (IKVD) – implemented an initial ESF project on developing the SQS and Improving Efficiency and Quality of VET. The aim of the project was to improve the quality and efficiency of VET to meet the development needs of economic sectors via restructuring, establishing a sectoral qualifications system, researching economic sectors, developing or improving basic occupational standards and specialised qualifications, as well as ensuring the recognition of skills acquired outside formal education. The results of the Project were subsequently embedded within the respective legal acts.

The SQF included the development of industry-specific descriptors for qualification levels (knowledge, skills and competencies) and references to qualification levels (EQF/LQF). At each qualification level, basic occupations specific to the sector and specialisations were described. The SQFs are publicly available on the website of the State Education Development Agency (VIAA 2012). The SQF covers all levels of qualifications, including HE, thus ensuring comprehensive information on various pathways and permeability between VET and HE. The qualifications within the SQF are clearly referenced to the NQF and its descriptors so there is a direct link and coherence with the design of the respective curriculum.

In Latvia the SQF must be updated at least every five years. The SQF was developed using a functional analysis approach, with the aim of creating a transparent, independent, yet interconnected structure of professional qualifications in each sector, including descriptions of the main professions. The qualifications included in the NQF have been equated to the corresponding LQF level starting from the most basic level of certification in the field to the highest level of credentialisation. The final document of the sectoral qualification structures is available on the VISC website (https://visc.gov.lv/profizglitiba/nozkval.shtml) and complies with the formal Regulation in force. The final version of the SFQ has been confirmed by the VET sub-council (PINTSA) of the Tripartite Co-operation Council.

The Ministry of Education and Science claims that Sector Qualifications Frameworks ensure a systemic approach in the offer of qualifications (Ministry of Education and Science 2020). They have been agreed with the social partners via their active involvement and the coordination of the Sector expert councils.

The necessary institutional settings are in place, but the key challenge is to encourage the work of Sector expert councils to increase their ownership of the process by regularly updating the Sector qualifications framework in collaboration with their respective counterparts from the education sector. The beneficial effect of the Sector Qualifications Frameworks is recognized by stakeholders in providing a comprehensive systemic overview of qualifications and enabling targeted continuous updating of occupational standards in line with labour market needs (Ministry of Education and Science 2020).

## Conclusion

VET reform in Latvia was almost complete by 2020, but it had taken more than two decades to transform the system, the years from 2010 having been decisive in introducing fundamental innovation and new paradigms regarding skill formation, embracing upgrading and reskilling in the context of lifelong learning. The VET system in Latvia has become mature and major policy interventions reforming the system are complete. No formal studies have yet been undertaken on the impact of the reform and it is too early for meaningful evaluation. However, the early results as described in this chapter suggest that the reform has had some success. A major achievement is the current legislative process on draft VET amendments, which at the time of writing is being considered by Parliament, following approval by the Cabinet of Ministers in early 2021. These amendments represent a complete legal transformation of previous approaches but were only possible because of major investment in financial and human resources during the previous two decades.

Latvia is closely following EU developments with respect to skill formation and lifelong learning. Major developments were related to the implementation of the Riga Conclusions (a mid-term EU VET policy document developed under the Latvian presidency of the EU Council). Currently the Osnabruck Declaration and the Council Recommendation on Vocational Education and Training for Sustainable Competitiveness, Social Fairness and Resilience highlight common European goals for improved approaches to skill formation and European competitiveness. Latvia has implemented the key measures regarding VET reform to become a relevant player in the EU context, having a skill formation system that is aligned to the labour market, relevant for citizens of all ages, which also promotes the personal and professional development and life satisfaction of individuals. This is also the leading objective underpinning the Education Development Guidelines of Latvia for the period 2021–2027.

## References

AIC (Academic Information Centre) (2021). 'National Observatory Reports on Professional Education and Labour Market',<http://www.aic.lv/portal/par-aic/nacionala-observatorija>, accessed 14 May 2021.

Brence, I. (2010). *Darba tirgu regulējošo faktoru piemērošana uzņēmējdarbības attīstības veicināšanai Latvijā [Implementation of Labour Market Regulating Factors for Promoting Entrepreneurship Development in Latvia]. PhD Thesis.* Riga: UL.

Buligina, I. (2015). *The Approaches by the Public Administration in the Development of Competitive Labour Force in Vocational Education and Training in Latvia. PhD Thesis.* Riga: UL.

Cabinet of Ministers of Republic of Latvia (2000). 'Noteikumi par prasībām pedagogiem nepieciešamajai izglītībai un profesionālajai kvalifikācijai' [Regulations on the required education and professional qualification of teachers], *Order of CM Nr. 347 03.10.2000*, <https://www.vestnesis.lv/ta/id/11488-noteikumi-par-prasibam-pedagogiem-nepieciesamajai-izglitibai-un-profesionalajai-kvalifikacijai >, accessed 14 June 2021.

Cabinet of Ministers of Republic of Latvia (2006). 'Par izglītības attīstības pamatnostādnēm 2007.-2013.gadam' [On the Education Development Guidelines for 2007–2013], *Order of the CM Nr. 742 27.09.2009*,<https://likumi.lv/ta/id/144686-par-izglitibas-attistibas-pamatnostadnem-2007-2013-gadam>, accessed 14 June 2021.

Cabinet of Ministers of Republic of Latvia (2007). 'Par Mūžizglītības politikas pamatnostādnēm 2007.-2013.gadam' [Guidelines for Lifelong Learning 2007–2013], *Order of CM Nr. 11 23.02.2007*, <https://likumi.lv/ta/id/153578-par-muzizglitibas-politikas-pamatnostadnem-2007-2013-gadam>, accessed 14 June 2021.

Cabinet of Ministers of Republic of Latvia (2009). 'Par koncepciju "Profesionālās izglītības pievilcības paaugstināšana un sociālo partneru līdzdalība profesionālās izglītības kvalitātes nodrošināšanā' [On the Concept "Increasing the Attractiveness of Vocational Education and Participation of Social Partners in Ensuring the Quality of Vocational Education"], *Order of CM Nr. 629 16.09.2009*, <https://likumi.lv/ta/id/197894-par-koncepciju-profesionalas-izglitibas-pievilcibas-paaugstinasana-un-socialo-partneru-lidzdaliba-profesionalas-izglitibas-kvalitates-nodrosinasana >, accessed 14 June 2021.

Cabinet of Ministers of Republic of Latvia (2010). *Guidelines for the Optimization of the Network of the Vocational Education Institutions 2010 – 2015 Order of CM N5, 06.01.2010*, <https://eacea.ec.europa.eu/national-policies/eurydice/content/organisation-vocational-upper-secondary-education-25_en>, accessed 14 May 2021.

Cabinet of Ministers of Republic of Latvia (2016). 'Profesijas standarta, profesionālās kvalifikācijas prasību (ja profesijai neapstiprina profesijas standartu) un nozares kvalifikāciju struktūras izstrādes kārtība' [Procedures for the Development of a Professional Standard, Professional Qualification Requirements (if a professional standard is not approved for a profession) and a branch qualification structure], *Order of CM Nr. 633 27.09.2016*, < https://likumi.lv/ta/id/285032-profesijas-standarta-profesionalas-kvalifikacijas-prasibu-ja-profesijai-neapstiprina-profesijas-standartu-un-nozares-kvalifikaciju-strukturas-izstrades-kartiba >, accessed 20 May 2021.

Cabinet of Ministers of Republic of Latvia (2016a). 'Nozaru ekspertu padomju izveidošanas, darbības un darbības koordinācijas kārtība' [Procedure for the establishment and operation of sector expert councils and the coordination of their activities], *Regulation of CM Nr. 485 15.07.2016*, <https://likumi.lv/ta/id/283737-nozaru-ekspertu-padomju-izveidosanas-darbibas-un-darbibas-koordinacijas-kartiba >, accessed 14 June 2021.

Cabinet of Ministers of Republic of Latvia (2016b). 'Darbības programmas "Izaugsme un nodarbinātība" 8.5.1. specifiskā atbalsta mērķa "Palielināt kvalificētu profesionālās izglītības iestāžu audzēkņu skaitu pēc to dalības darba vidē balstītās mācībās vai mācību praksē uzņēmumā" īstenošanas noteikumi' [On the implementation of specific support measure 8.5.1. "To increase the number of learners of VET institutions involved in work-based learning or training placements at enterprises" of the Operational program "Growth and Employment"], *Regulation of CM Nr. 483 15.07.2016*,

<https://likumi.lv/ta/id/283736-darbibas-programmas-izaugsme-un-nodarbinatiba-8-5-1-specifiska-atbalsta-merka-palielinat-kvalificetu-profesionalas-izglitibas>, accessed 20 June 2021.

Cabinet of Ministers of Republic of Latvia (2016c). 'Kārtība, kādā organizē un īsteno darba vidē balstītas mācības' [Procedure on the organisation and implementation of work-based learning], *Regulation of CM Nr. 484 15.07.2016*, <https://likumi.lv/ta/id/283680-kartiba-kada-organize-un-isteno-darba-vide-balstitas-macibas>, accessed 14 June 2021.

Cabinet of Ministers of Republic of Latvia (2021). 'Par izglītības attīstības pamatnostādnēm 2021–2027' [Education Development Principles for 2021–2027], *Regulation of CM Nr. 436 22.06.2021*, <https://likumi.lv/ta/id/324332-par-izglitibas-attistibas-pamatnostadnem-2021-2027-gadam>, accessed 20 June 2021.

Cedefop (2019). 'Latvia–European Inventory on NQS 2018', *Cedefop*, < https://www.cedefop.europa.eu/files/latvia_-_european_inventory_on_nqf_2018.pdf>, accessed 14 June 2021.

Cross Sectoral Coordination Centre Republic of Latvia (2012). 'National Development Plan of Latvia for 2014–2020', <https://www.pkc.gov.lv/sites/default/files/inline-files/NDP2020%20English%20Final_1.pdf>, accessed 21 June 2021.

Dorothee, B. & Greskovits, B. (2007). 'Neoliberalism, embedded neoliberalism and neocorporatism: Towards transnational capitalism in Central-Eastern Europe', *West European Politics*, 30 (3), 443–466.

Draycott, M. & Rae, D. (2011). 'Enterprise education in schools and the role of competence frameworks', *International Journal of Entrepreneurial Behaviour & Research*, 17 (2), 127–145.

European Commission (2007). 'Taking European Knowledge Society Seriously', *Report of expert group on science and governance to the Science, Economy and society Directorate of the Directorate-General for Research, European Commission*, <https://ec.europa.eu/research/science-society/document_library/pdf_06/european-knowledge-society_en.pdf>, accessed 25 June 2021.

European Commission (2009). 'Strengthening the participation of research teams in science, economy and society in an enlarged Europe', *Summary of the sessions at the research connection conference Prague 7-8.05.2009*, <https://danube-inco.net/object/document/10178/attach/ses-session-summary_en.pdf >, accessed 14 June 2021.

European Training Foundation (2018). *Financing Vocational Education and Skills Development: A Policy Area for etf Support*. Torino: European Training Foundation.

Ferrández-Berrueco, R., Kekale, T. & Devins, D. (2016). 'A framework for work-based learning: basic pillars and the interactions between them', *Higher Education, Skills and Work-Based Learning*, 6 (1), 35–54.

Fernández González, M. J., Pīgozne, T., Surikova, S. & Vasečko, Ļ. (2019). 'Students' and staff perceptions of vocational education institution heads' virtues', *Quality Assurance in Education*, 28 (1), 1–18.

Harris, M., Chisholm, C. & Burns, G. (2013). 'Using the Knowledge Transfer Partnership approach in undergraduate education and practice-based training to encourage employer engagement', *Education + Training*, 55 (2), 174–190.

IZM Ministry of Education and Science of Republic of Latvia (1996). Izglītības attīstības stratēģiskā programma 1998–2003 [*Strategic Programme for the Development of Education 1998–2003*]. Riga: The Ministry of Education and Science.

Jaunzeme, I. (2011). *Karjeras vadības un atbalsta sistēmas pilnveidošanas problēmas augstākajā izglītībā Latvijā [Problems of career management and support system improvement in the higher education in Latvia] PhD Thesis.* Riga: UL.

Kalvāns, R. (2012). *Izglītības iestādes vadītāja loma izglītības kvalitātes nodrošināšanā Latvijā [The role of the head of an educational institution in ensuring the quality of education in Latvia] PhD Thesis*. Riga: UL.

Kalve, I. (2008). *Vadības izglītība mūsdienu sabiedrībā [Management education in the modern society] PhD Thesis*. Riga: UL.

Kantāne, I. (2013). *Latvijas mazo uzņēmumu vadīšanas īpatnības [Peculiarities of Latvian small business management] PhD Thesis*. Riga: UL.

Kinta, G. (2013). *Mācīšanās rezultātu nozīme profesionālās vidējās izglītības vadībā [The role of learning outcomes in the vocational education and training governance] PhD Thesis*. Riga: UL.

Kulberga, I. (2013). *Uzņēmējdarbības vadītāja profesionālās kompetences pilnveidošana [Improving the professional competence of a business manager] PhD Thesis*. Riga: UL.

Lahiff, A., Li, J., Unwin, L., Zenner-Höffkes, L. & Pilz, M. (2019). 'Industrial standardisation as a driver for cross-national convergence in training processes: Aviation apprenticeships in England and Germany', *European Journal of Training and Development*, 43 (7/8), 752–766.

Lanka, A. & Mūrnieks, E. (2006). 'Vocational education and training in Latvia: The problems and solutions'. In Janewein, K. & Buenning, F. (eds.), *The Transformation of Vocational Education and Training (VET) in the Baltic States – Survey of Reforms and Developments*, pp. 47–68. Dordrecht: Springer.

Lapiņa, G. (2007). *Inovācijas pedagoģiskā izpratne augstskolā [Understanding of pedagogical innovation in the higher education] PhD Thesis*. Riga: UL.

Latvian Qualification Framework – National Coordination Point (2012). 'Latvijas izglītības sistēmas piesaiste Eiropas kvalifikāciju ietvarstruktūrai mūžizglītībai un Eiropas augstākās izglītības telpas kvalifikāciju ietvarstruktūrai [Linking the Latvian Education System to the European Qualifications Framework for Lifelong Learning]', *Latvian Qualification Framework – National Coordination Point*, <http://www.nki-latvija.lv/en>, accessible 14 June 2021.

Latvijas Republikas Saeima (1998). 'Izglītības likums 29.10.1998 [Education Law accepted 29.10.1998]', < https://likumi.lv/ta/id/50759-izglitibas-likums>, accessed 21 June 2021.

Latvijas Republikas Saeima (1999). 'Profesionālās izglītības likums [Law on Vocational Education]',<https://likumi.lv/ta/id/20244-profesionalas-izglitibas-likums>, accessed 21 June 2021.

Latvijas Republikas Saeima (2001). 'Par reglamentētajām profesijām un profesionālās kvalifikācijas atzīšanu 20.06.2001' [Law on the Regulated Professions and the Recognition of Professional Qualifications 20.06.2001], < https://likumi.lv/ta/id/26021-par-reglamentetajam-profesijam-un-profesionalas-kvalifikacijas-atzisanu>, accessed 21 June 2021.

Latvijas Republikas Saeima (2014). 'Izglītības attīstības pamatnostādnes 2014.-2020.gadam [The Education Development Guidelines for 2014–2020]',< https://likumi.lv/ta/id/266406-par-izglitibas-attistibas-pamatnostadnu-20142020gadam-apstiprinasanu>, accessed 21 June 2021.

Latvijas Republikas Saeima (2015). 'Grozījumi Profesionālās izglītības likumā 23.04.2015 [Amendments to the Law on Vocational Education accepted 23.04.2015]', < http://tap.mk.gov.lv/lv/mk/tap/?pid=40485457>, accessed 21 June 2021.

Latvijas Republikas Saeima (2017). 'Grozījumi Profesionālās izglītības likumā 22.06.2017 [Amendments to the Law on Vocational Education accepted 22.06.2017]', < http://tap.mk.gov.lv/lv/mk/tap/?pid=40485457>, accessed 21 June 2021.

Lavendels, J., Sitikovs, V. & Uhanova, M. (2012). 'Influence of Socio-demographic Characteristics to Attractiveness and Success of Initial Vocational Education and Training in Latvia', *Procedia – Social and Behavioral Sciences*, 55, 756–765.

Lester, S. (2015). 'A vocational qualifications system fit for adults? Revisiting some ideas from the university for industry', *Higher Education, Skills and Work-Based Learning*, 5 (2), 102–116.

Lice, A. & Sloka, B. (2019). 'Performance of vocational education in Latvia in developing employability of graduates. Society. Integration. Education', *Proceedings of the International Scientific Conference*, 5, 222–232.

Lindell, M. (2006). 'From formulation to realisation: The process of Swedish reform in advanced vocational education', *Education + Training*, 48 (4), 222–240.

Lindell, M. & Stenström, M. (2005). 'Between policy and practice: Structuring workplace learning in higher vocational education in Sweden and Finland', *Journal of Workplace Learning*, 17 (3), 194–211.

Luka, I. (2018). 'Summative evaluation of online language learning course efficiency for students studying tourism and hospitality management', *Quality Assurance in Education*, 26 (4), 446–465.

Ministry of Education and Science of Republic of Latvia (2020). 'Darba vidē balstītas mācības [Work – based Learning]', <https://www.izm.gov.lv/lv/darba-vide-balstitas-macibas>, accessed 21 June 2021.

Ministry of Education and Science of Republic of Latvia (2021). 'Prezentē jaunā absolventu monitoringa datus [Presentation of new graduate monitoring data], <https://www.izm.gov.lv/lv/jaunums/prezente-jauna-absolventu-monitoringa-datus>, accessed 21 June 2021.

Nikandrou, I., Brinia, V. & Bereri, E. (2009). 'Trainee perceptions of training transfer: An empirical analysis', *Journal of European Industrial Training*, 33 (4), 255–270.

Nikolou-Walker, E. & Curley, H. (2012). 'An examination, evaluation and analysis of work-based learning leadership within a higher education setting', *Higher Education, Skills and Work-Based Learning*, 2 (2), 186–200.

OECD (2001). *Reviews of National Policies for Education: Latvia 2001*. Paris: OECD Publishing.

OECD (2020). *OECD Skills Strategy Implementation Guidance for Latvia*. Paris: OECD Publishing.

Onstenk, J. & Blokhuis, F. (2007). 'Apprenticeship in The Netherlands: Connecting school- and work-based learning', *Education + Training*, 49 (6), 489–499.

Paisey, C. & Paysey, N. J. (2010). 'Developing skills via work placements in accounting: student and employer views', *Accounting Forum*, 34, 89–108.

Peiseniece, L. (2010). *Cilvēkresursu vadīšanas novērtēšanas metodes un to pilnveidošanas virzieni Latvijas lielajos uzņēmumos [Methods of Human Resource Management Evaluation and Directions for Their Improvement in Large Enterprises of Latvia] PhD Thesis*. Riga: UL.

Plump, C. M. (2010). 'Dealing with problem employees: A legal guide for employers', *Business Horizons*, 53, 607–618.

Ramina, B., Hodireva, V., & Silina, S. (2001). 'The modernisation of vocational education in Latvia', *Latvian National Observatory*, <http://www.aic.lv/Obs_2002/rep2001e/default.htm>, accessed 21 June 2021.

Riley, T. (2017). 'Work-based learning for the creative industries: A case study of the development of BA (Hons) web design and social media', *Higher Education, Skills and Work-Based Learning*, 7 (1), 79–91.

Rivera, C. A. (2010). *Building a Model of Leadership Development for Times of Change*. Riga: UL.

Romele, L. (2014). *Izglītības privātās un sociālās atdeves novērtējums Latvijā [Measuring the private and social returns to education in Latvia]*. Riga: UL.

Rusakova, A. (2011). *Recognition of Prior Learning within Higher Education in the Context of Lifelong Learning [Iepriekšējās izglītības atzīšana augstākajā izglītībā mūžizglītības kontekstā]*. Riga: UL.

Skilled-up (2018). *Project "Skills for the Baltic Wood industry – European Quality in Vocational Education and Training"*,< https://www.skilled-up.eu/>, accessed 21 June 2021.

Shaw, S. & Ogilvie, C. (2010). 'Making a virtue out of a necessity: Part time work as a site for undergraduate work-based learning', *Journal of European Industrial Training*, 34 (8/9), 805–821.

Smith, E. & Smith, A. (2011). 'Does the availability of vocational qualifications through work assist social inclusion?', *Education + Training*, 53 (7), 587–602.

Smith, S. & Martin, J. (2014). 'Practitioner capability: Supporting critical reflection during workbased placement – a pilot study', *Higher Education, Skills and Work-Based Learning*, 4 (3), 284–300.

Sommers, J., Woolfson, C. & Juska, A. (2014). 'Austerity as a global prescription and lessons from the neoliberal Baltic experiment', *The Economic and Labour Relations Review*, 25 (3), 397–416.

Talbot, J. & Lilley, A. (2014). 'Approaches to supervising work-based learning students' workplace research', *Higher Education, Skills and Work-Based Learning*, 4 (1), 44–65.

Tauriņa, Ž. (2011). *Jauniešu sasniegumu novērtēšanas procesa vadība vidējā izglītībā Latvijā [Managing the process of youth achievement assessment in secondary education in Latvia]*. Riga: UL.

Thomas, H. & Qiu, T. (2012). 'Work – related continuing education and training: Participation and effectiveness', *Journal of Workplace Learning*, 24 (3), 157–176.

Toledano-O'Farrill, R. (2017). 'Professional application projects: Work-based learning in the curriculum', *Higher Education, Skills and Work-Based Learning*, 7(1), 21–34.

Upenieks, A. (2008). *Jauno izglītības iestāžu vadītāju sagatavošana un adaptācija darbam izglītības iestādēs [Training and adaptation of new heads of educational institutions Training and adaptation of new heads of educational institutions]*. Riga: UL.

Vasiļevska, D. (2014). *Sociāli ekonomiskie faktori augstākās izglītības pieejamības nodrošinājumam Latvijā [Socio-economic factors for access to higher education in Latvia]*. Riga: UL.

VIAA (2012). 'Branch qualification system – recommendation', *State Education Development Agency of Republic of Latvia*,< https://www.viaa.gov.lv/lat/es_fondu_projekti/nozaru_kvalifikacijas_sistema/?tl_id=12561.&tls_id=14912>, accessed 21 June 2021.

Vilka, I. (2004). *Pašvaldību reformas un reģionālā attīstība Latvijā [Local government reforms and regional development in Latvia]*. Riga: UL.

Woolfson, C. (2008). 'Social dialogue and lifelong learning in new EU member states: "reform fit" in Latvia', *Journal of European Social Policy*, 18 (1), 79–87.

Zaļaiskalne, A. (2013). *Pārmaiņu vadība profesionālās izglītības satura pilnveidošanā Latvijā [Change management in the improvement of the vocational education and training content in Latvia]*. Riga: UL.

Zeibarte, L. (2011). *Pedagogu tālākizglītības pārvaldība nepārtrauktas profesionālās pilnveides nodrošināšanā [Managing teachers' continuing professional development]*. Riga: UL.

Krista Loogma

# 4. Estonia: expanding the institutional landscape

**Abstract:** This chapter discusses the main institutional developments of the skills formation system in Estonia with a particular focus on skills polarisation within the Estonian labour market. Furthermore, the chapter details the development of the institutions of skills formation in Estonia after the country regained independence in 1991, identifying four periods of change: (1) the liberal adjustment period, in the early 1990s was characterised by the transformation of the basic ideological principles underpinning education policy, (2) the EU pre-accession period, when the liberal adjustment was displaced by extensive standardization in education, particularly in VET and HE, (3) the post-accession crisis period, and, (4) the period of adoption of the comprehensive Estonian Lifelong Learning Strategy 2020. The development of the social dialogue on skill formation and the national qualifications system as the main institutional macro mechanism to coordinate skills supply and demand are explored. The chapter concludes with an assessment of future issues facing the skill formation system.

**Keywords:** Estonia, EU accession, institutional development, national qualifications system, skill formation system

## Introduction

Estonian students performed remarkably well according to the most recent PISA survey (at the end of the basic school) and the differences in attainment between students of different socio-economic backgrounds are low by international comparison. This could be seen as evidence that basic education is of high quality with school leavers having high levels of basic skills, such as maths, literacy and science alongside other general competencies. Attainment levels with respect to post-compulsory education and lifelong learning (LLL) are, however, becoming more polarised.

In Estonia, a relatively large proportion of young people (around 11 per cent of those between the ages of 18 and 24) do not complete compulsory education, and are thus likely to be not in education, employment or training (NEET) after school leaving age (Lauristin et al. 2020). Although the strategic goal for 2020 in the Estonian Lifelong Learning Strategy (ELLS) was to reduce this to less than 9 per cent, it has remained higher during recent years, at about 10.8 per cent. (HTM 2018). About 3 per cent of graduates do not continue studies after compulsory education and 20 per cent of those that do continue, do not complete the next educational level during the subsequent 4 years (HTM 2018). Although more than half the working-age population participates in adult education each year, participation levels are unequal and are influenced by prior educational attainment, employment status, gender and age (Saar et al. 2014). Additionally, in 2017 about 29 per cent of adults in the age group 25–64 have no professional or vocational qualification, making them particularly vulnerable in the context of crises and labour market transformations (HTM 2018). These trends suggest there is a risk of increasing polarisation of high and low skilled cohorts. The COVID-19 pandemic has also amplified the divide between the high skilled, with better positions in labour market and higher levels of participation in lifelong learning, and vulnerable groups (Lauristin et al. 2020). Men are over-represented within vulnerable cohorts.

The skills divide in Estonia begins with the pathways available to students after compulsory education. Whilst the majority (about 70 per cent since 1995) of graduates from basic school take the academic track, students with lower levels of attainment are directed to IVET. This approach prevents the improvement of VET quality and embeds a profound academic-vocational divide (Loogma et al. 2019).

A focus on core competencies is one approach that could be considered to address this situation. The COVID-19 pandemic underlined the importance of key competencies and skills, particularly the capacity for self-direction, and the digital skills needed for individualised distance learning. Such key competencies are not sufficiently supported nor developed systematically via formal education (Lauristin et al. 2020). The pandemic also revealed that while people can acquire digital skills relatively quickly, the capacity for self-direction takes longer to develop (ibid.).

Recent attention has focussed on the skills formation system (SFS) for several reasons. 'Free market forces' have been unable to balance skills supply against the backdrop of increasing demand (Schwalje 2011, 2), while growing uncertainty and rapid change within labour markets has emphasised the need for lifelong learning to enable individuals to upskill and re-skill. The SFS, therefore, is seen as an adaptive system (ibid.) embracing a complex set of actors such as governments, education and training (E&T) providers, business communities and individuals and their complicated relationships with the labour market. While E&T systems and government focus on skills supply the businesses, and individuals as lifelong learners, generate the demand for skills (Saar and Ure 2013; Schwalje 2011).

Estonia's SFS follows a neo-liberal or market model, similar to the model adopted in countries like the UK and USA, where E&T is orientated to the immediate needs of employers and adult training is seen as the responsibility of private actors (ibid.).

This chapter presents and discusses the main institutional developments in the SFS in Estonia, with a particular focus on skill polarisation within the Estonian labour market. The next section of this chapter details the development of the institutions of skills formation in Estonia after the country regained independence in 1991, identifying four periods of change.

## Institutional development and EU integration

The collapse of the Soviet Union and the re-establishment of independence in 1991 was a radical and complex regime change. Estonia adopted the most liberal and radical way of transitioning to a market economy, so-called shock therapy which was based on an expectation that the 'invisible hand of the market' would be a universal panacea. In the early 1990s, rapid change involving privatisation, foreign investments, and a reorientation from Eastern to Western markets impacted upon all sections of society. The transition resulted in rising unemployment and a significant mismatch with respect to the supply and demand for skills in labour market (Loogma 2004).

### The neo-liberal policy direction in education

During the period of Soviet rule in Estonia, education policy was highly centralised and ideologically determined. The first attempts to affect change within the sphere of education were initiated by the Estonian teachers of general education resulting in the generation of the new, independent and de-ideologised national curriculum for general education based on humanist and democratic values (Loogma et al. 2013). The new national curriculum was discussed at the Teachers' Congress in 1987 and later served as basis for education innovations in general education, although these had no impact on vocational education and training (VET) until the early 1990s when dramatic changes occurred within the labour market. The Soviet VET system in Estonia, was extremely centralised and tightly related to the centralised and planned economy, but this was reformed in the process of the transition to a market economy. In 1997, the first Development Plan for VET was drawn up by a partnership involving the state, employers and other social partners. This continued with work to establish the legislative framework for VET. An important milestone in the reform process was the adoption of the Professions Act in 2000, which provided the legal foundation for the National Qualifications Framework (NQF). Additionally, an informal agreement to co-operate in the development of VET was signed by the social partners (ibid).

Upper secondary education had become profoundly unequal by the end of the Soviet period, as there were differences in the quality of education between 'elite' schools, ordinary schools and vocational schools. From the viewpoint of skills development, the chasm between general and vocational education was the most significant divide. The vocational pathway was seen as inferior, and had a negative, determining influence on student progression. In the 1980s only 1 per cent of graduates from vocational secondary education had access to universities (Helemäe, Saar & Vöörmann 2000).

At least three factors influenced the adoption of a neo-liberal approach to education policy. Firstly, the direction of policy was influenced by external agents, international donors and development organisations, such as the International Monetary Fund (IMF), World Bank (WB) and others (Grootings 2009). Secondly, the adoption of a neo-liberal approach to education fitted with the overall transition strategy which was based on the introduction of a liberal market economy through the shock-therapy approach, as with many post-socialist countries. Thirdly, policy learning and transfer also influenced the adoption of the neo-liberal approach. After the re-establishment of Estonian independence, the country lacked both the finance and expertise necessary to build a new system. During the early 1990s, horizontal learning and the adoption of best practices from other (often random) systems took place (Toots & Loogma 2015). For example bilateral development programmes with Denmark, Germany and Finland made possible by the EU Phare programme dominated, yet many of these had a relatively narrow focus, (being directed at the training of vocational teachers, the adoption of new vocational curricula (e.g. commerce, banking, electronics, computer graphics) or finding partner schools from abroad, for instance).

## Periods of transformation of SFS

The Estonian education system has undergone four main waves of transformation during the post-socialist period (ibid). These are described in more detail below:

*1. The liberal adjustment period.* This period started in the early 1990s and was characterised by the transformation of the basic ideological principles underpinning education policy. The decentralisation and liberalisation introduced in Estonia meant that schools had significant freedoms to adjust to the new economic and social structures, although this process generated considerable instability.

Neoliberal principles such as cultivating student choice in relation to schools, competition between schools, the application of the NPM (New Public Management) model in school management and the decentralisation of the school network, alongside increasing standardization and accountability (Sahlberg 2010), were rapidly introduced in the late 1990s. League tables of gymnasiums were produced and 'elite' gymnasiums established, which exacerbated the divide between general and vocational education at upper secondary level and contributed to the continued negative status of VET (Loogma et al. 2019).

The extensive restructuring of large Soviet industrial enterprises which were closed or privatized rendered the previous system of training redundant. In this period, state intervention was minimal, and the social partners (employers, unions) were too weak to initiate and support reforms in VET and HE. In the mid-1990s Estonia's involvement in EU programmes, such as PHARE enabled the reform process to be kickstarted.

In 1995, the first legislative act regulating the activities of VET schools was developed ('*Kutseõppeasutuse seadus*'). At the same time the process of restructuring the VET schools network to adjust to the demand of new emerging economic structure began (Loogma 2010). During a very short period the VET system in Estonia has moved from the highly centralised 'distorted dual' Soviet system into a school-based system – the antithesis of the 'Soviet' model (ibid).

In 1999, Estonia signed the Bologna Declaration, which though not legally binding supported knowledge transfer via studies abroad, the creation of course structures more favourable to the needs of the labour market, and the harmonisation of quality standards. The Bologna Declaration quickly became an imperative with legal force as part of a plan for the reform of HE, institutionalised in the Universities Act, the Institutions of Professional Higher Education Act, and the Standards for Higher Education (Toots 2009). This meant transition to the 3+2 years HE system to make university studies more flexible and to accelerate students' transition to the labour market. The direction taken in the early 1990s toward neoliberal competition based HE resulted in considerable autonomy for the public universities and a boom in the establishment of private universities (ibid.). For example, in 2002, there were 49 institutions of HE in Estonia (including 23 private establishments) which competed more than they cooperated. Such fragmentation, however, resulted in the HE interest-groups becoming weak partners for the government (Toots 2009).

In the second half of the 1990s as accession negotiations with the EU proceeded, policy-learning in the education sector became more coordinated.

The initial desire to learn from the 'best' education policy and practice from abroad was replaced by the aspiration for EU membership, and thus policy transfer from the EU slowly became dominant (Toots and Loogma 2015), particularly in relation to VET and HE.

Finland's role in facilitating policy learning and transfer has been remarkable both at institutional level as well as through individual interactions between schools, teachers, public servants and others. However, policy transfer from Finland was relatively limited. Only some features of the Finnish education system were adopted by Estonia, such as greater autonomy for schools, the individualised approach to students and the establishment of system of state examinations at the end of gymnasium. Other aspects of Finnish system which the Finnish experts saw as key factors for their success in the PISA survey, such as free school lunches, social pedagogical support and less competition between schools, were not adopted (Toots 2009).

In 1996, prior to the commencement of the process of EU accession, the establishment of the Vocational Education Reform Foundation and the National Observatory of Vocational Education and the Labour Market by the European Training Foundation (ETF) marked the first steps in the creation of an institutional framework related to the Europeanization of education. Besides steering VET reform, the network of national observatories created for post-socialist countries by the ETF, served as horizontal learning mechanisms. In 2003, the Vocational Education Reform Foundation became the Innove Foundation with the aim to develop innovations in VET (Loogma 2016).

*2. The pre-accession period.* In the pre-accession period liberal adjustment was displaced by extensive standardization in education, particularly in VET and HE. The ratification of the Lisbon Strategy marked a new era in institutional development in education, and Estonia joined the Copenhagen Declaration for the development of VET policy in 2002, prior to joining the EU in 2004. For Estonian VET, the EU strategy toward a uniform, transparent vocational educational framework, set by the Copenhagen Declaration, provided the impetus for intense Europeanization (Loogma 2016), which in practice meant:

> the process of the construction, diffusion and institutionalization of formal and informal rules, procedures, policy paradigms, styles, ways of "doing things" and shared beliefs and norms, which are first defined and consolidated in the making of EU decisions and then incorporated into the logic of domestic discourse, identities, political structures and public policies. (Radaelli 2000, 213).

As the EU adopted the Open Method of Coordination to create a common educational framework in VET and HE, the process of Europeanization went hand in hand with policy learning from the EU (Toots & Loogma 2015). The Europeanization of education in Estonia in this period has manifested itself in the process of integrating with EU structures and joining the EU education strategies (Lisbon Strategy, Bologna Process) as well as a relatively uncritical transfer of EU education initiatives. This has become the driving force behind changes in education in Estonia in the 21st century (Loogma 2016).

The ratification of the EU Lisbon Strategy and participation in the Copenhagen Process changed the methods of policy learning and gave rise to new domestic institutions (Toots & Loogma 2015). In this period the Estonian Qualifications Authority was founded and a 5-level Estonian qualification framework (EstQF) was established. Whilst one of the main aims of the EstQF was to coordinate skills supply and demand, it also provided a strong impetus for standardization, particularly for VET and HE as well as a mechanism for implementing EU guidelines with respect to education. The standardization was most influential within VET and HE as those sectors were most affected by Europeanization in education.

3. *The Post-accession period.* Estonia became part of the European Union in May 2004. The period after that has also been referred to as the period of post-accession crisis (Agh 2010). The aspiration 'to turn to the West' (Lauristin & Vihalemm 1997) seemed to have been achieved on acquiring EU membership, NATO membership in 2004, and by joining the Eurozone in 2011. However, there was a lack of vision about the next 'grand goal' for the nation in the context of new challenges that arose as a result of the continuing dominance of the radical neo-liberal approach (Vetik et al. 2012). The rapidly worsening demographic situation, a declining and ageing population, was exacerbated by 'brain drain' caused by the free movement of labour to countries with higher salaries. The brain drain highlighted that demand for high-level skills was relatively limited in Estonia (Saar et al. 2014) chiefly because low value-added industry was over-represented in the Estonian economy, a situation that persists today.

The economic crisis of 2008 caused unemployment to increase, peaking in 2010. The crisis showed that individuals with higher qualifications coped better during periods of economic difficulty and so promoted increased interest in generic skills and key competencies (Loogma et al. 2019). Employees with backgrounds in basic and (vocational) secondary education (without HE) were most at risk from unemployment because of their lower capacity for mobility in the labour market. In 2009, just 54 per cent of graduates from VET were employed six months after graduation. Even though the overall employment rate increased after the economic crisis, those with general upper secondary education and/or HE found it easier to gain alternative employment than those with

**Table 4.1.** Unemployment rate by educational attainment (1997–2019)

| | Basic education or lower | Secondary education | HE (incl MA and PhD levels) |
|---|---|---|---|
| 1997 | 15.5 | 10.0 | 4.4 |
| 1998 | 15.4 | 10.5 | 4.3 |
| 1999 | 19.6 | 12.9 | 4.5 |
| 2000 | 23.6 | 15.3 | 7.2 |
| 2001 | 20.6 | 13.9 | 5.4 |
| 2002 | 19.8 | 11.4 | 4.9 |
| 2003 | 16.2 | 10.5 | 5.8 |
| 2004 | 16.6 | 10.7 | 4.3 |
| 2005 | 13.2 | 9.1 | 3.9 |
| 2006 | 10.9 | 6.2 | 2.5 |
| 2007 | 9.5 | 4.7 | 1.6 |
| 2008 | 10.4 | 5.8 | 2.5 |
| 2009 | 25.6 | 15.5 | 5.1 |
| 2010 | 27.6 | 19.1 | 8.4 |
| 2011 | 24.5 | 12.4 | 7.7 |
| 2012 | 21.6 | 10.3 | 4.9 |
| 2013 | 14.0 | 9.6 | 5.5 |
| 2014 | 12.9 | 8.1 | 4.6 |
| 2015 | 12.2 | 6.8 | 3.7 |
| 2016 | 12.7 | 7.8 | 3.8 |
| 2017 | 10.9 | 6.7 | 2.9 |
| 2018 | 10.3 | 5.8 | 3.4 |
| 2019 | 9.8 | 4.8 | 2.9 |

*Note.* Statistics Estonia https://www.stat.ee/en.

only a basic and/or vocational education after basic education (ibid.). The economic crisis also increased the wage gap in the labour market, as the wages of managers and professionals continued to rise, while those of workers in elementary jobs, and skilled agricultural workers decreased (Saar & Helemäe 2011).

The EU policy framework has addressed two significant policy goals with respect to education, and particularly VET and HE. Firstly, the goals, principles and instruments related to quality assurance (e.g. common European Qualification Framework, ensuring access to education for vulnerable groups) have had a considerable influence on the domestic regulative and formal education institutions. Secondly, tools were developed to popularise VET as the main mechanism for overcoming disparities between general and vocational education at secondary level. Raising the status of vocational education has been a central aim during the entire European cooperation process. However, in the Estonian context, despite extensive efforts around 70 per cent of basic school graduates move into the gymnasium, i.e. to the HE track to obtain general education and access to university.

The 8-level EU common EQF and outcome-based curricula for skills development was written into law in Estonia in 2013 for VET and HE. This change simultaneously marked a transition to a learner-centred and outcome-based model in education provision and skills formation.

*4. The adoption of the comprehensive Estonian Lifelong Learning Strategy 2020* marked the next stage in the development of skills formation system. This strategy regarded all parts of the E&T system (general education, VET, HE and adult education) as a strategic whole. Where previously there were separate development plans for general, vocational, HE and adult education, all education sectors were now integrated into common strategic framework that saw education and thus, skills formation as integrated processes continuing throughout peoples' lives. In the strategy five main goals and policies designed to achieve these by 2020 were elaborated:

1. The adoption of a student-centred approach. The principal measures to support this included: ensuring the content and volume of studies supported learning outcomes, including the development of key competences; introducing formative assessment; developing in-service training provision for teachers and principals; supporting collaboration in and outside formal education and developing Centres of Competence for educational sciences.
2. Developing competent and motivated teachers and school leadership. The objective was to make the evaluation and remuneration of teachers and school leaders reflect their professional qualifications and performance via evaluation, salary adjustments and increasing the status of the teaching profession.
3. Establishing 'a digital focus in lifelong learning' by incorporating a digital culture into the learning process and supporting digital learning resources in schools; accessing a modern digital infrastructure for learning; creating and implementing assessment models for digital competence and creating learning opportunities for adults to acquire digital competencies (HTM 2018).
4. Promoting equal opportunities and increasing participation in lifelong learning. The measures to support this goal focus on creating more flexible access and better quality opportunities in education; ensuring the provision

of good quality VET and HE that addresses the needs of the labour market; providing support services and opportunities for LLL participation for the socially excluded and providing support schemes and assistance for students and graduates of non-Estonian language basic schools.

5. Aligning lifelong learning opportunities with the needs of the labour market through establishing a more efficient work experience scheme embracing a quality guarantee providing information and counselling services; preparing employees for jobs in areas of economic growth; and developing a system for anticipating future skills needs to inform lifelong learning policy and provision. For the last measure the state-supported programme OSKA was introduced. OSKA is the state-supported programme that analyses skills and labour market needs necessary for Estonia's economic development over the next 10 years (https://oska.kutsekoda.ee/en/).

The progress review on the results of ELLS 2010 by the Ministry of Education and Research (MoER) concluded that progress had been made in some areas. VET graduate employment levels and remuneration had risen indicating rising demand for medium-level skills in the labour market and the drop-out rate from general and VET schools had fallen. More students were graduating in STEM subjects from HE, and at the same time, the proportion of foreign students in HE increased. Participation in adult education increased considerably, with the rate of increase being fastest amongst those with poor levels of education (HTM 2018). Whilst unlikely to have had a direct impact on the relationship between LLL and the labour market, the introduction of the OSKA system probably increased awareness about skills demands, and the various factors influencing that. The introduction of OSKA can therefore be seen as step forward in the development of the skills formation system.

## Implications of economic and social developments on skills needs

Inefficiency and low productivity were consequences of the socialist economic system which was characterised by a workforce generated by central planning with limited scope for movement between jobs, the ideology of zero unemployment, the prevailing paternalistic organizational culture that valued loyalty, administratively controlled unions whose main task was to allocate goods and services (especially those that were infrequently available within very limited markets, such as cars, living spaces etc.) to the workforce (Loogma 2004; Loogma et al. 2019). The alignment of skills needs with the economy was assured by the manpower planning system, and the relationships between vocational schools and enterprises were strong, as all apprentices were guaranteed training places in state companies that provided practical training and financial support to the schools and provided graduates with real workplaces via a planned work assignment scheme. Yet, the occupational profiles built in VET schools were narrow as they needed to correspond to the labour needs of a specific 'support company' (Liivik et al. 2013).

The economic transition after Estonia regained independence in August 1991 involved a complex set of restructuring programmes, particularly privatisation, but which also included restitution, land reform, the restructuring of markets, and a rapid re-orientation from Eastern to Western markets (Loogma 2004). Privatisation was followed by de-industrialisation and many large enterprises were reformed into SMEs. Employment in industry and agriculture declined, whilst the service sector grew rapidly. The transformation revealed the need for new qualifications, skills and competencies, although there was no clear vision or understanding of what kinds of occupational profiles the newly founded companies would need (Eamets & Phillips 2000). As a result of rapid de-industrialisation and restructuring, the traditional ties between education and the labour market were almost broken. Emerging SMEs were not able to co-operate with E&T providers in the early years of transition (Loogma 2004), so the main route to skills formation in the labour market was work based learning. There was increased labour movement between sectors, especially from declining industry and agriculture to the emerging service sector (ibid).

The public discourse regarding the 'winners' and 'losers' in the transformation reflected how skills were related to individual success or failure (Loogma 2004; Loogma et al. 2019). Highly educated individuals, and especially those educated within HE were considerably more likely to be 'winners' primarily because of the cultural capital they possessed and their capacity to transform this into social and economic capital within the new context. Workers with a vocational education background, by contrast, were more likely to become 'losers' (Õun 2002, 69; Saar 2002). Social stratification became explicitly linked to HE qualifications, which became a symbolic currency and key to success in the new Estonian market system (Pavelson & Karotamm 2001). Subsequent crises, however, demonstrated that general/key competencies and social capital acquired in HE (see Table 1), rather than specific skills, were the determining factor for labour market success. The COVID-19 pandemic in turn showed firstly, the need for more flexibility in implementing the standards of EstQS and secondly, the primary importance of key skills, particularly skills to facilitate self-directed, independent learning (Loogma & Sirk 2021).

## Social dialogue in skills formation

Social dialogue can be regarded as an important factor in the process of accommodating the interests of the different parties/social partners within the SFS, particularly those of state, employers and employees. Social dialogue with respect to the SFS in Estonia has taken two main institutionalised forms: (1) the involvement of employers and trade unions within the qualification system; and (2) co-operation at workplace level to provide practical VET, HE and apprentice training.

However, the role of unions in the SFS has been limited. Most of the Soviet trade unions collapsed, and since the early 1990s, those that survived underwent significant change. During the first years of independence, economic and societal changes were accompanied by a sharp fall in union density. In the Soviet period trade union membership was compulsory but when compulsion ceased density declined sharply and by 2010 it had stabilised at around 7–8 per cent (Eamets 2013). In many traditional sectors such as transport, trade unions were restructured. In new sectors, including some parts of the service sector, IT, and banking, unions never emerged. Indeed, some industries such as construction and banking are unorganized in Estonia. Furthermore, in many fields, particularly the high skilled sectors, the professional organizations have been involved in social dialogue rather than the unions representing employees. Currently, trade unions have lower levels of membership in the private sector than in the public and voluntary sectors. In 2015 just 5.2 per cent of those working in private enterprises were union members, compared to 11.6 per cent of employees in central and local government, and 17.2 per cent of those working in non-profit associations and foundations. This means that significant parts of the economy are unorganized.

In the period of liberal adjustment after the collapse of Soviet system the system of practical training collapsed. The new enterprises were mainly too small and weak to provide and support practical training in enterprises. The first informal agreement between employers, state and VET institutions was signed in 2001 (Loogma 2004). The agreement primarily concerned cooperation and the involvement of employers in VET by way of providing practical training, developing school curricula and, importantly, participating in the national qualification system, established after 2000. Social partnership was also supported by the Europeanization process, particularly via the Copenhagen Process and later, in the process and framework of the Qualification System. With the transition to the 8-level European Qualification System in 2013, cooperation between state, educational institutions, employers and professional organizations was strengthened as employers were involved in every part and level of EstQF. However, the social partnership is often employer dominated, and the limited resources and negotiating power of unions has contributed to low levels of membership (Eamets 2013).

## The development of the national qualifications system as the main institutional macro mechanism to coordinate skills supply and demand

In 2000, the Professions Act provided the keystone for the national qualification system, and in 2000/2001 co-operation between the state, employers and professional organisations laid the groundwork for developing professional/vocational standards. The Estonian Qualifications Authority Foundation (EQA) was established in 2001 to develop the national occupational qualifications (EstQF) system. Since then, vocational standards have influenced curricula development in VET and HE schools and the award of vocational certificates. The qualification system was also designed to recognise and legitimise prior and lifelong learning.

The EQA serves as a support for the occupational qualifications system and is responsible for developing, assisting, recognizing and comparing occupational competence, and for organising and coordinating the activities of sector skills´ councils. Most significantly, for the development of the NQF, the EQA is responsible for implementing EU policies through several European Social Fund (ESF) projects, such as Development of Professional Qualifications 2008–2013, The development of the Estonian Qualification Framework (EstQF) and many others. In 2008–2012, the EQA developed the system so the EstQF could be referenced to the European Qualification Framework (EQF). However, EstQF emerged from this process in a dominant position vis à vis EQF without any meaningful debate. The EQA has become an important agent, mediating between EU and national actors to improve the coherence between National and European Qualification Frameworks and the quality standards of VET (Loogma 2016). The implementation of the EstQF, and particularly the 2013 introduction of a competence-based approach, however, has introduced 'overstandardization' and inflexibility into the system, particularly with respect to VET and HE. Furthermore, the autonomy of teachers has decreased considerably as standardization has left little room for curricula innovation or teacher creativity (Erss 2018). The process of standardization was challenged by the COVID-19 pandemic, which necessitated developing innovative training methods (Lauristin et al. 2019; Loogma & Sirk 2021).

In the initial phase, the responsibility for organizing examinations and issuing certificates was primarily within the remit of professional associations and some VET schools. School leaving certificates of VET did not automatically give qualifications to school leavers. Gradually, the share of VET schools and HE institutions with the remit to organize exams and issue certificates has increased. In the context of rapid labour market change, it is a moot point whether the qualification system remains fit for purpose, especially given the lengthy process of updating standards. Moreover, research has shown, that not all employers are aware of the standards and/or do not consider qualifications during the recruitment process (Loogma 2020). Given the context of ever faster change in the labour market, the emergence of new, flexible forms of work and new types of working, the goals and functionality of the qualification system should be reconsidered.

## Future issues in skill development

The lack of alignment between the demand and supply of skills, and the skills based social polarisation described earlier in this chapter have persisted, with little improvement during the strategic period 2010–2015. This indicates that institutional developments guided by neoliberal principles are insufficiently robust to mitigate such tendencies.

There is a risk that skills gaps will increase within the labour market, and that skills based social polarisation will grow. Deficits in the numbers qualified to be doctors, nurses, engineers, teachers and IT specialists are growing, and some labour market forecasts suggest the same trends are visible with respect to automated applications and AI (artificial intelligence) across several fields. As a consequence, some occupations requiring higher education (HE) , are disappearing or being modified, alongside the emergence of new occupations, such as data analytics, logistics and robotics. Yet against this backdrop there remains an unacceptably large segment of the population whose participation in the labour market and lifelong learning (LLL) is still limited (Lauristin et al. 2019).

The OECD (2018) uses the term 'future-readiness' to describe a broad combination of knowledge, skills, attitudes and values necessary for success in an increasingly complex and uncertain world. An important facet of future-readiness is the importance of human agency, the implication being that individuals need to take responsibility for their own development (OECD 2018). From the standpoint of skills formation, this implies developing the capability not just to respond to skills demands but to anticipate these too. In line with this, five main ideas (Lauristin et al. 2019) have been elaborated to transform the E&T system over coming decades.

First, there should be increasing focus on the development of new, broad-based skills and competencies, including the systematic development of general skills, manifest in so called T-shape skills profile, designed to enable individuals to manage change, develop the capacity for self-directed learning and development, and thus reduce their risk of social exclusion. New mechanisms for utilising high level skill in the labour market should be introduced along with workplace learning, and support for lifelong learning should expand. Second, education should support learners' individual choices, and individualised learning pathways should be provided. Informal learning should be recognised, and the integration of separate learning spaces should mirror the integration of general and vocational education provision. Third, the quality of HE should rise considerably, while maintaining a balance between internationalisation and preserving the national culture and language. HE should provide more degree options including modular so-called 'nano-degrees' where learners can assemble an individual educational plan from different short courses. Fourth, more emphasis should be placed on the mobility of scientists, partnerships with business, and the establishment of science-based incubation centres. Fifth, the teachers' role should be transformed to that of learning facilitator.

Central to the Estonian new education strategy 2035 are the concepts of flexible, individualised learning pathways and open learning spaces. For institutions this implies providing open and flexible learning opportunities better suited to rapidly changing labour markets.

## References

Agh, A. (2010). 'Post-accession crisis in the new member states: Progressing or backsliding in EU?' *Studies of Transition States and Societies*, 2 (1), 74–95.

Eamets, R. (2013). 'Labour market and labour market policies during great recession: The case of Estonia', *IZA Journal of European Labor Studies*, 2 (4), 1–25.

Eamets, R., & Philips, K. (2000). *Eesti tööturu areng üleminekuperioodil. [The development of the Estonian labour market during the transition period].* Tartu: Elmatar.

Erss, M.(2018). 'Complete freedom to choose within limits' – teachers' views of curricular autonomy, agency and control in Estonia, Finland and Germany', *The Curriculum Journal*, 29(2), 238–256.

Grootings, P. (2009). 'Facilitating policy learning. Active learning and the reform of education systems in transition countries'. In R. MacLean & D. Wilson (eds.), *International Handbook of Education for the Changing World of Work*, pp. 499–512. Springer: Toronto.

Helemäe, J., Saar, E., & Vöörmann, R. (2000). *Kas haridusse tasus investeerida? Hariduse selekteerivast ja stratifitseerivast rollist kahe põlvkonna kogemuse alusel.* [Was it worth investing in education?: The selective and stratifying role of education based on the experience of two generations]. Tallinn: Teaduste Akadeemia Kirjastus.

HTM (2018). 'Haridus- ja Teadusministeeriumi valdkondade arengukavade 2017. A tulemusaruanded [Ministry of Education and Research sectoral development plans 2017. Performance reports]', *HTM*, <https://www.hm.ee/sites/default/files/uuringud/htm_tulemusvaldkondade_2017_aruanded.pdf>, accessed 25.03.2021.

Lauristin, M., Loogma, K., Vernik-Tuubel, E.-M., Kutsar, D., Erss, M., Kallas, K., Sildnik, A., & Käosaar, I. (2019). 'Heaolu ja sidususe visioon. Ekspertrühmade tulevikuvisioonid ja ettepanekud Eesti haridus-, teadus-, noorte-, ja keelevaldkonna arendamiseks aastatel 2021–2035 [A vision for prosperity and cohesion. Expert Groups' visions and proposals for the development of education, research, youth and languages in Estonia 2021–2035]', *Haridus- ja Teadusministeerium*, < https://www.hm.ee/sites/default/files/haridus-_ja_teadusstrat_2035_heaolu_ja_sidususe_visioon.pdf>, accessed 25.03.2021.

Lauristin, M., Loogma, K., Erss, M., Vernik, E.-M., & Sarv, E.-S. (2020). 'Õpilaste, õpetajate ja lastevanemate toimetulek koroonakriisi aegses kaugõppes [Coping of Student, Teachers and Parents in the context of distance learning in the time of Covid-pandemia]', *Estonian Education Forum*,<https://haridusfoorum.ee/images/2020/Distantsppe_uuring_EHF_250720.pdf>, accessed 29.03.2021.

Liivik, R., Karmin, L., Janulaitiene, N., & Montvilaite, S. (2013). 'Vocational education.' In I. Kestere & A. Ksuze (eds.), *History of Pedagogy and Educational Sciences in the Baltic Countries from 1940 to 1990: An Overview*, pp. 70–84. Riga: SIA Izdevniecība RaKa.

Loogma, K. (2004). *Töökeskkonnas õppimise tähendus töötajate kohanemisel töömuutustega. [The meaning of learning in the work environment for workers adapting to changes at work], PhD Dissertation.* Tallinn: TPÜ kirjastus.

Loogma, K. (2010). 'The situation of VET teachers in Estonia'. In S. Kirpal (ed.), *Changing Roles and Competences of VET Teachers and Trainers. Final Report/ Volum II. National Summaries of Interview Results,* pp. 97–116. Bremen: Institute Technik and Bildung (ITB), University of Bremen.

Loogma, K. (2016). 'Europeanization in VET policy as a process of reshaping the educational space', *International Journal for Research in Vocational Education and Training*, 3 (1), 16–28.

Loogma, K. (2020). 'Kutsehariduse sotsiaalne ökoloogia.' [Social Ecology of Vocational Education]. In M. Heidmats (ed.), *Haridusmõte [Educational Thought]*, pp. 236–261. Tallinn: TLÜ Kirjastus.

Loogma, K., & Sirk, M. (2021). 'Eriolukorrast tingitud distantsõppe kogemused ja mõju kutseharidusele [The Experience and Consequences of the CoVid Pandemia on Vocational Education]', forthcoming.

Loogma, K., Tafel-Viia, K. & Ümarik, M. (2013). 'Conceptualizing educational changes: A social innovation approach', *Journal of Educational Change*, 14 (3), 283–301.

Loogma, K., Ümarik, M., Sirk, M., & Liivik, R. (2019). 'How history matters: The emergence and persistence of structural conflict between academic and vocational education: The case of Post-Soviet Estonia', *Journal of Educational Change*, 20, 105–135.

OECD (2018). 'The Future of Education and skills 2030. Learning Framework 2030',<http://www.oecd.org/education/2030/E2030%20Position%20Paper%20(05.04.2018).pdf>, accessed 15.01.2021.

Õun, M. (2002). 'Subjektiivset edu ja ebaedu mõjutavad tegurid.' [The subjective factors infuencing success and failure]. In E. Saar (ed.), *Trepist alla ja üles: edukad ja ebaedukad postsotsialistlikus Eestis*, pp. 59–80. Tallinn: Eesti Teaduste Akadeemia Kirjastus.

Pavelson, M., & Korotam, N. (2001). *Muutuv töö ja teisenev tegija [Changing work and worker]*. Tallinn: TTÜ Kirjastus.

Saar, E. (2002). 'Kihistumise süvenemine Eestis 1990.aasatel – kas paratamatus?' [Aggravation of stratification in Estonia in 1990 – is it inevitable?]. In E. Saar (ed.), *Trepist alla ja üles: edukad ja ebaedukad postsotsialistlikus Eestis*, pp. 275–302. Tallinn: Eesti Teaduste Akadeemia Kirjastus.

Saar, E., & Helemäe, J. (2011). 'Conclusions and discussions'. In E. Saar (ed.), *Towards a Normal Stratification Order. Actual and Perceived Social Stratification in Post-socialist Estonia.* Frankfurt am Main: Peter Lang.

Saar, E., & Ure, O.-B. (2013). 'Lifelong Learning Systems: Overview and extension of different typologies'. In E. Saar, O. B. Ure & J. Holford (eds.), *Lifelong Learning in Europe*, pp. 46–81. Cheltenham: Edward Elgar.

Saar, E., Unt, M., Lindemann, K., Reiska, E., & Tamm, A. (2014). *Oskused ja elukestev õpe: kellelt ja mida on Eestil oskuste parandamiseks õppida? PIAAC uuringu temaatiline aruanne Nr 2 [Skills and lifelong learning: from whom and what can Estonia learn to improve skills? PIAAC survey thematic report No 2].* Tartu: Haridus- ja Teadusministeerium.

Sahlberg, P. (2010). 'Rethinking accountability in a knowledge society', *Journal of Educational Change*, 11 (1), 45–61.

Schwalje, W. (2011). 'A conceptual model of national skills formation for knowledge-based economic development. MPRA Paper No. 30302', *London School of Economics*, <https://mpra.ub.uni-muenchen.de/30302/>, accessed 01.03.2021.

Toots, A. (2009). 'Brussels comes via Helsinki: The role of Finland in Europeanization of Estonian education policy', *Halduskultuur*,10, 58–73.

Toots, A., & Loogma, K. (2015). Õppiv Euroopastumine Eesti Hariduspoliitikas [Learning Europeanization in Estonian Education Policy]. In *Estonian Human Development Report*, pp 259–264. Tallinn: Eesti Koostöö Kogu.

Vetik, R, Sootla, G., Kalev, L., Kattel, R., & Saarts, T. (2012). *Eesti poliitika ja valitsemine 1991–2011*. [Estonia policy and governance 1991–2011]. Tallinn: TLÜ kirjastus.

Horacy Dębowski and Wojciech Stęchły

# 5. Poland: striving for better governance and integration

**Abstract:** This chapter analyses skill formation reforms in Poland after the fall of communism. These reforms focussed on improving skills formation in the all sectors of education and on introduction of qualitative innovations. Decision-makers made a conscious effort to restructure education policies to meet contemporary challenges. These reforms were evidence based, with Poland drawing heavily on the lessons of skill formation in other countries. The main driver for reform of the system of skill formation in Poland was aligning this with labour market needs. Incentives and obligations were thus designed to stimulate employer cooperation and foster national and international competition. Skill formation reforms have been hampered by the absence of organized social partners, path-dependent capacity of all the actors within skills formation, the lack of coherence in coordination of stakeholder partnerships, as well as the backdrop of political turmoil. Economic growth reduced unemployment yet large-scale emigration caused sudden and significant skills and shifted thinking about the importance of vocational skills at upper secondary and higher levels, and employer attitudes towards their own role in education. All the reforms were supported by EU funds and initiatives which were of paramount importance in driving policy. EU funds were used, not only to finance systemic projects that prepared for the introduction of strategies and reforms, but also to finance the initial stages of implementation.

**Keywords:** Labour market needs, Poland, skill formation reforms, skill formation strategy, social dialogue, EU funding and support

## Introduction

The evolution of institutional infrastructure for skill formation in Poland between 1989 and 2019 is most appropriately described by considering the four main education and training sectors: general education (GE); initial and continuing vocational education (VET); higher education (HE) ; and non-formal adult education (AE).

In the socio-economic transformations after 1989, skills policies were not prioritised and public funds for the purpose were limited. Major reform of general education in 1999 established a sound institutional setting, but systemic reform affecting other skill sectors did not take place until the 2010s. In the past decade, the situation changed markedly, as Poland reformed all sectors contributing to skill formation and developed initiatives in areas that were previously unregulated, uncoordinated or otherwise neglected by policy makers. Firstly, the state introduced new quality assurance arrangements in HE, VET and AE to respond to domestic needs and to ensure that the Polish system met quality criteria in line with European recommendations for the European Higher Education Area, Copenhagen Process and European Qualifications Framework. Several financial and organizational mechanisms were also introduced, with the intention of ensuring the skills system was responsive to industry needs and had the capacity to contribute to the improvement of socio-economic conditions. Reforms were focussed on promoting work-based learning and facilitating industry involvement in VET and HE, while providing training for employees. In HE, structural reform was introduced to enhance internationalisation and research excellence at Polish universities. EU funding was a key driver with respect to policy development and reform, as well as with regards to education and training provision. Initially, the social partners were passive, had limited resources, and paid scant attention to skills development, but their involvement gradually increased, as outlined below.

A more recent policy innovation involved integrating formal education with non-formal adult education, which was designed to increase investment by adults and companies in skills development. The Integrated Qualifications System Act (2015) and the Integrated Skills Strategy (2019) are core elements in state-led integration of skills formation, with the IQS Act constituting a structure for skills system governance.

Socio-economic factors were important drivers of policy change. Continuing skill deficits in Poland had arisen because of the pace of economic development, changes in the structure of the economy and occupations, and significant levels of emigration, which motivated policymakers and employers to search for new solutions. It became evident that the system for vocational skills after years of inattention demanded renaissance and that wholesale reform was necessary with respect to adult learning.

This chapter draws upon an analysis of policy documents, as well as nine open-ended interviews with representatives of the Ministry of Education, central and regional examination boards, higher education, social partner organizations and teachers, and through collaboration with scholars in the field.

## Socio-economic factors affecting the skills formation system

Several factors influence skills formation in Poland. Economic growth exerts the greatest impact, since Poland has raised its real GDP per capita almost 250 per cent during three decades of transformation, with one of the fastest growth rates in the world (Piątkowski 2018; World Bank 2019, 24), largely as a result of manufacturing and exporting low-technology goods (Brandt 2018).

Rapid economic growth was accompanied by intense demand for labour which in turn necessitated structural change. Employment in agriculture fell from 35 per cent in 1990s to 9 per cent in 2019 and employment in services rose to over 58 per cent, although deindustrialisation in Poland has not yet matched Western 1970s and 80s levels (Lewandowski & Magda 2014). In Poland in 2019, over 30 per cent of the labour force was still employed in industry. These changes reflect increased demand for non-routine tasks requiring higher skills. However, as noted by Hardy et al. (2018), in contrast with other Western countries, Polish uptake for routine cognitive tasks has also increased over the last 30 years (mainly due to growth in employment for medium skilled, non-manual workers). As a result, as in some other CEE countries, a large proportion of the labour force still routinely supplies the necessary cognitive input which is typical for simple office and service jobs (Lewandowski 2018).

Poland remains a 'moderate innovator', with little public and business research and low development expenditure, as well as a weak tradition of commercialising research. The productivity gap with other OECD countries is considerable, particularly for small enterprises. While Poland is gradually approaching EU15 countries in terms of ICT capital intensity and automation, the gap remains substantial for technologies driving upskilling and the de-routinization of labour (Lewandowski 2018).

Between 2002 and 2019, unemployment fell from 21 per cent to 4.5 per cent, although economic activity is still below the OECD average. The legal retirement age and the effective labour market exit ages are also below the OECD average. This contributes to low adult economic and training activities (OECD 2019a, 179) despite Poland having one of the longest average working hours in Europe (OECD 2021).

After joining the European Union in 2004, emigration reached an unprecedented scale. According to Fihel and Okólski (2019), after 2004, one in five people between the ages of 25 and 34 left Poland on a long-term basis, with estimates suggesting 2.4 million had emigrated by the end of 2015. Today, Poland is still one of the greatest exporters of skilled labour, although emigration is now falling (OECD 2019b).

As a result of labour force outflows, the crisis in VET, the boom in academic education and strong economic growth, significant labour force deficits have affected almost all sectors of the Polish economy. This situation was not mitigated by the massive worker inflow, chiefly from Ukraine, after 2014. The exogenous migration shocks of the 2010s had a significant impact upon industrial and skills policies, motivating employers toward human capital investment and their willingness to contribute to vocational education (Reegård & Dębowski 2020).

Demographic change is another significant factor influencing skills formation. The Polish population is forecast to fall from 38 to 33.9 million by 2050 (GUS 2014), and the corresponding decline in labour supply will negatively impact public finance, the pension system and the welfare state (Levandowski & Rutkowski 2017). HE is, and will remain, the most affected by population decline and many private institutions are expected to close, despite the rising global trend for increasing private sector market share. The consequences for general and vocational education will be less profound, as these form part of compulsory education, so most institutions are state financed (Levitas 2017).

## Institutional change within the skills formation system

In Poland, systemic political and economic transition began in 1989. Skills policies were reactive and not prioritised. Public fund allocation for the purpose was also limited. We should however bear in mind, as noted by Piątkowski (2018, 186), that 'it is widely accepted by international observers and institutions that Poland's governments conducted pragmatic, responsible and effective economic policy during the whole post transition period maintaining macroeconomic stability, developing institutions and providing support to private sector development'.

### Formal general and vocational education

Changes in the formal education system began with the School Education Act of 7 September 1991 and were designed for gradual introduction (Sławiński et al. 2013, 113). Increased autonomy for schools and teachers provided the institutional framework for the functioning of educational institutions and school choice. The second wave of reform took place in 1999, when a coherent set of institutions was established (Herbst et al. 2015). Under these reforms, educational content and examinations were administered centrally (Ministry of Education and its agencies), whereas other aspects of governance were decentralised and delegated to municipalities and schools.

Aligned to the 1999 administrative reform, local government assumed responsibility for managing primary and secondary schools and received funds from the state budget for that purpose. Herbst and Wojciuk (2017) noted that Poland introduced a well-balanced division of tasks between the various tiers of education governance: 50 per cent of decisions were left to school principals, 25 per cent each to municipalities and central government. Schools gained freedom in developing their training programmes (curricula) and the autonomy to choose textbooks satisfying the requirements for the newly introduced national core curricula.

The reform of 1999 also introduced a new school structure (eight years in primary school and four years in secondary school were replaced by six years in primary school, three years in lower secondary school and three years in upper secondary school) and the external examination system was established, consisting of the central and eight regional examination boards, which became responsible for design and administration of general and vocational external examinations.

External standardized exams are now organized at the end of primary school (exam for 8$^{th}$ graders) and upper secondary school (*matura*), and for the award of vocational certificates. The *matura* replaces admission examinations to HE. Over the years, the general examinations have evolved, focussing increasingly on critical thinking and problem solving rather than the assessment of factual knowledge. VET examinations have also been significantly modified, with a pivot towards performance-based assessment in work situations.

The core curricula in general education and VET were reformed in 2009 and 2012 respectively. The reforms introduced learning outcomes, increased the visibility of key competencies within lifelong learning and the transparency of procedures for recognizing prior learning, and initiated modularisation in VET (Dębowski & Stęchły 2015).

In 2016, the general education system underwent further structural and curriculum reform. This addressed the poor reputation of 3-year lower secondary schools and aimed to strengthen secondary level education by returning to the 8-year model for primary schools and 4- or 5-year secondary schools. These changes were opposed by many stakeholders, including teachers, parents and local authorities (Wiśniewski & Zahorska 2020).

Early educational reforms focussed exclusively on general education, leaving VET marginalised and with outdated initial and continuing education programmes (ETF 2003, 46). Increasing educational aspirations and opportunities to complete HE, coupled with uncertain labour market prospects for VET graduates in the radically changing economy, decreased the attractiveness of VET in the 1990s, this being reflected by primary school leaver choices (see Table 5.1). It might be said that the Polish school system followed a path of 'de-vocationalization'.

Vocational education has, however, received more emphasis in national policies since 2010 (Chłoń-Domińczak et al. 2012; Sztanderska & Drogosz-Zabłocka 2019). Major changes in VET were introduced in 2017–2019, aimed at bringing VET closer to the world of work and increasing its responsiveness to labour market changes by linking public spending both to the actual costs of this type of education and to labour market demand (e.g., more funding for training in occupations affected by skills shortages). To this end, employers and VET school principals were invited to debate future changes. A council of 42 vocational school principals was formed and a series of seminars and debates with employer representatives was organized.

Polish stakeholders sought to learn lessons from other countries with respect to increasing employer involvement in VET, and from Germany in particular, known for its dual VET system. Knowledge collected during study visits and peer learning activities was adapted to reflect local contexts, with adjustment to suit social partner capacities resulting in, for example, new types of work placement (*staż uczniowski*) for students who are not employed by firms based on the job contract. During this work, the idea of extending obligatory employer membership in corporate self-government (*samorząd gospodarczy*) to vocational education was mooted, as inspired by German and French solutions. The Government, however, withdrew from the initiative owing to the strength of resistance from employers.

The heightened focus on VET has been supported by EU educational policies and funding since VET has a central role within EU strategies for competitiveness and social inclusion (Dębowski & Stęchły 2015). Employers have also pushed central and local governments in this direction. Nevertheless, Poland can be still regarded as a statist VET regime, as characterised by Busemeyer and Trampush (2012, 12), which obtains high commitment to VET from the public sector but implies relatively low employer involvement (Drogosz-Zabłocka & Stasiowski 2016).

Despite qualitative and quantitative improvements (detailed in the next section of this chapter), the institutional transformation in formal general and vocational education did not significantly alter educational practices in which instruction prevails, and pupils have a passive rather than active role in the learning process (Fazlagić & Erkol 2015; Federowicz et al. 2015; Jeruszka 2012; Kwiatkowski 2018). In the absence of strong grassroots improvement, the centralised examination system is pivotal to quality assurance for teaching and learning, and challenges remain with respect to the development of key and transferrable competencies within school-based general and vocational education (Fazlagić 2018; Dębowski et al. 2021). Furthermore, transformation did not increase the attractiveness of the teaching profession or its perceived prestige despite the high educational attainment of Polish teachers. Several studies have reported that the teaching profession is seen as a negative career choice amongst students in both general and vocational education, and that job satisfaction is declining amongst teachers (Smak & Walczak 2015), whose salaries have remained relatively low in Poland.

## Craft education

A significant portion of the vocational training system within formal education is organized through craft organizations with apprenticeship schemes (dual VET model) based on youth employment (Sławiński et al. 2013, 121). The sector is relatively stable, accommodating 75,000 learners, approximately half of the total attending basic vocational schools (since 2017, basic vocational schools have been transformed into stage I 3-year sectoral vocational schools) within formal VET (Cedefop 2019a). Vocational training in crafts has undergone continuous adjustment, but no significant institutional change has taken place during the last 30 years, and separate examination and certification systems leading to journeyman certificates and master craftsman diplomas have been retained (Stępnikowski 2020). Apprentices who are employed by the craftsmen can elect whether to take the VET examination organized by the Central Examination Board or the craft examinations organised by the chambers of crafts. Since 2015, craft qualifications have been gradually integrated into the qualifications system and referenced to the national qualifications framework. As a result, the master of crafts and journeyman qualifications are being progressively described in terms of learning outcomes which are accompanied by verification criteria.

## Higher education

In 1990, a liberal higher education law was introduced, which granted universities autonomy and independence from the state, but as noted by Antonowicz (2012, 100), to a much greater degree than in Western countries. The new law allowed state universities to offer paid part-time studies and facilitated the foundation of private universities. This was followed by the expansion of higher education, which accommodated increased Polish educational aspirations post-transformation (Siemieńska & Walczak 2012) and was to some extent enabled by permitting academic staff to hold multiple concurrent posts (moonlighting) and, prior to 2002, the presence of liberal and ineffective quality assurance mechanisms (Antonowicz 2015). Since 1989, a significant increase in the number of students undertaking higher education has been observed. The education boom was coupled with the opening of the sector to private HEIs. The number of HEIs rose from 112 in 1990 to 460 in 2011 (132 public and 328 private). Thereafter, both the number of students and institutions declined, so by 2019, there were 367 HEIs (133 public and 234 private). Currently the de-privatisation of study in Poland is being observed: publicly funded offers of study are increasing, while the private offer is decreasing (Kwiek & Szadkowski 2018).

The expansion of higher education was, however, restricted to specific fields: the social sciences, humanities, economics and law.

A spectacular and largely uncontrolled growth in private HE led to a relative decline in research activities and the 'deinstitutionalization' of the university research mission (Kwiek 2014).

Despite many issues relating to funding, quality of teaching and research, HE was not subject to any major governmental initiatives during the initial 15 years of transformation. This period was characteristically strongly market-driven with a policy of 'non-policy' (Antonowicz 2015). Since 2005, the state has been gradually reclaiming influence with the new law on HE introduced to implement the requirements of the European Higher Education Area and the Bologna Process (Kwiek 2018). The Polish Accreditation Agency, set up in 2002, also began to have a positive impact on quality (Antonowicz et al. 2017).

Further comprehensive reform was introduced in 2009–2012 when The National Qualifications Framework in Higher Education was implemented (using the field of study level descriptors as a tool for quality assurance of study programmes) and the central list of study programmes was abolished (Marciniak 2014). State supervision assumed a new form through establishing new intermediary coordinating institutions between higher education institutions (HEI) and the state, including two research councils for basic and applied research, an accreditation agency, and a committee for the evaluation of scientific units. Additionally, financing for public HE was linked more directly to measurable research outcomes. As noted by Kwiek (2018, 339), the state decided to leave most funding decisions to the quasi-market, institutionalised in the new intermediary agencies, where HEIs compete for national research grants. However, funding allocated to research grants was inadequate, significantly limiting the impact of the measures introduced and rendering HE less attractive as a career destination. To enhance the labour market relevance of HE, a nationwide graduate tracking system was introduced relying on linked administrative datasets to provide information on post-graduation employment and earnings (OECD 2019a, 59).

Another notable reform aimed at generating research excellence in Polish universities was introduced in the period 2016–2018. Promoted by the Government as a 'Constitution for Science' this had a broad scope and was designed to impact HEIs on different fronts. The reform increased the authority of chancellors (at the cost of collegiate bodies such as university senates) and introduced the university council as the new governing body. A university council must have at least 50 per cent of its members from outside the institution (it can include representatives from local government, business and employers' organizations) (OECD 2019a). Significant changes were introduced in the funding formula by creating a distinction between academic (*akademickie*) and professional (*zawodowe*) HEIs. Funding for professional HEIs was linked to the employment status of graduates according to the graduate tracking system and student-staff ratio (Lewicki 2018). The concept of dual studies was also introduced by this new legislation. The position and finances of academic HEIs became more dependent on research performance in which international publications were key. This might imply unintended negative consequences for teaching quality, as the ministerial evaluation criteria create incentives for HEIs and individual academics to concentrate exclusively on research at the expense of teaching. It is expected that these effects will be exacerbated within the top universities which are more research oriented.

This reform was prepared through a broad and innovative 2-year consultation process, although it did not achieve widespread acceptance (see: Antonowicz et al. 2020).

Since the onset of the transformation, the aspiration gap between families with differing levels of educational attainment, and between urban and rural populations has been steadily closing. In contrast to global trends, tuition fees (for full-time studies) have not been introduced in Poland largely because rising tertiary attainment was central to upskilling the Polish workforce. And it should be noted that this educational upgrading contributed significantly to the changes in task content structure and more rapid shift from routing and manual to non-routing cognitive jobs on the labour market in Poland (Dębowski et al. 2018).

Yet, despite the reforms, many issues remain unresolved. The HE structure is heavily biased towards the humanities and social studies with relatively little emphasis on science, technology, engineering, and mathematics (STEM), although this is growing. International collaboration between HEIs is weak, as is cooperation with industry. Both the quantity and quality of publications are comparatively low. One major shortcoming is also the underdevelopment of professional higher education, which is only weakly linked to the labour market. With the massification of HE, a professional education track with a strong practical component would be more compatible with many students' abilities and interests. This offer could also target adults in the short cycle studies, which are almost non-existent in Poland at present (Chmielecka & Trawińska-Konador

2014), although this situation may change. Anielska (2020) showed that demographic and economic pressures stimulate HEIs, especially in the private sector, to be more open towards adult learners by offering postgraduate programmes and more flexible training courses.

As in general education, teaching in HE is not regarded as an attractive career option due to poor remuneration, research underfunding and unstable employment in the early stages of an academic career. Furthermore, the lack of research opportunities undermines career development which paradoxically is then dependent on research achievement rather than teaching ability. In terms of teaching, classical lecturing also remains dominant in most institutions, focussed on knowledge transfer, with students taking a passive role, which may lead to a *didactic illusion*, as observed by Brdulak (2021). The 2016–2018 reform efforts are aimed at tackling most of these issues, but it is too early to assess their success.

## Non-formal adult education

The promotion of adult learning was not a priority during the first two decades of transformation and there was no established agency to ensure quality, conduct supervision in this area, or to promote adult learning. Private training companies have been operating according to *laissez faire* principles. Public institutions and agencies, usually under ministerial supervision also organize training, and award qualifications according to the relevant laws governing such qualifications (e.g., heavy machinery operation in the construction sector, electrical work or aviation), but practices and quality assurance mechanisms have varied.

More emphasis was placed on adult learning after Poland joined the EU. The first policy instruments financed by the European Social Fund were designed to support the supply side of the adult education market, i.e., private and public training institutions and labour offices, which organized training for the unemployed, although these instruments proved largely ineffective. Dębowski et al. (2010) suggested that distribution of public funds was not based on learners' or employers' expectations and the system was therefore unable to motivate training institutions to align their offers to labour market demands.

The lack of clarity over training outcomes and quality assurance undermined the decision-making processes of individuals and firms, which discouraged participation in learning or its finance. When the new EU programming period for 2014–2020 was in its planning stages, there was broad consensus that the state should act to reduce the asymmetry of information on the training market, increase the transparency of spending, and introduce quality assurance mechanisms (Kocór & Worek 2017).

The search for effective solutions coincided with the development of the European Qualifications Framework (EQF) and support for the development of national qualifications frameworks. The subsequent introduction of the Integrated Qualifications System (IQS) Act in 2015 resulted in a new institutional framework for the adult education sector. The IQS Act aimed to integrate formal general, vocational and higher education and non-formal adult education (including private training providers and providers operating under the auspices of ministries). The inclusion of market and regulated qualifications in the IQS is voluntary (see Dębowski et al. 2018, 411–423).

The development of various elements of the IQS was seen as a necessary policy initiative to enhance adult learning. Poland introduced the *Baza Usług Rozwojowych* – a register of providers and services (education, training, coaching) and the Integrated Qualifications Register (IQR) providing detailed information about all qualifications referenced to the National Qualifications Framework (NQF), discussed further below. It is expected that solutions within the IQS will be better linked to public employment and counselling services (Cedefop 2019b) and with the resources available from the National Training Fund, which was also established in 2015 (OECD 2019a, 106).

## Dynamics within the skills formation system

The trend of de-vocationalization within the skills system is starkly visible in the absolute numbers of learners entering basic vocational schools (Table 5.1 below) and is exacerbated by the high rates of technical school graduates attaining the *matura* (over 75 per cent) and entering higher education, over 37 per cent for 2016/2017 (Bulkowski et al. 2019). There has been a significant increase in the number of students entering HE since 1989 as discussed earlier in this chapter (Baranowska 2008).

Poland has one of the highest enrolment rates for upper secondary education in Europe but has very low rates of participation in adult education and training, and despite substantial increases in public spending, the level of participation has remained low. The involvement of Polish employers, particularly SMEs, in the finance and organization of training for employees is one of the lowest in Europe (Sienkiewicz et al. 2014), although this has been increasing. As noted by Górniak (2015), the human capital strategy for many SMEs was based on recruiting rather than developing worker competencies, but this approach is changing in the face of labour deficits. Lifelong learners in Poland are mostly

**Table 5.1.** Youth and adult participation in education and training 1990–2018 (thousands)

| | Youth – compulsory upper secondary education | | | Adult | | |
|---|---|---|---|---|---|---|
| | **Basic vocational / stage I sectoral schools** | **Technical and other vocational schools*** | **General secondary schools** | **Post-secondary non-tertiary institutions** | **Higher Education institutions** | **Participation in formal and non-formal adult education (% aged 25–64)**** |
| 1990 | 814.5 | 636.6 | 445.0 | 108.3 | 403.8 | - |
| 1995 | 721.9 | 838.0 | 683.0 | 161.0 | 794.6 | - |
| 2000 | 542.0 | 976.9 | 924.2 | 200.1 | 1,584.8 | - |
| 2005 | 232.5 | 743.8 | 738.6 | 313.5 | 1,953.8 | 4.9 % |
| 2010 | 224.9 | 595.7 | 634.5 | 298.8 | 1,841.3 | 5.2 % |
| 2015 | 178.8 | 518.9 | 501.2 | 255.1 | 1,405.1 | 3.5 % |
| 2018 | 146.2 | 529.2 | 470.3 | 218.6 | 1,230.3 | 4.8 % (2019) |

*Note.* Statistics Poland, Eurostat
*Including general art schools leading to professional certifications, in the 2002/03-2013/14 school years, including specialised general secondary schools and in the 2004/05-2013/14 school years – supplementary technical secondary schools.
** Participation rate in education and training (last 4 weeks), Eurostat: [trng_lfs_01], break in time series for 2018.

young, well-educated people, specialists and managers residing in large cities and employees of large firms. Whilst this pattern of participation is a concern in all countries, in Poland, this situation is worse than the EU average (Kocór & Worek 2017).

Poland is a high achiever in terms of the PISA basic skills assessment, with a significant increase in performance having been achieved since testing began. In 2018, it had risen from below the OECD average in 2000 to above average in all categories: reading literacy (Poland/OECD average: 512/487), mathematics (516/489) and science (511/489). A reduction in the proportion of low performing students, and decreased variation in performance between schools has been a particularly important development (Białecki et al. 2017).

By contrast, Poland was below the OECD average for countries participating in the IALS (International Adult Literacy Study) in 1993–1995, and Polish 16–65 average performance was close to the OECD average in the 2010–2018 rounds of the PIAAC study (Programme for the International Assessment of Adult

Competencies). These studies highlighted basic skills deficits among Polish adults, but subsequently the scores have significantly increased for all cohorts.

## Social dialogue in Poland

Social dialogue in Poland has been extensively addressed in the literature (Czarzasty & Mrozowicki 2018; Gardawski et al. 2012; Kozek 2004) with the salient characteristic from the perspective of the skills formation system being that dialogue between government and social partners depends primarily on governmental good will. Government and local authorities determine the intensity and authenticity of dialogue as a tool for the joint preparation of public policies. Dialogue mechanisms in Poland connect the government and corporate entities, which, though valuable, is insufficient to foster the modernisation of the skills formation system and implementation of long-term reforms (Bukowski & Dębowski 2010: 154–175; Gardawski & Meardi 2010).

### Social dialogue on skills

Until recently, there was little social dialogue relating to skills policy. Social dialogue both at central and enterprise level concerned employment and wage regulation but rarely addressed issues such as flexible working time, lifelong learning and other topics related to the skills agenda. This was the consequence of several factors. Firstly, the Government did not have an overarching skills policy and until recently, skills were not treated as an important policy goal. Secondly, the social partners had neither the capacity nor resources to develop a visionary skills policy in the absence of government initiative. Thirdly, the bulk of trade union members are employed in the public sector rather than in services and developing sectors of the economy where skill needs are most dynamic. Fourthly, many employers compete on price and therefore regard skill formation as cost rather than investment. Fifthly, the relatively high unemployment of 1990–2010 and the consequent availability of skilled labour encouraged employers to abrogate responsibility for skills formation, which was passed on to individual workers and/or the state.

In these circumstances social dialogue relating to the skills agenda was limited to consultations on legislation, in which the Ministry is obliged to seek the opinions of social partners but is not required to act on them. Whenever major changes are being prepared for formal education, the relevant minister establishes a group of experts or organizes consultations, but this occurs outside the institutions for social dialogue, and participants in consultations are selected according to their expertise, rather than as social partners. Employers were largely absent from discussion on skills policies during the transformation and were not pushing for changes in the skills formation system, other than occasionally voicing the view that VET should be more aligned with current labour market needs. This attitude changed substantially more recently when significant skills shortages emerged. Reegård and Dębowski (2020) noted increased activity by employers both at central and VET school levels. Employers have increasingly demanded reform and government action to provide a skilled labour force.

Within the VET system, the social partners have been involved in decisions about strengthening the training provided by schools. Since 2019, VET schools have been required to obtain approval from the *voivodeship* (regional) labour market council, which comprises local employers, representatives of trade unions, chamber of crafts and local authorities to provide training programmes relating to occupations not previously covered by existing provision. Previously, non-binding opinions were required from county labour market councils. At central level, the social partners have had an institutional role and are able to initiate the introduction of new occupations to VET programmes (Chłoń-Domińczak et al. 2016).

The trade unions were primarily involved in policy discussions relating to compulsory education and to a limited extent, HE (mostly related to teacher training). Each of the three central trade union organizations has its own dedicated unit or organization responsible for compulsory education. The teachers' trade unions are especially strong as education is the most highly unionised sector in Poland with 24 per cent of all unionised workers being employed in the education sector (CBOS 2014). The teachers' unions therefore have a strong bargaining position in negotiations with central and local government. Nevertheless, bargaining has largely been restricted to employment conditions, including rules for promoting teachers. Like the employers' organizations, trade unions are unable to influence core curriculum structure, content or the organization of exams, nor to influence the direction of systemic changes to the skills formation system. However, it should be emphasised that trade unions played a significant role in the modernisation of formal education in the late 1990s and early 2000s by promoting reforms within governmental structures to which they often belonged or were closely linked.

### Recent institutional changes augmenting the role of social partners and stakeholders in skills formation

The necessity of overcoming systemic barriers relating to the involvement and capability of social partners was recently recognized as key to ensuring quality of education, resolving labour market skill mismatches and to establishing a feedback loop in programme design and delivery.

The IQS Act established the Stakeholders Council, a new institution designed to strengthen the role of social dialogue. The Council plays an advisory and supportive role to the IQS minister coordinator and became the forum for employers and trade unions to express their expectations about the development of the IQS and skills formation policy. The position of the council is unique in skills formation owing to its gatekeeping power with respect to the ratification of the NQF level for new qualifications.

Sector Skills Councils (SSCs), established by the Polish Agency for Enterprise Development in 2016 through ESF co-funded projects, actively participate in skills development initiatives relating to initial and continuing VET, whilst also supporting adult education and the development of new qualifications in the IQS. By 2019, seventeen SSCs had been established, each having up to 40 members. SSCs are actively institutionalising dialogue between social partners, ministries and other stakeholders, including professional organizations, training providers, experts and research institutions. However, the impact of sector skills councils on skills policy and skills formation is limited because they do not have legal powers and their activities have not been legally formalised.

## The national qualifications system

### The rationale for the integration of the qualifications system and implementation of a national qualifications framework (NQF)

Changes in the various education sectors have been ongoing since the 1990s, as this chapter has already outlined. These modernisation efforts, however, were conducted without meaningful communication between sectors or indeed their input. The confluence of internal labour market pressures, reforms in formal education and EU lifelong learning policy, coupled with political will and funding, ultimately created the conditions facilitating the institutionalised integration of the qualifications system and the enhancement of adult learning policies.

The last decade has seen the concept of the NQF-based qualifications system become one of the most important lifelong learning policy tools, allowing a more adequate response to the challenges in Poland (Chmielecka et al. 2019; Sławiński et al. 2013).

## The NQF as an innovative policy tool

The national qualifications framework (NQF) and the concept of the integrated qualifications system (IQS) was developed on the back of reform to higher, general and vocational education and in response to the shift to learning outcomes. The term *national qualifications framework* (NQF) in this section is used in a narrow sense, as a policy tool built around level descriptors and procedures enabling assignment of a level to a qualification, whereas *Integrated Qualifications System* (IQS) refers to a wider concept, encompassing a wide set of regulations and practices in qualifications development, quality assurance and certification as well as system governance mechanisms. IQS in the Polish context is understood as a distinct part of the national qualifications system, governed by the regulations of the Act on the IQS. Qualifications not included in the IQS can function in Poland, but they are not assigned a NQF level and cannot be entered into the qualifications register.

These changes were in line with EU recommendations and were introduced to the entire formal education system before the IQS was established (Sławiński et al. 2013). Openness to learn from international experience was a relevant part of the process. Peer-learning activities, study visits and consultations with experts contributed to the final shape of solutions adopted. The inclusion of social partners and adult learning stakeholders was especially important when the proposed Act on the IQS went through the legislation process.

The innovation in the modernisation of qualifications systems using the national qualifications framework was made possible by authentic dialogue and the involvement of key stakeholders, an evidence-based approach and novel solutions relating to three elements. Firstly, the integration of the qualifications system. The IQS Act introduced uniform concepts and terminology related to qualifications across all sectors of the skills formation system (Sławiński et al. 2014), a qualifications description standard based on learning outcomes (Stęchły et al. 2016), external quality mechanisms (Dybaś et al. 2015) and a qualifications registry. Secondly, governance. The IQS is coordinated by the education minister. This represented an important paradigm shift since there was previously no leading ministry in this area and regulations on awarding qualifications were governed through inter-ministerial entities, which by their nature had relatively limited ability to respond quickly to changing circumstances. Another innovation is the formal inclusion of stakeholders in the governance structures through the Stakeholders Council, which holds gatekeeping power with respect to the inclusion of qualifications into the system. Thirdly, the construction of the NQF, which has two levels of descriptors. First stage generic (universal) descriptors relate to all education sectors, while second stage generic descriptors provide contextual detail (Sławiński et al. 2013). The IQS also uses third stage generic descriptors – known as 'sectoral qualifications frameworks' (Trawińska-Konador & Żurawski 2018).

The IQS in Poland could be described as 'tight and comprehensive' using the typology developed by Tuck (2007), as it applies common rules and procedures across all qualifications and aims towards wider social goals. It can also be characterised as a 'transformational' system (Raffe 2011), as it is expected to drive change, with the state in the leading role, and develop new systemic elements and mechanisms (e.g., establishing market qualifications, and the recognition of non-formal learning). With respect to scope and inclusiveness, the IQS could be described as 'coherent and providing limited incentives for the inclusion of qualifications', as qualifications included in the system become a public good and the specific regulations for inclusion have the character of required legal norms (Dębowski et al. 2018).

## Qualifications included in the IQS

By September 2020 more than 10,300 qualifications were included in the Register, of which 10,165 are now awarded in formal education (with over 9,000 HE diplomas) and 123 market qualifications with assigned NQF levels (as of May 2021). More than 200 market qualifications currently await acceptance.

In terms of skills formation, market qualifications are better tools for skills development than for building a wide knowledge base and social competence. In this sense, they resemble the narrow approach to training sometimes attributed to UK VET, rather than the holistic approach to professional competence associated with German VET. In the absence of widely accepted definitions of competence, the process of market qualification design was driven by the need for swift adaptation in response to skills needs, and for widespread application of criterion-based assessments (deemed adequate, given deficits in quality and trust in the non-formal training sector).

Despite growing numbers of qualifications included in the IQS (and referenced to the NQF) it is still too early to claim that the implementation of the IQS has had a broad impact on the adult education skills landscape in Poland. IQS, as an instrument for institutional change and policy innovation, should therefore be evaluated in the long-term and on qualitative grounds (e.g. by identifying whether the development of new qualifications solved skills issues).

## Future issues in skills development

During the transformation period, Poland conducted a thorough reform of general education creating new orders, and institutions including a system of centralised external examinations. The reforms left some issues unresolved but were generally successful, and the formal education system began to 'produce' some of the most competent students in Europe, with Poland being perceived as a 'rising star in education' (see Klatt & Elliott 2016).

Reform of other areas within the system of skill formation followed later. Significant reforms were introduced in vocational education (2012 and 2017–2018), higher education (2011–2012 and 2016–2018) and adult education (2015–2017), while earlier changes were less comprehensive and systemic. The most recent raft of reforms provide evidence that governments have started to regard skills as an important policy area that contributes to economic and social modernisation. The Strategy for Responsible Development (2017), Constitution for Science (2018) and the Integrated Skills Strategy (2019) represent major initiatives in this context.

Each reform focussed on improving skills formation at sector level (general education, vocational education, higher education and non-formal adult education), although common qualitative innovations were also introduced. Firstly, despite being outside traditional structures for social dialogue, extensive consultations with the main stakeholders and expert groups paved the way for each reform. Following Howlett et al. (2009), the policy response in Poland can be classified as 'redesign': decision-makers made a conscious effort to restructure education policies to meet contemporary challenges. Secondly, reforms were evidence based, with Poland drawing heavily on the lessons of skill formation in other countries. That said, a different approach was adopted with the reform of the school structure (2016), which abolished lower-secondary schools (*gymnasia)* and extended primary school to eight years. This change was opposed in many quarters (teacher unions, parents and research results).

The main driver for reform of the system of skill formation in Poland was aligning this with labour market needs. Incentives and obligations were thus designed to stimulate employer cooperation and foster national and international competition. In the absence of organized social partners, national authorities institutionalised skills dialogue through sector skills councils and the IQS Stakeholders Council. The capacity of all the actors within skills formation are, however, significantly path dependent (or prone to inertia), and the coordination of stakeholder partnerships lacks coherence, (Rapacki 2019) and often takes place against the backdrop of political turmoil.

The reorientation towards VET could be interpreted as policy reaction to an exogenous shock. As noted by Sabatier (1988), shocks such as new technologies or economic crises, can create a window of opportunity for new policy and new action plans. Economic growth reduced unemployment yet large-scale emigration caused sudden and significant skills problems – 'no one could find employees with the right skills.' This external shock shifted thinking about the importance of vocational skills at upper secondary and higher levels, and employer attitudes towards their own role in education, while simultaneously labour market segmentation moved towards internal markets, with increased significance placed on diploma credentials external to the conventional education path (Tomescu-Dubrow et al. 2018).

All the reforms were supported by EU funds and initiatives, and almost all the experts interviewed in preparing this chapter indicated that EU initiatives were of paramount importance in driving policy. EU funds were used, not only to finance systemic projects that prepared for the introduction of strategies and reforms, but also to finance the initial stages of implementation. The implementation of IQS (2010–2015) and its further development (2016–ongoing) in addition to the implementation of the Integrated Skills Strategy (2017–2019) can be regarded as model examples of how EU co-financing and OECD support can generate positive outcomes.

As for the future, it remains to be seen whether the reforms will yield the expected impact in the longer term, and whether they will be continued rather than reversed by future governments. Further investment in skills development by both public and private partners will undoubtedly be necessary. Greater institutional coherence and policy coordination within the various education sectors will also be of critical importance. These should align with industrial and innovation policies developed by the ministries responsible for technology and development. The better coordination of innovation policies, including the creation of a ministerial council for innovation and the involvement of the Polish Development Fund are positive developments.

The alignment of IQS solutions with public employment, counselling services and the training activities funded from the National Training Fund overseen by the Labour Ministry should be established. To date, the development of the IQS has been strongly geared towards embracing qualifications from the private market sector, but in the longer term it should also support further modernisation within formal education. In this context it is important to note that there is currently little public advocacy for continuing education: few people in Poland understand why this is socially desirable or how adult learning might benefit them personally. The importance of lifelong learning is also overlooked within schools.

The place and role of teachers remains unresolved across all branches of the education and skills formation system. The institutions regulating labour, social security and professional development of teachers are ineffective in raising the quality of teaching and learning. The development of systemic solutions for recruitment, retention, remuneration, and initial and continuing teacher training will continue to be a challenge in the medium term. Reversing the negative perception of the teaching profession as a career choice is also critical.

It is vital that links between research institutes and decision makers are strengthened to ensure the continuation of evidence-based policy development, and that mechanisms for the delivery of high quality data are developed. Efforts should continue to institutionalise employer and other stakeholder involvement in dialogue relating to the skills agenda (perhaps focussed within sector skills councils already established), even though the involvement of social partners organized within traditional structures of social dialogue will pose a challenge, demanding joint resolution by government in concert with the social partners.

## References

Anielska, A. (2020). *Szkolnictwo wyższe wobec studentów nietradycyjnych. Strategie uczelni w obszarze kształcenia dorosłych na przykładzie studiów podyplomowych. [Higher education towards non-traditional students. University strategies in the area of adult education on the example of postgraduate studies] PhD Thesis.* Toruń: Nicolaus Copernicus University in Toruń.

Antonowicz, D. (2012). 'External influences and local responses. Changes in Polish higher education 1990–2005.' In M. Kwiek & P. Maassen (eds.) *National Higher Education Reforms in a European Context: Comparative Reflections on Poland and Norway*, pp. 87–110. Frankfurt: Peter Lang.

Antonowicz, D. (2015). *Między Siłą Globalnych Procesów a Lokalną Tradycją. Polskie Szkolnictwo Wyższe w Dobie Przemian [Between the Power of Global Processes and Local Tradition. Polish Higher Education in a Time of Change].* Toruń: Wydawnictwo Naukowe Uniwersytetu Mikołaja Kopernika.

Antonowicz, D., Kulczycki, E., & Budzanowska, A. (2020). 'Breaking the deadlock of mistrust? A participative model of the structural reforms in higher education in Poland', *Higher Education Quarterly,* 74 (4), 391–409.

Antonowicz, D., Kwiek, M., & Westerheijden, D. F. (2017). 'The government response to the private sector expansion in Poland.' In H. de Boer, J. File, J. Huisman, M. Seeber, M. Vukasovic & D. F. Westerheijden (eds.), *Policy Analysis of Structural Reforms in Higher Education*, pp. 119–138. Cham: Springer.

Baranowska, A. (2008). 'Poland'. In I. Kogan, M. Gebel & C. Noelke (eds.), *Europe Enlarged. A Handbook of Education, Labour and Welfare Regimes in Central and Eastern Europe*, pp. 268–294. Bristol: The Policy Press.

Białecki, I., Jakubowski, M., & Wiśniewski, J. (2017). 'Education policy in Poland: The impact of PISA (and other international studies)', *European Journal of Education*, 52 (2), 167–174.

Brandt, N. (2018). *Strengthening Innovation in Poland*, OECD Economics Department Working Papers. Paris: Organisation for Economic Cooperation and Development.

Brdulak, J. (2021). *Jakość w szkolnictwie wyższym. Zapewnianie czy iluzja [Quality in higher education. Assurance or illusion]*. Warsaw: Szkoła Główna Handlowa w Warszawie.

Bukowski, M., & Dębowski, H. (2010). 'Social dialogue in the changing labour market'. In M. Bukowski (ed.), *Employment in Poland 2009. Entrepreneurship for Work*, pp. 154–175. Warsaw: Institute for Structural Research.

Bulkowski, K., Grygiel, P., Humenny, G., Kłobuszewska, M., Sitek, M., Stasiowski, J., & Żółtak, T. (2019). *Absolwenci Szkół Zawodowych z Roku Szkolnego 2016/2017. Raport z Pierwszej Rundy Monitoringu Losów Edukacyjno-Zawodowych Absolwentów Szkół Zawodowych [Vocational School Graduates from the 2016/2017 School Year. Report from the First Round of Monitoring the Educational and Professional Fate of Vocational School Graduates]*. Warsaw: Instytut Badań Edukacyjnych.

Busemeyer, M. R., & Trampush, C. (eds.) (2012). *The Political Economy of Collective Skill Formation*. Oxford: Oxford University Press.

CBOS (2014). *Związki Zawodowe i Prawa Pracownicze [Trade Unions and Employment Rights]*. Warszawa: Centrum Badania Opinii Społecznej.

Cedefop (2019a). *Vocational Education and Training in Europe – Poland 2018*. Luxemburg: Publications Office of the European Union.

Cedefop (2019b). *Coordinating Guidance and Validation*. Luxembourg: Publications Office of the European Union.

Chłoń-Domińczak, A., Dębowski, H., Drogosz-Zabłocka, E., Dybaś, M., Holzer-Żelażewska, D., Maliszewska, A., Paczyński, W., Podwójcic, K., Rucińska, M., Stęchły, W., Tomasik, M., Trawińska-Konador, K., & Ziewiec, G. (2012). 'Edukacja zawodowa w Polsce' [Vocational education in Poland].

In M. Fedorowicz & A. Wojciuk (eds.), *Raport o stanie edukacji 2011. Kontynuacja przemian [State of Education Report 2011. Continuing the transformation]*. Warszawa: Instytut Badań Edukacyjnych.

Chłoń-Domińczak, A., Dębowski, H., Żelażewska-Holzer, D., & Maliszewska, A. (2016). *Vocational Education and Training in Europe – Poland*, Cedefop ReferNet VET in Europe reports. Warsaw: Instytut Badań Edukacyjnych.

Chmielecka, E., Saryusz-Wolski, T., Sławiński, S., & Stęchły, W. (eds.) (2019). *Ramy Kwalifikacji, ECTS i ECVET Dla Uczenia Się Przez Całe Życie [Qualification Frameworks, ECTS and ECVET for the Lifelong Learning]*. Warszawa: Ministerstwo Edukacji Narodowej.

Chmielecka, E., & Trawińska-Konador, K. (2014). *Poziom 5-brakujące ogniwo [Level 5 – Missing link]*. Warsaw: Fundacja Rektorów Polskich.

Czarzasty, J., & Mrozowicki, A. (2018). 'Industrial relations in Poland', *Employee Relations* 40 (4), 674–691.

Dębowski, H., Lis, M., & Pogorzelski, K. (2010). 'Lifelong learning in a changing economy'. In M. Bukowski (ed.), *Employment in Poland 2008*. pp. 145–176. Warsaw: Institute for Structural Research/Human Resources Development Centre.

Dębowski, H., Poczmańska, A., Sławiński, S., & Walicka, S. (2018). 'Poland.' In *Including Non-Formal Sector Qualifications in National Qualifications Frameworks. The Experiences and Solutions of Seven European Countries. Volume I: Country Reports*, pp. 389–447. Warsaw: Instytut Badań Edukacyjnych.

Dębowski, H., Sławiński, S., Poczmańska, A., Walicka, S., & Przybylska, B. (2018). *Proposed Models of Including Non-formal Sector Qualifications in National Qualifications Frameworks.* Warsaw: Instytut Badań Edukacyjnych.

Dębowski, H., & Stęchły, W. (2015). 'Implementing ECVET Principles. Reforming Poland's Vocational Education and Training through Learning Outcomes Based Curricula and Assessment', *Warsaw Forum of Economic Sociology*, 6 (12), 57–88.

Dębowski, H., Stęchły, W., Tomengova, A., Reegård, K., & Valovic, J. (2021). *Development and Assessment of Transversal Key Competences in the VET Sector – Model Solutions and Practices in Six European Countries*. Warsaw: SGH Warsaw School of Economics.

Drogosz-Zabłocka, E., & Stasiowski, J. (2016). 'Praktyczna nauka zawodu pracowników młodocianych z perspektywy pracodawców. Koszty, korzyści i ryzyka' [Practical vocational training of young workers from the employers' perspective. Costs, benefits and risks], *EDUKACJA Quarterly* 2 (137), 5–31.

Dybaś, M., Rozenbaum, J., Saryusz-Wolski, T., & Stempień, M. (2015). *Zapewnianie jakości procesu nadawania kwalifikacji spoza systemów oświaty i szkolnictwa wyższego.* Warszawa: Instytut Badań Edukacyjnych.

ETF (2003). *Thirteen Years of Cooperation and Reforms in Vocational Education and Training in the Acceding and Candidate Countries: What Are the Lessons to Be Learned from the Perspective of the Lisbon Objectives?* European Training Foundation Report. Luxembourg: Office for Official Publications of the European Communities.

Fazlagić, J. (2018). *Szkoła dla innowatora: kształtowanie kompetencji proinnowacyjnych [School for innovators: developing pro-innovative competences].* Kalisz: Ośrodek Doskonalenia Nauczycieli.

Fazlagić, J., & Erkol, A. (2015). 'Knowledge mobilisation in the Polish education system', *Journal of Education for Teaching*, 41 (5), 541–554.

Federowicz, M., Biedrzycki, K., Karpiński, M., Rycielska, L., Sitek, M., & Walczak, D. (2015). *Dynamika przemian w edukacji i diagnoza problemów do rozwiązania [Dynamics of change in education and diagnosis of problems to be solved].* Warszawa: Instytut Badań Edukacyjnych.

Fihel, A., & Okólski, M. (2019). 'Population decline in the post-communist countries of the European Union'. *Population & Sociétés*, 567, <https://www.ined.fr/fichier/s_rubrique/29352/567.ang.population.societies.june19.depopulation.eastern.countries.en.pdf>, accessed 21 January 2022.

Gardawski, J., & Meardi, G. (2010). 'Keep trying? Polish failures and half-successes in social pacting', *Warsaw Forum of Economic Sociology*, 1 (1), 69–90.

Gardawski, J., Mrozowicki, A., & Czarzasty, J. (2012). *Trade Unions in Poland.* Brussels: European Trade Union Institute.

Górniak, J. (2015). *(Nie)Wykorzystany Potencjał: Szanse i Bariery Na Polskim Rynku Pracy: Raport Podsumowujący V Edycję BKL z 2014 Roku [(Un)Utilised Potential: Opportunities and Barriers on the Polish Labour Market: Summary Report of the 5th Edition of the 2014 BKL].* Warsaw: Polska Agencja Rozwoju Przedsiębiorczości.

GUS (2014). *Sytuacja Demograficzna Osób Starszych i Konsekwencje Starzenia Się Ludności Polski w Świetle Prognozy Na Lata 2014–2050 [Demographic Situation of the Elderly and the Consequences of Population Ageing in Poland in the Light of the Projections for the Years 2014–2050].* Warsaw: Główny Urząd Statystyczny.

Hardy, W., Keister, R., & Lewandowski, P. (2018). 'Educational upgrading, structural change and the task composition of jobs in Europe', *Economics of Transition*, 26 (2), 201–231.

Herbst, M., Herczyński, J., Federowicz, M., Smak, M., Walczak, D., & Wojciuk, A. (2015). *Bilans Zmian Instytucjonalnych. Polska Oświata w Okresie Transformacji [The Balance of Institutional Change. Polish Education in the Period of Transformation]*. Warszawa: Instytut Badań Edukacyjnych.

Herbst, M., & Wojciuk, A. (2017). 'Common legacy, different paths: The transformation of educational systems in the Czech Republic, Slovakia, Hungary and Poland', *Compare: A Journal of Comparative and International Education*, 47 (1), 118–132.

Howlett, M., Ramesh, M., & Perl, A. (2009). *Studying Public Policy: Policy Cycles and Policy Subsystems*, Vol. 3. Oxford: Oxford University Press.

Jeruszka, U. (ed.) (2012). *Unowocześnianie Metod i Form Kształcenia Zawodowego w Polsce. Diagnoza i Oczekiwane Kierunki Zmian [Modernisation of Vocational Education Methods and Forms in Poland. Diagnosis and Expected Directions of Changes]*. Warszawa: Instytut Pracy i Spraw Socjalnych.

Klatt, M., & Elliott, K. (2016). 'Education reforms in Central Eastern Europe and its impact on youth transitions – a case of Poland'. In S. Bohlinger, T. K. A. Dang & M. Klatt (eds.), *Education Policy: Mapping the Landscape and Scope*. Bern: Peter Lang.

Kocór, M., & Worek, B. (2017). 'Adult learning–providing equal opportunities or widening differences? The Polish case', *British Journal of Educational Studies*, 65 (2), 239–260.

Kozek, W. (2004). 'How far into implementation? Social dialogue in Poland for participation in the EES'. In B. Galgóczi, C. Lafoucriere & L. Magnusson (eds.), *The Enlargement of Social Europe. The Role of Social Partners in the European Employment Strategy*, pp. 301–344. Brussels: European Trade Union Institute.

Kwiatkowski, S. M. (ed.) (2018). *Kompetencje Przyszłości [Competencies of the Future]*. Warszawa: Fundacja Rozwoju Systemu Edukacji.

Kwiek, M. (2014). 'Structural changes in the Polish higher education system (1990–2010): A synthetic view', *European Journal of Higher Education*, 4 (3), 266–280.

Kwiek, M. (2018). 'Building a new society and economy: High participation higher education in Poland', In B. Cantwell, S. Marginson & A. Smolentseva (eds.), *High Participation Systems of Higher Education*, pp. 334–357. Oxford: Oxford University Press.

Kwiek, M., & Szadkowski, K. (2018). 'Higher education systems and institutions, Poland.' In P. N. Teixeira & J.-C. Chin (eds.), *Encyclopedia of International Higher Education Systems and Institutions*, pp. 1–10. Heidelberg: Springer.

Lewandowski, P. (2018). *How Does Technology Change the Nature of Work? Poland vs. the EU.* Warsaw: Instytut Badan Strukturalnych.

Lewandowski, P., & Magda, I. (eds.) (2014). *Employment in Poland 2013. Labour in the Age of Structural Change.* Warsaw: Institute for Structural Research (IBS).

Lewandowski, P., & Rutkowski, J. (eds.) (2017). *Population Ageing, Labour Market and Public Finance in Poland.* Warsaw: Institute for Structural Research (IBS).

Lewicki, J. (2018). 'Nowy algorytm podziału dotacji podstawowej dla uczelni akademickich. Pierwsze skutki zmian i wstępne wnioski [A new algorithm for the distribution of the basic subsidy to academic institutions. First effects of changes and preliminary conclusions]'. *Nauka i Szkolnictwo Wyższe*, 2 (52), 171–87.

Levitas, A. (2017). 'Local government reform as state building: What the Polish case says about 'decentralization', *Studies in Comparative International Development*, 52 (1), 23–44.

Marciniak, Z. (ed.). (2014). *Self-certification Report of the National Qualifications Framework for Higher Education.* Warsaw: Instytut Badań Edukacyjnych.

OECD (2019a). *OECD Skills Strategy Poland: Assessment and Recommendations.* Paris: Organisation for Economic Cooperation and Development.

OECD (2019b). *International Migration Outlook 2019.* Paris: Organisation for Economic Cooperation and Development.

OECD (2021). 'Hours worked (indicator)', <https://www.oecd-ilibrary.org/employment/hours-worked/indicator/english_47be1c78-en>, accessed 16 June 2021.

Piatkowski, M. (2018). *Europe's Growth Champion: Insights from the Economic Rise of Poland.* Oxford: Oxford University Press.

Raffe, D. (2011). 'Are "communications frameworks" more successful? Policy Learning from the Scottish Credit and Qualifications Framework', *Journal of Education and Work*, 24 (3), 283–302.

Rapacki, R. (ed.) (2019). *Diversity of Patchwork Capitalism in Central and Eastern Europe.* London: Routledge.

Reegård, K., & Dębowski, H. (2020). 'Exit, voice or loyalty? VET stakeholders' response to large scale skilled emigration', *International Journal for Research in Vocational Education and Training*, 7 (3), 325–43.

Sabatier, P. A. (1998). 'The advocacy coalition framework: Revisions and relevance for Europe', *Journal of European Public Policy*, 5 (1), 98–130.

Siemienska, R., & Walczak, D. (2012). 'Polish higher education: From state toward market, from elite to mass education'. In W. R. Allen, R. T. Teranishi & M. Bonous-Hammarth (eds.), *As the World Turns: Implications of Global*

*Shifts in Higher Education for Theory, Research and Practice*, pp. 197–224. Bingley: Emerald.

Sienkiewicz, L., Jawor-Joniewicz, A., Sajkiewicz, B., Trawińska-Konador, K., & Podwójcic, K. (2014). *Competency-Based Human Resources Management. The Lifelong Learning Perspective.* Warsaw: Instytut Badań Edukacyjnych.

Sławiński, S., Dębowski, H., Chłoń-Domińczak, A., Kraśniewski, A., Pierwieniecka, R., Stęchły, W., & Ziewiec, G. (2013). *Referencing Report. Referencing The Polish Qualifications Framework for Lifelong Learning to The European Qualifications Framework*, Warsaw: Instytut Badań Edukacyjnych.

Sławiński, S., Dębowski, H., Michałowicz, H., & Urbanik, J. (2014). *A Glossary of Key Terms related to the National Qualifications System.* Warsaw: Instytut Badań Edukacyjnych.

Smak, M., & Walczak, D. (2015). *Pozycja społeczno-zawodowa nauczycieli [Socio-professional position of teachers].* Warsaw: Instytut Badań Edukacyjnych.

Stęchły, W., Ziewiec-Skokowska, G., & Danowska-Florczyk, E. (2016). *How to Describe Market Qualifications for the Polish Qualifications System. A Guidebook.* Warsaw: Instytut Badań Edukacyjnych.

Stępnikowski, A. (2020). *Mistrz w rzemieślniczym przygotowaniu zawodowym. Kompetencje społeczne i pedagogiczne [Master in craftsmanship professional preparation. Social and pedagogical competences].* Radom: Instytut Technologii Eksploatacji.

Sztanderska, U., & Drogosz-Zabłocka, E. (2019). *Wykształcenie Zawodowe. Perspektywa Systemu Edukacji i Rynku Pracy [Vocational Education. Education System and Labour Market Perspective].* Warszawa: Fundacja Rozwoju Systemu Edukacji.

Tomescu-Dubrow, I., Słomczyński, K. M., Domański, H., Dubrow, J. K., Sawiński, Z., & Przybysz, D. (2018). *Dynamics of Class and Stratification in Poland.* Budapest: Central European University Press.

Trawińska-Konador, K., & Żurawski, A. (2018) 'Use of sectoral qualifications frameworks in a development of study programs', presented at *13th European Quality Assurance Forum. Broadening the scope of QA.* Vienna.

Tuck, R. (2007). *An Introductory Guide to National Qualifications Frameworks.* Geneva: International Labour Organisation.

Wiśniewski, J., & Zahorska, M. (2020). 'Reforming education in Poland'. In F. Reimers (ed.), *Audacious Education Purposes*, pp. 181–208. Cham: Springer Open.

World Bank (2019). *Return on Investment of Public Support to SMEs and Innovation in Poland.* Washington, DC: World Bank.

Dominik Dvořák and Petr Gal

# 6. Czech Republic: national and local perspectives

**Abstract:** Arguably, the Czech Republic experienced the least change in the macro structure of its training system, compared to all other countries in Central and Eastern Europe. Traditionally, as well as now, a very large share of Czech secondary students (more than 75 per cent) has entered and graduated from professional/technical or vocational tracks. At the local level, however, the network of providers and programs available has changed significantly. Tertiary education in the Czech Republic expanded significantly, but qualitative changes in the structure and content of education can be perceived as controversial as the growth was mainly concentrated in the social sciences and humanities. Life-long learning neither represents a priority of educational policy nor has it developed into a unified and interconnected system. A unique but significant exception has been the legal regulation of the recognition of prior learning through the National Qualifications Framework (*Národní soustava kvalifikací*, NSK) as a system of *partial* professional qualifications. In this chapter there are described the processes that led to the current situation in all areas of skill formation and their perceived logic at the national level and also at local scale in one specific area of Czechia.

**Keywords:** Czechia, life-long learning, post-socialist transformation, professional/technical education, tertiary education, qualifications

## Introduction

The communist regime in Czechoslovakia collapsed at the end of 1989. In 1993, Czechoslovakia split into two states: the Czech Republic (Czechia) and Slovakia. After the fall of communism, the available pool of cheap labour with decent technical skills attracted many foreign investors to the Czech Republic, and the important position of these employers/taxpayers now contributes to the very low unemployment rate, but also perpetuates demand for blue-collar workers and the wage gap between Czechia and its Western partners. This trajectory contributed to the present-day situation when, arguably, 'of all the CEE countries, the Czech Republic experienced the least change in the structure of its training system' (Šćepanović 2020). In this chapter, we describe the events that led to the current situation and their perceived logic at the national level and also at local level in one specific area of Czechia.

Traditionally, as well as now, a very large share of Czech secondary students (now 77.5 per cent) has entered and graduated from professional/technical or vocational tracks. The latter programme, mainly a 3-year secondary education leading to vocational certificates (ISCED 353, EQF 3) is commonly called 'apprenticeship' education, but it is essentially a school-based VET programme. Such a structure of education is highly controversial. On the one hand, educationalists and the non-profit sector point to growing inequalities in Czech society. Students in the vocational track are characterised by lower socio-economic status and worse academic achievement in comparison with students from the technical and academic tracks, and worse attitudes towards participation in politics (Straková 2015). In particular, the most popular 3-year vocational track is condemned as a dead-end educational path, because it does not allow for direct entry to post-secondary schools. Roma students are overrepresented in vocational tracks compared with general and professional programmes (European Commission 2020; Prokop 2020). On the other hand, major employer organizations strongly support the present dominant role of vocational and professional upper secondary education and criticise the structure of HE, where the share of students in technical/engineering fields has decreased.

In this chapter we follow suggestion that the complex network of actors taking part in education policy making and their interactions could be analysed by juxtaposing different narratives about the processes in different arenas or at various levels (Mikser and Goodson 2019). The national story is based mainly on analysis of policy documents, statistics, and secondary sources. For the local level, data from our studies of adolescent trajectories in different types of upper secondary schools are used (Dvořák et al. 2020, 2021).

## Institutional development

The post-socialist transformation of Czech schooling took place in the context of rhetoric about unconditional acceptance of the contemporary Western economic and political model of society (especially in its neoliberal form). At the same time, however, the skill formation system had returned to (rather idealised) education and training models that existed in the pre-communist era, often despite the recommendations of Western experts and despite considerably changed conditions. The first period after the fall of the communist regime was a window of opportunity for change. However, the policies available were mainly the recycling of older institutional models. Although more sophisticated proposals emerged at the beginning of this millennium as the *White Paper* (2001), *The Strategy of Lifelong Learning in the Czech Republic* (MEYS 2007), and the *White Paper on Tertiary Education* (Matějů et al. 2009), government ability to implement them has usually been lacking. It is worth examining the previous path of the Czech skill formation system to understand its apparent attraction.

## Origins

Some of the key events that led to the rise of the modern Czech educational system could be linked to mid-18th century conflicts between Prussia and Austria. As a result of three wars, Maria Theresa's Austrian imperium (of which Czechia was a part) not only lost the vast majority of Silesia – the richest part of imperium – to Prussia, but also suffered a significant damage to its prestige. Several waves of Theresian reforms followed the defeats, among them the establishment of a country-wide system of free public schools since 1774 (with compulsory primary school attendance introduced soon after). The loss of Silesia as the most developed province led to efforts to improve industry elsewhere in Austria (Komlosy 2010). J. L. von Chamaré, a Silesian aristocrat who had moved to Potštejn in Northeast Bohemia, founded not only linen manufacture, but in 1755 also a spinning and weaving 'school' (de facto several-week-long courses) that became a model for similar institutions in other Bohemian towns aiming to improve the quality of textile products. According to Kadlec (2019, 34), the establishment of the first modern skill training courses was connected to 'growing competition in the textile product market as well as with spinning and weaving being declared so-called free trades, which meant, among other things, that they were not subject to the guild organised system of professional training'. Indeed, the ultimate abolition of the guild organization almost one century later and the Trade Act of 1859 could be seen as an important step to the dual system of vocational training as the Act provided both for school education and apprenticeship training of future workers and tradesmen.

During the 19th century, the Czech lands took over the position of the most industrialised part of the Austrian Empire and the need for educated and skilled workforce was urgent. In the 1830s, the first secondary 'real' schools emerged (quasi modern secondaries combining practical and liberal education). Later, secondary real schools became more academically oriented, preparing students for study in colleges of technology (or technical universities), but in the meantime they contributed to the development of both professional/technical secondary schools and to trade continuing schools.

By 1883, the system of skill formation at the secondary level was almost completed in Czechia: lower, upper and incomplete professional/technical secondary schools (incomplete professional schools were an alternative to apprenticeship and led to vocational qualification) provided full-time initial professional or vocational education of varying duration. Trade continuing schools (affiliated mainly to general secondaries or to professional schools) provided part-time education for apprentices (Mašek 1882). Before the 1880s, professional education was a shared responsibility of the ministries of instruction and commerce, but from 1881 it was strictly centralised under the Ministry of Culture and Instruction. The long tradition of higher technical education dates back to 1707, when the Estates College of Engineering was established in Prague.

The first Czechoslovak Republic (1918–1938) retained the Austrian (Austro-Hungarian) educational system, but during the interwar period there was a quantitative expansion of schools and modernisation of curricula. *Contemporaneously, the famous system of* company education in Baťa's industrial city of Zlín (*Baťovy školy práce* – Baťa's schools of *work) was part of an* extraordinarily thriving *multinational firm, as well as a rather controversial social experiment.* Baťa's *educational project aimed far beyond training vocational skills and was an attempt to create men and women fit* for modern industrial life (Doleshal 2012; Kasper and Kasperová 2018). Zlín became a kind of myth and the elite character of Baťa's education perhaps contributed to the belief that professional education is not inferior and to its long-time popularity in Czechia.

During the Second World War, Czech lands were important for the industrial and agricultural supply of the German military, so secondary TVET education (unlike other types of Czech schools) did not face restrictions. Moreover, constriction of academic programs had led to a further increase in the number of students in secondary TVET tiers. Entire classes of students were often deployed into war production. Jews, however, were forbidden to attend any Czech (and even more so German) schools, while those of mixed ethnicity needed a special permit at TVET schools (Doležal 1996, 44).

## Under communist rule

In the years 1948–1989, the Czechoslovak school system shared many features with other countries in the Soviet bloc: unification of education and its subordination to the ideology of Marxism-Leninism, but also no tuition fee, free textbooks, subsidized school meals etc. The numbers of students of various programs were set by the State Planning Commission, which responded to fluctuations in economic development. The quotas for vocational or study fields were determined according to the needs of the workforce in enterprises. The communist regime also easily followed the inherited educational model and used it for its goals. On the other hand, even within the Soviet bloc, Czechoslovakia maintained some local traditions and a certain continuity of curricular policy and qualifications system.

We cannot go here into detailed description of the reforms mandated by no less than five Education Acts (1948, 1953, 1960, 1978, 1984) that changed the length of comprehensive school (from nine years to eight, back to nine, and to eight again), curricula and syllabi. The main reason for these changes was the labour market situation, when in some periods the need to accelerate the journey of young people to the extensively developing socialist economy prevailed. On the contrary, when the labour market failed to absorb strong cohorts, the educational trajectory was prolonged. Only the situation immediately preceding the fall of Communist rule will be presented in some detail.

The Education Act of 1984 extended compulsory school attendance to ten years. Every girl or boy aged fourteen had to enlist in an upper secondary school and attend it for at least two years. Simultaneously, vocational schooling was officially declared the main tier of secondary education favoured by the Party. About 55 per cent of comprehensive school graduates attended various types of vocational schools (the share of girls was 40 per cent), about 15 per cent of the population went through selective academic track (60 per cent girls), and about 23 per cent studied in professional/technical schools. (Pick 1990) The number of children admitted to academic and professional tiers was limited. Although the system of admissions to different tiers considered applicants' previous academic results, students' social background and/or parental Communist Party membership played key role (Šimáně and Kamanová 2020). The 14-year-old youngsters not admitted to school of their choice were administratively assigned by National Committees (municipal and regional governments) to unpopular schools/fields of study, as a rule to VET programmes which otherwise failed to attract pupils.

The road to secondary education graduation was shortened by one year compared to the previous situation and the curriculum was condensed. The boundaries between curriculum of technical/professional schools and vocational schools became blurred, with some vocational schools having a lot of theoretical subjects. Special 4-year vocational programs entitled their graduates to access to university and provided the firms highly qualified blue-collar workforce. Concurrently, academic school curriculum put an emphasis on STEM subjects and quasi-TVET was also introduced in academic track in accordance with the requirement of *polytechnization* of unified education. Academic schools (*gymnasium*) taught technical subjects 6 hours weekly in upper two grades and students spent a few weeks at *internship* placements in state companies. Youngsters in VET schools got the identical legal status with their peers in other upper secondary schools: they were no longer apprentices and became students (pupils).

Several ministries were involved in VET school governance. The Education Ministry centrally set instructional guidelines and detailed syllabi. The Ministry of the Interior administered finance to cover costs of the general component of education (called 'theoretical instruction') through regional committees, which also hired teachers and performed school inspections. Nursing, military, police or agriculture schools were subject to other ministries. Finally, there were VET schools serving students with special educational needs. School administration and apprenticeship facilities, however, were part of state-owned enterprises or cooperatives and were managed by relevant trade ministries and directorates-general of nationalised industry.

The situation of tertiary education was very different from secondary schools. Czechia had a long tradition of higher education institutions (HEIs), with Charles University (established 1348) the oldest in Central Europe. Although German universities in Prague and Brno perished after the Second World War, the communist regime created a new network of regional, mostly professionally oriented HEIs (without university status). The number of HE students thus increased significantly until the mid-1960s. As in other communist countries and unlike in the West, this trend did not continue, so the 1980s could be characterised as stagnation (Jareš 2012; Scott 2007). At the end of the communist rule (and unlike in the secondary TVET field), the number of HE students lagged significantly behind Western Europe with enrolment of only 10–15 per cent of the population. The share of STEM students was quite high (see Figure 6.2), which corresponded to an economy with a high share of industrial production.

## Transition to market economy and democratic society after the collapse of Communism

In Czechia, from the very first days of the Velvet Revolution (November 1989), a sizeable portion of teachers and experts demanded profound changes in the school system. Indiscriminate critique of socialist schooling was widely welcomed as a tool to bring about radical reforms. A decisive break with the previous tradition seemed inevitable (but it did not occur, of course).

The first phase of the transformation of the education system was mainly run by right-wing governments. While the neo-liberals focused on quick reforms of the economy, until the mid-1990s the Ministry of Education, Youth and Sports (MEYS) was controlled by academics and conservatives with links to former Catholic dissent. Hence Czech economic reform used 'shock therapy' inspired by radical neo-liberal thought (Machonin et al. 2006), but the top-down changes in the state/public school system came in the form of small steps, some aimed

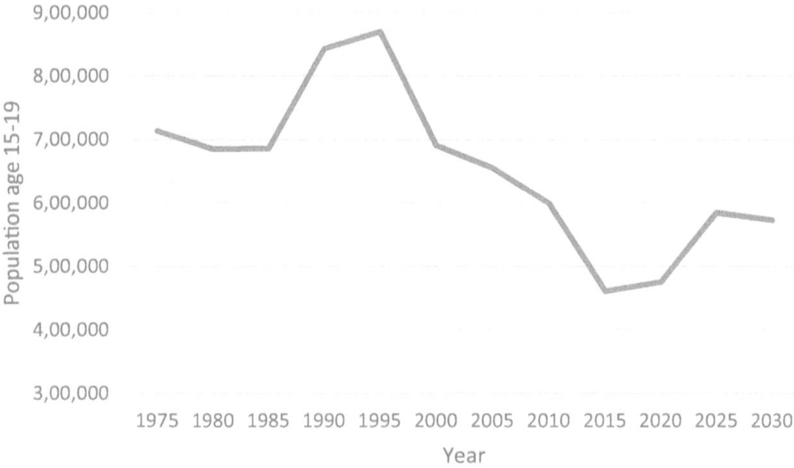


**Figure 6.1.** Number of young Czechs in typical age of upper secondary students (Source: Czech Statistical Office, 2018; data for 2020–2030 are predications).

at restoring the pre-Communist structure (as controversial early tracking of secondary students). The state-run system of skill formation was *caught between rapidly changing society and economy and* the conservative leadership of the Ministry of Education.

Despite the absence of comprehensive top-down reform of secondary schooling, some new measures (as newly introduced school choice policy together with per capita financing) opened a wide space for bottom-up initiatives. Secondary education was changing quite quickly.

The upper secondary education faced another major challenge in Czechia, because of unique demographic conditions (Figure 6.1). Just as birth cohorts from the 1970s baby boom reached upper secondary age, ample space was suddenly opened for non-state school founders and for individual initiative. The centralised system of creation, approval and implementation of both schools and TVET study fields and programmes was relaxed and private and church secondary schools were established, helping to compensate for insufficient capacity in academic and technical/professional tracks. After forty years of socialist rule, the education system was learning to respond again to the demands of students (or parents) and to changes in the job market and structure of the economy. The mismatch between demand and supply of programmes has largely narrowed, as proportions between intake into different types of schools changed (Koucký et al. 2008).

Not all changes were for the better, however. The quick transition from a central planning to a market economy including massive privatisation of state property, coupled with the lack of managerial experience and illegal practices resulted in the bankruptcy of many companies and the loss of many job opportunities. These problems were especially negatively reflected in the peripheral areas of Czechia (Jančák et al. 2008; see also the case study below). The demise of large state-owned factories severed the remaining links between businesses and vocational schools and VET drifted even further from a dual-like school-apprenticeship approach to a school-based model (West 2013), a trend that already started in the previous decades. Other problematic legacies of the early transition period include radical decentralisation without corresponding accountability policies, and fragmentation of qualification system, described below.

Schools have not shown much willingness to enter the field of non-formal and life-long learning (LLL); but several non-school organizations responded quite flexibly to the new needs of a transforming society, especially in the field of professional learning. As a result, there are many providers of LLL in Czechia, but most of them are small organizations that often cannot offer follow-up support activities. The supply of non-formal education for personal purposes is quantitatively smaller, but it has a relatively good institutional basis (Novotný 2010).

## Higher education

Shortly after 1989, tertiary education in the Czech Republic expanded significantly (Matějů et al. 2009), but qualitative changes in the structure and content of education can be perceived as controversial. The expansion was mainly concentrated in the social sciences and humanities. As with upper secondary education, the offer of fields such as business and management has increased sharply. However, the number of STEM students stagnated or declined (Figure 6.2). It is evident that new and newly trained staff were needed for management in both the private and public sectors, while concerns remain about the lack of technical specialists.

The key circumstance for changes in HE was the crucial role played by students of Czech HEIs in the Velvet Revolution, which made transformation of universities an absolute priority. While other levels of the education system had to wait for a completely new legal regulation until 2004, and for many years they had to be satisfied only with amendments to the old communist era laws, the new HE Law was passed in the summer of 1990 (Act No. 172/1990 Coll.).

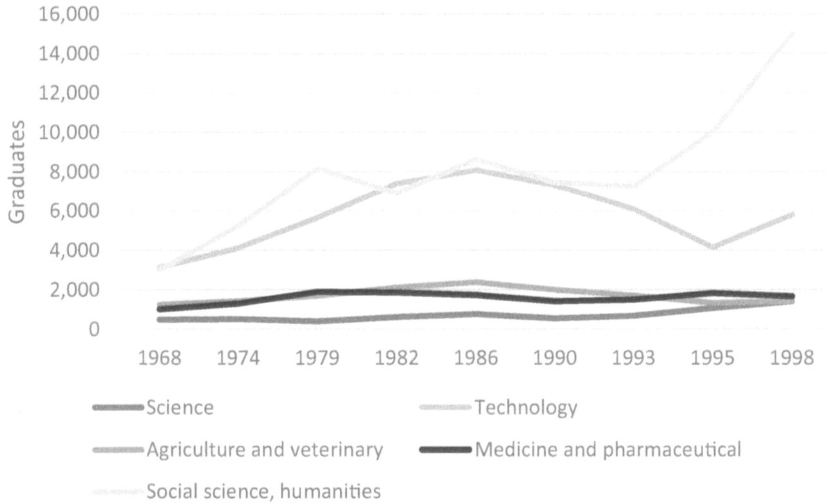


**Figure 6.2.** Number of university graduates according to the field of study in a given year.

This way and contrary to the advice of experts, 'higher education adopted an uncompromisingly Humboldtian character, governed by an academic oligarchy, shielded by academic freedom and institutional autonomy, and delivering curricula according to academic concerns' (Pabian, Šima and Kynčilová 2011: 96).

More practically trained professionals were expected to come to the labour market from a completely new type of tertiary schools in the Czech environment: post-secondary professional schools or higher professional/vocational programmes (ISCED level 5B; *vyšší odborné školy*, VOŠ). Pabian et al. (2011) emphasise the role of external (specifically Dutch) support in their creation in the early 1990s. Domestic actors were also interested in creating such institutions and played an important role. Some of them were intellectuals from anti-communist dissent, who before 1989 had been banned from universities. After the Velvet Revolution, some of them did not want to return to traditional universities, which previously often excluded them from their ranks. Instead, they conceived alternative HE institutions such as Academy of Social Pedagogy and Theology JABOK (jabok.cz) or The College of Media and Journalism (vosp.cz), both backed by Catholic Church.

Western European professional colleges like the German *Fachhochschulen* served as a model for the first VOŠ. From 1992, the VOŠ were first created in 'experimental mode'. In 1995, an amendment to the Education Act created legal ground for post-secondary professional programmes as strongly professionally/vocationally oriented alternative to university education.

## Accession to the European Union

Despite the original hopes in 1989, it took fifteen years before the new Education Act and a set of connected regulations were passed. It is no accident that it happened in 2004, the year when the Visegrád countries joined the EU. Around the time of EU accession, all the countries launched reforms emulating global trends (Corner 2015). It is sometimes argued that the main reason for the second wave of educational reforms in CEE was the desire to meet the rules for using EU cohesion and structural funds in education (i.e. external funding-driven reform, Halasz 2013; Surubaru 2021).

The Education Act (2004) deepened and institutionalised the previous trends to the wide autonomy of schools (Kučerová et al. 2020). As the PISA 2015 data (OECD 2016) show, the degree of autonomy perceived by Czech school principals is the highest of OECD countries. However, principals' administrative burdens significantly increased with new responsibilities (financial, legal, personnel management and public relations) leaving them little time for instructional leadership. This change was strongly influenced by neo-liberal ideologies of education with less state intervention and elements of the marketization. Decentralisation was an understandable reaction to previous state socialism and was inspired by trends of educational policy in Western countries from the 1980s. The market mechanism, however, was transplanted into a Czech system hostile to the idea of testing and accountability. The Czech School Inspectorate has only slowly shifted its focus from monitoring administrative and legal compliance to the quality of education provided in schools (Česká školní inspekce 2019). The key market assumption that parents have information on the quality of the school of their choice, was thus not fulfilled. While the quality of academic programmes is more even across schools, the differences between individual TVET schools are perceived as more important not only by students and parents (Kostelecký et al. 2018), but also by employers, as also our case study illustrates.

The number of HE students grew until the end of the first decade of the new century, when they reached 400,000. Then, the trend reversed due to demographic changes discussed above. In 2021, there were 28 public and state universities and around 30 private HEIs with 300,000 students in Czechia (SIMS database of MEYS). The government's strategy (Matějů et al. 2009) envisaged strengthening the influence of businesses/employers (and students) on the programmes of HEI, inter alia by increasing the share of private funding for universities (including the introduction of tuition fees). However, such a reform has not succeeded. The only significant change that has taken place in the last decade has been the strengthening of HEI autonomy in the accreditation of study programmes. Thus, HE remains deeply academic in nature. Despite that, it has been argued that Czech graduates

> imbued with Humboldtian academic education fare exceptionally well in the contemporary changing economy...Graduates themselves view their study experience as a good basis for their work even though (or because?) they identify their education as theory-oriented without extensive practical knowledge and experience. (Pabian, Šima and Kynčilová 2011: 95).

In 2020, there were also 156 VOŠ professional/vocational schools (including about 20 running only distance or hybrid programmes) with 11,500 students in on-campus programmes and 7,000 students in other types of programmes. While some schools have been built from scratch, most are now associated with upper secondary professional/technical schools that founded the VOŠ as their branch and a replacement for cancelled Communist-era post-secondary studies. Obviously, even this 'new' element of the education system is not so completely new.

While the early development of LLL institutions had the character of a bottom-up process in the first decade of the transformation, in the following period several government-issued documents on educational policy and skill formation generally or specifically on LLL appeared (Kalenda 2015). These activities were usually related to or driven by the availability of quite generous European funds (Kopecký, Šerák and Sycha 2018). At the same time, as in many other areas, the success of the implementation of these policies has been modest. Support is provided to selected areas only, such as retraining. Participation in LLL remains relatively low. Moreover, the differences in participation between groups with different initial educational attainment are significantly greater than in other European countries. Thus, LLL not only does not help to reduce undesirable differences of skill levels produced by initial school education (which is a general phenomenon), but it further deepens the gaps (Czesaná 2010, 374). Historically, the low share of people who did not achieve at least some professional qualifications could be one of the reasons for the relatively low interest in building the LLL system. However, the expected demographic development may bring about a greater relative importance of LLL compared to IVET (Kaňáková, Czesaná and Šímová 2019).

## Qualifications system

In the 1980s, a new system of upper secondary TVET qualifications was created. The new programmes featured a high share of general and foundational theoretical education as well as professional training. It was expected that this approach would support career adaptability and workplace flexibility. The number of vocational qualifications was reduced to 148, besides 62 secondary technical/professional qualifications. Following the requests of major state-owned companies, 48 new 4-year programs provided dual qualifications – both a high school diploma and an apprenticeship certificate.

Developments in skill formation immediately after 1989 went in the opposite direction. With the Ministry of Education neither able nor willing to guide the transformation, bottom-up processes prevailed, and newly emerging private schools became key agents of change. The need for new skills was met but the skill formation system was fragmented into the hundreds of qualifications (often almost identical) and the evaluation/quality control system decayed. Some schools opened new programmes without having adequate human or material resources. In the 1990s, Janyš (1997) estimated that 1,500 TVET qualifications were provided by Czech secondary schools. Class sizes dropped, and costs skyrocketed. Despite all these negatives, such development probably could not be avoided. It can be said that for the following 25 years, the Czech education system has been trying to deal with the problem of its qualification system.

Since the second half of the 1990s, the quantitative expansion of the qualification system was curtailed, and gradually stabilised. The creation of new programmes/qualifications was largely attenuated in connection with the 'optimization' of the school network (see next section) and by administrative measures of the Ministry of Education, as the recognition of new programmes became more difficult (Chamoutová et al. 2017).

Over the past decade, students have chosen from about 300 programmes leading to different qualifications (Decree 211/2010 Coll.) that can be grouped into three main tiers and about a dozen broad fields of education and training (e.g. mechanical engineering, health care, retail). Within the vocational tier, there is still rather complex structure (Table 6.1). Beyond the most popular 3-year VET programmes (referred as H-track) there are also 4-year craft programmes (L track) that lead to the *maturita*. The L track is part of the VET tier, but applicants must sit the obligatory national test to be admitted, and successful graduates are entitled to apply directly for tertiary education. On the other hand, the less demanding VET programmes (2–3 years E track) prepare students for simple auxiliary jobs. (The art tier differs and is not included here, nor are some lowest-profile VET tracks.)

After completion of four years academic and technical/professional programmes, an upper secondary school-leaving examination, *maturita* (like the German Abitur, roughly equivalent to A-levels) is taken and successful candidates are eligible to apply for tertiary education. VET students must pass a final apprenticeship examination (with a strong practical component) that traditionally facilitates transition to the labour market, but VET graduates cannot directly enter tertiary education. Graduates of 3-year VET programs need two or more additional years of study to gain *maturita*, but these follow-up programs are known to have very low completion rates.

Hence the typical 3-year vocational programme is often a dead-end educational trajectory.

So far in this section, *full* qualifications corresponding to a 2–4 years upper secondary programme (combination of a tier and field of study) have been discussed. The most recent analysis (S2030+) states that the IVET system still includes qualifications already losing their relevance, either due to their obsolescence or too narrow specialisation. Unfortunately, LLL cannot fix the problems as it neither represents a priority of educational policy nor has it developed into a unified and interconnected system (Kopecký and Šerák 2015). A unique but significant exception has been the legal regulation of the recognition of prior learning through the National Qualifications Framework (Národní soustava kvalifikací, NSK) as a system of *partial* professional qualifications. The NQF system has been under construction since 2005, largely due to two EU-supported projects. Priority was given the needs of low-skilled people. Of fundamental importance is the Act 179/2006 Coll., On Recognition and Validation of Continuing Education Results. On the one hand, this is indeed a rare case of a measure that is being implemented in a coherent way for a long time. Despite that, the ambition that the NQF would represent a bridge between the world of education and the world of work is yet to be fulfilled. Currently, the framework serves primarily to meet the legal requirements for a rather limited range of professions through recognition by examination, but far less supports education and skills development (Kopecký, Šerák and Sycha 2018).

**Table 6.1.** Main tracks in Czech upper secondary education

| Czech code | ISCED 97 | ISCED 2011 | Czech name(s), abbreviations and translation | Track characteristics | Share of students (%) |
|---|---|---|---|---|---|
| K | 3A | 344 | Gymnasium (G)<br>Grammar school | academic tier (4 years)<br>secondary education leading to a *maturita* certificate and preparing students for studies at any higher education institution | 22.5 |
| M | | 354<br>344 | Střední odborná škola (SOŠ)<br>Lyceum<br>Secondary Technical School | professional tier (4 years)<br>non-academic professionally oriented technical programmes leading to the *maturita* certificate | 37.5 |
| L(0) | | 354 | Střední odborné učiliště s maturitou (SOU)<br>Vocational School | VET tier (4 years)<br>*maturita* certificate (a small number of programmes lead to an apprenticeship certificate) | 6.0 |
| H | 3C | 353 | Střední odborné učiliště (SOU)<br>Vocational School | VET tier (3 years)<br>leads to an apprenticeship certificate and prepares students for direct entry into the labour market | 30 |
| E | | 353 | Střední odborné učiliště (SOU)<br>Vocational School | VET tier (2–3 years)<br>does not lead to an apprenticeship certificate; students are trained to perform simple auxiliary tasks in production or services | |

*Note.* The numbers refer to new entrants from the comprehensive lower secondary schools in the 2017/2018 school year. Students already in 8-year and 6-year academic programmes not included.
*Source:* Authors, based on (Vojtěch and Chamoutová 2018).

## Developing VET schools and their labour market relevance

At the beginning of the new century, fourteen territorial self-governing units – thirteen regions and city of Prague – were established in the Czech Republic and became the founders/operators of public upper secondary schools, i.e. also of most TVET schools. According to the Education Act (Act No. 561/2004), regions are obliged to ensure the provision of post-compulsory education and establish/abolish public upper secondary and post-secondary schools. The regions immediately faced new problems: parents' demands shifted to fields providing academic/professional education with *maturita* graduation exam (and some private schools have promised to provide it regardless of students' actual skills and knowledge). There were suddenly almost no pupils for expensive (yet still underfunded) VET schools. Several traditional craft qualifications were particularly affected, creating a risk that employers would not have enough skilled labour and move their investments elsewhere.

The VET situation was once again significantly affected by demographic developments and juggling with the length of compulsory education. During the early transformation stage, secondary schools had to absorb strong cohorts born in the 1970s, whereas the fall of Communism brought a sharp decrease in the number of births in the 1990s, followed by stagnation in the early 2000s and a slow rise thereafter. At the end of the millennium, the numbers of secondary students first returned to pre-boom levels, but it was clear that a dramatic decline would follow (Figure 6.3). Moreover, compulsory education was (again) cut down to nine years and, since 1995, the comprehensive basic school was (once again) extended to the same length, so its graduates can directly enter the job market at 15 years of age without enlisting in any upper secondary school.

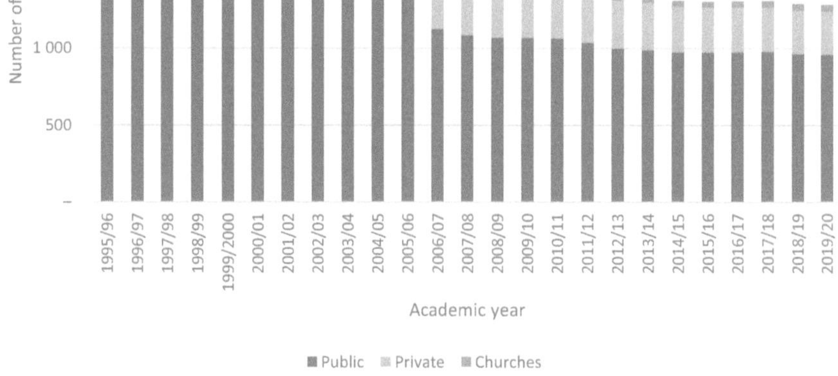


**Figure 6.3.** The number of Czech upper secondary schools by operator (Source: MEYS).

That posed even greater problem later, in the *period* of *good economic growth before the COVID-19 pandemic.*

## Policies to stimulate IVET

In the first half of the 1990s, changes took place mainly as bottom-up initiatives, but in the second half of the decade the question reemerged whether and how the central and regional governments should intervene in the situation to ensure the sustainability and quality of VET education. Efforts to address this situation first concerned regulation of the supply of TVET, and later also the demand for various types of education.

In 1997, the so-called 'optimization' process was launched. Some public secondary schools were shut down, mainly in first decade of the new century. To avoid closure, small or shrinking TVET schools merged in many places. Before 1989, there was strict between-school differentiation at the upper secondary level. So, the typical upper secondary school offered programmes/qualifications within just one field and single tier. Nowadays, many schools have two or even three tiers (level of programmes) and a rather heterogenous mix of qualifications from different fields. At present, the total number of secondary schools is almost stable (Figure 6.3).

The emergence of large upper secondary schools offering programmes at different levels and from different fields 'under one roof' could create the preconditions for a new integrated model of upper secondary education, such as in Sweden, for example. This development will be illustrated by a case study.

**Case study: The supply of TVET in Šluknov Hook**

In Northwest Czechia, the share of students enrolled in TVET secondary programmes is the largest in the whole of the EU (Eurostat 2020). This is also the only Czech area where demand for vocational education exceeds supply. The Šluknov Hook is a part of this region protruding deep into Germany. Until World War II, the area was settled almost exclusively by Germans and, besides agriculture, was famous for its textile industry. Annexed by Germany in 1938 and reclaimed back after the war, the area witnessed an almost complete exchange of population that never reached the pre-war size due to the expulsion of Germans from Czechoslovakia. Despite that, in the Communist era there was a dense network of large textile mills and other factories building on the regional industrial heritage. In the 1980s, at least ten vocational schools supplied skilled workers to enterprises in the Hook (Table 6.2), besides one academic and several professional/technical secondary schools.

Today, the Hook shares typical problems of peripheral regions (lacking opportunities and access to resources) compounded by its political history of ethnic clashes and partial collapse of textile mills since the 1990s. Educational achievement in Northwest

**Table 6.2.** Vocational schools in Šluknov Hook in 1980s (Source: author based on archive research)

| Fields of training | Company operating the school | Site of school |
|---|---|---|
| production of decorative objects / artificial flowers | Centroflor / Jablonecká bižuterie | Dolní Poustevna |
| printing | Polygrafia | Rumburk |
| farming / agriculture | State-owned farms | Šluknov |
| forestry CVET programs | State forest industry | Šluknov |
| energy distribution technologies | Czech Energy Enterprises | Varnsdorf |
| mechanical engineering | TOS | Varnsdorf |
| textile technologies | Elite | Varnsdorf |
| textile technologies | Velveta | Varnsdorf |
| telecommunications | State Post and Telephone Office | Varnsdorf |
| construction / roadbuilding | Silnice n. p. | Zahrady / Krásná Lípa |

Czechia systematically lags other regions (Česká školní inspekce 2019), which could explain the popularity of TVET programmes.

There are now seven upper secondary schools in Šluknov Hook: two academic schools (traditional public *gymnasium* in Rumburk and another new Catholic one in Varnsdorf) and five schools that offer various TVET programmes. In Rumburk, the former printing vocational school became a TVET school of media design and printing, while two other secondary schools merged into a professional school with two programmes in nursing and one in business administration. In Varnsdorf, all public secondary schools merged into one large organization offering programmes in many different fields and from short 2-year training courses to post-secondary TVET. The scope is very broad reaching far beyond the programmes of its predecessors. The school retained two textile-related qualifications, too: fashion design (4-year) and tailoring (3-year program).

The Šluknov school has now a dozen full-time programmes not only in forestry, but also in fields of security/paralegal and social services, and food processing/bakery. Adolescents with more severe impairments can attend several 'practical schools', attached to public or private elementary schools in the area.

Despite the broad scope of VET programmes available in the Hook, some local youth prefer to commute to more distant TVET schools. As one hairdresser student explained to us: 'I chose the vocational school in Varnsdorf but my mother told me that not to go to school here, that it was bad here, so I went to Děčín [the other school offering this program some 50 km away], and it was great, so I enrolled over there.' Probably due to the poor reputation of the programmes in Varnsdorf state run school, a new private secondary TVET school was founded in 2016 by a successful engineering company TOS in the same town. One student of this school participating in our research explained that selection criteria for the applicants are much more rigorous than in public schools.

In recent years, two important measures affecting upper secondary education have been implemented: (1) national admission test to more prestigious upper secondary tiers and (2) new *maturita* (graduation exam). These changes appear as a logical structural necessity in an overly decentralised school system. At the same time, however, both measures have been perceived by many as a substantial move towards the curtailment of access to HE. Exam reforms may include the hidden agenda of discouraging a significant share of youth from enrolling to academic and professional tracks, and hence increasing the demand for IVET programmes.

## National admission test

In accordance with the spirit of the Educational Law of 2004, the policy for the *admission of applicants* had been fully devolved to upper secondary school principals. Since 2016, however, the uniform centrally administered Czech Language and Mathematics tests has been mandated for applicants (Decree No. 353/2016 Coll.). So, to transit to the academic or professional tier, compulsory school graduates must sit the test. Students applying for most VET programmes do not sit the national test. At present, no cut-off test score/ minimal required level of knowledge has been set yet for the programmes leading to maturita exam. But introducing a cut-off score and raising entry barriers to more demanding (academic and professional) programmes has been strongly demanded by some regions (i.e. operators of upper secondary schools) and also by employers' organizations like the Confederation of Industry of the Czech Republic.

## New maturita exam

The reformed exam was to take place in the school year 2007/2008. The 2007 amendment to the Education Act postponed this date to the school year 2009/ 2010 on grounds of 'unresolved organizational and logistics issues for maturita graduation exam and missing funding for organization of pedagogical training' (see Long-term plan for education and development of the Czech education system from May 2007). In September 2009, another amendment to the Education Act postponed the date of the new form of the matura examination for the 2010/2011 school year. In the following ten years, however, the conditions under which the test took place changed almost every year.

Our research (Dvořák et al. 2021) confirms that some compulsory-school teachers discourage lower achieving students from applying to technical/professional programmes leading to *maturita* (and effectively channel them towards the 3-year VET programmes). The 4-year programmes with both the admission and graduation exams are seen as a rather risky career path for many teenagers. It is not uncommon for a student successfully to complete a 4-year programme and fail the *maturita* final examination e.g. in Czech language or mathematics. Such a student has learnt the entire professional curriculum, but according to current rules, has attained only lower secondary education and drops out without any professional or vocational qualification. In this way, national and local education policy ensures new cohorts of young IVET graduates continue to enter the labour market, without, however, having systematically developed the quality of VET schools and their labour market relevance.

## Regional scholarships

The regions as school operators are often blamed for not discontinuing some obsolete VET programs. Scholarships are one mechanism used by regions to increase enrolment in selected fields of education, in best case scenario the qualifications demanded on the labour market but taken by small numbers of students ("supported qualifications"). The scholarships may be perceived as a measure to promote equality, but VET schools could attract youngsters from poorer families who gain a short-term advantage at the cost of losing direct access to HE. Several studies show that vocational tiers are mainly attended by students with low socio-economic status, even after accounting for their abilities, and that home background has become increasingly important (Katrňák 2004; Straková 2015; Veselý 2006).

The regions are determined to increase the number of students taking supported qualifications so the average class size of 28–30 students in freshman grades of VET programmes is reached and maintained. Scholarships are expected to increase the number of successful graduates and decrease dropouts. They are usually awarded only the students residing in the given region and attending a school established by that region, so students commuting to schools in other regions are not eligible.

## Discussion and conclusion

In 2020, the Czech Government approved a new Education Policy Strategy for years 2021 to 2030 and beyond (Strategy 2030+), defining the vision, priorities and goals of education in the period beyond the horizon of 2030. In S2030+, TVET is conceived as an integral part of the education system, in which almost 80 per cent of upper secondary students are educated. The aim of secondary (and post-secondary non-tertiary) VET shall be 'preparing the graduates for the qualified performance of occupations and work activities, or for his further education. It should however also create the preconditions for a quality and full life, lifelong learning, independent decision-making and critical work with information.' How does the reality match these aspirations?

We have seen that the fundamental responsibility for TVET education / skill formation has increasingly shifted to the state in recent decades. At the same time, the Czech state failed in its role of providing the necessary conditions to fulfil this task. Specifically, schools in Czechia have been seriously underfinanced for a long time, as expenditures on primary through tertiary educational institutions were among the lowest of OECD countries (OECD 2020), despite recent increases in spending and a (temporary) demographic decline raising per-student expenditure. Probably the most serious negative consequence of underfunding is a significant shortage of teachers and trainers, particularly in STEM subjects.

Underfunding had very negative ramifications for attracting people into teaching, affecting not only the supply of teaching staff, but also their quality. As Münich and Smolka (2020) note, there is very low variability in teachers' salaries, so quality teachers are undervalued and insufficiently motivated, increasing risk of leaving the profession. Indeed, Ryška (2008) found the most severe problem in VET schools related to teachers: shortage of qualified teachers; work morale; relationship to students; and teaching methods. Staff shortages are even worse in peripheral areas.

Decline in demand for manual labour and for vocational training graduates was overestimated. The former state agency for TVET (Národní ústav odborného vzdělávání, NÚOV) has been merged with other educational agencies. Another serious problem of contemporary Czech education is the government's inability to create a stable legal and institutional framework for schools and students, as in the case of New Maturita. Are we witnessing just 'normal' complex, chaotic policy making or are the post-socialist countries, because of their history of constrained agency, stuck forever in a perpetual transition process (Greger 2011), or a capability trap (Pritchett et al. 2010) like the post-colonial world?

At the national level, the basic structure of Czech upper secondary education has not changed, whereas at the local level the network of providers and fields has changed significantly. Šćepanović (2020) attributes the slow development of the macrostructure, paradoxically, to the emergence of several successful local partnerships or new schools, when companies or non-profit organizations took education under direct control and lost interest in systemic reforms. Our study (Dvořák et al. 2021) also suggests that the supply of quality TVET education strongly depends on the role of specific local actors. The presence (or absence) of a successful manufacturing or service company brings a fundamental change to the situation. It provides for higher quality of IVET as well as future employment. The 'local' actor would be sometimes part of a multinational/global group, as in the case of car manufacturers in Czechia, or a successful player in a small niche of a global market, as with the engineering company in Šluknov Hook.

> Positive choices are not available to all young people, either due to spatial distance or due to low level of skills and aptitudes acquired in some compulsory schools. The involvement of employers and other social partners in IVET is insufficient and uneven. Above all, there is a lack of incentives or systemic support for their participation. (Koucký et al. 2008).

While the social, economic and demographic changes of recent decades have had a major impact on the development of skill formation, the Czech Republic essentially maintained an education system with an early tracking of youth and with a very high proportion of IVET at the upper secondary level, and academically oriented autonomous HEI. Post-secondary professional schools (VOŠ, ISCED 5B) could serve as a (relatively) exceptional case of policy borrowing. *Fachhochschulen* operate successfully in several countries of Western Europe, and their transfer to Czechia had significant external support. At the same time there were local actors who could use them to achieve their own goals. Although VOŠ became institutionalised as a relatively stable part of the Czech skill building system, at the same time they were also gradually assimilated to correspond more closely to domestic tradition. Contrary to the original ideas, the concept of VOŠ has gradually shifted from tertiary towards advanced upper secondary education. This situation became even more obvious since the 2004 Education Law. With the increasing availability of university programmes, VOŠ are becoming less and less attractive, also due to the still unresolved permeability between university and non-university programmes (Matějů et al. 2009) and lower prestige of the VOŠ graduates.

The Czech system of skill formation is considered obsolete by many experts at home and abroad. Current poor permeability creates dead ends, thus reducing or preventing the chances of further employment. Matějů et al. (2009: 11) warned that 'without the healthy development of its educational system, the Czech Republic will gradually become an assembly plant of Europe, pressured by long working hours and a deepening decline in real wages'. In the short term, however, the situation so far seems different. Accelerating wages, low unemployment rates, and the long period of economic growth in Czechia before the COVID-19 pandemic (Kaňáková, Czesaná and Šímová 2019) could have obscured some future problems and disparities between central and peripheral areas. The 2020 pandemic and the next economic crisis may reverse these trends, making socio-economic cleavages more serious once again. On the other hand, one outcome of the years 2020–2022 may be the renaissance of European production branches on which the Czech education system was oriented until now, or the arrival of radically different scenarios of education and skill formation.

## References


Act No. 561/2004 Collection of Law, On Pre-school, Basic, Secondary, Tertiary Professional and Other Education.

Česká školní inspekce. (2019). *Mezinárodní šetření PISA 2018. Národní zpráva. [PISA 2018. National Report PISA 2018. National Report].* Prague: ČŠI.

Chamoutová, D., Vojtěch, J., and Chomová, P. (2017). *Analýza realizované vzdělávací nabídky středních škol [Analysis of the satisfied educational offer of secondary schools].* Prague: Národní ústav pro vzdělávání.

Corner, T. (2015). *Education in the European Union: Post 2003 Member States.* New York, NY: Bloomsbury.

Czech Statistical Office. (2018). 'Projekce obyvatelstva České republiky [Population projections of the Czech Republic]', <https://www.czso.cz/csu/czso/projekce-obyvatelstva-ceske-republiky-2018-2100#>, accessed 14 May 2021.

Czesaná, V. (2010). *'Nerovnosti v účasti v dalším vzdělávání'.* In P. Matějů, J. Straková and A. Veselý (eds.), *Nerovnosti ve vzdělávání: od měření k řešení [Inequalities in education: from measurement to solutions],* pp. 353–373. Praha: SLON.

Doleshal, Z. A. (2012). *Life and Death in the Kingdom of Shoes: Zlín, Baťa, and Czechoslovakia, 1923–1941.PHD Thesis.* University of Texas at Austin.

Doležal, J. (1996). *Česká kultura za protektorátu: školství, písemnictví, kinematografie*. Prague: Národní filmový archiv.

Dvořák, D., Kučerová, S. R., Simonová, J., Meyer, P., Kučera, Z., and Šmíd, J. (2021). 'Coming of Age in the Czech Countryside: Life and Educational Transition Contexts for Rural Youth'. In: K. Schafft, S. Stanić, R. Horvatek and A. Maselli (eds), *Rural Youth at the Crossroads: Transition Societies in Central Europe and Beyond*, pp. 90–114. London: Routledge.

Dvořák, D., Meyer, P., Kučerová, S. R., Vyhnálek, J., and Šmíd, O. (2020). 'Changing Place, Changing Track: Inter-school Mobility of Czech Secondary Students', *Journal of Pedagogy*, 11 (1), 83–105.

Eurofound (2014). *Mapping Youth Transitions in Europe*. Luxembourg: Publications Office of the European Union.

European Commission. (2020). 'Country report Czechia 2020', <https://op.europa.eu/en/publication-detail/-/publication/6bc7ac28-5943-11ea-8b81-01aa75ed71a1>, accessed 16 June 2021.

Eurostat. (2020). 'Distribution of pupils and students enrolled in general and vocational programmes by education level and NUTS2 regions [Dataset]', < https://appsso.eurostat.ec.europa.eu/nui/show.do?dataset=educ_uoe_enra13&lang=en>, accessed 26 June 2021.

Greger, D. (2011). 'Dvacet let českého školství optikou teorií změny vzdělávání v post-socialistických zemích', *Orbis scholae*, 5 (1), 9–22.

Halasz, G. (2013). 'Educational Development through ESF Funding in the Central-Eastern European Region and in Hungary', <https://nesetweb.eu/wp-content/uploads/2019/06/2013-Educational-development-through-ESF-funding-in-the-central-eastern-European-region-and-in-Hungary.pdf>, accessed 19 June 2021.

Jančák, V., Havlíček, T., Chromý, P., and Marada, M. (2008). 'Regional Differentiation of Selected Conditions for the Development of Human and Social Capital in Czechia', *Geografie*, 113, 269–284.

Janyš, B. (1997). '*Kurikulum, hodnocení a certifikace / Hodnocení kvality / Vzdělávání učitelů* [Curriculum, Assessment and Certification / Quality Assessment / Teacher Training]'. In P. Grootings and J. Kalous (eds.), *Od pilotních škol k reformní strategii [From the pilot schools to the strategies of reforms]*, pp. 4–64. Prague: Fragment.

Jareš, J. (2013). '*Dějiny vysokého školství v Československu po roce 1945*: Otázky a podněty [History of Higher Education in Czechoslovakia after 1945: questions and suggestions]'. *Acta Universitatis Carolinae*, 52 (1), 13–24.

Kadlec, P. (2019). 'Changes in Education for Textile Production in the Industrialisation Process', *Fibres and Textiles*, 26 (4), 32–46.

Kalenda, J. (2015). 'Development of Non-Formal Adult Education in the Czech Republic', *Procedia – Social and Behavioral Sciences*, 174, 1077–1084.

Kaňáková, M., Czesaná, V., and Šímová, Z. (2019). *Vocational Education and Training in Europe –Czech Republic. Cedefop ReferNet VET in Europe Reports 2018.* Prague: National Institute for Education and National Training Fund (Cedefop ReferNet Czech Republic).

Kasper, T., and Kasperová, D. (2018). 'The Baťa Company in Zlín: A Shoe Company or a School Company?' *History of Education*, 47 (3), 321–348.

Katrňák, T. (2004). *Odsouzeni k manuální práci. Vzdělanostní reprodukce v dělnické rodině [Condemned to manual labour. Educational reproduction in a working-class family]*. Prague: SLON.

Komlosy, A. (2010). 'Austria and Czechoslovakia: The Habsburg Monarchy and Its Successor States'. In L. Heerma van Voss, E. Hiemstra-Kuperus and E. van Nederveen Meerkerk (eds.), *The Ashgate Companion to the History of Textile Workers, 1650–2000* [on-line], pp. 43–74. Abingdon: Routledge.

Kopecký, M., and Šerák, M. (2015). 'Adult Education and Learning Policy in the Czech Republic'. In M. Milana and T. Nesbit (eds.), *Global Perspectives on Adult Education and Learning Policy*, pp. 29–43. London: Palgrave Macmillan.

Kopecký, M., Šerák, M., and Sycha, M. (2018). 'Politika uznávání výsledků předchozího učení – případ České republiky [Policy of recognition of prior learning – the case of the Czech Republic]'. In M. Kopecký et al. (eds.), *Celoživotní učení a transnacionalizované veřejné politiky [Lifelong learning and transnationalised public policies]*, pp. 152–175. Prague: FF UK.

Kostelecký, T., Mikešová, R., and Bernard. J. (2018). 'Střední školy v regionech Česka: ovlivňuje periferní poloha nabídku škol, poptávku po nich a úspěšnost jejich studentů? [Secondary schools in the regions of the Czech Republic: does peripheral location affect school supply, demand and student success?]'. In J. Bernard (ed.), *Nic se tady neděje…Životní podmínky na periferním venkově [There's nothing going on here…Living conditions in the peripheral countryside]*, pp. 92–123. Prague: SLON.

Koucký, J., Kovařovic, J., and Ryška, R. (2008). *Evaluace, učitelé, a vývoj středního školství v ČR [Evaluation, Teachers, and the Development of Secondary Education in the Czech Republic].* Prague: Vydavatelství Pedagogické fakulty, Univerzita Karlova.

Kučera, Z., and Kučerová, S. (2012). 'Historical Geography of Persistence, Destruction and Creation: The Case of Rural Landscape Transformations in Czechia's Resettled Borderland', *Historická geografie*, 38 (1), 165–184.

Kučerová, S. R., Dvořák, D., Meyer, P., and Bartůněk, M. (2020). 'Dimensions of Centralization and Decentralization in the Rural Educational Landscape of Post-socialist Czechia', *Journal of Rural Studies*, 74, 280–293.

Machonin, P., Tuček, M., and Nekola, M. (2006). 'The Czech Economic Elite after Fifteen Years of Post-socialist Transformation', *Sociologický časopis / Czech Sociological Review*, 42 (3), 537–556.

Mašek, J. L. (1882). *O vývoji průmyslového školství v Rakousku, v Německu, ve Švýcarsku, v Holandsku, v Belgii, ve Francii a na Rusi: s dodavkem o pracovnách školních [On the development of industrial education in Austria, Germany, Switzerland, Holland, Belgium, France, and Russia: with an appendix on school offices]*. Prague: Tiskem a nákladem knihtiskárny Františka Šimáčka.

Matějů, P., Ježek, F., Munich, D., Slovák, J., Straková, J., Václavík, D., Weidnerova, S., and Zrzavý, J. (2009). *White Paper on Tertiary Education*. Prague: Ministry of Education, Youth and Sport.

MEYS. (2007). 'Strategy of Lifelong Learning in the Czech Republic', <https://www.msmt.cz/uploads/Zalezitosti_EU/strategie_2007_EN_web_jednostrany.pdf>, accessed 24 September 2021.

Mikser, R., and Goodson, I. F. (2019). 'The Concept of Refraction and the Narrative Approach to Exploring Multi-level Social Reform Initiatives: Conceptual and Methodological Issues'. In P. Vihalemm, A. Masso and S. Opermann (eds.), *The Routledge International Handbook of European Social Transformations*, pp. 84–97. London: Routledge.

Ministerstvo školství, mládeže a tělovýchovy (2010). 'Nové nařízení vlády o soustavě oborů vzdělání v základním, středním a vyšším odborném vzdělávání 211/210 [Decree 211/2010 Coll., on System of Qualifications in Basic, Upper Secondary and Post-secondary Education]', <https://www.msmt.cz/vzdelavani/stredni-vzdelavani/nove-narizeni-vlady-o-soustave-oboru-vzdelani-v-zakladnim>, accessed 16 June 2021.

Münich, D., and Smolka, V. (2020). 'Platy učitelů v roce 2019: Blýská se na lepší časy? [Teachers' salaries in 2019: Are better times ahead?]', *IDEA Studies*, < https://idea.cerge-ei.cz/files/IDEA_Studie_3_2020_Platy_ucitelu/IDEA_Studie_3_2020_Platy_ucitelu.html#p=1>, accessed 16 May 2021.

Novotný, P. (2009). 'Vzdělávání v institucích neformálního vzdělávání [Education in non-formal education institutions]'. In J. Průcha (ed.), *Pedagogická encyklopedie*, pp. 520–525. Praha: Portál.

OECD. (2011). *Lessons from PISA for the United States: Strong Performers and Successful Reformers in Education*. Paris: Organisation for Economic Cooperation and Development.

OECD. (2016). *PISA 2015 Results (Volume II): Policies and Practices for Successful Schools.* Paris: Organisation for Economic Cooperation and Development.

OECD. (2020). *Education Policy Outlook: Czech Republic.* Paris: Organisation for Economic Cooperation and Development.

Pabian, P., Hündlová, L., and Provázková, K. (2011). 'The Czech Republic Between Studentocracy, Academic Oligarchy and Managerialism: Are Students Powerful or Powerless?' *Tertiary Education and Management*, 17 (3), 191–203.

Pabian, P., Šima, K., and Kynčilová, L. (2011). 'Humboldt Goes to the Labour Market: How Academic Higher Education Fuels Labour Market Success in the Czech Republic', *Journal of Education and Work*, 24 (1–2), 95–118.

Pick, M. (1990). 'Ekonomická výzva ke vzkříšení kvalifikačního potenciálu ČSSR [The economic challenge to increase the qualification potential of the Czechoslovak Socialist Republic]', *Socialistická škola*, 30, 337–351.

Pritchett, L., Woolcock, M., and Andrews, M. (2010). *Capability Traps? The Mechanisms of Persistent Implementation Failure.* Washington, DC: Center for Global Development.

Prokop, D. (2020). *Slepé skvrny: O chudobě, vzdělávání, populismu a dalších výzvách české společnosti [Blind spots: on poverty, education, populism and other challenges of Czech society].* Brno: Host.

Ryška, R. (ed.) (2008). *Kvalita škol a hodnocení výsledků vzdělávání [School quality and assessment of learning outcomes].* Prague: Vydavatelství Pedagogické fakulty, Univerzita Karlova.

Šćepanović, V. (2020). 'Skills on Wheels: Raising Industry Involvement in Vocational Training in the Czech Republic, Slovakia and Hungary'. In V. A. Covarrubias and S. Ramírez Perez (eds.), *New Frontiers of the Automobile Industry*, pp. 401–428. Cham: Springer International.

Scott, P. (2007). 'Reflections of the Reform of Higher Education in Central and Eastern Europe'. In J. J. F. Forest and P. G. Altbach (eds.), *International Handbook of Higher Education*, pp. 423–441. Springer, Dordrecht.

Šimáně, M., and Kamanová, L. (2020). 'Přijímací řízení na středních odborných školách v období socialistického Československa [Admissions to secondary vocational schools in socialist Czechoslovakia]', *Studia paedagogica*, 25 (3), 69–101.

Straková, J. (2015). 'Strong Vocational Education – a Safe Way to the Labour Market? A Case Study of the Czech Republic', *Educational Research*, 57 (2), 168–181.

Surubaru, N.-C. (2021). 'European Funds in Central and Eastern Europe: Drivers of Change or Mere Funding Transfers? Evaluating the Impact of European

Aid on National and Local Development in Bulgaria and Romania', *European Politics and Society*, 22 (2), 203–221.

Ústav školských informací. (1989). *Vývoj a současnost středních odborných učilišť v ČSSR [The Development and Present of Secondary Vocational Schools in the Czechoslovak Socialist Republic]*. Prague: Ústav školských informací.

Veselý, A. (2006). 'Kdo a proč končí v učňovských oborech? [Who ends up in apprenticeships and why?]'. In P. Matějů and J. Straková (eds.) ‚*Nerovné šance na vzdělání. Vzdělanostní nerovnosti v České republice [Unequal educational opportunities. Educational inequalities in the Czech Republic]*, pp. 247–281. Prague: Academia.

Vojtěch, J., and Chamoutová, D. (2018). *Vývoj vzdělanostní a oborové struktury žáků a studentů ve středním a vyšším odborném vzdělávání v ČR a v krajích ČR a postavení mladých lidí na trhu práce ve srovnání se stavem v Evropské unii – 2017/18 [Development of the educational and occupational structure of pupils and students in secondary and higher vocational education in the Czech Republic and in the regions of the Czech Republic and the position of young people on the labour market in comparison with the situation in the European Union – 2017/18]*. Prague: Národní ústav pro vzdělávání.

West, J. (2013). *Vocational Education and Training in Eastern Europe: Transition and Influence*. London: Centre for Learning and Life Chances in Knowledge Economies and Societies.

White Paper (2001). *National Programme for the Development of Education in the Czech Republic*. Prague: Ministry of Education, Youth and Sport.

Wolter, A. (2013). 'Massification and Diversity: Has the Expansion of Higher Education Led to a Changing Composition of the Student Body?' In I. Repac and P. Zaga (eds.), *Higher Education Reforms: Looking Back – Looking Forward*, pp. 202–220. Ljubljana: University of Ljubljana.

Juraj Vantuch and Dagmar Jelínková

# 7. Slovakia: skill formation at the crossroads

**Abstract:** After the velvet divorce in 1993, Slovakia faced a triple challenge: transition to democracy, economic transformation and building institutions of an independent state. This chapter reflects the development of skill formation in Slovakia in three phases: post-communism (1989–1998), Europeanization (1998–2006), and the phase of 'softening capitalism' (2006–2020). Based on the history lessons, the reflection of the socio-economic background and ongoing revision of the national qualifications system, it also discusses the future of skills development. Czechoslovak institutionally well-developed and strong initial VET was at a crossroads because of long-term underestimation of incoherency of processes shaping the market-driven economy and public education and qualifications systems. The traditional school-based system deteriorated in the quality of graduates and faces increasing inefficiency in supplying skills to meet labour market needs. Because of the ill-conceived funding model and long-term underfunding of public education and training, there are two alternatives for skill formation going forward: a corporatist model and a market-driven model. The biased 'German-style' corporatist and biased 'Anglo-Saxon' market-driven alternatives, both weakening the national authorities' governance, are in conflict with traditional school-based VET. The 2017 Learning Slovakia strategy paper, therefore, suggested building on the existing school-based VET adjusted to labour market needs via strong spells of work-based learning and increased flexibility in the provision of qualifications. The corporatist model shifting power to sectoral and professional organisations representing employers' side however prevails. This is accompanied by insufficient balancing of employers' preferences, often dominated by their short-term specific needs, and national responses to forthcoming challenges of digitalisation, automation and robotization. Furthermore, the Slovak approach to the transition to a market economy led to the dominance of a 'race to the bottom' and 'rent seeking' behaviour in the economy instead of growth in innovation-based production.

**Keywords:** Corporatist model of skill formation, market-based model of skill formation, school-based VET, Slovakia, work-based learning

## Introduction

Institutionalised skill formation in Slovakia had its origins in the 19th century. At that time, the first VET schools were created by professional associations, although young people predominantly embarked upon individual apprenticeships serving the needs of a master and acquiring strictly job-related skills. The creation of the vocational education and training (VET) stream as part of the education system only commenced after the establishment of Czechoslovakia in 1918. This chapter reflects the development of skill formation in Slovakia in three significant phases: Post-communism, Europeanization, and the phase of 'softening capitalism'. *Two additional* sections, on the socio-economic background and revision of national qualifications system, complete the picture. The final section discusses the future of skills development in a country which is clearly at a crossroads.

## Development during early post-communist transformation in 1989–1998

The post-communist transformation of Slovakia started in 1991 with the 'shock therapy' of economic reform embracing price liberalisation and large-scale privatisation. The impact on Slovakia (-15 per cent GDP; 12 per cent unemployment; 61 per cent inflation, all in 1991) was extremely harsh compared to the Czech Republic (Vantuch et al. 2001). The collapse of industry, in particular sectors related to the military, the declining purchasing power of citizens (69.6 per cent real wage decline compared to 1989) and the restrictive fiscal and monetary policy of the federal government resulted in Slovakian and Czech citizens having different attitudes with respect to further economic reform. While Czech politicians preferred rapid and large-scale privatisation, Slovak politicians preferred gradual reform steps.

The dissolution of Czechoslovakia, a federal state since 1968, resulted in the termination of financial transfers to Slovakia from the Czech Republic which represented approximately 7 per cent of Slovak annual GDP in 1992 (Šujan & Šujanová 1994). Thus, between 1989 and 1998, Slovakia faced three challenges: undertaking the transition to democracy; developing a market economy; and establishing an independent state from 1 January 1993; each of which required substantial financial and human resources. Despite improving economic conditions between 1994–1998, Slovakia failed to fulfil the necessary political criteria and so was not included in the first group of candidates for integration into the EU.

Democratisation was the ultimate goal of 1990 education reforms. Together with changes in curricula designed to remove the influence of communist ideology, substantial flexibility was introduced. The election of school directors was established, schools could renew up to 30 per cent of the content, reallocate up to 10 per cent of weekly hours, and introduce new subjects without claims for additional funding by the state. Private and church-affiliated schools also emerged, supported by the government.

Secondary initial VET streams faced new challenges. The minority stream (accounting for about 25 per cent of upper secondary graduates) was represented by secondary specialised schools, offering pure school-based VET with a strong theoretical component and prepared students for entering middle-management jobs. These theoretically oriented VET programmes prepared students both for entering the labour market and higher education (HE) programmes corresponding to the respective VET school profile. As with the general education stream (15 per cent), this stream expected a bright future, freedom from ideology and learning environments with state-of-the-art educational technology.

The major VET stream (accounting for about 60 per cent of students) was represented by secondary vocational schools offering training for specific occupations in close cooperation with companies. It encompassed traditional craftsmanship training and generic blue-collar training. This pathway was severely compromised by economic reform, as schools lost the opportunity to use the premises of collapsing companies. The original 2-year programmes with a 50 per cent share of work-based learning, as well as the 2.5-year and 3.5-year programmes with a final 4-month period of workplace based professional development, had to be adapted in order to postpone the entry of students into the labour market.

The 1990s saw growing student interest in grammar schools and secondary specialised schools that offered VET with a strong theoretical component and wider profile compared to the secondary vocational schools that originally focussed on training for specific professions. Between 1989 and 1998, the number of graduates from grammar schools increased by over 50 per cent and from secondary specialised schools by over 60 per cent. The number of graduates from secondary vocational schools decreased slightly by 1 per cent (Vantuch & Jelínková 2002, Tables 41 and 42). But this was only the beginning of decline.

Fears of growing unemployment accompanying economic reform led in the 1990s to a loss of confidence in VET, particularly its early narrow specialisations. It was clear that initial VET with about 1,500 specialisations offered by a variety of programmes from 2 to 4 years duration needed to be reformed. International programmes (Vantuch & Jelinkova 2010, 202–203) explored 'occupational standards with consequently pursued educational standards', and the modularisation of initial VET was piloted in 20 schools, whilst efforts to create a stream of higher professional schools were piloted in 10 secondary VET schools and three higher education institutions. These promising reforms never translated into systemic changes, however, as they were overshadowed by other agendas and finally abandoned, with a lack of expertise having also played a role. The State Institute of Vocational Education in Bratislava, established in 1991, was not able to replace lost capacities after the dissolution of Czechoslovakia, due to insufficient funding from the state budget with fewer than 15 full-time specialists covering the core VET agenda.

In 1990, the government 'nationalized' all secondary vocational schools to prevent the sale of their buildings as part of industrial privatisations. Only five companies continued to run secondary vocational schools, with the other schools being taken over by sectoral ministries.

Subsequently, four regional educational authorities were established under the education ministry, with responsibility for grammar and secondary specialised schools. In 1996, 'ministerial' governance was substantially weakened in favour of territorial management. Autonomous regional educational authorities were abolished, and responsibility for establishing secondary vocational schools was transferred from the respective ministries to regional state authorities. Strengthened regional governance, however, simultaneously weakened the links of VET schools to specific sectors of the economy, and VET schools gradually accelerated provision of any kind of programmes regardless of their earlier sectoral profiles. Later evaluations of the development in the 1990s explicitly stated that VET suffered from a lack of labour market intelligence, the loss of staff employed in senior positions and insufficient interest on the part of entrepreneurs and other social partners, who were content to leave responsibility for curricular changes with schools (Group of education ministry experts 2000, 28–33).

Democratisation was also considered to be a priority in higher education: A new act on higher education (172/1990) re-introduced academic rights and freedom and allowed for the autonomy of higher education institutions (HEIs). The establishment of self-governing bodies within universities and self-governing representations of higher education restricted the power of the education ministry and highlighted the need for regulatory clarification. This, alongside impulses from abroad, resulted in the legislation being amended in 1996, although discrepancies in power-sharing between rectors and deans and university and faculty senates have persisted. Long-term strategies and priorities for development were also elaborated by the amendment. A 3-cycle model of tertiary studies was accepted, but the diversification of higher education was frozen because of the resilience of the assumption that all higher education institutions would become universities made during the initial phase of the transformation.

The idea of improving further education rather than improving lifelong learning was dominant in the 1990s. Slovakia inherited a strong network of further education institutions structured on three levels: education centres affiliated to companies; education institutions established on a sectoral basis; and institutions affiliated to central government authorities. In addition to further education addressing the need for the upskilling and reskilling of employees and the existence of a strong stream of adult education in part-time secondary and tertiary studies, there was also a pathway addressing individual learners' needs and civic, cultural, political and environmental awareness. Here, the major players were the culture ministry with so-called 'houses of culture' established in almost all municipalities, and the Socialistic Academia with a network of facilities nationwide. Nevertheless, this system collapsed in the process of dismantling the state-owned economy. New private institutions emerged offering services sensitive to the purchasing power of individual learners and companies and the Association of Adult Education Institutions was established in 1991 as a non-profit organisation to promote common interests of adult learning providers. The act on further education (386/1997) failed to create a new framework for adult education as none of the financial schemes to support adult education that had been considered was adopted. However, it did create a market for private tertiary education for individuals unable to access formal studies.

The transformation crisis quickly dampened initial euphoria around democratisation. This was felt most acutely by VET, as labour market shocks led to a decline in interest in VET qualifications in the at-risk sectors, and a commensurate increase in interest in general education or broad-profiled VET. The sharp rise in unemployment also led to a decline in employers' interest in both young workers and workplace training. During the years of political turbulence, the necessary structural reforms of VET were simply postponed. This had later consequences for the functionality of the national qualifications framework and delayed the diversification of tertiary education.

## Development in the phase of 'Europeanization' 1998–2006

A political change after the 1998 elections and the subsequent period of political stability was dominated by a right-wing political party, the Slovak Democratic and Christian Union (SDKÚ), which was a powerful driver of reform. There was swift progress in the processes of international integration: Slovakia became an EU candidate country in December 1999, joined the OECD in December 2000 and became an EU member state on 1 May 2004 together with the first group of former candidate countries.

Reforms, especially during the 2002–2006 period, were 'neoliberal' in character. The government doubted the effectiveness of social policies and intended to reduce economic inactivity with the threat of deregistration from the labour office registry. An act relating to employment services (5/2004) redefined labour market policies and created a new network of labour offices, which integrated social and employment policies under the labour ministry and strengthened its control. A new act relating to social protection (599/2003) resulted in the number of people receiving social support benefits falling significantly and a reduction in the value of those benefits. This had a particularly significant impact on the Roma minority. The Labour Code amendment supported greater flexibility in hiring/firing employees, leading to the expansion of overtime and part-time work. Privatisation of strategic companies and network industries, pension and healthcare reforms, all backed by a right-wing mantra that the state is an ineffective administrator, paved the way for the political swing to the left in 2006.

The first influential strategy paper, the National Programme of Education in the Slovak Republic for forthcoming 15–20 years (the Millennium), was adopted by the Government in 2001. The VET related chapter referred to the strategic recommendations of the study financed by the EU (Birks, Sinclair and Associates Ltd. 1993), but the paper had a stronger impact in general education. Only two initiatives were implemented with respect to VET, and these resulted from spontaneous developments rather than deliberate policies: reducing the stream of VET graduates to the lower limit of 70 per cent and merging both aforementioned types of VET schools into one in 2008.

Two other recommendations of the Millennium sought to draw from international experience: to modularise the provision of VET and to establish a unified general education programme with a strengthened focus on key competences in the first year of all VET programmes. In contrast to these two recommendations that are still relevant and under discussion, the recommendation to split VET into a theoretically based and a strongly practically oriented stream was seen as looking back to the 1930s. Millennium suggested awarding a certificate of apprenticeship 'within two-year and three-year studies strictly based on the enterprises' and traders' orders at schools established by enterprises or in a dual system (besides some branches, e.g. in agriculture)'. However, this proved to be unrealistic due to the weakness of professional associations and the reluctance of enterprises to assume responsibility for training young workers when there was a plentiful supply of qualified unemployed workers.

At the beginning of the 2000s, fiscal incentives to support cooperation between schools and business/industry became a topical issue, promoted by the Slovak National Observatory of VET (SNO). Studying international experience and reporting to ETF and Cedefop on VET, the SNO criticised the finance ministry's reluctance to consider fiscal incentives in support of VET and lifelong learning. Measures such as levies, tax incentives and learning accounts, were rejected, and this resulted in the last five companies ceasing to run their VET schools. The SNO's intervention nevertheless generated debate within the Millennium paper about the development of a new model of vocational and lifelong learning financed from more sources. Although the Millennium was adopted by the parliament, its recommendations have never been delivered. It is significant that the finance ministry was strongly opposed to the Millennium's initial proposals to increase investment in education up to a minimum of 5 per cent of GDP in 2006 and 6 per cent in 2010, and to increase the remuneration of pedagogical staff. The finance ministry declared that increasing investment in education should be made dependant on 'possibilities of the state budget'. Schools and the new education act became victims of austerity measures.

A new financing scheme based on per capita funding was introduced in 2004. This had positive features, as the allocation of funding was transparent, and the introduction of 'hard budget constraints' to public schools ended the practice of bailing out indebted schools. Less positively, continued underfunding decreased quality. A mix of academic naivety on the part of economists and a belated acknowledgement of the reluctance to stimulate quality assurance is exemplified in the following comment of a leading reformer:

> The link between the volume of financial resources allocated to the founders and the number of pupils represents a motivating means for more efficient use of the allocated financial resources and the rationalization of the school network. Schools are also motivated to provide a quality education because, with increased interest in the school and a higher number of students, they will have more funding (Mikloš et al. 2005, 35).

The SNO criticised this scheme as unbalanced and lacking incentives for achieving quality, as highlighted by their report written for Cedefop:

> Schools are dominantly input market oriented trying to attract as many students as possible to secure the richest possible budget. Financing per capita introduced without quality check of graduates resulted in gradual deterioration of their quality, as schools subordinated pedagogy to economy. Quality and employability of graduates became secondary. Insufficient financing from the state budget deepens the modernisation debt. (Vantuch & Jelinkova 2012, 32).

The HE legislation was adopted after a lengthy process. It encompassed the ideas of the Bologna process, but it failed in some important details. A credit system was implemented but was not fully compatible with European Credit Transfer System (ECTS). Similarly, the Accreditation Commission's status and accreditation procedures were not fully compatible with European Association for Quality Assurance in Higher Education (ENQA) requirements. Little emphasis was placed on the need to develop thorough internal quality assurance. The most significant weakness with respect to skill formation was the lack of support for the development of tertiary VET. Newly introduced bachelor studies were not designed to promote labour market entry, but as the first half of earlier higher education programmes, and the per capita funding scheme stimulated schools to push bachelors to pursue master studies. A similar phenomenon manifested itself in PhD studies and the professionalisation of teachers. Academic inbreeding (practice, when universities are hiring their own graduates to be professors) was inherent in the system and although it was intellectually harmful, schools had no reason to combat this practice. Per capita funding which undermined quality across the whole system, also resulted in the permanent postponement of investment in education. which remained amongst the greatest risk of cutbacks from austerity measures.

The lifelong learning agenda came to prominence in Slovakia following the publication in 2000 of the *Memorandum on Lifelong Learning*. The consultation process associated with this EU document was the first in history to involve all relevant stakeholders and reflected dissatisfaction with the act on further education (386/1997). It gave rise to consensus on the need to abandon the former restrictive focus on further education, in favour of a holistic approach encompassing formal, non-formal and informal learning from cradle to grave. In 2001, detailed rules for the accreditation of further education providers were introduced and the practice of paid tertiary studies offered in cooperation with universities, under the umbrella of lifelong learning but without any relevant quality monitoring was eliminated. In 2004, the Government adopted a concept paper on lifelong learning which reflected the ideas of the *Memorandum on Lifelong Learning* and initiated the preparation of a genuine act on lifelong learning. However, ministerial commitment to this agenda gradually waned, and lifelong learning continued to be subsumed within adult, and further education.

This important period, in which the democratic deficit was significantly reduced and structural reforms in the economy introduced, led to a remarkable growth of the national economy. However, the development of the education system was still neglected and necessary structural reforms relating to VET were postponed again. Both the new funding scheme and the decentralisation reforms, despite generating some improvements, were characterised by weaknesses which continued to undermine the development of the education system. The decentralisation reform disregarded the need to reconstruct links between VET schools and enterprises, and neither the new funding model nor the new governance model proved effective in reducing the mismatch between labour market needs and skills supply.

Although employer representatives were highly critical of the failure of schools to adjust to the market economy, their criticism were misplaced: school directors fully adjusted their behaviour to the market economy, but to the 'school market' rather than to the labour market, and as such were input, rather than output driven. The SNO contributed to the discussion raised by the Slovak Academy of Sciences' question 'Is the education system a driver or an obstacle to progressive structural changes in the economy of the Slovak Republic?' by referencing the 'perverted motivations' caused by reformers: schools accepted the 'capping' of their spending and focused on adapting to the conditions of the educational services market. Thus, their focus was not on the quality of graduates they produced nor the requirements of employers or schools providing education at a subsequent level, but the quantity of students enrolled; and the satisfaction of students' and parents' preferences in educational programmes became decisive for school budgets. Perversely, under the new arrangements, it was possible for a school to jeopardize its existence by focussing on the production of high-quality graduates. Competition for students in the education market was exacerbated by population decline, and deprived school managements of any ethical barriers. The gradual devastation of education is clearly a collateral loss of the Slovak form of economic transformation (Vantuch 2015, 24).

## Development in the phase of 'softening capitalism' 2006–2020

Public disenchantment with the libertarian principles and austerity of the right wing resulted in political change at the 2006 parliamentary elections. SMER declaring itself a third way social democratic party, initially made only moderate reversals of the earlier reforms and continued with efforts to fulfil the Maastricht criteria. Slovakia joined the Eurozone on 1 January 2009 on the eve of the global financial crisis. The crisis demonstrated the weakness of the national economy's lack of diversity and heavy dependence on the production of slow-moving goods. Despite solid GDP growth after the crisis, Slovakia did not return to the steep growth of the pre-crisis period and the catching-up process has gradually slowed down. Consequently, left-wing policies, with a short interruption in 2010–2012 prevailed. Furthermore, dissatisfaction with pro-capital policies of the right-wing governments and corruption scandals associated with privatisation resulted in the leading reforming political party SDKÚ having no parliamentary presence from 2012.

The marked West-East divide visible in unemployment rates made interventions aimed at reducing regional disparities inevitable. The act on the support of the least developed districts (336/2015) and subsequent action plans for district development, were adopted by the government. Many districts lagging in development have large Roma communities. Substantial improvement is therefore expected to be generated by alternative ways of retraining of adults, and from combining learning and working via social enterprises. In 2018, the parliament adopted the act on social economy and social enterprises (112/2018), which among other things addresses the low-skilled and long-term unemployed.

Some have argued that increasing regional disparities and growing vulnerability to the challenges of robotization, automation and digitalisation are a consequence of the economic transformation strategies in the post-communist era, which made the country attractive for foreign investors because of a cheap skilled workforce. The political left described this as a typical example of a 'race to the bottom' premised on reducing labour costs to favour manufacturing, while other segments of the economy, notably agriculture, stagnated or even declined. The extensive production of cars and electronic devices, as well as the reliance on heavy industry exposed to increasing competition from countries outside the EU, created the demand for a workforce with intermediate skills. As a consequence, increasing numbers of Slovaks with tertiary education have been forced to look for a career abroad, or accept positions for which they are over-qualified. Slovakia failed to support investment in favour of restructuring the economy towards goods and services with higher value added.

The postponed reform started with the education act (245/2008) and introduced a curricular reform that was also valid for secondary VET. National curricula ('state educational programmes') were designed by national authorities based on educational standards, creating a framework for the development of school curricula ('school educational programmes'). In VET, the first steps towards reform were taken in the early 2000s with the promotion of competence-based curricula over traditional syllabi, increased emphasis on key competencies and the promotion of graduate profile descriptions comprising key competencies, general competencies and vocational competencies in all VET programmes. National curricula for VET were more consistent when compared to the national curricula for general education programmes, but the reform as a whole was undermined by inadequate time being available for piloting, the preparation of textbooks, and retraining teachers to cope with the fundamental shift in focus towards learning outcomes.

The long-term underfunding of schools had a particularly severe impact on VET schools that were not able to adjust to technological progress. In addition, neither financial nor institutional support was given to VET teachers and trainers to enable them to adjust to labour market needs. The State Institute of Vocational Education and Methodological-Pedagogical Centre had insufficient personnel and financial capacity to organise retraining of VET teachers and trainers unless this was supported by ESF. The act on VET (184/2009) correctly recognised the need to strengthen cooperation with industry and commerce by introducing new VET governance architecture and 'sectoral assignees' empowering chambers and associations to intervene in VET (Vantuch & Jelinkova 2019, 38). In 2015, this act was replaced by a new act on VET (61/2015) introducing a Slovak version of dual VET, which met the requests of employers, notably in the automotive industry, yet this was criticised for its inflexibility. Ten measures were suggested (Group of education ministry experts 2017, 164), the most important of which concerned financial incentives to support not just dual VET, but all forms of work-based learning. However, this proposal was not reflected in 2018 amendments to the act, so the potential to support direct contacts between schools and businesses and the provision of short-term forms of in-company training remained unrealised.

Today, secondary VET can be delivered in three forms: via school-based programmes with practical training delivered mainly in school workshops; via a mixed scheme, with school-based learning along with in-company training within the framework of traditional school-company agreements; and via dual VET formats combining in-company training and school-based learning, where learners (or their parents) have a contract with enterprises for training, while companies and schools are contracted to deliver the shared provision of VET theory and practice. Dual learners however remain students of VET schools and do not have employee status within contracted companies. Because of this VET is not a salient issue with respect to social dialogue in enterprises.

Employers and economists viewed the dual VET format as a fundamental systemic change predicated on the assumption that employers know best how to train young workers. Employer representatives were very optimistic about the implementation of dual VET, but despite heavy promotion and the massive fiscal incentives available to enterprises involved in dual VET (Cedefop ReferNet Slovakia 2019) it is still marginal: 6.4 per cent of the newly enrolled VET students in the 2019/2020 school year, according to the calculation of SNO. There has been no resurgence of interest in apprenticeship type VET, despite good practice examples in some enterprises, and the flight to VET programmes entitling graduates to apply for higher education that started after 1989 persists. The number of grammar schools has almost doubled since 1989, despite a severe population decline. While in 1973–1985 more than 90,000 live births occurred each year, in 2000–2019 it was less than 56,000 on average. This situation has contributed to employer dissatisfaction with the structure of secondary schools and has led to repeated calls to reduce the number of secondary schools, especially those not delivering graduates with skills demanded by the labour market. This resulted in pressure for regulating the inflow of new entrants into secondary schools to meet the needs of employers, and ceilings setting a maximum number of new entrants for each school and each programme are prescribed. These ceilings are based on macroeconomic forecasting by the public employment services, and the outcomes of negotiations between stakeholders at regional level (Vantuch & Jelinkova 2019, 39 and Annex 2). This regulation is controversial, as macroeconomic forecasting data are not the most suitable basis for such a detailed regulation, which has caused conflicts between parents and schools, since forcing the early specialisation of 15-year-olds is counterproductive and ineffective. Labour market intelligence has significantly improved since 2018 thanks to newly available graduate tracking data. New robust datasets (Cedefop ReferNet Slovakia 2020) have the potential substantially to improve the regulation of secondary VET and could result in changes to the practice of using ceilings.

An alternative approach would be to improve career guidance and counselling to support student decision making and enrich the qualifications system by offering 'smaller' qualifications in addition to the 'large' qualifications, currently provided within formal initial VET lasting 3 to 5 years. The process of creating 'smaller' qualifications better addressing labour market needs began together with the creation of the fourth sub-framework of the national qualifications framework (discussed below). These processes have the potential both to increase the supply of qualifications offered by schools and to stimulate demand from adults looking for reskilling or upskilling opportunities.

Persistent criticism in relation to the decreasing quality of higher education resulted in a substantial change in legislation in 2018. The Slovak Accreditation Agency for Higher Education was created, and this body prepared three sets of standards: internal quality assurance system standards; study programme standards (accreditation standards); and standards for awarding professional titles for higher education teachers. These standards comply with the Standards and Guidelines for Quality Assurance in the European Higher Education Area (ESG) and were adopted on 2 July 2020 after public discussion of draft standards presented in 2019. In contrast to the past, the new accreditation agency is fully independent, and it is expected that within two years it will become a regular member of the European Association for Quality Assurance in Higher Education and will be registered on the European Quality Assurance Register for Higher Education.

A fundamental departure comes with the act on quality assurance in higher education (269/2018), which makes quality assurance processes a crucial instrument for accreditation. HE institutions have two years both to adjust their internal regulation to these standards, and to apply for accreditation of their internal system of quality assurance, processes which must be completed by 2024 at the latest. Robust internal quality assurance will allow freedom in curricular design that, in contrast to the past, will not be subject to a specific accreditation procedure.

Universities are, however, still subject to the ill-conceived per capita funding model, and so their focus remains on increasing student enrolments rather than on graduate quality. Furthermore, the ongoing reform is insufficiently flexible to support the diversification of tertiary education in the context of massification. The efforts of universities to offer labour market-oriented bachelor studies have been, with one exception, somewhat lacklustre. Vocational drift in HE is undermined both by the criteria of the quality standards, and the funding model, as well as by the reluctance of stakeholders to support legislation that would result in the establishment of universities of applied sciences.

The spirit of the *Memorandum on Lifelong Learning* was again evident in the Strategy of Lifelong Learning and Lifelong Guidance until 2015, which was adopted by the Government in 2007. However, the 2007 Action Plan remained the internal document and the act on lifelong learning (568/2009) marked a return to the established pattern. This placed lifelong learning within further education and placed learning activities outside the remit of the education ministry. A new impulse came from the 2011 Strategy of Lifelong Learning and the subsequent Action Plan. This suggested a one-stop-shop platform for lifelong learning and a specific financial instrument to increase adult participation which was extremely low compared to international LFS data. All options affecting the state budget, except for ESF, were rejected by the finance ministry.

The 2017 Learning Slovakia strategy paper again raised the need for financial stimulation of adult learning in the form promoted by the Association of Adult Education Institutions, which became a respected international player. Individual learning accounts (€200 annually for adults not in education and training) and tax relief for companies for retraining employees were suggested. This proposal was accepted by the National Programme for the Development of Education, and adopted by the Government in 2018, who identified the budget to implement individual learning accounts in the period 2020–2027.

The preparation of new legislation covering learning in all settings and supporting the validation of non-formal and informal learning and the new lifelong learning strategy was delayed by agreement of the education ministry and the OECD, to prioritise the elaboration of the national skills strategy. The 2020 National Skills Strategy (OECD 2020) published shortly before the beginning of the COVID-19 pandemic was critical of the way in which individual learning accounts had been implemented and recommended these should be focussed solely on SMEs and disadvantaged adults. This, alongside the COVID-19 crisis, put a stop to further efforts to stimulate lifelong learning and all related capacity building at the education ministry. The National Lifelong Learning Institute was abolished in 2019, following the conclusion of several problematic ESF projects supporting lifelong learning.

Although national curricula ('state educational programmes') contain a reference to the key competences of the European reference framework, schools needed more assistance in translating requirements expressed in national curricula into 'school educational programmes' and school practice. Yet VET schools were left alone to find the appropriate mix of general and vocational components within curricula and the balance between learners' general development and their employability. The authorities failed to supply teaching materials to support the development of key competences, and despite later improvements, this reform was, and remains, a reform in programming curricula rather than a curricular reform *per se*. Specific criticisms related to the lack of funding for ICT and digital educational content. The COVID-19 crisis and the difficulties associated with online learning confirmed the lack both of digital equipment and ready to use quality digital educational content.

Co-operation between the spheres of education and business/industry has improved substantially, although such improvements are most evident at the highest levels, as legislation and financial contributions from the state budget primarily support selected employer representatives, so-called 'sectoral assignees'. The same level of support is not available to many other employer representatives instrumental within VET or for autonomous co-operation involving schools and companies unless this is within dual VET. The emphasis put on the macro-level neglecting the micro-level is a systemic weakness, since local or regional players are best placed to identify the most favourable forms of cooperation in the provision of work-based learning. There is no reason to favour work-based learning based on the individual contract between students and companies ('Slovak' dual system) over the work-based learning of the same school students but based on the contract between the school and company (mainstream VET). Other programmes are also worthy of corporate support and co-operation. Financial incentives in support of cooperation between higher education institutions and companies have the potential to be the first step in the development of tertiary VET.

In 2020, the country entered a new phase of development. The dominant left-wing party lost power because the electorate was unhappy with the increasing influence of oligarchs, excessive profiteering on the part of landlords, and corruption in public administration and the judiciary. Large scale protests by citizens after the murder of an investigative journalist resulted in a swing towards centre-right government on the eve of the COVID-19 crisis. The pendulum of power has again swung from 'pro-labour' to 'pro-capital'. A small libertarian party in the coalition with centrist and populist parties has forced measures to 'improve the business environment', which was justified by the deteriorating position of Slovakia in various international rankings. For example, Slovakia ranked 45th among 190 economies in 2019 for ease of doing business compared to 24th in 2014, according to the World Bank.

A more flexible Labour Code is again under discussion and support for pro-labour measures is has diminished, the previous government, being more sensitive to trade union positions. Concepts such as the need for a 'small state' and faith in the market as the engine of all human progress have also returned. The new political context together with the COVID-19 crisis, makes stronger public financing of skill formation institutions increasingly unlikely. Furthermore, there is a high risk both that people will be reduced to the 'homo economicus' and that VET will focus on utilitarian workforce training.

## Implications for economic growth and social development

Slovakia is one of the most open and industrialised economies in Europe. Heavy dependence on the export of goods such as cars and electronics makes the economy very vulnerable, which is evidenced by sharp declines in GDP during times of crisis. It can be seen in the annual decline of -5.5 per cent in 2009 compared to +5.6 per cent and +10.8 per cent in 2008 and 2007, respectively. A marked decline is expected in 2020 due to a slowdown in manufacturing because of the COVID-19 pandemic.

The lack of diversity of the economy, resulting from the post-communist transformation is a serious risk, and reformers are resigned to policies aimed at intensifying the exploitation of workforce knowledge and skills. The lack of entrepreneurial expertise which resulted from the earlier prohibitions on private enterprise was used to justify the replacement of local managers and administrators with foreigners, and even hostile takeovers of competitive local companies by foreign firms. Shock therapy based on a rushed liberalisation of prices and the privatisation of state-owned companies paved the way for an inflow of foreign capital investment that was a major factor shaping the future economy. In the spirit of the Washington consensus, market forces were considered the best option for transition processes (see also Vantuch 2007). The decline of some traditional sectors of the economy was conceptualised as creative destruction, from which the new economy should have emerged.

The decline of sectors such as textiles, shoes and glass making followed a different pattern to that of the agricultural sector and the food industry. According to the indices of food self-sufficiency for EU countries estimated for 2016 by Kołodziejczak (2018, 141), Slovakia decreased significantly. This cannot be explained by a specialisation in manufacturing, because industrial Germany achieved 126 per cent in producing potatoes and 144 per cent in meat, while Slovakia 58 per cent and 52 per cent, respectively. The weak performance of the agricultural sector has also had a serious impact on VET and the employability of the rural population, especially for those with relatively low levels of educational attainment. The decrease in demand for specific knowledge and skills contributed to the decline of agricultural VET programmes, and VET schools originally specialising in agriculture were forced to re-profile and provide education and training for other sectors, often with insufficient experience.

Industrial production including military industries also declined severely in the early 1990s, but in contrast to other sectors of the economy, the influx of foreign capital led to a strong revival. The miracle boom of the automotive industry in Slovakia, a European champion in producing cars per capita, was fuelled by the availability of cheap skilled labour. The industrial boom increased demand for workers graduating from secondary VET programmes once the supply of unemployed skilled workers had been exhausted. Despite this, Slovak people were nevertheless reluctant to enrol in VET programmes preparing for blue-collar professions in the turbulent times of the 1990s and remain cautious of early specialisation, preferring programmes leading to a '*maturita*' certificate and postponing entry to the labour market.

The authors have calculated that the number of general education graduates in 2020 more than doubled to 33 per cent and the number of graduates from theory-focussed VET increased to more than 35 per cent compared with 25 per cent in the communist period. Over time, a VET stream offering a double qualification (19 per cent) has expanded, entitling 87 per cent of secondary school graduates to apply for HE with 13 per cent not doing so because they only received a certificate of apprenticeship (ISCED 353). However, since some VET graduates have a double qualification, a certificate of apprenticeship was awarded to 32 per cent of secondary school graduates. Despite this, the proportion of certificate of apprenticeship holders has halved since the 1980s. Moreover, comparing ISCED 3C and ISCED 353 programmes, it can be said that the stream of graduates with a secondary vocational qualification designed to facilitate direct entry into the labour market decreased to 22 per cent in 2019/2020 compared to 1989/1990.

Employment rates by level of education are also indicative of problems, since data on VET graduates show less favourable outcomes compared to secondary general education, and HE graduates. It is also significant that VET graduates with a '*maturita*' certificate have higher employment rates compared to VET graduates with only a certificate of apprenticeship. Furthermore, during the 2008–2012 crisis, employment in manufacturing dramatically decreased, while employment in public administration increased. The employment rate of people with ISCED 2 level education declined substantially (20.2 per cent in 2019) and the unemployment rate is much higher than those who are better educated (31.9 per cent compared to 5.8 per cent for all levels of education in 2019). It is likely that for rural inhabitants with low levels of education, jobs in agriculture, and particularly meat production, have not been replaced by alternative employment opportunities. The trend away from early departure from education and training (the share of 18–24-year-olds who only completed secondary education and are not in further education or training) established in the EU, has not been mirrored in Slovakia indeed the position has deteriorated. In 2010, with 4.7 per cent, Slovakia had the lowest proportion of early leavers in the EU, but this had risen to 8.3 per cent in 2019 that is worse than the 2020 national target (6 per cent).

Slovakia inherited education and qualification systems which steered school choice in favour of industrial programmes. Secondary general education, as well as tertiary streams, were very thin by international comparison, and tertiary studies in social science and humanities were harder to access. This contributed to the boom of such tertiary studies after 1989, in addition to tertiary studies preparing for jobs in industry declining in popularity.

Subsequently, the number of tertiary graduates increased dramatically, rising from 9,254 in 1989 (before bachelor studies existed in the country), to 29,134 graduates from bachelor and master studies in 2019, after a peak of 43,872 in 2010. The over-qualification of the tertiary educated in Slovakia is among the highest in the EU. Although Slovakia fulfils the target of over 40 per cent tertiary educated in the age cohort 30–34, almost all completed ISCED 7 university studies because bachelor studies adjusted to labour market needs are marginal.

The finance ministry rejected the Europe 2020 strategy target to invest 3 per cent of GDP in research and development by 2020. Despite heavy criticism by academics, the national 2020 target was set at 1.2 per cent GDP but even that was not achieved. Indeed, in one year investment fell well below 1 per cent of GDP. Furthermore, the ministry was hesitant to stimulate private investment in research and development. In 2015, a stimulus for enterprises was introduced allowing for an additional tax deduction of 25 per cent of the real costs of investment in research and development. In 2020 this was increased to 100 per cent, in line with other countries. Unsurprisingly, the share of tertiary graduates from science, technology, engineering and mathematics (STEM) programmes is only slightly above 20 per cent, which according to UNESCO is insufficient for a shift away from an economy based on manufacturing towards a knowledge-based economy with more opportunities for those with tertiary education. Because of questions relating to the quality of Slovakian universities, and because the tertiary-educated can find better jobs abroad, Slovakia suffers from a profound brain drain. The outbound tertiary mobility ratio increased from 4.3 per cent in 2000 to 20.8 per cent in 2017, meaning every fifth tertiary student studies abroad. This potential loss is not offset by the inflow of tertiary educated people as the inbound mobility rate was only 6.9 per cent in 2017 despite a solid growth compared to 1.2 per cent in 2000 (according to UNESCO). Slovakia has one of the highest levels of over-qualification among young people in the EU, and the strongest vulnerability to job loss from automation. The 2017 Learning Slovakia strategy paper was the first document to highlight the dramatic forecasts of Frey and Osborne (2013) and Arntz et al. (2016) and to discuss the vulnerability of the national economy and VET. The recommendation to conduct detailed analyses of labour market change in order to enable educational programmes more responsive to technological shifts has yet to be implemented, however.

The country also faces a serious human resources crisis because of demographic decline. Natural population increase is marginal (0.61 per thousand inhabitants in 2018) due to an unfavourable fertility rate. At the same time, Slovakia is relatively unattractive to foreigners. Only 645 citizens obtained Slovak citizenship in 2017, the second lowest number in the EU. With accession to the EU, outward migration increased. Kahanec and Kureková (2014) detailed short-term labour migration data, noting that migration fluctuates with the economic cycle and a higher migration propensity amongst the unemployed and from more depressed regions of Slovakia. This pattern remained evident in 2019, as inhabitants from the undeveloped north-east of the country accounted for a disproportionate share of people working abroad. More than 70 per cent of short-term migrants found employment in industry, construction, and in health and social care, all sectors where domestic demand for workers is high but wages significantly lower. It must be noted that the total number of workers abroad is damagingly high and in the peak year 2007, it represented up to 14 per cent of the economically active population, according to Kahanec and Kureková (2014, 8). Together with high levels of outflow of tertiary students, this illustrates a serious weakness of the national economy – insufficient creation of attractive jobs. Balancing the talents of the population with labour market needs by making qualifications systems more flexible and less sensitive to inward and outward migration is, therefore, the predominant challenge.

## Development of the National Qualifications System in Slovakia

Debates in relation to the National Qualifications System (NQS) are something of a novelty. The definition of qualification used in European discourse represents a paradigmatic change, which has yet to be fully absorbed. In Slovakia, there was traditionally a difference between certification for the attainment of a specific education level and a qualification certificate. Moreover, qualification was as a rule seen as a combination of education level and additional skills acquired through work, which were sometimes certified, sometimes uncertified, and were often represented by a prescribed number of years of practice. Differences in terminology and a kind of cultural clash resulted in a confused process of standards setting (Vantuch & Jelinkova 2019, 48).

Educational standards were developed under the responsibility of the education ministry and were composed of so-called content and performance standards, as stipulated by the education act (245/2008). Reflecting 'a shift to learning outcomes' and abandoning 'input' regulations they were embedded into 27 new national curricula ('state educational programmes') covering all major VET fields. According to the 2008 reform decentralising curriculum development, schools are obliged to use educational standards.

Occupational standards and the development the National System of Occupations (NSO) was initiated by the labour ministry, inspired by the Anglo-Saxon experience and backed by the act on employment services (5/2004). Over 1,500 standards were developed by Trexima company (a private company that was assigned to develop standards, among other services for the Ministry of Labour) in cooperation with newly created 24 sectoral councils and the Alliance of Sectoral Councils financed by ESF projects. Occupational standards however, serve only to provide information and do not contribute to the recognition of qualifications. Hence, qualification standards started to be developed under the supervision of the education ministry backed by the act on lifelong learning (568/2009) and supported by ESF.

The creation of the National Qualifications System and the National Qualifications Framework (NQF) aligned to the European Qualifications Framework (EQF) is undoubtedly a result of 'European' trends. Two comparative studies were therefore initiated. The first (Vantuch et al. 2013) which compared selected national qualifications systems, pointed out that that policy borrowing is not possible because all foreign models are deeply embedded in their national tradition, and that policy learning is not possible until the following questions have been resolved: 'Why are we creating the NQS and NQF and how should the formulation of qualification requirements based on learning outcomes contribute to the transformation of VET?' The study made ten recommendations which offered a conceptual framework for reforms. It warned about understanding learning outcomes as a sort of 'verbal game' and explicitly addressed four problems in identifying learning outcomes: the instability of concepts; the risk of reductionism; choices relating to the granularity of descriptions; and the adequacy of standardization, granularity and appropriate measurability (Vantuch et al. 2013, 38). Discussion and the sharing of experience were regarded as crucial for the identification of appropriate learning outcomes and standard setting. Standards without an assessment manual were seen as incomplete.

In 2014, a study analysing the NQFs of ten countries found the Scottish, Irish and Estonian versions most inspirational for the Slovak National Qualifications Framework (SKKR). Vantuch et al. (2014) suggested this should be composed of four sub-frameworks: general education; VET; higher education; and professional (occupational) qualifications. This proposal combined the traditional school-based system and the Anglo-Saxon objective of reflecting labour market needs. The fourth sub-framework was intended for containing 'smaller' qualifications to be developed to meet labour market needs and serve as building blocks for learner progression. This kind of NQF initiated discussions about units of qualifications and resurrected debates about the modularisation of initial VET programmes. The study formulated 12 recommendations for national authorities concerning the creation of the SKKR to make NQS flexible enough to meet labour market needs and holistic enough to preserve the tradition manifested in an adequate portion of general education within formal initial VET. The study re-emphasised the importance of agreement on terminology and clarified the reasons for the complexity in public discussion relating to qualifications.

Unfortunately, SKKR is still not fully functional. It has fulfilled some communications functions, but it is neither a reforming nor transformational framework in terms of the Raffe typology (Allais et al. 2009). Indeed, the referencing report (Pathóová et al. 2017) adopted by the Government and subsequently by the European Qualifications Framework Advisory Group in 2017 should be seen as referencing the education system (and respective levels of education) rather than referencing the fully functional NQF (and qualifications) to the EQF. The national register of qualifications contains 1,000 qualifications and qualification standards, but assessment manuals are absent, and only a few have been fully recognized by the education ministry. There is no systemic effort to fill the fourth sub-framework of professional qualifications based on a functional analysis of performance in the workplace. Supporting quality assurance and the validation of non-formal and informal learning expected via SKKR is still not in place.

The education ministry seemingly has no clear vision of how to respond to 'European' challenges concerning future VET. Educational standards offer norms for formal secondary initial VET (and 'large' qualifications only). NQS is not completed and has failed so far to make the qualification system more flexible via the SKKR fourth sub-framework. NSO and occupational standards only provide information about job requirements in terms of ISCO 4-digit codes and have no decision-making capacity concerning VET. Certainly, there is no need to have two fully functional platforms – NQS and NSO. Whilst the former is necessary, the education ministry's support for NQS is weak compared to the labour ministry's support for NSO. In parallel to NSO, Trexima also developed the information system on the labour market (ISTP) to report on vacancies, occupations and job requirements and a robust graduate tracking system (Cedefop ReferNet Slovakia 2020) and is currently working on human resource development strategies to address Industry 4.0 challenges. This should support the revision of NSO and identify the transversal competencies that will be needed in 2030.

It can therefore be seen that no agreement has been reached in relation to absorbing international experience and transforming the traditional education and qualifications systems. The education ministry focuses on maintaining traditional school-based VET inherited from Czechoslovakia, and implementing dual VET influenced by German-speaking countries and heavily promoted by employers and economists. The labour ministry, however, supports an Anglo-Saxon alternative with occupational standards and sectoral councils, and interestingly, a French approach to personal skills audits making use of the *bilan de compétences* methodology. However, all these approaches could be harmonised provided national authorities succeed in overcoming sectoral limitations.

## Future issues of skill formation in Slovakia

The skill formation system in Slovakia is at a crossroads. The traditional school-based system, weakened through long-term underfunding, has contributed to inefficiency in supplying skills to meet labour market needs. The VET system is in serious conflict. In the case of ISCED 354 programmes (currently over 75 per cent of secondary VET graduates annually), schools are pushed into the provision of education, which, legally, should be equivalent to that provided by grammar schools, as a '*maturita*' school-leaving certificate from VET school entitles students to apply for any higher education programme. Yet, at the same time, they must equip graduates with the competences required by the labour market. The only possible solution is to redefine the value of VET certificates: to introduce a new type of ISCED 354 vocational '*maturita*' school-leaving certificate which would limit the entitlement of students to apply for related, rather than all, higher education programmes, alongside new types of certificates equivalent to EQF 4 and EQF 6 for holders of apprenticeship certificates demonstrating professional progression. However, VET schools cannot abandon general education. Although employers demand 'just in time and work-ready' graduates, schools must also consider broader aspects of graduate employability and equip them with the competencies to enable future upskilling and reskilling.

Unfavourable economic conditions raise concerns over the ability of schools to adjust to the challenges of technological change and to secure the quality of teachers and trainers given the lack of in-service training opportunities. It is unlikely that the current model with the education ministry as the dominant national authority is sustainable in this context. There are two alternatives for skills formation going forward: a corporatist model and a market-driven model.

A corporatist model is gradually emerging, backed by acts on VET in 2015 and 2018 and it seems likely that Slovakia will continue in this direction. It is visible in the increasing roles of sectoral and professional organisations and in the heavy criticism levelled at the education ministry and VET schools (both secondary and tertiary level) by employers. Sectoral and professional organizations that were originally keen to participate in developing secondary initial VET (in a role of 'sectoral assignees') are more interested in restricting the responsibilities of the education ministry. Indeed, this ministry has already lost momentum in relation to continuing VET, as evidenced by the low interest in the lifelong learning agenda and the repeated postponement of work on new legislation. It is also visible in employers having full control of systemic national ESF projects (Development of Secondary VET, Dual Education and Increasing Attractiveness and Quality of VET, System of Verifying Qualifications). While one project builds on the traditional school-based system, a second focusses on the promotion of dual VET via media campaigns and piloting parallel supportive structures. A third reflects the Anglo-Saxon market-driven approach in awarding qualifications and should pilot validation of non-formal and informal learning related to 300 selected qualifications.

It is significant that ESF projects run under the umbrella of the education ministry largely failed to clarify the future of VET. Employers, interested in just-in-time delivery and a workforce perfectly aligned to their needs, have strongly supported the expansion of dual VET as the only efficient form of initial VET. Yet dual VET is not fully responsive to business cycles, has unresolved issues relating to quality assurance, and presents a risk of binding a young workforce to segments of the economy such as steel and automotive, which though currently strong, are nevertheless vulnerable to changing patterns of global trade. The argument that companies have detailed knowledge about skills needs and have the capacity to offer quality VET are questionable. Chambers and other sectoral assignees lack the capacity and experience in quality assurance and specialised training centres outside schools changing '2al' into '3al' are also insufficiently developed. Finally, the current model of dual is very inflexible, and, in fact, changing dual into the trial as well as offering in-company training to older learners is inevitable. The need to build the third pillar of trial, i.e. training centres, adjusted to offer training under better conditions compared to VET schools and companies, will soon create problems and lead to heated debates on financing.

In parallel to the 'German-style' approach, the Anglo-Saxon alternative is strongly supported by employers as well. The Alliance of Sectoral Councils with 24 sectoral councils dominated by employers are currently working, under the labour ministry, on the revision of occupational standards and on sectoral human resource development strategies within the ESF project Sector-Driven Innovations. Thus, the Anglo-Saxon market-driven model is the second alternative for future skill formation. It is, however, hampered by interruptions to the task of making the qualification system more flexible. Furthermore, no new professional qualifications related to the fourth sub-framework of the SKKR have been identified as yet. These qualifications envisaged as complementary to the 'large' qualifications currently offered by formal education are necessary if the qualifications system is to be more flexible.

Both the corporatist and market-driven alternatives are in in conflict with the existing school system. Unquestionably, there are too many secondary and tertiary schools to serve a declining population and there are programmes that are of doubtful quality or utility. The need to reduce the number of schools and programmes should, however, not be confused with the marginalisation of school-based VET. It is necessary to balance employers' preferences, often biased by their short-term specific needs, and national responses to future challenges.

The Learning Slovakia strategy paper detailed the systemic errors within the current approach to initial VET, but suggested building on the existing school-based VET and adapting this to the new context. Learning Slovakia recommended no changes to support for the provision of in-company training offered to learners based on individual learning contracts; contracts between school and company or based on a simple short-term arrangement for internships or tasters. The authors would argue that any type of work-based learning with clearly identified objectives or learning outcomes should be financially supported by the state rather than just work-based learning backed by individual learning contracts within the existing form of the 'Slovak' dual model. It is important to stress that dual learners in Slovakia are regular students of secondary schools and not employees and the final responsibility for quality of training and awarding qualification rests with the VET school.

Learning Slovakia endorses the commencement of well-designed new 'short' qualifications as part of the fourth sub-framework of SKKR, within VET schools that are currently almost exclusively focussed on young people and the delivery of 'large' formal qualifications set by school educational programmes. Qualification standards, regardless of whether based on occupational standards or derived from educational standards, could support modularised training and units of qualifications offered by a variety of providers and to learners of all ages, in addition to the validation of non-formal and informal learning.

Direct involvement of employers' organizations in the provision of initial VET is problematic because they lack the necessary personnel and financial resources since membership is not obligatory. However, there is potential for them to make a meaningful contribution to quality assurance processes with respect to corporate training if they were fully accountable and prepared for the role. Similarly, they could provide information about changes in the labour market. Learning Slovakia recommended transforming existing sectoral councils working as *ad hoc* bodies financed by ESF projects into permanent bodies backed by a contract between the state and strong sectoral institutions with a mandate from all the relevant sectoral players. At present, although employers constantly criticise schools for unsatisfactory performance, they are not obliged to provide quality information to improve the profile of school graduates. Contracts between the state and sectoral institutions mandating the financing of necessary tasks, periodic evaluation of their effectiveness, and delegating full institutional responsibility for results to the associated sector council have the potential to generate significant improvements, leading to a more valid inflow of information to schools on the future need for knowledge and skills, ensuring that qualifications in the SKKR and educational standards of VET programmes meet the needs of employers.

Slovakia is at a crossroads not only due to the challenges of digitalisation, automation and robotization, but also because of limits arising from the current principles of economic transformation. According to Piketty (2018), between 2010 and 2016, the annual outflow of profits and incomes from property (net of the corresponding inflows) represented on average 4.2 per cent of GDP in Slovakia, while the annual net transfers from the EU over the same period were only 2.2 per cent. For the time being, it is easier for foreign capital to exploit a reliable, low paid, and often overqualified domestic workforce, or to import talent from abroad, than to reinvest the profits generated in Slovakia and to strive for production with higher added value in Slovakia. The transition to a market economy has led to the dominance of a 'race to the bottom' and 'rent seeking' behaviours instead of growth in innovation-based production.

Periods of growth in population and education alternate with periods of decline in population and workforce quality, irrespective of formally higher level of education. The way forward lies in revitalizing the education system and exploiting the potential of the population in a transformed economy with a more equitable share of value added.

## References

Allais, S., Raffe, D., & Young, M. (2009). *Researching NQFs: Some conceptual issues.* Employment Sector, Skills and Employability Department. Geneva: International Labour Office.

Arntz, M., Gregory, T., & Zierahn, U. (2016). *The risk of automation for jobs in OECD countries: A comparative analysis. Social, Employment and Migration working papers, 189.* Paris: Organisation for Economic Cooperation and Development.

Birks Sinclair and Associates Ltd. (1993). *Strategic review of vocational education and training – Czech and Slovak Republics.* Prague: PHARE-Labour market restructuring.

Cedefop ReferNet Slovakia (2019). 'New financial incentive for companies involved in dual VET', <https://www.cedefop.europa.eu/en/news-and-press/news/slovakia-new-financial-incentive-companies-involved-dual-vet>, accessed 26 June 2020.

Cedefop ReferNet Slovakia (2020). 'Graduate tracking instrument launched in Slovakia', *Skillset and match*, 19, <https://www.cedefop.europa.eu/files/9146_en.pdf>, accessed 26 June 2020.

Food Chamber of Slovakia (2020). 'Výsledky prieskumu ponuky slovenských potravín na pultoch sú sklamaním [The results of a survey of the offer of Slovak food on the shelves are disappointing]', FCS Portal, <https://www.potravinari.sk/page7657sk.html>, accessed 26 June 2020.

Frey, C. B., & Osborne, M. A. (2013). *The future of employment: How susceptible are jobs to computerisation?* Oxford: Oxford Martin School.

Group of education ministry experts (2000). *Slovenské školstvo na križovatke tisícročí* [Slovak education on the crossroads of the Millennium]. Bratislava: Ministerstvo školstva SR.

Group of education ministry experts (2017). 'Učiace sa Slovensko [Learning Slovakia]', Ministerstvo školstva, vedy, výskumu a športu SR, <https://www.minedu.sk/data/files/7532_uciace-sa-slovensko2017.pdf>, accessed 26 June 2020.

Kahanec, M., & Mytna Kureková, L. (2014). 'Did post-enlargement labor mobility help the EU to adjust during the great recession? The case of Slovakia', *IZA Discussion Paper*, 8249, <http://ftp.iza.org/dp8249.pdf>, accessed 14 March 2021.

Kołodziejczak, M. (2018). 'Food self-sufficiency in EU countries: An attempted projection to 2080', *Proceedings of the 27th International Scientific Conference Agrarian Perspectives XXVII. Food Safety – Food Security*, 134–143, <https://ap.pef.czu.cz/en/r-12193-conference-proceedings>, accessed 14 March 2021.

Mikloš, I. et al. (2005). *Kniha reforiem* [Book of reforms]. Bratislava: Ministerstvo financií SR.

OECD (1992). *Review of higher education in the Czech and Slovak Federal Republic. Examiner's report and questions.* Paris: Organisation for Economic Cooperation and Development.

OECD (2020). *OECD skills strategy Slovak Republic: Assessment and recommendations.* Paris: Organisation for Economic Cooperation and Development.

Pathóová, I., Gállová, Ľ., & Junášková, A. (2017). *Referencing report of the Slovak Qualifications Framework to the European Qualifications Framework.* Bratislava: Štátny inštitút odborného vzdelávania.

Piketty, T. (2018). '2018, the year of Europe', *Le blog de Thomas Piketty*, <https://www.lemonde.fr/blog/piketty/2018/01/16/2018-the-year-of-europe/>, accessed 14 March 2021.

Rosa, V., Turek, I., & Zelina, M. (2001). *The national programme of education in the Slovak Republic for forthcoming 15–20 years (Millennium).* Bratislava: IRIS.

Sujan, I., & Sujanova, M. (1994). 'The macroeconomic situation in the Czech Republic', *CERGE-EI Working Paper Series*, 46, <http://dx.doi.org/10.2139/ssrn.1558106>, accessed 14 March 2021.

Vantuch, J. (2015). 'Je vzdelávací systém podporou alebo bariérou progresívnych štruktúrnych zmien v ekonomike Slovenskej republiky? [Is education system a driver or an obstacle to progressive structural changes in economy of the Slovak Republic?]', *Working papers*, 97, <http://www.ekonom.sav.sk/uploads/journals/325_wp79-vantuch_apvvmorvay2015.pdf>, accessed 14 March 2021.

Vantuch, J. (2007). 'Lisbon process and a knowledge Europe: A policy perspective of central and eastern European countries'. In O. Strietska-Ilina (ed.), *A clash of transitions: towards a learning society*, pp. 145–172. Frankfurt: Peter Lang.

Vantuch, J., Augustinská, D., Fonodová, I., Jelínková, D., Korbas, P., Rehúš, M., & Strakoš, J. (2013). *Analýza národných systémov kvalifikácií vo vybraných krajinách EÚ* [Analysis of national qualifications systems in selected EU countries]. Bratislava: Štátny inštitút odborného vzdelávania.

Vantuch, J., Fonodová, I., Jelínková, D., Korbas, P., Rehúš, M., & Strakoš, J. (2014). *Analýza Európskeho kvalifikačného rámca a Národných kvalifikačných rámcov vo vybraných krajinách EÚ* [Analysis of European Qualifications Framework and national qualifications frameworks in selected EU countries]. Bratislava: Štátny inštitút odborného vzdelávania.

Vantuch, J., & Jelínková, D. (2002). *Current status of vocational education and training in Slovakia: Vocational education and training on the verge of the millennium*. Bratislava: State Institute of Vocational Education.

Vantuch, J., & Jelinkova, D. (2010). *A bridge to the future: European policy for vocational education and training 2002–10: National policy report: Slovakia.* Bratislava: ReferNet Slovakia.

Vantuch, J., & Jelinkova, D. (2012). *Slovakia: VET in Europe: Country report.* Thessaloniki: Cedefop.

Vantuch, J., & Jelínková, D. (2016). *Key competences in vocational education and training – Slovakia.* Cedefop ReferNet thematic perspectives series. Thessaloniki: Cedefop.

Vantuch, J., & Jelinkova, D. (2019). 'Vocational education and training in Europe: Slovakia', *Cedefop ReferNet VET in Europe reports 2018*, <http://libserver.cedefop.europa.eu/vetelib/2019/Vocational_Education_Training_Europe_Slovakia_2018_Cedefop_ReferNet.pdf>, accessed 14 March 2021.

Vantuch, J., Kulich, D., Srnánková, Ľ., Šinka, L., & Jelínková, D. (2001). *Modernisation of vocational education and training in Slovakia.* Turin/Bratislava: SNO.

Andrea Laczik and Eva Farkas

# 8. Hungary: liberal and developmental choices

**Abstract:** This chapter offers an overview of the developments and trends in vocational education and training (VET) and adult education over time in Hungary. It reaches back to the pre-1989 times setting the scene for the post-socialist transition. The periods 1989–2010 and post-2010 will be discussed separately as they differ considerably in term of their contexts and characteristics; the first period covers the first free general election and the accession of Hungary to the EU in 2004, the latter period is discussed in the light of the political power of FIDESZ. These events greatly influence the developments and directions of skills formation in Hungary. Between 1989 and 2010 decentralisation, liberalisation and democratisation can be observed, whereas post-2010 is seen as moving towards centralisation, autocracy and nationalism. It is argued that post-1989, VET and adult education and training has experienced considerable and frequent system wide reforms to improve the quality of provision, to link VET to the skills demand and to improve the status of VET. These aspects are discussed in the context of political, economic and societal changes in Hungary. It is argued that VET in Hungary has been in a continual state of flux for several decades. Therefore we demand long term strategic planning of VET and adult education development, and a national skills strategy based on wide social consensus in order to support long-term economic development based on education and training.

**Keywords:** Adult education, centralisation-decentralisation of skill formation, Hungary, dual vocational education and training, economic change, VET 4.0 strategy

## Introduction

This chapter offers an overview of the developments and trends in vocational education and training (VET) and adult education over time. We argue that the Hungarian VET system and general education had deviated from the rigid centralised and autocratic system prior to 1989 establishing a benchmark for the discussion of post-1989 developments in initial and continuous VET. The period 1989–2010 will be discussed first, beginning with the first free general election and Hungary's accession to the EU in 2004. The period since 2010 will be discussed in light of the political power of FIDESZ as this greatly influences the frequent top- down policy changes in VET. FIDESZ is the leading political party in Hungary and has gained majority in Parliament since 2010. When set up in the 1980s it was the *'Alliance of Young Democrats' (direct translation), now 'Hungarian Civic Alliance'* suggesting a change in approach. The two periods witnessed considerable reforms that were both quantitative and qualitative in character. The first period is characterised by decentralisation, liberalisation and democratisation, whereas the second period is linked to the growing power of the FIDESZ party, and in general a move to centralisation, autocracy and nationalism.

We primarily discuss the developments of VET and adult education in the context of political, economic and societal changes in Hungary, but will also reflect on developments in adult education. We will demonstrate how VET is changing in Hungary to support economic growth and how changes in the economy, labour market and employment impact on VET provision. Targeted VET and adult education provision are often regarded as a remedy for economic failings. In Hungary, however, economic inefficiency remains, despite the relatively well- educated population, largely because of a lack of long-term strategic planning within VET, general and adult education systems. We therefore question the effectiveness of the VET system in Hungary.

## A different starting point for transition in Hungary

Hungary is a former Eastern bloc country with a history of association with the Soviet Union and shares some common characteristics with other former Eastern bloc countries in terms of VET provision (Laczik 2015) such as the well-developed vocational provision that supported the development of the working class. However, it is important to recognise the nuanced particularities of Hungarian skill formation systems from developments in other neighbouring countries. Although a Soviet type of education system was in place between 1945 and 1989, early deviation from the mainstream and centralised system 'reflected the impact of continuous economic and societal changes during the pre-1989 era' (ibid. p. 114). This period was a roller-coaster of developments in politics, education, economy and society. Kelemen (2003) and Laczik (2015) discuss four attempts of reform during the period 1945–1989, which were geared towards the establishment of an education system that was more responsive to economic and societal needs at the time. Examples of changes during this early period include the development of the upper-secondary school types and aligning vocational education with secondary education. Modern scientific content with balanced age differentiation was included in the new curricula (1963, 1965), and some allowances were built in to meet learners' individual needs (Hungarian on-line library 1996–2000). Economic reforms during the late 1960s weakened the planned economy and led to the development of the labour market. These changes led organically to changes in education which responded to societal and economic needs. Each period of reform was characterised by loosening political control and moving towards a liberal, democratic and pluralistic education system. The breadth and depth of reforms corresponded to the political, economic and societal contexts at that time. Each of these reform phases abruptly ended, after which the centralised system was reinstated, but they nevertheless paved the way for decentralisation and the steady decline of political control. The early 1960s saw the legitimisation of the state monopoly in relation to both education and the uniform school structure. While Hungary retained the highly academic *gymnasiums,* secondary education was overwhelmingly vocational. The three types of vocational schools served the purpose of educating the Hungarian working class, the main pillar of the socialist system. Economic reforms and the development of the labour market occurred later in the decade. Although these reforms were once again curtailed, it was increasingly clear that an education system more responsive to the economic and societal needs of the country was required. Kozma (2012) therefore considered these years as the opening of education policy. The most important milestone before the 1989 changes was the publication of the 1985 Education Act. The Act presented a compromise between the 'old' socialist rhetoric and nature of upbringing, and new curricula and teaching methods, including more independence for educational institutions and pedagogues, as well as an increased emphasis on the rights and responsibilities of learners, parents, teachers and the local community. However, some of the content could not be put into practice as it conflicted with the interests of the ruling Hungarian Socialist Workers' Party (MSZMP). Nevertheless, it started a 'radical decentralisation process' (Halász 2000a).

The continuing decentralisation of public administration was supported by changes in economic and social policy, and the early persistent and piecemeal processes of easing state power led to an accelerated transition from 1989 (Zachár 2002).

## Transition: 1989–2010

### Rapid transformation of politics, economy and society

Post-1989 politics in Hungary experienced several U-turns, with the Hungarian Socialist Party reappearing as Hungary's leading party after several elections. The political transformation of the country was not linear in the first 20 years of its democracy as party political powers changed at every general election. However, the political transformation in 1989 enabled a general movement towards a more democratic society and a market economy. The introduction of a market economy led to quantitative and structural changes in the labour market, with this being most evident in the huge growth of unemployment and the restructuring of the labour force. The labour market experienced the greatest shock between 1990 and 1993 when employment dropped from 64.5 per cent per cent to 48.9 per cent per cent and unemployment grew from 0.4 per cent to 12 per cent, whilst the proportion of economically inactive population significantly increased (Központi Statisztikai Hivatal 2010). The structure of the economy has also changed; industry sectors disappeared and new areas of economic activity were established, in particular within the service sectors. Large national enterprises, which previously dominated the planned market economy, gave way to micro-businesses. Ninety-five per cent of new enterprises that emerged at this time employed less than ten people and were therefore unable to absorb the people who were left without employment. Addressing the consequences of mass unemployment in Hungary became a state responsibility, and consequently, several job centres and nine *regional re-skilling centres* were established across the country supported by the World Bank in 1991. These centres were to develop a benefit system and programmes to re-skill those who were unemployed or were at risk of becoming so. Such centres played an important role in adult education, re-skilling existing employees and supporting career change from their inception.

The economic impact on society was remedied by new policies. For example, social security benefits were made more widely available, easing the pressure on the labour market, and voluntary early retirement was used to reduce the unemployment count (Farkas 2013). Two developments in the field of education policy also supported this aim; the extension of compulsory schooling to 18 years of age in 1998 (from 2012 this was reduced to 16 years of age) and individuals up to the age of 23 were given the opportunity to acquire two school based, full time, state accredited vocational qualifications free of charge. These developments impacted positively on unemployment. The former kept young people longer in education before joining the labour market; the latter encouraged them to obtain secondary and higher qualifications, and so become more competitive and have better chances for employment. However, these measures also reduced the proportion of Hungarians who were economically active from 74.9 per cent in 1990 to 51.5 per cent in 1998 (Farkas 2013).

## Changes in vocational education and training

In parallel with the new political, economic and societal developments after 1989, the structure, institutional ownership, control, maintenance and financing of education and skills formation changed considerably. The year 1993 was a milestone in Hungarian education; general education, VET and higher education were regulated separately. The 1993 Education Act concerning VET set out as its aim 'to develop a flexible and differentiated system of VET that adjusts to societal changes and to national economic and labour market demands'. This Act, however, did not regulate the operation of VET establishments, only the operation of the VET functions. According to Halász (2011) there were three particularly significant elements to this. Firstly, the state saved the VET educational establishments from collapsing together with the business sphere; secondly, adult education gained growing significance as a target group for VET, although it remained unregulated until 2001; and thirdly, enterprises became influential partners via the introduction of a unique, new tax-like contribution and so were directly financing VET. They also gained some influence by way of their inclusion within a tripartite decision-making board (Laczik 2015, 119). While employer engagement in VET can be observed through the involvement of the Chambers of Commerce and Industry and some employers' representation, wide-ranging social partner involvement in VET was absent. Trade unions were not involved in the dialogue, and the role of employers was defined by policy rather than being an organic employer-led development. Although all three 1993 Education Acts went through several modifications, the main characteristics of the institutional framework did not change until 2010 (Halász 2011, 5).

Changes in the economy and increasing competition in the labour market were reflected in the decreased proportion of young people attending vocational schools, which dropped from 44 per cent in 1990 to 25 per cent in 2010 (Ministry of Human Resources, Hungary 2012, 11). However, the proportion of young people favouring upper secondary education that ended with completed secondary education ('*Matura*'), which provided a gateway to higher education, increased. The upper secondary vocational school was the most popular route among young people, and by 2010 numbers enrolled at such schools increased by 54 per cent (Valuch 2013). This school type offered young people progression both to higher education and post-secondary vocational programmes, demonstrating the increased appetite amongst young people for higher level programmes and skills development opportunities.

Following considerable changes in the economy and its unexpected impact on employment during the early 1990s, considerable changes in VET can be observed. These changes were reactive rather than proactive system developments. Another significant milestone influencing skills formation was the publication of the National Vocational Qualifications Register (NVQR) in 1993. This set quality standards and embraced all state accredited VET qualifications, standardising all forms of VET. These internal organic developments were buttressed by external pressures from the EU and the World Bank and placed Hungary in a favourable position with regard to EU accession.

The European Commission's White Paper in 1995 outlined the criteria for accession with regard to education and training as learning was central to the document and the link between education and employment was strongly emphasised. According to the White Paper, education aims notably in relation to the development of ICT, language and entrepreneurial skills were designed to forge a close link between the economy and employment, and thus support the realisation of employment policies (Halász 2003). Halász (2001) argues that the question for Hungary was not whether education and training was ready for the EU accession, but whether education could contribute to the preparation of Hungarian society and economy for EU integration (Laczik 2015, 122), since the EU required legal harmonisation for the mutual acceptance of VET qualifications, which to some degree was already in place because of Hungary's regulatory framework. Earlier policy developments already supported employer engagement in training, the introduction of a competence based (outcome oriented) curriculum in VET and the institutionalisation of social partners' decision making in VET (Halász 2000a, 2000b).

Nevertheless, Hungary's accession to the EU in 2004 was a significant influence on VET policy developments. Unlike in other Central and East European countries, migration was insignificant in Hungary both before and after accession. Net migration rate per thousand inhabitants had decreased from 1.9 in 1995 to 0.62 in 2020, with the lowest rate of 0.50 recorded in 2010 (https://fuggelek.foldrajzmagazin.hu/nepesseg/migracio/). Migration had little impact on skill formation. However, EU accession gave the country access to considerable financial resources, which were used for the restructuring of vocational training and higher education systems. In 2004–2006 NVQR was modernised and re-developed as a competence based modular structure. This new structure served several purposes, for example, linking different VET qualifications, acknowledging prior learning thereby shortening training time, enabling mobility between different vocational programmes and quicker responses to labour market demand. Simultaneously with the NVQR development, the related Vocational and Examination Requirements (VER) were developed for each qualification. Consultation with employers ensured that relevant knowledge, skills and competencies particular to specific occupations were included in the NVQR and VER. This process also embedded employers as key players within the development of VET provision. The new NVQR was introduced in 2008 and is still being regularly updated although it now has a different structure.

In parallel with the renewal of the content and structure of qualifications, the previously fragmented institutional infrastructure of VET was re-structured and 88 Regional Integrated Vocational Centres were developed. This was a non-profit consortium of 6–8 vocational training providers. These centres provided school-based and non-school-based training as well as local economy and labour market driven vocational training, and they also contributed to the development and promotion of life-long learning. Local professional consultative bodies were set up within such centres to identify local skills needs, and influence both student choices and VET school provisions (Farkas 2013). In particular, they sought to encourage participation in less popular vocations, thus reducing the over-supply of skills in more popular areas. Given the great economic recession of 2008–2010, skills demand was increasingly difficult to predict. Employers themselves found it difficult to see six months ahead, while the local professional consultative bodies worked with data from the previous year. It was inevitable that skills predictions were inaccurate, and as a result, tensions built up between local professional consultative bodies and VET schools (Laczik and Farkas 2018).

By 2010, economic structures had stabilised in Hungary. Sectoral realignment meant that 65 per cent of employees worked in the service sector, 30 per cent in industry and 5 per cent in agriculture compared to 47, 38 and 15 per cent respectively in 1990 (Farkas 2013). Further, micro-enterprises accounted for 99.9 per cent of the economy, whilst large companies only had a share of 0.1 per cent. Large companies nevertheless employed 26.5 per cent of the active population and contributed 45 per cent of the added-value. Yet, the Hungarian labour market remained characterised by an extremely low level of economic activity (62 per cent in 2010) and employment (55.3 per cent in 2010), with an average level of unemployment (10.9 per cent in 2010) (Központi Statisztikai Hivatal 2020). By 2010 youth unemployment had become a serious problem standing at 26.4 per cent, long-term unemployment (over 24 months) stood at 21 per cent and economic inactivity among young people was 35 per cent (Eurostat 2020a), whilst 20.6 per cent of the 15–34 age group were not in education, employment or training (NEET). Encouragingly, the increased level of schooling among the population between 2001 and 2010, meant that the number of those who had not completed basic education (8 years of schooling) at all and those who had only completed basic education was decreasing. Further, there was an increase in the number of those who obtained '*Matura*' and vocational qualification. The greatest increase in numbers was among those who completed higher education.

VET underpins economic development and can also have a profound impact on personal and social mobility, and thus individual life trajectories, and indeed quality of life. So, the modernisation of professional/occupational structures was necessary, and as a result of the processes linked to on-going structural changes in the economy the reformation and renewal of VET was unavoidable. However, due to the continuous changes in VET in Hungary, monitoring and identifying consistent and linear trends is problematic. Changes in VET were made so frequently that any impact evaluation of the reform of the new structure or curriculum was impossible. For example, the government had already introduced the dual VET system in 2013, before the outcomes of the 2006 curriculum reforms could have been assessed.

## Main features of adult education

Following the 1989 transition and the development of the liberal market of education, non-formal, foundations, non-governmental organisations and for-profit educational institutions were established. From 1998 employment indicators were continuously improving due to better economic outcomes and the increasing average level of education of the population. Yet, whilst new jobs were created, the persistent high level of unemployment remained prevalent and youth unemployment became one of the biggest problems within Hungarian society. The importance of adult education had already been acknowledged across Europe, so Hungary also had to recognise that adult education had the potential to make a significant contribution in addressing the issues of (un)employment. It became apparent that schools were unable to teach the new generation everything they would need in their future lives and considerable learning would be necessary in adulthood. Both economic progress and trends in the labour market underlined this and increased the status of adult education. The first Adult Education Law which regulated provision external to the school system was published in 2001. This focused on governance, institutional and financial systems and curriculum requirements, aligning the Hungarian approach to adult education with the rest of Europe. It created standardised and coherent adult education provision which facilitated lifelong learning, as all adult learners could find provision reflecting their needs and interests and could engage with it flexibly. While the Act regulated provisions external to the school system, it focused both on training linked specifically to the labour market and on learning opportunities designed to support the cultural and social development of individuals. The latter development in particular demonstrates that the government was committed to improving the living standards of citizens not just via vocational training to increase employability, but also by providing non-vocational learning opportunities for self-enrichment. Participation in adult education increased significantly in 2007 and 2008, as a result of many European-funded programmes commencing in Hungary after EU accession.

The economic and financial downturn in 2008 led to a decrease in GDP by 6.9 per cent in 2009. Unemployment grew and the standard of living dropped. Despite this, in 2010 the number of participants in adult education grew by 200,000. According to the OECD (2011) analysis, education was seen as a remedy for unemployment, thus fuelling demand in adult education. EU resources were once again channelled to support programmes helping with the crises. Data from the National Data Collection Programme clearly shows a growing interest in adult education between 2003 and 2010, despite the fact that compulsory school age was increased to 18, and that young people generally had a higher level of education. Adults overwhelmingly participated in state-accredited vocational courses based on NVQR. Unsurprisingly, this type of training was prevalent until 2007 as they had clear labour market value.

## Skills formation after 2010 during the Orbán government

### Contextual issues

The 2010 election brought yet another change in the power dynamic in Hungary, as the FIDESZ, the Hungarian Civic Union won the general election with 56 per cent of the votes and gained an outright majority in the National Assembly. This ushered in significant changes in the Hungarian VET system. Halász (2011) argues that the roles and aims of VET did not change after the election, and a strong emphasis remained on VET being a tool to increase economic competitiveness, to improve the employability of individuals, and to integrate socially disadvantaged groups (p. 33). Extensive EU funding at the time also ensured that national and EU priorities of any developmental programmes clearly aligned, perhaps with the aim of securing and delivering on broader objectives. However, the directions of policy developments and major VET reforms, and the ways in which they were introduced, were very different to pre-2010 reform processes. During the time FIDESZ has been in power there has been a strong move to centralisation within education in general and within VET in particular, and a resurgence in top down, system-wide and blunt policy initiatives. The influence of politics came to the fore yet again. Other initiatives in the field of education at this time included a reversal to a state-maintained institutional structure, a reduction in financial resources, strict curriculum/content regulations, a reduction in the school leaving age, restricted access to educational provision and

VET itself being geared to meet the short-term needs of the labour market and economy.

Due to these structural changes, the macro-economy became more competitive and in 2013 there was an upturn of economic growth in Hungary, with economic and employer indicators growing significantly. By 2019 employment rate increased to 70.3 per cent among those 15–64 years old, which was better than the EU average (OECD 2019). Unemployment reached a record low of 3.4 per cent as opposed to over 10 per cent in 2009 (Központi Statisztikai Hivatal 2020). Similarly, youth employment improved but schooling indicators worsened, especially in comparison with EU trends. It is therefore necessary to consider whether such positive developments resulted not from the quality of the Hungarian education system, but from changes in other policy areas, including for example, increasing the retirement age, reviewing disability pensions, shortening the unemployment benefit payment period to 3 months, introducing public employment, reducing the school leaving age to 16 and shortening the duration of vocational training in the vocational schools.

After 2010 every education sector in Hungary was overhauled yet again, with general education, vocational education, adult education and higher education all experiencing a raft of reforms. The new Education Law was published in 2011 and contained separate provisions for each of the sectors, with adult education being regulated later, in 2013. The new law for VET came into force on 1 January 2012. Major changes were introduced impacting on institutional structures, governance, social partner's involvement, and content and delivery of VET. These will be discussed below.

## Skills formation and dual training

The Hungarian VET system was subject to extensive change after 2010. VET was of critical importance for the development of the Hungarian economy and it was also seen as a mechanism to alleviate social problems (Laczik and Farkas 2018). Changes were introduced to meet the needs of enterprises, to increase the popularity and reputation of VET and to increase participation in VET, in order to boost economic development in Hungary.

The autonomy of VET providers was curtailed in relation to curricula and textbooks, as well as with respect to financial and human resource management. By 2017, the state took over all operational responsibilities from local authorities, thus gaining direct control of financial management, maintenance and governance (European Commission 2019). This meant that vocational educational institutions became state maintained, with the responsible minister having oversight of both vocational and adult education; currently this is the Innovation and Technology Minister.

The changes are perhaps most visible within those vocational schools which do not provide the '*Matura*' school leaving certificate. The duration of provision in these vocational schools was reduced from 4 years to 3 years and learners could start a vocational programme at the age of 14. Before 2013 there was a greater emphasis on general education and young people were only able to start vocational training after 2 years of studying mathematics and Hungarian Grammar/Literature for 3 hours per week alongside a modern foreign language and nature studies (geography and biology). From 2013, vocational practical training was available to students at the age of 14 and the general education content was reduced as young people progressed through their programme, with there being no general education at all in the third year (Hermann Horn and Tordai 2020). The emphasis on vocational training was clearly at the expense of general education. Through these developments the government tried to prevent early school leaving while providing businesses with skilled workers.

The tendency of excluding general education, however, reinforced the existing problem of VET absorbing young people from lower socio-economic backgrounds, whose experience of basic school is characterised by underachievement. If young people do not develop their functional skills (at least mathematics and Hungarian) as part of their initial VET, this can become a barrier to later up-skilling and/or re-skilling, which consequently may become an obstacle to securing continuous employment.

Both vocational secondary schools without '*Matura*' and vocational grammar schools with '*Matura*' were organised and operated in large regional Vocational Centres from 2015. (Prior to this they were part of the Regional Integrated Vocational Centres.) There were 44 such centres across Hungary with 370 member institutions. These institution types and qualification offers are very similar to that which existed prior to 1998 including during the socialist era. General education for young people up to the age of 16 only existed between 1998 and 2010 when the compulsory school leaving age was 18 and VET could be started at 16 years of age.

The post-1989 Hungarian VET system has been characterised primarily by school-based provision where young people developed their practical skills mainly in workshops within a school setting. Post-2010 the system has moved towards an emphasis on practical skills development, especially through work-based training within enterprises. These developments have reflected the objective of aligning the VET system with employers' needs in terms of the quality and quantity of labour supply, thus supporting the economic development of

Hungary. Dual vocational training (we will refer to these as apprenticeships in the rest of the chapter) were introduced for precisely these reasons in 2013, and fundamentally changed the structure of provision. Since that time, apprenticeships are considered to be the benchmark for vocational provision in Hungary. The rationale for this was that apprentices would be more employable after graduation having gained experience in real work settings. As yet, however, this assumption is not borne out by an analysis of graduates' destinations, and in the short term, there is no significant difference in labour market outcomes between apprentices and those who have completed a school-based VET (Horn 2020).

The apprenticeship system in Hungary is based on the German model, although there are some fundamental differences. Prior to 2020 Hungarian apprentices signed a training contract with the company and were classed as students. Now they sign an employment contract and are employees of the company, but because of this change in status, apprentices are now entitled to employment rights. Another difference from German apprenticeships is that learners initially enrol in a vocational secondary school (not leading to '*Matura*') where they begin theoretical learning. However, not all learners will continue to an apprenticeship, as those who are unable to secure an employment contract with an employer, will complete a school-based VET. Both apprenticeship and school-based VET lead to a state-recognised vocational qualification, but this qualification is not sufficient for entering higher education. The government consequently introduced a 2-year academic programme in 2016 which provided the opportunity for such young people to prepare for a secondary school leaving examination. As a result of this initiative young people now have the option of entering the labour market, continuing further vocational training or pursuing higher education.

The strong emphasis on 'real' practical training and the general introduction of apprenticeships put considerable pressure on employers, and there are, and have been, clear barriers to employer engagement. These may include the economic climate, and employers' limited resources during unpredictable times and the demography and structure of enterprises. In Hungary, 95 per cent of enterprises employ fewer than 9 people (Központi Statisztikai Hivatal 2011). Hungary therefore faces similar issues to many European countries and there is a limited capacity for practical placements.

The cost of apprenticeships is shared between the state and economic partners, with the Hungarian Chamber of Commerce and Industry (HCCI) playing a key role as a mediator, process manager and co-ordinator between the VET schools and enterprises. Only the enterprises that are in the register of either HCCI or Hungarian Chamber of Agriculture can offer training contracts, and every new company wishing to be on the register is inspected to ensure that they have the necessary resources to offer high quality practical training. HCCI quality assure all practical training elements in the workplace and in the vocational schools. In-company trainers must pass a master craftsman examination that includes the development of teaching skills. However, the Hungarian Association for Vocational Training claims that Hungarian SMEs do not have the capacity and resources to offer young people training that meets the quality requirements of VET (ReferNet Hungary 2011). Trade unions are not engaged in the social dialogue about VET.

The Government aims to increase the number of apprentices and in 2015, the Chamber Guarantee was introduced meaning that the Chamber guarantees to find employers who are willing to sign training contracts. If it fails, the young person may receive school-based training in its workshops. This initiative, however, undermines the core principle of the apprenticeship – gaining practical experience in a real work setting. Despite government incentives, for example, the introduction of scholarship system and financial incentives for employers, the number of learners in 3-year vocational schools (not leading to the '*Matura*' examination) declined between 2010 and 2018 by almost 50 per cent (Ministry of Human Resources 2020). Whilst this can be explained partially by demographic changes, other reasons for the decline in participation include the reduced duration of VET courses, the lack of progression opportunities, the lack of interest in VET and the fact that the employment rate of those with '*Matura*' is significantly higher than in the group of those with only vocational qualifications. However, during the same period the proportion of young people in apprenticeships (work-based programmes) has grown from 32 per cent to 67 per cent.

This aim is further supported by the work of the 19 Sector Skills Councils (SSC), which were established in 2018. Each SSC is a voluntary association of employer representatives from the same sector. Their work is co-ordinated by the HCCI, and they are responsible for the development and updating of VET content and structure, as well as harmonising labour market demand and VET provision. SSCs advise both in their specific sector, and in different geographical areas on the demand for skills, thereby influencing VET provision.

We have demonstrated how enterprises have been offered increased opportunities to engage with VET, and how they are pressured into engagement. Yet preliminary analysis outlines some early challenges to this approach, including the difficulty of securing sufficient number of work-based placements and ensuring that all sectors and industries are represented within the VET system.

## Adult education

The year 2015 brought considerable changes in adult education. Following the modification of the 2011 Law for VET, adult learners were able to obtain a second state-accredited vocational qualification free of charge. This was valid for full-time, school-based courses for learners up-to the age of 25, and the over 25s could complete part-time and evening courses free of charge. The Government wanted to ensure that adult learners participated in programmes of high quality that were nationally accredited, were in the NVQR, and were offered in state maintained vocational institutes. The new regulation had a positive impact on participation in adult learning, and the number of learners almost tripled between 2015 and 2019 rising from 9,685 to 27,511 (Ministry of Human Resources 2020).

The objective of increasing participation in adult education was overwhelmingly supported by EU resources. During the last decade adult education received little state funding and most programmes were realised through EU funding. Adult education supported up-skilling and re-skilling beyond the school system. It also responds better to employers' needs because it is more flexible. Developing modern foreign language skills and digital competencies also impacts positively on the employability of adults in general. Special programmes were introduced aiming at those who were low-skilled and in public works employment and which specifically sought to promote digital skills development amongst adults. These non-school-based adult learners contributed to increasing participation from 650,000 learners in 2010 to 1 million in 2019 (National Statistical Data Collection Programme), with 17 per cent of learners choosing a state-accredited vocational qualification. Although adults may complete two school-based VET qualifications free of charge, there are three times as many adult learners in non-school-based state-accredited courses annually (National Statistical Data 2020). The reason for this popularity is that in adult education, training can be organised flexibly, it can start any time of the year, can be delivered on Saturdays and it can be short and intensive.

The 2001 Adult Education Law regulated the whole spectrum of adult education outside the school system. Adult education was re-regulated in 2013 and covered only VET provisions that are state-accredited and those which develop vocational, modern foreign language and transferable skills and competencies and which are financed by the state or EU programmes. These programmes can be offered only by authorised providers following the strictest rules. The government, however, did not guarantee either access to, or the quality of provision in those areas within adult education that were not covered by the new Law. However, in 2020 all adult education provision was brought within the Law.

## Some issues influencing skills formation

Although employment and unemployment indicators have been improving since 2013, the number of learners in training has been decreasing since 2012, unlike in the rest of Europe, where the opposite trend can be observed. This can be explained by the growing demand for labour and the most recent developments in VET policy, such as the centralisation of education and training, the decrease of compulsory school age to 16, the restructuring of VET and the restriction of state-funded higher education places (Csillag et al. 2020).

Other positive outcomes include the decrease in young people between the ages of 20 and 34 years who are not in education employment or training (NEET). Between 2010 and 2019 the proportion of NEETs fell from 27.6 per cent to 18.4 per cent. Less encouragingly, however, the proportion of young people who are NEET is still higher than the European average of 16.7 per cent, and the proportion of early school leavers remains high, especially amongst those who live in deprived areas and those who attend vocational programmes. The real problem, however, lies not with the absolute number of early school leavers, but the trend these numbers show, as in other European countries, the proportion of early school leaving shows a decrease, while in Hungary the proportion is growing (Eurostat 2020b). Hungary, therefore, is moving further away from the 10 per cent targeted objective of the EU2020 strategy to which Hungary is a signatory. Participation of 17 and 18 year olds in secondary education decreased sharply, from 98 per cent to 85 per cent, between 2011 and 2016 due to lowering the school leaving age from 18 years to 16 years. Those young people who have lower educational attainment, who are disengaged from education or who have disadvantaged family backgrounds opted for unqualified employment rather than training.

The distribution of early school leaving varies greatly by school type and region. Early school leaving correlates strongly with education outcomes, which are lowest in rural settlements. In rural communities the capacity to provide quality education and training services is more limited and teacher shortages are more pressing. Hungary has the largest urban/rural gap in education outcomes of all OECD countries (European Commission 2019) before accounting for socioeconomic status. Tackling early school leaving is therefore pivotal both for reasons of employment and equity. In Hungary, the lack of secondary school leaving certificate, the '*Matura*' or an accredited vocational qualification, leads to greatly unfavourable labour market opportunities and often to long term poverty (Hermann 2020).

The reduction in the school leaving age and the 2013 vocational law led to lower attainment in vocational secondary schools in terms of mathematics and reading comprehension. Data from the Hungarian National Competence Centre indicates that learners' basic skills are significantly lower after two years of vocational schooling than before the reform. Such an outcome could be explained by the reduced number of lessons of general education in the curricula of secondary vocational schools. Whilst graduates may successfully secure employment directly after finishing their schooling, the restricted curriculum may present challenges with respect to retaining employment and would certainly reduce the capacity of such individuals to engage in adult education successfully (Hermann, Horn and Tordai 2020).

Erasmus+ Mobility Projects present great opportunities for skills development. They contribute to knowledge generation, the acquisition of modern foreign languages, and the development of a deeper understanding of different cultures within the context of globalisation. They provide learners, in-school and in-company trainers with work experience in a multi-cultural environment through, for example, learning about new technologies and new machineries currently unavailable in Hungary. There is evidence that participants in Erasmus+ Mobility Projects have a better chance to secure employment (European Commission 2017). However, in Hungary in 2019 very few young people (3,961 learners) and school staff (1,577) had the opportunity to participate in such projects for VET (Tempus Közalapítvány 2020).

The Industry 4.0 era, which is likely to bring about fundamental changes to our lives, work and relationships, presents considerable challenges. Industry 4.0 is set to transform the labour market and work processes, requiring employees to possess different sets of knowledge, skills and competencies. Future jobs will require well-developed cognitive and creative abilities, higher skills and well-developed social and emotional competencies. We envisage that technical skills, problem solving in complex digital environment, critical thinking and creativity will become the most important employability skills of the future. According to McKinsey (2018), automation will have an impact upon 1 million jobs in Hungary, as it is already possible to automate processes and tasks representing 49 per cent of working hours. At the end of 2019 there were 74,824 vacancies advertised in Hungary and 51,144 were not filled (Központi Statisztikai Hivatal 2020b). Automation may provide part of the solution to the skills shortages that are now impeding Hungary's economic growth.

The importance of future skills development is widely recognised in Hungary. There is a clear need to develop the new skills and competencies to support the Industry 4.0 Strategy and improve the employability of learners and existing employees. Yet fulfilment of this strategy requires systemic change and new approaches to VET.

## Latest and future developments in VET and adult education – post 2020

In 2020, Hungary embarked upon another major reform of VET, and the 2020 Vocational Education Law fundamentally changed the system of VET and adult education yet again. It serves as basis for the mid-term strategic policy plan: *Vocational Training 4.0 Strategy*. This was necessary to align with employers' demand, macro-economic factors and labour market changes. Due to technological changes new professions are emerging that require different and higher skills sets, creating new challenges for VET. *Vocational Training 4.0 Strategy* aims to ensure that all VET learners develop the appropriate skills and competences to succeed in the changing labour market. The 2020 transformation of VET is markedly different in scale from previous transformation processes. The reforms have been systemic in character, and have encompassed the very concept of VET, as well as its structure, institutions, finances and curriculum content.

Following the Austrian and German example, the NVQR used in the past with its 700 qualifications was replaced in the Spring of 2020 with a new vocational register, containing 174 qualifications. These 174 broad vocational qualifications can only be delivered/obtained in school-based provision, and not in adult education outside the school system. Apprenticeships remain the same as in 2019 although the learner has an employment contract with the employer, gets employee status and receives wages both for time in the workplace and in school-based training. In September 2020 the 4+1 vocational grammar schools were replaced by the 5 year long '*technikums*' (this type of school existed between 1951 and 1973 and again between 1985 and 1993). Young people in '*technikums*' obtain both the '*Matura*' and a vocational qualification and so may progress to specialist higher education where they are treated favourably at the entrance examination.

A fundamental new element drawing on the Austrian and German models has now been introduced in the structure of vocational training. The process of obtaining a qualification now has two elements: a broad sector-based basic education; and specialist vocational education. The same broad sector-based basic education is provided for all occupations within the same sector and is delivered in every vocational institution. In the 3-year vocational secondary school this happens in year 9, in the '*technikums*' in years 9 and 10. This foundation concludes with a final national examination, which tests the basic vocational knowledge of young people and assesses whether they have the competencies necessary to carry out work within the sector. Young people are only able to continue to the apprenticeships programme after passing this exam, which relates to the transferrable skills and knowledge that permits permeability across occupations.

All qualifications are outcome-based, which is a new approach with a different content and methodology. Based on the profile of professions, outcomes are determined in terms of the skills, knowledge, attitude, and autonomy/responsibility necessary for competence, and link to the Hungarian Qualifications Framework. This offers teachers and trainers authority and flexibility in the choice of teaching and learning methods, processes, evaluation criteria and content. A learning outcomes-based curriculum is more effective if teaching is based on projects instead of the traditional subject system, and examination requirements have been changed accordingly. The development of this new set of curricula which replaced the input and process- based approach with the learning outcome-based curriculum was completed in May 2020 and operationalised from September 2020. This new development should enhance the quality of VET and provide a better alignment to industry needs. The key question is to what extent vocational schools and teachers can prepare themselves to deliver according to this new structure.

## Conclusion

The Hungarian VET system, including all sectors of education, moved from a highly decentralised system in the early 1990s to a highly centralised one by 2020. Decentralisation and liberalisation of VET provision (1989–2010) followed a more neoliberal Anglo-Saxon approach to VET, whereas the VET reforms post-2010 were characterised by a mixture of top-down collective skill formation and state-led skill formation.

The VET sector has experienced several system wide reforms and changes over time. These include for example, the introduction of NVQR in 1993, the modular and competency-based NVQR in 2006, the introduction of dual training and the establishment of the Vocational Training Centres in 2012. During this period the compulsory schooling age has increased (1998) and then decreased (2012) impacting on employment outcomes. The most recent changes were introduced from 2019, with the impact of these yet to be seen. It is then, fair to say that VET in Hungary has been in a continual state of flux for several decades. Each set of reforms was aimed at improving the quality of provision, linking VET to skills demand, and securing employers' contribution to VET in the form of both financial incentives and work-based training offers. Over the years employers have been offered opportunities and have been put under pressure to engage with VET to ensure this has labour market relevance. VET in Hungary is unpopular and does not enjoy a high status. Successive governments have been unable to remedy this, and young people with low socio-economic status and from deprived areas are often channelled to vocational courses.

VET and adult education experienced a short-lived revival in the late 1990s and early 2000s when general education was promoted within VET and adult education, which served to increase the cultural capital of the Hungarian population. As an integral part of any VET programmes at this time, more emphasis was placed on young people developing basic skills, digital skills and languages, and adults were offered programmes through which they could develop social and cultural skills, and through this, higher living standards. These changes were the result of national policy developments, combined with an increase in resources available for VET and adult education following Hungary's EU accession.

The Hungarian vocational policy orientation after 2010 became secondary school focused. 1. Changes were rapid and frequent, therefore the impact could not be evaluated. But the strong centralisation, the downgrading of general education within VET and the decrease in expenditure on VET suggest that the changes are unlikely to promote economic development. While the average level of schooling in Hungary is the same as in other OECD countries, Hungary is less economically developed. It is therefore possible to argue that education and training in Hungary are less effective, and their quality is poorer than in other OECD countries, since the same human capital indicators have led to lower economic development (Polónyi 2016). It would also be highly desirable to develop a national skills strategy based on wide social consensus. This could serve as the basis for a governance structure to support long-term economic development based on education and training.

## References

Csillag, M., Scharle, Á., Molnár, T., and Tóth, E. (2020). 'Young people in the labour market and in education – changes between 2002 and 2018'. In K. Fazekas, M. Csillag, Z. Hermann, and Á. Scharle (eds.), *The Hungarian Labour Market 2019*, pp. 37–44. Budapest: Institute of Economics, Centre for Economic and Regional Studies.

European Commission (2017). *Strengthening European Identity through Education and Culture.* The European Commission's contribution to the Leaders' meeting in Gothenburg, 17 November 2017. Strasbourg: EC.

European Commission (2019). 'Education and training monitor 2019 Hungary', <https://ec.europa.eu/education/sites/education/files/document-library-docs/et-monitor-report-2019-hungary_en.pdf>, accessed: 13 September 2020.

Eurostat (2020a). 'Young people neither in employment nor in education and training by sex, age and labour status (NEET rates)', <http://appsso.eurostat.ec.europa.eu/nui/show.do?dataset=edat_lfse_20&lang=en>, accessed: 13 September 2020.

Eurostat (2020b). 'Early leavers from education and training by sex and labour status', <https://appsso.eurostat.ec.europa.eu/nui/show.do?dataset=edat_lfse_14&lang=en>, accessed: 13 September 2020.

Farkas, É. (2013). A láthatalan szakma. Tények és tendenciák a felnőttképzés 25 évéről. [The invisible vocation. Facts and tendencies during the 25 years of adult education.]. Pécs: Typiart Médiaműhely.

Halász, G. (2000a). 'A magyar integrációs felkészülés kérdései', [Questions concerning the preparation for the Hungarian integration], *Új Pedagógiai Szemle*, 10, 110–121.

Halász, G. (2000b). 'Az oktatás és az európai integráció'. In A. Blahó (ed.), Tanuljunk Európát. [Let's learn Europe], pp. 297–340, Budapest: Budapesti Közgazdaságtudományi és Államigazgatási Egyetem..

Halász, G. (2003). Tanulás és európai integráció. OKI konferencia előadás a Gyulai Felnőttoktatási Akadémián: A tanuló felnőtt – a felnőtt tanuló [Learning and European integration. Based on the presentation at the Gyula Adult Education Academy: The learning adult – adult learning] Gyula, 2003 September 10–12.

Halász, G. (2011). Az oktatáspolitika két évtizede Magyarországon: 1990–2010. Kézirat. 2011 október. [Two decades of the Hungarian education policy: 1990–2010. Manuscript. October 2011], < http://halaszg.elte.hu/download/Policy_kotet.pdf >, accessed 15 November 2017.

Hermann, Z. (2020). 'The impact of decreasing compulsory school-leaving age on dropping out of school'. In K. Fazekas, M. Csillag, Z. Hermann, and Á. Scharle (eds.), *The Hungarian Labour Market 2019*, pp. 70–77. Budapest: Institute of Economics, Centre for Economic and Regional Studies.

Hermann, Z., Horn, D., and Tordai, D. (2020). 'The effect of the 2013 VET reform on student achievement'. In K. Fazekas, M. Csillag, Z. Hermann, and Á. Scharle (eds.), *The Hungarian Labour Market 2019*, pp. 64–69. Budapest: Institute of Economics, Centre for Economic and Regional Studies

Horn, D. (2020). 'The short-term labour market effects of apprenticeship training in vocational schools.' In K. Fazekas, M. Csillag, Z. Hermann, and Á. Scharle (eds.), *The Hungarian Labour Market 2019*, pp. 82–85. Budapest: Institute of Economics, Centre for Economic and Regional Studies.

Kelemen, E. (2003). 'Oktatáspolitikai irányvátozások Magyarországon a 20. század második felében (1945–1990).' [Changes in the educational policy in the second half of the 20th Century in Hungary (1945–1990)], *Új Pedagógiai Szemle*, 53(9), 25–32.

Kozma, T. (2012). 'Nyitás az oktatáspolitikában. Egy rendhagyó nyári egyetem. [Opening of education policy. An unconventional summer school.]', < https://www.academia.edu/1476317/Nyit%C3%A1s_az_oktat%C3%A1spolitik%C3%A1ban_-_A_Forgotten_Moment_in_the_Hungarian_Educational_Policy?auto=download>, accessed: 15 March 2013.

Központi Statisztikai Hivatal (2010). Magyarország 1989–2009 a változások tükrében. [Hungary 1989 -2009 in the light of changes]. Budapest: Központi Statisztikai Hivatal.

Központi Satisztikai Hivatal (2020). 'A 15–64 éves népesség gazdasági aktivitása. [Economic activity rate of the population aged 15–64]', <https://www.ksh.hu/docs/hun/xstadat/xstadat_evkozi/e_qlf034.html>, accessed: 13 September 2020.

Központi Statisztikai Hivatal (2020a). 'Üres álláshelyek száma. [Job vacancies]', <http://www.ksh.hu/docs/hun/xstadat/xstadat_evkozi/e_qli027c.html>, accessed: 13 September 2020.

Laczik, A. (2015). 'Education in Hungary: Recent history, changes and trends.' In T. Corner (ed.), *Education Around the World*. London: Bloomsbury Publishing Plc.

Laczik, A., and Farkas, É, (2018). 'Past and present developments in vocational learning in Eastern Europe: The case of Hungary.' In S. McGrath, M. Mulder, J. Papier, and R. Suart (eds.), *International Handbook of Vocational Education and Training for the Changing World of Work*, pp. 1089–1105. London: Springer.

McKinsey & Company (2018). 'Transforming our jobs: Automation in Hungary', <https://www.mckinsey.com/~/media/McKinsey/Locations/Europe%20and%20Middle%20East/Hungary/Our%20Insights/Transforming%20our%20jobs%20automation%20in%20Hungary/Automation-report-on-Hungary-EN-May24.pdf>, accessed: 13 September 2020.

Ministry of Human Resources (2012). Oktatás-statisztikai évkönyv. 2011/2012. [Statistical yearbook of education. 2011/2012]. Budapest: Emberi Erőforrások Minisztériuma.

Ministry of Human Resources (2020). 'Köznevelési statisztikai évkönyv 2018/2019. [Statistical Yearbook of Public Education 2018/2019]', <https://www.kormany.hu/download/4/5b/d1000/K%C3%B6znevel%C3%A9si%20statisztikai%20%C3%A9vk%C3%B6nyv%202018-2019.pdf#!DocumentBrowse>, accessed: 13 September 2020.

National Statistical Data Collection Programme (2020). 'Statistics of adult education', <https://statisztika.mer.gov.hu/>, accessed: 13 September 2020.

OECD (2011). *Education today Crisis Survey 2010. The Impact of the Economic Recession and Fiscal Crisis on Education in OECD Countries*. Paris: OECD Directorate for Education.

OECD (2019). 'Employment rate. Total % of working age population, Q2 2019', <https://data.oecd.org/emp/employment-rate.htm#indicator-chart>, accessed: 13 September 2020.

Polónyi I. (2016). Emberi erőforrásaink 21. százada. [The 21st century of our human resources]. Budapest: Gondolat Kiadó.

ReferNet Hungary (2011). 'Hungary – Restructuring VET to better meet labour market demands',<http://www.cedefop.europa.eu/EN/articles/19185.aspx>, accessed 15 October 2013.

Tempus Közalapítvány (2020). 'Éves beszámoló a Tempus Közalapítvány 2019. Évi tevékenységéről. [Annual report on the activities of the Tempus Public Foundation in 2019]', <https://tka.hu/docs/palyazatok/tka_eves_jelentes_2019.pdf>, accessed: 13 September 2020.

Valuch, T. (2013). 'A társadalomszerkezet változásainak néhány jellegzetessége a rendszerváltás Magyarországán. [Characteristics of the changes in social structure during the period of the change of system]'. *AETAS*, 28 (4), < http://acta.bibl.u-szeged.hu/32918/1/aetas_2013_004_101-118.pdf >, accessed: 13 September 2020.

Zachár, L. (2002). 'From a unified to a flexible vocational system: The Hungarian transition case'. In W. J. Nijhof, A. Heikkinen, and L. F. M. Nieuwenhuis (eds.), *Shaping Flexibility in Vocational Education and Training*, pp. 113–126 Dordrecht: Springer.

Samo Pavlin, Klara Skubic Ermenc and Branko Bembič

# 9. Slovenia: segmentation and sectoral disparities

**Abstract:** This chapter explores key skill formation processes in Slovenia in the past decades until the present, and compares sectoral particularities. It starts with analysis of institutional developments in four periods: Yugoslavia and the socialist system, when Slovenia as a part of former Yugoslavia rejected the Eastern type of communism, post-socialist transformation period, period related to joining the EU in 2004 and global financial crisis of 2008 and its aftermath. Like in the other EU countries, skill formation developments in the latest period includes implementation of the national qualification framework discussed in this chapter. In this context, we disclose similarities and differences in the overarching skill-formation strategies pursued in the four sectors: the well-regulated health sector, the export-oriented metal industry that demands sector and firm-specific skills, and the two labour-intensive, mostly unskilled, sectors of hospitality and retail. Differences between these sectors include the proportion of workers in standard employment, the average gross wage and the proportion of workers receiving the minimum wage. Skill formation in these sectors faces significant and highly diverse challenges related to ageing population, the need of expansion of employment, improvement of working conditions and wages, and preparation to technological change. The chapter is concluded with a notice of the increasing need for a strong involvement of all social partners in skill formation.

**Keywords:** Qualification framework, sectoral skill formation strategies, skill formation, Slovenia, social dialogue

## Introduction

In recent years, the Slovenian labour market has been characterised by increasingly weak social dialogue and dependence on supranational institutions. Major challenges to achieving a collective approach to skill formation include insufficient corporate responsibility among the social partners, too high expectations of state interventions and the lack of long-term strategic vision within companies. In this chapter we look at how the main skill formation processes that led to this situation changed over the past decades, and how they have been reflected in sectoral particularities.

After the transition from socialism, one of the biggest problems facing skill formation in Slovenia is the segmentation of the labour market, a challenge that is not alien to many other European countries. By labour market segmentation we refer to the labour market being divided into distinct segments each characterised by diverse conditions relating to employment and job quality (Pavlin 2018). Labour market dynamics cannot therefore be viewed in isolation from sectoral conditions or Slovenia's broader development. Following Stanojević and Furlan (2018, 17), the key trend in Slovenia's labour market since independence 'is the gradual and systematic increase in the common share (sum) of non-standard (precarious) workers and unemployment of the active population.' One might assume this issue is largely related to the inherent institutional logic of developing competencies in education and the world of work. Segmentation may be viewed on various dimensions: workers who (i) have completed vocational or general education; (ii) completed secondary or tertiary education; (iii) with long or short seniority; and (iv) who work in differently regulated sectors. While the level of educational attainment and quality of education has gradually improved in Slovenia, low skills are especially prevalent among older adults (OECD 2017, 58). Moreover, while worker participation in CVT courses is relatively high in Slovenian companies, and the resources invested per participant are comparatively generous according to the Continuing Vocational Training Survey (Eurostat, data for 2015), data on adult learning (collected by the Adult Education Survey) show that formal and non-formal adult learning is quite unevenly spread across various levels of educational attainment. While adults with a tertiary education benefit from having good access to formal and non-formal education opportunities, with levels considerably above the EU average, those with ISCED levels 1–2 record much lower levels of both formal and non-formal education and training, hovering at levels far below the EU average (Eurostat, data for 2016).

After Slovenia gained its independence, the system of skill formation experienced three about-turns: from attempts to devise a collective skill-formation system resembling those in German-speaking countries; over a more state-led skill-formation system; to the current model that attempts to re-introduce a collective skill-formation system with neoliberal elements. To some extent we agree with Le Deist and Tūtlys (2012) who state that skill-formation systems and regimes remain in a phase of evolution and without sharp boundaries. However, our view is that skill-formation cannot just be viewed from an evolutionary perspective as some monolithic black box but should also be understood within a sector-specific context. The characteristics of a sector represent a special set of relations between curricular and programme features as well as various factors specific to the labour market and industry.

In this chapter, we look for similarities and differences in the overarching skill-formation strategies pursued by four sectors: the well-regulated health sector; the export-oriented metal industry that demands sector and firm-specific skills; and the two labour-intensive, mostly unskilled, sectors of hospitality and retail. The first two are characterised by more stable employment conditions, while the prevalence of basic and general skills in the two private service sectors allow adjustments to be made to market demand through laying off staff (Boyer 2014) and relying on labour markets outside Slovenia. If a stable sector experiences employment turbulence, workers find it easier to move to a less technologically developed sector, yet the reverse is much more difficult. Some sectors are also better able to plug skills gaps with migrant workers than others.

The VET system has not responded dynamically to the labour market challenges and Slovenia has now arrived at the point where the future development of educational programmes requires stronger cooperation between various elements of the national skill-formation system as well as better integration of migrant workers, adult learning and retraining. It is likely that state protection of occupational labour markets will maintain the considerable sectoral differences in terms of job security, earnings and the work environment, and limited public resources mean that some sectors will always be more protected than others. The Slovenian HE system faces several challenges related to graduate employability and connection with the world of work, but this chapter focuses mainly on VET related labour market segments. Before considering in greater depth the sectoral particularities we have briefly discussed, we first describe the main aspects of industrial relations in Slovenia and outline the changes to education and training systems.

## Institutional developments

### Yugoslavia and the socialist system

Slovenia was a Socialist Federal Republic of Yugoslavia and became an independent country a decade after the death of Tito. After World War II, Slovenian industrial relations were strongly determined by the Tito–Stalin conflict during which Yugoslavia rejected the Eastern type of communism. Although Yugoslavia had big state-owned companies and constant political intervention in the economy, like 'real socialist' societies, it was unlike other communist countries. In particular, there were more decentralised and autonomous decision-making systems, a limited private sector, a non-formal economy, a flow of workers to Western countries, and certain attempts to develop the export sector (the best known example being the attempt to export Zastava cars to the USA). 'The Slovene economy was not only the most liberalized but also the most developed and western-oriented economy of former Yugoslavia and of the whole Soviet bloc' (Bohle & Greskovits 2007, 452). The period was, however, dominated by an industrial low-skilled economy. Companies made decisions based on the 'socialist self-management' or 'self-governing socialism' system that anticipated management of companies by workers that was meant to be different from both capitalist countries and those within the Soviet Union. Even though the system was introduced by the Communist Party of Yugoslavia its principles were relatively open to economic and political cooperation in international relations, yet the inability to introduce new technologies and utilise highly skilled labour meant they resulted in a deep economic recession in the 1980s (Svetlik 2009, 1).

After World War II, the development of industry saw vocational education expand. In the late 1970s the 'career-oriented' educational system was introduced, the reform creating a special comprehensive secondary education model based on two general principles. Firstly, enabling the entire population to obtain a common basis for further education, personal development and greater cultural appreciation, and secondly, directing students towards work or an appropriate branch of further education (Ermenc 2011). These principles made the model progressive, yet its implementation was plagued by many problems that led to it being dismantled. The model was criticised for inadequately preparing students to enter employment, yet employers did not cooperate with the reforms (Ermenc 2009). Such 'career-oriented' education was also introduced to higher education (HE) with the aim of bringing it closer to the needs of labour market. This approach failed, however, and it is claimed that the lowering of educational standards in secondary education led to a significant fall in the number of university graduates (Milharčič-Hladnik & Šušteršič 1986).

## Post-socialist transformation period

Slovenia declared independence in 1991 following military conflict (The Ten Day War or Slovenian War of Independence). The loss of Yugoslav markets soon after independence, however, led Slovenia into an economic crisis, resulting in a large fall in GDP.

> Since 1993 the Slovenian economy has been in the process of permanent restructuring characterised by labour saving measures and productivity growth, introduction of new technologies, penetration of global market niches, takeovers by foreign companies and by reorganisations in terms of outsourcing, slimming down organisations and making or joining bigger corporations' networks. (Svetlik 2009, 10).

These years may be described as bringing a (re)constellation of social and political institutions and a (re)orientation of the economy towards new European markets. Following the loss of the Yugoslav market, the capital-intensive part of the export sector, including motor vehicles and medicinal and pharmaceutical products, managed to reorientate to foreign markets. However, sectors based on unskilled labour, which were an important source of trade union membership and mobilisation power found the transition more problematic (Crowley & Stanojević 2011, 276). The transition process was firmly marked by economic and political elites readjusting to the unique mix of cultural and entrepreneurial traditions.

> The hegemony of the old political elite was replaced by new parties already in the early 1990s, while after 1992, the Liberal Democracy of Slovenia – a new, relatively strongly market-oriented political party – was the leading faction of an essentially changed, mostly new political elite. (Stanojević 2018, 720).

Following the German example, these connections produced a Slovenian type of neo-corporatism characterised by economic growth, the formation of a pluralist and strong trade union movement which all impacted on employment relations and social policies. 'Legally enforced negotiated management–labour relationships, and extended collective agreements have …been able to deliver the compromises required for a balanced and inclusive agenda' (Bohle & Greskovits 2007, 462).

Svetlik (2009, 5) argues that a paradigm shift from the socialist self-management system to more traditional industrial relations transferred a large part of responsibility for job design, employment, remuneration, education and training, promotion and working conditions from employees and workers' representative bodies to managers. This was particularly the case in privatized enterprises that focused on their core and knowledge-based activities.

> In the old socialist regime training was considered to be one of the workers' rights that was supported by special education and training funds, financial support for studies, long-term recruitment schemes, own training centres or strong cooperation with vocationally-oriented educational institutions (Svetlik 2009: 19).

However, in the transition period, companies involved in skill formation started to contract. Labour-intensive industries like metals, shoes and textiles were primarily faced with labour surpluses, and restructuring was a protracted process due to tripartite negotiations. During the transition, the state played a key coordinating role in establishing the skill-formation system because, for a variety of reasons, social partners and other stakeholders lacked capacity. In 1991, the Slovenian Institute for Adult Education (Andragoški center Republike Slovenije) was established, and in 1995 the Institute of the Republic of Slovenia for Vocational Education and Training (Center Republike Slovenije za poklicno izobraževanje) (CPI) was created, as the central national institution based on social partnership principles. The CPI has been coordinating the work of employers as well as other institutions such as the Chamber of Commerce and Industry, the Chamber of Crafts, and the Chamber of Agriculture and Forestry. The National Agency for Quality Assurance in Higher Education was established more than a decade later.

Economic changes revealed problems of skills and education mismatches. As in other CEE countries (West 2013) VET experienced a substantial loss of status in Slovenia during the transition period. While changing markets were reflected in structural unemployment, this was accompanied by high demand for industry-specific skills. The institutional response, led by the state, was slow and occasionally superficial in terms of (re)introducing a competence-based approach to skill formation, which in several respects lagged behind labour market needs. However, as Kureková (2012) noted, these reforms repositioned the status and power of skill providers in Slovenia and saw various (new) stakeholders become formally involved in skill formation and design. Building on the experience accumulated from career-oriented education, the conceptual design of a new VET system in Slovenia was developed in 1992. In 1996, new legislation on education and schooling was passed. The role of the labour market in education gradually strengthened (Muršak 2010). The major aims of the reform were to embed principles of social partnership within vocational education, as a way both of ensuring basic VET for all, and of establishing a complete educational ladder, with each occupational field required to develop all levels, including both post-secondary and tertiary (Medveš & Muršak 1992). Two forms of alternance were introduced: a typical dual system and a school-based system of teaching vocational and technical skills within upper and post-secondary levels of education including on-the-job training. In both pathways responsibility for providing education was partially delegated to employers: in the first case, individual contracts were signed; and in the second, collective contracts were signed. Programmes of 2 and 3 years were available within each pathway, with 4-year programmes also possible in the school-based pathway. Svetlik and Barle (2000, 59–62) describe how the curricular changes were coordinated by the National Curriculum Council (NCC) with the principal goals being to increase the autonomy and professional responsibility of schools and teachers and to raise the interconnectedness of disciplines. Curriculum content with general value and utility was to be given priority. An evaluation prepared during the MOCCA (Modernisation of Curricula, Certification and Assessment in Vocational Education for Youth and Adults) project (as a part of the PHARE Programme) in 2000 showed the reforms had met with only limited success.

The need for greater flexibility, deregulation and decentralisation was obvious, and in 2001, amendments to the Guidelines for Elaboration of Educational Programmes in VET were approved. The document marked the beginning of a new period of reform as it introduced important changes with a particular focus being on ensuring the new educational programmes conformed to European development policies pursued by Slovenia. Reform peaked in 2006 when a new Vocational Education and Training Act was adopted. One of the crucial initiatives included in the reforms of the 2000s was the introduction of occupational standards. Since then, all social partners have been involved in developing occupational standards at national level: occupations and the content of qualifications were defined according to labour market needs and their levels of complexity were determined accordingly. In addition, certification was introduced in the national vocational qualifications (NVQ) system. The system comprises a network of institutions and bodies enabling individuals to obtain formal recognition for knowledge and competencies acquired through non-formal and informal learning (Šlander 2007). Changes were also seen in HE, where Zgaga (2002, 325) noted during the transition that 'there was an urgent need to make a systemic legislative adaptation of the higher education system to the new social and political reality'. This was related:

> to defining institutional autonomy, the national system of higher education (higher professional education along traditional university studies, enrolment procedure, etc.) and its financing; private higher education institutions; accreditation, quality assessment and assurance procedures, broadening access to higher education; strengthening international cooperation etc. (Zgaga 2002, 325).

The HE system therefore, was a significant catalyst for the change from a socialist to a market economy and society, although some challenges remain. 'Bologna reforms in higher education, aimed at providing students with attractive courses rather than ones with civic relevance, or evidence-based interrogations of social problems, will not rectify the situation' (Kramberger & Stanojević 2015, 660). The shift towards aligning professional development with the needs of the job market came later.

## Joining the EU in 2004 and thereafter

Before joining the EU, Slovenia displayed many of the features of coordinated market economies that according to the VoC typology (Hall & Soskice 2001) included the tradition of employers' involvement in skill formation, high union membership, centralised wage bargaining, social dialogue and long job tenure (in some sectors). Slovenia enjoyed relatively stable economic growth in the pre-accession period after 1993. However, it has been claimed that with 'Slovenia's entry to both the EU and the Eurozone, its neo-corporatist system – in the form that occurred in the 1990s – has been becoming dysfunctional' (Stanojević 2018, 709).

> In 2004, a change of government introduced a new approach to policy formation: In autumn 2004 the domination of a centre-left political coalition of more than a decade ended. The new centre-right government started with radical criticism of a so-called gradualist approach. It prepared a reform programme strongly inspired by neoliberal ideas […]. Social partners have been ignored whenever and wherever possible. (Svetlik 2009, 3).

The following period was characterised by the second wave of privatisation often through selling state companies to managers using state-backed loans and workers' demonstrations supported by the trade unions, reflecting decreasing support for the centre-right Government. Issues relating to skill formation and its integration with education were not prioritised by employers at this time and concerns over curricular developments were left within the sphere of national and supranational institutions. Principles for deploying skills, including high performance work practices, competence-based management, teamwork, autonomy, mentoring, job rotation, incentive pay and flexible working hours, received insufficient consideration (OECD 2017: 99). After the Bologna and Copenhagen processes, attention was paid to designing new educational programmes for secondary and tertiary education, that could attract enough learners and better reflect specific workplace needs. These developments were influenced by EU and OECD terminology like 'knowledge-based society', 'competencies', 'learning outcomes', 'credit point system' and 'qualification frameworks'. Moreover, membership of the EU facilitated further development of recognition and validation of non-formal learning and national qualifications outside the jurisdiction of the Ministry of Education or the universities. Several EU programmes and frameworks supported these changes. Paradoxically, the reputation and status of VET continued to fall in this period. Due to a shortage of apprenticeship positions and lower interest from employers, young people and trade unions, the dual system was abolished in 2006, with schools and education authorities again becoming isolated VET providers. Despite these unfavourable developments for skill formation, since 2006 the issue of work-based training has remained important and a better solution is still being sought (Cedefop 2017).

## Global financial crisis of 2008 and its aftermath

Slovenia experienced a sharp fall in gross domestic product (GDP) of 8 per cent in 2009, with modest growth of 1.4 per cent in 2010 and 0.6 per cent in 2011 (Feldman 2017, 33, 38). However, the country's economic growth resumed in 2014 (ibid). During the crisis the social partners worked together in the tripartite Economic and Social Council, and the subsequent economic and social reforms moved Slovenia further towards the liberal market economy model due to entry into the Eurozone (Stanojević 2018, 721). The OECD noted:

> about one-third of working-aged adults in Slovenia – almost 500,000 people – are either unemployed or not participating in the labour market [...] Slovenia has the highest proportions of young (15–24 years-olds) and older (65+ year-olds) workers in temporary employment in the OECD' (OECD 2017, 71, 77).

Slovenia has one of the highest numbers of regulated professions in the EU. Nevertheless, attempts to reduce regulation following the advice of the European Commission generated mixed results, and arguably were detrimental to skill formation in some scenarios (see below).

From the crisis period onwards, the formal education system has, in theory, been aligned with the labour market to improve youth employability. However, the Slovenian education system, in common with other EU countries, has been characterised by extended schooling, postponing educational choices and orientation towards general knowledge rather than specific skills (Markowitsch & Hefler 2019). The shortage of apprenticeship positions coupled with the declining interest of employers, young people and trade unions was especially problematic with regards to collective approaches to skill formation. According to the Special Eurobarometer Survey in 2011 (European Commission 2011, 22–23), the public image of VET in Slovenia was the lowest among all EU-27 countries, which was also demonstrated by the Cedefop (2017b, 53, 56) opinion survey. However, this survey also indicated that the share of people who would recommend VET programme enrolment to a young person and believed that government should increase investment in VET was among the highest in EU. Even though Slovenia has significantly improved in terms of student skill performance and tertiary attainments in recent years, the OECD (2017, 5, 41) noted that skill-formation systems continue to face problems such as the concentration of low-performing and disadvantaged students in VET, the low completion rates of tertiary students, the lack of tertiary graduates' cognitive and socio-emotional skills, and weak university-business cooperation, including work-based learning. A further point of concern is low literacy and numeracy skills among the adult population.

Slovenian literacy, numeracy and problem- solving skills in technology-rich environments score significantly below the OECD average (OECD 2019).

Against this backdrop, work-based training attracted renewed interest after 2012 when the EC and Cedefop recognized apprenticeship and work-based learning as vital tools for addressing the issues of skills shortages and high youth unemployment in Europe. Apprenticeships became a Slovenian government priority, leading to preparation of a new law on apprenticeship that was adopted in 2018. A Cedefop (2017a) study revealed that many stakeholders continued to see education as a state responsibility, this being especially the case within the education sector itself, with concerns being conveyed primarily to the ministry responsible for education, rather than other ministries (e.g. those responsible for labour or the economy) and the social partners. Since the key stakeholders have not widely embraced the concept of social partnership, the Act on Apprenticeship does not show a clear vision and the conditions for its implementation are not being met. Tellingly, the latest national evaluations showed that the most positive views on apprenticeship were expressed by a small number of companies that had engaged with the apprenticeship programme (Klarič 2019). It may therefore be the case that better support to those companies who have embraced the notion of 'cultivating' human resources for the future, might serve to reduce hesitancy in relation to apprenticeships among others (Cedefop 2017a).

With respect to HE, the discrepancy between expectations arising from quality principles, the lack of public funding and precarisation of academic work has begun to accompany all major developments in teaching and research. The Slovenian HE system was not performing well by international standards, especially given the European objective of orientating HE more towards the labour market (Pavlin 2014), as HE graduates did not experience a smooth transition into working life (Pavlin & Svetličič 2012), and the role of social partners in skill formation in HE was similar to the situation in VET.

## The role of the NQF

Between 2009 and 2014 Slovenia developed its national qualifications framework (the SQF) and referenced it to the EQF. It is a comprehensive framework which includes qualifications from all subsystems of initial and further education and training and three types of qualifications: (1) formal educational qualifications; (2) vocational qualifications that can also be obtained outside the formal education system and consist of (a) national vocational qualifications (NVQs) and (b) qualifications obtained under continuing vocational training or study programmes for continuing education; and (3) supplementary qualifications, i.e. qualifications that supplement an individual's competencies in a specific professional field and are tied to labour market needs. Its formally stated main objectives are: to support lifelong learning; to connect and coordinate Slovenian qualifications subsystems; and to improve the transparency, accessibility and quality of qualifications in relation to the labour market and civil society. Despite these ambitious objectives, the SQF was conceptualized primarily as a communication framework, and was not intended to change either existing attitudes towards qualifications or established practices (Mikulec & Ermenc 2016). By introducing a new type of qualification, it has modestly incorporated some reform elements into the SQF, as with the supplementary qualifications, the education authorities provided state recognized visibility to those qualifications generated by the labour market. The SQF also recognized new vocational qualifications (i.e. qualifications obtained under continuing vocational training programmes or study programmes for continuing education), which supported lifelong learning opportunities and fostered greater integration of the labour market and education.

In 2019, ten years after its development began, the first evaluation of the SQF was undertaken and the SQF Register created (Ermenc, Mikulec & Biloslavo 2020). The findings showed that the initiative was well received, with respondents positively evaluating its contribution both to the transparency and orderliness of the education system, and the transparency of qualifications. The transparency of qualifications was improved because of the introduction of the Register of the SQF, a public information system that provides information on all individual qualifications covered by the SQF. The information on qualifications includes learning outcomes, which also acted to strengthen the learning outcomes approach to curriculum design. Respondents, however, detected no difference regarding assessment of competencies and award of qualifications. The SQF's impact on the labour market has been limited to its integration into sectoral legislation, and regulations regarding the definition of training conditions for skilled personnel in individual sectors within the defined SQF levels. In terms of reform, SQF has not proved successful, and it has not become the driver of change intended. The evaluation indicated that it can only be a useful tool when supporting other relevant policies related to education–labour market cooperation.

## Skill formation in different sectors

This sub-section considers details of training in three sectors of the Slovenian economy: retail and hospitality as two branches that fall within private sector

**Table 9.1.** Sectoral shares (per cent) of standard employment, 2017

| | | Health and social work activities (Q) | Metal (C24–C30, C33) | Hospitality (I55, I56) | Retail (G47) |
|---|---|---|---|---|---|
| Share of standard employment | | 76 | 79 | 48 | 64 |
| Average gross wage (€) | | 1973 | 1699 | 1226 | 1378 |
| Share (%) of workers receiving the minimum wage | | 4.8 | 4 | 5.5 | 10 |
| Share (%) of workers with academic qualifications | secondary | 45 | 71 | 74 | 73 |
| | tertiary | 50 | 18 | 15 | 24 |
| CVET expenditures per employee (€) | | 290 | 202 | NA | 102 |

*Note.* Statistical Office of the Republic of Slovenia (SURS). By standard employment we mean permanent, full-time contracts of employment.

services, where basic general skills dominate; health, which remains mostly organized within the public sector with heavily regulated occupations that demand high skills; and the core of the country's export sector – the metal sector, which calls for sector-specific and company-specific skills. Issues relating to skill formation and provision in these three sectors are closely connected to the level of non-standard employment in each sector. The strong demand for highly skilled workers is due either to state regulation (health sector) or to the requirements of the labour process (metal sector), which tends to make employment patterns stable, stimulating and enabling skill formation that further bolsters long-term employment relationships. In the deregulated private sector, services like retail and hospitality, where a market-based system for skill formation prevails, the reverse seems to apply. The deregulated labour market here discourages skill formation in schools and allows firms to resort to a contingent labour force, this in turn impeding development of high-quality services and giving a bigger competitive advantage to companies relying on an unskilled labour force. The result is that skill formation is segmented along sectoral lines.

Historically, the development of the four sectors has not neatly followed the reforms of the skill-formation system. While educational policies clearly had an impact on skill formation, at sectoral level skill formation reflects interactions between the broad reforms described above and sector specific paths of development.

**Table 9.2.** Historical developments in the three sectors

| | | Post-socialist transformation period | | EU accession | Post-2008 recession and aftermath | |
|---|---|---|---|---|---|---|
| **Period** | | **1992–1996** | **1997–2004** | **2005–2008** | **2008–2013** | **2013–2019** |
| Developments in relative wages[1] | Health | -1 | -1 | -1 | -3 | +2 |
| | Metal | 0 | +5 | +1 | +6 | +2 |
| | Hospitality | +2 | -12 | -1 | -2 | -1 |
| | Retail | -5 | -12 | -2 | +2 | +2 |
| Change in the level of employment[2] | Health | +3 | +3 | +5 | +10 | +17 |
| | Metal | -34 | +11 | +14 | -13 | +27 |
| | Hospitality | -10 | +13 | +14 | -6 | +30 |
| | Retail | -17 | +17 | +10 | -8 | +11 |
| **Academic year** | | **1990/1991** | **1995/1996** | **2005/2006** | **2007/2008** | **2014/2015** |
| Share of secondary students (%)[3] | Health | 3.8 | 4.3 | 5.8 | 6.2 | 6.6 [b] |
| | Metal | 17.8 | 11.3 | 7.1 | 7.4 | 8.5 [b] |
| | Hospitality | 5.5 | 5.6 | 5.2 | 4.8 | 5.8 [b] |
| | Retail | NA | NA | NA | 2.1[b] | 1.6 |

*Note.* [1] Cumulative change (in percentage point) of average sectoral wage expressed as a share (%) of average national wage during a period given. [2] Cumulative percentage change during a given period. [3] Share of secondary students enrolled in courses for key occupations in the sector. [b] Break in time series. Source: Statistical Office of Republic of Slovenia.

## Health sector

Historically, skill formation in the health sector appeared to follow a stable path determined by the trend towards professionalization on the one hand and opportunities for employment and wage developments on the other. Throughout the three periods of post-socialism, there was a continuous development of the expertise that defined nursing and delineated this from medicine. The tasks and competencies required for particular jobs provided the basis for developing formal educational courses (cf. Ažman & Prestor 2019). With expanding employment opportunities and wages that increased in line with other sectors, enrolment in secondary education courses increased steadily until late 2000s and the share of pupils continued to increase (Table 9.2).

The health sector has a relatively low level of non-standard employment, relatively high average wages and a comparatively low level of workers on the minimum wage (Table 9.1). The sector is mainly publicly funded and supplemented with quasi-mandatory private insurance. It is heavily regulated by the state in terms of skills, with considerable input from professional associations and (to a lesser extent) by the social partners. Initial vocational training is school based so the skill formation system in the health sector can be characterised as state-led with elements of neo-corporatism. Nurses acquire basic skills in school but develop occupation-specific competencies in continuous vocational training where the role of work experience and on-the-job training is indispensable (Trobec, Čuk & Istenič Starčič 2014). The latest changes tighten educational requirements for nursing staff but allow work experience to be counted as a substitute for formal educational attainment (Ažman 2019), confirming the importance of on-the-job training. Research in other EU countries (Crouch 2015) indicates that strong demand affected by public beliefs that access to health services should be widely shared, coupled with labour shortages limits employers' room for manoeuvre. In addition, strict educational requirements and the nature of work requiring trained and experienced nursing staff further strengthen the basis for stable employment patterns (Bembič et al. 2016, 33). Indeed, according to Employment office ZRSZ data, workers with a degree in health sciences enjoyed some of the shortest waiting periods for their first job in the Slovenian labour market in 2019, second only to those with a degree in natural sciences.

## Metal sector

In contrast to the health sector, the development of the metal sector was not linear. A sharp drop in employment as a result of restructuring, coupled with relatively low wages (around 80 per cent of the national average) probably contributed to students being less attracted to VET opportunities in related subjects during the 'transformation period'. The share of secondary students enrolled in metallurgy and mechanical engineering courses plummeted during this period (Table 9.2). Once restructured, however, employment in the sector recovered substantially and wages rose to some 90 per cent of the national average by the end of the second period. Enrolments in the secondary courses of mechanical engineering stabilised after 2000. After a sharp fall in employment following the post-2008 recession, employment levels surged after 2013, reaching levels not seen since early 1990s while wages showed stable growth. The post-2008 period saw a gradual increase in the proportion of secondary students enrolled in mechanical engineering and similar courses (Table 9.2). Furthermore, while the uptake of apprenticeship opportunities is very low in Slovenia (less than 30 per cent of available places were filled in 2020), 60 per cent of open places registered with the Chamber of Industry and Commerce and 67 per cent of filled vacancies were in the metallurgy and mechanical engineering courses.

The share of standard employment in the metal sector slightly exceeds that in the health sector and the share of workers on the minimum wage is lower, yet the average wage is also lower (Table 9.1). In this sector product demand is determined by the market and firms face tough global competition. We should thus expect pressures for de-standardization and quite unstable employment patterns. Yet, as research in other EU countries shows (Crouch 2015), the need for skill retention is a countervailing force to market pressures for greater flexibility. This does not, however, mean firms rely on traditional skills based on manual dexterity and sensory perception. With the spread of computer-based technologies, the tacit knowledge which remains crucial to company performance complements codified know-how since it relates to problem-solving, controlling and improving processes while finding new technical solutions and designs (Balconi 2002, 346). In Slovenia, companies in the sector demand a multi-skilled workforce, but new entrants only receive basic training at a vocational school so must constantly learn in the workplace to develop the requisite competencies to plan and service automated production lines (Bembič et al. 2016, 27). Although skill formation here is mainly state-led, elements of neo-corporatism may be found with social partners' influence on school boards and on-the-job skill formation. For instance, the sectoral collective agreement provides for the elimination of job demarcation, enabling the formation of a broadly skilled, *polyvalent* labour force (ibid.). Recent research shows the very nature of production in the Slovenian metal sector restricts the use of non-standard arrangements since high labour turnover increases training costs, so many companies prefer to foster relationships with their employees to promote stability and long service (ibid., 24, 27).

Considerable challenges nevertheless remain with respect to skill-formation in the metal sector as not all employees possess the digital skills required to use computer-based technology, giving rise to concerns about the workforce of the future. The problem of low skills is especially pronounced among older workers (OECD 2017, 58) and the preference of companies to train workers who already have a certain degree from formal education (see above) exacerbates this situation. Employers are aware of the scale of the challenge represented by low-skilled older workers given the pace of technological change. Nevertheless, rather than dealing with this issue through social dialogue, they primarily regard it as a matter for companies' human resource departments. The trade unions seem to be much more attentive to this problem since they fear a large proportion of older, low-skilled workers will be rendered unemployable by recent technological changes, fearing that employers will elect to retain the most highly skilled workers and leave the low-skilled older workers behind. Such concerns stem, firstly from the fact that low-skilled older production workers represent a large proportion of their membership and secondly, that mass redundancies in the sector would seriously disturb the labour market more generally, because the displacement of this group would overwhelm welfare state programmes.

## Private services – retail and hospitality

The historical trajectory of retail and hospitality has been one of steadily deteriorating working conditions, including wages. Secondary courses linked to the two branches of the private services sector were consequently less attractive. The decline in employment in retail and hospitality was less pronounced than in the metal sector during the transformational depression and the subsequent expansion was stronger (Table 9.2). Nevertheless, except for the first half of the 1990s when wages were around the national average, wage developments in the two branches of private services lagged behind the growth of national average wages during the three periods (Table 9.2). This, coupled with poor working conditions, especially concerning working time, made associated fields of study less attractive for potential students. Thus, despite vigorous growth of employment opportunities, the proportion of students enrolled in catering and tourism secondary courses declined from the mid-1990s. The deregulation of occupations undertaken by the government in hospitality during the second period and retail during the third, expanded the pool of potential candidates for jobs in these sectors, but further undermined the attractiveness of educational courses.

In contrast to the health and metal sectors, both hospitality and retail are characterised by a greater proportion of the workforce employed in non-standard employment arrangements, and considerably lower wages, with a high concentration of staff receiving the minimum wage in retail (Table 9.1). In these sectors demand for labour is market based, with this fluctuating considerably in hospitality, which appears to be increasingly characterised by precarious employment: in 2017 less than half the labour force was in regular employment (Table 9.1) and average wages were among the lowest in Slovenia. This mirrors developments across the EU, because the hospitality sector is characterised by temporary employment in part reflecting its seasonality (Gerogiannis, Kerckhofs & Vargas 2012). Furthermore, multinational investors that increasingly dominate the sector are interested in short-term profits, so downward pressure on wages has grown substantially throughout the sector and become the main path to achieving greater profitability (Jany-Catrice & Ribault 2010). In

Slovenia, under pressure from the European Commission and with the aim of making employment more flexible and the sector more competitive, educational requirements for key occupations in the sector were deregulated in 2005. Trade unions and employers' organizations objected to this deregulation, arguing that workforce quality would deteriorate as vocational education would lose its appeal; fears that were subsequently justified. Skill formation has therefore been negatively affected by the combined impact of deregulation, low pay, and the absence of stable working conditions. The shortage of trained employees has forced employers to provide in-house training, but pressure to cut the wage bill means that employers are unable to retain employees in periods of slack demand, and staff are often laid off just a few months after completing their elementary training.

Skill levels and service quality in Slovenian tourism have been profoundly, and negatively, affected by the discontinuous approach to training, which has been influenced by the neo-liberal market model. A similar picture emerges in the retail sector, which also has a high share of non-standard employment (Table 9.1) and relatively low wages. This is consistent with analyses emphasising reliance of retail chains on elementary skills which enables them to utilise external flexibility to manage fluctuations in demand (Boyer 2014). The main occupations in the sector were deregulated in 2015 as Government reform plans aligned with the EU approach. Only one of the sectoral social partners, the Slovenian Chamber of Commerce, favoured deregulation, reflecting the influence of the large retail chains. The Chamber of Craft and Small Business of Slovenia, the Chamber of Industry and Commerce, and trade unions in the education and retail sectors, by contrast, were opposed, arguing that the quality of skills would deteriorate. Deregulation appears to have had a negative impact on skill formation. The system of skill provision is moving closer to a market-based model and interest in vocational education programmes by prospective students has decreased and the costs of training have shifted to the employers. Yet sharp price competition, especially from discount retailers, who primarily employ easily replaceable unskilled workers, has exerted considerable pressure on traditional retail chains to cut costs to stay competitive. Traditional retailers rely on service quality, and cost-cutting measures are undermining their ability to fund training (Interview with a trade union representative, 2020). The outcome of these developments is a lower skill level within the workforce and a deterioration in service quality in the sector.

## Conclusion

Once a member of the Federative Socialist Yugoslavia, Slovenia has passed through various stages of institutional development: from self-managed socialism where major company decisions were based on state governance, self-management and workers' councils, to different stages of post-socialist transformation and social partner cooperation. In this transition, the education system and the mainly state-led VET system attempted to introduce collective approaches to skill formation based on social partnership principles. This chapter has questioned the extent to which the Slovenian skill formation system can be viewed as a national monolith. The system is becoming increasingly segmented and the quality of employment at sector level is determined by the state's involvement and competitive strategies of companies. Differences between sectors include the proportion of workers in standard employment, the average gross wage and the proportion of workers receiving the minimum wage.

There seems to be a link between patterns of skill-formation and the level of non-standard employment and quality of work. Several factors like market stability and strict regulation of educational requirements ensure steady employment conditions thereby stimulating investment in continuous skill formation. One example of this is the health sector in which a state-led skill-formation system with elements of collective skill-formation prevails. In the metal sector, requirements for multi-skilled workers are associated with stable employment. Schools still provide basic skills that are then deepened by continuous vocational training. Companies have incentives to ensure stable employment relations for their workers. Non-standard employment, poor working conditions and low wages have penetrated the retail and hospitality sectors, diminishing the attractiveness of educational courses required for employment in both branches. Educational requirements were deregulated when the skill-formation system moved from being state-led to a more market-based neoliberal system. This shift is encouraging employers to adopt low-cost strategies: they call for basic skills or rely on unskilled workers to help them adjust to fluctuating demand by resorting to numerical flexibility. Effective skill formation in the two sectors is undermined by both deregulation and the flexible employment regime.

Each of the sectors considered here faces significant challenges. With an ageing population there is a need to expand employment in the health sector, but this should not be at the expense of professional standards or service quality. Conditions within both retail and hospitality demand a significant rethink of the sectoral approach to skill formation but this must be accompanied by improving working conditions and wages to attract students to the appropriate educational courses. The metal sector, by contrast, faces the challenge of retraining older workers to prepare them for technological changes. Thus, the need for a collective approach to skill formation and the strong involvement of all social partners is more pressing than ever.

## References

Ažman, M. (2019). 'Dokument Poklicne kompetence in aktivnosti izvajalcev v dejavnosti zdravstvene nege: nastanek, odzivi in izzivi [Documenting vocational competencies and activities of nursing service providers: origins, responses and challenges]', *Obzornik zdravstvene nege*, 53 (4), 264–268.

Balconi, M. (2002). 'Tacitness, codification of technological knowledge and the organisation of industry', *Research Policy*, 31 (3), 357–379.

Bembič, B., Stanojević, M., Hrženjak, M., Ignjatovič, M., & Breznik, M. (2016). *PRECARIR Project Report, Slovenia*. Ljubljana: Fakulteta za družbene vede.

Bohle, D., & Greskovits, B. (2007). 'Neoliberalism, embedded neoliberalism and neocorporatism: Towards transnational capitalism in Central-Eastern Europe', *West European Politics*, 30 (3), 443–466.

Boyer, R. (2014). 'Developments and extensions of '"Régulation theory" and employment relations.' In A. Wilkinson, G. Wood & R. Deeg (eds.), *The Oxford Handbook of Employment Relations: Comparative Employment Systems*, pp. 114–153. Oxford: Oxford University Press.

Cedefop (2017a). *Apprenticeship Overview: Slovenia. Introduction of Apprenticeships in Slovenia*. Thematic reviews by countries. Luxembourg: Office for Official Publications of the European Union. <https://www.cedefop.europa.eu/files/4157_sl.pdf>, accessed 8 February 2021.

Cedefop (2017b). *Cedefop European Public Opinion Survey on Vocational Education and Training*. Cedefop Research paper No 62, Luxembourg: Office for Official Publications of the European Union.

Crouch, C. (2015). 'Labour market governance and the creation of outsiders', *British Journal of Industrial Relations*, 53 (1), 27–48.

Crowley, S., & Stanojevic, M. (2011). 'Varieties of capitalism, power resources, and historical legacies: Explaining the Slovenian exception', *Politics & Society*, 39 (2), 268–295.

Ermenc, K. S. (2009). 'From de-tracking to re-tracking in Slovenian upper secondary education.' In J. Hopfner & E. Protner (eds.), *Education from the Past to the Present: Pedagogical and Didactic Lessons from the History of Education*, pp. 122–138. Bielsko-Biała: Filozofska fakulteta, Mednarodna založba

Oddelka za slovanske jezike in književnosti, Zora, 62, Mednarodna knjižna zbirka Zora.

Ermenc, K. S. (2011). 'Vocational education and training in Slovenia between 1974 and 2010: developments and dilemmas.' In J. Bergland Holen & A. Phillips (eds.), *Studies in Education from Diverse Contexts*, pp. 11–26. Grand Forks, ND: University of North Dakota.

Ermenc, K. S., Mikulec, B., & Biloslavo, R. (2020). *Evaluation of the Slovenian Qualifications Framework and the Register of Qualifications of the SQF*. Ljubljana: Institute of the Republic of Slovenia for Vocational Education and Training.

European Commission (2011). *Attitudes towards Vocational Education and Training Special Eurobarometer 369*. Conducted by TNS Opinion & Social at the request of Directorate-General Education and Culture.

Feldmann, M. (2006). 'Emerging varieties of capitalism in transition countries industrial relations and wage bargaining in Estonia and Slovenia', *Comparative Political Studies*, 39 (7), 829–854.

Feldmann, M. (2017). 'Crisis and opportunity: Varieties of capitalism and varieties of crisis responses in Estonia and Slovenia', *European Journal of Industrial Relations*, 23 (1), 33–46.

Gerogiannis, E., Kerckhofs, P., & Vargas, O. (2012). *Employment and Industrial Relations in the Hotels and Restaurants Sector*. Dublin: Eurofound.

Hall, P. A., & Soskice, D. (2001). *Varieties of Capitalism: The Institutional Foundations of Comparative Advantage*. Oxford: Oxford University Press.

Jany-Catrice, F., & Ribault, T. (2010). 'The hotel industry in service economies: from one "service world" to another', *Work Organisation, Labour & Globalisation*, 4 (1), 120–135.

Klarič, T. (2019). *Podjetja pozdravljajo vajeništvo: prvo evalvacijsko poročilo o poskusnem izvajanju vajeništva*. Ljubljana: Center RS za poklicno izobraževanje.

Kogan, I., & Unt, M. (2008). 'The role of vocational specificity of educational credentials for labour market entry in Estonia and Slovenia', *International Sociology*, 23 (3), 389–416.

Kramberger, A., & Stanojević, M. (2015). 'Class concepts and stratification research in Slovenia', *East European Politics and Societies*, 29 (3), 651–662.

Kureková, L. (2012). 'Success against all odds? Determinants of sectoral rise and decline in Central Europe', *East European Politics and Societies*, 26 (3), 643–664.

Markowitsch, J., & Hefler, G. (2019). *Future Developments in Vocational Education and Training in Europe. Report on Reskilling and Upskilling through*

*Formal and Vocational Education Training*, JRC Working Papers Series on Labour, Education and Technology, 07.

Medveš, Z., & Muršak, J. (eds.) (1992). *Sistemsko urejanje poklicnega izobraževanja. [Regulation of the system of vocational education]*. Slovensko društvo pedagogov. Andragoško društvo Slovenije. Ministrstvo za šolstvo in šport.

Mikulec, B., & Ermenc, K. S. (2016). 'Qualifications frameworks between global and European pressures and local responses'. *SAGE open*, <doi: 10.1177/2158244016644948>, accessed 8 February 2021.

Milharčič-Hladnik, M., & Šušteršič J. (eds.) (1986). *Šolska reforma je papirnati Tiger*. Ljubljana: KRT.

Muršak, J. (2010). *Vocational Education and Training between School and Labour Market: The Case of Slovenia*. Horlivka: Ministry of Education and Science of Ukraine: Horlivka state pedagogical institute of foreign languages.

OECD (2017). *Skills Strategy Diagnostic Report Slovenia*. Paris: Organisation for Economic Cooperation and Development, <https://www.oecd.org/skills/nationalskillsstrategies/Skills-Strategy-Diagnostic-report-Slovenia.pdf>, accessed 8 February 2021.

OECD (2019). *Skills Matter: Additional Results from the Survey of Adult Skills*, OECD Skills Studies. Paris: Organisation for Economic Cooperation and Development.

Pavlin, S. (2018). 'Time to reconsider the strategic role of system(s) for monitoring higher education graduates' careers?' *European Journal of Education*, 54 (2), 261–272.

Pavlin, S., & Svetličič, M. (2012). 'Higher education, employability and competitiveness', *Hacettepe Egitim Dergisi*, 43, 386–395.

Šlander, V. (2007). 'Certification of national vocational qualifications.' In M. Zevnik, K. S. Ermenc & M. Kovač (eds.), *National Institute for Vocational Education and Training in Development of a Common European VET Area*, pp. 35–37. Ljubljana: Center RS za poklicno izobraževanje.

Stanojević, M. (2018). 'Slovenia: Neo-corporatism under the neo-liberal turn', *Employee Relations*, 40 (4), 709–724.

Stanojević, M., Kanjuo-Mrćela, A., & Breznik, M. (2016). 'Slovenia at the crossroads: Increasing dependence on supranational institutions and the weakening of social dialogue', *European Journal of Industrial Relations*, 22 (3), 281–294.

Svetlik, I. (2009). 'Managing HR in Slovenia'. In M. J. Morley, N. Heraty & S. Michaelova (eds.), *Managing Human Resources in Central and Eastern Europe*, pp. 219–242. London: Routledge.

Svetlik, I., & Barle Lakota, A. (2000). 'Curriculum reform Slovenia'. In S. Gabrščcek & N. Dimc (eds.), *Strategies of Educational Reform in South East Europe Countries*. Proceedings of the Seminar Bled, Slovenia. CPZ-International Centre for Knowledge Promotion 8–10 June, <http://www.cpz-int.si/Assets/pdf/Strategies.pdf>, accessed 8 February 2021.

Trobec, I., Čuk, V., & Istenič Starčič, A. (2014). 'Kompetence zdravstvene nege ter opredelitev strategij razvoja kompetenc na dodiplomskem študiju zdravstvene nege [Nursing competences and the definition of strategies for competence development in undergraduate nursing studies]', *Obzornik zdravstvene nege*, 48 (4), 310–322.

West, J. (2013). *Vocational Education and Training in Eastern Europe: Transition and Influence*. London: Centre for Learning and Life Chances in Knowledge Economies and Societies.

Zgaga, P. (2002). 'Changes in Slovenian higher education: Governance, autonomy, admission, quality', *Higher Education in Europe*, 27 (3), 325–332.

Teo Matković and Nikola Buković

# 10. Croatia: impact of Europeanization on skill formation

**Abstract:** This chapter sets out to elaborate how Europeanization fits in the current institutional state of the Croatian skill formation regime, qualified as predominantly statist, with partial collectivism in training for occupations in skilled trades. Text provides outlines of demographic and industrial context, followed by depiction of linkages between the education system and labour market. Main features of the social partnership and its role in functioning of the national skill formation system are also explored. The chapter contains two important cases studies on Europeanization in the national system: on development of apprenticeship schemes and introduction of the national qualification system. Both indicate that role of Europeanization can be understood as the one of "great accelerator". On one hand it pushes policymakers to 'play catch-up' with more developed member states, while on the other functions as a repository of (re)usable policy idea and source of funding to back up their implementation. However, institutional change remains sluggish as layering, rather than displacement, represents the dominant mechanism of institutional change in the Croatian skill formation system. This can be interpreted by three lines of argument: (1) path dependence, creating a dominant position of the central state in early 1990s which was not coupled with adequate policymaking capacity; (2) lack of interest, capacity and ambition of non-state actors to assume more prominent role and (3) structural factors, primarily protracted abundance of qualified labour force, hindering employers' investment in innovation and human capital.

**Keywords:** Croatia, post-communist transition, Europeanization, VET, qualifications, layering

## Introduction

The development of the Croatian education policy from independence onwards can best be understood in terms of it having two successive phases, each shaped by the dominating political paradigms at the time (Žiljak 2013; Žiljak & Molnar 2015). In the first phase, which spanned the 1990s, the education system was primarily seen as a tool of (re)creating national identity and the nation-state. The second phase began in the 2000s and is still in effect. This phase is characterised by the paradigm of Europeanization and its key features: lifelong learning, competitiveness, and employability. This has entailed harmonising national policy with the education policy of the European Union, while also implementing policy learning from other member states.

A recent analysis of the institutional features of the Croatian skill production regime (Buković 2019) classified it, following Busemeyer and Trampusch (2012, 12), as 'predominantly statist, with partial collectivism in training for occupations in skilled trades.' This means that the central state and its subsidiaries control, deliver, and fund most aspects of skill formation in Croatia, with general education tracks enjoying more prestige than their vocational counterparts (Buković & Matković 2018). The critical exception – which inserts a measure of hybridity into the system – comprises programmes for skilled trades occupations (in Croatian: *programi za obrtnička zanimanja)*, which include apprenticeships. Here, the Croatian Chamber for Trades and Crafts (CCTC) plays a significant role in programme design, delivery, and administration. This cannot be considered an example of corporatism in the sense of developed industrial democracies, however, since it lacks a sustained and equitable partnership between the state, employers, and trade unions in delivering programmes.

This chapter aims to deepen understanding of the dominant forces shaping and maintaining the Croatian skill production regime over time. It will set the scene by offering a demographic and industrial context for this, and by describing the education and labour market linkages across the spectrum of education. It will then describe the institutional particularities of the social partnership in Croatia, regarding governance of the skill production regime. In the two central sections, we present cases of policy transfer that characterise the functioning of the Croatian skill production regime. These are: (i) the struggle related to apprenticeship-based VET, which has been ongoing for two and half decades, and the succession of solutions and actors involved; and (ii) the policy transfer process and challenges around the implementation of the Croatian Qualification Framework which has been proclaimed by policymakers as the main instrument for overcoming skill mismatches within the labour market. The final section offers some conclusions.

## Demographic and industrial context

Any changes in the system of skill formation must be analysed within the context of broader structural developments over the past three decades: (1) declining cohort size, (2) labour migration, and (3) changes in the industrial structure.

## Demographics

Demographic developments present the first set of challenges to the functioning of the Croatian skill production regime. With birth cohorts steadily on the decline – from 69,000 in 1979 to 41 thousand in 2001 – Croatia's education system has faced a diminishing number of pupils at the upper secondary education level since the late 1990s (Figure 10.1). The size of the generation entering the labour market has also begun to shrink since the early 2000s. Throughout the 2010s the size of the cohorts leaving the labour market was about 20 per cent larger than the cohorts completing their education. This makes for a substantial cohort replacement challenge.

## Work immigration

In the 1990s, a flood of Croatian nationals immigrated from the other ex-Yugoslavian countries (particularly from Bosnia and Herzegovina), with 30–50,000 people settling in Croatia annually. This workforce had experienced similar education systems but was generally less qualified than the resident population. This inflow declined to 15–20,000 in 2002–2008. It then mostly ended, with the prolonged economic crisis and with Croatia's accession to the EU in 2013, as many Croatian nationals residing in neighbouring countries opted to move directly to other EU Countries. Recently the work immigration quota system for non-nationals has become more salient. Only established in 2003 – and effectively frozen over the crisis period (2010–2015) – the immigration quota exploded thereafter, increasing from 7,000 in 2017 to 55,000 in 2019. This is an important development for the skill formation regime, since up to 90 per cent of the quota was specified for skilled, VET-related occupations. Thus, in recent years, the level of immigration of skilled workers has dwarfed the annual output of the national VET system.

The annual level of youth emigration (aged 20–29) seems to have stabilised at about 9,000 in 2018–2019 – after the initial post-accession wave relented – or at about 1.9 per cent of the population. The brain drain appears to have had most impact amongst tertiary education graduates; the pilot 2018 Eurograduate survey identified 5–6 per cent of Croatian graduates as living abroad a year after graduation (Meng et al. 2020, 238).

## Industrial structure

In the decades since the transition began, Croatia's industrial structure has followed a long-term shift towards services, coupled with deindustrialisation

**Table 10.1.** Mid-term changes in broad sectoral employment

| | 1981 | 1991 | 2001 | 2011 |
|---|---|---|---|---|
| Total employment (in 000s) | | | | |
| Agriculture | 449 | 265 | 175 | 80 |
| Manufacture, construction, mining | 631 | 590 | 386 | 377 |
| Other (services) | 783 | 892 | 847 | 1,004 |
| Total employment | 1,863 | 1,747 | 1,408 | 1,461 |
| Structure of employment (per cent) | | | | |
| Agriculture | 24.1 | 15.2 | 12.5 | 5.5 |
| Manufacture, construction, mining | 33.9 | 33.8 | 27.4 | 25.8 |
| Other (services) | 42.0 | 51.1 | 60.2 | 68.7 |

*Note.* Census (1981–2011 rounds)

and a reduction in total employment (Table 10.1). During the decade 2009–2019, the absolute number of people employed bounced back to about the pre-crisis level (1.56 million vs. 1.57 million), but the structure of employment changed substantially. There has been strong growth (over 20 per cent) in all personal service sectors, ICT, and professional and support business services; modest growth in health and education; and a decline in finance, in most transformative industries, and – particularly – in the extractive sector (Matković 2020, 15).

Current (2018) Cedefop skills forecasts indicate that the trend may change again. The strongest growth is projected to be in health, education, professional activities, and green jobs, whereas hospitality services may join manufacturing and agriculture as a declining sector.

It is important to mention employment in sole proprietorships (non-incorporated businesses), as they are main providers of workplace training for skilled trades occupations. Sole proprietorships also gain the most from the occupational labour market and standardised workplace training since they lack the resources and size to train internally. The share of employment in such entities steadily increased from 9.6 per cent of all employment in 1991 to 17.5 per cent in 2008. Yet this sector was badly affected during the 2009–2015 crisis and has not recovered since. By 2019, employment in the sector had shrunk to 194 thousand, or 12.5 per cent of all employment. This has implications for both the sector's labour demand and its training provisions.

## Education system and labour market linkages, 1990–2020

The skill production regime that emerged during the transition must be understood as a reaction to the one that preceded it. In 1975, Yugoslavia implemented a sweeping national education reform, setting up a system called vocational-oriented education (in Croatian: *usmjereno obrazovanje*). This was not just characterised by vocationalized curricula, localised links between the education and productive sectors, and a focus on learning through work; it was also explicitly designed to facilitate the emancipation of the working class and the suppression of the (white-collar, critical intellectual) middle class. This made the concept toxic during the democratic transition. Dismantling the pre-transition system was made easier by the fact that VOE did not reach its proclaimed skill matching goals, and that industry itself only partially embraced its principles (Baćević 2016).

### Upper secondary education and VET

The main features of the current system were introduced in 1992. They clearly reflected the dominant paradigm of the time, which favoured a clean break with the socialist era. To be more precise, this break was with *the late socialist era*, since the system set up in 1992 closely resembles the one put into place by the earlier socialist reform of 1958. After eight years of compulsory education, most students choose from three main tracks, which differ considerably in prestige and social selectivity (Buković & Matković 2018; Matković et al. 2013), duration, horizontal differentiation, vocational specificity, approach to workplace training, labour market linkages, and vertical permeability (Matković 2011). The most selective – accounting for 29 per cent of entrants in the year 2019/2020 – is the general secondary, or grammar school, track. This track concludes with a matriculation exam (*matura*), with 87–88 per cent of graduates entering higher education (HE) outright (Šabić 2019). The other two tracks are vocational.

The first group of VET programmes takes four years (five in the medical field) and prepares entrants for a group of occupations whose practitioners are usually referred to as 'technicians'. This is the largest track overall (accounting for 44 per cent of the enrolments in 2019/20) and it represents a middle ground between general education and pure VET, with the curricula containing a significant share of general content during the first two years. These curricula usually entail no, or very little, workplace learning (up to two weeks, often only in the final years of study). There is also no standardization in terms of execution, monitoring, or pupil-employer matching regarding workplace learning. Such programmes are prevalent in sectors such as economics, electronics and engineering, health, and hospitality. This track has a hybrid nature since, apart from providing vocational credentials, it allows students to apply for a matriculation exam and enter any tertiary education programme. Many do; 43–45 per cent of the 2015–2017 cohort of technical education graduates (and as many as 56 per cent of economics course graduates) immediately enrolled in HE after graduation (Šabić 2019).

The lower tier of VET programmes in Croatia lasts just three years. It could be qualified as purely vocational with a high degree of vocational specificity, a strong practical orientation, very narrow general curriculum and no direct access to tertiary education or a matriculation exam (Buković 2019; Matković et al. 2013). This track is in long-term decline, shrinking from 39 to 24 per cent of overall enrolment between 1999 and 2019 (Figure 10.2); the available places in 3-year VET programmes are rarely filled (Christiaensen et al. 2019). There are two sub-groups within this track. In one, students are trained for skilled occupations. The other sub-group provides a workforce for retail and industry. Workplace learning is far more prevalent within the skilled trades segment. The decline in the upper-secondary education cohort size began in the late 1990s. Yet, until 2011, the 3-year VET track bore the brunt of this decline – dropping from 21.0 to 13.5 thousand entrants. As the entrant cohort size continued to decline over the 2010s, the sharp contraction within the 3-year vocational track has continued (from 13.5 in 2011 to 9.2 in 2020). This time around, however, some decline in enrolment has also appeared in the technical (22.1 to 17.6) and gymnasium (13.6 to 11.1) programmes.

On the output side, the number of pupils graduating annually from 3-year vocational tracks declined from 20.4 to 8.4 thousand between 1999 and 2019. Over the same period, the decline in the number of graduates was lower for technical tracks (19.3 to 17.4 thousand) and stagnant for gymnasium tracks (11.9 to 12.0 thousand), with some contraction occurring after 2016. Consequently, while the share of upper secondary graduates completing vocational education declined from 77 per cent to 68 per cent of the cohort, the share of purely vocational 3-year VET graduates almost halved from 40 per cent to 22 per cent.

## Higher education

Higher education was the last segment of the Croatian education system to be reformed during the transition. The Act on Higher Education Institutions (AHEI) was fully implemented only in 1995. Based on the constitutional guarantee of autonomy for universities, academic self-management (i.e., the ability to determine their own programmes, rules, and criteria) was guaranteed to

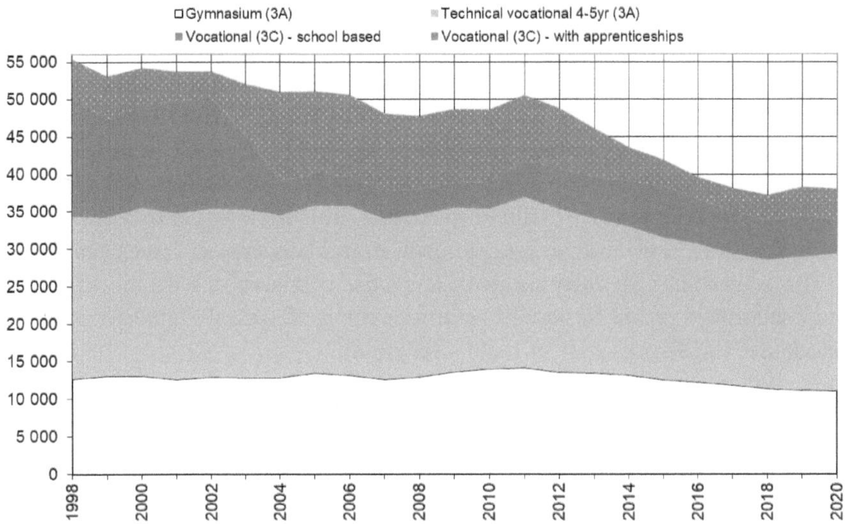


**Figure 10.1.** Enrolment in upper secondary education tracks, 1998–2020. (Sources: CBS first releases 'Upper secondary schools.' Apprenticeships: CCTC statistical reports (up to 2012), *Školski e-rudnik (since 2013)*. Note: first-year entrants, no repeaters. Regular art and design programmes displayed among technical schools. Special needs education track not displayed.)

higher education institutions (HEI). Tertiary education was re-established as a binary single cycle 'diploma' system, with strongly separated academic and professional tertiary education (PTE) tracks. Unlike the pre-transition regulations, workplace-based training or involvement of firms was not mentioned in the AHEI, while connection to the labour market was mentioned only via the notion that programmes ought to be 'appropriate to needs of employers.'

The more comprehensive Act on Scientific Activity and Higher Education was introduced in 2003 and remains in force as of 2020. With respect to linkages with employers, the only remaining vestige of the fundamental principles was the 'unity of professional and education work for the purpose of training for specific professional knowledge and skills.' Neither the labour market nor employers are otherwise mentioned, indicating a significant decoupling from the labour market. However, this Act also set up the groundwork for the implementation of the Bologna sequential study regime (Bachelor – BA / Master MA) starting in 2005, and for an external assessment and accreditation process.

The Agency for Science and Higher Education (ASHE) has had responsibility for the HEI assessment since 2010. An overview of the 2010–2016 cycle (Petrušić 2017), indicated the weak to non-existent involvement of labour market stakeholders (institutions or firms) in strategic planning, quality assurance, and revision of study programmes. Internships and practical work were sporadic, and the assessment of labour market needs, alumni organizations, and graduate tracking practices were virtually non-existent. This is common to assessments regardless of field of study or type of institution. Many appeals have been made in the assessments for institutions to formalise cooperation with industry. Yet the conclusions of the National Committee for Professional Higher Education Excellence (NCPHEE) state its main strength as

> the well-established link between PHE and the world of work seen through the fact that programmes are developed in cooperation with the world of work and the education process is connected with practical exercises. The perception of the world of work regarding PHE students' competences is positive (Poličnik et al. 2017, 14).

Indeed, four of the nine PHE strengths identified via a SWOT analysis pertain to cooperation with industry. As for evidence of work-based learning, Botrić (2017) identified that in 2015–2016 just 49 per cent of university students attended programmes that involve work placements, along with 73 per cent of students in professional programmes. Within university programmes, there is a higher prevalence of work placements in the medicine and biotechnical fields (83–96 per cent) and a lower prevalence in social sciences and humanities (36–37 per cent). The average annual duration – for those who attended the work placement – averaged a modest 65 hours in academic courses and 95 hours in professional programmes. Such placements were commonly based on bilateral agreements between the HEI and employers. As for employer linkages via career guidance services, a recent analysis showed that just one in five HEIs reported offering a career guidance centre, yet most HEIs reported their intention to open such a centre (Đorđević 2017).

With HEIs being legally positioned to determine the number of placements and retain the income – yet without enforceable staffing standards or external assessment prior to late 2000s – the number of enrolled students increased rapidly from the mid-1990s to the mid-2000s, particularly in PTE and the social sciences (Babić et al. 2007). Consequently, by the late 1990s the number of graduates recovered to the levels achieved in early 1980s (Matković 2009). It then increased sharply from 2001 to 2008, levelling off at about 21 thousand thereafter (Figure 10.2). Initially, PTE courses were the major contributor to the growth, as the number of graduates from professional courses almost equalled those

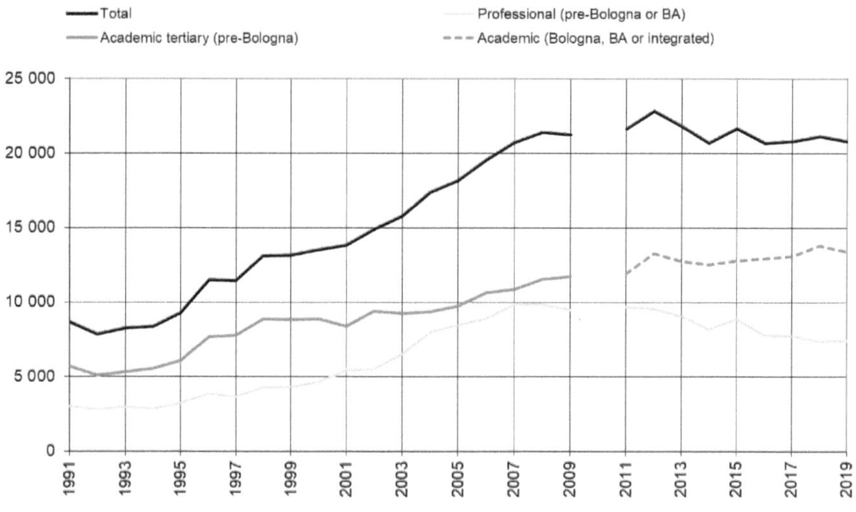


**Figure 10.2.** Graduates from professional and academic tertiary education. (Source: CBS First Releases 'Students who Graduated from University Study or Completed Professional study'. Note: 2010 break due to the 'overlap year' of pre-Bologna and Bologna.)

from academic courses in the 2004–2008 period. While the supply of placement positions in PTE has remained high, the number of entrants and graduates has decreased strongly since then. By 2018–2019, the share of professional graduates (at the BA level) dropped again to about 35 per cent, similar to the early 1990s.

While the number of graduates declined slightly since 2012, the cohort size has declined dramatically (cf. Figures 10.1 and 10.2). Consequently, according to the Labour Force Survey (LFS), the share of 25–34-year-old workers with tertiary education doubled from 18 to 35 per cent between 2002 and 2019.

## Adult education and lifelong learning

During the 1990s 'adult education was marginalized and the key actors of its implementation were presented as redundant remnants of the old socialist education system' (Žiljak 2018, 55). The area was initially regulated via bylaws, with comprehensive regulation introduced only through the Adult Education Act in 2007. The Agency for Adult Education was set up in 2006, and was tasked with monitoring, developing, evaluating, and running the registry of adult education. It merged into the Agency for Vocational Education and Training and Adult

Learning (AVETAE) in 2010, institutionally framing adult education as continuous vocational education.

Adult education courses are provided by a patchwork of public open universities, VET schools, HEIs, language schools and private firms, with the number of registered entities doubling from 345 in 2009 to 618 in 2018. Providers are organized under the umbrella of the Croatian Association of Open Universities (1954), the Association of Institutions for Adult Education (2009) and the Association of Employers in Education within the Croatian Employers' Association (2011), but none has power of representation. There is a possibility, but no mandate, for providers to associate with firms to provide courses (including provision of work-based training). About 800–900 courses are registered annually across the country, with 11,309 entries in the registry by the end of 2018. (Christiansen et al. 2019, 315). Some providers are private, some are established by local governments, but there is little publicly funded provision. Local governments fund some operational expenses, while central government (and EU instruments such as Erasmus+ and ESF) funds some development activities. Yet apart from provision of elementary education, all the courses are paid for by attendees (or their employers), with few placements being offered by the Croatian Employment Service and occasional opportunities being provided by NGOs or funded by towns or municipalities.

Despite recent developments, such arrangements led to low and stagnant participation in lifelong learning, especially in non-formal education. The monthly participation rate in education and training for population aged 25–64, as measured by the Labour Force Survey, remained stagnant at 2.5–3.5 per cent for the entire 2006–2019 period, and was among the lowest in the EU. The findings of the 2016 Adult Education Survey were similar, with only around a third of adults participating in education during the previous year. Both sources indicate that the participation is particularly low among those aged over 45, those without tertiary education and the unemployed. When it comes to corporate HRD policies, training makes up an average 1.3 per cent of the labour costs of Croatian firms (EU average 1.7 per cent) as per the 2015 Continuous Vocational Training Survey. Furthermore, only 55 per cent of Croatian firms provide training (cf. 73 per cent EU average), with the incidence of externally provided courses declining over the 2010–2015 period. Any business-driven initiative to upgrade the system of skill formation seems unlikely, as 79 per cent of employers claimed that qualifications, skills and competences correspond to the current needs of their enterprises, while 65 per cent assessed the level of training they provide as appropriate (cf. 52 per cent EU average).

Adult education holds a prominent place in the Strategy for Science, Education and Technology (Hrvatski sabor 2014), but public and political interest has remained lukewarm, while the amendments to the Adult Education Act and improvements in quality assurance stalled during the 2015–2020 period (Žiljak 2018).

## Social partnership and skill formation in Croatia

Several factors have affected the current state of social partnership within the Croatian system of skill formation. The first is weak co-ordination, exemplified by the various advisory councils established since the 2000s. This includes the Council for VET (2009), the National Council for Science, Higher Education and Technological Development (NCSHETD 2004) and the National Council for Human Potential Development (NCHPD 2014). The latter is a central forum established to monitor and improve the implementation of reforms, revolving around the national qualification framework. A common feature of all these forums is their broad membership: their 18 (NCSHETD), 21 (Council for VET), and 25 (NCHPD) members are usually drawn from state administration, business associations (including chambers), and trade unions. Academic professionals are also represented – as are, sometimes, other stakeholders such as NGOs or individual entrepreneurs. Another important feature of such national councils is their strictly advisory role, even though the members of the NCSHETD and NCHPD are elected by the Croatian Parliament (CVET members are appointed by the minister in charge of education). These bodies sometimes face prolonged periods of inactivity, usually because new appointments have yet to be confirmed by the competent bodies. Unlike proactive examples such as Austria's Federal Council for Apprenticeships (Bundesberufsausbildungsbeirat, BABB), which all but autonomously put forward a proposal for a key bylaw governing the delivery of apprenticeships (BMA 2012, 21), the existing literature shows little evidence of those bodies significantly influencing policy in Croatia. This could be attributed primarily to lack of tradition and institutional capacity for participative policymaking, but also reflects the nature of social partnership in Croatia, which is elaborated in the following paragraphs.

Second, with respect to tripartite social dialogue, the national-level Economic and Social Council (ESC) represents a key forum for coordination among social partners: the central state, the representative association of employers, and three trade union federations. One of the ESC working groups, the Commission for Employment, Education and Alignment with the Labour Market, regularly produces opinions and recommendations on legislative proposals and draft strategies relevant to the field of skill production. Yet the work of this commission, and of the ESC in general, is also characterised by discontinuities. These dynamics are framed by Bagić (2013) as 'an unproductive balance of power' between social partners. He argues that the central state usually holds enough political power to pass policies – regardless of disagreements among the social partners – but that it is sometimes blocked by the mobilisation of trade unions, via protests, referendum petitions, strikes and withdrawal from the ESC. The central state also often requires some involvement from employers for policy to have any tangible impact; the national employers' association has only a limited capacity to organise and, particularly, to sanction employers who break the rules. According to Bagić, such a balance is 'unproductive' because it is unlikely to facilitate compromises and joint stakeholder action, as opposed to confrontations and unilateralism from the central state.

Third, the current economic structure itself does not seem to be conducive to bilateral and sectoral collective bargaining. Economic sectors usually consist of just a few major firms and many small ones, impeding the development of mutual interests and undermining the organization of employers at sectoral level (Bagić 2010).

The situation is even more complicated in the field of VET, the workings of which strongly influence the nature of Croatia's system of skill formation. The national trade union federations and national employers' association do not possess the capacity to directly influence policymaking. Trade unions that organize workers in the education sector are relevant and influential but seem to place more emphasis on issues crucial to the interests of their members (such as wages, teacher training, and teaching hours) rather than on the direction of education policy. Nevertheless, issues related to the functioning of the education systems and those related to trade union members' interests can overlap – particularly in relation to discussions on the network of schools, as these can directly influence the sustainability of teaching jobs. There is some involvement of chamber bodies: the CCTC continuously assumes a prominent role in VET development and delivery, while the Croatian Chamber of Economy (CCE) has recently discovered an interest in VET policy, particularly around expanding apprenticeships into other sectors of the economy. Yet the relationship between the chambers and the central state could be better described as a sort of 'outsourcing', rather than social partnership (Buković 2022). It seems that the central state, and particularly the ministry in charge of education, is willing to relinquish some control of the skilled trades programmes to minimise its operational involvement in this segment of the education system – which is not usually considered to be particularly prominent, from the economic and political perspectives. However, contrary to the practice of corporatist skill production regimes, the position of the CCCT remains highly precarious and subject to unilateral action from the central state aimed at curbing its role in the apprenticeship provision.

These factors result in a near-absence of meaningful social dialogue within governance arrangements for the system of skill formation in Croatia, both at the bipartite and tripartite levels.

## Policy transfer: Apprenticeship learning in VET

This case was selected primarily because the introduction of apprenticeship learning gives the entire Croatian system of skill formation a distinctively hybrid character. It is also worth looking at in more detail because the governance and implementation of apprenticeship learning established in Croatia functions quite differently to the institutional models of developed industrial democracies. Apprenticeships, as a form of intensive work-based instruction, were introduced in Croatia through legislative changes in 1993 and 1996. The former introduced the possibility of delivering skilled trades programmes through apprenticeships but left out many elements vital to its practical implementation. The latter represented an attempt to address these omissions. This initiative is an example of early Europeanization, as the apprenticeship system of the Federal State of Bavaria was used as a model and source of policy transfer. It was also an example of policy entrepreneurship by the CCTC which was the primary instigator of this scheme but also its primary beneficiary.

This initiative also created a parallelism within the VET system, with apprenticeship-based and school-based programmes for the same craft vocations running in parallel. Apprenticeships initially failed to expand in other sectors (e.g. VET training for industry) or solidify their position *vis-à-vis* the school-based variant of education for skilled trades (Figure 10.1, dotted area). Therefore, in 2003, the dual model was changed into the Joint model of education (in Croatian: *jedinstveni model obrazovanja*; JMO). This change was introduced through a series of changes at the curricular level, without larger legislative and institutional reforms. The JMO model was less ambitious in terms of workplace training but resulted in apprenticeships becoming more prevalent between 2004 and 2012.

Throughout the JMO programmes, there is balance in terms of instruction time allocated towards three main components (general education, professional theory, and the practical component) is similar. In a typical example, the still-active 2003 curriculum for the occupation of pedicurist, 77 per cent of the total instruction time is allocated to vocational content, combining 'professional theory' (17 per cent) and the practical component (60 per cent). The remaining 23 per cent is allocated to general education content. The education plan sets the ceiling for practical training delivered in schools, as well as for the minimum amount of workplace training. Apprentices should spend a minimum of 36 per cent of total instruction time with licensed businesses in their first year, increasing gradually to 48 per cent in the third/final year. The actual intensity of workplace learning is relatively low, in the context of similar programmes in other countries. In Austria, for instance, apprentices spend around 80 per cent of their instruction time in workplace/company training (BMA 2012, 5), whereas among their Croatian counterparts the minimum rarely exceeds 50 per cent, even in their final years of study.

The second key feature of apprenticeships within the JMO is remuneration. Because apprentices do not have the status of employee but are regarded as students and apprentices in their trade, only some provisions of labour legislation apply. Compensation is also set at a minimal 10 per cent of the average net wage in the Republic of Croatia for first-year students, 20 per cent for second-year students, and 25 per cent for third-year students (in 2019, 87.3, 174.6 and 218.3 EUR, respectively), although employers have the discretion to compensate apprentices more generously. These sums are paid in a net amount, without contributions for social insurance. A recent Council of Europe (2017, 5) report has established that Croatia is in breach of the European Social Charter on this issue, exposing the country to a collective complaint procedure. Moreover, research indicates that even this (relatively) low level of financial commitment is fully upheld by only a minority of employers (Cedefop 2019, 17; Herceg 2010, 26). However, there is increasing financial support for apprenticeship programmes from public sources. For example, more affluent local governments often provide stipends for students enrolling in occupations classified by the Croatian Employment Service as being in high demand. More recently, the central state has begun to offer grants disbursed via the ministry in charge of entrepreneurship, mostly funded through the European Social Fund (ESF). This includes student stipends and compensation of employer apprenticeship expenses for VET programmes that train students in skilled trades that are in high demand. Such schemes began about 2010, with HRK 2–5 million disbursed annually, escalated between 2015 and 2018 with annual disbursements of about €1.6–3.6 million, and boomed in 2019, with €10.5 million, about €200 monthly allocated to 4,165 pupils in skilled trades programmes (Ministarstvo gospodarstva, poduzetništva i obrta 2020). Following the CCE initiative, in 2018, another element was introduced to the 3-year VET track: experimental 'dual education' programmes. Overall instruction time has been reduced in the new dual model, compared to the JMO, at 3,845 versus 4,334 class contact hours on the basis of a full-time 3-year programme. Dual programmes are less focused on general educational content, compared to the JMO (784 versus 848 hours), with more emphasis being placed on vocational theory (921 versus 886 hours). Dual programmes contain more practical instruction at schools (513 versus 475 hours), but less workplace training (1,627 versus 2,125 hours) (HOK 2019). Contrary to the abovementioned legal provisions on remuneration, the dual model allows for remuneration to be determined at company level. The pilot started with four programmes, 10 schools, and 147 pupils. In two years, by 2020/1, the dual model expanded modestly to nine programmes, 25 schools, and 451 pupils (cf. JMO crafts: 39 programmes, 100 schools, 4,120 pupils). All but one of the newly introduced dual programmes were already delivered as JMO programmes with apprenticeships.

The number of pupils entering work-based training arrangements (Figure 10.1, dotted area) has been subject to great variation – accounting for about 3–5,000 placements (up to 10 per cent of the total cohort) in 1998–2002, then increasing to about 10–12 thousand in 2004–2010 (about a fifth of the cohort). Apprenticeships declined sharply from 2012 and were down to under 3,000 in 2015. Since then, there has been a slight recovery rising to 4,571 in 2020. All apprenticeship arrangements are affected within the rapidly contracting 3-year VET track, which currently stands at about nine thousand entrants. Apprenticeships now comprise about half of all placements in this track, while all other pupils attend school-based VET programmes, as do all 4-year technical VET pupils.

The key features of the apprenticeship model and its implementation in Croatia can be summarised thus:

- it is limited to a relatively narrow sector of economy (trades and crafts);
- it was negatively impacted by demographic decline;
- there is a prominent role of the CCTC in delivery and administration, but with a status that is vulnerable to abrupt political intervention by the central state;
- there is a relatively low intensity of workplace learning, compared to similar programmes in developed industrial democracies;
- there is weaknesses in monitoring and rule enforcement, as evidenced by the case of sub-standard financial compensation for apprentices, with the bulk of employers apparently unwilling to pay even such low amounts;
- it can be characterised as an educational dead-end, with links towards HE largely disrupted and limited opportunities in the field of continuing VET.

Deeper understanding of these outcomes, particularly in terms of their causality, is necessary and requires additional empirical research. Below, we outline several explanatory tracks that could provide the foundation for such research.

The first explanation relates to the central state, which avoids expanding apprenticeship into other fields of education/economy because it is potentially a very demanding and politically risky reform. This interpretation would see maintaining the current *status quo* as a way of satisfying the basic needs of the most prominent apprenticeship advocate in Croatia (namely, the CTCC), while delegating some accountability for unfavourable outcomes to it. In this context, it will be interesting to observe whether the recent resurgence of interest within the CCE could lead to a more coherent push from employers' side. However, initial evidence (Cedefop 2019, 81) indicates that the two chambers have thus far not coordinated their positions – with the CCE being interested in establishing its own apprenticeship system, under the 'dual education' trademark, and the CTCC being primarily interested in protecting the JMO.

The second set of factors relates to the transformation of the economic structure – characterised by industrial decline (Table 10.1) and the prolonged recession (2009–2014). This decimated the number of sole proprietors and radically limited many firms' capacity to retain such a demanding and relatively expensive learning scheme as apprenticeships (Matković et al. 2013). Persistently high unemployment also weakened trade unions in the private sector – while the relatively low mobility of the workforce (prior to Croatia's accession to the EU) allowed firms to build their competitiveness based on the price of labour, rather than on investing in knowledge and innovation (Mršić 2018). It may thus not be surprising that both the central state's and the CCE's renewed interest in apprenticeships emerged only after the EU labour market was open to Croatian workers seeking employment. This resulted in significant workforce migration and, consequently, in shortages in some key economic sectors with widespread apprenticeship training, like tourism and construction. It remains to be seen whether these developments will incentivise key actors to adopt a more favourable view of apprenticeship in Croatia.

Europeanization can influence policy through other important channels, apart from the common market. The apprenticeship model is, in Croatia, associated with the tradition of German-speaking states that often served as institutional models. It is thus not surprising that apprenticeship was (re)introduced in Croatia based on the German/Bavarian model. These ties persist. For instance, many German-speaking companies doing business in Croatia provide direct funding for VET reforms, as does the Swiss-Croatian Cooperation Programme. Austrian institutions are also involved as partners in the 2016 Cap4App capacity building project, supporting the most recent introduction of the dual system. Yet other elements of Europeanization may have adverse effects on the development of apprenticeship in Croatia. Some authors (Powell & Trampusch 2012, 285–286) emphasise tensions between national qualification frameworks and the collectivist approach to skill formation, which is particularly prominent in the case of apprenticeships. This is primarily due to their focus on learning outcomes, rather than on the overall educational experience of 'becoming' a member of the occupational community through an intensive mentorship programme, which is fundamental in the case of apprenticeships.

Finally, the government's political orientation is likely to play a role, with centre-right/conservative parties being more open to apprenticeships than social democrats. It seems that the latter often perceive apprenticeships as overly skill-specific, which in the long run favours the interests of employers over those of workers (Busemeyer & Trampusch 2012, 26). The evidence from Croatia is consistent with this pattern, as apprenticeships were introduced and reinforced only during the rule of the centre-right Croatian Democratic Union (in Croatian: *Hrvatska demokratska zajednica*; HDZ). It was then scaled down and weakened, via the JMO framework, during the 2000–2003 coalition rule of the Social Democratic Party of Croatia (*Socijaldemokratska partija Hrvatske*; SDP). A robust expansion of JMO apprenticeship took place during another HDZ mandate (2004–2011). Yet the trend was then halted during the SDP tenure (2012–2015), as the 2013 legal changes stripped a number of powers in the delivery and administration of skilled trades programmes from the CTCC in favour of central state agencies. During the HDZ's most recent period in government (since 2016), most powers have been reinstated to the CTCC by legislative changes of 2019. The number of apprenticeships ticked up and investment intensified, a considerable part of this coming from the European Social Fund.

## Policy transfer: The Croatian Qualifications Framework

In the mid-2000s, the process of developing the European Qualification Framework gained much traction in the Croatian education policy sphere, just as Europeanization had gathered momentum. This case was selected due to its transformative potential for the functioning of the entire system of skill formation in terms of stakeholder involvement, the balance of power between stakeholders, and possible changes to curricular design, validation and instruction.

The process of adoption of the Croatian Qualification Framework (hereafter CROQF) was initiated in 2006, by a Minister-led committee producing the CROQF founding principles, which were adopted by the Government in 2007.

Those steps preceded adoption of the EQF recommendation in 2008. An operative support team was established in 2008, which engaged about 5,000 people with presentations and consultations (Beljo Lučić et al. 2009). The process has introduced a competence framework into the national education discourse, while reinforcing notions of learning outcomes and European learning credit mechanisms. Yet the early focus of the process was mostly directed towards defining the levels of learning outcomes and allocating existing education programmes accordingly.

Originally planned to be implemented in 2010, the process survived several changes of ministers, election cycles, and a change of government. The Croatian Qualifications Framework Act was eventually adopted in 2013. The Act was made operational with a bylaw on the register of the Croatian Qualification Framework in 2014 – which defined 25 sectors and sectoral councils as instrumental in managing the CROQF, as well as the sub-registers of (a) occupational standards, (b) qualification standards, and (c) learning outcomes.

Sectoral councils were originally established by the 2009 VET reform, which essentially introduced the instruments of qualification framework, national macro-coordination and educational profiles based on labour market needs. With some changes, the Act on CROQF extended these instruments to the entire education system. The first sectoral councils were established in November 2014. Yet the majority were founded only in July 2017, after repeated calls, and the final three came as late as February 2018. The CROQF register itself went online in 2016. The first occupational standard was adopted in September 2017 and the first qualification standard in January 2020. As of September 2020, 35 occupational standards and 8 qualification standards (with 329 learning outcome sets) had been adopted (SRCE 2020). Considerable bottlenecks were evident within the process by the end of 2020, with over 350 pending submissions. As sectoral councils themselves were evidently failing to fulfil their competence of reviewing proposals and issuing recommendations for individual standards, the recent amendments of Act on CROQF (February 2021) were set to address the situation by transferring this task to independent commissions set up by ministry in charge of labour (occupational standards) and educational agencies (learning outcomes and qualification standards): AVETAE (VET and Adult Education), ASHE (tertiary education) and the Teacher Training Agency (general education). Sectoral councils retained the strategic role of providing recommendations on sectoral development to the ministries involved. At the time of writing, it is still too early to assess the effectiveness of this shakeup, but the new qualification standards, and the learning outcomes they are designed to deliver, are meant to be the main reference points for corresponding educational programmes, which should consequently undergo adequate revisions.

This is stressed at the strategic level, as CROQF figures prominently within the Strategy for Science, Education and Technology (Hrvatski sabor 2014). It is stressed in the preamble and is then highlighted in the context of the recognition of informal learning (lifelong learning, 3); curricular reform (pre-tertiary education, 2); assessment of learning outcomes (pre-tertiary, 8.6); as a tool for the adaptation of the content of HEI programmes with clearly defined learning outcomes (tertiary, 1.2); and the internationalisation and European integration of HE (tertiary, 7). CROQF has, additionally, featured heavily in every National Reform Programme (NRP) that the Government of Croatia has submitted – between the country's EU accession in 2013 and 2020 – with 7–47 mentions per year. Within the NRPs, the CROQF and its standards have been consistently touted as key instruments for aligning Croatia's education system with its labour market needs, at all levels of education.

While its name is suggestive of national ownership, the CROQF has been strongly linked with the European level initiatives since its inception. It has drawn support from the European Training Foundation and Instrument for pre-accession assistance. Since accession, the development of CROQF was supported by a total of nine ESF operations, initiated in the 2013–2019 period (Ministarstvo znanosti i obrazovanja 2020) for a total of HRK272 million (€36.8 million), or about 7 per cent of total ESF education investments. The ESF operations provided support to the implementation of the CROQF – such as in the development and management of sectoral councils, registers, survey methodology, and labour market tools. There were also four open calls for education system stakeholders to develop standards and programmes. These resulted in a total of 97 projects worth HRK231 million, which have included several hundred partners and education programmes over the decade. One of the calls was used by the ministry in charge of labour, for the definition of 200 occupational standards. A separate HRK234 million VET modernisation project, led by the AVETAE, aims to develop 108 occupational and 195 qualification standards by 2022.

There is little evidence that the CROQF is regarded as a threat by any stakeholder. This is somewhat unexpected because chambers and employers' association(s) in some more collectively oriented skill production regimes have perceived qualification frameworks as mechanisms that diminish their own role in skill formation (Powell & Trampusch 2012). Furthermore, trade unions – especially those with significant private sector worker membership, organized around the Union of Autonomous Trade Unions of Croatia – saw CROQF as an opportunity to establish a more fruitful cooperation with employers and the state, compared to the processes of traditional social dialogue (Buković 2022). Such support for the CROQF, shown by key non-state actors, is indicative of their attitude towards the existing policy coordination mechanisms. In the context of the CCTC, it could also represent a pragmatic acceptance of necessary change which could nevertheless be made compatible with existing organizational interests.

Furthermore, some actors are clear winners of the 'CROQF reshuffle'. The ministry in charge of labour is one such 'winner', as it established itself as a key stakeholder in the skill production process through its coordinating role in developing occupational standards and its control of the EU funding underpinning the reform process. Similarly, the state agency in charge of VET (AVETAE) strengthened its role – not just as administrator of the EU funding propelling the CROQF reforms, but also as a driving force of its implementation in the VET domain. Yet despite this, it does not seem that the introduction of CROQF has diminished the position of the ministry in charge of education, as this ministry retained *de facto* veto actor position, while becoming significant beneficiary of EU funding pertaining to CROQF.

Finally, it is interesting to regard the policy re-framing of the CROQF as a key instrument of 'aligning education with the labour market needs' in the 2010s. This discourse has mostly replaced the initial focus on defining learning outcomes, their levels, and positioning of educational programmes within the qualification framework. The period over which the CROQF was taking shape in Croatia was defined by protracted economic crises and high rates of unemployment. Croatian policymakers were immersed in a frenetic search for mechanisms to alleviate this problem, with the idea of supply-side intervention gaining traction. This was similar to the paradigm promoted at the time by the European Commission within the 2010 *Agenda for New Skills and Jobs*. The finalisation of the CROQF occurred against the backdrop of Croatia's accession to the EU in 2013, which also marked the high point of European influence on national policymaking. Within this context, (re)aligning the CROQF with EU- policy priorities provided an acceptable roadmap and allowed for substantial funds to be drawn down from EU sources.

## Conclusions

The analysis in this chapter validates our basic assumption that *Europeanization mattered* with respect to the development of the Croatian system of skill formation. However, it suggests a highly specific type of impact, as Europeanization seems to function as a sort of 'great accelerator': It pushed national policymakers to respond to policy initiatives coming from the EU level, 'playing catch-up' with more developed member states, whilst also providing a selection of 'oven ready' institutional solutions, often coupled with considerable funding to facilitate their implementation.

However, it would be wrong to assume that this has led to significant structural changes in Croatia's skill production regime. In the terminology of historical institutionalism, the dominant mechanism of institutional change, from Croatian independence onwards, was the layering, rather than displacement, of existing arrangements (Fioretos et al. 2016, 8–13). The analysis of both cases in this chapter – the development of apprenticeships and the introduction of CROQF – indicates that, despite their ambition, they did little more than create additional institutional layers over what is still a predominately statist regime. In the case of apprenticeships, they remain constrained to a sort of 'corporatist oasis' of training for skilled trades occupations – failing to expand into other educational tracks, while remaining precariously sensitive to the central state's unilateralism (making it resemble outsourcing, more than fully-fledged corporatism). In the case of the CROQF, it has thus far done little to 'align education to the labour market needs' – and, while not necessarily representing a zero-sum game, it most certainly has not weakened the central state vis-a-vis other actors.

There are at least three overlapping lines of argument that may be helpful in interpreting such outcomes. *The first* is the classic path dependence argument, with the institutional state-building setup of the early 1990s proving difficult to disrupt in the later phases of development. The economic and political transition, having taken place under conditions of war, created a lasting framework with a powerful central state that can always function as a 'veto actor.' Yet, compared to the statist regimes of developed industrial democracies like Sweden or France, the Croatian state acts as a successful policy instigator and implementer less frequently. *The second* line of argument is that non-state actors – particularly employers' associations – generally lack the interest, ambition, and capacity to assume a greater role in skill formation and thus to challenge central state dominance. The absence of functioning mechanisms of social dialogue presents an additional difficulty. *Third*, there are several structural elements that must be taken into consideration when analysing the development of the Croatian skill production regime. Throughout the 1990–2015 period, Croatian employers enjoyed an abundance of qualified labour, this being particularly the case in the context of industrial decline and the rise of unskilled and semi-skilled roles within personal and distributive services revolving around tourism. In this context, it is not surprising that the focus was primarily on cost reduction rather than on innovation and the development of human capital. Demographic change has had little impact on this situation, because the decreasing number of young people enrolling in 3-year VET programmes was offset by immigration from neighbouring countries (Bosnia and Herzegovina, in particular).

All these factors have created a dynamic of 'constant change that changes precious little'. Yet two important developments are now evident, which have some potential to disrupt the *status quo*. First, labour market shortages – which have impacted numerous sectors of the economy – seem to have changed the climate within a segment of the employer community, in terms of their willingness to take a more active role in skill formation. As a corollary, the CCE's interest in developing and deploying infrastructure to support workplace training in the initial VET may be a game changer. Yet the recent rise in unemployment, due to the COVID-19-induced recession in 2020, may tempt many Croatian businesses to proceed with business as usual – pushing for (further) flexibilization of the labour code and tax exemptions, rather than more demanding reforms such as the development of a joint infrastructure to deliver skill formation. Second, it remains to be seen whether substantial sums invested via EU funding (both in CROQF and in VET) will have a substantive impact on the workings of the skill production regime. In theory, it could improve the quality of the initial VET teaching through equipment modernisation; incentivise a further expansion of workplace learning; and support the development of standards and curricula. Finally, the effects of the recent amendments of the Act on CROQF should be monitored and assessed. They are likely to be successful in resolving the institutional gridlock and improving the average time needed for approving new occupational and/or qualification standards. However, they will probably further consolidate the statist nature of the Croatian skill-production regime, raising broader questions over strategic directions within this policy domain.

## References

Babić, Z., Matković, T., & Šošić, V. (2007). 'Structural Changes in Tertiary Education and Impacts on the Labor Market', *Croatian Economic Survey*, 9, 125–165.

Baćević, J. (2016). 'Education, conflict and class reproduction in socialist Yugoslavia'. In R. Archer, I. Duda & P. Stubbs (eds.), *Social Inequalities and Discontent in Yugoslav Socialism*, pp. 89–106. London: Routledge.

Bagić, D. (2010). *Industrijski odnosi u Hrvatskoj – društvena integracija ili društveni sukob [Industrial relations in Croatia – social integration or social conflict]*. Zagreb: Tim press.

Bagić, D. (2013). 'Neproduktivna ravnoteža moći: Zašto nema kompromisa „socijalnih partnera“ u Hrvatskoj i zašto je malo vjerojatno da će ga uskoro biti [Unproductive balance of power: Why there is no compromise between the "social partners" in Croatia and why it is unlikely to be soon]'. In N. Pološki Vokić & A. Obadić (eds.), *Zbornik radova okrugloga stola 'Uloga sindikata u suvremenome društvu'*, pp. 15–35. Zagreb: Ekonomski fakultet Sveučilišta u Zagrebu.

Beljo Lučić, R., Buntić Rogić, A., Dubravac Šigir, M., Dželalija, M., Hitrec, S., Kovačević, S., Krešo, M., Lekić, M., Mrnjaus, K., Rašan Križanac, M., Štajduhar, M., & Tatalović, M. (2009). *Hrvatski kvalifikacijski okvir-uvod u kvalifikacije [Croatian Qualifications Framework – Introduction to Qualifications.* Zagreb: Vlada Republike Hrvatske i Ministarstvo znanosti, obrazovanja i športa.

BMA (2012). *Apprenticeship: Dual Vocational Education and Training in Austria. Modern Training with a Future.* Wien: Federal Ministry of Economy, Family and Youth.

Botrić, V. (2017). *Studija o stručnoj praksi u visokom obrazovanju [Study on professional practice in higher education].* Zagreb: Ministarstvo znanosti i obrazovanja.

Buković, N. (2019). 'Razvoj institucionalnog ustroja hrvatske politike strukovnog obrazovanja [Development of the institutional structure of Croatian vocational education policy]'. *Političke perspektive : časopis za istraživanje politike*, 9 (2), 99–122.

Buković, N. (2022). 'Institucionalni ustroj i formulacija politike srednjeg strukovnog obrazovanja u Hrvatskoj: Preliminarna analiza [Institutional structure and policy formulation of secondary vocational education in Croatia: Preliminary analysis]'. *Suvremene Teme: Međunarodni Časopis Za Društvene i Humanističke Znanosti* (forthcoming).

Buković, N., & Matković, T. (2018). *Cedefop opinion survey on vocational education and training in Europe: Croatia.* Thessaloniki: Cedefop ReferNet Thematic Perspectives Series.

Busemeyer, R. M., & Trampusch, C. (2012). 'The comparative political economy of collective skill formation'. In R. M. Busemeyer & C. Trampusch (eds.), *The Political Economy of Collective Skill Formation,* pp. 3–40. Oxford: Oxford University Press.

Cedefop (2019). *Apprenticeship Review: Croatia. Improving Apprenticeships through Stronger Support and Care.* Thematic Country Reviews. Luxembourg: Publications Office of the European Union.

Christiaensen, L., Ferre, C., Rubil, I., Matković, T., & Sharafudheen, T. (2019). *Jobs Challenges in Slavonia, Croatia – A Subnational Labor Market Assessment.* Jobs Working Paper 35. Washington, DC: World Bank.

Council of Europe. (2017). *Croatia and the European Social Charter.* Council of Europe.

Đorđević, M. (2017). *Izvješće o istraživanju aktualnog stanja i izazova u pogledu djelovanja centara karijera i profesionalnog usmjeravanja na visokim učilištima [Report on the research of the current situation and challenges regarding the operation of career centers and vocational guidance at higher education institutions].* Zagreb: Agencija za znanost i visoko obrazovanje.

Fioretos, O., Falleti, T. G., & Sheingate, A. (2016). 'Historical institutionalism in political science'. In O. Fioretos, T. G. Falleti & A. Sheingate (eds.), *The Oxford Handbook of Historical Institutionalism,* Vol. 1, pp. 3–30. Oxford: Oxford University Press.

Herceg, I. (2010). *Survey on Appropriateness of VET for Craft Occupations Quality and Employability. Report.* Torino: European Training Foundation and Hrvatska obrtnička komora.

HOK (2019). *Dualni model obrazovanja vs. Jedinstveni model obrazovanja [Dual model of education vs. unified model of education].* Working document. Zagreb: Hrvatska obrtnička komora.

Hrvatski sabor (2014). *Strategija znanosti, obrazovanja i tehnologije [Strategy of knowledge, education and technologies].* Narodne novine, 124/2014.

Matković, T. (2009). 'Pregled statističkih pokazatelja participacije, prolaznosti i režima plaćanja studija u Republici Hrvatskoj 1991.-2007. [Overview of statistical indicators of participation, pass rates and payment regimes in the Republic of Croatia 1991–2007]' *Revija Za Socijalnu Politiku,* 16 (2), 239–250.

Matković, T. (2011). 'Screens and credentials: Education and labor market entry in Croatia in the early 2000s'. In I. Kogan, C. Noelke, & M. Gebel (eds.), *Making the Transition: Education and Labor Market Entry in Central and Eastern Europe,* pp. 110–140. Stanford, CA: Stanford University Press.

Matković, T. (2020). 'Trendovi tržišta rada i javni sektor: Ponuda i potražnja radne snage u desetljetnoj perspektivi [Labor Market Trends and the Public Sector: Labor Supply and Demand in a Decade Perspective]'. In M. Kroflin (ed.), *Projekcije podudarnosti dostupne radne snage i potreba tržišta rada do 2030. Godine. Izazovi demografskih promjena i četvrte industrijske revolucije,* pp. 12–39. Zagreb: Matica hrvatskih sindikata.

Matković, T., Lukić, N., Buković, N., & Doolan, K. (2013). *Croatia — Destination Uncertain? Trends, Perspectives and Challenges in Strengthening Vocational*

*Education for Social Inclusion and Social Cohesion*. Torino: European Training Foundation.

Meng, C., Wessling, K., Mühleck, K., & Unger, M. (2020). *Eurograduate Pilot Survey: Design and Implementation of a Pilot European Graduate Survey*. Luxembourg: Publications Office of the European Union.

Ministarstvo gospodarstva, poduzetništva i obrta (2020). 'Poduzetnički impuls. Objava dodjeljenih sredstava [Entrepreneurial impulse. Publication of allocated funds]', *Dataset*, <http://poticaji.mingo.hr/objava.aspx>, accessed 2 October 2020.

Ministatstvo znanosti i obrazovanja (2020). 'O projektima [About projects]', *HKO Portal*, <http://www.kvalifikacije.hr/hr/projekti/o-projektima>, accessed 2 October 2020.

Mršić, A. (2018). *Procesi definiranja problema i prioriteta u stvaranju inovacijske politike u Hrvatskoj iz perspektive diskurzivnog institucionalizma [Processes of defining problems and priorities in creating innovation policy in Croatia from the perspective of discursive institutionalism]*. PhD disertation. Zagreb: Sveučilište u Zagrebu, Fakultet političkih znanosti.

Petrušić, I. (2017). *Analysis of the Five-year Cycle of Re-accreditation of Higher Education Institutions*. Zagreb: Agencija za znanost i visoko obrazovanje.

Poličnik, J., Sauli Miklavčič, A. L., Alupei-Durach, F., Nožica, Ž., Chrást, O., Voldánová, I., Karpíšek, M., Dinya, L., Medve, A., Wéber, G., Racsko, R., Perényi, P., & Camilleri, A. F. (2017). *Policy Challenges for Professional Higher Education in Central and South-Eastern Europe*. PROCSEE Consortium.

Powell, J. W., & Trampusch, C. (2012). 'Europeanization and the varying responses in collective skill regimes'. In R. M. Busemeyer & C. Trampusch (eds.), *The Political Economy of Collective Skill Formation*, pp. 284–313. Oxford: Oxford University Press.

Šabić, J. (2019). 'Populacijska perspektiva — Visokoškolski odabiri hrvatskih srednjoškolaca u razdoblju od 2010. Do 2017. godine [Population perspective - Higher education selections of Croatian high school students in the period from 2010 to 2017] '. In Z. Ristić Dedić & B. Jokić (eds.), *Što nakon srednje? Želje, planovi i stavovi hrvatskih srednjoškolaca [What after high school? Wishes, plans and attitudes of Croatian high school students]*, pp. 136–185. Zagreb: Agencija za znanost i visoko obrazovanje.

SRCE (2020). 'Standardi. Informacijski Sustav Hrvatskog Kvalifikacijskog Okvira [Standards. Croatian Qualifications Framework Information System]', <https://hko.srce.hr/registar/standardi>, accessed 2 October 2020.

Žiljak, T. (2013). 'Dvije faze obrazovne politike u Hrvatskoj nakon 1990. Godine [Two phases of education policy in Croatia after 1990]'. *Andragoški glasnik: glasilo Hrvatskog andragoškog društva*, 17 (1), 7–23.

Žiljak, T. (2018). 'Adult education in Croatia after 1990', *Andragoška spoznanja*, 24 (4), 53–68.

Žiljak, T., & Molnar, T. (2015). 'Croatian education policy in the EU context'. In Z. Petak (ed.), *EU Public Policies Seen from a National Perspective: Slovenia and Croatia in the European Union*, pp. 279–297. Ljubljana: Faculty of Social Sciences.

Ralitsa Simeonova-Ganeva, Kaloyan Ganev and Radostina Angelova

# 11. Bulgaria: skill imbalances and policy responses

**Abstract:** The chapter explores the skill-formation processes in Bulgaria over four periods: two periods of the communist regime, the transition to market economy and EU integration. For all of them, it reviews the sizable human capital imbalances faced by governments and their policy responses for the long term. The issues inherited from central planning regarding the qualification of the labour force are identified. Their analysis focuses on the alternation of periods of large skill shortages and surpluses and their effects on economic dynamics. A major finding is that for a substantial part of the periods under scrutiny, skill formation policies have been incoherent with technological and sector-specific developments. It is substantiated by means of the observed recurrence of sizable skill supply and demand imbalances. We also present evidence that systematic and strategically focused policies were largely absent. We identify exceptions to this rule that concern only two periods. The first one spans from the late 1950s to the beginning of the 1970s. It is characterised with high intensity of measures primarily driven by economic (rather than political) considerations in response to the acute skill shortages in the economy. The second one covers the mid-2010s to the present. It is featured by similar labour market issues, though the political context is completely different. What we find different for this second period is that the social dialogue was among the main drivers of decision-making. We arrive at the conclusion that policy responses in Bulgaria have not been influenced by the differences in the alternating political regimes but rather by the severity of economic issues. The findings help to better understand the long-term drivers of skill formation policies and outcomes. They also provide a basis for policies targeted at the mitigation of future skill imbalances.

**Keywords:** Bulgaria, EU integration, post-communist transition, skill demand and supply, skill mismatch, skill formation policies

## Introduction

This chapter presents an analytical exploration of skill-formation processes in Bulgaria over the last seven decades. Four periods are distinguished: two periods of the communist regime, the transition to markets and EU integration. By studying the historical developments, the issues inherited from central planning regarding the qualification of the labour force are identified. The perspective chosen is economic rather than political, however: it focuses on the alternation of periods of large skill shortages and surpluses, their effects on economic dynamics and policy responses. The analysis leads us to conclude that in a substantial part of the periods under scrutiny, skill formation policies were incoherent with technological and sector-specific developments. This finding is corroborated by the observed recurrence of sizable imbalances concerning skill supply and demand. The results help to better understand the long-term drivers of skill formation policies and outcomes. They could also serve as a basis for policies targeted at the mitigation of future skill imbalances.

It is particularly noteworthy that the policy responses to issues relating to skill formation were largely unrelated to the different political regimes in Bulgaria. In all four periods governments faced sizable imbalances concerning human capital availability, and so under both communism and democracy they had to assess objectively the economic circumstances and to design and implement adequate policy responses for the long term.

The first of the identified periods spanned the 1950s and the 1960s. After WW2, the communist governments were faced with a population characterised by extremely low levels of literacy and educational attainment. That meant a very low starting level of the human capital stock. The initial conditions concerning overall economic development were also unfavourable, despite the progress of the preceding decades. At the same time, governments were strongly determined to quickly build a solid industrial base. This objective was reflected in the first central plans, however the failure of this undeniably indicated that drastic changes in the quantity and qualification of the labour force were needed. The obvious solution that was pursued entailed the investment of enormous resources to form the required human capital. Impressive results in this respect were achieved over a relatively short period of time (about two decades), reflecting the low starting point.

The remarkable success in human capital accumulation engendered a degree of complacency stemming from obvious quantitative improvements. At the same time, this success entailed major quality issues, and policies had to be adjusted correspondingly. However, the economic decline of the Eastern Bloc that started in the 1970s resulted in tighter budget constraints and thus substantially limited the policy response options. Subsequent developments were therefore left almost entirely to the momentum of the past. Eventually, this caused Bulgaria to fall behind other CEE countries in the area of skill formation, a situation which persisted until the end of the regime.

It is assumed here that the period of transition covers the years 1990–2002. The end of transition to market economy is associated with the acknowledgement that Bulgaria is functioning market economy in European Commission's

2002 Regular Report on Bulgaria's Progress towards Accession (EC 2002). During the transition to a market economy, public opinion was dominated by the conventionally adopted and largely unchallenged view that highly skilled human capital was one of the achievements of the communist regime in Bulgaria (Blanchard 1997; Sachs 1999), yet there was little evidence to substantiate such a view (Simeonova-Ganeva 2012). Nevertheless, this argument was used to substantiate a claim that the available human capital presented a good starting point for economic restructuring and progress (Bojkov 1999). This partially explains why little concentrated effort was made to formulate and implement long-term strategies and policies targeted at skill formation. The inertia inherited from communism largely remained.

Effective EU integration is assumed to have started in 2003 as by the end of that year Bulgaria managed to close twenty-six out of thirty negotiation chapters. The economic expansion during the EU integration period and the associated rise in employment, alongside decreasing unemployment, was accompanied by a higher demand for skilled labour. Yet options for hiring qualified workers were constrained by the continuously shrinking supply of such labour due to the negative demographic trends. The situation was further aggravated by the considerable migration outflows evident from the beginning of transition. This process led to the manifestation of skills-related issues which were previously not obvious. As a result, the conventionally adopted view that the supply of human capital was sufficient, started to gradually change (Simeonova-Ganeva et al. 2015). The mismatch between demand and supply in relation to specific skills (especially in industry and construction) became one of the major topics in debates which intensified in the mid-2010s. This logically spurred the process of modernisation of the qualification system that was launched in the context of EU integration. Also, policy making gained a well-defined focus on addressing skill shortages, quality and long-term outcomes.

Section which follows, contains a critical review of policy responses to economic challenges related to skill availability under communism and democracy. Afterwards there are considered the evolution of social dialogue and development of the modern qualification system. After that, there is discussed human capital dynamics in the period under review and summarised the available evidence on the impact of skill formation on economic developments in Bulgaria. The chapter concludes with an outline of several likely scenarios concerning future labour market developments and the challenges associated with skill formation policies.

## Skill formation and institutions: Central planning vs. markets

### Skill shortages after WW2 and the policy response

After WW2, the qualification level of the labour force in Bulgaria was comparable to neighbouring Balkan states but considerably worse than in other CEE countries. According to 1946 census data, 23.4 per cent of the Bulgarian population was illiterate. This cohort was concentrated in the rural parts of the country, working mainly in low-tech, low-productivity subsistence farming. The working-age population was largely inactive in the labour markets and the number of employees was very low. In 1948, for example, their share equalled about 14.5 per cent (own estimate based on CSO yearbook data (CSO 1948-1990). The labour market was characterised by low levels of female participation. The situation concerning the quantity and quality of labour was further aggravated by the fact that the share of highly educated population decreased by about one half after the war due to the persecution of intellectuals by the communist authorities (in 1944, intellectuals represented 2.09 per cent of the population which was also low). Yet, at the same time, the stated government goals of industrialisation and high productivity required not only a literate but also a well-qualified workforce. In such a context, the high levels of illiteracy presented major obstacles to the realisation of socialist plans. Therefore, policies and measures were required to address this quickly.

As deep-rooted behavioural patterns could not be easily altered in the short run by mere propaganda, in the years following WW2, government policies for human capital formation had to rely mainly on coercive measures. In order to reduce illiteracy and inactivity, all unemployed and/or uneducated people were forced to participate in literacy training and to become economically active. A Law on the Liquidation of Illiteracy was submitted to Parliament in 1950 to oblige the illiterate persons to enrol in free literacy courses. In addition, it imposed a sentence of a year in prison for persons who refused to attend or created barriers that prevented illiterate people attending. After 1945, similar measures for the liquidation of illiteracy were taken by many communist countries like the USSR, Poland, Romania, Albania and Vietnam (Ministry of Education 1952). To address the extremely low number of higher education students and graduates especially in engineering and related sciences, the government issued numerous decrees to establish new higher educational institutions in the large cities, with a pronounced focus on technical education. In that period, there were fewer than 700 qualified engineers in the country and most of them had graduated abroad (mainly in Germany and Czechoslovakia). The first Higher

Technical School in Bulgaria opened in 1942. The number of students enrolled increased enormously and this raised significant issues in relation to education quality (Marcheva 2016). Nevertheless, due to the very low starting point and despite quality issues, the strategy of increasing the number of people with technical skills had a positive impact on economic development.

At the end of the 1950s, the rates of industrial development accelerated, supported by the labour force inflow from agriculture to industry (Berov 1994). However, quantitative improvements resulting from the initial policy response had already reached the limit of their potential. The continuation of economic growth at high rates required still higher human capital inputs. At the beginning of the 1960s, the State Planning Committee reported that the shortage of skilled workers had been the most important reason for the failure to fulfil the economic plans in many key industries: there were around 65,000 jobs, particularly in construction, agriculture and some manufacturing activities which remained unfilled due to the lack of skilled labour. (Council of Ministers 1960d). Another problem that impeded the planning process and the implementation of the central plans was labour mobility which resulted in the abandonment of many agricultural units followed by drops in yields and revenues in the sector. The free movement of the labour force, the free choice of workers to work or not, the 'headhunting' (although the term was not used at the time, almost every management team had effectively recruit skilled labour in order to fulfil their plan; the political pressure to fulfil plans was high enough to motivate headhunting, and intensive searches across the entire country) by managers to recruit skilled workers were all issues before central planning. Furthermore, the size of the economically active population was still relatively small.

The quick solutions that emerged were to train and activate women and young people who were not in employment, education, or training. The government implemented two major complementary policies: one imposing restrictions on the functioning of labour markets and labour movement and another focused on vocational training and education. In the area of labour markets, an information system involving regular and detailed compilation of labour balance sheets was developed and used in policy making (this practice was abolished after the end of socialism and most of the compiled balance sheets were lost). Central and regional bureaus were assigned the task of controlled recruitment and allocation of the labour force on the basis of central economic plans. In the area of Vocational Education and Training (VET), the institutional framework was substantially advanced as follows (Council of Ministers 1960a, 1960b, 1960c, 1960d, 1960e):

- Vocational schools were established and started operating in collaboration with enterprises. Study duration was from 1 to 3 years. Graduates acquired only worker qualification and not an educational degree. Later on, in 1964, these schools started being transformed into secondary vocational technical schools.
- Centralised labour allocation to industries was adopted: graduates from specialised and professional schools and institutions were supposed to start working in the role and industry they had been allocated to. This also meant guaranteed employability.
- Urgent training programs for qualified labour in the most demanded specialties were launched (mostly for skilled workers in construction, metal-working, etc.).
- Orders were issued to transfer men in good health performing light work to jobs implying harder labour and to replace them with women. Intensive training and recruitment of women in enterprises and organizations where female labour could be used were introduced.
- The Ministry of Education was ordered to give priority to female applicants for jobs implying light work conditions in specialised and professional secondary schools.
- An order for obligatory recruitment as workers or trainees of all inactive young people who were not in training and education was issued and implemented. Their employment was often preceded by non-formal training provided by enterprises.

In addition, vocational trainings of employees, including on-the-job trainings, were intensively implemented on a mass scale. In 1956–1975, such training covered from one fifth to one quarter of the employed population (own estimate based on CSO Yearbooks data (CSO 1948–1990); for a broader perspective on lifelong-learning developments, see Boyadjieva et al. 2013).

## The economic slowdown and its impact on skill formation in the late 1970s and in the 1980s

The late 1970s and the 1980s were marked by the economic slowdown and the growing external indebtedness in all Eastern Bloc countries including Bulgaria. Tighter budget constraints meant that the government could not afford large investments including those in the field of education.

Lower growth rates led to a situation where skill shortages turned into skill surpluses: the accumulated human capital started exceeding the demand for it. Government administration and enterprises, which were obliged to employ new graduates according to the central plans, did not have vacant positions for them in the late 1970s. For example, in 1977 the number of engineering and technical sciences graduates was 6,626, but 3,429 of them (52 per cent) could not be employed (Council of Ministers 1977). This led to the emergence of hidden unemployment: some employees had labour contracts but in fact had nothing or very little to do at work. The problem continued in the 1980s as official unemployment was not an option for authorities and this was their way to conceal it. Official information on the under-employment of qualified labour was not available. Nevertheless, the under-employment issue is revealed to some extent from 1986 sociological data. The shares that follow are calculated using the survey data from Institute of Sociology (BAS 1988): 91.5 per cent of the employed with tertiary education occupied positions related to their field of study; the respective share of vocational training school graduates was 67.5 per cent. These shares were much higher than the average concerning all in employment (44.6 per cent) but still suggested that vocational training was not congruent with the labour market at this time. A predominant part of secondary vocational training graduates was employed in industry (34.5 per cent), construction (8.1 per cent), trade (7.9 per cent) and agriculture (7.0 per cent). Those with tertiary education were mainly employed in industry (18.1 per cent), public services and administration (17.4 per cent), education (12.8 per cent) and science (9.5 per cent). Due to the low demand, at the end of the communist regime the share of students in secondary vocational education decreased to 13–14 per cent (almost 6 p.p. lower than in the early 1970s and similar to the early 1960s levels).

Still, the upskilling of the employees remained a government priority. The 'special qualification' (i.e. narrow specialisation related to a job) of an employee was considered highly important for labour productivity. Therefore, the share of employees included in vocational training constantly increased in the period 1975–1985. The share of employees who participated in on-the-job vocational training increased from 22.5 per cent in 1975 to 29.3 per cent in 1985. Despite the considerable coverage of training, in 1986 a quarter of employees had a low level of special qualification, half had a medium level, whilst a further quarter had a high level (own estimates based on CSO Yearbooks data). This signalled that the problem with labour productivity persisted. Also, it indicated that the issues could not be solved by training having the same scope and content as that already provided.

## The limited demand for skills during the transition period

At the beginning of transition, capital ownership in Bulgaria was almost entirely in the hands of the government. Most state-owned enterprises were however in a catastrophic condition. Due to the breakdown of Comecon (Council for Mutual Economic Assistance (CMEA), an economic organization of the Eastern bloc established in 1949 and led by the Soviet Union until its breakdown in the beginning of the 1990s), markets were lost, purchase orders diminished and/or became less secure and access to finance was largely absent. Many of these enterprises had to scale down operations, restructure and some were even forced to close with significant layoffs. The private sector was feeble and was therefore unable to offer alternative employment to redundant workers, who were also unable to seek work outside Bulgaria. This development resulted in considerable structural unemployment, especially of skilled labour and professionals (technicians, engineers, scientists, etc.) leading to a growing perception that vocational training did not provide a route to employability.

The financial distress of state-owned enterprises combined with the shrinking demand for vocational training triggered the dissociation of large production facilities and vocational schools and made vocational training even less relevant with respect to the labour market.

One explanation for such negative developments and the falling status of vocational qualifications is rooted in the view that the quality of education was high in communist times but deteriorated in transition (Bekhradnia 2005). Such an explanation is however only partially true. It is hard to deny that the turbulence of transition adversely affected some aspects of the quality of the education system, yet at the same time, it is necessary to recognize that the education system under the communist regime was far from perfect. On the contrary, the quality of training of specialists that it offered was insufficient and it had drastically lagged behind the scientific and technological developments in advanced economies in some respects. In addition to the overall technological underdevelopment of the country, other major factors that contributed to the lower quality of vocational education were the limited accesss of teachers, trainers, industry managers to contemporary knowledge and insufficient investments in vocational training infrastructure during the 1980s.

Because of this, the overall perception of vocational training was relatively unfavourable during the years of transition. Students and parents assessed the level of preparation in vocational schools as unsatisfactory and vocational school diplomas as not prestigious. Instead, they preferred foreign-language, mathematical, or other types of high schools, which they considered more relevant to

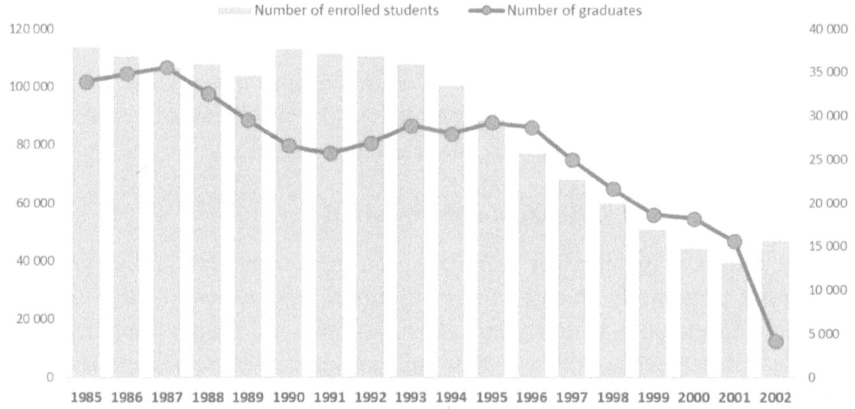


**Figure 11.1.** Secondary vocational education: enrolled students and graduates (right-hand scale). (Source: CSO and NSI statistical yearbooks.)

university level study. This is consistent with the change in attitudes and behaviour during transition in other CEE countries. Kogan et al. (2012), for example, discuss the issues of growing unpopularity of vocational schools, the irrelevance of their curricula in the new economic context, and the consequences of privatisation on school-industry collaboration amongst other issues.

As a result of the lower demand for vocational education, the number of secondary vocational schools dropped by almost two thirds, from 297 to 105 between 1980 and 2002 (NSI 2001; NSI 2019). A similar development was observed in relation to teachers: their number shrank from 9,400 to 2,900. Accordingly, the number of the enrolled students decreased from 149,700 to 47,000 and that of graduates fell from 48,000 to 4,100 (the calculations are based on CSO and NSI Yearbooks data; see also Figure 11.1). The contraction of vocational education commenced in the 1980s but it was largely contained by the specifics of the economic and political system at that time, however, liberalisation during the transition period accelerated this trend.

The high unemployment rates observed in the 1990s and in the beginning of the 2000s encouraged many young people to postpone their entrance to the labour market by enrolling as university students. This process was facilitated by institutional change such as the lifting of strict state controls which until 1989 limited student numbers and the range of specialisms that were available. Young people consequently had the opportunity to study for majors which were considered to offer good employment prospects and the potential to achieve high social status (such as law, management, finance, etc.). As a result, the share of young people with university degrees increased substantially, especially in social and humanitarian sciences. All this, combined with the lower importance of VET, led to specific skill shortages at a time when the economy had already experienced major restructuring and its growth rates started accelerating.

## EU integration and skill shortages revisited

As was the case in all other transition countries, democratisation and EU integration profoundly changed the institutional framework of the Bulgarian economy. Specifically, labour demand and supply and labour mobility were liberalised, and access to tertiary education was significantly improved. The transition to a market economy and EU integration should not, however, be deemed the sole determinants of the expansion of the tertiary education in Bulgaria. The latter is also in line with the globally observed processes transforming higher education systems from being elitist to becoming mass ones. These global changes affected considerably skill formation, employability and labour market outcomes in the country (Boyadjieva and Ilieva-Trichkova 2016). The process of EU accession considerably influenced labour market policies in Bulgaria. A comprehensive labour market information system was developed (including the information system of the Employment Agency, the labour market surveys of the NSI/Eurostat, the administrative data of the Ministry of Education and Science and the labour market forecasts produced by the Ministry of Labour and Social Policy). Many national and EU-funded programmes focused on improving the professional qualifications of the unemployed and the vocational training of adults. The collaboration between vocational schools and businesses was also re-established. Modern approaches to vocational training were introduced in secondary education, and the VET system was strengthened, in particular by the establishment and development of VET centres, which were few in number during the years of transition. Initially the VET centres were funded with the support from international programmes with 971 being active as of 2019, nevertheless, the combination of reforms could not compensate for the legacy of labour market mismatches of the preceding decades.

Skill mismatches turned out to be more acute in times of economic growth when the demand for labour considerably outpaced supply. In 2008, when the Bulgarian economy was still growing and the unemployment rate was 5.7 per cent (below the EU average according to Eurostat data), over 20 per cent of the employers reported that labour shortages presented obstacles to their activities (compared to an EU-28 average of less than 10 per cent). Most of the businesses

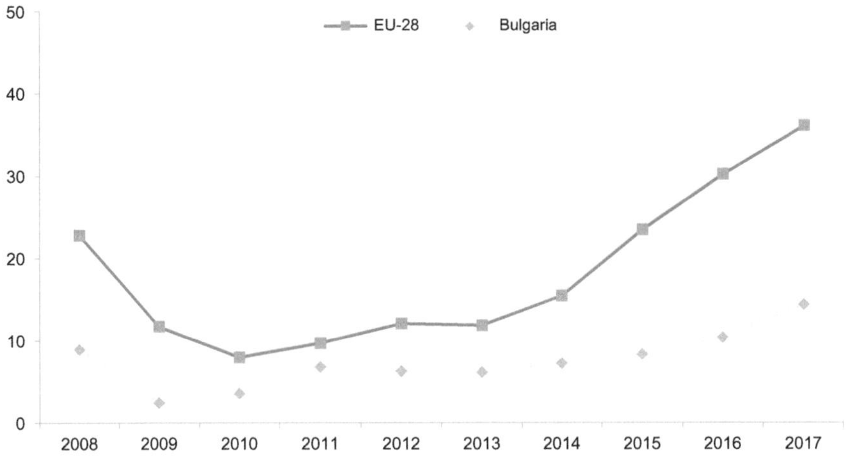


**Figure 11.2.** Comparison of shares of employers reporting labour shortages as an obstacle to their activities in Bulgaria and in EU-28 (per cent). (Source: NSI, Eurostat, own calculations.)

which experienced problems were in industry or construction and the shortages were mainly of skilled workers. After the start of the economic downturn in 2009 (in that year real GDP fell by 3.4 per cent on an annual basis according to Eurostat data), the unemployment rate increased, peaking in 2013 (13.0 per cent) and the labour shortages decreased (NSI 2019). In 2014, a period of positive development began and employment quickly started increasing. According to NSI LFS data between 2016 and 2019 the unemployment rate decreased rapidly amongst those aged fifteen and over, reaching its lowest value of 4.2 per cent in 2019. Labour shortages increased correspondingly, with approximately half of construction enterprises and every third industrial company experiencing this problem in 2019.

Labour shortages remain a persistent problem in Bulgaria, but despite this many enterprises in Bulgaria are still not committed to the development of their human resources to the same degree as enterprises in other EU Member States. For example, in 2018, the share of SMEs that had trained their employees was 42.2 per cent while the EU average share was 72.6 per cent (European Commission 2019).

There is an essential aspect of skill shortages which has been consistently observed in every phase of the business cycle of the Bulgarian economy. This results from long-standing issues related to the on-going pivot towards high-tech

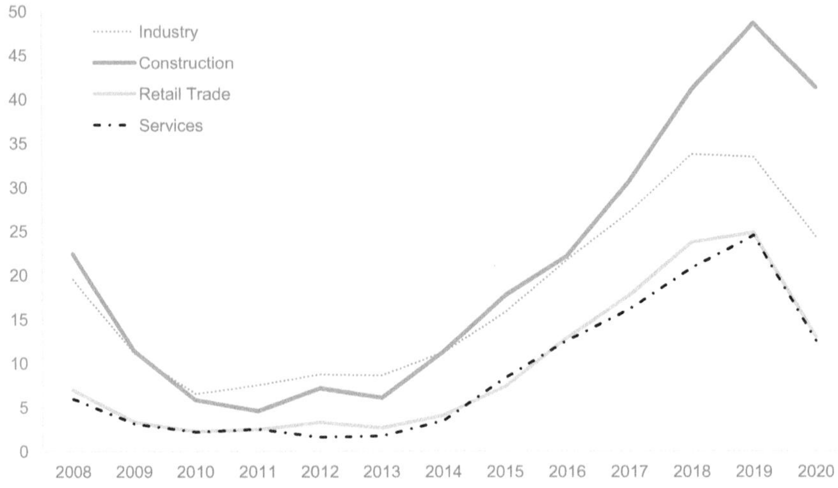


**Figure 11.3.** Share of employers in Bulgaria reporting labour shortages as an obstacle to their activities (by economic sector, per cent). (Source: NSI, Eurostat, own calculations.)

production, the existing gaps between the wages of qualified workers in Bulgaria and those in the other EU Member States and the fact that the Bulgarian workforce continues to lag behind those of other EU Member States in terms of key competences.

As a result, a considerable number of jobs requiring upper secondary education (in particular, vocational education) are taken by people with primary or tertiary education. For example, in 2018, when the employment totalled 2,900,000, there was a shortage of 185,300 workers with upper secondary education (NSI 2019). This resulted in the under-employment of around 32,900 university graduates who were appointed to the respective positions to fill in the gap. The businesses most affected by such developments were those concerned with the manufacture of textiles, apparel and shoes as well as hotels and restaurants. At present, substantial skill shortages are also associated with specific occupations requiring vocational training in transport, construction and manufacturing (sectors which are expected to account for 37.3 per cent of employment in 2024; Simeonova-Ganeva et al. 2019).

On the basis of this, an imbalance is clearly visible: the structure of the Bulgarian economy implies higher demand for professional workers, rather than for university graduates, which provides an explanation for the underemployment of university graduates. Other determinants of their employability include individual background and merits, as well as the quality of their qualification (Boyadjieva and Ilieva-Trichkova 2015). In this respect, another clearly identifiable structural issue is that the educational system still fails to provide tertiary education of constant high quality (Boyadjieva et al. 2020).

Overall, there are two challenges that policy makers face at present. Firstly; there is a need to further strengthen VET and to improve its image among parents and students. At present, most parents and students perceive secondary vocational education to be less prestigious and a bad career-related choice (PwC 2020). Secondly; there is a need to alleviate the issues stemming from the low quality of tertiary education. A solution to these issues is unlikely to be formulated by government alone, however, and the pro-active involvement of social partners is also critical.

## Social dialogue

The social dialogue started formally in 1992 with the establishment of the National Council for Tripartite Cooperation (NCTC). One of the legal rules that it pushed through required that regulatory amendments concerning labour and social issues are subject to consultation with the social partners (trade unions and employers' organisations). In the years of transition, some of the governments sought to limit the content and mechanisms of social dialogue and trade unions responded with strikes and protests. Social dialogue was normalised and became effective only with the approach of EU membership. Over the years, NCTC focused mainly on social insurance issues, minimum wages and taxation. Issues concerning skills and qualifications became one of its priorities only relatively recently.

At the sectoral and horizontal policy levels, there are also specialised councils (such as the Economic and Social Council, the National Economic Council, the National Employment Promotion Council, the National Working Conditions Council, the Smart Growth Council, etc.) and working groups. All of them, along with NCTC, are involved in the development of key strategic documents and legislation, in policymaking and in the allocation of national and EU funds.

With the EU accession of Bulgaria in 2007, the participation of social partners in skill formation policies deepened and became more effective, and their importance in decision-making processes regarding vocational guidance, training and education increased substantially. In particular, their formal representation in the Management Board of the National Agency for Vocational Education and Training ensured their direct involvement in the licensing activities in the system of vocational education and training. Their engagement in issues related to VET is however not limited to the latter but also includes participation in the respective advisory council at the Minister of Education and in the relevant sectoral councils. Responsibilities related to the formulation of labour market measures followed from their participation in the National Employment Council and the regional employment councils.

Through the years, the national skill formation policies had to consider both the business cycle and the labour market projections. Nevertheless, until 2015 governments could not efficiently implement long-term skill formation strategies. A change in the institutional approach to the problem was initiated in 2014, when long-term forecasts were added to the labour market information system, and a gradual improvement in the collaboration among relevant ministries (namely, the Ministry of Labour and Social Policy, the Ministry of Education and the Ministry of Economy) began. Long-term labour market forecasting in the country started in 2013–2014, when the Labour Market Forecasting Model for Bulgaria compliant with the international practice was developed. In 2018–2019, the model was updated and upgraded. Its current methodological framework consists of nine modules, able to generate forecasts for 120 occupations, thirty-five economic activities, twenty-eight provinces, three educational attainment levels and demographics. A simulation module allows for labour market modelling based on different scenarios for economic growth, investments, convergence rates and other criteria.

This process was further supported by improved social dialogue and more effective involvement of the social partners. Within a couple of years, the estimation of skill demand and supply enabled the social partners and the policy makers to identify the riskiest segments of the labour market and to formulate evidence-based measures to overcome the expected structural imbalances. As a result, the scope of the current skill-formation policy aimed at overcoming those imbalances is as follows:

- Medium-term measures to mobilise labour market reserves including training and support targeted at improving the employability skills of those unemployed and inactive.
- Long-term measures consisting of investments in higher education and VET narrowly tied to the redefinition of curricula, access rules, mechanisms of financing, etc. Presently, education and healthcare are priority areas.

## Modernising the qualifications system

At the onset of transition, the qualifications system in Bulgaria appeared unsophisticated and under-developed, and looked unfit to meet the needs of the market or future development. The key players (policymakers, educators, employers and trade unions) that were responsible for reform and modernisation were badly prepared for this task, since most of them were educated in that same system their careers were built in the context of a planned economy, and their knowledge and experience was difficult to adapt to the new circumstances. They also faced a large degree of uncertainty concerning the future and were to a great extent unaware of the nature of demand for and supply of skills in future years. In the 1990s, the first attempts to change the old system were made with the support of external institutions such as the World Bank. Most of the measures were confined to short-term, partial solutions only largely as a result of the high degree of political and economic instability in that decade.

The more intensive evolution of the current qualifications system in Bulgaria started in the years of EU integration, as a natural consequence of the evolution in the perceptions, views and values of the key players involved. Alongside a more general growth in the private sector, numerous private educational institutions, including VET centres and universities opened. Public administration underwent significant modernisation and educators gained access to contemporary knowledge and practices. The macroeconomic turbulence which characterised the past eased, and the new environment allowed for making longer-term plans for the future.

The process of EU integration boosted modernisation through the Bologna process and the commitment of governments to the implementation of the Lisbon Strategy, Europe 2020, and other policies.

In the domestic setting, the late 2000s and the 2010s the issues related to skill shortages were acknowledged by all key players and within society more broadly. The modernisation of the qualification system became an important item in the social dialogue agenda: specifically, the social partners demanded a closer linkage between the educational system and the labour market.

The development of the Bulgarian National Qualifications Framework (NQF) started in 2007 when the European Qualifications Framework (EQF) was put forward for consultations. Its formalisation was completed with its adoption in 2012.

The NQF is designed to ensure transparency of qualifications and thus allow their comparability and transferability both domestically and internationally facilitating the mobility of workers, students and educators. It additionally provides mechanisms to facilitate the process of validation of knowledge and skills acquired through formal, non-formal and informal education, and as such is also a tool to incentivise and promote lifelong learning.

One of the initial purposes of NQF was to align the national policies in the field of skill formation with the EU. On a broader scale, however, it also significantly contributed to the overall process of modernisation. Its focus on learning outcomes and the clear definition of the knowledge, skills and competencies that should be acquired at each level of qualification was highly beneficial in this respect. In particular, it forced all parties involved in the development of qualification programmes and curricula to align their practices with the requirements of the markets. In effect, this fostered improvements in the quality of education and training, and the direct involvement of employers in this process enabled the issue of skills shortages to be addressed.

Modernisation was strongly supported by the development of relevant information systems such as the NAVET database, the university rankings system and the various Ministry of Education and Science registers amongst other initiatives. The active use of those systems by the key players involved has contributed to the effective implementation of the NQF principles and standards and to the resolution of existing problems.

Despite the positive role of NQF, this was not a panacea for all the problems within Bulgaria's education and training system, since many issues remain unresolved. For instance, additional incentives need to be created so that higher participation in lifelong-learning activities is ensured. In 2019, the share of the population aged 25–64 which participated in training was 2.0 per cent compared to an EU-28 average of 11.3 per cent. With respect to continuing vocational trainings, in 2015 the share of participants was 26.5 per cent of all employed while the EU-28 average was 40.8 per cent.

Also, modernisation has been a necessary but not a sufficient condition for quality improvements. More work is needed in the area of VET to boost the efficiency of quality assurance systems, to finalise the restructuring of the State Educational Standards for VET qualifications and to improve the cooperation with employers and their organizations. In higher education, the reforms targeting quality improvements should be consolidated and their sustainability should be guaranteed for the long term. In this respect, proper budget financing incentives should be tied to educational outcomes. Also, the extension of public resources to higher education institutions should be aligned to macroeconomic and sector-specific policy objectives.

## Implications for economic growth and social development

An analysis of the entire period under review reveals that the reform of the education and training system in Bulgaria after WW2 was a slow and gradual process. Documents and data show that both the communist regime and the democratisation of the country contributed substantially to human capital accumulation.

In the period 1946–1985, significant changes occurred with respect to level of education within the population (Simeonova-Ganeva 2005). The share of the population with upper secondary and higher education increased almost seven times, mainly because of the considerable increase in the number of students in vocational education. This change is associated with increasing expenditures on education. For example, for the same period the number of schoolteachers doubled and were over 70.5 thousand in 1985–1986. This outcome is consistent with the results of the mass education processes that took place in CEE. It follows from the adoption of compulsory education rules and the ongoing institutional, political, cultural and economic processes (see Boli et al. 1985; West 2013). For example, the number of technicians with such training increased from 22,000 in 1953 to over 201,000 in 1974 (Michev 1978). Nevertheless, by the end of the communist regime, more than half of those aged sixteen years and over had not completed upper secondary education and almost a quarter had not completed primary education (Institute of Sociology 1988), the latter being particularly indicative of unfavourable conditions for skill formation to facilitate industrial development.

Substantial changes also took place in the years of transition. There was a significant increase in the number of those with tertiary and graduate level education, despite the number of young people within the population falling. At the same time, vocational training and education experienced slowdowns. Those processes were among the main causes of the labour imbalances observed in the 2010s.

Skill formation and deployment had positive impacts both for the individual and at macroeconomic level. Various studies of the net effects at the individual level confirm that skill formation expenditure led to an increase in employment of the vulnerable groups. (For a review, see Simeonova-Ganeva and Angelova 2018). During the socialist period, the policy response to skill shortages led to a considerable improvement of the qualification of the labour force through intensive training programmes and the strengthening of vocational education. The traditionally lower educational attainment of females was overcome and the wide inclusion of women in the labour market led to a significant reduction in gender inequality. Human capital investments boosted economic growth. During the

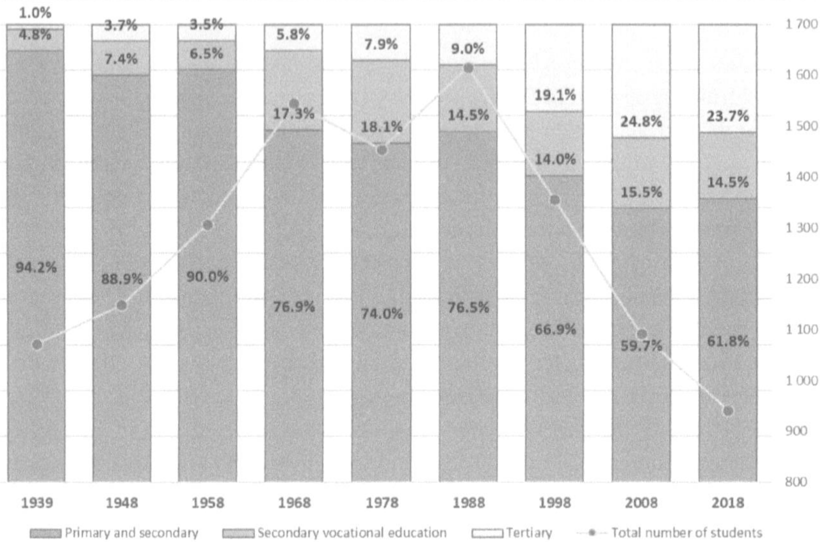


**Figure 11.4.** Total number of students (thousands, right-hand scale) and shares of tertiary (PhD level not included), primary and secondary (excl. VET) and secondary vocational education (per cent). (Source: CSO and NSI statistical yearbooks, own calculations.)

period 1950–1989, the increase in the number of vocational school graduates by 1 permille accelerated the growth of national income by 0.89 percentage points with a lag of two years (Simeonova-Ganeva 2006).

Estimates show that during the transition, each one-year increase of the educational attainment of the population led on average to a 3 per cent growth of total factor productivity (TFP). The decline in TFP, and, respectively the decline in output in the 1990s, can be largely explained by the slowdown in skill formation and education observed in the late 1970s and in the 1980s. In other words, the economic problems of transition can be also attributed to the human capital inherited from the communist regime. Empirical evidence for the period 1990–2005 shows that 80 per cent of the TFP growth was explained by the educational attainment in the preceding fifteen years (ibid.).

In the 2000s, macroeconomic dynamics were also positively affected by labour market interventions which were predominantly funded by national sources. The employment rate and the income levels of the most vulnerable groups increased. Policies contributed to maintain and develop the employability of the (long-term) unemployed. Indirectly, these measures served to increase the labour market participation rate and the social inclusion of vulnerable groups (Simeonova-Ganeva 2015), although the overall impact on GDP was low, if positive.

After accession, numerous skill-formation policies were implemented under the EU-funded programmes, most notably the Operational Programme Human Resources Development (OPHRD). The estimates calculated with the SIBILA model (Ganev et al. 2015) using data from the Council of Ministers and the Ministry of Finance show that the net effect of OPHRD on real GDP for the end of 2019 was 4.2 per cent. The total employment for the same year was evaluated to be by 8.3 per cent greater than in a scenario with no such skill formation spending; the unemployment rate was projected to be by 3.8 percentage points lower and the average gross wage 4.3 per cent higher. The social effect of vocational training and lifelong learning with respect to vulnerable groups in the labour market was equally important, especially its impact on young people (Ilieva-Trichkova and Boyadjieva 2018) and on reducing gender inequalities (Bieri et al. 2016).

## Future issues in skill development

This review of skill formation processes and related issues over the last seven decades points to the conclusion that systematic and strategically focused policies were largely absent. Only two periods were exceptions to this rule. The first lasted from the late 1950s to the beginning of the 1970s and the high intensity of measures and investments were primarily driven by economic rather than political considerations, and responded to acute skill shortages in the economy. The second commenced in the mid-2010s and, ironically, was determined by the same economic factors, despite the different political context.

As to the future; different scenarios for economic development produced using a simulation tool outlined in Simeonova-Ganeva et al. (2019) imply different issues related to skill formation and availability. But, irrespective of which scenario materializes, the structural shortage of specialists with vocational education will persist in the long term. The relative technological backwardness of the Bulgarian economy will continue determining the concentration of employment in sectors like manufacturing, wholesale and retail trade, construction, and others. Therefore, a key challenge for policy making is to train and qualify workers for those industries.

An undesirable but likely scenario is that technological advance in the country slows down and output growth decelerates significantly. Given such a development, the above-mentioned skill shortage is expected to intensify. Policy would then have to address a larger surplus of university graduates by including them in vocational training and providing them with opportunities to obtain well-remunerated employment in Bulgaria.

An alternative scenario assumes that selected key professions related to human capital accumulation and maintenance (e.g. medical staff, educators, etc.) will continue being underpaid compared to their counterparts abroad and to other professions in Bulgaria. Given the high degree of labour mobility within the EU, which is further facilitated by EQF, the outflow of such specialists is expected to continue, thus leading to even deeper skill shortages. To prevent this, policies should be designed and implemented so that adequate working conditions and attractive remuneration packages are guaranteed. Failure to do so will mean the failure of any strategy for skill formation in the country.

Policy discussions often attribute substantial weight to the development of high-tech and knowledge-intensive sectors. In a third scenario, where the relative share of those industries increases sizably, two major effects are expected. First, the skill shortages concerning workers with vocational training will persist. Second, skill shortages would also emerge with respect to university graduates in sectors like education, public administration, low-tech industries, etc. Hence, policies aimed at fostering the development of Industry 4.0 need to be supplemented by measures to secure skill formation and deployment in sectors other than the high-tech ones, too, to prevent unfavourable economic outcomes.

To successfully manage the risks that these different scenarios imply, social dialogue should take into account the lessons of the past, alongside possible future trajectories. This, combined with a clear set of strategic goals, would enable the identification, formulation and implementation of specific skills formation measures to become feasible, relevant and effective in the long term.

## References

Bekhradnia, B. (2005). A Review of the Higher Education in Bulgaria (prepared for the Ministry of Education and Science). Oxford: Higher Education Policy Institute.

Berov, L. (1994). Economic History: The World Economic Development from Antiquity to Modern Times. Sofia: Open Society Foundation.

Bieri, F., Imdorf, C., Stoilova, R. and P. Boyadjieva (2016). 'The Bulgarian Educational System and Gender Segregation in the Labour Market', European Societies, 18(2), 158–179.

Blanchard, O. (1997). The Economics of Post-Communist Transition. Oxford: Oxford University Press.

Bojkov, A. (1999). 'The Potential for Growth of the Bulgarian Economy'. In CED, Factors for Economic Growth in Bulgaria. Sofia: CED.

Boli, J., Ramirez, F., and Meyer, J. (1985). 'Explaining the Origins and Expansion of Mass Education', Comparative Education Review, 29(2), 145–170.

Boyadjieva, P., and Ilieva-Trichkova, P. (2015). 'Institutional Diversity and Graduate Employability: The Bulgarian Case'. In Pritchard, R. M. O., Klumpp, M., and Teichler, U. (eds.), Diversity and Excellence in Higher Education, pp. 153–171. Boston, MA: Brill Sense.

Boyadjieva, P., and Ilieva-Trichkova, P. (2016). 'Expansion of Higher Education and Graduate Employability Data and Insights from Central and Eastern Europe'. In Delteil, V., and Kirov, V. (eds.), Labour and Social Transformation in Central and Eastern Europe: Europeanization and Beyond, pp. 207–227. New York, NY: Routledge.

Boyadjieva, P., Milenkova, V., Gornev, G., Petkova, K., and Nenkova, D. (2013). 'The Lifelong Learning Hybrid: The Case of Bulgaria. In Saar, E., Ure, O. B., and Holford, J. (eds.), Lifelong Learning in Europe, pp. 304–326. Northampton, MA: Edward Elgar Publishing.

Boyadjieva, P., Ilieva-Trichkova, P., Milenkova, V., and Stoilova, R. (2020). 'The Local Embeddedness of Graduates' Education-Job Mismatch and of Lifelong Learning Policies for Its Overcoming', International Journal of Lifelong Education, 39(1), 104–118.

Council of Ministers (1960a). 'Decree №108: Further Improvement of the System of Planning of the Economy'. Sofia: CSA.

Council of Ministers (1960b). 'Decree №129: The Proper Recruitment and Allocation of the Labour Force for the Needs of the Economy'. Sofia: CSA.

Council of Ministers (1960c). 'Decree №151: Approval of New Wage Rates'. Sofia: CSA.

Council of Ministers (1960d). 'Decree №166: Surmounting the Shortage of Labour Force in Some Industries and Approval of a Regulation for Organized Recruitment and Allocation of the Labour Force'. Sofia: CSA.

Council of Ministers (1960e). 'Decree №174: Professional Training and Provision of Work for the Youth under 18 Who do not Continue Their Education'. Sofia: CSA.

Council of Ministers (1977). 'Report by the Labour Committee Concerning the Adoption of an Ordinance on the Terms and Conditions for the Allocation and Placement of Young Professionals, Graduates of Higher Education Institutions and Semi-higher Institutes'. Sofia: CSA.

CSO, Statistical Yearbooks of the People's Republic of Bulgaria, 1948-1990. Sofia: CSO.

European Commission (2002). 'Regular Report on Bulgaria's Progress towards EU Accession'. Brussels, 02.10.2002.

European Commission (2019). '2019 SBA Fact Sheet Bulgaria'. Brussels.

Ganev, K., Simeonova-Ganeva, R., Vasileva, I., and Vasilev, A. (2015). Methodology for Net Impact Assessment of European Funds on Economic Development (SIBILA 2.0: Methodological Framework and Technical Documentation). Sofia: ECORYS, Sigma Hat, Ministry of Finance.

Ilieva-Trichkova, P., and Boyadjieva, P. (2018). 'Educational Systems Matter: Differences Across European Countries in How Young People with Secondary Education Experience Job Insecurity', Journal of Education and Work, 31(7–8), 595–610.

Institute of Sociology, BAS (1988). An Empirical Sociological Survey: "The Town and the Village-86". Sofia: CSO.

Kogan, I., Gebel, M., and Noelke, C. (2012). 'Educational Systems and Inequalities in Educational Attainment in Central and Eastern European Countries', Studies of Transition States and Societies, 4 (1), 69–83.

Marcheva, I. (2016). The Policy for Economic Modernization in Bulgaria During the Cold War. Sofia: Letera.

Michev, N. (1978). Population in Bulgaria (Economic-Geographic Study). Sofia: BAS, Institute of Geography.

Ministry of Education (1952). 'Report and Draft Law on the Liquidation of Illiteracy'. Sofia: CSA.

NSI (2001). Statistical Yearbook. Sofia: NSI, National Satistical Institute.

NSI (2019). Statistical Yearbook 2018. Sofia: NSI, National Statistical Institute, < https://nsi.bg/sites/default/files/files/publications/God2018.pdf>, accessed 21 January 2021.

NSI, Statistical Yearbooks of the Republic of Bulgaria, 1992–2018. Sofia: NSI.

PwC (2020). Analysis of the SMEs in Bulgaria, Report for the Purposes of the National Strategy for Small and Medium-Sized Enterprises 2021–2027. Sofia: PwC, commissioned by DG REFORM, and the Ministry of Economy of the Republic of Bulgaria.

Sachs, J. (1999). Economic Growth – Models and Approaches. CED, Factors for Economic Growth in Bulgaria. Sofia: CED.

Simeonova-Ganeva, R. (2006). The Impact of Human Capital on Economic Growth (Bulgaria, 1949–2005). PhD Thesis. Sofia: FEBA, Sofia University St. Kliment Ohridski.

Simeonova-Ganeva, R., and Angelova, R. (2018). 'The Impact Assessment of Active Labour Policy at Individual Level in Bulgaria: Review of Completed Evaluations and Lessons Learnt', Vocational Education Journal, 20(4), 368–384.

Simeonova-Ganeva, R., Vassilev, A., Ganev, K., and Dimitrov, L. (2019). Medium-Term and Long-Term Forecasts for the Development of the Labour Market in Bulgaria: Factors of Labour Demand, Employment Trends, Regional and Educational Imbalances (2008–2032). Sofia: Ministry of Labour and Social Policy, Human Capital.

Simeonova-Ganeva, R., Vassilev, A., Ganev, K., Dimitrov, L., and Vassileva, I. (2015). Ex-post Assessment of the Net Impact of the Active Labour Market Policy on the Dynamics of Selected Indicators of Economic and Social Development in Bulgaria for the Period 2000–2011. Sofia: Ministry of Labour and Social Policy, ECORYS South East Europe, Sigma Hat.

Simeonova-Ganeva, R. (2005). 'Education and Labour Force in Bulgaria: 1944–2004', Conference Proceedings, Conference on Medium-Term Economic Assessment, Sofia Edition. Sofia: Agency for Economic Analysis and Forecasts.

Simeonova-Ganeva, R. (2012). 'Human Capital Formation during Communism in Bulgaria', Sociological Problems Journal, 3–4, 303–326.

West, J. (2013). 'Vocational Education and Training in Eastern Europe: Transition and Influence', LLAKES Research Paper, 41.

Zoica Elena Vladut

# 12. Romania: between statist and collective approaches

**Abstract:** This chapter presents evolution of skill formation in Romania after 1990, with the main steps taken, the determining factors and results in two important stages, before and after EU accession, in the transition from a centralised system to a market economy.

In this period the Romanian skill formation system experienced significant positive changes, which refer to the development of institutions and legislation, standardization of qualifications and the curriculum based on competencies, knowledge, skill and attitudes. There have also been established mechanisms for involving the social partners in the process of development and validation of qualification and fostering evolution of social dialogue in this field. The development of mechanisms and tools for planning the training offer also took place, starting from the introduction of the forecasts of labour market needs in the short, medium and long term as well as the introduction of quality assurance elements in skill formation to increase confidence in the system's capacity to support economic and social development.

Some issues related to the ability of the skill formation system to develop remain problematic and can profoundly influence it's future development. These issues include the effectiveness of the lifelong learning, the comprehensive approach at the level of the skill formation system, the financing, the relevance of the social dialogue institutions and their capacity to support the challenges related to competitiveness, globalisation and negative demographic development of society.

**Keywords:** Competitiveness, demography, financing, functional illiteracy, Romania, stakeholders, standardization

## Introduction

The evolution of skill formation in Romania after 1990 was not a comprehensive process involving initial vocational education and training (IVET), continuing VET and higher education (HE). Change in these sectors of skill formation was very often influenced by many internal and external factors, sometimes affecting only one sector. In some educational sectors the transformations were slow, while in others transformation was more rapid, due to reform programmes and projects supported by external funds. No comprehensive study has been undertaken in the field but skill formation in Romania in the post-communist period is a consequence of market-oriented reforms and socio-economic and political transformations largely influenced by external factors.

During the last 30 years skill formation in Romania was affected by frequent changes in institutional and legislative frameworks, these being defined by political changes. De-synchronisation in institutional development interventions (dictated by the funding schedule of various international institutions) has inevitably affected the timing of policies in the field, with implications on the quality and efficiency of skill formation. For example, a lack of updated occupational standards prevented the definition of qualifications, while delay in the establishment of a national authority for qualifications had a knock-on effect on the development of a comprehensive national qualifications framework. The fragmented governance of skill formation, with functions divided between the Ministry of Labour (MoL) and the Ministry of Education (MoE) and many overlaps, also delayed policy design and implementation.

The prevailing idea shared by civil society and policy makers, that academic higher education presents an elite pathway to skill formation, whereas VET offers a professional route delivering low-level qualifications, prevented real collaboration between subsystems of skill formation and led to the lack of a consistent approach and communication.

## Institutional development pathway of skill formation in Romania

### Institutional change and development of skill formation during the early post-communist transition 1990–2007

The period from 1990 to 2007 was marked by the establishment of new institutions, regulatory frameworks and pathways of skill formation. These transformations, summarised in Table 12.1, were largely defined by European and international developments in the field of skill formation and its institutionalization.

During the socialist period, VET schools were organized in partnership with state-owned enterprises and coordinated by the ministries responsible for economy and education. VET schools operated according to a system like dual education and provided the necessary workforce for state-owned companies.

After 1990, the transition to a market economy and democratic society led to changes in institutions and governance. The modernisation of economy and society was slowed down by the political environment, which was characterised by the persistence of former mind sets and attitudes. Policy makers retained the former centralised institutions and mechanisms and tried to use them in

**Table 12.1.** Institutional change and development of skill formation during early post-communist transition 1990–2007: critical interventions

| | |
|---|---|
| Initial VET | ➢ 1995- a new law of education approved.<br>➢ 1995–1998 reform (supported by the EU Phare fund) of the vocational school and post high school by redefining qualifications, introducing training standards and a new curriculum, and starting to organize social partnership for VET support at zones level and sectors implemented.<br>➢ 1998 – the National Centre for Technical and Vocational Education and Training Development (NCTVETD) established by following recommendations of the Phare VET reform programme.<br>➢ 2003- amendment to the law of education and ten years of compulsory education introduced.<br>➢ 2001–2003- reform of initial VET (supported by the EU Phare fund), for 3 qualifications levels implemented. |
| Continuous VET | ➢ 1994 the Council for Occupational Standards and Qualifications (COSA) established with the support of the World Bank.<br>➢ 1994–1997 –the methodology for occupational standards development and first occupational standards designed.<br>➢ 1999 –the National Adult Training Board (NATB) established as a tripartite structure.<br>➢ 2000 the legal framework of vocational training for adults, which regulated the accreditation of the adult training providers approved by Government Ordinance.<br>➢ 2005 –the law on apprenticeship introduced. |
| Higher education | ➢ 1993 – the National Council for Academic Evaluation and Accreditation (NCAEA) which introduced a system for evaluation and accreditation of HE institutions established.<br>➢ 2004- 3 cycles-based HE qualifications framework introduced in line with the European Higher Education Area Qualifications Framework (Dublin descriptors).<br>➢ 2005 – the Authority for Qualifications in Higher Education and Partnership with the Economic and Social Environment (AQHEPESE) established. |

*Note.* Prepared by author.

promoting evolutionary economic and social transformation. Institutional changes regarding skill formation were mostly determined by learning and implementing policies developed by Western European countries (United Kingdom, Germany, France) because of Romania's involvement in different programmes and projects supported by the EU.

In the years immediately after 1990, skill formation continued to be very centralised (especially in the field of allocation of human and material resources), and without a clear strategy for development. Stoica (2003) distinguishes the stages of deconstruction (1990), stabilisation (1991–1992) and restructuring (1993–1996) in the early post-communist VET reforms of Romania. Meaningful reform came with the establishment of relevant legislation on education (Law of Education in 1995, the Law of University Accreditation in 1993, the Law of the Teaching Staff in 1997) and more systemic governance arrangements for skill formation, which focused on linking the governance of educational institutions with labour market developments and involving social partners in co-financing education reform.

The key problems for initial VET schools were inadequate infrastructure and outdated technologies, and equipment unsuitable for developing the new skills needed in the labour market, along with a lack of competent managers of schools, and low opportunities for professional development of school managers and teachers. All of these contributed to the negative image of VET in society and led to a continued decrease in student enrolment and graduation in VET. Continuing VET was almost non-existent, and ill-suited for retraining the unemployed workforce.

The first years of post-communist transformation were marked by significant technological stagnation within workplaces and workforce de-skilling (Tarlea and Freyberg-Inan 2018).

These factors contributed to employers having little interest in hiring VET graduates, as well as graduates from HE in different specialisations (especially engineers) and by students having little interest (in general influenced by their parents) in following VET training pathways. The low interest in VET qualifications was also influenced by controversies surrounding the slow and complicated privatisation of state-owned companies. Small and medium sized enterprises in Romania have been characterised by very reductionist and fragmented investment in continuing vocational training (Lafuente and Robetino 2011). Local enterprises preferred to compete through cost reduction, while multinational enterprises also had limited commitment to investing in skills (Tarlea 2017). Unemployment increased significantly following the closure of many state companies. After 1990, VET schools were reorganized under the governance of the MoE. With general economic decline, demand for skilled workers fell significantly, while vocational qualifications developed in the communist period became increasingly obsolete.

The first reform programme supported by EU Phare funds in the field of initial VET was implemented in the period 1995–1998. The main interventions were focused on restructuring vocational schools and post-high-schools, although this was completed without reference to high-school, general and HE establishments. The main transformations involved introducing a progressive pathway for vocational schools by eliminating narrow specialisation and providing students with a choice of specialisation closer to the moment of graduation.

The reforms of curricula in VET in the first decade of post-communist transformation were targeted on the introduction of competence-based curricula and aimed to reduce the volume of narrow qualifications and specialisations (Stoica, 2003).

New competence-based VET standards provided information about required knowledge, skills, and social competencies, and served as a reference for developing new curricula. The employers' associations and trade unions started to organize and restructure themselves but suffered from having relatively little power as well as being unrepresentative (Trif 2013). New private companies started to appear but their influence and interest in the VET system was very low because high unemployment meant an abundant workforce was available (Stanica and Aristigueta 2019; Tarlea and Freyberg-Inan 2018).

The MoE developed and introduced a strategic planning model for the VET offer. The model was designed in 2000, by capitalising on the experiences from 1996 to 2000, and the first tools that informed the strategic planning decisions of the initial VET offer were made in 2004.

Nevertheless, such strategic planning was not effective in solving many important problems related to the sequential and non-systemic approach of VET reform, an isolated approach to initial and continuing training, low interest of youth in VET, a lack of student career guidance towards VET pathways, reduced horizontal and vertical mobility within the VET system, and insufficient capacity of the system to operate with continuous change strategies (Musset 2014; Tarlea and Freyberg-Inan 2018).

After the first reform programme affecting initial VET it was recommended by the project final report to establish a specialised institution under the coordination of the MoE to coordinate initial VET, and the National Centre for TVET Development was established in 1998. School-based VET continued to be dominant because the engagement of companies in the training processes was limited. Due to a lack of financial resources, the remaining VET providers continued to provide training in workshops with outdated equipment and teachers who were not motivated to pursue a career in the education system (Musset 2014).

Educational institutions applied mainly reactive survival strategies during the transitional reforms, by lowering the standards of admission of potential students, lowering the quality of instruction and catering to a market for higher degrees (Chiaburu and Chiaburu 2004). This led to a skills offer that was fragmented and incoherent, as well as to deep problems with the quality of skill formation, manifest in education providers giving temporary accreditation, an increasing supply of questionable or low value credentials, and overlap in the contents of available curricula (ibid.).

A new Phare-TVET Programme (Social and Economic Cohesion-Technical and Vocational Education and Training) was launched in 2001 aimed at rationalizing the VET system, strengthening social dialogue in VET and developing vocational qualifications (Stoica 2003).

In 2003 the Law on Education was modified, and the duration of compulsory education increased from 8 to 10 years. In parallel, the possibility of vocational training within the last two years of compulsory education was introduced. 'Schools of arts and crafts' (*scoala de arte si meserii*- SAM), were introduced with courses lasting 2 years (after the 8th grade) providing the possibility for students to continue studies for other 2 years within high-school, before the baccalaureate (after finalising compulsory education and an additional year to recover general education). This new pathway was named the 'progressive pathway' because it enabled students to accumulate 3 levels of qualifications in 5 years of schooling. However, this new pathway did not gain the trust of employers or students.

An alternative for the 8th grade graduates available at the same time was to follow a 'direct pathway' of training, which entailed 4 years at technological high school, the first 2 years of which enabled compulsory education to be finalised. This gave students the opportunity to acquire a vocational qualification and/or to acquire general secondary education at the end of schooling.

The institutional reform of the VET system described above was influenced by a range of external conditions notably unfavourable demographic trends. A high level of emigration was accompanied by an inability of local employers to attract skilled workers from both the Romanian and especially the European labour market (Chiaburu and Chiaburu 2004; Musset 2014; Tarlea 2017; Tarlea, Freyberg-Inan 2018).

Several factors supported the implementation of the new system. The EU's promotion of education and training as a mechanism for developing a knowledge-based society convinced local policymakers and stakeholders of the need to blur the differences between general and vocational education so that all participants in education could benefit from VET. Furthermore, Romania was open to learning from, and adopting the policies of international donors and foreign companies, especially from the UK, Germany and France, which established subsidiary operations in the country.

EU agendas also influenced the development of the VET system and the character of provision. In line with suggestions for restructuring the VET system, the MoE agreed to restructure VET qualifications, starting with redefining the core qualifications comprising key and general competencies. The aim of providing a pathway from VET to HE was framed within the debates at EU level for the descriptors of the EQF (European Qualifications Framework for Lifelong Learning) reference levels. In parallel a system for quality assurance in initial VET was introduced, which aligned with the requirements for EU accession. The adoption of liberal approaches and policies with regards to skill formation did not, however, bring the changes that were anticipated, largely because of the lack of institutional support and because the new system of skill formation was difficult to access. For example, the apprenticeship law was approved in 2005 under the initiative of the MoL to support people without vocational qualification leaving compulsory education. Yet an extremely small number of employers engaged with this approach, because of cumbersome bureaucratic regulation, their limited capacity to guarantee meaningful training to committed learners, and the fact that a large number of qualified people were unemployed, and thus available in the labour market. The 2000 Law on adult training also introduced the possibility of assessment and recognition of competencies acquired in non-formal and informal contexts, but very few people were able to take advantage of this, as there was no provision for public funding, leaving beneficiaries to fund themselves. Pirciog et al. (2015) and Planas and Benus (2006) also highlight the lack of active labour market measures based on vocational training in Romania, and the lack of alignment to the needs of employers.

The post-communist transformation of HE in Romania has been characterised by rapid expansion under conditions of democratisation and economic openness (Tarlea and Freyberg-Inan 2018). According to Tarlea and Freyberg-Inan (2018) institutional change within HE was influenced by the low skills equilibrium which was exacerbated by the brain-drain of high-skilled workers, the decreasing sophistication of economic activity, accompanied by increasing demand for formal degrees, rather than higher level skills.

According to Stanciu and Banciu (2012) institutional developments within HE also involved the de-ideologisation of HE studies, the introduction of curriculum reforms inspired by the Bologna process, and attempts to optimise the number of HEIs. One of the key implications of these institutional developments has been the decreasing quality of higher education, as well as decreasing credibility and competitiveness in universities (Stanciu and Banciu 2012). The growth of private universities with significant numbers of students, as well as orientation of the HE system and universities to student flows and the transmission and reproduction of knowledge rather than learning and research outcomes, exacerbated the divergence between the HE system and labour market needs. Serban (2012), however, claimed that HE expansion helped people adjust to the changing skills needs of the economy, thus increasing their employability and mobility within the labour market.

From 2004 HE began to implement the Bologna process and simultaneously HE qualifications were revised and a national framework was introduced. In 2006 the Law on the quality of education was introduced, establishing basic principles applicable for all levels of pre-university education, initial VET and HE. These principles involved focusing on learning outcomes, promoting quality improvement, protecting education beneficiaries (first of all learners), and centring on the internal evaluation process (self-assessment) of education providers.

The quality assurance of continuing training was coordinated by the MoL and regulated by the adult training law. The lack of a coherent approach in terms of quality assurance in initial and continuing VET, as well as HE, demonstrated lack of trust between the stakeholders in these systems, and this became an important external factor for development of the skill formation system.

## Institutional change and development of skill formation from 2007

After 2007, when Romania joined the EU, reforms of the skill formation system continued with a stronger focus on the development of a coherent system of qualifications (Table 12.2). During the EU accession process, national authorities in the field of education and labour designed a range of strategies to eliminate gaps in education and employment, and to align education and labour market policies. Strategies in the field of employment were targeted at supporting employment and helping the unemployed, whilst strategies in education aimed to reduce the volume of early school leavers, and support lifelong learning, VET and HE developments. These strategies served as a basis for implementation of the national projects financed by EU structural funds, but they did not entirely achieve their proposed targets.

In 2009 the MoE decided to stop allocating funds for 'schools of arts and crafts' and only to maintain technological high schools. The new structure of technological high schools envisaged a change to a direct and progressive training route. At the end of the lower cycle of the technological high school (compulsory education), students had limited options: – either to continue their studies in the upper cycle and obtain a vocational qualification referenced to EQF level 4, whilst also having the opportunity to obtain the baccalaureate diploma; or, to obtain a level 3 EQF vocational qualification certificate after completing a practical training

**Table 12.2.** Institutional change and development of skill formation during 2007–2018: critical interventions

| | |
|---|---|
| Initial VET | 2007–2009, implementation of the Phare 2004–2006 VET programme, continuing the IVET reform by involving the VET schools in the rural areas, supporting the social partnership in VET by developing and periodically revising the planning instruments of VET at regional, county and local levels, supporting the development of the national qualifications framework and initial VET quality assurance instruments.<br>2009- decision to provide initial vocational training only through high-school, and giving up the progressive pathway of training<br>2012- reintroduction of vocational schools<br>2016- introduction of dual education as an alternative to vocational school |
| Continuous VET | 2007–2008, implementation of a Phare project to develop the NATB and transform it into National Authority for Qualifications (NAQ) |
| Higher education | 2011 establishment of the National Council for Attestation of Titles, Diplomas and University Certificates (NCATDUC) |

*Note.* Prepared by author.

course lasting 720 hours (6 months). This pathway was strongly criticised by multinational companies facing difficulties in obtaining skilled workers with qualifications referenced to level 3 EQF due also to high levels of emigration of skilled workers and high volume of retirement among older skilled workers. The number of students choosing graduation after the 6 months of practical vocational training remained very low, and companies complained that the competencies of graduates from this programme did not meet their needs.

After introducing a new Law on Education in 2011, the MoE assumed responsibility for organizing lifelong learning. Simultaneously with the introduction and implementation of the EQF, ECVET and EQAVET instruments at EU level, negotiations started to develop a National Authority of Qualifications (NAQ), which was established in 2011 by reorganizing the National Adult Training Board. At the same time, the MoL assumed additional responsibilities for continuing VET.

In 2012, a former type of vocational school was re-introduced: Starting from the school year 2012–2013, two years of vocational education were tacked on to the end of nine years basic general education. This initiative was also strongly criticised by different stakeholders because it created a disincentive for students enrolled in the ninth grade of general education to choose training at the vocational school (due to the lack of attractiveness of VET to young people), furthermore, the number of hours of practical training was considered too low for the award of a vocational qualification referenced to EQF level 3.

Starting from the school year of 2014–2015, vocational education commenced after completion of the $8^{th}$ grade of general education, and was extended to 3 years.

In 2016, after long debates with companies (especially foreign companies) and social partners the law of education was amended to introduce 'dual vocational education' starting from the 9th grade and based on a partnership contract concluded between the VET school, the company and the student (or their legal representative). This stipulated the duality of training in separate locations, the proportion of practical training from the total number of training hours: on average 50 per cent (differentiated by the year of study: 20 per cent in the ninth grade, 57 per cent in the tenth grade, 72 per cent in the eleventh grade), and the roles and responsibilities of the company in relation to the appointment of tutors, on-site training, the final exam and certifying the acquisition of the qualification.

Dual vocational education provides vocational qualifications referenced to EQF level 3 and presents an alternative to 'school-based' vocational education.

These changes in initial VET were influenced by the German model but also by general trends within the EU.

As a result of these institutional changes and reforms, enrolment of students in high school fluctuated with a trend of decreasing numbers in recent years. The demographic trends and parents' emigration (sometimes leading to students dropping out of school) also contributed to this situation. A significant decline in enrolment at vocational schools was strongly influenced by political decisions taken in 2009 which were thwarted by the decision to reintroduce vocational schools in 2012, while the decision to introduce dual vocational schools in 2016 resulted in an increasing number of enrolments (as presented in Table 12.3).

The main reform in HE after 2007 aimed to improve quality of education by exploiting the tools of ranking and international benchmarking. A national ranking of universities and study programmes was introduced after the publication of the new law of education in 2011. This ranking was designed to redistribute budgetary funds of HE 'according to performance criteria', but it was not applied in practice. The reports on the quality of higher education in Romania, also known as the Quality Barometers (2009, 2010, 2011) provided an unequivocal diagnosis of the poor quality of university education. Referring to the indicators that measure quality in terms of the relationship between universities and the labour market and the content of educational processes, the authors of the reports indicated the increasing risk of widening 'diploma disease', poor

**Table 12.3.** Changes in the number of students enrolled in high-school and vocational school in the period 2000–2018 (thousands)

| School year | Total number of students in high schools | Total number of students in vocational schools or schools of arts and crafts |
|---|---|---|
| 2000–2001 | 684.4 | 239.5 |
| 2007–2008 | 788.8 | 220.3 |
| 2009–2010 | 835.3 | 115.4 |
| 2012–2013 | 829.5 | 19.7 |
| 2015–2016 | 673.6 | 68.6 |
| 2016–2017 | 647.9 | 84.3 |
| 2017–2018 | 637.7 | 90.2 |

*Note.* National Institute for Statistics Romania https://insse.ro/cms/en.

performance of universities, and their decreasing competitiveness in Europe (The Romanian Agency for Quality Assurance in Higher Education 2010).

After 1990 the volume of enrolments in HE increased rapidly, with Romania registering the highest growth rate of all EU member states. But the evolution of HE had its own dynamic and had no correlation with the needs of the economy. The quality of studies and performance of the HE system was not driven by output indicators and there were no mechanisms of accountability of universities for failures in the field of skill formation.

The total number of universities and faculties decreased during the period 2011–2018. There was a decrease in the number of private universities and faculties, simultaneously with maintaining, in approximately the same parameters, the state HE network (Table 12.4). The decreasing trend registered by HE institutions correlates with trends registered at the level of student enrolment (Table 12.5). Thus, the number of students enrolled for Bachelor degrees decreased significantly in 2011–2016 (from 539,900 to 405,600) and began to increase slightly from 2017 (408,200).

Romanian HE institutions could not enter international rankings for a long period, and when they did, none occupied high positions. Some disciplines achieved respectable rankings, suggesting islands of superior performance. Although there were more than 100 HE institutions in Romania, only 5 or 6 feature in rankings that involve a substantial number of universities (1,000). The expansion of HE has not only been associated with a decrease in the quality of education but has also brought a relative saturation of the labour market in some fields (Nicolescu 2003). In recent years there has been an increase

**Table 12.4.** The network of the national higher education system

| | 2011/ 2012 | 2012/ 2013 | 2013/ 2014 | 2014/ 2015 | 2015/ 2016 | 2016/ 2017 | 2017/ 2018 |
|---|---|---|---|---|---|---|---|
| Number of accredited and provisionally authorised higher education institutions, of which: | 108 | 107 | 103 | 101 | 98 | 96 | 93 |
| - public universities | 56 | 55 | 55 | 55 | 55 | 55 | 55 |
| - private universities | 52 | 52 | 48 | 46 | 43 | 41 | 38 |
| Number of faculties, of which: | 614 | 596 | 590 | 583 | 567 | 515 | 508 |
| - public faculties | 410 | 405 | 405 | 403 | 409 | 372 | 372 |
| - private faculties | 204 | 191 | 185 | 180 | 158 | 143 | 136 |

*Note.*
1. Raport privind starea invatamantului superior din Romania 2017–2018- MEN.
2. Government Ordinance no. 140/2017 with subsequent amendments.
3. Învățământ Superior. Raport UEFISCDI 2017–2018.

in unemployment and inactivity of the population with higher educational qualifications, especially in younger age groups. Bălan (2019) noticed that the rapid expansion of participation in HE in the first two decades after the 1990 did not solve the problems of tertiary and higher education accessibility, especially for the most socially vulnerable population groups. Besides the high emigration rates, reducing volumes of young people with pre-higher education implied significant restructuring and the 'optimization' of HE provision in the country was illustrated by a decrease in the number of universities and private faculties (Bălan 2019).

## Implications of skill formation for economic growth and social development in Romania

Economic policies were not generally supportive of skill formation as long as substantial numbers of qualified unemployed were available on the labour market. The employment rate of VET graduates has been very low due to the high level of over-qualification exacerbated by massive recruitment of HE graduates by international companies operating in Romania.

Romania has experienced strong productivity growth since 1990, but overall productivity remains low compared with other EU member states. Although in the period 2007–2018, labour productivity growth in Romania was 53 per cent (being the highest in the former communist European countries, according

**Table 12.5.** Number of students enrolled for Bachelor degrees (thousands)

| | 2011/ 2012 | 2012/ 2013 | 2013/ 2014 | 2014/ 2015 | 2015/ 2016 | 2016/ 2017 | 2017/ 2018 |
|---|---|---|---|---|---|---|---|
| No. Bachelor degree students, of which: | 539.9 | 464.6 | 433.2 | 411.2 | 410.7 | 405.6 | 408.2 |
| Public universities | 399.5 | 364.9 | 354.0 | 345.3 | 351.5 | 350.1 | 352.3 |
| Private universities | 140.4 | 99.7 | 79.2 | 65.9 | 59.2 | 55.5 | 55.9 |

*Note.*
1. Raport privind starea invatamantului superior din Romania 2017–2018- MEN.
2. Government Ordinance no. 140/2017 with subsequent amendments.
3. Învăţământ Superior. Raport UEFISCDI 2017–2018.

to Eurostat), its level remains low due to several factors, including the preponderance of outdated technologies and the shortcomings of the skill formation system.

Demographic changes have had an impact on the development of VET. Participation in secondary education has been decreasing, leading to the consolidation of the school network via the merger and closure of schools. Indeed, since 2012/2013, the number of VET upper secondary schools has decreased by 8.5 per cent (Cedefop 2019).

The merger and closure of schools required the provision of additional transport services for learners. This was the responsibility of local authorities, but not all provided transport. Participation in education and training at various levels is much lower among the rural population than among those living in urban areas. Roughly 45 per cent of all Romanians under the age of 25 live in rural areas, but according to current data from the National Institute of Statistics, rural communities provide only 24 per cent of students (Strategia privind reducerea părăsirii timpurii a şcolii în România 2015). At the secondary school level, the dropout rate in rural schools was about 1.5 times higher than in urban ones (Strategia privind reducerea părăsirii timpurii a şcolii în România 2015), and there is significant under-representation of rural youth in HE.

Romania had its worst results for 9 years in the 2018 PISA (the OECD Program for International Student Assessment) tests. The score was worse than either of the two previous tests in which Romania participated (2012 and 2015), and in all three areas of assessment: reading, mathematics and science, according to

"*PISA 2018 Results, What students know and can do, volume I*", published by the Directorate for Education of the OECD. Functional illiteracy has increased to 44 per cent (OECD 2019a). Romania also continued to face a wide performance gap between students from the most and least disadvantaged socio-economic groups.

Inequality of opportunity based on socio-economic status has a significant impact on the academic achievement of children in Romania. For example, disparities between Roma and non-Roma students are considerable with minority language speaking students underperforming. Yet at least half the gap in relation to reading could be eliminated, especially by reducing social segregation in schools. Students living in big cities and urban centres are more likely to experience a favourable school environment than those living in rural areas. Expanding access to pre-primary education and improving the quality of teaching practices in rural schools could partially reduce the gap.

Initial VET enrols many students with low performance in reading, mathematics and science from disadvantaged areas and this translates into low performance of initial VET graduates. Although it has declined, Romania's poverty rate is still among the highest in the EU, at 40.4 per cent in 2013 (World Bank 2015).

Popescu and Roman (2018) have highlighted a positive impact of VET on employability in Romania, where VET courses have increased the employment chances of the unemployed by about 15 per cent, but VET still suffers from being ineffective, and poorly targeted to the most relevant sub-categories of unemployed. Andrioni and Popp (2012) have highlighted the importance of vocational education and training for the social and labour market integration of the most deprived and disadvantaged groups, especially Roma women.

Pantea (2020) claims that the severe underfunding of the education system has led to a significant growth in functional illiteracy among young people. The pressure from industry and an economic climate shaped by a growing service sector and foreign investment in car and textile manufacturing forced the state to attempt to make VET more attractive. It led to a heterogeneity of development in VET with the co-existence of underfunded and weakly developed VET provision alongside isolated cases of high-quality dual VET (Pantea 2020).

During the period 2011–2017, Romania registered relatively constant economic growth, in tandem with an increasing budget deficit. A variety of reasons lay behind these developments, but economic growth increased interest in skill formation amongst numerous stakeholders.

After 2017, economic growth declined this being attributed to consumption funded largely by remittances sent to families by the diaspora rather than to internal investment by businesses in leading economic sectors. As a consequence, economic growth did not increase demand for labour nor the attractiveness of VET. Enrolment in VET stagnated even when new international enterprises entered the market and created new workplaces.

There was an uptick in interest in the dual education pathway, however, as this provided qualifications referenced only to the EQF level 3, although its impact on productivity and competitiveness has been negligible.

Unemployment increased rapidly during the initial stage of economic transition in 1993–1994, and again in the period 1998–2000, but decreased significantly before and after EU accession as can be seen in Figure 12.1. Decreasing unemployment at this time, however, has been largely attributed to workforce emigration rather than economic growth.

Statistical data showing a high employment rate for graduates with HE qualifications, hide significant levels of underemployment. According to one study, 86 per cent of HE graduates (total sample 5576) stated that they learned mostly at work (Voici et al. 2010). Universities tailored their provision based on enrolment of students. The risks of unemployment or underemployment were transferred exclusively to students, with the universities abrogating all risk in this regard (Voici et al. 2010).

The field of lifelong learning is under-developed in Romania. The level of participation is the lowest in the EU, and unlike in other member states, is not increasing.

Only 1.6 per cent of adults (aged 25–64) in Romania participated in lifelong learning (LLL), compared with the EU27 average of 8.9 per cent, in 2011. Between 2007 and 2013, the adult participation rate in LLL increased very marginally, from 1.3 per cent to 1.8 per cent. Romania's national goal for lifelong learning was to increase participation to 10 per cent by 2020 (World Bank 2015). The low participation in adult education in Romania can be explained by the lack of partnership and cooperation between employers, workers, and education and training providers. This results in an unresponsive, under-performing lifelong learning system, in which employers, workers, and education and training providers make choices and act in isolation. The expansion of lifelong learning in Romania requires the factors responsible for underdeveloped social partnership to be addressed: (i) imperfect and asymmetric information among actors; (ii) weak incentives to participate in education and training activities; and (iii) inadequate capacity of actors (World Bank 2015).

Against this backdrop population migration is a very important factor and a direct outcome of weaknesses in the skill formation system. Over 2 million people of working age (25 per cent of the workforce) are estimated to have

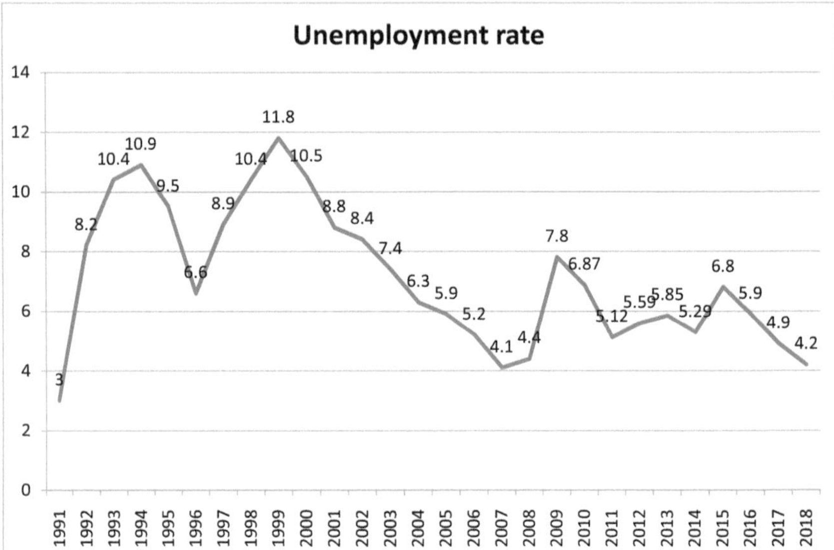


**Figure 12.1.** Unemployment rate in Romania between 1991 and 2017. (Source: National Agency for Employment.)

emigrated in search of better job opportunities in Europe and elsewhere (OECD 2019b).

The Romanian Diaspora is the fifth largest in the world (OECD 2019b). Indeed, the OECD (2019b) report shows that the population of Romania declined by 12.9 per cent (from 22.4 million to 19.5 million) between 2000 and 2018 largely because of emigration (OECD 2019b). Romanian emigrants work mostly in low-skilled jobs, and those with higher education are often over-qualified for the jobs they do, according to the OECD report. In OECD countries, Romanian emigrants are three times more likely than citizens of the host country to work in unskilled or semi-skilled jobs and half as likely to work in highly-skilled jobs. Almost half of Romanians with HE qualifications who emigrated to OECD countries took up low-skilled jobs, with limited employment opportunities in Romania being the main reason given by Romanians who leave their country. The educational level of the Romanian diaspora in OECD countries is on average relatively high, with a quarter having HE qualifications.

## Social dialogue in the field of skill formation

From the early years of post-communist transition, many quasi-governmental and non-governmental organizations emerged within the fields of skill formation and employment, but their activities were highly fragmented (Chiaburu and Chiaburu 2004). Given this, only government had the capability to initiate changes in skill formation and in some situations it even supported the institutional development of social partnership.

The slow development of social dialogue in relation to skill formation, and especially the low involvement of employers' organizations, can be explained by the high level of unemployment, and the tendency of employers to regard skill formation as expenditure rather than investment in business development. The subsequent organization and more active involvement of employers was largely because this gave them some capacity to influence political decisions.

For many years employers regarded the state as being responsible for skill formation, whilst the trade unions that existed during the communist period lacked credibility and wielded insufficient power to represent the interests of the employees effectively (Adăscăliței and Guga 2017; Trif 2013).

Skill formation was not a primary concern for trade unions during the initial years of the post-communist transformation, and did not feature in their demands (Ghebrea 2005). At this time, trade unions, as communist-era organizations, were beset by fragmentation, a lack of representativeness, de-unionisation and concentration in the public sector. They also experienced difficulties in clarifying their identity and purpose in the new economic and social context, while employers failed to appreciate their legitimacy (Ghebrea 2005). The role and activity of trade unions in industrial relations and social dialogue were changing: from 1990 to 2003 the unions were very militant, influential and effective in protecting the rights of employees, whereas after 2009 under the influence of EU and international organizations, policies that weakened trade unions and led to the deregulation of employment relations were implemented (Adăscăliței and Guga 2018). National collective agreements developed in the first two decades of transition specified pay-rates linked to training and education levels, and prevented the payment of minimum wages to higher qualified workers (Trif 2013). The 2008 crisis triggered an extreme and disorganised decentralisation of collective bargaining in Romania by a 'frontal assault' on multi-employer collective bargaining and the transformation of the regulatory framework from a statutory system that supported collective bargaining at national, sectoral and company levels to a so-called 'voluntary' system that made it almost impossible to negotiate new national and sectoral collective agreements after 2011 (Trif 2016).

The increasing power of individual employers in defining terms and conditions of employment after 2008 was manifested in the imposition of revisions to the Labour Code permitting the engagement of new recruits on flexible contracts. The decline in national and sectoral collective agreements led to an increase in the importance of regional collective bargaining (Trif 2016).

Accession to the EU fostered social dialogue by implementing the norms of *acquis communautaire*, but it did not succeed in overcoming the formal character of social dialogue or solve the problems of low engagement of the social partners in this period, which was characterised by passive discussions between the government and trade unions, which excluded the employers (Ghebrea 2005).

Social partner organizations with limited institutional capacity had no financial resources to support their activity (although the trade unions possessed important material legacy from the communist period) and so later mainly relied on public funds to support their activity in relation to skill formation.

The biggest challenge for the social partners has been to develop a new model of social dialogue to ensure the skill formation system reflected the qualifications and competencies needed by labour market both at national and local levels. Beginning in 2003, specific partnership structures were established for the initial VET system: Local Committees for Social Partnership Development (LCSPD) and Regional Committees for Social Partnership Development (RCSPD). Their institutional development was supported by Phare projects in the field of VET. They developed with the support of the National Centre for TVET Development, a strategic planning model for VET supply, approved by the MoE (Cedefop 2019). Strategic planning is characterised by the collective action of stakeholders, including associations, trade unions, organs of public administration, relevant government and civil society organizations. The model combines top-down and bottom-up decision-making processes, involving consortia at regional level, local committees for development of social partnership at county level, and school boards at local area level. In some respects, strategic planning at regional level included HE provision. Other partnership structures were created following the models of other European countries, for example, the Chamber of Commerce and Industry of Romania and county chambers. However, these have limited capacity for involvement in skill formation.

Another important step was the establishment of tripartite social partnership structures at national level that had a consultative, rather than decision-making, role, such as the National Adult Training Board. The establishment of sector committees in 2005, with the support of the Phare TVET programmes, and their involvement in identifying and validating qualifications was an important step in the development of social dialogue over skill formation. However, the amendment of the social dialogue legislation in 2009 introduced uniform collective labour contracts in the public sector at national level and meant a step back in the development of the institutional capacity of social partners.

The reform programmes supported by the EU Phare funds, and later by the structural funds, which facilitated the introduction of the national qualifications framework and the development of vocational training standards for initial VET, increased the institutional capacity of the social partners, but this has developed slowly and is still insufficient. In recent years, especially under the pressure and initiative of multinational companies (which have both financial capacity and know-how in the field), social partner involvement in skill formation and implementation of dual education has increased.

The involvement of social partners in HE has also been limited. In 2005 the Authority for Qualifications in Higher Education and Partnership with the Economic and Social Environment – ACPART – was established. This institution was designed to promote cooperation between HE institutions and the social partners to adapt the educational offer to the economic and social environment. The sectoral committees were not really involved as partners in HE qualifications revision procedure.

## Development of the national system of qualifications

The introduction of the EQF enabled some national level decision-making processes in the national system of qualifications, but at national level skill formation nevertheless remains quite fragmented. The slowness of the development of a coherent skill formation system has resulted from reduced institutional capacity within public institutions and the institutions of social dialogue, and frequent legislative change. Whilst there is currently a transparent system of qualifications in initial VET and HE, there is less transparency in continuing VET.

The introduction of competence-based approaches and quality elements to the description of qualifications (for example their validation by the social partners) is a process that requires an active and balanced involvement of all stakeholders. Institutional arrangements after 1995 were characterised by formality, limited institutional development of social partner organizations, and a lack of mutual trust between partners. Under such conditions, the national qualifications system was not fit for purpose, especially as it lacked mechanisms for recognizing competencies obtained in non-formal and informal ways. Since 2000, legislation relating to the national system for the validation of non-formal and informal learning has been gradually developed and implemented but it does not embrace the entire system of skill formation. The National Authority for Qualifications, including the National Centre for Accreditation of the competence assessment centres coordinates and monitors the validation process.In 2011, governmental approval was given for the organization, structure and functioning of the National Authority for Qualifications, which was established as a national coordination point for the National qualifications framework (NQF) in relation to EQF. In 2013 the NQF also received governmental approval following exactly the levels and descriptors established by the EQF.

In general, the design of qualifications followed the 'Anglo-Saxon' approach in relation to the NQF design, with a modular initial VET curriculum, and the technical elements created by ECVET (in defining training standards).

Initial VET qualifications are based on training standards. Training standards (*standard de pregatire profesionala*) describe learning units consisting of learning outcomes and are based, in general, on occupational standards when they exist. Training standards are developed by representatives of companies from the respective sectors and VET providers, with the methodological support of the NCTVETD, endorsed by the NAQ. They are validated by employers and other social partners through sector committees. The revision of standards is carried out ideally at least every five years or at the request of economic operators.

The share of national and local curricula varies by qualification level (Cedefop 2019). Continuing VET qualifications are based on occupational standards, validated by the sector committees and approved by the NAQ (Cedefop 2019). Qualifications in HE are defined by learning outcomes, expressed in terms of knowledge, skills and competencies, and are related to the respective level of university studies. The description of qualifications takes into account that professional activity presupposes the existence of professional and transversal competencies. The implementation of the national system of qualifications, and the introduction of the NQF in Romania have been focussed on the development of lifelong learning and continuing training possibilities. Popescu (2012) suggested that continuing vocational training and lifelong learning in Romania were institutionalised with the implementation of the NQF and the establishment of the National Qualifications Authority in 2011. This coincided with major liberalisation with respect to the supply of continuing vocational training, enhanced by the availability of funding for CVT measures from the EU (Popescu 2012). The development of CVT and the implementation of the NQF in Romania were also greatly influenced by the trends of growing emigration of skilled workers to the other EU member states, since this created the need to institutionalise the recognition of skills and qualifications and social security of the migrant workers.

## Future issues in skill development in Romania

At present two core gaps in skill formation remain.

1. The lack of quality and low attractiveness of vocational qualifications is caused by insufficient practical and dual training, as well as low levels of involvement by the social partners. The technological high school is not providing a real EQF level 4 qualification because the duration of practical training is insufficient and the dual education for EQF levels 4 and 5 is not yet operational. The involvement of SMEs (especially national) in the VET process remains low due to financial problems and limited human resources available to act as tutors. Additionally, even if the companies involved in dual education are encouraged by some fiscal facilities, these facilities remain difficult to access.
2. The lack of transparent and effective institutionalization of lifelong learning and higher education provision is the result of the absence of consistent and clear approaches to lifelong learning and supply-oriented higher education provision.

Possible scenarios for the institutional development of skill formation depend on a clear vision for the economic and social development of the country in the context of EU membership, and on a conscious and responsible involvement of all stakeholders. The development of the qualifications system has already created a series of premises but lacks a coherent approach at system level.

For the immediate future we present a pessimistic scenario, since maintaining the status quo is more feasible than proposing positive changes. The lack of financing of the system also militates against optimistic change, and even the maintenance of the status quo, as this serves to exacerbate existing problems.

Analysing the current situation of skill formation in Romania and the absence of clear programmes for economic and social development, in the context of the new crisis of 2020, we consider that the only viable solution may arise from political interest in increasing Romania's competitiveness since this could provide an impetus to improve the skill formation system.

Potential solutions might include: investing in competitive sectors of the economy; and especially in sectors that can generate added value and in which Romania has a competitive advantage; further aligning the system of skill formation with the skills needs of competitive sectors in particular, and enterprises more generally; continuing to develop the institutional capacity of social partnership; and investing in education and training.

But as it stands, Romania remains strongly dependent on global value chains. Continued demographic decline, the unattractiveness of the skill formation system in the eyes of the country's youth and in many cases its lack of relevance to labour market needs, as well as continuing economic decline, is unlikely to result, at least in the short term, in a change in the skill formation system. It also seems likely that the evolution of skill formation will be negatively impacted by the lack of realistic measures to reduce poverty and functional illiteracy.

## References

Adascalitei, D. & Guga, Ş. (2016). 'Taking stock of the crisis: A multilevel analysis of the Romanian trade union movement', *CELSI Discussion Paper No. 39, June 2016*< https://www.researchgate.net/publication/311650530>, accessed 24 November 2020.

Adăscăliţei, D. & Guga, Ş. (2018). 'International actors and trade unions during postsocialism and after: The case of Romania', *Employee Relations*, 40 (4), 692–708.

Andrioni, F. & Popp, L. (2012). 'Plea for the development of human resources through professional training in Romania', *Procedia – Social and Behavioral Sciences*, 62, 413–417.

Bălan, M. (2019). 'Particularities of the recent evolution of higher education in Romania. Analysis and forecasts', *Journal of Intercultural Management*, 11 (3), 87–104.

Cedefop (2019). *Vocational Education and Training in Romania- short description*. Luxembourg: Centre for Publications of the European Communities.

Chiaburu, D. & Chiaburu, V. (2004). 'Institutional influences on change in Romanian educational organisations: Strategic, evaluative and discursive responses', *SEER: Journal for Labour and Social Affairs in Eastern Europe*, 6 (4), 85–100.

Diaconu (Maxim), L.(2014). 'Education and labour market outcomes in Romania', *Eastern Journal of European Studies*, 5, 99–112.

Ghebrea, G. (2005). 'The role of social dialogue in Romania: Impressive form, deficient content'. In Lafoucriere, C. & L. Magnusson (eds.), *The Enlargement of Social Europe. The Role of Social Partners in the European Employment Strategy Part II*, pp. 149–201. Brussels: ETUI-REHS.

Lafuente, E. & Rabetino, R. (2011). 'Human capital and growth in Romanian small firms', *Journal of Small Business and Enterprise Development*, 18 (1), 74–96.

Monitorul Oficial al României (2000). 'Ordonanta nr.129/2000 privind formarea profesionala a adultilor' [Ordinance No. 129/2000 on the vocational training of adults],<http://www.mmuncii.ro/j33/images/Documente/MMJS/Legislatie/Munca/2017-03-03-OG_nr._129_din_2000_privind_formarea_profesionala.pdf>, accessed 24 July 2020.

Monitorul Oficial al României (2011a). 'Legea educatiei nationale, nr. 1/ 2011, cu modificarile si completarile ulterioare' [National Law on Education No. 1/2011 with further modifications], <https://edu.ro/sites/default/files/_fi%C8%99iere/Legislatie/2019/Legea%20nr%201%20Educatiei%20Nationale%20actualizata%202019.pdf>, accessed 24 July 2020.

Monitorul Oficial al României (2011b). 'Legea nr.279/2005 privind ucenicia la locul de munca' [Law no. 279/2005 on apprenticeships at workplace]< http://www.mmuncii.ro/j33/images/Documente/MMJS/Legislatie/Munca/2018/20181207-Lege-279-2005_ucenicia_la_locul_munca.pdf>, accessed 24 July 2020.

Monitorul Oficial al României (2015a). 'Strategia nationala pentru invatamant tertiar 2015–2020' [National Strategy of the Tertiary Education 2015–2020], < https://www.edu.ro/sites/default/files/fisiere%20articole/Strategie_inv_tertiar_2015_2020.pdf>, accessed 26 July 2020.

Monitorul Oficial al României (2015b). 'Strategia privind reducerea părăsirii timpurii a şcolii în România' [Strategy for reducing early school leaving in Romania], < https://www.edu.ro/sites/default/files/_fi%C8%99iere/Invatamant-Preuniversitar/2015/Strategie-PTS/Strategia-PTS-2015.pdf>, accessed 26 July 2020.

Monitorul Oficial al României (2015c) 'Strategia nationala privind invatarea pe tot parcursul vietii 2015–2020' <https://www.edu.ro/sites/default/files/fisiere%20articole/Strategie%20LLL.pdf>, accessed 24 July 2020.

Monitorul Oficial al României (2016). 'Strategia educatiei si formarii profesionale din Romania pentru perioada 2016–2020' [Vocational education and training strategy of Romania for the period 2016–2020], < https://www.edu.ro/sites/default/files/_fi%C8%99iere/Minister/2016/strategii/Strategia_VET%2027%2004%202016.pdf>, accessed 26 July 2020.

Monitorul Oficial al României (2017). 'Planul de implementare a Garantiei pentru Tineret 2017–2020' [Youth Guarantee Implementation Plan 2017–2020],< http://www.mmuncii.ro/j33/images/Documente/MMJS/Legislatie/Munca/Plan_implement_Garantie_pt_tineret_2017-2020.pdf>, accessed 24 July 2020.

Monitorul Oficial al României (2018a). 'Strategia nationala pentru ocuparea fortei de munca 2014–2020' [National employment strategy 2014–2020], < https://mmuncii.ro/j33/images/Documente/Munca/2018/SN_Ocupare_forta_munca_2018.pdf>, accessed 26 July 2020.

Monitorul Oficial al României (2018b). 'Raport privind starea invatamantului superior din Romania 2017–2018- Ministerul Educatiei Nationale' [Report on the state of higher education in Romania 2017–2018- Ministry of National Education], < https://www.edu.ro/sites/default/files/Raport%20privind%20starea%20%C3%AEnv%C4%83%C8%9B%C4%83m%C3%A2ntului%20superior%20din%20Rom%C3%A2nia_%202017%20-2018.pdf>, accessed 26 July 2020.

Monitorul Oficial al României (2018c). 'Raport privind starea invatamantului preuniversitar din Romania, 2006–2018' [Report on the state of pre-university education in Romania, 2006–2018],<https://www.edu.ro/rapoarte-publice-periodice>, accessed 24 July 2020.

Monitorul Oficial al României (2019). 'Repere pentru proiectarea, actualizarea si evaluarea curriculumului national – document de politici educationale, Ministerul Educatiei Nationale' [Landmarks for designing, updating and evaluating the national curriculum – educational policy document, Ministry of National Education], <https://www.edu.ro/sites/default/files/DPC_31.10.19_consultare.pdf>, accessed 24 July 2020.

Musset, P. (2014). *A Skills Beyond School Commentary on Romania*. OECD. Paris.

Nicolescu, L. (2003). 'Higher education in Romania: Evolution and views from the business community', *Tertiary Education and Management*, 9, 77–95.

OECD (2019a). *PISA 2018 Results (Volume I): What Students Know and Can Do*. Paris: OECD Publishing.

OECD (2019b). *Talent Abroad: A Review of Romanian Emigrants*. Paris: OECD Publishing.

OECD (2019c). *Pogramme for International Students Assessment Reports, PISA 2018 Results*. Paris: OECD Publishing.

Olesia, L. & Simona, M. (2006). 'Work and education in transition', *Journal of Organizational Change Management*, 19 (6), 775–779.

Pantea, M.-C. (2020). 'Perceived reasons for pursuing vocational education and training among young people in Romania', *Journal of Vocational Education & Training*, 72 (1), 136–156.

Petrescu, C. (2016). 'Invatamantul profesional si tehnic, provocari si perspective de dezvoltare, raport de politica publica, Academia Romana, Institutul de Cercetare a Calitatii Vietii, 2016' [Vocational and technical education, challenges and development perspectives, public policy report, Romanian Academy, Quality of Life Research Institute, 2016], < https://www.researchgate.net/publication/310609289_Invatamantul_profesional_si_tehnic_Provocari_si_perspective_de_dezvoltare>, accessed 22 July 2020.

Pirciog, S., Ciuca, V. & Popescu, M. E, (2015). 'The net impact of training measures from active labour market programs in Romania – Subjective and objective evaluation', *Procedia Economics and Finance*, 26, 339–344.

Popescu, A. I. (2012). 'Continuing training in Romania: Reasons and benefits from the perspective of the knowledge economy', *Economics & Sociology*, 5 (2), 35–49.

Popescu, M. E. & Roman, M. (2018). 'Vocational training and employability: Evaluation evidence from Romania', *Evaluation and Program Planning*, 67, 38–46,

Rodriguez-Planas, N. & Benus, J. (2006). 'Evaluating active labor market programs in Romania'. Discussion Papers Series IZA DP No. 2464, < http://ftp.iza.org/dp2464.pdf >, accessed 22 November 2020.

Serban, A. C. (2012). 'A Better Employability Through Labour Market Flexibility. The Case of Romania', *Procedia – Social and Behavioral Sciences*, 46, 4539–4543.

Stanciu, S. & Banciu, V. (2012). 'Quality of higher education in Romania: Are graduates prepared for the labour market?', *Procedia – Social and Behavioral Sciences,* 69, 821–827.

Stanica, C. M. & Aristigueta, M. (2019). 'Progress toward new public governance in Romania', *International Journal of Public Leadership*, 15 (3), 189–206.

Stoica, A. (2003). 'Vocational education and training reform in Romania and Bosnia-Herzegovina: Strategy, legislation, and implementation'. *European Journal of Education,* 38 (2), 213–222.

Tarlea, S. (2018). 'Low- and high-skills equilibria in Central and Eastern Europe: What role for the government?', *Eastern European Politics, Societies and Cultures*, 33 (1), 157–175.

Tarlea, S. & Freyberg-Inan, A. (2018). 'The education skills trap in a dependent market economy. Romania's case in the 2000s', *Communist and Post-Communist Studies*, 51 (1), 49–61.

The Romanian Agency for Quality Assurance in Higher Education (2019). 'Quality Barometer 2010. The State of Quality in Romanian Higher Education', < https://www.aracis.ro/wp-content/uploads/2019/08/sinteza-barometru-en.pdf>, accessed 24 July 2020.

Trif, A. (2013). 'Romania: Collective bargaining institutions under attack', *Transfer: European Review of Labour and Research*, 19 (2), 227–237.

Trif, A. (2016). 'Surviving frontal assault on collective bargaining institutions in Romania: The case of manufacturing companies'. *European Journal of Industrial Relations*, 22 (3), 221–234.

Voicu, B., Tufis, C. & Voicu, M. (2010). 'Recent graduates of higher education and their integration into the labor market', <https://www.academia.edu/11513368/Absolven%C8%9Bii_recen%C8%9Bi_de_%C3%AEnv%C4%83%C8%9B%C4%83m%C3%A2nt_superior_%C8%99i_integrarea_lor_pe_pia%C8%9Ba_muncii>, accessed 24 July 2020.

World Bank (2015). *The National Strategy for Lifelong Learning 2015–2020*. Washington, DC: World Bank.

Sergii Melnyk

# 13. Ukraine: late and iterative institutionalization

**Abstract:** This chapter analyses the problems, risks and prospects of the institutional settings of skill formation in Ukraine. It starts by reviewing the historical pathway of skill formation since the collapse of the Soviet system, then analyses the legal and institutional regulation of skill formation by focussing on key socio-economic and political factors affecting training providers. Finally, the chapter analyses the development of the national system of qualifications and offers insights into possible scenarios for the future. The institutional development of the system of skill formation in post-Soviet Ukraine is marked by the resilience of the Soviet legacy in the structures and functioning of institutional settings, behaviours and methodological approaches. It resulted to complex and iterative institutional methodological transformations against the backdrop of diversity. Specificities of socio-economic and cultural-historical development, such as revolutions of 2004 and 2014 have significantly influenced skill formation both in the regions and in sectors of economy, especially in regard to challenging and iterative involvement of civil society and interest groups in the processes of skill formation. Highly challenging and problematic socio-economic context of the reforms defined by important economic and humanitarian transformations and the emergence of a nation state and civil society in the period after the Dignity Revolution of 2014.

**Keywords:** Civil society, qualifications, revolutions, skill formation, socio-economic transformation, Soviet legacy, Ukraine

## Introduction

Ukraine presents a unique case of institutional transformation of skill formation in Central and Eastern Europe (CEE) in terms of the scope of political, ideological and institutional transitions: from the Soviet planned approach and centralisation, through radical market approaches, decentralisation and neoliberalism, and finally, to the development of coordinated social partnership based 'European' approaches to skill formation. As one of the core regions of the former Soviet Union, industrialisation, collectivisation and Soviet indoctrination left a far more powerful legacy (Applebaum 2017; Plokhy 2016) and therefore Ukraine also underwent a longer and more intensive process with respect to the formation of institutions compared to other CEE countries. Furthermore, Ukraine is probably the most diverse country analysed in this book in terms of regional disparities. Overall, the country experienced a significant modernisation of skill formation institutions and infrastructure, shifting to competence-based and work-based learning approaches in vocational education and training (VET) and higher education (HE) , in a highly challenging socio-economic, and political context, where the personal safety of individuals was compromised.

This chapter analyses the problems, risks and prospects of the institutional settings of skill formation in Ukraine. It starts by reviewing the historical pathway of skill formation since the collapse of the Soviet system, then analyses the legal and institutional regulation of skill formation by focussing on key socio-economic and political factors affecting training providers. Finally, the chapter analyses the development of the national system of qualifications and offers insights into possible scenarios for the future.

## Historical pathway of skill formation in post-Soviet Ukraine

The post-Soviet era in Ukraine shares many typical features and critical junctures with other CEE countries such as radical socio-economic transformation characterised by abrupt and iterative privatisation of the big Soviet industrial enterprises by their former managers ('red directors'). Such privatisation involved no significant investment or restructuring and was later followed by the oligarchization of the economy and widespread corruption (Plokhy 2016). Kuczabski and Michalski (2014) noted the conflict between the new social values and priorities brought by post-communist transformation on the one hand, and the continued totalitarian methods of public administration and policy making on the other. The strong military specialisation of Ukrainian industry during the Soviet period created multiple challenges for economic restructuring after the collapse of the Soviet Union (Kuczabski & Michalski 2014). This restructuring was very often accompanied by de-skilling, because former high-skilled industries turned to low-skilled production of mass consumption goods, or were subcontracted for low-skilled manufacturing by foreign enterprises. The collapse of the planned economy also disrupted workforce demand, while industrial employment shrank significantly, it began to grow in the tertiary sector. Thus, the post-soviet transition and economic restructuring enhanced de-industrialisation, fostered a shift from high-skilled to middle- and-low-skilled work processes and promoted a low-skill equilibrium (Kupets 2015).

The oligarchization of the economy suppressed the emergence of a middle class and reinforced trends of patronage of different clans, thus limiting access to decision making for most of the population and hindering the development of civil society (Minakov 2018; Plokhy 2016). It also increased power and influence of big enterprises and employers, weakening social dialogue and reducing the participation of trade unions and professional organizations in skill formation policies.

The development of civil society in Ukraine was strongly influenced by the massive and abrupt protest movements and revolutions in 1990 and 2004 (the Orange Revolution), and 2013–2014 (Dignity Revolution or Euromaidan), which channelled societal discontent and, at least temporarily, fostered democratic reforms. These movements prevented complete social and political inertia and the erosion of democratic institutions (Plokhy 2016). However, the outcomes of the reforms brought by these protest movements and revolutions were often stuck in the closed and highly bureaucratised system of public administration and dysfunctional institutional settings of direct democracy (Kuczabski & Michalski 2014). Such circumstances limited the potential of these revolutions to result in effective institutional development, although the Dignity Revolution consolidated civil society and strengthened the pro-European orientation of institutional development, marking a decisive shift away from the Russian model of socio-economic and institutional development (Plokhy 2016).

Another important specific feature of institutional development in post-Soviet Ukraine is regionalization caused by the cultural and socio-economic divisions of the regions. The strongest division can be noticed between Western regions, where the population was keen to accept the pro-European pathway of socioeconomic development, and the Eastern regions with closer ties to Russia and CIS countries (Plokhy 2016). Some authors even claimed a 'civilizational split' between the Western, Central and Eastern parts of Ukraine (Kuczabski & Michalski 2014). The authoritarian regime of Russia played a highly active role in interfering into the socio-economic and political development of Ukraine and in fostering this civilisational split, which was very evident after the Dignity Revolution of 2014.

The collapse of the Soviet socio-economic model and subsequent liberalisation and restructuring of economy after 1991 involved important changes in the system of skill formation, requiring re-orientation away from the skills of traditional industrial sectors, and towards the skills demands of tertiary sector. The period 1995–1998 was marked by a shift of VET policy towards social inclusion and labour market integration, addressing the challenge of growing structural youth unemployment. In the first decade of the independent state, two dominant routes of skill formation, VET and HE, reflected key needs of different stakeholders and interest groups.

More systemic and comprehensive development of institutions of skill formation started with economic stabilisation and growth towards the end of this period, resulting in the introduction of the legal framework on VET with the Order 'On the Reforms of VET in Ukraine' in 1996, the Law on VET in 1998 and the Law on Amendment of Legal Acts in VET in 2004. The new economic conditions, especially economic stabilisation and the beginnings of growth, were favourable for the differentiation of VET qualifications in terms of their types and levels. Different types and levels of VET provision were introduced in 1999, such as higher vocational schools alongside existing vocational technical schools, vocational technical schools in arts, VET centres, training centres for work-based learning in enterprises and centres for training and retraining employees. Significant efforts were made to standardize curricula by introducing and periodically reviewing the methodological guidelines of VET curriculum design in 2005, 2012, 2013, 2017 and 2018. New instruments of curriculum design and management were introduced, such as VET standards, typical training plans and programmes, working/operative plans, and programmes of training at the level of VET providers. These instruments embedded a competence-based approach and simultaneously sought to establish compromise between providing specialised vocational competencies and generic knowledge and skills to increase mobility of learners in the turbulent transitional labour market.

The institutional changes described above can be regarded as a strategy for modernising VET provision by bringing curricula closer to labour market needs. The focus of this modernisation was on strengthening workplace and work-based learning in initial VET, stronger involvement of business stakeholders in managing and funding VET, decentralising governance of VET and delegating more autonomy to VET providers.

However, one of the key challenges and problems with this modernisation process was a lack of coherent and comprehensive involvement of the social partners, especially trade unions and representatives of small and medium enterprises (SMEs). The second decade of the independent state also showed increasing regional differences relating to skill formation processes and policies in Ukraine. The differences between bigger cities and rural areas, as well as between the Western regions with faster development of market economy structures and SMEs, and the Eastern regions with the legacy of Soviet industrial enterprises, were especially significant.

The third decade of the independent state can be regarded as the period of Europeanization of skill formation processes. This was especially prominent after the Dignity Revolution of 2014, which marked a decisive shift towards adopting and adapting EU standards in different fields. Two key features in this period are particularly noteworthy: extensive policy borrowing and policy learning facilitated through implementing various EU projects and programmes, and the focus of reforms on systemic improvement of designing, providing and awarding of qualifications.

## Institutional development and adapting the skill formation system to EU requirements

### Current features of skill formation in Ukraine

After 2016, significant steps towards the decentralisation of governance of further education were taken by reducing the power of the Ministry of Education and Science and other Governmental bodies in the sector. For instance, VET governance was decentralised, bringing further (pre-higher) professional education under the control of regional councils. Universities were granted greater autonomy via the introduction of independent national bodies of governance, such as the National Agency on Quality Assurance of Higher Education. The processes of decentralisation of governance helped to introduce new forms of education and training, such as the dual approach in VET and HE, modular curricula, and ICT enhanced education. Ukraine adopted a comprehensive series of new fundamental legal acts for systemic reform in skill formation. (The Law 'On Education' was introduced in 2017, amendments to the Law 'On Higher Education' in 2018–2019, the Law 'On Special Higher Education' in 2019, the Law 'On Full General Secondary Education' in 2020. Draft laws were prepared 'On Vocational (Vocational and Technical) Education' in 2019, 'On the National Qualifications System' in 2019, 'On Adult Education' in 2019.). The country's first occupational standards were also developed and implemented (Register of Occupational Standards 2020, Register of Applications 2020).

Dual education has become widespread in both VET and HE along with competence-based approaches to curricula design. The recognition of non-formally acquired skills has started to function in the system of vocational education centres of the State Employment Service (Recognition of the outcomes 2020). The National Qualifications Agency has been established. The National Agency for Quality Assurance of Higher Education conducts independent accreditation of study programmes. General education curricula have also been reformed by implementing profiled education for senior students. However, these achievements are attenuated by vast and complex institutional challenges and problems.

Firstly, the government's attempts since independence to optimise the network of educational institutions of all types were undermined by the expansion and commercialisation of educational provision. This led to the formation of a

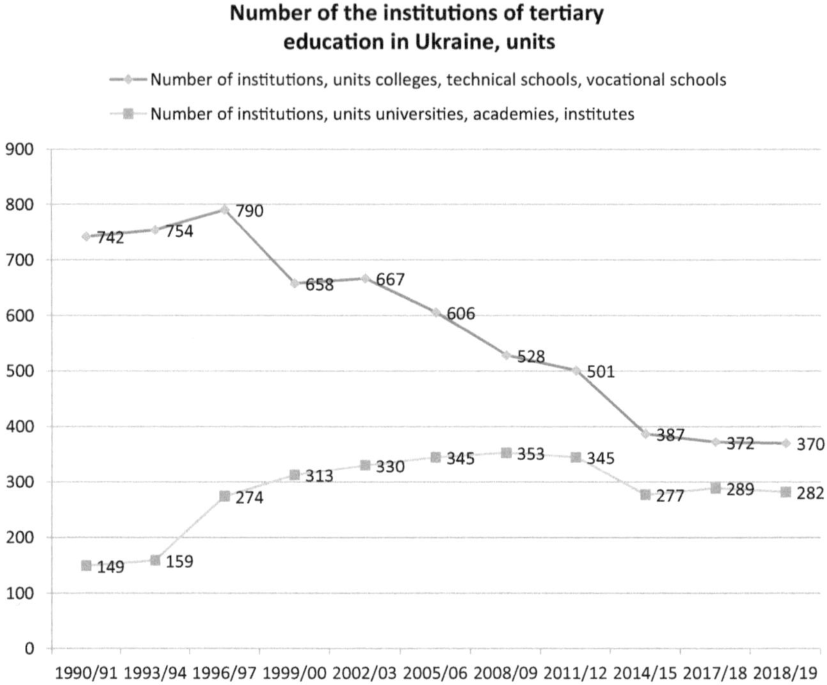


**Figure 13.1.** Number of the institutions of tertiary education in Ukraine. Source: State Statistics Service of Ukraine (http://www.ukrstat.gov.ua).

'diploma market' in the country, which precluded the sustainable development of the qualifications system.

Secondly, the increasing flows of students to HE was at the expense of enrolments in initial VET. This trend did not correspond to the skills demanded in the labour market and so fostered skills mismatches and over-qualification. The result was a significant imbalance between the skills required by employers, and those held by employees, with over-qualification being a major problem (Monitoring of the Provision 2020). During the period 1990–2019, the number of VET institutions decreased by 42 per cent, and technical schools/colleges by 55 per cent, while the number of universities increased by 89 per cent (Figure 13.1).

Thirdly, the expansion of HE and the implementation of the Bologna reforms failed to improve the quality of studies, because of the inertia and strong centralisation inherited from Soviet times (Kupets 2005). Fourthly, due to the decentralisation of management and funding, educational institutions of all

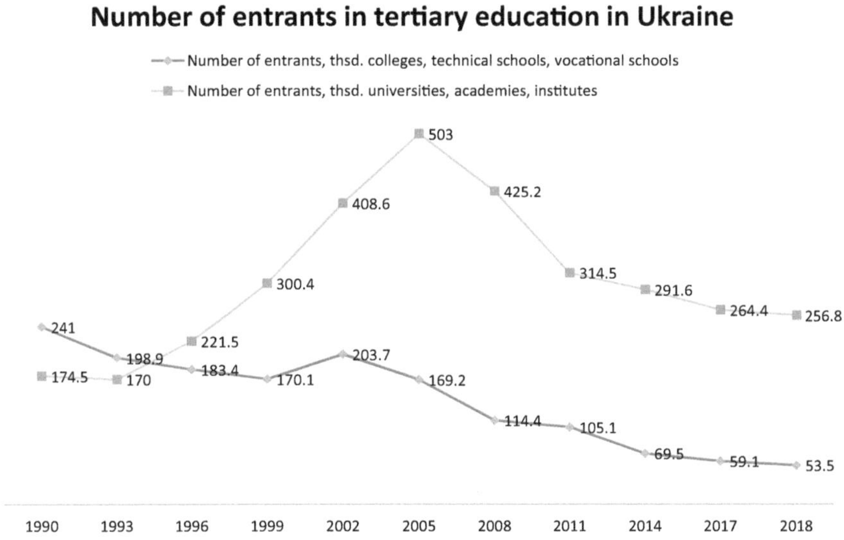


**Figure 13.2.** Number of entrants in tertiary education in Ukraine. Source: State Statistics Service of Ukraine (http://www.ukrstat.gov.ua).

types and forms of ownership have increased, and become larger, especially HE institutions. A similar trend is evident with respect to the number of students in post-secondary education institutions (Kupets 2005). The number of students in VET institutions from 1990 to 2018 decreased by 78 per cent, while students registered in universities increased by 47 per cent (Figure 13.2).

These changes were accompanied by a general reduction in the level of public funding allocated to education, and the inefficient use of those funds, primarily due to the failures of the distribution and cost management mechanisms. Overall public funding for education declined by 1.7 per cent of GDP (from 7.1 per cent to 5.4 per cent) between 2010 and 2016. Despite these reductions, Ukraine continues to occupy a leading position in Europe and worldwide according to the level of funding for education (close to the UK and ahead of the USA).

Finally, there is a large and persistent mismatch between the qualifications offered and labour market demand. In 2013–2019, holders of HE diplomas were disproportionately over-represented among the unemployed (about 50 per cent of the total) because vacancies were mainly in jobs demanding vocationally skilled workers (70–75 per cent) (Analytical paper 2019). The distribution of graduates of tertiary education institutions also evidences significant

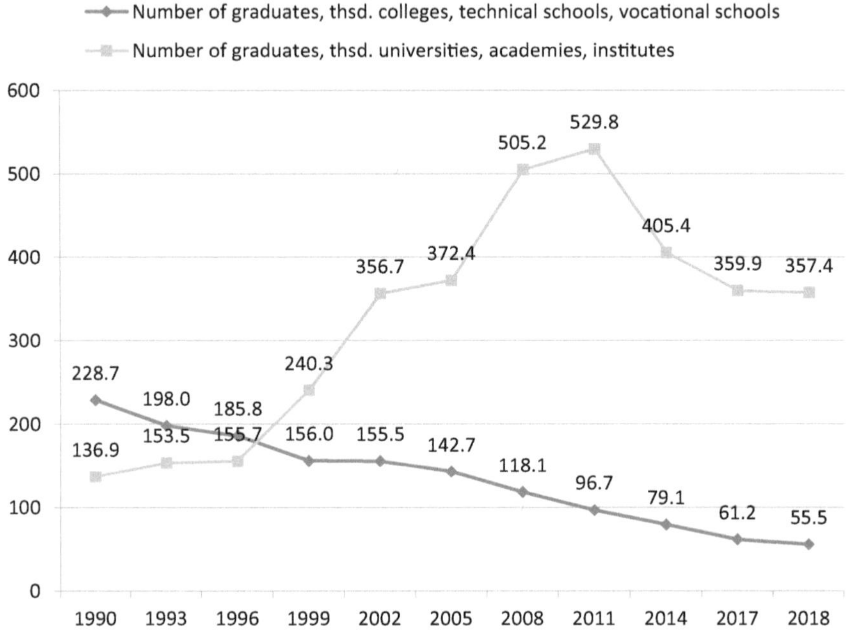


**Figure 13.3.** Number of graduates of tertiary education in Ukraine. Source: State Statistics Service of Ukraine (http://www.ukrstat.gov.ua).

disproportion of graduates of HE institutions, especially at the beginning of the second decade of this century (Figure 13.3).

The existing processes for skills forecasting in Ukraine continue to be mostly formal, corporate-departmental, and socially oriented, but not aligned with the real demands of the economy. The adoption in November 2012 of the Law of Ukraine 'On the formation and placement of a state order for the training of specialists, scientific, pedagogical and working personnel, advanced training and retraining of personnel' was not followed by the establishment of a clear, transparent, and accessible mechanism for educational providers which would help to implement it. The current system of vocational guidance and skill forecasting does not facilitate the acquisition of professional skills that would facilitate employment and career growth (Law on Formation and Placement of the State Order 2017).

Despite significant efforts to reform the VET system emergent policy has experienced significant iterations and blockages with respect to implementation, for several reasons. At the national level, no model or mechanism has been implemented to generate high-quality VET policy and practice oriented towards the acquisition of professional skills demanded by the labour market. There is also a latent conflict of interests of big enterprises and employers' organizations which have sought to advance their own agendas in both national VET policy and over qualifications in areas like development of occupational standards, independent assessment of competence and award of vocational qualifications. This also explains the reluctance to involve trade unions in these processes.

Despite such shortcomings, meaningful improvement in the institutional development of skill formation can nevertheless be discerned. There has been a noticeable reduction in bureaucratic barriers and restrictions over access to education and training, via increased autonomy of education and training providers, especially universities. The dual form of vocational training has expanded, especially in continuing training provided by the State Employment Service, as has recognition of non-formal education. For example, in the period 2017–2018 dual vocational training was launched in the 52 VET schools located in the 25 regions, covering 54 occupations (Ministry of Education and Science of Ukraine, 2020). Thirdly, there was an extension of corporate training by transnational corporations (McDonald's Ukraine, Coca-Cola, Bosch and many others).

## Contextual factors affecting the development of skill formation and VET systems

Several factors have influenced the development of the country's skill formation system. Firstly, demographics, the importance of which cannot be overstated. Ukraine was one of the ten countries in the world experiencing the highest population decline between 1991 to 2018, having lost over 18 per cent of the population during this time (Demographic and Social Statistics 2020). In 2018, there were 54 births per 100 deaths, and this has limited the entrant base for education providers. The labour force is rapidly ageing, and in many organizations, especially in the public sector, the average age of employees is approaching retirement. There is, therefore, a huge challenge to replace those about to retire with younger workers, which is exacerbated by the relatively low wages and low prestige of work in the public sector.

Secondly, there is a challenging labour market situation. Between 2010 and 2019 the workforce decreased by 9.3 per cent, the employed workforce by 13.6 per cent, and the number of hired employees by 27.5 per cent (Demographic and Social Statistics 2020). All this was accompanied by a redistribution of the workforce with a significant reduction in the number of employees in high-tech activities requiring high qualifications. In the economic downturn highly skilled workers and specialists very often sought alternative employment in the informal economy, especially in small businesses or as market traders, and enterprises found it difficult to encourage them to return to their former workplaces even when more attractive salaries and working conditions were offered. Thirdly, it is estimated that about 7 million citizens left Ukraine over the entire period of its independence, more than 70 per cent of whom do not plan to return (Вінокуров 2019).

Fourthly, the political processes of forming a new independent state following the collapse of the Soviet Union failed to generate dynamic, effective and irreversible forms of socio-economic development. The efforts to introduce the best examples of democracy, welfare systems and market economy models faced both internal challenges, such as dominance of oligarchic influence in governance institutions, and external ones, including military aggression by Russia. This, in turn, undermined the implementation of medium-term strategies to promote socio-economic development, establish welfare and social protection systems, and develop competitive systems for flexible provision and the acquisition of skills and qualifications.

Fifthly, the impact of historical legacies has proved to be resilient within a highly diversified and fragmented economy. A long and iterative transitional period in the formation of market relations, and a slow shift in the mentality of the population, especially in attitudes towards the paradigm of ownership, entrepreneurship and individual success, have required patience from policy makers introducing different reforms, as well as a long-term orientation in policy making. This has been difficult to achieve because of the factors described above.

An additional factor which must be considered in analysing challenges to skill formation in Ukraine is the impact of the military aggression of the Russian Federation in the Donbas region and its annexation of Crimea. While the extent of negative impact of this relatively new factor is difficult to estimate precisely, it is clearly colossal. Estimated losses constitute about 20 per cent of the country's economic potential. (Calculated by the author from statistical information for the respective regions). Many VET and HE providers operated in the occupied and uncontrolled territories: 53 institutions of vocational and technical education in Donetsk and 60 in Lugansk regions, plus dozens of universities and technical schools. The aggressor country expropriated the equipment from more than 40 leading engineering enterprises. More than 120 educational and industrial complexes, and 45 scientific and design institutions suspended their activities. Higher education and research institutions have been relocated to the other regions of Ukraine (about 30) but continue to suffer from lack of financial support from the state and weak logistical assistance from local authorities.

## Key challenges for skill formation in different sectors of the education system

### Lifelong learning

So far, educational institutions have paid little attention to creating conditions for lifelong learning (LLL). There are several reasons for the iterative and difficult development of LLL. Over the past two decades, universities have adapted to the mass education of young people, who have been motivated to work towards educational qualifications without reference to subsequent employment. Tertiary pre-university educational institutions in many cases are in a state of stagnation with an 'impoverished' training infrastructure. Easy access to higher education diploma studies, especially in the private sector, has reduced youth interest in VET. The liberalisation of industrial relations and decreased regulatory and supervisory mechanisms in the field of labour have led to deskilling, and a decrease in the proportion of qualified workers in a number of economic sectors as well as in many small and medium enterprises, provoking a knock-on drop in demand for educational and professional qualifications.

Most VET providers operate with solid but outdated training programmes and curricula which do not meet labour market needs, while enterprises are oriented to short-term training provision with partial qualifications. Furthermore, low incomes among the population prevents employees from investing in their career growth and increasing their professional skills and qualifications. Yet despite these challenges and difficulties, there have been some positive trends in the development of lifelong learning. For example, the Ministry of Social Policy introduced the practice of recognizing non-formal education in workers' occupations and successfully introduced a voucher system for funding training of unemployed for 30 occupations and 23 specialisations.

### Design of vocational qualifications and VET curricula

One of the key obstacles in the development of VET is the outdated national system of classification of occupations and vocational qualification standards. Almost half of the entries in the National Classification of Occupations of Ukraine relate to outdated and irrelevant occupations and professions. Despite various attempts made since 2016, the responsible governmental bodies and social partners have not succeeded in implementing the new National Classification of Occupations aligned with contemporary international approaches to occupational classification and standardization (ISCO-08, ESCO). A significant challenge for the implementation of competence-based vocational and higher education is the lack of benchmarks and guidance tools for identifying the skills and competencies needed in the different occupations.

Another outdated regulatory approach to determining qualifications is the system of qualification characteristics inherited from the Soviet period. So far about 6,100 qualification characteristics have been developed for almost 9,200 positions in the National Classification of Occupations (Melnyk 2020). Most of these qualifications are obsolete or refer to obsolete occupations, their key disadvantages being the absence of clearly defined criteria and requirements. In most cases, apart from individual qualification characteristics for occupations in the healthcare sector, there is no functional separation of competencies in the different labour functions. The description of qualifications in the qualification characteristics is presented in a generalised form without division into labour functions, and without a combined competence-based approach.

Nevertheless, due to the gradual design and implementation of the national occupational standards, qualification characteristics continue to be a key reference for the development of educational standards, which significantly impairs the quality of these standards and their relevance to the labour market requirements for competencies and skills. For example, at the beginning of 2020, the country approved 73 standards of higher education for bachelor's degree and 27 standards for master's degree studies. None of them were developed based on occupational standards due to their absence for the corresponding professions.

Over the past decade, nearly 400 national standards of vocational (vocational and technical) education in specific occupations have been developed and implemented, of which more than a third follow a competence-based approach (Melnyk 2020). Due to the absence of occupational standards, these educational standards have been prepared by following outdated qualifications characteristics (Melnyk 2020).

## Management and funding of VET

Although the decentralisation of the management and funding of the VET system emerged in policy discourse in the early years of post-communist transition, the practical implementation in policy started in 2016 in a very 'top-down' way and without extensive consultations with the relevant stakeholders. This process faced several problems, including the absence of an adequate regulatory framework, and the underfunding of VET providers in certain regions, primarily in the regional centres. Dismantling the existing vertical governmental control has not been followed by the development of new arrangements. There were also complications relating to horizontal relationships between VET providers in the different regions, which created obstacles for student mobility. The cooperation between employers, regional authorities and VET providers in the field of curriculum design and skills needs identification is very formal.

## Higher VET

Another important problem within the VET system of Ukraine is higher vocational education and training, which in the Soviet time was provided by so-called '*technikums*', designed to develop middle level skills and qualifications. The former *technikums* were transformed into professionally oriented higher education institutions and incorporated into the higher education system through the Law on Higher Education in 2002. More than one hundred *technikums* and higher vocational education schools (colleges) were integrated into universities to improve the image and quality of this type of further education. However, this solution was neither sustainable nor effective for policy makers. With the adoption in 2014 of the norms and provisions of the Law of Ukraine 'On Higher Education', higher vocational education institutions (technical schools, colleges, etc.) were excluded from the system of HE. The procedure introduced for their 'return' to HE is complicated, leaving many with the problem of finding the optimal place in the education system and market. Such uncertainty leads in many cases to falling enrolments and deteriorating prospects for the development of staff and infrastructure, which makes the training of technicians, technologists and other middle-level specialists more complicated.

## Policy borrowing and policy learning from EU

Skill formation, and especially VET in Ukraine was influenced by the policy borrowing and policy learning from both Anglo-Saxon and continental European (mostly German) models. Since the beginning of the new millennium until the adoption of the new Law of Ukraine 'On Education' in 2017, and thanks to broad international assistance (UN Program, World Bank, UNESCO programmes, European Training Foundation, British Council, Friedrich Erhard Foundation, etc.) and the assistance of many individual countries (USA, Canada, Japan, Finland, Germany and others) different foreign models, approaches and mechanisms for the formation / reform of the skill formation and VET were actively studied by the policy makers and stakeholders.

The introduction and implementation of competence-based VET curricula can serve as a good example in this respect. In the first decade of the 21st century, when VET curriculum reform began, it was supported by the different international donors, promoting Anglo-Saxon approaches to VET curriculum design, with a focus on functional analysis and task-based competencies. Trials of this approach were sporadic and had contradictory results due to resistance from VET providers and teachers and their lack of preparedness to accept such a radical turn from the school-based to competence-based education. This changed at the beginning of the 2nd decade with greater EU input, and especially the support of the European Training Foundation. In this period ETF and other international donors, such as GTZ from Germany began providing assistance and knowledge to facilitate the systemic reform of VET curricula and qualifications involving competence-based curriculum design (development of the occupational standards, VET standards and the standards of competence assessment), implementation and promotion of work-based learning. The German model of skill formation became increasingly attractive for policy makers and stakeholders in this period. These policy learning activities also involved engaging with, and building the capacity of, the social partners, especially employers' organizations.

As a result of policy borrowing and policy learning, a liberal, market-oriented model of the national qualifications system was designed in Ukraine before the establishment of the National Qualifications Agency, and higher education institutions were granted some level of autonomy. Yet at the same time, many issues relating to the activities of educational service providers, especially their responsibility for high-quality of education and training and its relevance to labour market needs, were either ignored or highly bureaucratised by the state. As a result, a hybrid model of skill formation developed in Ukraine, which was sub-optimal in terms of efficiency, effectiveness and the quality of training provided.

International experts and donors assisted in shaping an effective system of skill formation in the country. For example, in the period 2015–2019, the European Training Foundation conducted eight sociological and analytical studies and thirteen international practical seminars. More than 270 reports based on analysis of experience and developments in other countries were transferred to the relevant central authorities and domestic experts (European Training Foundation 2020), making a significant contribution for policy learning in the field of skill formation. Such developments included the preparation and dissemination of recommendations for the development of occupational standards, the organization of training for almost 200 VET teachers/trainers in 6 regions of the country on the development of occupational standards, the development of the website and the development of the National Register of Qualifications with their subsequent transfer to the National Qualifications Agency (Melnyk 2020).

The EU Project 'U4Skills: Best Skills for Modern Ukraine' was launched in 2019. This is a joint programme involving the EU, Germany, Finland, Poland and Estonia to support the reform of vocational education and training in Ukraine, to make training relevant to the requirements of the labour market, and to help young people and adults achieve their potential. The project is expected to be completed in 2023 by significantly upgrading the equipment and infrastructure of public VET providers and contributing to the implementation of competence-based curricula (EU4SKILLS 2020).

Although international cooperation and the consequent policy learning have aided the design and implementation of policies of skill formation, VET and qualifications, this was not without risk or problems. One of the key risks is that insufficient coordination of different initiatives will lead to a fragmentation of policy and methodology. Such projects also often lack the necessary public and private support to ensure continuity and sustainability.

## Social dialogue in the field of skills formation

### Social dialogue and the participation of social partners in skill formation

The views of employers and trade unions on the skills agenda in Ukraine do not differ much from the positions of social partners in the other countries, especially with respect to the economic, social, employment and entrepreneurial benefits of improving skills. Yet the good intentions of the social partners have been less evident with regards to implementation, which has always been very difficult and iterative.

One of the key areas of employer involvement in policy making has related to the development of the national system of qualifications. In 2010, big companies became the initiators and founders of the national qualifications system in Ukraine. The Federation of Employers of Ukraine developed and tested a draft procedure for referencing the requirements of learning outcomes for existing educational and professional qualifications to descriptor levels of the National Qualifications Framework (NQF). The joint representative body of employers' associations created the first industry councils in the country, which aimed to design and develop competence-based occupational standards and qualifications. These bodies developed about 70 per cent of the occupational standards that are currently approved. The Federation of Employers of Ukraine, with the support of German partners implemented dual higher education studies in the technical universities. This Federation has also taken an active part in the annual national competitions of professional excellence WorldSkills Ukraine.

Enterprises have also implemented a variety of different internal systems for assessing, assigning and describing vocational qualifications (mainly partial ones), with businesses operating with links to, or subsidiaries of, foreign corporations implementing international corporate qualification systems (BOSCH, McDonalds, etc.). The key disadvantage of the activities of employers and their associations in the field of skill formation is the disproportionate power of the Federation of Employers of Ukraine at national level, and of the Federation of Metal Production Industry of Ukraine at sectoral level. These organizations have monopolised social dialogue over skills and qualifications, and, although they have made positive contributions to employment relations, their excessive power has marginalised other less-powered employer's bodies and professional associations preventing their participation in social dialogue. The power of these bodies has also impeded enterprise access to resources, and the transfer of innovation to other businesses, notably the small and medium sized business sector.

Trade unions are the weak link in the development of social dialogue over skill formation. The low-profile of trade unions in skill formation, primarily at the sectoral, regional and local levels, stems from the general crisis of trade unions in the country. While unions have their own financial and human resources which would facilitate engagement with the skills agenda, trade union activities need a complete reset, in common with the entire system of social partnership, primarily at the sectoral and regional levels. At national level trade unions have faced the problems of a falling membership base, the emergence of alternative labour movements, which are often very aggressive; ageing leaders and their strong dependence on employers (there are many examples of this at the enterprise level). Unions are also focused on the need to 'preserve' property inherited from Soviet times, as they were strongly involved in the different violations that took place involving the mismanagement, appropriation and privatisation of property. More recently, the state authorities and big business have adopted aggressive policies towards trade unions.

Analyses of developments in the skill formation system during the last decade suggest that the system overall, and social partners in particular, do not fulfil their full potential (National Qualifications Framework 2020). There are many reasons for this situation. Employers often need to spend additional funds on 'retraining' graduates of educational institutions due to their lack of professional skills. This is a clear outcome of the 'diploma market' that has arisen, where learners seek a document confirming completion of education, but not of concrete professional skills and qualifications demanded in the labour market.

The work-based and in-service training of workers, with rare exceptions, is divorced in practice from formal education. Employers and providers of educational services do not act as equal partners, largely because of legislative barriers. The training of workers in more than 1,200 so called 'industrial training factories' (centres for in-service training) creates intense competition between formal education institutions for access to practical training infrastructure, yet to date these centres have not been recognized as equivalent 'players on the field' of the educational services market (National Qualifications Framework 2020).

## Development of skills needs forecasting system

While the design and development of skill needs forecasting instruments is advanced in the EU and other post-industrial economies, in Ukraine only the initial elements of such instruments and measures are emerging and their development is hindered by unresolved 'post-Soviet' problems.

First, there is no up-to-date statistical base for forecasting skills needs by occupations or qualifications. Enterprises, business stakeholders and government bodies lack information and data for strategic planning relating to economic activities and human resources in different segments of the labour market. The system of qualifications and occupational standards is at a preliminary stage of development. Neither enterprises nor government are sufficiently motivated and engaged to design a national system to forecast skills needs. Moreover, the Government is reluctant to implement effective skills needs forecasting, because this might reveal important policy failures with respect to skill supply and create pressure for remedial action. In an environment of political uncertainty and populism, policy makers prefer to make attractive, vague and unattainable promises about development of national human capital without assuming any real responsibility for it. Employers also do not want to invest in skills needs forecasts, arguing that this is a state responsibility. A latent self-interest of monopoly-oligarchic capital is to have an obedient and dependent workforce, whereas objective skills needs forecasts involving employee representatives might reveal the need for general social and personal competencies, the acquisition of which might make employees less dependent and obedient.

On the skills supply side, there is no clear link between occupations, educational standards, and programmes with professional qualifications. This has resulted in skill mismatches and over-qualification in certain fields. National level policy makers have insufficient information about skills gaps within the current workforce as well as demand for qualifications in national, regional and local labour markets. The forecasting of skills needs is also largely missing, as are algorithms for comparing standards and diplomas issued by universities, with labour market skills needs.

Over the past decade research has been undertaken to develop a model for forecasting the need for vocational qualifications (Analytical report 2017). The methodology for assessing medium-term skills needs at national level was developed by experts of the Ukrainian Ministry of Economic Development, and scientists of the Institute of Demography and Social Research of the NAS of Ukraine, with the participation of other stakeholders and direct support from the European Training Foundation (ETF). A methodology of skill needs forecasting based on statistical analysis of trends was designed in 2012–2013. In 2014–2015, Ukrainian experts, with the advisory and financial support of the ETF, Cedefop and other expert organizations, developed and tested the basic elements of the forecasting model for medium-term skills needs. Currently, scientists of the Institute of Demography and Social Research of the National Academy of Sciences of Ukraine are refining the model for implementation.

The research study 'Skills for modern Ukraine' conducted between 2014 and 2017 by World Bank staff indicated that Ukraine needs advanced cognitive, socio-emotional and technical/technological skills in almost all sectors of the economy and types of enterprises (Del Carpio et al. 2017). It also concluded that the current system of skill formation delivers a high level of basic cognitive skills and a significant number of people with tertiary qualifications.

In 2019, under the auspices of the United Nations, studies were undertaken of the activities of the State Employment Service and their impact on the vocational education system and labour market in the Luhansk and Donetsk regions (Complex analysis Donetsk 2019; Complex analysis Luhansk 2019). These studies involved methodological approaches to statistical forecasting and indicated that it is both straightforward and affordable, relying as it does solely on official data of the State Employment Service, regional (Kyiv city) and local employment centres and MES of Ukraine. This approach considers supply and demand over the long term and is thus able to predict the demand for education and training in relation to groups of professions. It also allows for annual adjustments after receiving official statistics for the previous year and can therefore be used to develop recommendations for all types of institutions of skill formation on the level of provision required with respect to different types of training.

## Formation of the national system of qualifications

Although discussions about the formation and development of the national system of qualifications started in 2020, it remains at the initial design stage. The policy focus has been on establishing the legal framework, institutional settings and methodological tools related to qualifications. The institutional framework, which is under development, and governance arrangements applied in the design and implementation of qualifications are relatively centralised, although traditionally employers' organizations play an important role and implement their own initiatives, especially in the field of design of qualifications and occupational standards.

The Ministry of Education and Science of Ukraine has played a key governance role in the development of the national system of qualifications. The Interdepartmental Working Group of Government on the development and implementation of the National Qualifications Framework was established in 2017, and this group executed an Action Plan for the Implementation of the National Qualifications Framework for 2016–2020. On 5 December 2018, the National Qualifications Agency (NQA) was created in Ukraine (Issues of the activity 2018).

Currently, the NQA is working on the formation of the legislative and regulatory framework necessary for the functioning of the national qualifications system, whilst also organising training for the developers of occupational standards and experts on accreditation of qualification centres, as well as for specialists in forecasting demand for skills and qualifications. There are approved procedures for the accreditation of qualification centres, a methodology for the examination of accreditation of qualification centres, and a training programme for experts on the accreditation of qualification centres. Prior to the creation of the NQA, governance arrangements for qualifications were neither permanent, nor collegial. The relevant ministries (education, economy and social policy) have faced a lot of long-standing problems, which are, in some cases, getting worse. For example, there is a mismatch between the supply of, and demand for, skills, there is a lack of institutions with the capacity to assess and award vocational qualifications and obsolete former Soviet approaches to vocational training remain in use. The functions of the NQA defined by the new Law 'On Education' are expected to enable and support the formation of new independent stakeholders in the national system of qualifications. First, the NQA supports and coordinates a nation-wide network involving sectoral and regional councils of qualifications, awarding centres, experts working in the assessment of competencies and the award of qualifications, developers of occupational, educational and assessment standards. Altogether, this network is expected to enable the launch of a new national qualifications system.

The NQA takes over the regulation of design and implementation of occupational standards, and the maintenance of the national register of qualifications from the Ministry of Economy. It also assumes the function of accrediting centres awarding qualifications, a function which has been delegated to different governmental bodies.

Policy makers and experts expected that the establishment of the independent NQA based on equal representation of state authorities and social partners would significantly reduce the risks of centralisation and bureaucratisation of the national system of qualifications. The work of the Agency was designed to simplify the administration of the accreditation processes for qualification awarding centres, whilst ensuring the subsidiarity-based coordination of the design and approval of occupational standards.

However, at the time of drafting, there is a real threat that the risks of increasing centralisation and bureaucratisation of the national system of qualifications will become a reality. A bill has been submitted to the Ukrainian parliament to transform the National Agency for Quality Assurance in Higher Education and the National Qualifications Agency into central government institutions. This demonstrates the resilience of the tendency towards institutional centralisation with respect to skill formation in Ukraine.

## Conclusions

The development of the system of skill formation in post-Soviet Ukraine presents an interesting study of institutional development marked by: (1) the resilience of the Soviet legacy in the structures and functioning of institutional settings, behaviours and methodological approaches; (2) complex and iterative institutional methodological transformations against the backdrop of diversity; of socio-economic and cultural-historical development both in the regions and in sectors of economy; (3) the challenging and iterative involvement of civil society and interest groups in the processes of skill formation, against the backdrop of the prevailing role of Government in policy making, fragmented social dialogue, the increasing power of employers in the processes of skill formation and the lack of transparency in policy making; and (4) the highly challenging and problematic socio-economic context of the reforms defined by both economic and humanitarian crisis and the emergence of a nation state and attendant civil society.

An analysis of the development of the system of skill formation in Ukraine within the context of broader international developments leads us to suggest four possible scenarios for skills formation in the future.

(I) *The modernisation scenario* foresees a systemic transformation of the fields of education, training, and skill formation, and the emergence of a clearly developed model compatible with the approaches to skill formation taken by other European countries and the EU. This scenario involves a detailed plan for the implementation of the adopted strategy, with a clear roadmap and lines of accountability for on-going reform.

(II) *The scenario of radical reform based on policy borrowing* would be realised when a successful model of skill formation developed in another country, or countries has been wholly 'imported'. Such a scenario would need to reference the ongoing 'competition' between the 'Anglo-Saxon' and 'Continental/German speaking countries' approaches to skill formation.

(III) *The scenario of iterative and regressive transformation* would be evident when the training system gradually adapts to changes in the economy and the labour market. Legislative and regulatory measures would be introduced, but due to insufficient funding and bureaucratic delays, would not be implemented. With insufficient financial incentives the state would not attract a critical mass of stakeholders. The government and central executive bodies would initiate and implement different measures of skill formation haphazardly, without following a systemic approach. Skill formation processes would be time consuming and ineffective and would not contribute to economic development due to irrational use of stakeholder resources. This is the most likely scenario, given the current trajectory of reform in Ukraine.

(IV) *The mixed scenario* combines elements of the three scenarios outlined above. In this scenario the development of skill formation system would result in the decentralisation and redistribution of funding, governance and the national system of qualifications. This would be achieved through the engagement of major stakeholders within the system of skills formation, and the promotion of public-private partnerships. This scenario foresees an important role both for policy learning from foreign (international) approaches and the removal of legislative and regulatory barriers that impede the recognition of acquired skills, and professional qualifications obtained through formal, non-formal and informal training (Melnyk 2017).

## References

Applebaum, A. (2017). *Red Famine. Stalin's War on Ukraine*. New York, NY: Doubleday.

Deissinger, T., & Melnyk, O. (2019). 'Reform perspectives for the Ukrainian VET System – a critical analysis'. In F. Marhuenda & M. J. Chisvert-Tarazona (eds.), *Pedagogical Concerns and Market Demands in VET*. Proceedings of the 3rd Crossing Boundaries in VET conference, Vocational Education and Training Network (VETNET), pp. 50–55. Valencia: University of Valencia.

Del Carpio, X., Kupets, O., Muller, N., & Olefir, A. (2017). *Skills for a Modern Ukraine. Directions in Development*. Washington, DC: World Bank.

European Training Foundation (2017a). *Децентралізація професійно-технічної освіти в Україні [Decentralisation of the vocational education and training in Ukraine]*,<http://pedpresa.ua/wp-content/uploads/2017/04/ukraine-vet-reform-steps-v5-sp-ua-1.pdf>, accessed 20 July 2020.

Kupets, O. (2016). 'Education-job mismatch in Ukraine: Too many people with tertiary education or too many jobs for low-skilled?' *Journal of Comparative Economics*, 44 (1), 125–147.

Libanova, E., Cymbal, A., Lisogor, L., Marchenko, I., & Iarosh, O. (2014). *Labour Market Transitions of Young Women and Men in Ukraine*. Geneva: International Labour Organization.

Lücke, M., & Saha, D. (2019). *Labour Migration from Ukraine: Changing Destinations, Growing Macroeconomic Impact*. Berlin, Kyiv: German Advisory Group.

Pieńkowski, J. (2020). *The Impact of Labour Migration on the Ukrainian Economy*. Luxembourg: Publications Office of the European Union.

Plokhy, S. (2016). *The Gates of Europe. A History of Ukraine*. London: Penguin Books.

United Nations Ukraine (2019a). *Комплексний аналіз регіонального ринку праці Луганської області [Complex analysis of the regional labour market of Luhansk region]*,<https://www.ua.undp.org/content/ukraine/uk/home/library/recovery-and-peacebuilding/comprehensive-analysis-of-the-regional-labour-market-in-luhansk-.html>, accessed 9 March 2020.

United Nations Ukraine (2019b). *Комплексний аналіз регіонального ринку праці Донецької області [Complex analysis of the regional labour market of Donetsk region]*,<https://www.ua.undp.org/content/ukraine/uk/home/library/recovery-and-peacebuilding/comprehensive-analysis-of-the-regional-labour-market-in-donetsk-.html>, accessed 9 March 2020.

United Nations Ukraine (2019c). *Комплексний аналіз системи професійно-технічної освіти в Луганській області 18 лип. 2019 року [Complex analysis of the system of vocational education and training in the Donetsk region, 18*

*July 2019]*, <https://www.ua.undp.org/content/ukraine/uk/home/library/recovery-and-peacebuilding/analysis-of-the-vocational-education-and-training-system-in-luha.html>, accessed 9 March 2020.

Верховна Рада України (2017). *Закон України «Про формування та розміщення державного замовлення на підготовку фахівців, наукових, науково-педагогічних та робітничих кадрів, підвищення кваліфікації та перепідготовку кадрів» [Law on Formation and Placement of the State Order for Preparation of Specialists, Scientific Research and Teaching Staff, their Continuing Training and Retraining]*,< https://zakon.rada.gov.ua/laws/show/5499-17#Text>, accessed 14 April 2020.

Верховна Рада України (2020). *Закон України «Про освіту» [Law on Education of Ukraine]*,<https://zakon.rada.gov.ua/laws/show/2145-19#Text>, accessed 14 April 2020.

Верховна Рада України (2020). *Закон України «Про внесення змін до деяких законів України стосовно удосконалення освітньої діяльності у сфері вищої освіти» [Law on Amendment of the Acting Laws of Ukraine on the activities of higher education institutions]*,<https://zakon.rada.gov.ua/laws/show/392-20#Text>, accessed 14 April 2020.

Верховна Рада України (2019).*Закон України « Про фахову передвищу освіту» [Law of Ukraine on the vocational further education]*,<https://zakon.rada.gov.ua/laws/show/2745-19#Text>, accessed 14 April 2020.

Верховна Рада України (2020). *Закон України «Про повну загальну середню освіту» [Law of Ukraine on the general secondary education]*,<https://zakon.rada.gov.ua/laws/show/463-20#Text>, accessed 14 April 2020.

Верховна Рада України (2018). *Деякі питання Національного агентства кваліфікацій. [Issues of the activity of the National Agency of Qualifications]*,< https://zakon.rada.gov.ua/laws/show/1029-2018-%D0%BF#Text>, accessed 9 March 2020.

Вінокуров, В. (2019). *Майже 10% населення: В уряді підрахували, скільки українців виїхало за кордон від початку десятиліття [Almost 10 percent of population: Government calculated the volume of Ukrainians who emigrated since the beginning of decade]*,<https://hromadske.ua/ru/posts/pochti-10-naseleniya-v-pravitelstve-podschitali-skolko-ukraincev-vyehali-za-granicu-s-nachala-desyatiletiya>, accessed 9 March 2020.

Гаврицька, М., Гречушкіна, Т., Косухіна, Т., Мельник, С. (2010). *Національний класифікатор України ДК 003 «Класифікатор професій» [National Classification of Ukraine DK 003 Classification of Occupations]*. Кіив: Держстандарт України, Видавництво «Соцінформ».

ГНУ «Институт образовательной аналитики» (2020). *Мониторинг обеспечения педагогическими работниками заведений образования Украины: методологические подходы к прогнозированию [Monitoring of supply of educational providers of Ukraine with teching staff: methodological approaches to forecasting]*,<https://iea.gov.ua/wp-content/uploads/2020/06/1-na_sajt_AZ_Monitoring_potrebi_ZO_u_pedpratsivnikah-final.pdf>, accessed 14 June 2020.

Державна служба зайнятості (2020). *Аналітики та статистика. [Analytics and statistics]*,<https://www.dcz.gov.ua/analitics/67>, accessed 11 March 2020.

Державна служба зайнятості (2019). *Аналітична записка про стан ринку праці та діяльності Державної служби зайнятості у 2019 році [Analytical paper on the labour market and activities of the National Employment office in 2019]*,< https://www.dcz.gov.ua/analitics/67file:///D:/%D0%97%D0%B0%D0%B3%D1%80%D1%83%D0%B7%D0%BA%D0%B8%20Google%20Chrome/analitychna_zapyska_shchodo_sytuaciyi_na_rynku_praci_ta_diyalnist_derzhanoyi_sluzhby_zaynyatosti_u_2019_roci%20(2).pdf>, accessed 9 March 2020.

Державний центр зайнятості (2019). *Визнання результатів неформального навчання. [Recognition of the outcomes of non-formal education]*, <https://www.dcz.gov.ua/storinka/pidtverdzhennya-neformalnogo-navchannya>, accessed 12 April 2020.

Держстат України (2020). *Демографічна і соціальна статистика / Ринок праці / Зайнятість и безробіття [Demographic and social statistics/Labour market/Employment and unemployment]*,<http://www.ukrstat.gov.ua/operativ/menu/menu_u/rp.htm>, accessed 11 March 2020.

Держстат України (2020). *Демографічна і соціальна статистика/освіта. Коледжі та університети [Demographic and Social Statistics / education. Colleges and universities]*,<http://www.ukrstat.gov.ua/operativ/operativ2005/osv_rik/osv_u/vuz_u.html>, accessed 11 March 2020.

Держстат України (2020). *Демографічна і соціальна статистика/освіта. Заклади професійної (професійно-технічної) освіти [Demographic and Social Statistics / education. Vocational education (vocational and technical education) institutions]*,< http://www.ukrstat.gov.ua/operativ/operativ2005/osv_rik/osv_u/ptu_u.html>, accessed 11 March 2020.

ДНУ «Інститут омвітньої аналітики». (2020). *Моніторинг забезпечення педагогічними працівниками закладів освіти України: методологічні підходи до прогнозування [Monitoring of the provision of educational institutions of Ukraine with the teaching staff: methodological approaches of forecasting]*, <https://iea.gov.ua/wp-content/uploads/2020/06/1-na_sajt_AZ_Monitoring_potrebi_ZO_u_pedpratsivnikah-final.pdf>, accessed 11 March 2020.

ДНУ «Інститут омвітньої аналітики». (2018). *Освіта в Україні: базові індикатори. [Education in Ukraine: basic indicators]*,<https://mon.gov.ua/storage/app/media/nova-ukrainska-shkola/1serpkonf-informatsiyniy-byuleten.pdf>, accessed 11 March 2020.

ДНУ «Інститут освітньої аналітики» (2019). *Методологічний підхід щодо обґрунтування оптимізації мережі закладів професійної (професійно-технічної) освіти [Methodological approaches for optimization of the network of vocational education and training providers]*,<https://iea.gov.ua/naukovo-analitichna-diyalnist/analitika/rezultati-naukovih-doslidzhen-2/rnd_2019/>, accessed 11 March 2020.

ДНУ «Інститут освітньої аналітики» (2019). *Освітня реформа: результати і перспективи [Reform of Education: results and perspectives]*,<https://iea.gov.ua/naukovo-analitichna-diyalnist/materiali-komunikatsijnih-zahodiv/2019-2/>, accessed 11 March 2020.

Українске Право (2019). *Проєкт Закону України «Про освіту дорослих» [Draft Law of Ukraine on the Adult Education]*,<https://ukrainepravo.com/news/ukraine/osvita-dlya-doroslykh-shcho-peredbachaye-zakon-pro-fakhovu-peredvyshchu-osvitu/>, accessed 14 April 2020.

Євро Освіта (2016). *Фінансування освіти: скільки, кому і як? НДІ прикладних технологій [Financing of Education: how much, to whom and how?]*, <http://www.euroosvita.net/prog/print.php/prog/print.php?id=4879&category1&id1092>, accessed 11 March 2020.

Мельник, С. (2017). 'Ключові підходи до реформування сфери підготовки кадрів в Україні [Key approaches of the reform of vocational education and training in Ukraine]', *Освітня аналітика України*, <https://science.iea.gov.ua/wp-content/uploads/2018/12/94_106_Melnyk-1.pdf>, accessed 9 March 2020.

Мельник, С. (2020). 'Моніторинг виконання Плану заходів із запровадження Національної рамки кваліфікацій на 2016–2020 роки [Monitoring of the execution of the Action Plan for Implementation of the National Qualifications Framework in 2016–2020]', *European Training Foundation bridging support to Ukraine's vocational education and training system and qualifications system in 2016–2019*, <https://openspace.etf.europa.eu/blog-posts/etf-bridging-support-ukraines-vocational-education-and-training-system-and>, accessed 9 March 2020.

Мельник, С. (2020). 'Рекомендації з розроблення професійних стандартів [Recommendations for development of occupational standards]', *European Training Foundation bridging support to Ukraine's vocational education and training system and qualifications system in 2016–2019*, <https://openspace.etf.europa.eu/blog-posts/etf-bridging-support-ukraines-vocational-education-and-training-system-and>, accessed 9 March 2020.

Міністерство Освіти і Науки України (2020). *Дуальна освіта [Dual Education]*,<https://mon.gov.ua/ua/osvita/profesijno-tehnichna-osvita/dualna-osvita>, accessed 15 May 2020.

Міністерство Освіти і Науки України (2019). *Проєкт Закону України «про професійну (професійно-технічну) освіту» [Draft Law of Ukraine on the vocational (vocational technical) education]*,<https://mon.gov.ua/ua/news/yakoyu-maye-stati-profosvita-v-ukrayini-uryad-uhvaliv-zakonoproyekt-pro-profesijnu-profesijno-tehnichnu-osvitu>, accessed 14 April 2020.

Міністерство Освіти і Науки України (2019). *Проєкт Закону України «Про Національну систему кваліфікацій» [Draft Law of Ukraine on the National System of Qualifications]*,<https://mon.gov.ua/ua/news/mon-proponuye-do-gromadskogo-obgovorennya>, accessed 14 April 2020.

Міністерство розвитку економіки, торгівлі та сільського господарства України (2020). *Реєстр професійних стандартів [Register of Occupational Standards]*,<https://www.me.gov.ua/Documents/Detail?lang=uk-UA&id=22469103-4e36-4d41-b1bf-288338b3c7fa&title=RestrProfesiinikhStandartiv&isSpecial=true>, accessed 12 April 2020.

Міністерство розвитку економіки, торгівлі та сільського господарства України (2020). *Реєстр заявок на розроблення професійних стандартів. [Register of Applications for Development of Occupational Standards]*,< https://www.me.gov.ua/Documents/Detail?lang=uk-UA&id=c5e6262d-5b44-4894-8b09-4e1e5da04dbd&title=RestrZaiavokNaRozroblenniaProfesiinikhStandartiv>, accessed 12 April 2020.

Міністерство Освіти і Науки України (2020). *Національна рамка кваліфікацій. [National Qualifications Framework]*,<https://mon.gov.ua/ua/tag/natsionalna-ramka-kvalifikatsiy>, accessed 9 March 2020.

Міністерство Освіти і Науки України (2017). *Аналітичний звіт щодо професійно-кваліфікаційного прогнозування в Україні. Робочий проєкт для обговорення 9 листопада 2017 р. у м. Києві. [Analytical report on professional qualification forecasting in Ukraine. Working project for discussion on November 9, 2017 in Kyiv]*, <https://mon.gov.ua/storage/app/media/nrk/Analitychni-materialy/2-analitichniy-zvit-shchodo-profesiyno-kvalifikatsiynogo-prognozuvannya-v-ukraini.pdf>, accessed 9 March 2020.

Кабінет Міністрів України (2020). *План заходів із запровадження Національної рамки кваліфікацій на 2016–2020 роки. [Plan of measures for implementation of the National Qualifications Framework in 2016–2020]*, <http://search.ligazakon.ua/l_doc2.nsf/link1/KR161077.html>, accessed 9 March 2020.

Центр продуктивності (2005). *Довідник кваліфікаційних характеристик професій працівників. Вип. 1. [Handbook of the Qualification Characteristics of Employees. Vol.1]*. Краматорськ: Центр продуктивності.

Emma Wallis and Jonathan Winterton

# 14. Social dialogue and skill formation systems in the CEE

**Abstract:** A brief review of social dialogue over skill formation in some EU15 countries is provided as a benchmark and location point for exploring the role of social dialogue in the skill formation systems of Central and Eastern Europe (CEE). Conclusions attempt to make sense of commonalities and differences in social dialogue and collective bargaining over the developing skill formation systems of CEE countries. Except for Slovenia, the CEE countries share weaknesses of social partner institutions and especially trade unions as part of the Soviet legacy. Far from overcoming these weaknesses, the adoption of neo-liberal approaches is further marginalising the role of trade unions in skill formation as in other areas, so there is little scope for optimism that meaningful dialogue will be established in the foreseeable future.

In all, there is no evidence that the idealised European model of social dialogue over skill formation is being replicated in CEE countries. More significantly, perhaps, nor is there any evidence that this was the intention with the criteria for EU accession. The Europeanization of CEE economies was designed to improve living and working conditions in those countries, and despite the disruptive restructuring of obsolete heavy industries, social and economic progress was evident at least until the economic crisis in 2008. The aim of reducing the risk of social dumping, however, appears somewhat inconsistent with the neoliberal approach promoted by the EU and international bodies, which all appear to have been serving the interests of international capital.

**Keywords:** Social dialogue, skill formation systems, neo-liberal approaches

## Introduction

Social dialogue refers to discussions between trade unions and employers or employers' associations (collectively known as social partner organizations) and is distinguished from collective bargaining because it does not necessarily involve negotiation, although there is an expectation that something more than consultation is involved. When the state joins as a third party, this is normally referred to a 'concertation', and the social partner organizations expect to have some influence on the policy that is being discussed. Social dialogue is one of the pillars of the European social model and plays a key role in European approaches to regulating labour markets and employment issues. In practice it is difficult to maintain a clear distinction between social dialogue and collective bargaining and both are captured in the country accounts in this collection and the wider literature on which this chapter draws.

Skill formation is often regarded as one of the areas where social dialogue is particularly appropriate, for three principal reasons. First, involving unions and employers in decisions about training ensures its relevance to the world of work. Second, when the social partners are involved in its design and delivery, skill formation has more legitimacy than if training providers alone determine curricula. Third, training is often viewed as an area where there are shared interests, making for partnership and cooperation.

Although these three reasons are widely accepted, each merits critical examination. What union representatives and employers identify as priorities for the content of training reflect their different respective perceptions of the world of work and these priorities may be driven more by economic interests than any logic of learning or pedagogy. The collaboration of social partners with training providers and experts in curriculum design does, of course, bring legitimacy, and should ensure training is grounded in the world of work and reflects workplace needs. However, the skills employers demand do not always match those that can be deployed in the jobs on offer, which is reflected in over-qualification and under-employment, especially among graduates. Employers frequently complain that graduates do not have appropriate skills, but often these are elaborated in terms of motivation and commitment, thinly veiling their quest for an acquiescent workforce (Winterton & Turner 2019).

On the third point, employers and unions often declare skill formation an area of consensus, but their interests are not entirely congruent (Winerton & Winterton 1994). Employers want a workforce with the competencies to support their business strategies, while workers want to develop skills that will lead to higher remuneration and better career opportunities. Employers are likely to emphasise firm-specific skills that will reduce employee mobility, whereas employees want the opposite in the form of portable qualifications that will enhance their mobility in the labour market. Employers' associations may have broader agendas around work restructuring to support flexibility and reduce demarcation, while unions are more likely to see training as a way of maintaining control over an occupation and reducing employers' opportunities for labour substitution. These interest differences are not entirely irreconcilable but justify the necessity of social dialogue to reach compromises over skill formation.

Adequate social partner organization is necessary, but not sufficient, for social dialogue, which also requires consent and even support from the state. Opportunities for social dialogue over skill formation are profoundly affected by labour market regulatory frameworks and the nature of the skill formation

**Table 14.1.** Typology of skill formation systems

| | *Regulation:* | *Market* | *State* |
|---|---|---|---|
| Focus | | | |
| Workplace | market-work | state-work | |
| School | market-school | state-school | |

*Note.* J. Winterton (2007). 'Building social dialogue over training and learning: European and national developments', *European Journal of Industrial Relations*, 13 (3), 281–300.

system even in countries where social partners institutions are well developed and free from state obstruction. Where skill formation systems are under development and labour markets less well regulated, social dialogue is unlikely to play a major role in training and development. Following this brief introduction, the chapter is organized in three sections. The first section offers a brief review of social dialogue over skill formation in some EU15 countries to act as a benchmark and location point for exploring in the second section; the role of social dialogue in the skill formation systems of Central and Eastern Europe (CEE). The third section offers conclusions that attempt to make sense of commonalities and differences in social dialogue and collective bargaining over the developing skill formation systems of CEE.

## Social dialogue over skill formation in the old EU15

Different country contexts are important, and two variables are particularly relevant: training systems and employment relations regimes. Training systems differ in focus (rather than locus) of training (school or work) and regulatory mechanisms (state or market). Combining these two dimensions produces a typology with four possibilities as shown in Table 14.1.

State-regulated, school-focussed skill formation systems predominate in EU15 countries, whether vocational education and training (VET) is delivered through specialist VET schools (as in France, Portugal and Spain) or integrated into mainstream schools (as in several Nordic countries). The exception among continental countries are those with state-regulated, work-focussed systems of skill formation, notably Germany with the dual system, also adopted in Austria, Denmark and Switzerland. The stereotypical form of market-led, work focussed skill formation is in the Western liberal market economies of UK and Ireland (also to a degree the Netherlands), while Italy had the unusual combination of a market-led, school-focussed skill formation system (Winterton 2000), also found in Greece, though in both cases more state regulation has been introduced in recent decades.

Social dialogue over skill formation was a defining characteristic of the European Union in the 1990s (EC/UNICE/CEEP/ETUC 1996; Heidemann et al. 1994), although the extent of dialogue varied substantially between countries. The main factor determining the extent of social dialogue over skill formation, and most other employment issues, was the labour market regulatory framework (using Amable's 2003 categories) and the associated employment relations regime. Unsurprisingly, while there was extensive social dialogue in the Nordic and Continental coordinated market economies (CME), in the Western liberal market economies (LME) this was the exception, Heidemann et al. (1994, 11) commenting on the 'almost total absence of social dialogue over VET' in the UK. Coordinated labour market regimes were associated with state-regulated skill formation systems, which invariably defined social partner involvement, often with significant statutory rights (Winterton 2007, 285). However, where skill formation was school-based, social dialogue tended to be at a more remote policy level compared with in the work-focussed dual system countries, where union involvement is embedded in the system. In market-led systems, the extent of social dialogue over training matters was more contingent upon the level of trade union organization (Winterton 2006) but in LMEs with work-focussed skill formation systems, as in the UK, social dialogue was extensive in unionised sectors. The skill formation system influenced the nature and extent of social dialogue over and above the labour market regime. Moreover, while the level of union organization had a determining influence over social dialogue in market-led systems, in state coordinated systems social dialogue structures were often established irrespective of the capacity of the trade unions to play an active role. Such a situation is evident in France and parts of Southern Europe, which has important implications for CEE, where trade union capacity is also in many cases limited.

Looking across the old EU15, in the last two decades there have been some outstanding examples of social dialogue over skill formation and three are worthy of mention. In France, the 2003 *Accord Nationale Interprofessionelle* constituted the most comprehensive national framework agreement for skill formation ever negotiated which, despite the limitations of union organization, resulted in more than 400 agreements at sector level and further enterprise level enhancements to training opportunities (Le Deist & Winterton 2012). In Germany, corporatist traditions at sector level have led to jointly managed skill formation systems that deliver what is often considered the gold standard of VET in the form of the dual system (Deissinger 2015). In the UK workplace initiatives such as *unionlearn*, which was built on the strength of workplace organization, for many years partnered successfully with employers to engage workers with few qualifications in learning at work (Stuart et al. 2013). It is no coincidence that these examples are drawn from the levels where social dialogue and collective bargaining in each country is most effective and each example reflects the country context. The paradox is that where unions have most state support, as in France, they remain weak at workplace level and where there is a hostile state, as in the UK, they survive only in well-organized workplaces or where they can contribute to workplace restructuring (Winterton & Winterton 1994). By contrast, the Scandinavian and German employment relations regimes left space for the unions without making them dependent on state support. Stuart and Wallis (2007) found innovative partnerships around learning in seven EU15 countries and noted the form of partnership reflected those different institutional contexts. The importance of context needs to be reiterated since it imposes serious limitations to the possibilities for policy borrowing either between the old EU15 countries or from them to the CEE countries. While there has been substantial comparative research on social dialogue and on VET, there have been relatively few systematic comparative studies of social dialogue *over* VET (Winterton 2008). This lacuna is even more evident in relation to social dialogue over skill formation in the CEE countries, addressed in the next section.

## Social dialogue in CEE countries

Social dialogue in the CEE countries is relatively underdeveloped and an earlier study of the unions' involvement in the European Employment Strategy found that although all candidate countries had established tripartite machinery as a condition of EU accession, social partner organizations in countries that were formerly part of the Soviet bloc often lacked resources and were relatively ineffective, allowing governments to dominate economic and social committees (Winterton & Strandberg 2004). In the transition economies that are the focus of this collection, trade unions lacked popular support because in the Soviet era they were linked to the Party and struggled to secure recognition from employers. Monitoring by the ICFTU (International Confederation of Free Trade Unions) revealed blatant union-busting by employers two decades ago (for details, see Winterton & Strandberg 2004) and the *2021 ITUC Global Rights Index* lists Estonia, Latvia, Lithuania and Slovakia as countries with repeated violations of workers' rights (ITUC 2021, 15), while Ukraine has also been mentioned for failing to respect freedom of association. Intimidation of union officials has been alleged in Romania (Trif 2013, 236), which ICFTU monitoring reported as widespread in Bulgaria, Hungary and Poland.

Tripartite structures had to be created as part of the accession process, without the foundation of bilateral 'autonomous social dialogue' (Lado & Vaughan-Whitehead 2003, 82), particularly in the form of underpinning collective bargaining, so union officials had little experience of negotiation and were often ineffective in social dialogue within concertation institutions. Two decades ago, there was a substantial gap between the transition economies and the EU15 in terms of national social dialogue (Casale 1999; Eurofound 2003) as well as sectoral dialogue (Ghellab & Vaughan-Whitehead 2003) and especially in influencing skill formation at enterprise level (Geororgica & Luttringer 1997). While the emphasis on social dialogue at that time was clearly part of a strategy of Europeanization of the unions (Dølvic 1999) and labour relations (Kirton-Darling & Clauwaert 2003), some observers were concerned about the reverse influence and the effect the new member states might have upon social dialogue throughout Europe: 'The lack of preparedness of the social partners from candidate countries for the social dialogue process could well lead to its progressive delegitimization.' (Lado & Vaughan-Whitehead 2003, 86).

At the time of the 2004 enlargement of the EU, the prevailing view was of serious limitations to the effectiveness of social dialogue in CEE countries, and relatively little effective involvement of social partner organizations in skill formation systems. Since that time, the 2007–2008 Global Financial Crisis (GFC) caused profound restructuring throughout Europe (Winterton & Forde 2013) and an increase in precarious work (Burgess, Connell & Winterton 2013). The banking crisis coupled with macroeconomic imbalances in the euro area led inexorably to the European Sovereign Debt Crisis, which began to unfold from 2010. The combined effect of these financial and economic crises emboldened employers to roll back collective bargaining and reinforce managerial prerogative throughout Europe and it is difficult to assess what effect, if any, this had on the 'social dialogue gap' between CEE and EU15 countries. The economic effects of the COVID-19 pandemic are still emerging, but it has evidently caused a deeper recession than either the GCF or the Great Recession of 1932 and CEE economies were among the most affected. While the specific impact of the pandemic on social dialogue is difficult to assess, the cumulative effects are expected to have further weakened trade unions.

Union density fell substantially in CEE countries, especially in Latvia and Hungary (Korkut et al. 2017, 67). However, union weakness is not simply a function of low union density, but of wider issues of credibility in overcoming the Soviet legacy and of capacity for effective involvement in social dialogue institutions. Union effectiveness is also affected by the extent to which the state supports social partner participation institutionally. France, for example, has one of the lowest rates of union membership in Europe, but social dialogue institutions exist at all levels because of state support. Where both the state and employers are hostile, unions are effectively hobbled even if they can develop internal capacity.

From the contributions to this book, the weakness of trade unions in CEE has continued to be a major limiting factor, but this has varied in both spatial and temporal terms. There have been some changes in the extent of social dialogue over skill formation in CEE countries but also substantial continuities with respect to limitations. Unsurprisingly, social dialogue arrangements remain least developed in the Baltic and Southeast Europe (Balkans and Ukraine), most robust in Slovenia and between these polar cases in the Visegrád countries. Drawing on extant literature and the country chapters in this collection, each group of countries is considered below.

## Baltic countries

Social dialogue is least developed in the Baltic countries with unionisation particularly low in Estonia and Lithuania, while bargaining coverage is low in Latvia and Lithuania compared with the other CEE countries (Kalanta 2020). There is no historical institutional legacy of social dialogue in the region and economic reforms after independence focussed on radical liberalisation and flexible labour markets (Kallaste & Woolfson 2013). EU accession required the establishment of social dialogue mechanisms, which Woolfson and Sommers (2016) argue were formally adopted but not effectively operationalised in the Baltic countries. In addition to low union density and weak institutional capacity, the strategies of Baltic enterprises were to resist multi-employer bargaining, a precondition for effective social dialogue according to Kalanta (2020). The contributors to this collection confirm that social dialogue remains particularly underdeveloped in these countries.

In Estonia, Vali (2004, 227) noted the predominance of tripartite national negotiations, explaining this by the relative weakness of collective bargaining at lower levels and the need for stronger state involvement. While social dialogue had increased it remained relatively weak, reflecting the low level of unionisation and coverage of collective bargaining (ibid., 225). Kallaste (2019) confirmed the decline in trade union density and coverage of collective bargaining but noted bargaining that survived transition was well established. At national level tripartite social dialogue arrangements include negotiation over VET (ibid., 178) but most agreements are single employer, notwithstanding employers' 'general aversion to collective bargaining' (ibid., 181). Loogma in this collection argues that the collapse of the Soviet trade unions led to low union density. In the social dialogue institutions promoted by the EU, employers dominate, and professional bodies have more influence in skill formation than the unions.

In Latvia, Ozola (2005) explained how a low level of employee trust in trade unions led to low unionisation rates and low coverage of collective agreements, which are predominantly at enterprise level. The weak finances of the unions makes it difficult to develop internal competence, which in turn limits capacity for effective involvement in tripartite social dialogue even though the structures have been formally established. Social dialogue has clearly been driven by the Europeanization agenda and Woolfson (2008, 80) argued that in the context of the liberal market reforms adopted in Latvia, the attempt to use social dialogue 'to promote policy goals of vocational training and adult learning' represented a 'lack of domestic reform fit.' Lulle and Ugure (2019) confirmed the weakness of social dialogue, falling coverage of collective agreements and predominance of company level bargaining, noting that 'lifelong learning' (ibid., 373) and 'study for qualifications' (ibid., 374) are sometimes covered in company agreements. In this collection, Buligina and Sloka suggest that the most significant social dialogue has been around the establishment of work-based learning (WBL), which was a key priority in the reform of skill formation. European initiatives under Erasmus+ and ESF projects facilitated more extensive social dialogue and the involvement of stakeholders was important for successful innovation in WBL.

In Lithuania, Gruzevskis and Blaziene (2005) noted that domestic employers were less amenable to negotiating collective agreements than foreign companies and that the weakness of bipartite negotiations limited the progress made with tripartite social dialogue, even though the institutions were established as part of preparations for EU accession. Similarly, Tūtlys, Kaminskienė and Winterton (2016, 391) attributed the adoption of LME approaches in designing the qualifications system in Lithuania to a lack of alternatives owing to the limited capacity of social partners and the underdeveloped state of social dialogue. The CME approach to qualifications and skill formation is predicated upon effective social partner organizations and well-developed collective bargaining and social dialogue. Blažienė, Kasiliauskas and Guobitė-Kirslienė (2019) confirmed that Lithuania has one of the least developed industrial relations systems in the EU, with low union density and bargaining coverage. There is nonetheless multilevel collective bargaining and agreements do often include training issues (ibid., 394). In this collection, Tūtlys et al. note that the inadequacy of social dialogue is evident in skill formation and that although tripartite institutions were created, these were largely driven by government because of the low capacity of social partners. Challenges of demographic trends and emigration led to a fragmentation of social dialogue over skill and employment which allowed employers more influence than the unions (see the chapter of Tūtlys et al. in this collection).

## Southeast Europe

The Balkan countries represented in this collection, along with Ukraine, are also marked by weaknesses in social dialogue arrangements for various reasons.

Bulgaria established tripartite institutions in 1992 but these were limited to consultations with employers' organizations and trade unions, mostly on economic and employment questions. Daskalova-Nikova (2004, 119) noted that tripartite social dialogue was delimited by the negotiations with the IMF and World Bank and marked by tension between the trade unions and government. From 2001 employment action plans, and most legal regulations were drafted without consulting social partners. The low employment rate, growing unemployment and emigration further constrained the economy and social partner involvement became token without any opportunity of real influence over policy. Kirov (2019) reported a drop in union membership in the early years of transition in Bulgaria and decreased bargaining coverage, although still relatively high among CEE countries. The 2008 economic crisis had a severe effect on Bulgaria and despite social partner agreement to wide ranging crisis measures, mass protests brought down a succession of governments. In this collection, Simeonova-Ganeva, Ganev and Angelova argue that skill formation was not a priority for a country with a low level of technological sophistication and limited labour market demand for skills. This in turn fed into lower demand for technical training, increasing negative perceptions of VET, growing demand for HE and underemployment of HE graduates. Following EU accession in 2007, there was increased involvement of social partners and more social dialogue over skill formation (see the chapter of Simeonova-Ganeva, Ganev & Angelova in this collection). More effective social dialogue is needed to improve labour market forecasting and modernise qualifications.

Croatia retained some of the strength of labour organization like Slovenia after the break-up of the former Yugoslavia, but, like Serbia, nationalism was prevalent (Kokanović' 2001) leading to a more conflictual and weaker institutionalised model of labour relations (Grdešić 2008). Bagić (2019) emphasised the stability of collective bargaining structures that are quite heterogenous between sectors and the maintenance of relatively high trade union density despite declining membership and fragmented union structure. In this collection, Matković and

Buković note that despite an apprenticeship model based broadly on the German dual system, the state is the dominant player in skill formation. Social partners lack the interest and capacity for greater involvement leading to the 'absence of functioning mechanisms of social dialogue.'

Romania in the early years of transition was marked by unstable labour relations, with strong trade unions and weak employers' associations and tripartite bodies dominated by government (Ghebrea 2005, 159). Unusually, this neoliberal country was characterised by weak state institutions and strong trade unions, involving centralised collective bargaining, high coverage of agreements and strong mobilisation power (Bohle & Greskovits 2012). The comprehensive industrial relations system included national tripartite arrangements, and multilevel bipartite collective bargaining (Trif 2013). Romania was badly affected by the 2008 economic crisis and in successive years governments restructured the system, promoting decentralisation and undermining collective bargaining institutions (Trif 2013). Some trade unions succeeded in using the crisis as an opportunity to introduce innovations such as moving from collective bargaining to servicing members and to organizing peripheral workers (Trif & Stoiciu 2016) but the overall picture is of severely weakened unions. Trif and Paolucci (2019, 520) contrast path-dependent institutional changes up to the 2008 economic crisis, with the 'frontal attack on collective bargaining institutions' through legal changes enacted in 2011. It was noted that the 2010 agreement in the retail sector mentioned training (ibid., 518). The chapter in this collection paints a picture of fragmented institutions of skill formation dominated by government and slow development of social dialogue because employers viewed training as a state responsibility and high unemployment made skills shortages less evident (see the chapter of Vladut in this collection). Trade unions, lacking credibility and with diminishing power, similarly do not regard skill formation as a priority.

Ukraine is characterised in this collection by a lack of involvement of social partners, especially trade unions and SMEs, in the modernisation of skill formation from 1999 onwards (see the chapter of Melnyk in this collection). In the period of Europeanization from 2014 large enterprises and employers' associations were reluctant to involve the unions, allowing government to drive policy implementation in a top-down fashion without stakeholder consultation. Employer involvement in the National Qualifications Framework was dominated by big companies and strongly influenced by external agencies. Policy borrowing and policy learning in ETF and EU projects failed to establish effective social dialogue and initiatives to develop skills forecasting were driven by government with involvement of the ETF, Cedefop and the World Bank. Trade unions remained the weak link in skill formation activities, suffering declining membership, competition from alternative representative movements, and employer aggression.

## *Visegrád countries*

Studies of Visegrád countries in the early years of transition noted all had developed tripartite fora but confirmed weaknesses in union organization. Mason (1995) noted the unions suffered from fragmentation in Hungary and that the union *Solidarność*, which led the protest movement in Poland during the 1980s, lost credibility. While the unions were less fragmented in the Czech Republic and Slovakia, in all four countries non-unionism increased with privatisation and the growth of SMEs. Pollert (1999) similarly noted that despite militancy in Poland in the early 1990s over economic 'shock therapy' and industrial unrest in the mid-1990s in the Czech Republic, restructuring leading to unemployment, coupled with the growth of SMEs and self-employment, led to weak tripartism and fragmented industrial relations in all the Visegrád countries.

In the Czech Republic the old trade unions were replaced with new ones that arose out of the 'Velvet Revolution' and tripartite social partnership was established in 1990, but the neo-liberal right marginalised the unions thereafter (Pollert 1997). Social dialogue was hindered by the immaturity of social partner organizations and government criticism of the EU as 'too socialist', favouring neo-liberal labour market approaches (Zeman 2004, 148). The Social Democratic Government elected in 1998 re-established social dialogue but social partners continued to leave employment policy to government officials. Casale (2001) described social dialogue in the Czech Republic as a 'success story', but Kroupa (2006) was more circumspect, addressing the need for 'capacity building for social dialogue'. Myant (2013, 194) by contrast noted that even after the election of a right-wing coalition Government in 2010, there was 'no significant attempt to reduce existing legal protection of employee or trade union rights.' Myant (2019) attributed the decline in trade union membership to the effects of economic transformation and restructuring of private services and to a degree employer hostility. Bargaining coverage declined less than unionisation but enterprise agreements increased, while sector agreements decreased. Notwithstanding, the country experts in this collection give no attention to social dialogue in the Czech skill formation system, from which we may infer there is still little involvement of the social partners in this domain (see the chapter of Dvořák and Gal).

Hungary experienced increased unemployment post 1989 and increased company-level influence on pay determination that revealed union ineffectiveness in pay bargaining (Neumann 2002). Galgóczi (2004, 292) described the tripartite fora established in preparation for EU accession as 'consultative' with social partner institutions, especially trade unions, not always invited, a situation that improved after the election of a social-liberal Government in 2002. The economic crisis of 2008 had a damaging effect on the unions in Hungary but the election of the Orbán Government in 2010 had a bigger impact, accelerating neoliberal reforms and 'attacking the remnants of labour incorporation' (Szabó 2013, 207). Borbély and Neumann (2019) attribute falling unionisation (under 10 per cent) and collective bargaining coverage to the challenges of privatisation, unemployment and austerity measures. Three levels of bargaining exist but employers' organizations are weak, so agreements are predominantly at company and establishment level. Almost half of agreements include provision on training (ibid., 310), but the contributors to this collection conclude that whereas employers via the Chamber of Commerce and Industry play as role in the skill formation system, trade unions are not involved in social dialogue over VET (see the chapter of Laczik and Farkas in this collection).

Poland, on the eve of EU accession, was portrayed as accepting social dialogue as part of the democratic transition (Kozek 2004, 312) and as having adopted a tripartite approach to employment policy, although bipartite dialogue was acknowledged to be weak (ibid., 314–5). Declining union density and union de-recognition, coupled with divisions and rivalry between national unions, limited the effectiveness of social dialogue in institutional terms (ibid., 340–1). Following the economic crisis of 2008, Poland was the only EU country to avoid recession and the 2008 economic crisis had the initial effect of 're-legitimizing social dialogue' (Meardi & Trappmann 2013, 196). While the crisis did not have a major impact in Poland, it did help consolidate the Polish socio-economic model, characterised as 'neoliberalism that includes decentralisation, flexibility and a residual welfare state, but which counterbalances its inherent insecurity through strong political intervention in the economy and through a relatively high degree of self-reliance, internal demand and monetary sovereignty.' (Meardi & Trappmann 2013, 203). Czarzasty (2019, 478) noted 'collective bargaining coverage is very low (18 per cent), the system is very decentralised, employers are reluctant to engage in collective bargaining and to sign collective agreements' and there are only 'minor references' to training in agreements (ibid., 477). Dębowski and Stęchły in this collection suggest that limited social dialogue over skills in Poland is partly because this was not a policy priority of the government and the government sponsors social dialogue, but also because unions lack capacity and are concentrated in the public sector. Moreover, employers competing on price are less interested in developing employees and relatively high levels of unemployment have assured the availability of skilled labour, although increased emigration is an issue. The Stakeholders' Council introduced under the IQS Act is expected to increase the role of social partners.

Slovakia was described as 'problematic' with respect to national level tripartite social dialogue in the preparation of national action plans for employment (Cziria 2005). Tripartite structures were restarted in 1999, floundered in 2001 then restored but with social partner involvement limited and formal. The economic crisis of 2008 initially strengthened national tripartite social dialogue (Kahancová 2013, 177) but ultimately weakened it, with the unions becoming 'bystanders' (ibid., 181) in policy making. At sector level, however, coordinated bargaining was consolidated, leading Kahancová (2013, 182) to conclude that 'a reasonably well-established and functioning sector-level bargaining system can contribute more to a sustainable coordinated bargaining system than any formal but "illusory" tripartism at national level.' Several factors contributed to deficiencies with social dialogue, including the relative weakness of employers' organizations. Employers were preoccupied with economic issues, while the trade unions focussed on opposing unpopular economic and social reforms. Kahancová, Martišková and Sedláková (2019, 525) note the disconnection between national tripartite structures that are consultative and collective bargaining at industry and company levels. Declining unionisation is matched with declining bargaining coverage and further decentralisation of bargaining to company level, but no mention is made of training within the scope of collective agreements. Vantuch and Jelínková in this collection confirm that with schools dominating the VET system, skill formation is not a topic for social dialogue in enterprises (see the chapter on Slovakia).

## Slovenia

Before EU accession, Stanojević (2003) argued that the unions were relatively powerful in Slovenia, partly because of the legacy of Yugoslav worker management. As noted earlier, although they shared the same history, Serbia and Croatia followed different trajectories, where nationalism and conflict were primary influences (Grdešić 2008). It should also be remembered that Slovenia was the most highly developed Republic of Federal Yugoslavia. With relatively strong trade unions and the employer side dominated by the Chamber of Commerce, social partners played an active role in the development of action plans for employment (Stanojević 2004). Stanojević and Klarič (2013) argued that the economic crisis of 2008, coupled with the inflow of FDI and privatisation damaged social dialogue such that the Government acted unilaterally, which ultimately broke up the coalition. The 2011 elections brought the centre-right party to power, but it quickly lost public support for structural reforms and austerity measures. Social dialogue in Slovenia steadily weakened under the increasing influence of supranational bodies (Stanojević, Mrčela & Breznik 2016). Stanojević and Poje (2019) noted that the centralised bargaining that produced an exceptional coverage of collective agreements in the early years of transition gave way in the private sector to more decentralised arrangements after EU accession in 2004. Following the 2008 economic crisis unionisation decreased further and bargaining coverage fell to under 80 per cent, while a series of political crises produced considerable instability. The contributors to this collection recognize that tripartite institutions were well developed before transition but note social dialogue is becoming increasingly weak and dependent on international institutions (see the chapter of Pavlin, Skubic Ermenc and Bembič). Social partner organizations have been extensively involved in developing occupational standards but lack capacity. Traditionally a neo-corporatist economic system close to the CME model of skill formation, the centre-right Government in 2004 marginalised the social partners and adopted neo-liberal LME principles.

## Conclusions

The above summaries, the country chapters and extant literature confirm the continued limitations of social dialogue over skill formation, and employment issues in general, in CEE countries overall. Overall, in comparison with the old EU15, social dialogue over skill formation in CEE countries is, rather like the dog that didn't bark, most significant by its absence. Differences between the Baltic countries, Balkan region (and Ukraine), Visegrád countries and Slovenia are quite nuanced but in line with expectations, confirming the polar positions of Estonia and Slovenia. Those differences are reflected in labour entry patterns: the Baltic countries are close to the Mediterranean model with weak employment and income sustaining policies but strong employment protection legislation; the Visegrád countries cluster with LME also having weak employment protection and sustaining policies; and Slovenia is the only CEE state that was put in the same cluster as the CME German model with strong employment protection and average employment and income sustaining policies (Saar, Unt & Kogan 2008). Such differences are best explained not by path dependency or strategic choice as alternative models (Regini 2003) but by the interaction of both, coupled with the overlayered compromises of agencies involved (Traxler 2003). Path dependency is evident in the geographic and historic influences on institutions, but strategic choices, especially by governments, have been a major influence. To the extent that governments' choices have been moderated through compromises with other agencies, international bodies, including the EU, have had more influence than social partners, especially the trade unions. The accounts summarised above suggest other common factors affecting social dialogue over skill formation, which are considered below.

Governments continue to exert most influence over skill formation in CEE countries, and to some extent this is explicable by the weakness of social partner organizations: the state must step in because of the lack of capacity of trade unions and employers' associations. That skill formation is also not high on the agenda of social partner organizations is understandable given the scale of restructuring and issues like workers' living standards and enterprise competitiveness that preoccupy the unions and employers respectively. In many countries, however, governments seem only to have introduced tripartite social dialogue to comply with EU accession requirements, maintaining token involvement of trade unions and using the new institutions for top-down information sharing and, at best, as consultative fora. In the Baltic and Balkan countries, the institutional weakness of social partner organizations left a vacuum easily occupied by the state, but developments in other CEE countries are of particular concern. In some Visegrád countries, social partner organizations were already weak but in others, governments have deliberately sought to marginalize and weaken the unions as part of a strategy of embracing LME approaches. Even in Slovenia, which had the most powerful trade union organizations and strongest tripartite institutions, social dialogue has been systematically undermined in moving from neo-corporatism to neo-liberalism.

Trade union organizations are, paradoxically, after governments the next most important players limiting social dialogue over skill formation and wider labour market issues in CEE. Cox and Mason (2000) argued that contrary to expectations the old communist trade unions did not all disappear, but in many cases transformed themselves. Unions were politically weak in both the Czech Republic and Hungary, which like Poland was also characterised by inter-union competition. Fragmented trade unions in Poland established decentralised territorial structures (Gardawski, Mrozowicki & Czarzasty 2012, 34) that were inappropriate for national social dialogue or sector restructuring. Conditions in the Czech Republic were regarded as more conducive to the development of social partnership than in Hungary, although Hungary did achieve a more peaceful transition than Poland (Cox & Mason 2000). Trade unions in all CEE countries face an enormous challenge of transforming from communist instruments of state control over the workplace into institutions representing worker interests and face problems of legitimacy in Romania and Ukraine (Varga 2013). Korkut et al. (2017, 66) note trade unions in both Hungary and Latvia lack capacity and have become unattractive to workers, but unions in each country pursued different strategies. While union leadership in Hungary 'ossified' and remained dominated by the old guard, Latvia's unions adopted a modern professional approach designed to appeal to younger workers (ibid., 77). As already noted, Slovenia remains the only country with relatively robust trade unions capable of playing a major role in skill formation.

The extensive informal economy in CEE countries (Kornai 1980) has thrived with market deregulation and liberalisation advocated by the World Bank, undermining labour market regulatory mechanisms of states, trade unions and international bodies like the ILO. Social dialogue is largely irrelevant to the hidden economy, which thereby reduces the relevance of social dialogue to the wider economy. Sik (1994) reported an increase in the informal economy in Hungary on the eve of transformation and predicted it would remain after transition to a liberal market economy. In Romania, Neef (2002) described a wide range of forms of 'unofficial labour' and undeclared activities, which were also found in Latvia (Sedlenieks 2003). Undeclared work in Ukraine involved self-employed, unemployed and retired workers avoiding tax liabilities as well as employees receiving cash payment 'off the books' to supplement formal wages (Williams 2007). Partly a reaction to severe economic problems and widespread perceptions of corrupt state officials, such practices undermine formal labour relations and trade unions. The informal economy partly explains why Romania has a very high degree of informalisation of employment relations, whereas Slovenia is highly formalised, and Bulgaria falls mid-way between the two (Williams et al. 2013).

Labour mobility is also an important factor and for countries experiencing emigration of a significant proportion of their workforce, skill formation can replace lost human capital but potentially exacerbate the 'brain drain' as countries seek to attract skilled workers. EU accession made it easier for individuals to migrate to the West and emigration increased from all CEE countries post-2004 (Galgóczi, Leschke & Watt 2012) but there were marked differences. The outflow from Baltic countries was particularly significant following the GFC and the austerity measures introduced. Juska and Wolfson (2015) note that austerity measured in Lithuania accelerated labour market segregation and those disadvantaged were most likely to emigrate. It has been suggested that migration and resulting labour shortages in CEE countries represented an opportunity for unions in CEE (Kaminska & Kahancová 2011), but Stan and Erne (2016, 179) noted there was no automatic link between migration, labour shortages and collective wage increases in Romania. East-West migration has been reduced by

Brexit and COVID-19, while intra-CEE migration has increased, adding further complexity to labour mobilities.

Capital mobility has always been more significant than labour mobility and has had a major influence on economic development in CEE countries to such an extent that the transition agenda has served the interests of foreign capital. Kirov (2019, 89) claimed transition has been driven by the 'neoliberal agenda of international institutions and foreign investors.' This is most evident in countries that depend upon FDI, such as Poland (Czarzasty 2019, 469) and Romania (Trif 2013, 229; Trif & Paolucci 2019). Transnational companies also play a major role in the Hungarian economy (Borbély & Neumann 2019) and where foreign companies have production facilities serving transnational supply chains, they are unlikely to be in favour of social dialogue or labour market regulation. In the Czech Republic transnational companies weakened employers' associations, preferring to negotiate independently (Myant 2019, 135). Nevertheless, there is evidence that foreign firms pay higher wages than domestic companies in Bulgaria (Kirov 2019, 86), Hungary (Earle, Telegdy & Antal 2018) and Poland (Broniatowska & Straviński 2021), where unionisation is also higher in foreign-owned enterprises (Czarzasty 2019, 467).

Policy borrowing, and to a lesser extent policy learning, has been a feature of innovation in skill formation in CEE countries, which have drawn both on the Continental CME approach and, increasingly, on the 'Anglo Saxon' LME model. The LME approach may, or may not, have been most appropriate for transitioning from communist to capitalist economies, but irrespective of their suitability or efficacy, liberal market principles were widely associated, if not conflated, with the development of political democracies (Holman 2001). The LME model was promoted by international bodies like the World Bank and IMF, as well as the EU and its agencies Cedefop and the ETF, as outlined in another chapter in this collection (see the chapter on 'Anglo-Saxon' influences and the market-based model of skill formation). Whereas social dialogue is endemic to the CME model of skill formation, the LME model as developed in the UK was associated with removing union influence from training (Rainbird 1990). Liberal market approaches to developing capitalist economies in CEE were designed to attract FDI by competing on cost (Drahokoupil 2009) and the LME model of skill formation was consistent with this.

It should not be assumed that tripartite structures in CEE countries will result in the sort of corporatist outcomes with which they are associated in Western European countries. The evidence from most of the countries considered in this collection supports the conclusion of Ost (2000, 503) that tripartite neocorporatist forms were used in CEE 'to generate neoliberal outcomes.' This 'illusory corporatism' Ost (2000, 504) attributed to 'communist-era legacies producing weak class identity [and] pro-capitalist predilections'. Bernaciak (2013, 240) argued that the flurry of tripartite activity in Poland and Bulgaria after the economic crisis was due to a combination of uncertainty over the magnitude of the downturn and instability in the party systems of the two countries. Labelling this 'PR corporatism', Bernaciak (2013, 249) argued that the measures were principally designed to boost the popularity of the respective ruling parties, but at the same time they widened the scope of tripartite social dialogue and opened the way for bipartite dialogue.

In all, there is no evidence that the idealised European model of social dialogue over skill formation is being replicated in CEE countries. More significantly, perhaps, nor is there any evidence that this was the intention with the criteria for EU accession. Meardi (2007), commenting on the failed export of EU models to CEE soon after accession, noted the responses of 'voice' in an upsurge of grass roots revolt, and 'exit' in the form of emigration. Of course, a simpler explanation is that the mobility afforded by EU membership enabled workers to seek higher earnings and send remittances to family members at home as well as the opportunity to experience other cultures after years of restrictions of movement under the Soviet regime. The Europeanization of CEE economies was designed to improve living and working conditions in those countries, and despite the disruptive restructuring of obsolete heavy industries, social and economic progress was evident at least until the economic crisis in 2008. The aim of reducing the risk of social dumping, however, appears somewhat inconsistent with the neoliberal approach promoted by the EU and international bodies, which all appear to have been serving the interests of international capital.

## References

Amable, B. (2003). *The Diversity of Modern Capitalism*, Oxford: Oxford University Press.

Bagić, D. (2019). 'Croatia: Stability amidst heterogeneous collective bargaining patterns.' In T. Müller, K. Vandaele & J. Waddington (eds.), *Collective Bargaining in Europe: Towards an Endgame Vol. I*, pp. 93–108. Brussels: European Trade Union Institute.

Bernaciak, M. (2013). 'Social dialogue revival or "PR corporatism"? Negotiating anti-crisis measures in Poland and Bulgaria', *Transfer*, 19 (2), 239–251.

Blažienė, I., Kasiliauskas, N., & Guobitė-Kirslienė, R. (2019). 'Lithuania: Will new legislation increase the role of social dialogue and collective bargaining?' In T. Müller, K. Vandaele & J. Waddington (eds.), *Collective Bargaining in*

*Europe: Towards an Endgame Vol. II*, pp. 381–401. Brussels: European Trade Union Institute.

Bohle, D., & Greskovits, B. (2012). *Capitalist Diversity on Europe's Periphery*. Ithaca, NY: Cornell University Press.

Borbély, S., & Neumann, L. (2019). 'Neglected by the state: The Hungarian experience of collective bargaining.' In T. Müller, K. Vandaele & J. Waddington (eds.), *Collective Bargaining in Europe: Towards an Endgame Vol. II*, pp. 295-. Brussels: European Trade Union Institute.

Broniatowska, P., & Strawiński, P. (2021). 'Foreign and domestic firm ownership and its impact on wages. Evidence from Poland', *European Journal of Industrial Relations*, 27 (4), 445–466.

Burgess, J., Connell, J., & Winterton, J. (2013). 'Vulnerable workers, precarious work and the role of trade unions and HRM', *The International Journal of Human Resource Management*, 24 (22), 4083–4093.

Casale, G. (ed.) (1999). *Social Dialogue in Central and Eastern Europe*. Budapest: International Labour Organization.

Casale, G. (2001). *Social Dialogue: The Czech Success Story*. Geneva: International Labour Organization.

Cox, T. M., & Mason, B. (2000). 'Interest groups and the development of tripartism in East Central Europe', *European Journal of Industrial Relations*, 6 (3), 325–347.

Czarzasty, J. (2019). 'Collective bargaining in Poland: A near-death experience.' In T. Müller, K. Vandaele & J. Waddington (eds.), *Collective Bargaining in Europe: Towards an Endgame Vol. II*, pp. 465–481. Brussels: European Trade Union Institute.

Cziria, L. (2005). 'The role of social dialogue in Slovakia's accession to the European Union.' In C. Lafoucriere & L. Magnusson (eds.), *The Enlargement of Social Europe. The Role of Social Partners in the European Employment Strategy Part II*, pp. 203–235. Brussels: European Trade Union Institute.

Daskalova-Nikova, N. (2004). 'The implications of the EES for Bulgaria.' In B. Galgóczi, C. Lafoucriere & L. Magnusson (eds.), *The Enlargement of Social Europe. The Role of Social Partners in the European Employment Strategy*, pp. 95–134. Brussels: European Trade Union Institute.

Deissinger, T. (2015). 'The German dual vocational education and training system as "good practice"', *Local Economy*, 30 (5), 557–567.

Dølvic, J.-E. (1999). *An Emerging Island? ETUC, Social Dialogue and the Europeanisation of Trade Unions in the 1990s*. Brussels: European Trade Union Institute.

Drahokoupil, J. (2009). *Globalization and the State in Central and Eastern Europe: The Politics of Foreign Direct Investment.* Abingdon: Routledge.

Earle, J. S., Telegdy, A., & Antal, G. (2018). 'Foreign ownership and wages: Evidence from Hungary, 1986–2008', *Industrial & Labor Relations Review*, 71 (2), 458–491.

EC/UNICE/CEEP/ETUC (1996). *Compendium: Vocational Training – Innovation and Diversity in Dialogue Practices between Social Partners.* Luxembourg: European Commission.

Eurofound (2003). *Social Dialogue and EMU in the Candidate Countries.* Dublin: European Foundation for the Improvement of Living and Working Conditions.

Galgóczi, B. (2004). 'Employment policy in Hungary with a view to the EES.' In B. Galgóczi, C. Lafoucriere & L. Magnusson (eds.), *The Enlargement of Social Europe. The Role of Social Partners in the European Employment Strategy*, pp. 263–299. Brussels: European Trade Union Institute.

Galgóczi, B., Leschke, J., & Watt, A. (2012). *EU Labour Migration in Troubled Times. Skills Mismatch, Return and Policy Responses.* Farnham: Ashgate.

Gardawski, J., Mrozowicki, A., & Czarzasty, J. (2012). *Trade Unions in Poland*, Report 123. Brussels: European Trade Union Institute.

Ghebrea, G. (2005). 'The role of social dialogue in Romania: Impressive form, deficient content.' In C. Lafoucriere & L. Magnusson (eds.), *The Enlargement of Social Europe. The Role of the Social Partners in the European Employment Strategy Part II*, pp. 149–202. Brussels: European Trade Union Institute.

Ghellab, Y., & Vaughan-Whitehead, D. (eds.) (2003). *Sectoral Social Dialogue in Future EU Member States: The Weakest Link.* Budapest: International Labour Office.

Gierorgica, P., & Luttringer, J.-M. (1997). *The Influence of the Social Partners on Training at Enterprise Level in the Member States of the European Union.* Turin: European Training Foundation.

Grdešić, M. (2008). 'Mapping the paths of the Yugoslav model: Labour strength and weakness in Slovenia, Croatia and Serbia', *European Journal of Industrial Relations*, 14 (2), 133–151.

Gruzevskis, B., & Blazienė, I. (2005). 'EES implementation promoting the development of social dialogue in Lithuania.' In C. Lafoucriere & L. Magnusson (eds.), *The Enlargement of Social Europe. The Role of the Social Partners in the European Employment Strategy Part II*, pp. 61–100. Brussels: European Trade Union Institute.

Heidemann, W., Kruse, W., Paul-Kohlhoff, A., & Zeuner, C. (1994). *Social Dialogue and Further Education and Training in Europe: New Challenges for the Trade Unions*. Berlin: Hans Böckler Stiftung.

Holman, O. (2001). 'The enlargement of the European Union towards Central and Eastern Europe: The role of supranational and transnational actors.' In A. Bieler & A. D. Morton (eds.), *Social Forces in the Making of the New Europe: The Restructuring of European Social Relations in the Global Political Economy*, pp. 161–84. Basingstoke: Palgrave Macmillan.

ITUC (2021). *2021 ITUC Global Rights Index*. Brussels: International Trade Union Confederation.

Juska, A., & Woolfson, C. (2015). 'Austerity, labour market segmentation and emigration: The case of Lithuania', *Industrial Relations Journal*, 46 (3), 236–253.

Kahancová, M. (2013). 'The demise of social partnership or a balanced recovery? The crisis and collective bargaining in Slovakia', *Transfer*, 19 (2), 171–183.

Kahancová, M., Martišková, M., & Sedláková, M. (2019). 'Slovakia: Between coordination and fragmentation.' In T. Müller, K. Vandaele & J. Waddington (eds.), *Collective Bargaining in Europe: Towards an Endgame Vol. III*, pp. 525–544. Brussels: European Trade Union Institute.

Kalanta, M. (2020). 'The Weakness of Social Dialogue in the Baltic Countries: An Employer-Centric Political Economy Perspective', *European Journal of Industrial Relations*, 26 (3), 227–242.

Kallaste, E. (2019). 'Estonia: Simultaneous institutionalisation and waning of collective bargaining.' In T. Müller, K. Vandaele & J. Waddington (eds.), *Collective Bargaining in Europe: Towards an Endgame Vol. I*, pp. 173–195. Brussels: European Trade Union Institute.

Kallaste, E., & Woolfson, C. (2013). 'Negotiated responses to the crisis in the Baltic countries', *Transfer*, 19 (2), 253–266.

Kaminska, M. E., & Kahancová, M. (2011). 'Emigration and labour shortages: An opportunity for trade unions in the New Member States?' *European Journal of Industrial Relations*, 17 (2), 189–203.

Kirov, V. (2019). 'Bulgaria: Collective bargaining eroding, but still existing.' In T. Müller, K. Vandaele & J. Waddington (eds.), *Collective Bargaining in Europe: Towards an Endgame Vol. I*, pp. 77–92. Brussels: European Trade Union Institute.

Kirton-Darling, J., & Clauwaert, S. (2003). 'European social dialogue: An instrument in the Europeanisation of industrial relations', *Transfer*, 9 (2), 247–264.

Kokanovic´, M. (2001). 'The cost of nationalism: Croatian labour, 1990–1999.' In S. Crowley & D. Ost (eds.), *Workers after Workers' States: Labor and Politics in Postcommunist Eastern Europe*, pp. 141–57. Lanham, MD: Rowman and Littlefield.

Korkut, U., de Ruyter, A., Maganaris, M., & Bailey, D. (2017). 'What next for unions in Central and Eastern Europe? Invisibility, departure and the transformation of industrial relations', *European Journal of Industrial Relations*, 23 (1), 65–80.

Kornai, J. (1980). *Economics of Shortage*. Amsterdam: North Holland Publishers.

Kozek, W. (2004). 'How far into implementation? Social dialogue in Poland for participation in the EES'. In B. Galgóczi, C. Lafoucriere & L. Magnusson (eds.), *The Enlargement of Social Europe. The Role of Social Partners in the European Employment Strategy*, pp. 301–344. Brussels: European Trade Union Institute.

Kroupa, A. (2006). *Capacity Building for Social Dialogue in the Czech Republic*. Dublin: European Foundation for the Improvement of Living and Working Conditions.

Lado, M., & Vaughan-Whitehead, D. (2003). 'Social dialogue in candidate countries: What for?' *Transfer*, 9 (1), 64–87.

Le Deist, F., & Winterton, J. (2012). 'Trade unions and workplace training in France: Social partners and VET.' In R. Cooney & M. Stuart (eds.), *Trade Unions and Training: Contemporary International Perspectives*, pp. 77–100. London: Routledge.

Lulle, A. & Ugure, E. (2019). 'Latvia: Post-Soviet legacy and the impact of neoliberal ideology on collective bargaining.' In T. Müller, K. Vandaele & J. Waddington (eds.), *Collective Bargaining in Europe: Towards an Endgame Vol. II*, pp. 361–379. Brussels: European Trade Union Institute.

Mason, B. (1995). 'Industrial relations in an unstable environment: The case of Central and Eastern Europe', *European Journal of Industrial Relations*, 1 (3), 341–367.

Meardi, G. (2007). 'More voice after more exit? Unstable industrial relations in Central Eastern Europe', *Industrial Relations Journal*, 38 (6), 503–523.

Meardi, G. & Trappman, V. (2013). 'Between consolidation and crisis: Divergent pressures and sectoral trends in Poland', *Transfer*, 19 (2), 195–204.

Myant, M. (2013). 'The impact of the economic crisis on collective bargaining in the Czech Republic', *Transfer*, 19 (2), 185–194.

Myant, M. (2019). 'Czechia: Bargaining supplements legal protection.' In T. Müller, K. Vandaele & J. Waddington (eds.), *Collective Bargaining in Europe: Towards an Endgame Vol. I*, pp. 131–149. Brussels: European Trade Union Institute.

Neef, R. (2002). 'Aspects of the informal economy in a transforming country: The case of Romania', *International Journal of Urban and Regional Research*, 26 (2), 299–322.

Neuman, L. (2002). 'Does decentralized collective bargaining have an impact on the labour market in Hungary?' *European Journal of Industrial Relations*, 8 (1), 11–31.

Ost, D. (2000). 'Illusory corporatism in Eastern Europe: Neoliberal tripartism and postcommunist class identities,' *Politics & Society*, 28 (4), 503–530.

Ozola, I. (2004). 'Social dialogue in Latvia: A challenge for the social partners.' In C. Lafoucriere & L. Magnusson (eds.), *The Enlargement of Social Europe. The Role of the Social Partners in the European Employment Strategy Part II*, pp. 25–59. Brussels: European Trade Union Institute.

Pollert, A. (1997). 'The transformation of trade unionism in the capitalist and democratic restructuring of the Czech Republic', *European Journal of Industrial Relations*, 3 (2), 203–228.

Pollert, A. (1999). 'Trade unionism in transition in Central and Eastern Europe', *European Journal of Industrial Relations*, 5 (2), 209–234.

Rainbird, H. (1990). *Training Matters: Union Perspectives on Industrial Restructuring and Training*. Oxford: Blackwell.

Regini, M. (2003). 'Tripartite concertation and varieties of capitalism', *European Journal of Industrial Relations*, 9 (3), 251–263.

Saar, E., Unt, M., & Kogan, I. (2008). 'Transition from educational system to labour market in the European Union: A comparison of new and old members', *International Journal of Comparative Sociology*, 49 (1), 31–59.

Sedlenieks, K. (2003). 'Cash in an envelope: Corruption and tax avoidance as an economic strategy in contemporary Riga.' In K.-O. Arnstberg & T. Boren (eds.), *Everyday Economy in Russia, Poland and Latvia*, pp. 37–52. Stockholm: Almqvist & Wiksell.

Sik, E. (1994). 'From the multicoloured to the black and white economy: The Hungarian second economy and the transformation', *International Journal of Urban and Regional Research*, 18 (1), 46–70.

Stan, S., & Erne, R. (2016). 'Is migration from Central and Eastern Europe an opportunity for trade unions to demand higher wages? Evidence from the Romanian health sector', *European Journal of Industrial Relations*, 22 (2), 167–183.

Stanojević, M. (2003). 'Workers power in transition economies: The cases of Serbia and Slovenia', *European Journal of Industrial Relations*, 9 (3), 283–301.

Stanojević, M. (2004). 'The EES: Challenges and perspectives for the social partners in Slovenia.' In B. Galgóczi, C. Lafoucriere & L. Magnusson (eds.), *The Enlargement of Social Europe. The Role of Social Partners in the European Employment Strategy*, pp. 345–383. Brussels: European Trade Union Institute.

Stanojević, M., & Klarič, M. (2013). 'The impact of socio-economic shocks on social dialogue in Slovenia', *Transfer*, 19 (2), 217–226.

Stanojević, M., Mrčela, A. K., & Breznik, M. (2016). 'Slovenia at the crossroads: Increasing dependence on supranational institutions and the weakening of social dialogue', *European Journal of Industrial Relations*, 22 (3), 281–294.

Stanojević, M., & Poje, A. (2019). 'Slovenia: organised decentralisation in the private sector and centralisation in the public sector.' In T. Müller, K. Vandaele & J. Waddington (eds.), *Collective Bargaining in Europe: Towards an Endgame Vol. III*, pp. 545–562. Brussels: European Trade Union Institute.

Stuart, M., Cutter, J., Cook, H., & Winterton, J. (2013). 'Who stands to gain from union-led learning in Britain? Evidence from surveys of learners, union officers and employers', *Economic and Industrial Democracy*, 34 (2), 227–246.

Stuart, M., & Wallis, E. (2007). 'Partnership approaches to learning: A seven-country study', *European Journal of Industrial Relations*, 13 (3), 301–321.

Szabó, I. (2013). 'Between polarization and statism – effects of the crisis on collective bargaining processes and outcomes in Hungary', *Transfer*, 19 (2), 205–215.

Traxler, F. (2003). 'Bargaining, state regulation and the trajectories of industrial relations', *European Journal of Industrial Relations*, 9 (2), 141–161.

Trif, A. (2013). 'Romania: Collective bargaining institutions under attack', *Transfer*, 19 (2), 227–237.

Trif, A., & Paolucci, V. (2019). 'Romania: From legal support to frontal assault.' In T. Müller, K. Vandaele & J. Waddington (eds.), *Collective Bargaining in Europe: Towards an Endgame Vol. III*, pp. 505–523. Brussels: European Trade Union Institute.

Trif, A., & Stoiciu, V. (2016). 'Turing crisis into opportunity: Innovation within the Romanian trade union movement.' In M. Bernaciak & M. Kahancová (eds.), *Innovative Union Practices in Central-Eastern Europe*, pp. 161–177. Brussels: European Trade Union Institute.

Tūtlys, V., Kaminskienė, L., & Winterton, J. (2016). 'Policy borrowing and policy learning in initial VET reforms of Lithuania after 1990.' In S. Bohlinger, T. K. A. Dang & M. Klatt (eds.), *Education Policy: Mapping the Landscape and Scope*, pp. 377–402. Frankfurt: Peter Lang.

Vali, M. (2004). 'Preparations towards participation in the EES: Estonia's progress in involving social partners.' In B. Galgóczi, C. Lafoucriere & L. Magnusson (eds.), *The Enlargement of Social Europe. The Role of Social Partners in the European Employment Strategy*, pp. 211–262. Brussels: European Trade Union Institute.

Varga, M. (2013). 'Refocusing studies of post-communist trade unions', *European Journal of Industrial Relations*, 19 (2), 109–125.

Williams, C. C. (2007). 'Tackling undeclared work in Europe: Lessons from a study of Ukraine', *European Journal of Industrial Relations*, 13 (2), 219–236.

Williams, C. C., Kedir, A., Nadin, S., & Vorley, T. (2013). 'Evaluating the extent and nature of informalization of employment relations in South-East Europe', *European Journal of Industrial Relations*, 19 (2), 91–107.

Winterton, J. (2000). 'Social dialogue over vocational training in market-led systems', *International Journal of Training and Development*, 4 (1), 26–41.

Winterton, J. (2006). 'Social dialogue and vocational training in Europe: Are we witnessing the emergence of a European model?' *Journal of European Industrial Training*, 30 (1), 65–76.

Winterton, J. (2007). 'Building social dialogue over training and learning: European and national developments', *European Journal of Industrial Relations*, 13 (3), 281–300.

Winterton, J. (2008). 'VET research and social dialogue.' In F. Rauner and R. Maclean (eds.), *Handbook of Vocational Education Research*, pp. 104–114. Bonn: Springer International.

Winterton, J., & Forde, C. (2013). 'L'Europe en crise: vers un modèle heuristique de la restructuration.' In F. Le Deist (ed.), *Restructurations et santé au travail: regards pluridisciplinaires*, pp. 27–46. Toulouse: Octarès.

Winterton, J., & Strandberg, T. (2004). 'European social dialogue: Evaluation and critical assessment.' In B. Galgóczi, C. Lafoucriere & L. Magnusson (eds.), *The Enlargement of Social Europe: The Role of Social Partners in the European Employment Strategy*, pp. 21–76. Brussels: European Trade Union Institute.

Winterton, J., & Turner, J. (2019). 'Preparing graduates for work readiness: An overview and agenda', *Education + Training*, 61(5), 536–551.

Winterton, J., & Winterton, R. (1994). *Collective Bargaining and Consultation over Continuing Vocational Training*. Sheffield: Employment Department Research Report RM.7.

Woolfson, C. (2008). 'Social dialogue and lifelong learning in new EU member states: "reform fit" in Latvia', *Journal of European Social Policy*, 18 (1), 79–87.

Woolfson, C., & Sommers, J. (2016). 'Austerity and the demise of social Europe: The Baltic model versus the European social model', *Globalizations*, 13 (1), 78–93.

Zeman, F. (2004). 'The EES and challenges and prospects for the social partners in the Czech Republic.' In B. Galgóczi, C. Lafoucriere & L. Magnusson (eds.), *The Enlargement of Social Europe. The Role of Social Partners in the European Employment Strategy*, pp. 135–156. Brussels: European Trade Union Institute.

Jörg Markowitsch and Horacy Dębowski

# 15. Education systems and qualifications frameworks

**Abstract:** This chapter discusses major developments in the education and training systems of post-socialist European countries since the fall of the Iron Curtain, focussing on the years following the financial crisis to date, and on the role of national qualification frameworks (NQFs) within these developments. Despite an enormous body of research on NQFs, the role of NQFs in post-socialist countries has not been a topic of comparative research beyond selected countries. This is all the more remarkable because, unlike some Western European countries, the instrument of qualifications frameworks, in its modern form, was completely new and was introduced by all CEE countries without exception. The chapter highlights three major developments in different education sectors and examines to what extent NQFs have played a role in them. In the area of vocational education, we looked at the 'renaissance' of vocational education which has followed more than a decade of de-vocationalization in almost all CEE countries. In the area of higher education, we looked at the rise and fall of private universities which has followed the trend to mass higher education. In the area of adult learning, we show how lifelong learning has only recently emerged in the CEE countries as a policy field. In the chapter we synthesise the main changes in qualifications systems in CEE countries related to NQFs implementation and conclude that NQFs have had little significant impact on systems of skill formation or on educational practice and institutions. For a variety of reasons however, this has not been considered a failure.

**Keywords:** Skill formation, qualification frameworks, Central and Eastern Europe (CEE), devocationalisation, private universities, lifelong learning

## Introduction

The aim of this chapter is to consider the major developments, or big picture changes, in the education and training systems of post-socialist European countries since the fall of the Iron Curtain, focussing on the years following the financial crisis to date, and on the role of qualification frameworks within these developments. Why is that of interest?

Firstly, the post-socialist countries represent the largest European sub-region ranked by population, and number of countries. Besides their Communist past, economic transition towards a market economy and candidature or accession to the European Union, these countries share a number of characteristics which have posed challenges to their education and training systems that differ from those in other European regions. Each experienced strong economic growth (compared to Western Europe) following independence, unemployment, especially youth unemployment, is relatively low (compared to Southern Europe), and most importantly populations are shrinking, and ageing faster due to low fertility rates and emigration (compared to the rest of Europe). Such commonalities are nevertheless overlaid by significant differences. For instance, the Baltic countries were hit harder by the Great Recession, and South-Eastern Europe has been facing more unfavourable economic conditions from the beginning of the transition than the Visegrád countries, while Ukraine and the countries of former Yugoslavia face on-going war and the legacy of previous conflict respectively.

Secondly, the great comparative narratives and larger European research projects (Kogan, Gebel, & Noelke 2008; Kogan, Noelke, & Gebel 2012; Saar, Ure, & Holford 2013; West 2013), only covered the period before the financial crisis yet developments since then cannot be simply extrapolated from preceding trends.

Thirdly, within the field of education, the launch of the European Qualifications Framework (EQF) including the subsequent establishment of national qualifications frameworks (NQF) can be considered as 'the' major EU policy intervention of the recent past besides the Bologna process. However, until recently knowledge about its impact has been incomplete (Bohlinger 2019). Furthermore, despite an enormous body of research on NQFs, the role of NQFs in post-socialist countries has not been a topic of comparative research beyond selected countries (e.g. Tūtlys & Aarna 2017). This is all the more remarkable because, unlike some Western European countries, the instrument of qualifications frameworks, in its modern form, was completely new and was introduced by all CEE countries without exception.

The challenge in discussing qualifications frameworks together with changes in education and training systems is that the related research and policy discourses seem to be split into parallel universes, like in superhero comics. Galactic fights are fought and potentially all life on earth destroyed, while life on earth goes on without anyone noticing. Similarly, debates about qualifications frameworks have often been framed in such a way that one might think the outcome would determine the fate of future education systems. However, even years after the implementation of qualifications frameworks, the impact of these mechanisms often remains unclear. Seen in this light, the EQF, as the much-vaunted super tool could take a similar course as in any superhero story. After its successful mission, life goes on as before.

Based on the analysis provided in the country chapters in this book we will scrutinize the relationships between qualifications frameworks and changes in education and training in general from two angles using two guiding questions. When looking at the major changes in the education and training systems in the CEE countries to what extent were these related to changes in the design, governance and awarding of qualifications and the introduction of qualifications frameworks? When looking at the introduction of qualifications frameworks in the CEE countries what impact on the delivery or outcomes of education and training can be identified? This approach acknowledges that qualifications frameworks can either be seen as a driver of change or as the outcome of reforms.

Our approach to these questions is firstly to examine the available literature on qualifications frameworks. Particular attention will be paid to the methodological challenge of assessing the impact of these arrangements. Next, we review the major developments in education and training in the CEE countries focusing on recent changes. The introductory chapter to this book has already explored these issues to some extent, with a focus on secondary, vocational, higher and adult education, but this chapter takes a more thematic approach. Finally, we analyse the comments made by the authors of individual country chapters in this book on the modernisation of qualifications system in their country. As part of this analysis, we also look at the role and implications of policy borrowing and policy learning (see also Bohlinger & Tūtlys in this collection). We conclude with some reflections on future challenges and problems in the development of national systems of qualifications.

## A brief review of research on qualifications frameworks

Although research on qualifications frameworks has grown over the last two decades, it has never been a well-researched topic within education or political science. There is little research tradition on which to build and such a 'fuzzy' topic, by nature interdisciplinary, does not align well with criteria for mainstream academic funding. Most of the research on qualifications systems that has been published in academic journals builds on development projects or research contracted by international organizations, notably the European Centre for Development of Vocational Training (Cedefop), the International Labour Organization (ILO) and the Organisation for economic Cooperation and Development (OECD). It is worth noting that there has been more debate on qualifications frameworks within educational administration and at various political events than at research conferences.

An examination of the research in international journals reveals three broad phases. Until 2004 research focussed on the early implementation of national qualifications frameworks (NQFs) in the "Rugby nations": England, Scotland, Wales, Ireland, France, Australia, New Zealand and South Africa (Keating 2003; Raffe 2003; Young 2003). The second phase of research from 2005 to 2010 was characterised by the development and launch of the EQF (Bjørnåvold & Coles 2008; Hanf & Rein 2008; Markowitsch & Luomi-Messerer 2008) and a growing criticism of this, based on first 'impact studies' of NQFs in South Africa, Australia and Scotland (Allais 2007, 2010; Raffe 2009a, 2009b; Young 2007, 2008, 2009). During this phase the first articles on the diffusion of NQFs were published (Chisholm 2007), which led Fernie and Pilcher (2009) to speak of a 'global tsunami' of NQFs. The number of reports and publications on qualifications frameworks exploded after 2010, with some focussing on specific countries (e.g. Romania, Russia, Thailand, Botswana), sectors or professions (qualifications frameworks for radiology, for music teachers, etc.). Besides these phases, the literature on qualifications frameworks which Bohlinger (2012) argues cannot be separated from research on learning outcomes, can be structured into three broad categories each with a specific perspective.

1. Research on the design of qualifications frameworks, the descriptors used and the types of frameworks, which fluctuates between technological and educational perspectives and discusses questions such as: 'How to develop descriptors? How to write learning outcomes? What type of frameworks exist?' (Lester 2015; Markowitsch & Luomi-Messerer 2008; Méhaut & Winch 2012; Mile & Mislav 2012; Young 2007).
2. Research on the implementation, success factors and impacts of qualifications frameworks mainly from the perspective of sociology and political science which asks: 'What worked? What did not work? Is it possible to measure impact at all?' (Allais 2010, 2017; Pilcher, Fernie & Smith 2017; Raffe 2013; Tau & Modesto 2011; Young 2009; Young & Allais 2016).
3. Research on the diffusion of qualifications frameworks, Europeanization and globalisation from the perspective of political economy and sociology which questions the diffusion and adoption of global or European norms and the standardization of education (Elken 2015a, 2015b, 2016a, 2016b; Kleibrink 2011; Mikulec 2017; Mikulec & Ermenc 2016).

Although much of the research on qualifications frameworks is descriptive, it has nevertheless generated tools to identify differences and classify qualifications frameworks. These tools, in turn, have found their way into handbooks on NQFs and were used by policy consultants to support the development of qualifications frameworks. Another strength of the research has been its critical position in analysing the relationship between qualifications frameworks and more profound societal changes. For instance, some authors claimed that qualifications frameworks and the trend towards learning outcomes and competencies undermined the role of education institutions, intensified the marketization of education and as such are a signal for the expansion of neo-liberalism (e.g. Allais, 2014). While this rightly points to the insidious influences of qualifications frameworks, the extent to which this has happened remains unclear. Certainly, the systemic breaks that some had hoped for have failed to materialise. Recent research, going more into detail for some European countries actually shows the opposite. Both the robustness and path dependency of education systems seem to ensure that the idea of NQFs is translated into existing systems but that their general character remains largely unchanged (Elken 2016b; Mikulec 2017). Based on a comparison of NQF implementation in Denmark, Portugal, Germany and Slovenia, Mikulec concluded:

> However, the data gathered through comparative analysis also revealed that the impact of the EQF is rather limited as the core concept and philosophy of learning outcomes from the VET policy of Anglo-Saxon dominant educational model did not result in the fulfilment of the neoliberal objective to separate educational outcomes from the educational institutions and programmes lying beneath them.... Therefore, the normative resonance (Sedelmeier 2011) between EQF (Anglo-Saxon) ideas and established NQFs in Scandinavian, Germanic, Mediterranean and Post-communistic contexts remains rather low. (Mikulec 2017, 19).

The main weaknesses of research on qualifications frameworks are the lack of empirical studies and misunderstandings about the object of research. What is considered as empirical data are policy documents, legislation and expert opinions. Data at the micro level in terms of the opinions of learners or individual employers is largely missing (compare also the levels in our model of skill formation in the first chapter of this book). The overemphasis on descriptions and types of frameworks has been recognised by researchers themselves as producing artefacts:

> Focusing on types of qualifications frameworks may prevent researchers from really seeing what is happening with the education/labour market interface, and result in no more than descriptive studies of what policy makers wish was happening...Focusing attention on them, through further research or further development and application of typologies, may reinforce the idea that they are something which exist in their own right, and can be studied as such; the existing research suggests this is not the case. (Allais 2017, 775).

There is certainly confusion over the purpose of researching NQFs and there are at least three different understandings of NQFs: (1) as a regulation or regulatory mechanism; (2) as a political or administrative process; or (3) mistakenly, as a synonym for qualifications or education systems (see our working definitions below). Also, it often remains unclear whether the education and training system or a particular representation of the system is being studied. In this sense, researching NQFs is like studying immune systems in medical science irrespective of a specific disease. We do have a notion of strong and weak immune systems, but no yardstick by which this could be measured objectively, and it makes no sense to study them in isolation of the actual diseases.

In our analysis we are particularly interested in two of the three research strands mentioned above: the question of impact and diffusion. Both issues were recently subject to a mid-term review by long-time observer, Sandra Bohlinger, who has used the theoretical concepts of policy borrowing and institutional isomorphism for this purpose. In her view, the EQF and the European NQFs are both examples of policy borrowing ('travelling reforms around the globe') and an example of institutional isomorphism (Bohlinger 2019, 401). Educational institutions at national level have adopted the EQF recommendation due to technical pressures (i.e. annual reporting, monitoring and public naming and shaming) and also due to a belief that this is expected by EU organizations, society and other EU Member States, despite the lack of evidence on the effectiveness of the EQF with respect to its principal objectives such as promoting a learning outcomes orientation, increasing the comparability of qualifications or fostering educational and occupational mobility.

## Clarifying key concepts and our approach

These brief remarks on previous research make clear that analysing the role of NQFs on the development of skill formation systems in the post-communist countries is not a simple undertaking. We begin with clarifying some basic concepts. We define national *skill formation systems* as the totality of all individual, organizational and collective learning processes in a country, including informal learning processes such as on-the-job learning, shaping national labour potentials, and the relationships between these elements. By national *education and training system* we mean the complete spectrum of educational provision, in terms of institutions, programmes and courses, as commonly depicted in popular overview diagrams by education ministries. Such representations usually show both typical educational ages and educational ladders. They sometimes include non-formal provision, but commonly exclude informal provision.

We define national *qualification system* as the set of nationally recognized qualifications within a country and any related institutions. It should be noted that there are exceptions to the rule that the successful completion of an educational programme leads to a qualification. For example, qualifications can be obtained without course attendance in some scenarios (for instance through validation of prior learning or external examinations). Also, there may be educational provisions not linked to qualifications, as is the case, for instance, for preschool education. Finally, *qualifications frameworks* are systems of hierarchical structuring of qualifications with the aim of fostering transparency within or between qualification systems. It should be also noted that we focus on *national* qualifications frameworks, but the term is also used for sector, regional or international frameworks, such as the European Qualifications Frameworks (EQF).

Assessing the impact of national qualifications frameworks in terms of traditional policy evaluations can be frustrating, as few effects can be interpreted as direct impacts of NQFs, and cause and effect often remains unclear. This is related to the desired impacts and objectives of NQFs having usually been exaggerated, which is evident in the country chapters in this book.

For Lithuania, Tūtlys and colleagues note that the 'Qualifications reform was highly ambitious', and that 'the wide and far reaching idealistic ambitions of the architects of reform' stood in contradiction to the actual institutional capacity to implement change. Matković and Buković have chosen the introduction of the Croatian Qualifications Framework in their chapter as a case study 'due to its transformative potential for the functioning of the entire skill production regime'. Nevertheless, they concluded that, despite its ambition, the CROQF did:

> little more than create additional institutional layers over what is still a predominately statist regime....it has thus far done little to 'align education to the labour market needs' — and, while not necessarily representing a zero-sum game, it most certainly has not weakened the central state vis-a-vis other actors. (Matković and Buković in this collection)

The concept of a qualifications framework is certainly seductive within the context of a deep reform of education and training. However, regarded more prosaically one could also ask: What impact on learning, training, teaching or recruiting practices can be expected from a simple re-classification of qualifications on paper? The approach we suggest here to evaluate any changes engendered by qualifications frameworks is to look closely at where those changes have occurred within the qualifications system, and whether they have in turn resulted in changes in education and training systems or skill formation systems. For this purpose, we ask questions such as: Did the implementation of the NQF lead to a change in the types of qualifications that are included to the national qualifications system? Did the NQF change the methodological approaches applied in designing qualifications, assessing competencies and learning outcomes, or awarding qualifications? Did the NQF lead to changes in the coordination between general, vocational, higher and adult education? Did the NQF bring to the fore any challenges and problems in the development of the national system of qualifications? Before outlining the results of this analysis, we briefly explain the context within which such changes have taken place and remind ourselves of the key developments in education and training in the CEE countries since the fall of the iron curtain.

## Key issues in education and training in Central and Eastern Europe since 1989

The economic, social and political developments of the CEE countries since the fall of the Iron Curtain show a dynamic and extent of change that cannot be observed in any other European region during that period. The development of the national skill formation systems, especially the vocational education and training (VET) systems, has been characterised by multi-directional changes that are unparalleled in Europe. Despite different starting positions and despite different political settings and approaches to reform (Bouckaert, Nakrosis & Nemec 2011), the country-specific contributions in this book highlight a number of common lines of development resulting from common challenges: the transition to independence; the integration into the European Union; the financial and economic crisis; and, most recently, the COVID-19 crisis.

It is beyond the scope of this chapter to provide a full summary of these developments. Nor is this the place to repeat what has already been said about the changes in the individual educational segments general, vocational, higher and adult education – in the introduction of this book. Instead, we want to take a closer look at some specific phenomena that have been neglected in previous comparative analyses or have only recently become more apparent. We are particularly interested in turning points in the recent history of skill formation which is most commonly presented as a linear and irreversible process of skills growth and skills upgrading.

In the area of VET, we are interested in the 'renaissance of VET'[1] which has followed more than a decade of de-vocationalization in almost all CEE countries.

1 A term used to denote the strengthening of VET and the political attention it has received in the aftermath of the financial crisis and the title of a respective conference (Gonon 2017).

In the area of higher education (HE) , we will look at the rise and fall of private universities which has followed the trend to mass HE. In the area of adult learning, we are going to show how lifelong learning has only recently emerged in the CEE countries as a policy field even though the European year of lifelong learning dates back to 1996. Before we turn to these topics, we review the big picture to set the context.

## The big picture: Education and training in Central and Eastern Europe 1989–2021

Considering the period since 1989, it is an open question whether it should be considered as two, three or even four distinct periods. For Lithuania, Tūtlys and colleagues distinguish in their chapter on Lithuania between two phases, the phase up to EU accession in 2004, and the phase after. Most other authors have differentiated between three phases, the transition period, the pre- and post-EU accession period up until the financial crises and the post-crises years. However, if one considers the political developments in the course of the European refugee crisis of 2015, for example in Poland or Hungary, one could also argue that we are already at the beginning of a fourth period characterised by a strengthening of nationalist tendencies and a departure from the European canon[2]. With regard to the development of the economy and skill formation systems, a fourth phase is not yet so clearly discernible, which is why we will content ourselves here with three main periods (see Table 15.1).

In the years of transition which were characterised by mass unemployment, hyperinflation and repeated recessions, national education reforms focused on de-ideologisation of curricula, decentralisation, and increasing the autonomy of universities. Limited labour market options for school leavers together with the opening of the universities resulted in mass HE, a surge of private universities and decline of vocational training. Increasing foreign investment, strong economic growth, increasing employment rates and ongoing emigration in the following

2 As for instance Randma-Liiv and Drechsler (2017) did when looking at the development of public administration. They distinguish the immediate post-communist transition (1989–1996) characterised by the New Public Management (NPM) paradigm, the EU-accession period (1997–2004/2007) with several reform initiatives strongly impelled by the EU accession criteria, a post-EU-accession period of finetuning, and a most recent phase (from 2016 onwards) during which some CEE countries have even become models for the "First World" regarding e-Governance and related concepts (ibid.).

**Table 15.1.** Overview on main changes in Education and Training in CEE 1989 to 2021

| | *Collapse and transformation 1989–1999* | *EU accession and global economic crisis 2000–2010* | *Rapprochement and COVID-crisis 2011–2021* |
|---|---|---|---|
| Key Education and Training Trends | Decline of VET, mass HE, surge of private universities | Ongoing de-vocationalization, increasing professional HE, reluctance of employer engagement | Decline of private universities, re-emphasis on VET and adult education |
| Major Education and Training Reforms | Autonomy of HE and VET providers, decentralisation, de-ideologisation of curricula | Bologna reform, modernising HE and VET, introducing quality assurance systems | Qualifications frameworks, Development of dual VET |
| Drivers of Change, Political and Economic Context | Privatisation and economic restructuring, hyperinflation, mass unemployment, establishment of statehood institutions (in some countries) | Strong economic growth, large scale emigration, increasing foreign investment, consolidation of state and societal institutions and social dialogue | Ongoing growth, skill shortages, immigration (pos. net migration), nationalist and developmental socio-economic policies in some countries. |
| Timeline, key facts | Dissolution of Soviet Union 1991 | Accession 2004/2007/2013, Economic Crisis 2009 | Ukrainian Revolution 2014, Refugee Crisis 2015, Pandemic 2020/21 |

*Note.* Prepared by authors.

years prepared the ground for an initial rethinking of policies which finally began after the economic crisis or the refugee crisis at the latest. Persistently increasing employment rates, positive net migration and skill shortages resulted in a re-emphasis on vocational and adult education which were additionally impelled by European policies such as the promotion of qualifications frameworks for lifelong learning and the development of dual VET. Of course, this is a simplified picture that shows neither the frictions involved nor the exceptions to the rule. We will turn to those in the following sections when trying to identify possible turning points.

## De-vocationalization and the renaissance of VET

The years of transition following the collapse of the Soviet Union and the associated economic and social upheavals had a dramatic impact on VET within post-communist European countries, much of which is still evident today (Markowitsch & Hefler 2019). For almost all the countries covered by this book the dissociation of large firms and VET schools, the growing unpopularity of VET schools and a shrinking demand for VET has been reported. The parallel expansion of the universities sharply contrasts with the decline of VET schools which faced numerous disadvantages including: outdated technologies and equipment unsuitable for developing the new skills that were needed; declining opportunities for adequate apprenticeship places or internships; a lack of competent school managers able to adapt to the new conditions and requirements; and few opportunities for teachers to engage in professional development. In the context of high unemployment and in the race for better labour market opportunities, VET was clearly outranked by HE, further exacerbating the difficult transition from VET to work. Against this background and compared to HE, the new autonomy of VET providers (as for instance in Poland or Lithuania) was a further obstacle rather than an advantage.

In Estonia the collapse of practical training previously linked to Soviet state enterprises, has led to a distrust of VET, which has a poor image and low status ('VET is only for weak learners'). In Croatia the previous vocational-oriented education (VOE) was abolished to achieve a clean break with the socialist era. As a consequence, and due to changes in demand, a long-term decline of shorter and practical school-based VET began and has persisted to date. In Slovenia, attempts were made to attenuate the decline of the reputation of vocational education by introducing a dual system alongside the school-based one, but this had to be abolished after a few years because it did not have the buy in of employers, young people or the trade unions. In Ukraine de-industrialisation and de-skilling was observed and VET policy shifted towards social inclusion and labour market integration during that first period. This is especially notable given the context of the oligarchization of the economy, widespread corruption and continued totalitarian approaches in public administration and policy making.

VET did not experience such a collapse in Hungary or in the Czech Republic as in the other CEE countries although the number of VET learners in basic VET (which does not provide access to maturity) did decrease in Hungary. In the Czech Republic high enrolment in VET remained, but a fragmentation of school provision became visible, as evidenced by the emergence of new VET qualifications which reached 1,500 in number compared to 250 qualifications before 1990.

An indicator of the low political importance attached to VET during this period is that in practically all countries new legislation was first introduced in respect of general education and HE, with legislation to reform VET being introduced after this. For instance, in Slovakia the *New Act on Higher Education* came into force in 1990 (amended in 1996), the *Renewal of the Education System* in 1992 and the *VET Reform* in 1994. In Romania the *National Council for Academic Evaluation and Accreditation* (NCAEA) was established in 1993, five years before the *National Centre for Technical and Vocational Education and Training Development* (NCTVETD). Also, in Bulgaria, the *National Agency for VET* (NAVET) was only established in 1999. In Lithuania, the *Law on Higher Education and Science*, which regulated the decentralisation of governance and autonomy of providers and which in turn resulted in the massification and market orientation of HE, was implemented in 1991, while the new law on VET was not introduced until 1997.

These years could perhaps be described as a period of academic drift, pointing towards the massification of HE (which also characterised developments in Western Europe and other parts of the world). However, in the case of most CEE countries it would be more appropriate to speak of a 'de-vocationalization' of the education system (see especially the chapter on Poland), in the sense that it was a deliberate move away from VET as an essential component of national skills strategies.

In the subsequent period, the years immediately before and after EU accession, de-vocationalization initially continued in many CEE countries, despite further reforms of the VET systems. In Slovenia the reputation of VET continued to fall despite EU initiated and funded modernisations (such as recognition of prior learning, credit points, learning outcomes, qualifications frameworks). In Estonia too, efforts to change the negative image of VET had little success. In Slovakia, necessary structural reforms of VET were postponed despite the ongoing economic growth and the decline of the working population. In fact, the financing ('per capita financing') and the decentralisation reform of 2013 in Slovakia further increased the mismatch in supply and demand because schools were incentivised for the number of students they enrolled, and not for increasing quality in teaching, graduation rates or graduate labour market entry.

The rise of employment and increasing demand for skilled labour alongside negative demographic trends and migration outflows however, led to a rethinking of skills polices in most CEE countries, and EU policies also encouraged further comprehensive reforms in VET. In Bulgaria, a process of modernising the VET system by re-establishing links between VET schools and businesses was initiated. In Poland, a process of restoring the importance of VET began and the negative trend in VET enrolments came to an end. In Latvia, a major reform of VET came into force in 2010 which aimed to modernise and modularise curricula, introduce learning outcomes and RPL, better involve social partners and establish VET competence centres which were designed to play an important regional role. In Hungary, FIDESZ won the general elections in 2010 which as well as bringing a significant shift in educational policy towards centralisation, also brought a new increased emphasis on VET. Even in Ukraine new instruments for curriculum design were introduced (e.g. VET standards) and competence-based approaches and work-based learning in initial VET were strengthened.

The promotion of work-based learning and apprenticeship training by the European Commission as a means to combat youth unemployment and alleviate the consequences of the economic crisis certainly contributed to these shifts in national policies[3]. This political re-emphasis on VET may have taken place in the CEE countries at different times, either before or after the economic crisis, before or after the refuge crisis, and influenced by EU policies or not, but there is no doubt that it occurred in all countries to some extent.

In all countries national qualifications framework have been established (and will be discussed further in the following section), the involvement of social partners and social dialogue in VET has been enhanced and methods of labour market and skills forecasting improved (see especially the chapters on Bulgaria, Estonia and Ukraine). In some countries sectoral skills councils have been established (e.g. Croatia, Latvia, Estonia, Poland), in others attempts to establish new, or reform existing apprenticeship tracks were made (e.g. Latvia, Lithuania, Slovenia, Croatia, Hungary, Romania, Ukraine).

The turning point from de-vocationalization to re-vocationalization was arguably most pronounced in Poland. In the aftermath of the economic crises, with new skill shortages on the horizon, and a massive influx of Ukrainian workers, employers were pushing for reforms in VET. Finally, the 2017–2019 VET reform was introduced. This, essentially reformed the curriculum and introduced a moderate form of modularisation both to bring VET closer to the world of work and to increase the responsiveness of VET to labour market changes.

---

3 It has to be noted that the effects of the crisis were quite different among the CEE countries. For instance, Poland was not hit severely by the crisis while it resulted in a deep recession in Estonia with unemployment especially high among VET graduates.

However, some of the reforms to strengthen VET were unsuccessful. For instance, the introduction of dual VET within formal VET in Romania in 2016 was ultimately not implemented. A Slovak version of dual VET introduced to meet employers' requests, especially from the automotive industry, was enabled by a New Act on VET in 2015, but the new track has remained marginal. In Poland, Sectoral Skills Councils (SSC) which were established with EU funds in 2016 to institutionalise social dialogue have had little impact so far, despite 17 SSCs becoming operational. In Slovenia, work-based training and apprenticeships became a government priority from 2012 onwards and in 2018 a new law on apprenticeship was established. But most Slovenian employers remain reluctant to employ apprentices as education is still seen as the responsibility of the state.

So, while there is clear evidence of political support for VET, the impact of reform is less clear. Many reforms to strengthen and improve VET have not been in place long enough to assess whether they have actually led to a sustainable *vocational turn*. In some countries, such as Poland or Hungary, re-vocationalization is more evident than in others. What is clear, however, is that the trend towards de-vocationalization has ended.

## The rise and fall of private universities

While de-vocationalization in the post-communist European Countries between independence and the onset of the economic crisis has received little academic attention, the parallel massification of HE is well documented (Dobbins 2011; Kogan, Gebel & Noelke 2012; Kogan et al. 2008; Scott 2007), and so only the key aspects are summarised here. It was universal (i.e. took place in all countries); was particularly strong in social and economic disciplines, less so in technology and natural sciences; was based strongly on the expansion of professional HE either by transforming former soviet *technikums* (such as in Lithuania or Ukraine) or establishing new universities of applied science; and was fostered by the financialisation, marketization and privatisation of HE as well as by methods of new public management adopted in public administration during that period.

Interestingly, the de-vocationalization of upper-secondary VET during the 1990s and 2000s coincided with a remarkable vocational drift in post-secondary and higher education. Of course, the patterns in the extent to which privatisation and vocational drift took place vary between countries. For instance, enrolment in professional HE courses increased very strongly in Croatia. In Lithuania the growth of private universities was modest due to strong competition from public universities, while on a much larger scale in Ukraine and Poland. The new

Republic of Poland granted universities autonomy and independence from the state to a much greater degree than Western countries (Antonowicz 2012) and essentially left development to the market. A decline of research activities (Kwiek 2012) and a huge growth in private HE were the consequence (see details in the chapter on Poland).

These developments have taken place in parallel to the Bologna process and were to large extent fostered by this. In fact, privatisation, financialisation and vocational drift in HE are closely related to the implementation of the new Bologna study architecture and the Europeanization of quality assurance in HE. Changes in financing, new forms of accreditation and quality assurance, the establishment of private universities and universities o applied science, usually resulting in binary HE structure and the strengthening of the influence of external stakeholders (e.g. by introducing university councils) have been almost universal.

Although globalisation and the politics of neoliberalism had a short setback by the economic crisis, it was to be expected that the trends described above for HE would continue. However, there were remarkable signs of change in some CEE countries. For instance, in Poland, in the aftermath of the crisis the number of students and number of HE institutions, in particular private ones began to decrease. As Dębowski and Stęchły stated in their chapter with reference to Kwiek and Szadkowski (2018): 'We are currently observing the de-privatisation of studying in Poland: the offer of publicly funded studies is increasing, while the privately funded offer is decreasing'.

Poland might be an extreme case when it comes to the trajectory of private universities[4]. However, decreases in the number of university students which cannot be attributed to demographics can be found in other CEE countries too. According to OECD data the share of enrolment in private tertiary education institutions (ISCED2011 levels 5–8) decreased between 2013 and 2018 in all Baltic states and Visegrád states while it increased in most Western European countries[5]. Rather than being the result of national HE policies however, this pivot away from private universities may reflect market developments, with forms of over-qualifications and 'diploma disease' being reported in some countries (compare for instance the chapter on Lithuania or Bulgaria).

---

4 Despite the relative decrease in student enrolments at private universities, Poland still has higher numbers of students (around 25 per cent) in private institutions than all other CEE countries with comparable to levels of France, Australia or the US.

5 Own calculations based on OECD Education at a Glance.

## Discovering lifelong learning and adult learning as a policy field

The third example of turning points we examine relates to the emergence of adult learning as a field within education and skills policies. During the years of transition, adult education[6] had even greater difficulties in gaining political attention than VET. It was viewed as market oriented and consumerist and was essentially left to private providers and voluntarist initiatives of NGOs. Policy makers focussed on compulsory and HE as strategic to the formation of human capital. In the absence of governmental support, the institutionalization of adult education and the professionalization of adult education providers and adult educators was slow. However, considering the economic difficulties and the enormous challenges for restructuring of the education systems of the CEE countries after 1989, it is perhaps understandable that adult education was not prioritised.

Only the steady economic growth of the 2000s, the targets set by the Lisbon process and the establishment of the European, and subsequently national qualifications frameworks, has raised awareness of the non-formal training sector. With the exception of Slovenia[7], new policies and regulations for non-formal adult education where not introduced before 2000. For instance, in Croatia, during the 1990s adult education was marginalised and the so-called people's universities were considered redundant remnants of the old socialist education system. A comprehensive new regulation, the Adult Education Act, had to wait until 2007 (see the chapter on Croatia). In Lithuania, the Law on Non-formal adult education and continuing training, which, among other things regulated the accreditation of prior learning, came into force only in 2015. In Poland, the promotion of adult learning was 'not at all a priority in the first two decades of transformation' as Dębowski and Stęchły state in their chapter. There was thus no agency ensuring quality, and adult education was left to private training companies. Public policy shifted its attention towards adult learning only after joining the EU and with European Social Funds becoming available to support the supply side of the adult education market, i.e. private and public training institutions and labour offices, which were organizing training for unemployed persons. However, it took another ten years for major structural

6 Understood here as an education sector rather than lifelong learning in general which usually also includes informal and on-the-job learning.

7 The Slovenian Institute for Adult Education was established in 1991 and Slovenia stood out in many respects when it comes to adult learning. It used to have participation rates in Lifelong Learning far above all other CEE countries, and partly also above many Western countries. See also Ivancič and Radovan (2013).

reforms in adult education to be implemented in Poland (compare the introduction of the Integrated Qualifications System (IQS) Act in 2015 in the chapter on Poland).

Policies promoting adult learning have gained momentum in all CEE countries in recent years, as evidenced by the development of national lifelong learning and skills strategies (Milana, Klatt & Vatrella 2020). In Estonia, the participation rate in adult lifelong learning has risen to an all-time record level recently. In 2019 20 per cent of Estonian citizens aged 25–64 participated in adult learning, which is far above the EU average and means a doubling of the rate within only one decade and closing the gap with the Scandinavian front runners. It remains to be seen if other CEE countries will follow this trend.

## Modernising qualification systems and qualifications frameworks in Central and Eastern Europe

In the previous section we suggested that national qualification frameworks (NQFs) had some influence on adult learning policies and participation, while other important developments, such as the re-emphasis on VET and the decline of private universities, would probably have taken place irrespective of NQFs. This section analyses the evolution of NQFs and examines the impact of the implementation of NQFs and broader educational developments, mainly by comparing qualification and education systems over time.

### Rationale for the implementation of national qualifications frameworks

In most CEE countries, developments in relation to NQFs started around 2006 when the first governmental working groups were established to consult on the proposal of the EQF Recommendation. The process gained momentum soon after EQF adoption in 2008 and resulted in the implementation of NQFs as early as 2012 although some frameworks took several more years to become operational (Cedefop 2020a).

Socio-economic conditions in the CEE countries were favourable for the implementation of NQFs by the first decade of the new millennium for a number of reasons. To begin with, growing skills demand due to economic growth, changes in the occupational structure and emigration had put strong pressure on governments to find solutions to skills deficits. Because NQFs were being presented as universal labour market tools national decision makers received social partners' commitment for their design and implementation process quite easily – a situation which was not common in other spheres of education and labour market policies. Secondly, it was the first instrument covering all education sectors in which CEE countries participated together with the old EU Member States. The integration of national education sectors with the rest of Europe and the visibility of national qualifications referenced to the EQF evoked natural enthusiasm among policymakers and social partners. Thirdly, NQF implementation was strengthened by the availability of substantial EU funds dedicated not only to central agencies but also to social partners and training institutions in all CEE countries. The scale of support is well illustrated by Matković and Buković who indicate in their chapter that the development of the Croatian Qualifications Framework was supported by numerous ESF projects involving several hundred institutions and the sum of almost €100 million.

It is significant to note that EU financial aid later came to be perceived as a carrot and stick mechanism; for whilst it provided funds and positive incentives for the NQF implementation, it also introduced external pressure into national policy making – as not implementing or delaying the NQF implementation may have resulted in negative financial consequences (e.g. returning funds or cutting future budgets). For instance, in Poland the implementation of NQF as was among the ex-ante conditionalities (EC 2017) defined in the partnership agreement with the EU. This means that if the NQF was not implemented, the launch of the whole human capital operational programme for 2014–2020 within the ESF funds would have been at risk.

## Character and scope of national qualifications frameworks in CEE countries

NQFs vary with respect to their objectives and the changes they intend to drive and consequently in their design and implementation (Raffe 2013). In most CEE countries NQFs are fulfilling an informative role and their implementation was therefore meant to complement existing reforms rather than to be agents of change in themselves. An exception is the qualifications framework in Poland where the NQF was expected to introduce new systemic elements and mechanisms particularly for the non-formal education sector.

The influence of NQF implementation was most evident within the VET sector in line with the observations by Allais (2017) for other parts of the world. Changes in general education resulting in the introduction of learning outcomes were driven by NQFs to a minor extent, and similarly in HE the modernisation of programmes was primarily driven by the Bologna process and the implementation of the European Higher Education Area (EHEA) guidelines rather than by the EQF itself.

The greater impact of NQFs on VET may stem from the fact that VET qualifications were often outdated and in need of reformulation when work on EQF started in the mid-2000s. In this sense, NQF implementation was a catalyst for the modernisation of VET qualifications and provided a useful format for their restructuring. Competence-based qualifications standards derived from professional practice were introduced in many countries with explicit linkages to occupational standards which were either updated or newly formulated. Almost all authors in this book have referenced the adoption of the European Credit System for Vocational Education and Training (ECVET) in relation to qualifications design (often labelled as Anglo-Saxon approach), in which VET qualifications were described with the usage of learning outcomes (LO) and often grouped into units of learning.

Linking the modernisation of qualifications with the adoption of a LO approach was assessed positively in most of the countries as this resulted not only in updated content, but also contributed to better transparency and clarity of qualifications within formal VET. Reformulating qualifications in the form of LOs allowed better alignment to NQF levels. Furthermore, the process revealed gaps within national qualifications systems, especially with respect to missing qualifications at EQF level 5. As a result, some countries (e.g. Estonia, Lithuania, Latvia, Croatia and Poland) began to develop dedicated level 5 qualifications either within formal VET or within HE short cycles.

Despite the effort put into reformulating the content of qualifications, LOs had limited effect on teaching practice, assessment, certification and quality assurance – with a few exceptions. Buligina and Sloka indicate in their chapter on Latvia that the implementation of LOs allowed better balancing between occupational specific skills, general subject knowledge and transversal skills within VET qualifications. Similarly, Laczik and Farkas contend that the implementation of LOs in Hungary allowed teachers and trainers to gain authority and flexibility in the choice of teaching and learning methods, processes, evaluation criteria and content. In contrast, Loogma in her chapter assesses the implementation of LOs and the NQF in Estonia negatively stating that they resulted in over-standardization and limited the autonomy of VET and HE teachers.

Better linking of formal and non-formal education sectors was rarely achieved, and validation of non-formal learning, one of the NQF flagship initiatives, was implemented only to a limited extent in most CEE countries. Only in Poland and Slovenia was it possible to align qualifications awarded outside the formal education sectors to the NQF. In, Poland, Slovakia, Slovenia and Ukraine, the need for including smaller, complementary or partial qualifications which are usually provided in the non-formal sector was noted. Vantuch suggests that in the case of Slovakia 'smaller' qualifications better address the needs of the labour market than 'large' qualifications provided within formal initial VET and could increase the availability of qualifications for adults looking for reskilling or upskilling. In Latvia, Lithuania, Poland and Croatia the development of sectoral qualifications frameworks has commenced. Sectoral qualifications frameworks embrace their own set of level descriptors to facilitate better transparency and alignment to NQF levels using sector-specific terminology and concepts. The concept of national level sectoral qualifications frameworks is a relatively new development in this part of Europe.

## Changes within the institutional landscape

The implementation of NQFs was accompanied by various shifts in the responsibilities of ministries and between ministries aiming at enhanced coordination of NQF development and lifelong learning policies. This aim was only partially achieved, however. In Poland, the Ministry of Education became the coordinator for NQF development which represented an important shift in the paradigm of governance, since there was previously no leading ministry in this area and regulations on awarding qualifications were governed through inter-ministerial entities which by their nature had relatively limited ability to respond quickly to changing circumstances. In Croatia, the NQF implementation significantly improved the position of the ministry of labour within skills policies, as this ministry became responsible for development of occupational standards and had responsibility for the disbursement of substantial EU funding. In Slovakia, the division of responsibilities for skills formation caused tensions at ministerial level. As Vantuch describes, the education ministry focused on maintaining the traditional school-based VET inherited from Czechoslovakia, whilst introducing a German style dual VET system. The labour ministry, however, supported an Anglo-Saxon alternative with occupational standards and sectoral councils, and interestingly, a French approach to personal skills audits making use of the *bilan de compétences* methodology.

The problem of coordination of skills policies, in many CEE countries, as highlighted by Vladut in her chapter on Romania was the result of inadequate institutional capacity within public institutions and underdeveloped social dialogue but was also a consequence of frequent changes in legislation. So, the major barriers to the integration of skills systems were unaffected by NQF.

The implementation of NQFs was accompanied by institutional changes, either via the establishment of new agencies (e.g. in Bulgaria, Croatia, Ukraine, Poland) or extending competencies of existing agencies (e.g. in Estonia, Slovenia, Latvia). The new institutions were usually given the task of managing NQF implementation within or across education sectors, and in some countries these agencies were also tasked with accrediting education programmes. However, new institutions rarely had sufficient prerogative to influence the functioning of education sectors, and their remit was generally confined to a single sector. Institutional change, though widespread, therefore did not necessarily lead to better integration and coordination of the skills formation system.

One of the key policy innovations was related to the institutionalization of social dialogue, which was achieved primarily via the introduction of *sector skills councils*. The alignment of qualification content with labour market needs was attributed to these bodies, which were also actively involved in developing occupational and vocational qualifications standards. In some countries (e.g. Latvia, Croatia), they also played a role in the accreditation of qualifications referenced to NQF or the accreditation of education programmes. However, the impact of sector skills councils has been limited, with their influence being most strongly felt in the sphere of macro level policy making. They have seldom had any influence with respect to the quality of education provision, probably because in most cases they operate as voluntary non-governmental organizations so lack specific funding and expertise.

However, even without the formal establishment of sector skills councils, employers' organizations were increasingly involved in the development of qualifications systems, especially in the design of occupational standards and qualifications, in many CEE countries in the last decade (e.g. the Baltic countries, Slovenia, Hungary and Ukraine). In the Baltic countries employers' organizations (or related bodies) have been involved in the design of occupational standards and qualifications, while in the Ukraine they have actively contributed to developing the methodology designing qualifications. In most cases this has resulted in imbalanced social dialogue on qualifications and VET curricula, with this being clearly dominated by the employers (and the state). The engagement of trade unions and professional organizations has remained weak and primarily formal in character due to their lack of capacity and expertise.

Another policy innovation adopted in almost all CEE countries relates to the development of *qualifications registries* containing information about qualifications and education and training provision. The transparency that NQFs aimed for was frequently achieved by the introduction of qualifications registries available to learners via electronic portals rather than by the implementation of

LOs. Such registries are often intended to be linked with labour market intelligence, career guidance and counselling. For instance, in the Czech Republic and Hungary qualifications registries were functioning before 2008, but NQF implementation provided the stimulus to develop this instrument further.

## Analysing the impact of national qualifications frameworks

The various country analyses in this book suggest that NQFs have had little significant positive impact on systems of skill formation or on educational practice and institutions. For a variety of reasons however, they do not argue that the NQFs have been a failure.

Firstly, implementation of NQFs was an uneven process in the CEE countries. In some countries, such as Estonia, the process of NQF adoption was quick and the framework reached operational stage by 2013, whereas in others it took many more years, and it is therefore too early to assess the impact. Moreover, the process of implementation was not successfully completed in all countries (Cedefop 2020). The meanders and timeline of the NQF adoption process is well illustrated by Matković and Buković in their chapter on Croatia. The development of the Croatian NQF was initiated in 2006 by the establishment of a minister-led committee and adopted by law in 2013. Sectoral councils were established in November 2014, but the first occupational and qualification standards were adopted only in 2017 and 2020 respectively.

Secondly, even though NQFs are presented as lifelong learning policy instruments, with the exception of Slovenia and Poland the country chapters suggest their scope is limited to formal education. NQFs in the CEE countries have thus far had little impact on the adult education sector and have not facilitated the integration of formal and non-formal education.

Thirdly, NQFs had most impact at the level of macro policy, in the way qualifications are designed and developed at ministerial or central agency level especially within the VET sector, but they did not result in new practices concerning how skills are developed or assessed by education providers. It can thus be concluded that in most CEE countries NQFs have had little impact on the experiences of learners.

It is difficult to assess from the country chapters whether decision makers in CEE were unaware that implementation of 'informative' NQFs which are limited to formal education was unlikely to have any profound impact, or whether they in fact intended NQFs to become agents of change. It might have been a conscious decision of policymakers that NQFs needed to be well embedded within formal education in the first instance, before extending their scope to the non-formal sector and beyond.

Irrespective of which interpretation is correct, CEE countries were able to avoid the major pitfalls of NQF implementation. The country chapters, even if mentioning that expectations were not met (e.g. in Lithuania, Croatia, Slovenia, Estonia), do not share the pessimism of other comparative studies (such as Allais 2010, 2014; Bohlinger 2019) describing examples of NQF failures. It is also appropriate to conclude that the development and implementation of NQFs neither distracted decision makers from reforming other areas of skills formation nor took resources from areas that needed them most, despite Raffe (2013) and Young & Allais (2016) suggesting this might be the case. This difference might be explained by the availability of substantial EU funding for NQFs. The real *stress test* for the sustainability of NQFs in the Eastern part of Europe will occur when EU funding devoted to NQFs is no longer available, although this is not an immediate concern.

The role of policy learning and policy transfer also needs to be underlined in the context of NQFs. Several country chapters highlight the positive effects of peer-learning activities organized at EU level, which embraced study visits and consultations with international experts. EU funded projects enabling social partners and education providers to participate in the exchange of ideas were also positively assessed. However, the implementation of NQFs was presented as one-dimensional policy transfer in some countries such as Croatia and Estonia.

Overall, it is difficult to assess the future direction of NQFs in CEE countries. If the character of the respective NQFs does not change and remains limited to formal education with only an informative role and no direct impact on educational practice, NQFs will become little more than tools facilitating the referencing of existing national qualifications to transnational meta-frameworks.

## Current and future challenges for national qualifications frameworks in CEE countries

Our analysis has largely highlighted the limited transformative potential of qualifications frameworks with regard to major changes in education in the CEE countries, although some consequence cannot be denied (e.g. stronger involvement of employers' organizations in standard setting, modernised curricula and more flexible pathways to attaining qualifications). In many cases, major changes and reforms in the education systems have taken place independently of the establishment of qualifications frameworks and it may be assumed that this will continue to be the case. Nevertheless, discussions about current and future

**Table 15.2.** Summary of main changes in qualifications systems related to the NQF implementation in CEE

| *Changes within the education system* | *Aims and reasons for changes* | *Intended and unintended effects* |
|---|---|---|
| Establishing or appointing agencies to coordinate NQF implementation and development<br>Establishing accreditation centres or other external quality assurance bodies<br>Institutionalization of social dialogue<br>Renewing occupation standards, restructuring VET curricula<br>Creating new types of qualifications (e.g. supplementary, partial qualifications)<br>Changing assessment, implementing RPL procedures<br>Developing qualifications registries | Integrating qualifications system<br>Coercive pressure from EU<br>Modernising skill formation<br>Enhancing quality of qualifications<br>Increasing the flexibility and transparency of VET<br>Improving coordination and involvement of social partners<br>Reducing asymmetry of information on the labour market<br>Alleviating growing skills deficits | Stronger involvement of employers' and employees' organizations in standard setting<br>Modernised curricula and qualifications structures<br>Emergences of sectoral frameworks<br>Better coordination of qualifications system<br>Various shifts in the responsibilities of ministries and between ministries and various governmental agencies<br>More flexible pathways to attaining qualifications<br>Increased participation in Lifelong Learning |

*Note.* Prepared by authors.

skills needs are increasingly centred on learning outcomes, assessment criteria and certification procedures. As a result, qualifications became the principal element in thinking about the organization of education provision across all sectors of education. This was already the case to some extent, but NQFs certainly made this process more explicit and structured.

The acceptance of the social partners, EU funding and the willingness to become part of the European area of lifelong learning have created favourable conditions for the implementation of NQFs in the CEE countries. NQFs as a policy tool aimed at improving the structuring of qualifications within qualifications systems could continue to play an important role in both formal and non-formal education, but remaining challenges still need to be addressed. For instance, non-formal adult education has not been sufficiently related to formal education and left largely to market forces. The question is whether and how this sector should be integrated into formal education, and clearly NQFs will play an important role in this process. The inclusion of qualifications from the non-formal sector in the NQF is a complex and resource-intensive process that requires new legislation, changes in the institutional framework and additional quality assurance mechanisms. Yet thus far, we have not seen the will in CEE countries to extend the scope of NQFs beyond the formal education sector. It has also become apparent that the introduction of NQFs has to date had only a limited impact on teachers and assessment practices.

Currently, it seems that CEE countries do not have clear strategies on what role the NQF should play in either formal or non-formal education going forward. Little effort has been made to improve up-skilling and re-skilling opportunities for adults by providing incentives, e.g. through providing subsidies, time off from work, tax breaks, or individual learning accounts. Mechanisms to encourage employer involvement in sharing the cost and provision of training are also insufficiently developed in CEE countries.

In the view of the substantial funding for the development and implementation of NQFs provided by the EU so far, an important question relates to the sustainability of these mechanisms when funding ends. The extent to which decision-makers, and especially the social partners, will be willing to engage in the NQF process without external funding remains to be seen.

The next few years will also reveal the impact of the COVID pandemic on education sectors and, more broadly, skill formation. An increased focus on self-directed learning, in non-school contexts can be expected, as well as a greater variety of assessment methods going beyond the traditional classroom examination. In this context, past efforts and research related to the recognition of prior learning could be useful for implementing more diverse assessment methods in the school context. In this respect NQFs could become essential devices to navigate through an increasingly heterogenous and pluralised education landscape as illustrated in one of three possible scenarios for the future of VET by Cedefop (2020b). Compared to the situation ten years ago, and the terminological confusion regarding qualification frameworks (and related concepts) the country chapters in this volume demonstrate that a respective *lingua franca* seems to be at the horizon, at least in Europe, which would be a prerequisite for such a development.

## References

Allais, S. (2007). 'Why the South African NQF Failed: Lessons for countries wanting to introduce national qualifications frameworks', *European Journal of Education*, 42 (4), 523–547.

Allais, S. (2010). *The Implementation and Impact of National Qualifications Frameworks: Report of a Study in 16 Countries*. Geneva: International Labour Organisation.

Allais, S. (2014). *Selling Out Education. National Qualifications Frameworks and the Neglet of Knowledge*. Rotterdam: Sense Publishers.

Allais, S. (2017). 'What does it mean to conduct research into qualifications frameworks?' *Journal of Education and Work*, 30 (7), 768–776.

Antonowicz, D. (2012). 'External influences and local responses. Changes in Polish higher education 1990–2005.' In M. Kwiek & P. Maassen (eds.), *National Higher Education Reforms in a European Context: Comparative Reflections on Poland and Norway*, pp. 87–110. Bern: Peter Lang.

Bjørnåvold, J., & Coles, M. (2008). 'Governing education and training: The case of qualifications frameworks', *European Journal of Vocational Training*, 42–43, 2007/3-2008/1 (Thematic Issue: The European Qualifications Framework), 203–235.

Bohlinger, S. (2012). 'Qualifications frameworks and learning outcomes: Challenges for Europe's lifelong learning area', *Journal of Education and Work*, 25 (3), 279–297.

Bohlinger, S. (2019). 'Ten years after: The "success story" of the European qualifications framework', *Journal of Education and Work*, 32 (4), 393–406.

Bouckaert, G., Nakrosis, V., & Nemec, J. (2011). 'Public administration and management reforms in CEE: Main trajectories and results', *Network of Institutes and Schools of Public Administration in Central and Eastern Europe. The NISPAcee Journal of Public Administration and Policy*, 4 (1), 9–29.

Cedefop (2020a). *National Qualifications Frameworks Developments in Europe 2019. Qualifications Frameworks: Transparency and Added Value for End Users*. Luxembourg: Publications Office of the European Union.

Cedefop (2020b). *Vocational Education and Training in Europe 1995–2035. Scenarios for European VET in the 21st Century*. Luxembourg: Publications Office of the European Union.

Chisholm, L. (2007). 'Diffusion of the National Qualifications Framework and outcomes-based education in southern and eastern Africa ', *Comparative Education*, 43 (2), 295–309.

Dobbins, M. (2011). *Higher Education Policies in Central and Eastern Europe: Convergence towards a Common Model?* Bern: Springer.

Elken, M. (2015a). 'Developing policy instruments for education in the EU: The European Qualifications Framework for lifelong learning', *International Journal of Lifelong Education*, 34 (6), 710–726.

Elken, M. (2015b). 'New EU instruments for education: Vertical, horizontal and internal tensions in the European qualifications framework', *Journal of Contemporary European Research*, 11 (1), 69–83.

Elken, M. (2016a). '"EU-on-Demand": Developing national qualifications frameworks in a multi-level context', *European Educational Research Journal*, 15 (6), 628–643.

Elken, M. (2016b). *Standardizing education? The development of the European Qualifications Framework and national qualifications frameworks.* Doctoral thesis.

Fernie, S., & Pilcher, N. (2009). 'National qualification frameworks: Developing research perspectives', *Quality in Higher Education*, 15 (3), 221–232.

Gonon, P. (2017). 'Renaissance der dualen Berufsbildung durch Modernisierung'. In P. Schlögl, M. Stock, D. Moser, K. Schmid & F. Gramlinger (eds.), *Berufsbildung,eine Renaissance? Motor für Innovation, Beschäftigung, Teilhabe, Aufstieg, Wohlstand*, pp. 44–60. Bielefeld: W. Bertelsmann Verlag.

Hanf, G., & Rein, V. (2008). 'European and national qualifications frameworks– A challenge for vocational education and training in Germany', *European Journal of Vocational Training*, 42 (3), 113–128.

Ivancič, A., & Radovan, M. (2013). 'Implementation oflifelonglearningin Slovenia'. In E. Saar, O. B. Ure, & J. Holford (eds.), *Lifelong Learning in Europe: National Patterns and Challenges*, pp. 258–279. Cheltenham: Edward Elgar.

Keating, J. (2003). 'Qualifications frameworks in Australia', *Journal of Education and Work*, 16 (3), 271–288.

Kleibrink, A. (2011). 'The EU as a norm entrepreneur: The case of lifelong learning', *European Journal of Education*, 46 (1), 70–80.

Kogan, I., Gebel, M., & Noelke, C. (eds.) (2008). *Europe Enlarged – A Handbook of Education, Labour and Welfare Regimes in Central and Eastern Europe.* Bristol: Policy Press.

Kogan, I., Gebel, M., & Noelke, C. (2012). 'Educational systems and inequalities in educational attainment in Central and Eastern European countries', *Studies of Transition States and Societies*, 4 (1), 69–83.

Kogan, I., Noelke, C., & Gebel, M. (eds.) (2012). *Making the Transition – Education and Labor Market Entry in Central and Eastern Europe*. Stanford: Stanford University Press.

Kwiek, M. (2012). 'Universities and knowledge production in Central Europe', *European Educational Research Journal*, 11 (1), 111–126.

Kwiek, M., & Szadkowski, K. (2018). 'Higher education systems and institutions, Poland'. *Encyclopedia of international higher education systems and institutions*, pp. 1–10.

Lester, S. (2015). 'The European qualifications framework: a technical critique ', *Research in Post-Compulsory Education*, 20 (2), 159–172.

Markowitsch, J., & Hefler, G. (2019). *Future Developments in Vocational Education and Training in Europe. Report on Reskilling and Upskilling through Formal and Vocational Education Training*. JRC Working Papers Series on Labour, Education and Technology (2019/07).

Markowitsch, J., & Luomi-Messerer, K. (2008). 'Development and interpretation of descriptors of the European qualifications framework', *European Journal of Vocational Training*, 42–43 (2007/3–2008/1), 33–58.

Méhaut, P., & Winch, C. (2012). 'The European qualification framework: Skills, competences or knowledge? ' *European Educational Research Journal*, 11 (3), 369–381.

Mikulec, B. (2017). 'Impact of the Europeanisation of education: Qualifications frameworks in Europe ', *European Educational Research Journal*, 16 (4), 455–473.

Mikulec, B., & Ermenc, K. S. (2016). 'Qualifications frameworks between global and European pressures and local responses', *SAGE Open*, DOI: 10.1177/2158244016644948.

Milana, M., Klatt, G., & Vatrella, S. (2020). *Europe 's Lifelong Learning Markets, Governance and Policy.* Bern: Springer.

Mile, D., & Mislav, B. (2012). Theoretical base for multidimensional classification of learning outcomes in reforming qualifications frameworks. *Interdisciplinary Description of Complex Systems,* 12 (2), 151–160.

Pilcher, N., Fernie, S., & Smith, K. (2017). 'The impact of National Qualifications Frameworks: by which yardstick do we measure dreams?' *Journal of Education and Work*, 30 (1), 1–12.

Raffe, D. (2003). '"Simplicity Itself": The creation of the Scottish credit and qualifications framework', *Journal of Education and Work*, 16 (3), 239–257.

Raffe, D. (2009a). *Can National Qualifications Frameworks Be Used to Change Education and Training Systems?* Brifing No. 48, Centre for Educational Sociology, University of Edinburgh.

Raffe, D. (2009b). National qualifications frameworks in Ireland and Scotland: A comparative analysis. Paper presented at the European Conference on Educational Research, Vienna.

Raffe, D. (2013). 'What is the evidence for the impact of National Qualifications Frameworks?' *Comparative Education*, 49 (2), 143–162.

Randma-Liiv, T., & Drechsler, W. (2017). 'Three decades, four phases: Public administration development in Central and Eastern Europe, 1989–2017 ', *International Journal of Public Sector Management*, 30 (6–7), 595–605.

Saar, E., Ure, O. B., & Holford, J. (eds.) (2013). *Lifelong Learning in Europe: National Patterns and Challenges*. Cheltenham: Edward Elgar.

Scott, P. (2007). 'Higher Education in Central and Eastern Europe'. In J. J. F. Forest & P. G. Altback (eds.), *International Handbook of Higher Education*, pp. 423–441. Berlin: Springer.

Tau, D., & Modesto, S. T. (2011). 'Qualifications frameworks: Implementation and impact in Botswana', *Journal of Education and Work*, 24 (3–4), 359–373.

Tūtlys, V., & Aarna, O. (2017). 'Competence-based approach in the education reforms of Lithuania and Estonia'. In M. Mulder (ed.), *Competence-based Vocational and Professional Education: Bridging the World of Work and Education*, pp. 381–406. Berlin: Springer.

West, J. (2013). *Vocational Education and Training in Eastern Europe: Transition and Influence*, LLAKES Research Paper 41, London: Institute of Education.

Young, M. (2003). 'National qualifications frameworks as a global phenomenon: A comparative perspective', *Journal of Education and Work*, 16 (3), 223–237.

Young, M. (2007). 'Qualifications frameworks: Some conceptual issues', *European Journal of Education*, 42 (4), 445–457.

Young, M. (2008). 'Towards a European qualifications framework: Some cautionary observations', *Journal of European Industrial Training*, 32 (2/3), 128–137.

Young, M. (2009). *Learning from the First Qualifications Frameworks*. Geneva: International Labour Organization.

Young, M., & Allais, S. (eds.) (2016). *Implementing National Qualifications Frameworks Across Five Continents*. London: Routledge.

Sandra Bohlinger and Vidmantas Tūtlys

# 16. EU implications for skill formation in the CEE

**Abstract:** This chapter seeks to disclose the consistent EU skills formation policy approaches and their main characteristics. It also discusses the existence of the European integration in relation to skills formation and VET and the implications of EU skills formation and VET policy for the institutional development of skill formation in the CEE countries. The chapter starts with an overview of European integration from a policy perspective and summarises the most important regulations and principles. It then outlines European integration from a theoretical perspective and identifies three 'grand theories' that are relevant to European integration in all European member states. Afterwards it questions whether and how the CEE countries are an exceptional example of EU enlargement which differs from previous enlargements, and aims to disclose its specificity both in general and with respect to VET and skill formation. Finally, some conclusions are presented, and suggestions are made as to ways in which the CEE countries might further develop. One of the key outcomes of EU accession for skill formation processes and institutions in the CEE countries was the development of a systemic approach towards reform which was commonly compromised by the fragmentation and lack of capacity on the part of providers, underdeveloped social dialogue and the low status of skill formation institutions resulting from skill mismatches in the labour market and rapid economic restructuring during the post-Communist transition.

**Keywords:** Central and Eastern Europe countries, EU policies of skill formation, Europeanization of skill formation policies, skill formation reforms, vocational education and training (VET) policy

## Introduction

One of the starting points of this book is a statement by Busemeyer and Trampusch who consider the VET systems of Central and Eastern Europe to be "dynamic, but vulnerable or even fragile institutional arrangements" (Busemeyer and Trampusch 2011, 4). The authors of the first chapter of this collection also identify three critical junctures common to VET and skill formation in the CEE countries: legacy of the communist past, economic transition towards a market economy and accession to the European Union (see the first chapter of this book).

When analysing skill formation and deployment in Post-Socialist countries and in the light of European integration there are several issues to be considered.

First, given the diversity of the CEE countries and their differing approaches to these three challenges, one might argue that the 'old' Western EU Member States have more in common than the CEE countries who "share many commonalities, while forming an increasingly diverse region of the world" (Silova 2009, p. 295).

Second, the term 'EU skills formation policy' assumes there is one EU skills formation policy followed by (almost) all EU countries. However, this is not the case as research on EU policy in the field of VET has shown (Ante 2015; Milana and Klatt 2019; Milana et al. 2020; Rasmussen 2014).

Third, research on European integration commonly focuses on those policy areas in which the integration process is regulated by substantive law, i.e. by decisions (by the Court of Justice), by regulations and by directives. Examples are the European Single Market, the Customs Union or the Common Agricultural Policy. In comparison, VET, HE and adult education used to be of lesser interest within the process of European integration. Research on the relationship between European integration and processes of skill formation is therefore commonly seen as a means to realise dominant policy aims such as competitiveness or freedom of movement (Ante 2015, pp. 52–80). VET remains, in accordance with the 1957 treaty establishing the European Economic Community (EEC), at least de jure under the sovereignty of its member states. Similar considerations hold true for the political science perspective. It is precisely because VET is outside the scope of EU regulations, and because it is caught up in a tangle of interests between economic, social and education policies, that it is not fully recognized as an independent policy area of fundamental importance to research on European integration.

Against this background, this chapter aims to illuminate the following questions: (1) Are there any consistent EU skills formation policy approaches and what are the main characteristics of these? (2) Is there any European integration in relation to skills formation and VET? (3) What are the implications of any EU skills formation and VET policy for the institutional development of skill formation in the CEE countries? In order to address these questions, this chapter starts with an overview of European integration from a policy perspective and summarises the most important regulations and principles. It then outlines European integration from a theoretical perspective and identifies three 'grand theories' that are relevant to European integration in all European member states. Next, it questions whether and how the CEE countries are an exceptional example of EU enlargement which differs from previous enlargements, and aims to disclose its specificity both in general and with respect to VET and skill formation. Finally, some conclusions are presented, and suggestions are made as to ways in which the CEE countries might further develop.

## What is European integration?

European integration refers to the voluntary collaboration and cooperation between European states. It is reflected in common institutions, regulations, politics and policies all designed to facilitate the 'harmonisation' of states and societal structures. It is a long-term project in which the term itself "reflects the [...] premise that we are witnessing a process that has a direction" (Hooghe and Marks 2019, 1115). As the cooperation between states is voluntary, states are able to act independently with regards to many issues including national economic policies and migration; the natural differences between states (e.g. due to an imbalance of natural resources, size, climate, social structure, values, prejudices) determines intergovernmental bargaining and negotiation (Hoffmann 1966, 868; Hooghe and Marks 2019, 1116). As European Integration has economics at its core, it "leaves state sovereignty untouched or it strengthens the national state" (Milward 1992, 2–3) and against this background, this

> functional integration's gamble could be won only if the method had sufficient potency to promise a permanent excess of gains over losses, and of hopes over frustrations. Theoretically, this may be true of economic integration. It is not true of political integration (in the sense of 'high politics') (Hoffmann 1966, 882).

Because European integration primarily refers to economic integration the success of the European project is commonly assessed by examining EU-openness to and importance of goods, services, capital and labour, labour costs, per capita income, consumer tax rate, economic growth, inflation, Schengen participation or infringement proceedings on the single market, environment and consumer protection and other sectors via the European Court of Justice.

However, there are few indicators that have a direct or indirect linkage to skills formation and VET; these refer to openness and importance of labour and change in unemployment (König and Ohr 2013, 1082). Moreover, there are attempts to measure the public support for European integration (the so-called "European Mood Indicator") referring to questions like "Generally speaking, do you think that (country's) membership of the European Community (common market) is a good thing, a bad thing, or neither good nor bad?" (Guineaudau and Schnatterer 2017, 1188).

Silova (2009) has pointed out that European integration seen from the perspective of the Post-Socialist States' represents an approach for catching up with the 'old' EU15 countries (EU member states prior to the accession of ten candidate countries on the 1st of May 2004) and that "the basic logic and most objectives of the EU educational initiatives – promoting international cooperation, enhancing the quality of education, encouraging social integration, and increasing employability of graduates – have generally corresponded to national development goals, and have formed the cornerstone of education policies in the new accession countries" (ibid, p. 302). Such objectives derive from the EU's general policy aims in education and its mode of governing VET policy at European level.

## Governing European VET policy

The European Union, as it is now known, was conceived in the immediate aftermath of World War Two as a peace project. The notion that the integration of European economies would render another war between European powers impossible underpins all other objectives including those relating to economic development and social cohesion. In order to facilitate those objectives, the jurisdiction of the EU has expanded into other socio-political spheres.

The Treaty of Rome is the cornerstone of the EU, which guarantees the free movement of goods, services, people and capital. In this respect, the so-called freedom of establishment is of particular relevance as, under Article 39, this warrants the abolition of any discriminatory treatment of workers within member states on the basis of national origin with respect to employment, and conditions of employment.

Protecting these 'four freedoms' has been at the core of European policy ever since, and is embedded within it is its operational and governance logic. Accordingly, European policy followed the strategies of harmonisation and convergence with respect to vocational education and training systems of the member states well into the 1960s as the Treaty of Rome seemed to demand this.

This is illustrated by a Council Resolution of 2 April 1963, which set out general principles for a common policy for vocational education and training, with principle number eight being perhaps, the most pertinent

> In particular, the common policy for vocational education and training must be constituted so as to permit the gradual convergence of academic standards. As required, the Commission jointly with the Member States will draw up harmonized descriptions of the basic requirements for admission to the various educational and training step stones for vocations requiring specialized education and training. Using these descriptions, the convergence of the objective requirements for passing final exams will be aimed at in order to make possible the reciprocal recognition of certifications and

other documentation of vocational education and training completed. (Council of the European Economic Community 1963.)

Against this background, EEC member states did not delay in launching initiatives designed to facilitate convergence, comparability, the consolidation of occupational profiles and training courses. Germany's mapping analysis ("establishing 'equivalencies' by comparing individual occupations", (Ante 2015, p. 48) of more than 10,000 distinct vocational training objectives and contents (Schmiel 1971) perhaps exemplifies this.

However, a harmonisation of VET systems turned out to be an unrealistic goal, since VET impacts free movement indirectly rather than directly (and, in a wider sense, the free movement of services). Consequently, in the 1970s there was a move away from the concept of harmonisation towards subsidiarity (the concept of respecting national and regional authorities within the EU) and the recognition of qualifications. In this context, the Dahrendorf Memorandum of 1973, in which Dahrendorf describes the harmonisation of education systems – at least in its entirety – as neither realistic nor necessary and instead sketches the elaboration of the educational policies of the national states as the Union's key mission going forward. This emphasises both the unity-in-diversity-principle (unitas multiplex) as well as the necessary creation of a "European dimension" in the educational system.

Since then, the EU has elaborated numerous measures and programmes for establishing a European area of lifelong learning, whilst simultaneously respecting the variety and heterogeneity of national qualification pathways and structures. Since 1980, numerous education and training programmes to support education, training youth and sports, such as Leonardo da Vinci, Erasmus, Comenius, Twinning and Jean Monnet have been set up that by now have been consolidated under the umbrella programme Erasmus+ which spans nearly all areas of general education, VET and higher education, and also permits collaboration with non-European countries. Voluntary participation by member states is the core principle of all the programmes; support or intervention by EU institutions takes place only if the member states give their explicit consent.

In the meantime, the key principle of subsidiarity has been embedded within the framework of EU treaties, for example, as Article 130 within the Single European Act (1987). It became the foundation of European policy when it was embedded within the Maastricht Treaty (1992), and the Treaty of Nice (Article 149) (2001). The principle of subsidiarity rests upon decision making taking place at the lowest possible level, with the EU having jurisdiction in specifically defined spheres. In areas such as VET which are not under EU jurisdiction the

EU will only become actively involved if and when the aims or measures being considered cannot be achieved satisfactorily at member state level and are more suited to implementation at European Union level.

When the Post-Socialist countries joined the EU15 the new member states endeavoured to quickly adopt EU principles and objectives (Silova 2009; p. 305). When the transformation process was formally finished, the "EU accession process has triggered major educational changes (either structural or rhetorical) in the new accession countries, but the accession itself has not meant the end of educational transformations" (Silova 2009, p. 304).

## European integration from a theoretical viewpoint

This section draws from a previously published article by one of the authors (Bohlinger & Münk 2020). European integration refers to the process of long-term voluntary institutionalised and structured cooperation between European national states. Over the years, a number of theoretical approaches were developed to frame this process analytically with some of these approaches dominating the field. They became known as the 'grand theories' of European integration: functionalism and neo-functionalism, liberal intergovernmentalism and multi-level governance.

While skill formation and VET are mostly not seen as part of the integration process and are thus largely overlooked by theoretical approaches, we assume that it is a paradigmatic case of the integration process (and thus, of the integration theories).

### Functionalism and neo-functionalism

Functionalism and neo-functionalism within the international policy discourse is focussed on peace building – far beyond European borders. The core idea refers to voluntary cooperation between states. Such cooperation, however, should be restricted to those policy fields that are relevant to peace building. David Mitrany, the main exponent of functionalism assumed that such necessary 'functional' collaboration would lead to a rational and utilitarian cooperation to guarantee peace. Moreover, he assumed that, if successful, such cooperation would lead to a dynamism generating further successful cooperation (Mitrany 1943, 20 ff.; 1944). However, this presupposes a strict separation of technical-administrative and political problems. While political problems stem from high politics, i.e. foreign affairs and home security which are addressed by professional and ambitious agents, technical and administrative problems comprise low politics including e.g. sports, culture, and education which are mostly addressed by technocrats, as such problems are less controversial and thus would lead to more successful co-operations, (Mitrany 1943, 1944).

However, as such strict separation between high and low politics proved to be somewhat unrealistic, neo-functionalism emerged in which European integration was seen as a gradual process of inter-state co-operation. In this process, it was no longer the networks of technical-administrative elites that dominated inter-state co-operation but rather the institutionalisation of co-operation (Knodt & Corcari 2012, p. 25). Also at the core of this process was the establishment of security and welfare regimes via the expansion of supranational decision making systems.

European VET policy is a paradigmatic case of both functionalism and neo-functionalism: When the European Coal and Steel Community was established in April 1951, its objective was to place a single sector of six states (Belgium, France, Germany, Italy, Luxembourg and the Netherlands) under a system of common governance, in order to make any war between France and Germany "not merely unthinkable, but materially impossible" according to the 1950 Schuman Declaration. VET played a minor role in this process until the 1957 (Treaty of Rome) which guaranteed the four basic rights, i.e. freedom of establishment, services, capital and goods. From then on, VET emerged as a separate policy field even though it was mostly functional-technocratic in its beginnings. Ever since, EU VET policy has supported the maintenance of the four basic rights.

## Liberal intergovernmentalism

(Liberal) intergovernmentalism is a further development of functionalism and neo-functionalism. It emerged in the 1960s when EU member states began challenging attempts to transfer additional statutory power to the European institutions.

Intergovernmentalism builds on the assumption that states are rational agents who observe and calculate actions and strategies based on cost-benefit-analyses that reflect their own interests. An additional assumption is that states observe the behaviour of other actors (rationality assumption). Moravcsik (1993, p. 481) assumes that state behaviour is built on domestically constrained preferences and

> governments first define a set of interests, then bargain among themselves in an effort to realize those interests. Metaphorically, these two stages shape demand and supply: functions for international co-operation. A domestic preference formation process identifies the potential benefits of policy co-ordination perceived by national

> governments (demand), while a process of interstate strategic interaction defines the possible political responses of the EC political system to pressures from those governments (supply) (Moravcsik 1993, p. 481).

As a consequence, so-called policy arenas emerge which are based on three factors. First, voluntary intergovernmental co-operation. Second, the bargaining environment of member states is information-rich and negotiators possess information about the preferences and opportunities facing their foreign counterparts, as well as the technical implications of policies that are of the greatest interest to them. Third, the transaction costs of intergovernmental bargaining are low, and side-payments and linkages can be made (Moravcsik 1993, p. 498–507).

Intergovernmentalism is closely linked with neoliberalism as both focus on the (motives of) co-operation among states as "egoistic agents in the international system" (Auth 1995, p. 95). Also, they both address the role of international organisations (Lemke 2018, p. 26), the ability to co-operate and the meaning of maximising usefulness in relation to their own position (Keohane and Nye 1987, p. 728 ff.).

Neoliberalism has a relevance with respect to European integration as it focuses on the role of international agents: their role being to ameliorate power imbalances among agents (states) in negotiations. This objective is realised by establishing common institutions, regulations, norms, communications and negotiation systems which act as binding mechanisms for all states and which establish mutual trust and ongoing cooperation – even in case of failed negotiations (Auth 1995, p. 97).

The development of EU VET policy since the 1970s has struck a balance between national and supranational sovereignty. On the one hand, EU VET policy has expanded its jurisdiction and influence by means of the Bruges-Copenhagen-Process, the Riga Conclusions, the European Alliance for Apprenticeship and the targeting of aims to strengthen VET's role in the Lisbon agenda, in Europe 2020 and Europe 2030. This has also been manifested in the establishment of central institutions for VET (CEDEFOP, ETF, DG Employment and DG Education and Culture) which have established common aims, norms, regulations, and processes in co-operation with the member states. As a consequence, member states align their VET policy with the EU VET policy's common aims. On the other hand, the EU has gained access to national VET policy despite the prohibition of harmonisation (Scharpf 2009). It has massively increased the number of expert groups and consultancies (Blomeyer et al. 2015, p. 27–28.), and an intergovernmental functionalisation of European VET policy has provided access to national VET systems which manifests in "[…] indicators of economies-of-scale and linkage to economic policies […]; controlling mechanisms and competition-orientation signify marketization" (Walkenhorst 2008: 569).

Kohl (2015, p. 286) even points out that

> [t]he European Commission's concentration on 'improving competitiveness' ignores the primary need for more active labour market policies and the maintenance and extension of social cohesion in Europe. One negative result of the clearly neoliberal approach that has been followed is the constant EU intervention in national social dialogue and collective bargaining in certain countries.

## Multilevel governance

At the core of this integration approach is the understanding and the identification of patterns of decision-making, bargaining and negotiation in political processes (Börzel 2018, p. 7; Héritier 2002) which aim to create welfare-oriented social conditions. In (vocational) education, it is particularly the interplay of European and national agents that is of interest, while the interaction between supranational and regional levels receives less emphasis (Strebel et al. 2019).

An important characteristic of multilevel governance in the EU in theory and practice is the distribution of power. Next to common modes of governance such as hierarchy and legitimacy, it is competitiveness, market orientation and welfare orientation as well as negotiation that are of importance. All of these are based on an assumption that actors are relatively equal. The outcome of negotiations depends on many factors including the reputation of actors, the number and sequence of strategically necessary steps, the system and structure of institutions, the volume and scope of information, information symmetry and asymmetry, distribution and distributability of negotiation subjects and bargaining chips including alternative options and coalitions, credibility of concessions, cost efficiency and side-payments, preferences of agents, risk propensity, expectations, patience and impatience and negotiation ability (Elgström and Jönsson 2000; Harsanyi 1977; Moravcsik 1993, p. 497 f.). It is the latter aspects (negotiation ability, patience and impatience) that are of particular importance to the modes of governance in (vocational) education policy because with little hierarchical governance options or competition, debate and negotiation become the most important instruments with respect to the development of policy. Moreover, research on decision-making and negotiations provide one more option to understand VET policy. There are similarities between multilevel governance and policy transfer as part of VET policy, since policy transfer is also characterised by debate, negotiation and bargaining.

## Policy transfer and its linkage with European VET policy

Policy transfer refers to the process of transferring knowledge, ideas, structures and elements from one context into another – either with or without adaptation to local (regional, national) specificities (Dolowitz/Marsh 2000, 5; Phillips/Ochs 2003, 451 ff.; Rose 1991; Stone 1999). Though most studies on policy transfer in (vocational) education refer to transfer from the Global North to the Global South (Portnoi 2016; Steiner-Khamsi 2004, 2014), there are linkages between policy transfer and European integration, as both fields have their origins in politics and in political science and within the European Union, the establishment of a single market presupposes discussions on harmonisation, standardization and regulation of markets (Stone 1999, 53).

Research on EU VET policy mostly focuses on the emergence, implementation and implications of reform ideas and recommendations for member states and regions. Moreover, research on the governance of education in the EU is often restricted to the role of softer policy tools ('soft law') such as the Open Method of Coordination, the European Semester, the National Action Plans or monitoring (Milana and Klatt 2019; Rasmussen 2014).

In parallel and with respect to EU VET policy, the idea of voluntary policy transfer has dominated the discourse. As a result, analysing governance by soft law is overemphasised while "the potential of supranational EU institutions for coercive transfer" (Bulmer and Padgett 2005, 104) is neglected. It is often assumed that the national implementation of European reform ideas represents voluntary policy transfer per se, yet this overlooks the fact that many policy transfers derive from former national or regional reform ideas, many of which have their origin in the Anglosphere, and their transfer was encouraged either by financial incentives and/or the threat of public naming and shaming. Examples of this are the EQF/NQF and the learning outcomes orientation (stemming from Scotland, Australia and New Zealand), the Bologna Process (stemming from Italy, France, Germany and the UK) and the implementation of tertiary certificates below Bachelor level (short cycle tertiary qualifications; Steiner-Khamsi 2014) as well as guidelines for quality assurance and for the validation of prior learning.

With respect to the Post-Socialist countries of Central and Eastern Europe, Silova (2009) has identified numerous examples of policy transfer all originating in the Western States of Europe (e.g. the Bologna Process, the joining of the European Council, secondary school reforms etc.).

Member states joining European Action Programmes almost always adopt European recommendations and statements with little knowledge of the added value. Apart from monetary incentives which, particularly in the case of Action

Programmes, are promised for successful participation, the symbolic power of such actions underpin participation

> Political manoeuvres might lead to governments adopting policies without the intention of implementing them. Policies that serve a strategic purpose such as political expediency are symbolic. Symbolic policies are typically abstract and lack concrete language for implementation (Portnoi 2016, 124).

Additional linkages between the 'grand theories' of European Integration and policy transfer can be found with respect to the origin of many reform initiatives. Just as processes of policy transfer beyond the EU, EU reforms are often "quasi-market, neo-liberal, or hyper-liberal reforms that originated during the Thatcher-Reagan era" (Steiner-Khamsi 2014, 160) and these reforms are similar to the often-criticised economic-neo-liberal approaches that derive from New Public Management. In parallel, the recourse on "successful" reforms offers a legitimation fundament for adopting them and thus serves to stabilise and expand the power those agents in the field of skill formation, and they, in turn, legitimise additional activities and reforms. Legitimacy, here, is another expression of power (in the sense of authority) and overlaps with fundamental ideas of governance.

## The implications of the EU accession to the skill formation policies and practices of the CEE countries

In this section we return to our third research question: What are the implications of the EU skills formation and VET policy for the institutional development of skill formation in the CEE countries?

EU accession brought to CEE countries a significant support for the implementation of the skill formation policies which facilitate the attainment of the socio-economic development goals raised by the EU strategies. Such support can have different forms, including financial support (EU structural funds, ESF), the provision of expertise support and policy learning opportunities in reforming skill formation systems, institutions and processes. The experience of the CEE countries shows, that this support enabled and strengthened two main directions in the reforming of skill formation systems. First of all, skills formation institutions and processes became stronger oriented to the needs of the market and human capital development in seeking for "catching-up" with the EU 15 member states. The examples of such orientation include the introduction of outcomes- and competence-based qualifications and curricula, implementing of work-based learning, strengthening involvement of employers in the field of qualifications and provision of training, fostering and supporting continuing vocational training in the enterprises, provision of the financial support for the modernisation of the VET and HE systems and infrastructure. Secondly, the skill formation becomes a more important measure of the social policy by following principles of the 'European Social Model' and other EU ideas fostering "rights-based" approach to education and skill formation (e.g., European Social Rights Pillar). The examples of this development include implementation of Youth Guarantees, usage of the ESF funding for the provision of social support and incentives for the at-risk groups of learners and other measures.

EU accession also facilitated some kind of convergence of skill formation approaches, processes, practices and instruments resulting from the targeted comparability of the qualification systems, qualifications and curricula, as a necessary condition of the mobility of workforce and learners. For example, implementation of the EQF led to similarity of approaches, methods and forms in implementing outcomes and competence-based qualifications and curricula in the CEE countries. Implementation of apprenticeship in the school-based VET systems of these countries under the ESF funded projects led to quite similar approaches in this field.

Finally, the EU accession enhanced and enabled systemic institutional change and reforms of skill formation in these countries by initiating agendas of long-term systemic skill formation reforms from the one side and providing access to resources and capacity building for implementation of these systemic changes from the other side. These new systemic issues and perspectives in the skill formation policies of the CEE countries were targeted to development of lifelong learning and national systems of qualifications. Capacity building of policy makers and institutions, as well as easier access to the expertise from the EU enabled a gradual shift from the policy borrowing to the policy learning. The open coordination of these reform agendas and implementation of the EU guidelines required higher comparability and benchmarking of policy making, what also fostered processes of policy learning.

Distinguishing and displaying these common implications of the EU accession to skill formation policies and institutions in the CEE countries does not mean that these implications shared only common features and have been uniform across all these countries. There can be distinguished rather important specificities of these implications, which are further discussed by referring to the key regional clusters of the CEE countries: Baltic countries, Visegrád countries, former Yugoslavian countries, South Eastern Europe / Balkan countries and EU candidate countries.

## Baltic countries

Unlike the other CEE countries covered in this book (with the exception of the Ukraine) the post-communist reforms of skill formation in the Baltic countries involved more radical institutional change and restructuring, because these countries had to re-establish their national (state) institutional framework after the collapse of the Soviet Union (Kogan 2008; West 2013). This has significantly influenced the reforms of skill formation brought by the EU accession of these countries. The early post-communist reforms were necessarily fragmented, because the newly established governance institutions and providers lacked both the orientation and capacity for operation in both a market economy and a democratic society. This created a favourable climate for an uncritical acceptance of the EU policy guidance on the part of local policy makers (Saniter and Tūtlys 2015). The drive of policy makers in the Baltic countries to catch-up with the old EU member states in terms of socio-economic development (neoliberal shock therapy economic and social reforms) has also chimed with the ambitious goals of the EU reforms like the Lisbon strategy, enabling the launch and implementation of several radical reform projects. This process also strengthened the role of the state and its agencies via the governance of EU funded national projects and programmes. The implementation of the acquis communautaire also strengthened the legitimacy and importance of VET amongst policy makers (Loogma 2016). Additionally, the resources provided by the EU to support skill formation have provided an impetus for the involvement of the social partners in policy formation. There have nevertheless been some significant differences between the countries.

In Lithuania and Latvia, there is a strong focus on the implementation of state regulated reforms leading to standardization in the curriculum design of VET and (to some extent) higher education, whereas in Estonia EU support was used to strengthen the liberal and more decentralised pathway of reform.

In Lithuania, EU support via ESF funded projects was an important enabler of an incremental improvement in the quality of VET, because it strengthened the links between the supply and demand of skills and improved the image of VET providers (Tūtlys, Kaminskienė and Winterton 2016). Project-based implementation of EU driven skill formation reform measures resulted into ambitious yet fragmented implementation of the new instruments, starting with the approval of the Lithuanian Qualifications Framework in 2010, the introduction of occupational standards and the modularisation of the VET curricula in 2013–2019 and ending with the introduction of new institutional practices such as efforts to implement the dual VET pathway and work-based learning in 2007–2019

(Tūtlys and Spūdytė 2011; Tūtlys and Aarna 2017). As has been discussed in the Lithuanian chapter, accession to the EU facilitated a systematic transformation of policy relating to skill formation, however this did not translate into sustainable practical measures. For example, the establishment of the sectoral practical training centres via investment in the infrastructure and equipment of selected public VET providers in 2014–2018 was expected to support the implementation of the dual VET and apprenticeship, but lack of human resources and administrative capacity prevented the realisation of the full potential of such centres. Similarly, the introduction of occupational standards and national modular competence-based curricula in 2013–2019 faced some resistance from VET teachers and trainers unwilling to change their teaching practices (Tūtlys and Vaitkutė 2022). The implementation of the dual apprenticeship was also hampered by the passive involvement of both VET providers and social partners (as detailed in the Lithuania chapter).

In Latvia too, EU support was crucial for the implementation of the major reforms during the first decade of independent state. The Latvian National Observatory to support VET developments was established in 1994 with the assistance of ETF (Lanka and Mūrnieks 2006). EU membership brought large scale investment in skill formation from the European Regional Development Fund (ERDF) and the European Social Fund (ESF) which provided the financial basis for the most significant reforms in the fields of VET, HE and the system of qualifications (Lice and Sloka 2019). The European influence on the Latvian reforms has been most evident in the decentralisation of the provision of skills and qualifications, manifest in the creation of regional VET hubs based on bigger VET schools (OECD 2019), the optimisation of the network of providers and efforts to align supply and demand for skills, especially after 2011 (OECD 2019).

EU funding significantly contributed to the updating of VET infrastructure and helped VET providers adjust to the new demographic realities created by the emigration and falling population levels following the 2008–2009 financial crisis (Lice and Sloka 2019).

In Estonia, EU accession was preceeded by pro-active and intensive Europeanization (e.g. joining the Copenhagen Declaration in 2002) and a liberal adjustment of the skill formation policy to the EU acquis communautaire in the pre-accession period. Implementation of EU policy instruments, such as EQF enabled skill formation policies to orientate towards quality assurance and social responsibility whilst maintaining a focus on employability and labour market needs whilst also increasing the status of VET (Loogma 2016). Implementation of EU policy instruments also strengthened the liberal pathway of reforms in the skill formation by investing in already implemented institutional settings of the liberal and flexible system of qualifications, for example, an independent national institution responsible for the governance of qualifications, Kutsekoda, occupational standards developed by the independent multilateral bodies (Loogma 2016; Tūtlys and Aarna 2017). Reforms introduced after accession, especially with respect to the national system of qualifications fostered the development of social partnership, and in particular facilitated the involvement of employers' organizations in the development of qualifications. Other reforms facilitated the incremental development of market-oriented practices and instruments in qualification design (e.g. occupational standards of occupational qualifications), education and training (e.g. development of apprenticeship and work-based learning schemes) and the independent assessment of competencies and learning outcomes in the lifelong learning pathways (as detailed in the Estonia chapter).

### *Visegrád countries*

The primary influence of EU accession in terms of skill formation in the Visegrád countries has related to the implementation of the modernisation agenda in relation to systems and processes which have chimed with strong industrial policies.

In Poland, like in many other CEE countries the EU focus on the LLL perspective has been transferred to policy through the mechanism of ESF priorities, which encouraged and incentivised governments to introduce reforms (Klatt and Eliott 2016). Some EU accession related pressures, notably increased emigration to other EU countries increased the importance of VET within national policies designed to address growing skill shortages (Reegård and Dębowski 2020). Efforts to modernise the VET system included introducing mechanisms to support lifelong learning, overcome systemic barriers to social partner involvement and seeking to deal with skills mismatches. However, these were primarily manifest in infrastructure improvement, increasing the transparency of qualifications and training for teaching staff (as detailed in the Poland chapter). The impact of EU support in other areas of skill formation (especially in the teaching and learning practices) have been undermined by the lack of capacity and passive stakeholder involvement.

In the Czech Republic EU accession generated a 'second' wave of skill formation reforms (after the first wave launched after the Velvet Revolution) supported by the structural funds. These reforms strengthened the autonomy of VET and HE providers and other educational institutions (Corner 2015). However, this was not accompanied by the establishment of meaningful governance mechanisms, and accountability was regarded as a matter for the market (as detailed in the Czech Republic chapter). This, in turn had a negative impact on the image of VET. Overall then, EU support resulted in improvements to the existing system rather than radical change to the existing fragmented skill formation model governed by the state.

In Slovakia, EU support played a significant role in the institutionalization of skill formation by enabling and strengthening national expert bodies and governing institutions ETF (European Training Foundation), for example, supported the establishment of the Slovak National Observatory of VET in 1997 (Vantuch and Jelinkova 2010), contributing to strong support within the country for the EU's ambitious reform agenda. The lack of institutional capacity however, resulted in reform being fragmented and incomplete this was especially the case for outcomes-based and competence-based curriculum reforms in VET and HE (detailed in the Slovakia chapter). Reform began later than in many other new EU Member States, commencing in 2013 with an ESF funded project (Vantuch and Jelinkova 2019), but instead of following the EU promoted outcomes-based and market-led curriculum reforms in VET, the Ministry of Education favoured the "German" style approach to initial VET in seeking to return to the old foundations of VET provision in cooperation with companies (Vantuch and Jelinkova 2019).

When Hungary joined the EU the country's skill formation system was already well developed, and embraced the mutual acceptance of VET qualifications, employer engagement in training, institutionalization of social partner involvement in VET and competence-based VET curricula (Laczik and Farkas 2018). VET reforms supported by the EU embedded stakeholder participation for example, modular VET curricula were introduced in 2008 with the active involvement of employers. EU funded programmes also facilitated improved access to adult education and continuing vocational training programmes as so increased participation (Refernet Hungary 2011). Policy changes in 2011 marked a shift from the "European" agenda of decentralisation towards greater centralisation via increasing the role of the state with respect to the governance of skill formation (Laczik and Farkas 2018). The aftermath of economic crisis has been marked by the ambitions of the national "developmental" reforms introduced by the ruling Fidesz party which were based on the restitution of a centralised and state-controlled approach to skill formation (as detailed in the Hungary chapter). This arguably reflects the implementation of a national industrial policy which aims to respond to the economic and social challenges of globalisation, and the needs of specific sectors, notably car manufacturing.

## Former Yugoslavia countries

One of the key and distinguishing outcomes of EU membership for Slovenia and Croatia is that this chimed with the "early Europeanization" of skill formation which was facilitated both by pre-accession EU support and ambitious reforms of skill formation processes following accession.

In Slovenia, the modernisation of skill formation policies and practices to reflect the country's market orientation and neo-corporatist approach following independence enabled the smooth implementation of systemic reform that accompanied EU accession (Muršak 2010; Ermenc 2011). During this process, skill formation policy shifted from the gradual neo-corporatist development pathway characteristic of the post-socialist reforms (partially inherited from the former Yugoslavia) to neoliberal reforms focused on aligning skills demand and supply. This resulted in some iterative developments of skill formation, for example, the abandonment of the dual apprenticeship model in 2006, and its later re-introduction. EU support enabled the implementation of new practices especially in the field of recognition of informal and non-formal learning. As in the other CEE countries, EU accession strengthened the legitimacy of the national government institutions – the Ministry of Education and Science and the National Agency of Vocational Education and Training as these followed EU guidelines, and had the authority to co-ordinate the provision of funding from the EU structural funds. Slovenia's reforms shared features of both the developmental and neoliberal approaches to skill formation. For example, the development of a competence-based system of qualifications sat alongside occupational deregulation at sectoral level which the public provision of VET and CVET (as detailed in the Slovenia chapter).

In Croatia too, the early Europeanization of skill formation policy focussed on the alignment of demand and supply of skills by fostering work-based learning and apprenticeships. The support of the ETF and later ESF was strongly focussed on the development of outcomes-based curricula and qualifications (Žiljak and Molnar 2015), with national policy makers needing to respond to EU policy initiatives both by following a catch up strategy, and by using existing institutional solutions and funding to facilitate their implementation. EU accession resulted in emigration and exacerbated labour shortages. This increased employer and government interest in work-based learning and apprenticeships resulting in the introduction of apprenticeship schemes in 2010, via the mechanism of subsidised apprentice wages (as detailed in the Croatia chapter). EU accession also enhanced policy learning which was essential for the implementation of the competence-based system of qualifications within the Croatian

Qualifications Framework, and occupational standards between 2013 and 2020. As in Slovenia, the implementation of EU driven reforms significantly increased the power of the government bodies and agencies responsible for the coordination of the EU support.

## South Eastern European (Balkan) countries

One of the key commonalities of EU accession in Bulgaria and Romania is the strong emphasis placed by policy makers on ensuring that the market orientation underpinning reforms was balanced by efforts to widen access to the skill formation system especially for socially vulnerable groups.

In Bulgaria, EU accession sharpened the focus of skill formation policies on issues related to skills shortages. EU support was used to improve the status and quality of VET, to strengthen social partnership in VET, and to promote the integration of VET and secondary education, as well as the modernisation of the system of qualifications following the Bologna and Copenhagen processes (Boyadijeva et al. 2013). The policies implemented after EU accession significantly strengthened the capacities of the social partners and thus their involvement in VET and skill formation processes. Other major outcomes of of EU accession flowed from the provision of ESF funding to pathways such as higher education, adult education and continuing training, which served to widen access (as detailed in the Bulgaria chapter). However, as in many other CEE countries, EU accession strengthened the power of central government institutions (Ministry of Education and Science, National Agency of VET) as they were responsible for coordinating reform following EU guidance.

In Romania, EU funding supported policy borrowing and learning with respect to the development of institutions of skill formation and facilitated the decentralisation of governance. Following the EU agenda of promoting lifelong learning and a systemic approach to qualifications, the education system was both aligned with the labour market needs and utilised to address social exclusion. The introduction of targeted measures to widen participation amongst the Roma population exemplifies this approach (Popescu and Roman 2018). However, EU supported policies and reforms have not significantly enhanced the capacity of VET and HE providers and stakeholders which has proved to be one of the core obstacles to reform. The influence of the EU and other international donors with respect to the implementation of the neoliberal reform agenda significantly weakened the social dialogue and especially the involvement of trade unions (Trif 2016). (as detailed in the Romania chapter).

## Ukraine

The outcomes of EU support in Ukraine, have been somewhat different to those experience by the other countries considered by this book. Ukrainian skill formation institutions have received significant assistance from a variety of EU initiatives that have variously supported capacity building projects relating to VET teacher training, VET curriculum design, equipment and infrastructure upgrades, and the implementation of the dual apprenticeship system (Deissinger and Melnyk 2019). The building of capacity also engaged the social partners, especially employers' organizations enabling them to play active role in the curriculum design, and the organization and provision of training. European integration then, became the major driver in the development of skill formation institutions and processes after the Euro-Maidan revolution in 2014 – a popular rising which removed the corrupt regime supported by the Russian Federation and enhanced strong pro-European reforms in many fields of socio-economic development. The new political regime launched ambitious and radical reforms aimed at an "EU-oriented" modernisation of the system of skills formation which focussed on the decentralisation of governance (Мельник 2017). However, the reforms have been undermined by the lack of social dialogue and stakeholder capacities, and by the strong oligarchization of public policies during the post-communist transition as well as by the concentration of power by the government after the Revolution of 2014 in an attempt to counter the military aggression of the authoritarian Russian regime and the resultant socio-economic crisis.

The Europeanization of skill formation after the 2014 Revolution has had contradictory implications for skill formation in Ukraine. EU support (e.g., the projects implemented by the ETF in implementation of the National Qualifications Framework and development of competence-based qualifications and curricula) facilitated the development of a more systemic approach to skill formation reforms at national, regional and sectoral levels, via the involvement of different institutions and stakeholders in these processes. However, the Europeanization of skill formation processes generated a multi-vector approach of policy learning with respect to the formation of the National Qualifications System which drew upon examples from different countries. For example, the functional analysis and DACUM method of curriculum design were chosen for development of occupational standards and VET curricula, while the consolidation of vocational qualifications, the modularisation of VET curricula and institutional reforms were developed by learning from the experience of France, Finland, Germany and Estonia (as detailed in the Ukraine chapter). Such multi-vector policy learning is expected to facilitate the faster Europeanization of the institutions and practices of skill formation in Ukraine by helping to remove the Soviet legacy which remains resilient (e.g., Soviet systems of ranking of qualifications, the old descriptor of qualifications, etc.). Policy learning and Europeanization is also designed to counteract residual attachment of the part of staff within skill formation institutions to the methodological approaches of the Russian Federation; now considered inappropriate because of their orientation to resource-based economy and centralised skill formation institutions.

## Conclusion

EU accession represents a critical juncture in the institutional development of the skill formation systems of the CEE countries and has defined the trajectory and pace of future development after the initial stage of the post-communist transition. EU support was critical in terms of capacity building with respect to both the institutions of skill formation and the involvement of the social partners.

The policy of generating economic competitiveness via the mechanism of skill formation and the development of human capital which underpinned EU strategies during the 4th and 5th waves of enlargement (Lisbon strategy) coincided with reforms to systems of skill formation in the CEE countries being driven by the objective of catching-up with Western economies and a strengthening of their market-related orientation. As a consequence, the EU agenda was widely accepted in the reforms of skill formation systems in the run up to, and immediately after these countries joined the EU.

One of the key outcomes of EU accession for skill formation processes and institutions in the CEE countries was the development of a systemic approach towards reform which was commonly compromised by the fragmentation and lack of capacity on the part of providers, underdeveloped social dialogue and the low status of skill formation institutions resulting from skill mismatches in the labour market and rapid economic restructuring during the post-Communist transition.

The principle of workforce and learner mobility underpinning the EU skill formation agenda and its associated instruments was accepted by policy makers and stakeholders in the CEE countries as both a challenge and a necessary cost of the EU integration. Many new EU members consequently focussed their investments in skill formation (supported by the EU) to address these challenges.

CEE countries widely used EU support for ambitious and systemic reforms of skill formation systems, but were often faced with the challenge of insufficient institutional and social partner capacity. As a result, the implementation of reform often lagged behind the design and development of policy measures at national level.

Although it is claimed that the EU agenda in relation to skill formation is strongly influenced by neoliberal ideology (liberal intergovernmentalism, focus on competitiveness, decentralisation and new public management approaches), this has not implied a unification of the ideological underpinning reforms of systems of skill formation across the CEE countries. The influence of neo-liberalism is most evident in the countries with a neo-corporatist orientation of skill formation (Slovenia, Slovakia, Croatia, Romania, Poland), where the main focus of the post-accession skill formation reform agendas was on aligning supply and demand for skills and the decentralisation of skill formation. Neoliberal approaches in the EU agenda naturally enhanced highly proactive approaches to adopting and applying EU policy measures related to skill formation (implementation of the Bologna and Copenhagen processes, development of NQFs, etc.) in the countries which followed neoliberal agendas during the post-communist transition. These policy measures were regarded by policy makers as suitable for market-based and bottom-up practices and approaches of skill formation (Estonia, Czech Republic). In Hungary and Slovakia, the neoliberal agenda adopted in the aftermath of the financial-economic crisis of 2008–2009 was abandoned in favour of a developmental approach to the reform of skill formation which prioritised national industrial policies over EU strategies.

There is a wide range of unexplored issues relating to the "Europeanization" of skill formation policies and practices in CEE countries. The trade-offs between both the ambitious scope of systemic skill formation reform and the changes enabled by EU accession and their fragmented implementation caused by the lack of local institutional capacity could be further explored; as could patterns of convergence and divergence in terms of ideological orientation and socio-economic trajectory, and the relationship between this and systems of skill formation. Another potential area of research might focus on the extent to which the CEE countries which joined the EU in 2004 will provide models and reference points for policy learning for current and potential EU candidate countries (Ukraine, Moldova, Georgia, North Macedonia).

## References

Ante, C. (2015). The Europeanisation of Vocational Education and Training. A Political Economy of Skills Perspective. Berlin: Hertie School of Governance.

Auth, G. (1995). Theorien der Internationalen Beziehungen kompakt. 2., aktualisierte und erweiterte Auflage. Berlin: u.a.

Blomeyer, R., Sanz, M., Kubekova, V., Beke, M. (2015). 'Composition of the Commission's expert groups and the status of the register of expert groups.', European Parliament, <https://www.europarl.europa.eu/RegData/etudes/STUD/2018/621793/IPOL_STU(2018)621793_EN.pdf>, accessed 14 May 2021.

Börzel, T. (2018). 'Governance Approaches to European Integration. KFG Working Paper Series', 84, Berlin,< https://nbn-resolving.org/urn:nbn:de:0168-ssoar-57628-2>, accessed 29 July 2020.

Boyadjieva, P., Milenkova, V., Gornev, G., Petkova, K., and Nenkova, D. (2013). 'The Lifelong Learning Hybrid: The Case of Bulgaria. In E. Saar, O. B. Ure and J. Holford (eds.), Lifelong Learning in Europe, pp. 304–326. London: Edward Elgar Publishing.

Bulmer, S., and Padgett, S. (2005). 'Policy Transfer in the European Union: An Institutionalist Perspective', British Journal of Political Science, 35(1), 103–126.

Busemeyer, M., Trampusch, C. (2011). 'Review Article: Comparative Political Science and the Study of Education', British Journal of Political Science, 41, 413–443.

Corner, T. (2015). Education in the European Union: Post 2003 Member States. London and New York: Bloomsbury.

Council of the European Economic Community (1963). Council Decision of 2 April 1963 laying down general principles for implementing a common vocational training policy, 63/266/EEC, Brussels.

Deissinger, T. and Melnyk, O. (2019). 'Reform perspectives for the Ukrainian VET System – a critical análisis'. In F. Marhuenda and M. J. Chisvert-Tarazona (eds.), Pedagogical Concerns and Market Demands in VET. Proceedings of the 3rd Crossing Boundaries in VET conference, Vocational Education and Training Network (VETNET), pp. 50–55, Valencia: University of Valencia.

Dolowitz, D. P., and Marsh, D. (2000). 'Learning from Abroad: The Role of Policy Transfer in Contemporary Policy-Making', Governance, 13(1), 5–23.

Elgström, O., and Jönsson, C. (2000). 'Negotiation in the European Union: Bargaining or Problem-Solving?', Journal of European Public Policy, 7(5), 684–704.

Ermenc, K. S. (2011). 'Vocational education and training in Slovenia between 1974 and 2010: developments and dilemmas'. In J. Bergland Holen and A. Phillips (eds.), Studies in Education from Diverse Contexts, pp. 11–26. Grand Forks, ND: University of North Dakota.

Guineaudau, I., and Schnatterer, T. (2017). 'Measuring Public Support for European Integration across Time and Countries: The 'European Mood' Indicator', British Journal of Political Science, 49, 1187–1197.

Harsanyi, J. C. (1977). Rational Behaviour and Bargaining Equilibrium in Games and Social Situations. Cambridge: Cambridge University Press.

Héritier, A. (2002). 'New Modes of Governance in Europe: Policy-Making without Legislating?', Institut für Höhere Studien (IHS), Wien, <http://aei.pitt.edu/236/1/pw_81.pdf>, accessed 29 July 2020.

Hoffmann, S. (1966). 'Obstinate or Obsolete? The Fate of the Nation-state and the Case of Western Europe', Daedalus, 95(3), 862–915.

Hooghe, L., and Marks, G. (2019). 'Grand Theories of European integration in the Twenty-First Century', Journal of European Public Policy, 26(8), 1113–1133.

Keohane, R. O., and Nye, J. S. (1987). 'Power and Interdependence', International Organization, 41 (4), 725–753.

Klatt, M. and Elliott, K. (2016). 'Education reforms in Central Eastern Europe and its impact on youth transitions – a case of Poland'. In S. Bohlinger, K. Dang, M. Klatt (eds.), Education Policy: Mapping the Landscape and Scope, pp. 353–376. Bern: Peter Lang Publishers.

Knodt, M., and Corcari, A. (2012). Europäische Integration. Anleitung zur theoriegeleiteten Analyse. Wien.

Kogan, I. (2008). 'Education systems of Central and Eastern European Countries'. In I. Kogan, M. Gebel and C. Noelke (eds.), Europe Enlarged: A Handbook of Education, Labour and Welfare Regimes in Central and Eastern Europe, pp. 7–34. Bristol: The Policy Press.

König, J., and Ohr, R. (2013). 'Different Efforts in European Economic Integration: Implications of the EU Index', Journal of Common Market Studies, 51(6), 1074–1090.

Kohl, H. (2015). 'Convergence and Divergence – 10 Years since EU Enlargement', Etui, 21(3), 285–311.

Laczik, A., and Farkas, É, (2018). 'Past and Present Developments in Vocational Learning in Eastern Europe: The Case of Hungary.' In S. McGrath, M. Mulder, J. Papier, and R. Suart (eds.), *International Handbook of Vocational Education and Training for the Changing World of Work, pp. 951–962.* Cham: Springer.

Lanka, A., and Mūrnieks, E. (2006). 'Vocational Education and Training in Latvia: The Problems and Solutions'. In The Transformation of Vocational Education and Training (VET) in the Baltic States – Survey of Reforms and Developments. Technical and Vocational Education and Training: Issues, Concerns and Prospects, vol. 4, pp. 47–68. Dordrecht: Springer.

Lemke, C. (2018). Internationale Beziehungen. 4., überarbeitete und ergänzte Auflage. Berlin, Boston.

Lice, A., and Sloka, B. (2019). 'Performance of Vocational Education in Latvia in Developing Employability of Graduates. Society. Integration. Education', Proceedings of the International Scientific Conference, 5, 222–232.

Loogma, K. (2016). 'Europeanization in VET Policy as a Process of Reshaping the Educational Space', International Journal for Research in Vocational Education and Training, 3(1), 16–28.

Мельник, С. (2017). 'Ключові підходи до реформування сфери підготовки кадрів в Україні [Key approaches of the reform of vocational education and training in Ukraine]', Освітня аналітика України, <https://science.iea.gov.ua/wp-content/uploads/2018/12/94_106_Melnyk-1.pdf>, accessed 9 March 2020.

Milana, M., and Klatt, G. (2019). 'Governing Adult Education Policy Development in Europe'. In S. McGrath, M. Mulder, J. Papier, and R. Suart (eds.), Handbook of Vocational Education and Training: Developments in the Changing World of Work, pp. 1–25. Cham: Springer.

Milana, M., Klatt, G., and Varella, S. (2020). Europe's Lifelong Learning Markets, Governance and Policy. Using an Instruments Approach. London: Palgrave Macmillan.

Milward, A.S. (1992). The European Rescue of the Nation-State. London: Routledge.

Mitrany, D. (1943). A Working Peace System. London: Royal Institute of International Affairs.

Mitrany, D. (1944). 'The Functional Approach to World Organization', International Affairs, 24(3), 350–363.

Moravcsik, A. (1993). 'Preferences and Power in the European Community: A Liberal Intergovernmentalist Approach', Journal of Common Market Studies, 31 (4), 473–524.

Muršak, J. (2010). Vocational Education and Training between School and Labour Market: The Case of Slovenia. Horlivka: Ministry of Education and Science of Ukraine, State pedagogical institute of foreign languages.

Phillips, D., and Ochs, K. (2003). 'Processes of Policy Borrowing in Education', Comparative Education, 39(4), 451–461.

Popescu, M. E., and Roman, M. (2018). 'Vocational Training and Employability: Evaluation evidence from Romania', Evaluation and Program Planning, 67, 38–46.

Portnoi, L. (2016). Policy Borrowing and Reform in Education. Globalized Processes and Local Contexts. New York: Palgrave Macmillan.

Rasmussen, P. (2014). 'Adult Learning Policy in the European Commission'. In M. Milana and J. Holford (eds.), Adult Education Policy and the European Union, pp. 17–35. Rotterdam: Sense.

Reegård, K., and Dębowski, H. (2020). 'Exit, Voice or Loyalty? VET Stakeholders' Response to Large Scale Skilled Emigration', International Journal for Research in Vocational Education and Training, 7(3), 325–343.

ReferNet Hungary (2011). Hungary – Restructuring VET to better meet labour market demands, <http://www.cedefop.europa.eu/EN/articles/19185.aspx>, accessed 29 April 2021.

Rose, R. (1991). 'What Is Lesson-Drawing?', Journal of Public Policy, 11(1), 3–30.

Saniter, A., and Tūtlys, V. (2015). 'Comparison of Historical Development Pathways of Initial Vocational Education and Training in Lithuania and Germany: How Does History Matter for Policy Learning?' In E. Berner and P. Gonon (eds.), History of Vocational Education and Training in Europe. Cases, Concepts and Challenges, pp. 511–530. Bern: Peter Lang.

Scharpf, F. W. (2009). 'Legitimität im europäischen Mehrebenensystem', Leviathan, 37, 244–280.

Schmiel, M. (1971). 'Deckungsanalysen der Ausbildungsordnungen von Ausbildungsberufen', Mitteilungen aus der Arbeitsmarkt- und Berufsforschung, 4(3), 253–331.

Silova, I. (2009). 'Varieties of Educational Transformation. The Post-Socialist State of Central/Southeastern Europe and the Former Soviet Union.' In R. Cowen and A. M. Kazamias (eds.), International Handbook of Comparative Education, pp. 295–320. Dordrecht: Springer.

Steiner-Khamsi, G. (2004). The Global Politics of Educational Borrowing and Lending. New York, NY: Teachers College Press.

Steiner-Khamsi, G. (2014). 'Cross-National Policy Borrowing: Understanding Reception and Translation', Asia Pacific Journal of Education, 34(2), 153–167.

Stone, D. (1999). 'Learning Lessons and Transferring Policy across Time, Space and Disciplines', Politics, 19, 51–59.

Strebel, A., Engelage, S., and Baumeler, C. (2019). 'Der Beitrag der institutional work-Perspektive zu Educational Governance'. In R. Langer and T. Brüsemeister (eds.) Handbuch Educational Governance Theorien, pp. 201–2018, Wiesbaden.

Trif, A. (2016). 'Surviving Frontal Assault on Collective Bargaining Institutions in Romania: The Case of Manufacturing Companies', European Journal of Industrial Relations, 22(3), 221–234.

Tūtlys, V. and Aarna, O. (2017). 'Competence-based Approach in the Education Reforms of Lithuania and Estonia'. In M. Mulder (ed.), Competence-based

Vocational and Professional Education. Bridging the Worlds of Work and Education, pp. 381–406. Cham: Springer International Publishing.

Tūtlys, V., Kaminskienė, L. and Winterton, J. (2016). 'Policy borrowing and policy learning in initial VET reforms of Lithuania after 1990'. In S. Bohlinger, T. K. A. Dang and M. Klatt (eds.), Education Policy: Mapping the Landscape and Scope, pp. 377–402. Frankfurt: Peter Lang.

Tūtlys, V., and Spūdytė, I. (2011). 'Implementing a National Qualifications Framework in Lithuania', Journal of Education and Work, 24 (3/4), 429–448.

Tūtlys, V., and Vaitkutė, L. (2022). 'Knowledge Formation Practices in the Context of the VET Curriculum Reform in Lithuania', Journal of Vocational Education & Training, 74(1), 126–145.

Vantuch, J., and Jelinkova, D. (2010). A Bridge to the Future: European Policy for Vocational Education and Training 2002–10: National Policy Report: Slovakia. Bratislava: ReferNet Slovakia.

Vantuch, J., and Jelinkova, D. (2019). Vocational Education and Training in Europe: Slovakia. Cedefop ReferNet VET in Europe reports 2018.

Walkenhorst, H. (2008). 'Explaining Change in EU Education Policy', Journal of European Public Policy, 15(4), 567–587.

West, J. (2013). Vocational Education and Training in Eastern Europe: Transition and Influence. London: Centre for Learning and Life Chances in Knowledge Economies and Societies.

Žiljak, T., & Molnar, T. (2015). 'Croatian Education Policy in the EU Context'. In Z. Petak (ed.), EU Public Policies Seen from a National Perspective: Slovenia and Croatia in the European Union, pp. 279–297. Ljubljana: Faculty of Social Sciences.

Jonathan Winterton

# 17. Liberal market influences on CEE

**Abstract:** After outlining the Anglo-Saxon approach and briefly tracing its origins, this chapter explores the extent to which transition economies have embraced the market-based skill formation model, assesses the roles of policy borrowing or policy learning, and discusses the suitability of market-based approaches for human capital formation in these countries. The arguments of proponents and detractors of the British model of skill formation are considered along with the perspectives of those adopting (or not adopting) that approach in the CEE countries. The ways in which the Anglo-Saxon model has featured in transition economies is considered before a concluding section explains its provenance and the processes involved. The primary driver for CEE countries adopting the Anglo-Saxon approach was that these were promoted by the EU through processes including Lisbon and Copenhagen, and mechanisms exemplified by Programmes such as PHARE and Leonardo da Vinci. Although the EU promoted limited harmonisation of VET, such programmes along with ECVET and the European Area of Lifelong Learning involved substantial 'Europeanization'. Without this influence of the EU, the skill formation regimes of CEE countries could have diverged even more than they do already, mirroring the outliers Estonia and Slovenia. Whether the resulting hybrid arrangements for skill formation that now characterise much of CEE are sufficiently robust to deliver the human capital needed for reconstruction and development will only be apparent in the future.

**Keywords:** Market model of skill formation, Anglo-Saxon approaches, Europeanization

## Introduction

For reasons of history and geography, countries of Central and Eastern Europe (CEE) might be expected to have a logical affinity with the German system of skill formation as outlined by Saniter and Eberhardt (2022) in this collection, yet most have developed systems closer to the market-based skill formation model of Anglo-Saxon countries. Is this because the Anglo-Saxon model offers the most suitable approach for 'catching-up' strategies of skill formation in the post-communist countries or are there more plausible explanations? After outlining key features of the Anglo-Saxon approach and briefly tracing its origins, this chapter explores the extent to which transition economies have embraced the market-based skill formation model, assesses the roles of policy borrowing or policy learning, and discusses the suitability of market-based approaches for human capital formation in these countries. The arguments of proponents and detractors of the market model in the UK are considered along with the perspectives of those adopting (or not adopting) that approach in the CEE countries. After examining the ways in which the market model has featured in transition economies, a concluding section explores its provenance and the processes involved.

## Anglo Saxon models of skill formation

At the outset it is important to make the caveat when using the term 'Anglo Saxon' that this is a convenient shorthand rather than a defining characteristic. It is rather like labelling new variants of COVID-19 according to where they were first discovered: viruses do not have passports and the millions of mutations that occur can happen anywhere. The adoption of a neo-liberal market model of skill formation in the UK, however, was not random but a result of the permissive environment created by the Thatcher Conservative Government that made the UK the quintessential liberal market economy (LME) in Europe. There have always been elements of neo-liberalism within the coordinated market economies (CME) of Continental Europe, but it never gained such political traction as in Thatcher's Britain. A second caveat is that there is no single model of skill formation that can be labelled Anglo-Saxon, although it is true that some, but not all, Anglophone countries adopted a similar approach to the version pioneered and promoted in the UK during the 1980s.

Within the context of a LME, the first defining element of the Anglo-Saxon model of skill formation is its market focus, with decisions about training left to individual employers. The second element, the adoption of competence-based qualifications underpinned by occupational standards, was a direct consequence of the first since employers prioritised training for narrow work tasks rather than occupations more broadly. Another consequence of the first element is frequent skills shortages and employers 'poaching' skilled workers. The employer-led nature of the system dramatically reduced trade union influence over skills, contributing to the deconstruction of labour relations institutions. How this model developed during the 1980s is outlined below after briefly considering the origins of skill formation in the UK.

The skill formation system in the UK, like Continental Europe, originated with Medieval Guilds regulating apprenticeships from the 12th century, which ended in England with the *Statute of Artificers 1563*, an Elizabethan law shifting control to the state and forming the legal basis of apprenticeship (Snell 1996, 304). Apprenticeships originally involved seven years servitude, learning through working alongside a master (Williams 1957). In 1814, the repeal of certain clauses of the 1,563 Statute reflected the fact that in the intervening 150 years the average length of apprenticeship had diminished to around five years but also marked the retreat of the state and the emergence of 'voluntary' apprenticeships. Once trade unions were sufficiently organized, they became involved in regulating apprenticeships, partly, like the Medieval Guilds, to control the number of skilled workers and maintain wage rates. Even with reduced duration, there was an element of 'time serving' where apprentices were kept on low wages and socialised into the craft (Liepman 1960).

With the expansion of construction and manufacturing in the post-WW2 boom, traditional apprenticeships in the UK did not keep pace with demand for craft workers and shortages of skilled workers were reported throughout the 1950s and 1960s (Haskel & Martin 1993). In 1963 the Conservative Government, concluding skill shortages were the result of 'leaving training to the discretion of individual employers' (Winterton & Winterton 1994, 3), enacted the *Industrial Training Act 1964*. The Act established tripartite Industry Training Boards (ITBs) empowered to raise funds through a levy on employers and disburse grants to companies providing training in accordance with sector requirements and to prescribed standards. The ITBs slowed the decline in apprenticeships and introduced important sectoral quality controls but did little to resolve chronic skills shortages. In 1966, believing employers to be hoarding skilled labour and deploying it inefficiently, the Wilson Government introduced selective employment tax to provoke a 'shake-out...[to] release the nation's manpower, skilled and semi-skilled' (*Hansard* 20 July 1966). Shortages of scientists, engineers and traditional craft occupations were reported through the 1970s and 1980s (Bosworth 1981; Hunter 1978; Meager 1986) and Britain was characterised by a 'low skills equilibrium' (Finegold & Soskice 1988). Studies by the National Institute for Economic and Social Research showed Germany had a higher proportion of skilled workers, particularly at intermediate level (Daly & Jones 1980; Prais 1981; Steedman, Mason & Wagner 1991).

Despite evidence of persistent skills shortages, the Thatcher Government disbanded most of the tripartite arrangements for training in response to lobbying from a small group of employers linked to the Conservative Party. Introducing a market-based system of training, sector ITBs were replaced by employer-led Industry Training Organisations, later becoming National Training Organisations (NTOs). In England and Wales, competence-based National Vocational Qualifications (NVQs), based on occupational standards grounded in functional analysis of occupations in a range of contexts, were introduced. Occupational standards established key roles, broken down into units of competence and sub-divided into elements of competence. For each element, performance criteria were defined as a basis for assessment and range indicators provided for guidance, based on actual work situations (Mansfield 1993). Assessment against occupational standards was undertaken in the workplace, keeping the system grounded in the world of work. Scotland adopted the same approach with Scottish Vocational Qualifications (SVQs, for brevity, NVQ hereafter includes both). This national system of vocational qualifications (VQs) and the underpinning competence framework became the focus of UK influence on EU policy.

In addition to insufficient workers with intermediate skills, British managers were also poorly qualified. The Handy Report (1987) described development for British managers as 'too little, too late for too few', arguing they were poorly trained in comparison with other industrialised nations (Handy et al. 1988). The Management Charter Initiative (MCI) was launched in 1988 by companies to address the issue and in 1990 the MCI was made lead body responsible for developing occupational standards for managers and promoting Management NVQs, which proved particularly controversial. Grugulis (1997, 2000, 2003) explored the implementation of Management NVQs in three organizations, concluding that the process involved no development and was overly bureaucratic. Thompson and Carter (1995) were more positive about Management NVQs, and the evaluation undertaken for the Department for Education and Employment found significant business benefits in sixteen organizations (Winterton and Winterton 1996, 1997). Case studies of the sixteen organizations published in the fuller version showed triangulated evidence of performance improvements of individual managers, teams and organizations where the MCI standards were comprehensively adopted (Winterton & Winterton 1999). The author discussed these different findings with Irena Grugulis in January 2022 and the key explanation was that the MCI evaluation focused on organizations that were involved in significant management development activity, whereas the other study was of companies accrediting individuals against the standards without any development. The emphasis on validation of experience reflected the UK problem that few managers had been trained for their role but had learned on the job, and the Management NVQ was designed to fix this qualification deficit. The Chartered Management Institute (established in 2002 following the merger of the British Institute of Management and Institute of Industrial Manager) is now responsible for professional standards for management and leadership.

Detractors of NVQs, mainly from education, argued they were reductionist, narrowly focussed on functional competencies for job tasks, and had insufficient underpinning knowledge and theory. Young (2008, 141) claimed 'the standards-based approach began by identifying and stating curriculum outcomes in terms of competences or what an employee would be expected to do, not what he or she needed to know.' Senker (1986) suggested the competence-based approach of NVQs led to a neglect of theory, making it inappropriate as a route for intermediate skills in engineering. Others argued that level 2 NVQs had no labour market value and further lowered the status of vocational education and training (VET) compared with higher education (HE) (Brown 2011; Hyland 1994). Notwithstanding the problems with Management NVQs, such claims cannot be supported in relation to level 3 craft qualifications like electrical contracting and chemical process control, which continued to involve substantial testing of underpinning knowledge.

Proponents of the NVQ system emphasised the advantages for employers of in-house training and assessment and the attraction for employees, especially those without accredited learning, of an experiential route to qualification (Jessup 1991). The NVQ approach was adopted in much of the Commonwealth (Young 2008). Towards the end of the Conservative era, the UK was notoriously associated with low skills, low pay and bad jobs (Snower 1996). Holman (2013, 494) showed Western Liberal economies lagged Nordic and Continental ones but were ahead of Southern European and Transition economies in terms of job quality.

With the succession of Blair's Labour Government in 1997, there was no change of approach to NVQs, but chronic skills gaps and shortages were recognized. Around 20 per cent of British adults were functionally illiterate and an even higher proportion lacked numeracy skills (STF 2000, 22). Research for the Skills Task Force confirmed British managers were under-qualified, with only 18 per cent having a degree (Johnson & Winterton 1999). Research into managers' future skills needs demonstrated a need for substantial development (Winterton et al. 2000). Labour governments during the first decade of the millennium made institutional changes aimed at reducing learning inequalities, but the Leitch Review (2006) highlighted continued poor performance in basic skills, with the UK ranking 12th out 18 OECD countries. Numbers achieving qualifications did not increase with the introduction of NVQs, but they became the dominant qualification because government funding was directed towards NVQ attainment (Young 2008, 131). The chronic deficit of intermediate skills continued, with Germany having four times the proportion of engineering employees with intermediate qualifications in the UK. University enrolments grew to exceed 60 per cent of cohorts after 2000 (Wolf 2020), so employers recruited graduates for jobs at intermediate skills levels, using a degree as a 'sorting device' (Crouch, Finegold & Sako 1999, 6) while exhorting universities to improve graduate work readiness (Winterton & Turner 2019).

The May 2010 General Election resulted in a Conservative-Liberal Democrat Coalition Government, which prioritised deficit reduction through cutting public spending. UK skill formation was extensively reviewed: the *Wolf Review of Vocational Education* (2011, 44) finding 'serious problems in current provision'; the *Richard Review of Apprenticeships* (2012, 4) describing modern apprenticeships as 'a government-led training programme, shaped by training professionals not employers'; and the *(Whitehead) Review of Adult Vocational Qualifications in England* (2013, 17–20) identifying 'weak accountabilities in the vocational qualifications system', 'overly narrow occupational standards', a 'proliferation of vocational qualifications' and limited 'employer ownership'. Despite substantial changes made under Labour, these reviews suggested the UK skills formation system was broken. Additionally, the systematic destruction of much of the adult learning infrastructure since 2010 left the UK without the capacity to provide learning opportunities for the increasing numbers of vulnerable workers including migrants, refugees and survivors of slavery and trafficking (Wallis, Nacua & Winterton 2022).

Successive Conservative governments were preoccupied with 'Brexit' and the COVID-19 pandemic which arrived early in 2020 and masked the economic impact of the former. After years of neglect and under-funding of adult training, in September 2020 Prime Minister Boris Johnson announced the introduction of a Lifetime Skills Guarantee, recommended by the Augar Review, the Interim Conclusion of which was published in January 2021 (DfE 2021). Supported by a £2.5 billion National Skills Fund, administered by the Education and Skills Funding Agency (ESFA), the aim is to enable adults to gain a level 3 qualification in areas with acute labour market shortages. In December 2020, the House of Commons Education Committee (2020, 47–48) recommended that the Government 'commission analysis to identify where the nation's immediate and longer-term skills needs lie', 'set out an ambitious long-term strategy for adult skills and lifelong learning', and 'work with sector bodies to develop a modular offer for skills qualifications at all levels.' Those recommendations show that the LME approach to skill formation has failed to cure the UK skills deficit. The UK still lags comparable continental CME countries in the proportion of the workforce qualified to VQ 3, which begs the question as to why the EU promoted LME approaches apparently modelled on the UK.

## Adopting the liberal market model

Allais (2016, 435) describes occupational standards developed in the UK as a 'dysfunctional product for export' and proceeds to question the validity of the approach, even suggesting that employers in the UK did not buy into the standards. It is not the purpose of this chapter to defend the UK skills system, but it must be acknowledged that the standards were developed systematically from extensive functional analysis and employers were widely involved (Mansfield & Mitchell 1996). Allais also commented that qualification reform alone was insufficient to reform labour markets and on the lack of correspondence between work and education. It was never claimed that qualifications would reform labour markets and the lack of alignment between education and work was precisely the motivation for a competence-based approach. More contentious is the notion of 'export', as if the adoption of competence-based approaches (and by extension the LME approach to skill formation) in other countries could be attributed to UK influence. Key individuals and institutions from the UK and Ireland promoted elements of VET associated with the LME model of skill formation, but their role should not be exaggerated. Mike Coles and Tim Oates from the National Council for Vocational Qualifications (NCVQ) as well as Bob Mansfield of Prime Research and Development were heavily involved in promoting the NVQ model, within and beyond Europe, which Irena Grugulis jokingly described in our conversation in January 2022 as 'a pyramid VET scheme'.

Bohlinger and Tūtlys in this collection note that competence-based approaches to skill formation in CEE were part of the EU alignment agenda under the accession process. Chakroun (2010), noting the importance of qualifications frameworks for VET reform, suggested that 'policy borrowing' and emulation gave way to 'policy learning', where the emphasis was on capacity building rather than emulation. Kleibrink (2012, 108) noted that the European Training Foundation (ETF) was extensively involved in organizing 'policy learning events' and providing resources to CEE countries to promote the adoption of EU approaches to skill formation. That EU agenda is unsurprising because the overarching aim of the single European market was to promote a neo-liberal economy and increase competitiveness and capital accumulation. As Jessop (2009, viii) noted in the immediate wake of the global financial crisis (GFC), the 'crisis of mass political legitimacy' was symptomatic of 'the fundamental economic limits of the neoliberal project, whether in its more disembedded Anglo-Saxon form or its more embedded Continental European variants.' The Washington Consensus around the need for trade liberalisation and deregulation was taken up not only by international financial institutions, foreign advisors and consultants, but crucially by transnational bodies like the ILO, OECD and the EU, which all played a role in shaping regulatory frameworks in CEE countries (Holman 2001). Simultaneously, the pursuit of foreign direct investment (FDI) subordinated countries in CEE to the global economy (Drahokoupil 2008). The

World Bank (Taylor 1997) promoted the liberalisation agenda and other supranational institutions developed education policies in line with this (ILO 1997; OECD 1999). The European Employment Strategy launched at the Luxembourg Summit in November 1997 was about competitiveness, while the Lisbon Summit in March 2000 established the key objective of making Europe by 2010 'the most competitive and knowledge-based economy in the world capable of sustainable growth and better jobs and greater social cohesion.' (European Council 2000, para. 5). European integration explicitly adopted liberal market mechanisms to increase competitiveness.

Global policy consensus over competence-based approaches to skill formation reflected three aims. First, to make education and training more relevant to labour market needs; second, to promote geographical mobility through a common framework of competencies underpinning qualifications; and third, to increase permeability between VET and HE. The competence movement began in the UK, and when France and Germany developed competence models, each was rooted in the different systems of VET and cultures of work (Brockman, Clarke & Winch 2009; Le Deist & Winterton 2005). Other countries adopted competence models approximating to one of these three dominant approaches and increasingly aligned with an emerging European model, rather than the UK version (Winterton 2009). European companies like Airbus were also actively developing competence-based approaches to managing human capital (Winterton & Turnbow 2020). In the Copenhagen Declaration (2002), Directors-General for VET announced a strategy to support developing qualifications and competences at European level, committing to a European Credit Transfer System for VET (ECVET). The parallel European Credit Transfer Systems (ECTS) for HE had been extended to all Member States under the Bologna Declaration (1999) but was based on notional workload input (European Commission 2003) rather than competence outcomes, which were regarded as more appropriate for VET (Cedefop 2008). A Technical Working Group was established to develop the principles with the secretariat provided by Cedefop, who commissioned three pieces of underpinning research to design the ECVET architecture. A team from Kassel University developed the credit transfer system (Le Mouillour 2005); colleagues from the Qualifications and Curriculum Authority in London designed the vertical dimension of reference levels (Coles & Oates 2005); and the team at Toulouse Business School established the horizontal dimension, a typology of knowledge, skills and competence (Winterton, Le Deist & Stringfellow 2006). From the recommendations of these three studies, the ECVET system was designed and adopted at the Maastricht summit on 14 December 2004.

Experience with ECVET revealed the political processes involved in designing European instruments and the development of the European Qualifications Framework (EQF) proved even more complicated (Markowitsch & Loumi-Messerer 2008; Sellin 2008). The adoption of competence-based qualifications within the EU has been problematic and imperfect, with major contradictions identified in different EU policy instruments (Winterton 2011), which again raises questions on the motivation for CEE countries to adopt key features of the liberal market approach to skill formation embodied in EU policy and practice.

## CEE perspectives

The country chapters in this collection are relatively circumspect about the reasons for adopting instruments of skill formation either associated with the 'Anglo-Saxon' LME model or the 'German' CME model. Explanations inevitably vary between countries and one of the tasks of this chapter is to explore whether there are discernible patterns that are amenable to explanation by history or geography. Since the CEE countries are far from homogeneous, a starting point is to explore similarities between countries grouped according to distinct regulatory frameworks, institutional characteristics and economic structure.

In the original version of Varieties of Capitalism (VoC) the dichotomous classification of countries into LME and CME (Hall & Soskice 2001) was of limited value analytically. Amable (2003) offered a more nuanced version with Diversity of Capitalism (DoC) but treated all CEE countries as 'transition economies', or as Hancké et al. (2007, 13) termed them, 'emerging market economies.' The World Bank promoted the US version of capitalism in CEE countries, involving deregulation and liberalisation to promote market competition and privatisation of state assets, but the EU was less prescriptive (Hanson 2007), respecting subsidiarity principles (see the chapter of Bohlinger & Tūtlys in this collection). As a result, the transition economies of CEE displayed considerable diversity in moving from centrally planned to market economies (Lane 2007), the different paths reflecting specific economic conditions and institutional legacies (Knell & Srholec 2007).

Ahlborn, Ahrens and Schweickert (2016) used cluster analysis to compare CEE countries with the LME and CME models between 1995 and 2009. The Visegrád countries and Slovenia were consistently associated with the CME model, but from 2004 Slovakia moved towards LME, whereas Croatia moved to the CME model from LME. The Baltic countries similarly were consistently associated with the LME model, along with Bulgaria and Romania, and from 2004, Slovakia. Ahlborn, Ahrens and Schweickert (2016) found no evidence of the underperforming mixed market model associated with Mediterranean countries within CEE. Berber et al. (2020) used the same classifications, finding training practices aligned with the attributed regulatory models.

Attempting to fit transition economies into VoC (or DoC) categories is questionable, since CEE countries are subject to rapid change and have varying degrees of economic stability (Leszczynski 2015; Rapacki et al. 2020). Drawing on Polanyi's (1944) work, Bohle and Greskovits (2007) developed a typology of CEE countries independent of the VoC/DoC categories, arguing that their transformation reflects conflicts and compromises between marketization and social protection, which each country 'pursued and institutionalised with different amounts of vigour and in varied forms.' (ibid., 445). Whereas the Baltic states adopted neoliberalism 'in a rather radical and uncompromising fashion', the Visegrád countries were characterised as 'embedded neoliberal regimes' and Slovenia as 'neocorporatist' (ibid.) In terms of marketization, the Baltic states were most market radical and Slovenia least, with Visegrád countries between these extremes (ibid., 446). The Baltic states were marked by de-industrialisation, deskilling and inequalities, Slovenia the opposite and Visegrád countries a mix (ibid., 447).

Transnational corporations (TNCs) were involved in post-socialist restructuring of heavy industries. Whereas Slovenia and the Visegrád countries had highly skilled labour able to handle complex production technologies, the Baltic states depended on light industry subcontracting where TNCs expected governments to keep 'labour markets flexible, wages low, work conditions unregulated, and workers docile' (ibid., 461). Nölke and Vliegenthart (2009) identify external dependency on TNCs and FDI as a key feature of the Visegrád countries, characterising them as 'dependent market economies' (DME) distinct from LME or CME. Saar, Ure and Desjardins (2013, 221) provide a useful synthesis of the distinctions between LME, CME and DME in relation to education and training systems and welfare state characteristics (see also Saar & Ure, 2013).

The country studies in this collection largely conform with these three distinct groups. As noted in the first chapter of this collection, the Baltic states lacked sufficiently robust institutions for CME approaches so adopted 'shock therapy' to bring about radical changes and pure neoliberalism along the lines of LMEs (Maszczyk & Rapacki 2012). Drahokoupil and Myant (2015) labelled the Baltic states (along with and Bulgaria and Romania) as 'peripheral market economies.' At the opposite extreme is Slovenia, widely regarded as neo-corporatist (Bohle & Greskovits 2012) and following a trajectory that predated transition (Stanojevic 2018). Several studies confirmed Estonia and Slovenia as polar extremes of the CEE countries (Buchan 2007; Feldman 2006). The Visegrád countries (Czech

Republic, Hungary, Poland and Slovakia) fell between these extremes, converging towards a model of 'Competition State' (Drahokoupil 2009), centred on attracting FDI, although this proved insufficient to accelerate industrial restructuring (ibid., 188). Each of these groups is discussed below.

## The Baltic states

Accounts from the three Baltic states in this collection display substantial conformity to the neo-liberal model suggested above. Estonia is characterised by Loogma (see the chapter on Estonia) as involving shock therapy and privatisation to reform VET from a Soviet system to a market model. Three principal reasons are highlighted for the choice of a neo-liberal approach: the influence of external agencies including the World Bank and International Monetary Fund (IMF); the recognition that a neo-liberal approach was a better fit with the marketization strategy; and the influence of policy learning from Denmark, Germany and Finland. While such policy learning might have suggested adopting elements of the CME model of skill formation, Loogma in her chapter confirms that the major influence was 'Europeanization'.

For Latvia, similarly, the priorities of developing a skills formation system that would better meet labour market needs required VET efficiencies through 'optimization' of institutions and curricular reform (see the chapter of Buligina & Sloka). The neo-liberal model was evident in the choice of a competence-based approach to qualifications and modularisation of content, and while these were consistent with the influence of the World Bank and OECD, it was primarily alignment with European strategy and the specific influences of the Leonardo da Vinci and PHARE programmes, and later ESF funded initiatives. As with Estonia, policy choices on skill formation in Latvia seem to have been most influenced by the European agenda rather than directly by LME countries.

Tūtlys et al. in their chapter explain that in Lithuania the adoption of abrupt radical neoliberal marketization was driven by the need to achieve rapid changes in the skill formation system and build new institutions to replace Soviet infrastructure. EU support through the Leonardo da Vinci and PHARE programmes was crucial during the early stages of transition, as were structural funds after accession. The failure of school-based VET system to meet enterprise needs demanded education and training be more closely aligned with the labour market, initially using policy borrowing (imitation) to construct a competence-based qualifications system, for example. That approach conformed very much with policy transfer, which Dolowitz and Marsh (1996, 354) noted is 'dependent upon the transferring political system possessing the political, bureaucratic and economic resources to implement the policy.' Such constraints were explicitly recognized in using a policy learning approach to develop deeper structural changes through projects funded by the Leonardo da Vinci Programme to develop regional VET networks (Winterton, Bukantaitė & Tūtlys 2008) and an apprenticeship system (Tūtlys, Saniter & Winterton 2012). In those projects, elements of practice in France, Germany, The Netherlands and the UK were examined in terms of quality, cost and transferability, while the conditions in Lithuania were assessed to establish whether an element was likely to succeed (Tūtlys, Kaminskienė & Winterton 2016). The analogy was drawn of whether a particular *cépage* can be transplanted abroad, which depends upon soil and climate being conducive. The approach adopted was essentially that advocated by Toepper, Zlatkin-Troitschanskaia and Khüling-Thees (2021, 148), who noted that successful VET transfer depends on elements being adapted to the context of the recipient country.

## *The Visegrád countries*

The Visegrád countries, characterised above as 'competition states' or 'dependent market economies', would be expected to exhibit more similarities with CME than LME, but the situation described by contributors to this collection is more complicated. Such complexity is unsurprising given how these multi-ethnic countries were born from the dissolution of Central European empires and settlements after the two world wars (Fitzmaurice 1998). In the transition era that is the focus of this collection, these four countries began as pro-liberal and pro-European, and GDP per capita almost quadrupled between 1990 and 2015. However, the 2008 economic crisis and particularly the 2013 immigration and refugee crisis, undermined liberal politics, with pro-nationalist mobilisations in the Czech Republic and Slovakia and 'illiberal turns' in Hungary and Poland (Pakulski 2016, 10).

Dvořák and Gal in their chapter portray the Czech Republic as traditionally having a strong VET system with elements of a German dual system in some regions producing a more skilled workforce than the average Soviet model and HEIs producing substantial numbers of graduates in STEM subjects to support industrial production. With the collapse of Communism, privatisation and marketization flourished. Industrial restructuring was driven by FDI, and the existing education and training system struggled to meet labour market needs so private sector providers filled the gap. VET moved away from a dual system to a school-based system and the 'optimization' of institutions amounted to a rationalization and contraction of provision. The expansion of HE was driven by social sciences, business and humanities, further weakening the technical human capital base. EU support for developing the Czech NQF brought additional elements of the LME approach resulting in a mixed model of skill formation, with much local variation, fragmentation and substantial confusion with multiple ministries involved.

Laczik and Farkas in their chapter describe Hungary before transition as having a Soviet education system and elements of the German dual system in VET. The early years of transition were marked by political instability, significant restructuring, growing unemployment and a fall in VET enrolments. The school leaving age was raised to reduce labour market pressure, which raised the qualification level of the workforce, increasingly with HE graduates. The school leaving age was subsequently lowered as enterprises struggled to find workers, one of the consequences of which was increasing numbers of early school leavers, particularly in rural areas. Education was liberalised and decentralised in the early reforms, but VET was brought back under centralised state control in 2017. The influence of the LME approach, evident in modularisation and competence-based qualifications, is attributed to the World Bank and EU rather than any direct influence from Anglophone countries. Laczik and Farkas in this collection doubt that the current skill formation system in Hungary is adequate to support the economic development that the country needs to raise the standard of living of the population.

Dębowski and Stęchły in their chapter describe a complex skills formation system in Poland, with the end of the Soviet era marked by serious skills deficits driven by the rapid pace of economic development, industrial restructuring and emigration on an unprecedented scale. Despite significant growth in real GDP per capita and a substantial fall in unemployment over the past two decades, Poland has a significant productivity gap with the EU15 and has experienced a crisis in VET. As Dębowski and Stęchły stated in their chapter, the early years of transition involved 'devocationalization' of skill formation and HE marketization driven by private HEIs. HE massification involved social sciences, humanities, economics and law, exacerbating skills shortages caused by population decline and leading to increased attention to VET. The statist VET regime had little employer involvement and its redesign, involving competence-based modular training and the NQF, was driven by the EU agenda.

Vantuch and Jelínková in this collection describe the initial 'shock therapy' in Slovakia as involving liberalisation and privatisation, leading to collapse of some industries and reduced purchasing power. Arguing that Slovakia adopted a more gradual approach than the Czech Republic, they nonetheless associate increased unemployment and reduced confidence in VET with these changes, primarily aimed at establishing democracy, a market economy and an independent state. Democratisation involved reforming curricula to remove the ideological content in VET and granting universities autonomy in HE. Marketization led to the collapse of companies, which badly affected craft training and in the 1990s the government 'nationalized' secondary VET schools to protect them during company privatisation. The period 1998–2006 is characterised by 'Europeanization', involving the adoption of competence-based approaches and modularisation of VET, but the changes did not deliver the skills needed in the labour market (see the chapter on Slovakia in this collection). Public disenchantment with the liberal agenda of right-wing governments brought the social democratic party to power in 2006, but the centre-left government fell after a series of corruption scandals and control returned to the right in 2020. In addition to this political instability, the several ministries involved in skills formation are aligned with different stakeholders, backing different models, adding to the complexity. Concluding that Slovakia is at a crossroads in terms of skill formation, structural weaknesses in the economy, declining population and significant emigration of those with tertiary qualifications, are not grounds for optimism.

## Slovenia

Slovenia is depicted by the experts contributing to this collection (Pavlin, Skubic Ermenc, & Bembič) as being the most liberalised, economically developed and westernized of the whole Soviet bloc, but having a low skill economy that career-oriented education in the 1970s failed to improve. The skill formation system has undergone three phases of development since independence. The first period involved reorientation towards EU markets and an attempt to develop a neocorporatist collective skills formation system like the German model, in which the state played a major role because companies most involved in training were contracting. The second period from 2001 involved deregulation, decentralisation and adopting occupational standards. EU accession in 2004 was followed by a second wave of privatisation and the abolition of the piloted dual system in 2006. The third period following the 2008 GFC involved developing the NQF and the state-led VET system developed into a hybrid system involving a collective model with neoliberal elements. Workforce qualifications have increased, but there are sectoral disparities, labour market segmentation and precarisation, with older adults having lower skills, further exacerbated by the 'Matthias effect' (McCracken & Winterton 2006, 56). Sectoral differences necessitate contextualising national skill formation strategies but depend upon social partner engagement and capacity.

## Southeast Europe and Ukraine

Of the remaining four countries considered in this book, three (Bulgaria, Croatia and Romania) are part of the Balkan peninsula of Southeast Europe, while Ukraine neighbours four of the countries in this collection as well as Russia, Belarus and Moldova.

In Bulgaria, lack of attention to skill formation in the early years of transition is explained by complacency and the misplaced belief that human capital development in the Soviet era provided adequate foundations for building a strong economy (see the chapter of Simeonova-Ganeva, Ganev & Angelova in this collection). Under transition, restructuring of state enterprises led to substantial unemployment, particularly for skilled, technical and professional workers, while exposing the low level of technological development in the existing economy, which had compromised VET quality. Increased participation rates in HE, mainly in social sciences and humanities, coupled with demographic trends and emigration, led to labour market shortages in technical areas. Although EU accession improved VET provision, with economic growth those skill shortages became more acute and persist to this day, in part because enterprises are reluctant to train, and to fill the intermediate skills gap, HE graduates take posts for which they appear overqualified. Many initiatives, such as VET modernisation and NQF development, followed the LME approach but were driven by EU programmes as part of the Europeanization agenda. As in previous eras, human capital development in Bulgaria has been widely associated with economic growth (the chapter of Simeonova-Ganeva, Ganev & Angelova in this collection).

Croatia, like Slovenia, declared independence from the former Yugoslavia in 1991 and education policy focused on the task of (re-)establishing national identity (see the chapter of Matković & Buković in this collection). Since the early 2000s, the focus of skill formation has been Europeanization, which included developing an NQF in line with the EQF. Issues affecting skill formation include demographics, labour migration and changing economic structure. The birth rate fell by more than 40 per cent between 1979 and 2001, and over the last decade cohorts retiring have been 20 per cent larger than those completing education. In recent years more skilled workers have entered the labour market through immigration than from the VET system, although there has been some emigration, mostly of those with tertiary qualifications. In the past decade the economy has restructured away from agriculture, manufacturing, construction and mining, with significant growth of the service sector, which by 2011 represented 69 per cent of employment. The 'vocationalized' education system of Yugoslavia was designed to ensure sufficient blue-collar workers but since transition the 3 years VET pathway has fallen to 24 per cent of the cohort, the 4–5 years VET path providing intermediate skills has grown to 44 per cent and the gymnasium route to HE increased to 29 per cent of the cohort. However, of those taking the intermediate skills route 25 per cent enter the labour market as technicians and 19 per cent progress to HE studies, so the tertiary route totals 48 per cent of the cohort. Reform of HE involved increasing the autonomy of HEIs but links with enterprises are weak and there is little opportunity for work placements, so universities are not well aligned with labour market needs. An apprenticeship system developed in the 1990s was modelled on the dual system operated in the Federal State of Bavaria but involves much less workplace learning. The Croatian NQF was accelerated as part of the Europeanization process and supported by EU funds, but the authors conclude that the skill formation system has remained fundamentally statist and has not changed significantly, although skill shortages may disrupt the continuity (see the chapter of Matković & Buković in this collection).

Romania in the communist era had a dual system of VET where schools partnered with state enterprises to provide training but the privatisation programme that started with transition in 1990 effectively removed opportunities for learning at work. The transformation involved establishing new institutions, characterised as 'Europeanization' and largely funded by the PHARE VET reform programme, but progress was slow partly because of fragmented governance involving the Ministries of Labour and Education (see the chapter of Vladut). VET schools were restructured, and new competence-based curricula developed but without enterprise engagement the system became school-based. VET continued to have low prestige and with high unemployment, local enterprises competed on cost and TNCs equally showed little interest in investing in workforce skills. HE was transformed, undergoing democratisation and removal of ideological content, and expanded rapidly in response to student demand although 'decreasing sophistication of economic activity' suggested fewer opportunities for graduates in the labour market, which fuelled the 'brain drain' (see the chapter on Romania). EU accession in 2007 brought a more strategic approach with access to EU finance but the adoption of liberal approaches to skill formation had little success and in 2016 a dual system modelled on Germany was established involving a contract between the VET school, enterprise and learner. Unemployment fell after EU accession, but this was in part a result of emigration and the relatively high employment rate of those with tertiary qualifications masks significant underemployment as graduates take jobs that do not require a university education. Another persistent problem is the performance gap between students according to socio-economic background, which is most marked between Roma and non-Roma and between rural and urban areas. There is little room for optimism that the skill formation system can address such inequalities and poverty until there is a more coherent programme of socio-economic development to reverse labour migration and economic decline.

Ukraine adopted abrupt radical changes with the collapse of the Soviet Union in 1991, liberalising the economy and privatizing state enterprises, the restructuring of which brought de-industrialisation and deskilling to focus on low-skilled production, so skill formation was not high on the agenda (see the chapter of Melnyk in this collection). The country has major regional divisions and has been marked by protest, state bureaucracy and corruption. Modernisation of skill formation effectively began towards the end of the 1990s under more stable economic conditions, with the introduction of VET standards and competence-based training designed to align training with labour market needs. From 2016, extensive Europeanization and decentralisation of the Ukrainian skill formation system led to the adoption of a dual approach in both VET and HE, modularisation of curricula and introduction of occupational standards. Attempts to optimise education were undermined by commercialisation and the growth of a 'diploma market' where HE enrolments grew at the expense of VET leading to skills mismatch and over-qualification. Bologna reforms failed to improve HE quality so 50 per cent of unemployed hold tertiary qualifications and labour market vacancies are for those with VET qualifications. Most recent reforms have been driven, and funded, by international bodies and EU projects promoting an Anglophone competence-based approach to VET curricula with hybrid dual models of delivery. Contextual problems for skill formation include challenging socio-economic context; demographics (population decline, ageing workforce and emigration); political instability because of regional differences and Russian aggression; the resilience of the Soviet legacy, exemplified in bureaucracy and an outdated classification of occupations; and limited stakeholder involvement.

## Conclusion

One of the aims of this chapter was to explore the extent to which 'Anglo-Saxon' (LME) approaches to skill formation had been adopted in the transition economies of CEE and to offer explanations for the direction of travel. Taking stock across the countries covered in this collection, the most obvious conclusion is that there is no single approach to skill formation in the transition economies of CEE and that the influence of the LME model has mainly been through its adoption by European institutions. Vliegenthart and Overbeek (2009) claimed that the CEE countries were used as a 'template' for deepening neoliberal reform, and that lower tax regimes in CEE lured FDI and intensified tax competition putting pressure on the EU15 countries to reduce the tax burden on business.

Another observation is that the characterisation of the different countries by the experts contributing to this collection, while largely corresponding with the distinctions identified in the extant literature between the four groups (Baltic, Visegrád, Slovenia and the Balkans), show nuanced differences when explored in more detail. The country accounts also confirm the observation that different paths followed by CEE countries (Myant & Drahokoupil 2011) exacerbated differences experienced in the impact the GFC (Myant & Drahokoupil 2012).

All three Baltic countries adopted radical 'shock therapy' approaches involving privatisation and marketization, adopting LME approaches through a combination of Europeanization and policy learning driven by the need to replace the Soviet skill formation system. Visegrád countries had Soviet skill formation systems with elements of CME dual arrangements, and Europeanization introduced LME elements leading to hybrid arrangements. In all cases, loss of prestige of VET and HE expansion in social sciences and humanities led to skills mismatches and underemployment of university graduates. Slovenia maintained its distinctive neo-corporatist skill formation system, moving away from the CME model and introducing LME elements influenced by Europeanization, then restoring dual arrangements to arrive at a hybrid model. The respective experts for the remaining (Southeast European) countries also describe Europeanization driving agendas for modernizing skill formation, resulting in hybrid combinations involving modularisation and competence-based approaches based on LME models and elements of the dual system associated with CME models. These countries faced challenges of Soviet legacy, demographic developments and emigration, which combined with the low prestige of VET and expansion of HE, led to skills deficits and overqualification. Governments in Southeast Europe adopted elements of LME approaches and Kleibrink (2012, 104) suggested they 'unreflectively emulated EU lifelong learning policies because they strove for more legitimacy on their way to EU membership.'

In summary, LME approaches to skill formation have become more influential, but not entirely dominant, in the CEE countries represented in this collection and the remaining aim of this chapter is to explain the provenance and processes involved. Anglo-Saxon countries are undeniably 'ideal typical' examples of the LME approach and the provenance of competence and modularisation, which might be seen as appropriate for countries transitioning towards market economies. It is not difficult to explain why the LME approach was so attractive to CEE countries. First, it was the best fit with the 'shock therapy' market transitions of the Baltic states, Romania and Slovakia and closest to the increased marketization of the other countries, with perhaps the exception of Slovenia. Second, the LME model of skill formation is easier to adopt than the CME collective skills formation model, which depends upon effective social partner organizations and institutions of social dialogue. Third, for most CEE countries, Anglophone models were more accessible because English was already the second language of choice above German or French (even in countries like Hungary and Romania, where those languages were, respectively, widely spoken).

Nevertheless, it was the adoption of LME approaches by the EU that was the main driver of their appearance in CEE, through processes including Lisbon and Copenhagen, and mechanisms exemplified by Programmes such as PHARE and Leonardo da Vinci. Although the EU promoted limited harmonisation of VET, such programmes along with ECVET and the European Area of Lifelong Learning involved substantial 'Europeanization' (see the chapter of Bohlinger & Tūtlys). Indeed, the influence of the EU was sufficient for Bohle and Greskovits (2007, 456) to argue that 'left on their own, the CEE regimes would have perhaps ended up as even more divergent: the Baltic states more market-radical, politically and socially more exclusive, the Visegrád states less macroeconomically stable, and Slovenia more protectionist.' Whether the resulting hybrid arrangements for skill formation that now characterise much of CEE are sufficiently robust to deliver the human capital needed for reconstruction and development will only be apparent in the future.

## References

Ahlborn, M., Ahrens, J., & Schweickert, R. (2016). 'Large-scale transition of economic systems – do CEECs converge toward western prototypes?' *Comparative Economic Studies*, 58 (3), 430–454.

Allais, S. (2016). 'Occupational standards in the English-speaking world: A dysfunctional product for export?' In: S. Bohlinger, T. K. A. Dang & M. Klatt (eds.), *Education Policy: Mapping the Landscape and Scope*, pp. 435–459. Frankfurt am Main: Peter Lang.

Amable, B. (2003). *The Diversity of Modern Capitalism*. Oxford: Oxford University Press.

Berber, N., Slavic, A., Strugar Jelača, M., & Bjekić, R. (2020). 'The effects of market economy type on the training practice differences in the Central Eastern European region', *Employee Relations*, 42 (4), 971–998.

Bohle, D., & Greskovits, B. (2007). 'Neoliberalism, embedded neoliberalism, and neocorporatism: Towards transnational capitalism in Central-Eastern Europe', *West European Politics*, 30 (3), 443–466.

Bohle, D., & Greskovits, B. (2012). *Capitalist Diversity on Europe's Periphery*. Ithaca, NY: Cornell University Press.

Bosworth, D. L. (1981). 'The demand for qualified scientists and engineers', *Applied Economics*, 13 (4), 411–429.

Brockmann, M., Clarke, L., & Winch, C. (2009) 'Competence and competency in the EQF and in European VET systems', *Journal of European Industrial Training*, 33 (8/9), 787–799.

Brown, A. (2011). 'Lessons from policy failure: The demise of a National Qualifications Framework based solely on learning outcomes in England', *Journal of Contemporary Educational Studies*, 62 (5), 36–55.

Buchan, C. (2007). 'Estonia and Slovenia as Antipodes.' In D. Lane & M. Myant (eds.), *Varieties of Capitalism in Post-Communist Countries*, pp. 65–89. Basingstoke: Palgrave MacMillan.

Cedefop (2008). *The Shift to Learning Outcomes: Conceptual, Political and Practical Developments in Europe*. Luxembourg: Publications Office of the European Union.

Chakroun, B. (2010). 'National Qualification Frameworks: From policy borrowing to policy learning', *European Journal of Education*, 45 (2), 199–216.

Coles, M., & Oates, T. (2005). *European Reference Levels for Education and Training: Promoting Credit Transfer and Mutual Trust*. Cedefop Panorama series 109, Luxembourg: Office for Official Publications of the European Communities.

Copenhagen Declaration (2002). Declaration of the European Ministers of Vocational Education and Training, and the European Commission, convened in Copenhagen on 29 and 30 November 2002, on enhanced European cooperation in vocational education and training. 'The Copenhagen Declaration' 30 November 2002.

Crouch, C., Finegold, D., & Sako, M. (1999) *Are Skills the Answer? The Political Economy of Skills Creation in Advanced Industrial Countries*. Oxford: Oxford University Press.

Daly, A., & Jones, D. T. (1980). 'The machine tool industry in Britain, Germany and the United States', *National Institute Economic Review*, 92, 53–63.

DfE (2021). *Interim Conclusion of the Review of Post 18 Education and Funding*, CP 358. Department for Education, London: Stationery Office.

Dolowitz, D., & Marsh, D. (1996). 'Who learns what from whom? A review of the policy transfer literature', *Political Studies*, XLIV, 343–357.

Drahokoupil, J. (2008). *Globalization and the State in Central and Eastern Europe: The Politics of Foreign Direct Investment*. London: Routledge.

Drahokoupil, J. (2009). 'The rise of the Competition State in the Visegrád Four: Internationalization of the state as a local project.' In B. van Apeldoorn, L. Horn & J. Drahokoupil (eds.), *Contradictions and Limits of Neoliberal European Governance. From Lisbon to Lisbon*, pp. 187–208. Basingstoke: Palgrave Macmillan.

Drahokoupil, J., Myant, M. (2015). 'Putting Comparative Capitalisms Research in Its Place: Varieties of Capitalism in Transition Economies.' In M. Ebenau, I. Bruff & C. May (eds.), *New Directions in Comparative Capitalisms Research. International Political Economy Series*, pp. 155-171. London: Palgrave Macmillan.

European Commission (2003). 'ECTS – European Credit Transfer System', *CEC, Brussels*, <http://europa.eu.int/comm/education/programmes/socrates/ects_en.html> accessed 24 January 2022.

European Council (1997). 'Extraordinary European Council Meeting on Employment, Luxembourg, 20 and 21 November, Presidency Conclusions', <http://www.consilium.europa.eu/uedocs/cms_data/docs/pressdata/en/ec/00300.htm>, accessed 24 January 2022.

European Council (2000). 'Lisbon European Council 23 and 24 March 2000 Presidency Conclusions',<http://www.europarl.europa.eu/summits/lis1_en.htm>, accessed 24 January 2022.

European Union (2010). 'New Skills for New Jobs: Action Now', *A report by the Expert Group on New Skills for New Jobs prepared for the European Commission, February 2010*, <http://ec.europa.eu/social/main.jsp?catId=568&langId=en>, accessed 24 January 2022.

Feldmann, M. (2006). 'Emerging Varieties of Capitalism in Transition Countries: Industrial Relations and Wage Bargaining in Estonia and Slovenia', *Comparative Political Studies*, 39 (7), 829–854.

Finegold, D., & Soskice, D. (1988). 'The failure of training in Britain: Analysis and Prescription', *Oxford Review of Economic Policy*, 4 (3), 21–52.

Fitzmaurice, J. (1998). *Politics and Government in the Visegrad Countries*. Basingstoke: Macmillan.

Grugulis, I. (1997). 'The consequences of competence: A critical assessment of the Management NVQ', *Personnel Review*, 26 (6), 428–444.

Grugulis, I. (2000). 'The management NVQ: A critique of the myth of relevance', *Journal of Vocational Education and Training*, 52 (1), 79–99.

Grugulis, I. (2003). 'The contribution of National Vocational Qualifications to the growth of skills in the UK', *British Journal of Industrial Relations*, 41 (3), 457–475.

Hall, P. A., & Soskice, D. (eds.) (2001). *Varieties of Capitalism. The Institutional Foundations of Comparative Advantage*. Oxford: Oxford University Press.

Hancké, B., Rhodes, M., & Thatcher, M. (eds.) (2007). *Beyond Varieties of Capitalism: Conflict, Contradictions, and Complementarities in the European Economy*. Oxford: Oxford University Press.

Handy, C. (1987). *The Making of Managers. A Report on Management Education, Training and Development in the USA, West Germany, France, Japan and the UK*. London: National Economic Development Office.

Handy, C., Gordon, G., Gow, I., & Raddlesome, C. (1988). *Making Managers*. London: Pitman.

Hanson, P. (2007). 'The European Union's influence on the development of capitalism in Central Europe.' In D. Lane (ed.), *The Transformation of State Socialism. System Change, Capitalism or Something else?* pp. 95–112. Basingstoke: Palgrave Macmillan.

Haskel, J., & Martin, C. (1993). 'The causes of skill shortages in Britain', *Oxford Economic Papers*, 45 (4), 573–588.

Holman, D. (2013). 'Job types and job quality in Europe', *Human Relations*, 66 (4), 475–502.

Holman, O. (2001). 'The enlargement of the European Union towards Central and Eastern Europe: The role of supranational and transnational actors.' In A. Bieler & A. D. Morton (eds.), *Social Forces in the Making of the New Europe: The Restructuring of European Social Relations in the Global Political Economy*, pp. 161–84. Basingstoke: Palgrave Macmillan.

House of Commons Education Committee (2020). *A Plan for an Adult Skills and Lifelong Learning Revolution*. Third Report of Session 2019–21, HC 278, House of Commons, 19 December.

Hunter, L. C. (1978). *Labour Shortages and Manpower Policy*. London: HMSO.

Hyland, T. (1994). *Competence, Education and NVQs. Dissenting Perspectives*. London: Cassel.

ILO (1997). *Competence Based Training*. International Labour Organisation, Montevideo: Cintefor.

Jessop, B. (2009). 'Foreword.' In B. van Apeldoorn, L. Horn & J. Drahokoupil (eds.), *Contradictions and Limits of Neoliberal European Governance. From Lisbon to Lisbon*, pp. viii–xi. Basingstoke: Palgrave Macmillan.

Jessup, G. (1991). *Outcomes: NVQs and the Emerging Model of Education and Training*. Brighton: Falmer Press.

Johnson, S., & Winterton, J. (1999). *Management Skills*. Skills Task Force Research Paper 3. London: Department for Education and Employment.

Kleibrink, A. (2012). 'Lifelong learning policies in Southeastern Europe: From emulation of life-long policies to tailor-made reforms?' In M. Arandarenko & W. Bartlett (eds.), *Labour Market and Skills in the Western Balkans*, pp. 103–128. Belgrade: FREN (Foundation for the Advancement of Economics).

Knell, M. & Srholec, M. (2007). 'Diverging pathways in Central and Eastern Europe.' In D. Lane & M. Myant (eds.), *Varieties of Capitalism in Post-Communist Countries*, pp. 40–64. Basingstoke: Palgrave MacMillan.

Lane, D. (2007). 'Post state socialism: A diversity of capitalisms?' In D. Lane & M. Myant (eds.), *Varieties of Capitalism in Post-Communist Countries*, pp. 13–39. Basingstoke: Palgrave Macmillan.

Le Deist, F. D., & Winterton, J. (2005). 'What is competence?' *Human Resource Development International*, 8 (1), 27–46.

Le Mouillour, I. (2005). *European Approaches to Credit (transfer) Systems in VET: An Assessment of the Applicability of Existing Credit Systems to a European Credit (transfer) System for Vocational Education and Training (ECVET)*. Cedefop dossier series 12. Luxembourg: Office for Official Publications of the European Communities.

Leszczynski, D. (2015). 'Emerging varieties of capitalism in transition countries: Literature review', *International Journal of Management and Economics*, 48 (1), 101–124.

Liepman, K. L. (1960). *Apprenticeship: An Enquiry into Its Adequacy under Modern Conditions*. London: Routledge and Kegan Paul.

McCracken, M. and Winterton, J. (2006). 'What about the managers? Contradictions in lifelong learning and management development', *International Journal of Training and Development*, 10 (1), 53–64.

Mansfield, B. (1993). 'Competency-based qualifications: A response', *Journal of European Industrial Training*, 17 (3), 19–22.

Mansfield, B., & Mitchell, L. (1996). *Towards a Competent Workforce*. London: Gower.

Markowitsch, J., & Loumi-Messerer, K. (2008). 'Development and interpretation of descriptors of the European Qualifications Framework', *European Journal of Vocational Training*, 42/43, 33–58.

Maszcyk, P., & Rapacki, R. (2012). *Varieties of Capitalism in Transition Countries*, Warsaw: Collegium of World Economy at the Warsaw School of Economics (SGH).

Meager, N. (1986). 'Skill shortages again and the UK economy', *Industrial Relations Journal*, 17 (3), 236–248.

Myant, M., & Drahokoupil, J. (2011). *Transition Economies: Political Economy in Russia, Eastern Europe and Central Asia*. Hoboken, NJ: Wiley.

Myant, M., & Drahokoupil, J. (2012). 'International integration, varieties of capitalism and resilience to crisis in transition economies', *Europe-Asia Studies*, 64 (1), 1–33.

Nölke, A., & Vliegenthart, A. (2009). 'Enlarging the varieties of capitalism: The emergence of dependent market economies in East Central Europe', *World Politics*, 61 (4), 670–702.

OECD (1999). *Definition and Selection of Competencies. Projects on Competencies in the OECD Context: Analysis of Theoretical and Conceptual Foundations*. Organisation for Economic Cooperation and Development, Neuchâtel: Swiss Federal Statistical Office.

Pakulski, J. (ed.) (2016). *The Visegrad Countries in Crisis*. Warsaw: Collegium Civitas.

Polanyi, K. (1944). *The Great Transformation*. New York, NY: Farrar & Rinehart.

Prais, S. J. (1981). 'Vocational qualifications of the labour force in Britain and Germany', *National Institute Economic Review*, 98, 47–59.

Rapacki, R., Gardawski, J., Czerniak, A., Horbaczewska, B., Karbowski, A., Maszczyk, P., & Prochniak, M. (2020). 'Emerging varieties of post-communist capitalism in Central and Eastern Europe: Where do we stand?' *Europe-Asia Studies*, 72 (4), 565–592.

Richard, D. (2012). *The Richard Review of Apprenticeships*. London: Department of Business, Energy & Industrial Strategy.

Saar, E., & Ure, O. B. (2013). 'Lifelong learning systems: Overview and extension of different typologies.' In E. Saar, O. B. Ure & J. Holford (eds.), *Lifelong Learning in Europe: National Patterns and Challenges*, pp. 46–81. Cheltenham: Edward Elgar.

Saar, E., Ure, O. B., & Desjardins, R. (2013). 'The rôle of diverse institutions in framing adult learning systems', *European Journal of Education*, 48 (2), 213–232.

Sellin, B. (2008). 'The proposal for a European Qualifications Framework. Making it a reality – possibilities and limitations', *European Journal of Vocational Training*, 42/43, 4–18.

Senker, P. (1996). 'The development and implementation of National Vocational Qualifications: an engineering case study', *New Technology, Work and Employment*, 11 (2), 83–95.

Snell, K. D. M. (1996). 'The apprenticeship system in British history: The fragmentation of a cultural institution', *History of Education*, 25 (4), 303–321.

Snower, D. J. (1996). 'The low-skill, bad job trap.' In A. L. Booth & D. J. Snower (eds.), *Acquiring Skills: Market Failures, Their Symptoms and Policy Responses*, pp. 109–124. Cambridge: Cambridge University Press.

Stanojevic, M. (2018). 'Slovenia: neo-corporatism under the neo-liberal turn', *Employee Relations*, 40 (4), 709–724.

Steedman, H., Mason, G., & Wagner, K. (1991). 'Intermediate skills in the workplace: Deployment, standards and supply in Britain, France and Germany', *National Institute Economic Review*, 136, 60–76.

STF (2000). *Skills for All: Proposals for a National Skills Agenda*, Final Report from the National Skills Task Force. Sheffield: Department for Education and Employment.

Taylor, L. (1997). 'Editorial: The revival of the liberal creed – the IMF and the World Bank in a globalized economy', *World Development*, 25 (2), 145–152.

Thompson, J. E., & Carter, S. (1995). 'The development of competence: National standards for managers.' In M. Mulder, W. J. Nijhof & R. O. Brinkerhoff (eds.), *Corporate Training for Effective Performance*, pp. 13–32. Dordrecht: Springer.

Toepper, M., Zlatkin-Troitschanskaia, O., & Khüling-Thees, C. (2021). 'Research in international transfer of vocational education and training – A systematic literature review', *International Journal for Research in Vocational Education and Training*, 8 (4), 138–169.

Tūtlys, V., Kaminskienė, L., & Winterton, J. (2016). 'Policy borrowing and policy learning in initial VET reforms of Lithuania after 1990.' In S. Bohlinger, T. K. A. Dang & M. Klatt (eds.), *Education Policy: Mapping the Landscape and Scope*, pp. 377–402. Frankfurt: Peter Lang.

Tūtlys, V., Saniter, A., & Winterton, J. (2012). *Implementation and Development of Apprenticeship in the Vocational Education and Training System of Lithuania*. Kaunas: Vytautas Magnus University.

Vliegenthart, A., & Overbeek, H. (2009). 'Corporate tax reform in neoliberal Europe: Central and Eastern Europe as a template for deepening the neoliberal European integration project?' In B. van Apeldoorn, L. Horn & J. Drahokoupil (eds.), *Contradictions and Limits of Neoliberal European Governance. From Lisbon to Lisbon*, pp. 143–162. Basingstoke: Palgrave Macmillan.

Wallis, E., Nacua, L., & Winterton, J. (2022). 'Vulnerable workers and the demise of adult education in England', *Education + Training*, 64 (2), 244–258.

Whitehead, N. (2013). *Review of Adult Vocational Qualifications in England*. Wath Upon Dearne: UK Commission for Employment and Skills.

Williams, G. (1957) *Recruitment to Skilled Trades*. London: Routledge & Kegan Paul.

Winterton, J. (2009). 'Competence across Europe: Highest common factor or lowest common denominator?' *Journal of European Industrial Training*, 33 (8/9), 681–700.

Winterton, J. (2011). 'Competence in European policy instruments: A moving target for developing a National Qualifications Framework?' *Journal of Contemporary Educational Studies*, 62 (5), 72–87.

Winterton, J., Bukantaitė, D, & Tūtlys, V. (2008). 'Historical development of vocational education and training in Lithuania and implications for designing and implementation of regional VET partnerships', *Profesinis Rengimas: Tyrimai ir Realijos*, 16, 180–191.

Winterton, J., Le Deist, F. D., & Stringfellow, E. (2006). *Typology of Knowledge, Skills and Competences: Clarification of the Concept and Prototype*. Cedefop Reference series 64. Luxembourg: Office for Official Publications of the European Communities.

Winterton, J., Parker, M., Dodd, M., McCracken, M., & Henderson, I. (2000). *Future Skill Needs of Managers*, Research Report RR182. Sheffield: Department for Education and Employment.

Winterton, J., & Turnbow, T. (2020). 'What is competence? Theory, policy and practice.' In T. Dundon & A. Wilkinson (eds.), *Case Studies in Work, Employment and Human Resource Management*, pp. 123–128. Cheltenham: Edward Elgar.

Winterton, J., & Turner, J. J. (2019). 'Preparing graduates for work readiness: An overview and agenda', *Education + Training*, 61 (5), 536–551.

Winterton, J., & Winterton, R. (1994). *Collective Bargaining and Consultation over Continuing Vocational Training*, RM.7. Sheffield: Employment Department.

Winterton, J., & Winterton, R. (1996). *The Business Benefits of Competence Based Management Development*, RS16. Department for Education and Employment, London: HMSO.

Winterton, J., & Winterton, R. (1997). 'Does management development add value?' *British Journal of Management*, 8 (Special Issue), S65-S76.

Winterton, J., & Winterton, R. (1999) *Developing Managerial Competence*. London: Routledge.

Wolf, A. (2011). *Review of Vocational Education – The Wolf Report*. London: Department for Business, Innovation and Skills and Department for Education.

Wolf, A. (2020). 'Political context. "One size fits all" – A default policy that is serving no one well', *European Review*, 28 (Special Issue), S28–S43.

Young, M. F.D. (2008). *Bringing Knowledge Back In: From Social Constructivism to Social Realism in the Sociology of Education*. London and New York: Routledge.

Andreas Saniter and Christiane Eberhardt

# 18. Skill formation: policy learning from Germany ?

**Abstract:** Collective skill formation in Germany is both highly complex and unique. Even the dual systems of other German-speaking countries show considerable differences. Focusing on four underpinning pillars (*political consensus, involvement of companies, collective skill formation, vocational principle*) of German IVET, the chapter raises the question if the German model is suitable as an example or blueprint for the development of VET in other countries. The authors address the topic from a historical perspective and refer to the experiences of the last thirty years of IVET-cooperation between Germany, the European Union and CEE countries that played a crucial role for developments. Cooperation programmes and the connected funding streams reflect the historical context and the role assigned to IVET in CEE countries: IVET was understood and supported as an instrument to promote the market economy (1990s), it played an essential role for EU accession (2000s) and afterwards to reduce youth unemployment via apprenticeship (2010s). The chapter concludes with an attempt to align the developments of skill formation in the CEE countries with the German collective skill formation system by comparing key features of these developments with the four main pillars of the German IVET system.

**Keywords:** Collective skill formation, dual apprenticeship system, internal flexibility of curricula, support of CEE countries with TRANSFORM and PHARE, EU accession

## Introduction

This book focusses on "directions of development" in "skill formation in Central and Eastern European (CEE) countries". Educational reforms or developments never occur in empty spaces. Firstly, developments are dependent on existing structures and are embedded in the traditions, beliefs and vested interests in reforming countries. Secondly, they are influenced by educational trends and examples of apparent good practices in other countries. Thirdly, in the case of financial support from third parties, reforms are affected by the policy aims and interests of those parties. The first chapters of this book refer to the first aspect, they describe the traditions, challenges, interests and solutions chosen by CEE countries and the pathways they pursued since 1989.

With regard to the second aspect, Germany, due to geographical and cultural proximity and its economic strength, could offer an example for policy learning. Following Moyson et al. (2017) the authors of this chapter differentiate "three approaches to policy learning that operate at micro-, meso- and macro-levels" (Moyson et al. 2017, p. 163) and assume that, due to the complete breakdown of the former socialist structures in CEE countries, policy learning on the macro (systemic) level is most relevant. This chapter also refers to chosen examples in the meso (organisational) level, whilst the micro (individual) level is disregarded. But how should the German Dual Initial Vocational Education and Training (IVET) system be described given that the whole system is both highly complex and unique, with even the dual systems operating within other German speaking countries differing substantially. The other extreme, breaking the system down to "eleven essential elements of a dual vocational training system" (Euler 2013) like "funding" or "qualifications of teachers and training personnel" and looking for similarities with other IVET systems is too detailed and therefore some similarities might be found between almost all IVET-systems. The authors of this chapter decided on an intermediate approach, focussing on four key pillars of the German system, which underpin the system.

In the case of CEE countries the third aspect; implicit or explicit policy aims of donors, have also played a crucial role, following the collapse of socialist regimes. The huge economic gap between Western Europe and CEE countries in the 1990s must also be taken into account. The main bilateral (Germany – CEE countries) and European Union (EU) programmes must be considered here.

This chapter consists of four sections. Following this brief introduction, the next section presents an overview of the collective skill formation model of Germany, by highlighting the chosen key pillars of German IVET qualifications ("qualifications" refer to state-recognised, nationwide established, IVET programmes lasting between 2 and 3.5 years and leading to a qualification on European Qualification Framework (EQF) level 3 or 4).

Even if collective skill formation is seen by CEE countries as an example of good practice or as an attractive system for mirroring the own national IVET system, any reforms need financial, administrative and political support. The third subsection therefore drafts the schemes of IVET-cooperation between Germany, the European Union and CEE countries that played a crucial role for developments, and which referenced German or other West-European practices. Cooperation programmes and the attached funding streams reflect the historical context and the role assigned to IVET in CEE countries: IVET was understood and supported as an instrument to promote the market economy (1990s), it played an essential role for EU accession (2000s) and to reduce youth unemployment via apprenticeship (2010s). The last subsection attempts to align the developments of the skill formation in the CEE countries with the German collective skill formation system by comparing key features of these developments with the four main pillars of the German IVET system.

## Pillars of the German Dual System

There are various approaches to analysing and describing the German Dual System (e.g. Münk 2010; Bosch 2010; Greinert 1995a; Fürstenau, Pilz, and Gonon 2014; Euler 2013, Saniter 2020) in a transnational context. In this chapter, the use of "dual system" is synonymous with company-based apprenticeship.

This chapter does not intend to analyse the German Dual System in detail. It refers to four underpinning pillars (political consensus, involvement of companies, collective skill formation, and holistic approach) which are responsible for the stability of the dual system in Germany. This selection might be considered incomplete, but, from the perspective of the authors, the pillars described are the ones most crucial for the success of the dual system in Germany. All the pillars of the German dual VET system nevertheless have weaknesses and potential threats, which are also considered in this section.

### Evolution not disruption – political consensus

According to Greinert, (1995b, 2006) three periods of the development of the German IVET system since industrialisation can be distinguished:

1. the "period of the establishment" of initial VET institutions from 1870 to 1920;
2. the "period of institutional structuring and consolidation" of the dual VET system in 1920–1970;
3. the "period of further construction and rationalisation" of the dual VET system; initiated by the Federal Law of Vocational Education (Berufsbildungsgesetz) in 1969.

Other authors, for example Busemeyer and Thelen (2012), argue that in the year 2000 another period, the one of "decentralisation of the provision of IVET" started. This period was characterised by an experimental approach that led to a re-consolidation. Since industrialisation, Germany has experienced a sequence of serious political disruptions:

- The end of the emperors regime 1918;
- The first (Weimar) republic (1918–1933);
- The national socialist regime (1933–1945);

- Post-war Germany under allied occupation (US, UK, France and USSR (1945–1949));
- The German division (GDR and FRG (1949–1989));
- German reunification (1990).

A comparison of the dates of Greinert`s periods and the changes of the political systems suggests that none of these (radical) political changes were accompanied by a disruption of the basic structures of IVET. Even more, the periods of development of the German IVET system are characterised by incremental verbs like "establishing", "consolidation" and "further construction".

Nowadays, all stakeholders, including the political parties agree on the principles of the approach to skill formation, with only variants of some of the elements (f. e. length of IVET programmes, level of apprentice wages) being under discussion. For example, the principle that apprentices in the Dual System receive wages is undisputed, but the level of wages is the subject of sectoral collective negotiations. Another broad discussion in Germany refers to the question of whether refugees without confirmed right of residence are eligible to apply for an apprenticeship.

Consensus, however, led to a certain level of inertia within the system. This can be illustrated by the response to the 3rd industrial revolution, when the Information Technology (IT) sector arose in the1980s. The curriculum of the only IVET vocation in this sector, the "management assistant in data processing" (Datenverarbeitungskaufmann) from 1969 was valid until 1997 before it was replaced by three modern (by the standard of the 1990s) vocational profiles (cf. BIBB 2021). A whole generation of career seekers in the IT sector therefore had no option of starting their VET qualification according to the curricula of a modern, state-recognized IT-profile and had to qualify via standards set by big IT companies ("company-certified professional").

## Involvement of companies – no alternative qualification pathways

This chapter does not aim to make a contribution to the industrial-cultural debate nor to questions of whether an "apprenticeship culture" (Deissinger 2004) exists and, if so, what role it plays within Human Resource Development (HRD) strategies. The first priority of German companies, in common with companies from other countries, is to generate profit rather than to support the educational system. Yet, in a high-income country like Germany, value creation strongly depends on qualified skilled workers, and the only way to qualify young people is via company-based apprenticeship, as in most sectors no state funded school-based IVET-system exists. Thus, the involvement of companies in

German IVET is an instrumental rather than altruistic action. According to the results of a representative BIBB survey on the costs and benefits, the investment pays off, particularly when the apprentice is employed after finishing their dual training: recruitment costs are saved, reliance on the external labour market is reduced and potential downtime costs due to personnel bottlenecks are avoided. The majority (59 per cent) of the more than 3,000 companies surveyed claim they are "very satisfied" or "satisfied" with the cost-benefit balance of training (BIBB 2009). Whilst generating some costs, apprentices also contribute to the production of goods and services through their work. The same survey also asked about the reasons why companies participate in training. Most responses highlighted economic benefits: Training young workers to meet the requirements at the work place, and reducing recruitment costs (84 per cent). A further important issue for 58 per cent was to prevent instability within the workforce with 55 per cent suggesting it was advantageous to deploy the apprentice as a worker during their training.

The apprenticeship market functions are comparable to the labour market and strongly depend on the economic situation and expectations. This became very clear during the summer of 2020 when recruitment was influenced by the Covid 19 pandemic; new apprenticeship contracts decreased by 9.3 per cent, the highest decrease since statistics began to be collected in 1977. Not surprisingly the decrease in hospitality (-31 per cent) and tourism (-61.1 per cent) were amongst the highest (cf. Statistisches Bundesamt 2021). No company invests in future staff in times of great uncertainty. State-driven IVET-systems could potentially negate such cyclical trends.

## Collective skill formation

Curriculum design and examinations within the German apprenticeship system are strictly dual: Public bodies (the sixteen federal regions (Bundesländer) represented by VET-teachers) are responsible for the curricula of the educational institutions which provide approximately one quarter of the learning time, whilst the social partners (employers organisations and trade unions) have responsibility for workplace curricula. Both social partners nominate an equal number of delegates for the committees that restructure/design VET-profiles and for the final examination boards. The central state only organizes and supervises the negotiations, and validates new IVET-profiles when the stakeholders have reached agreement on content and structure. German chambers support companies in their region in all aspects of apprenticeship and of organising the final examinations (cp. Saniter 2020).

This approach succeeds in sectors with strong trade unions. If trade unions are weak in a sector, and are unable to nominate an equal number of delegates to the examination boards they can be overwhelmed by the joint pressure by the employers, chambers and state concerning the structure of IVET profiles. In such circumstances, whilst consensus is required, decisions might nevertheless be taken without one of the stakeholders (cp. IGM 2004). For example, most of the "assistant" vocations, where IVET lasts only two (instead of three or three and a half) years were established without confirmation by trade unions.

## Holistic approach (Vocational principle, Berufsprinzip) – internal flexibility

The principle of recognised vocations or occupations (Berufsprinzip) refers to an "universal principle for the regulation of initial vocational training content and qualification standards" (Reuling 1998). The Vocational Training Act (Berufsbildungsgesetz, BBiG) sets the legal framework for all dual training vocations. The relation between vocational qualifications and the labour market is symbiotic, as one structures and governs the other – and vice versa. "Recognised vocations" therefore are both education-related and employment-related. A basic element of this governance is the limited number of recognized dual vocational profiles: in 2021, 323 vocations for all sectors were in force a number that has been very stable in the last decades, varying by just plus or minus 5 per cent. The rationale for the limited number of recognised profiles is that vocational qualifications should permit successful apprentices to work in different companies, sectors and regions. Thus "occupational proficiency" or "vocational ability to act" (berufliche Handlungsfähigkeit) is the backbone of the German holistic approach. Modern VET-profiles for the workplace are structured via twelve to twenty "time-frames" (Zeitrahmen) that draft the content only briefly and offer variable time-spans for each time-frame (for example, between 1 and 3 months). This internal flexibility allows companies to reflect their main business and work-processes without neglecting the other time frames and prevents the modularisation of German IVET profiles.

Unfortunately, the close link between the labour market and IVET profiles often results in qualifications from other countries and informal acquired skills being neither valued nor recognised. To "upgrade" foreign qualification or informal skills to a recognized qualification is often a time-consuming, bureaucratic and expensive procedure – but generates long term rewards as German wages are usually linked closely to formal qualifications.

## Assistance of Germany for the CEE countries in skill formation: Preconditions, interventions and implications

The collapse of communism at the end of the 1980s led to profound social, economic and political changes in all CEE countries. New legal and political infrastructures, new public financial mechanisms, social security and welfare systems were required. The move from planned to market economies implied the liberalisation of prices, the lifting of trade barriers and – first and foremost – the loss of the most important trading partner of all of them, the former Soviet Union.

The CEE countries were different in many respects including their approaches to initial vocational education and training, although, from West European perspective, they were often subsumed under "eastern bloc" or characterised as members of the Council for Mutual Economic Assistance (COMECON), which comprised East Germany (ex-GDR), Bulgaria, Hungary, Poland, Romania, Czechoslovakia, the USSR, Mongolia, Cuba and Vietnam.

### IVET in CEE countries before 1989

In order to illustrate the extent of transformation with respect to IVET after 1989, it is helpful to review the situation after 1945. Most of the COMECON countries were agricultural states with little developed industry. In the 1950s and 1960s, the "socialist state-owned large-scale industry" emerged and needed an increasing amount of at least semi-skilled workers. The labour force (mostly former agricultural workers) was trained via short-term courses. At the same time, the states took responsibility for the initial education and training of young people. They established vocational education in full time schools, which had little contact with the world of word. This situation started to change with the introduction of "partner companies" which cooperated with local IVET schools. Partner companies offered internships for students and equipped training centres at the schools. In addition, they often gave simple production orders to the schools and expressed their qualification needs to the school administration. This led to more, but still not enough, practice-orientation of vocational curricula (Laur-Ernst 2008). It should be kept in mind that education was an important strategy to strengthen and sustain the "socialist construction" after World War II. Education aimed at the formation of a "socialist personality" who serves state and society best by working. Labour was interpreted as the most important field of personal development (Leontjew 1977). From this point of view, education and labour were closely connected. There are three typical patterns of IVET provision which had been developed in CEE countries before the great educational reform in the Soviet Union from the 1980s (BIBB 1997):

- Fulltime vocational schools with in-house training centres: companies took over supporting schools ("partner companies") and provided opportunities for short-term internships,
- School-based "dualised / cooperative" vocational education and training in the modified form of company vocational schools, i.e. adapted to the large-scale state industry,
- Company-based "dual" vocational education and training in small companies and collectives (mainly in crafts), partly linked to inter-company training centres.

The reform of education and VET launched in the Soviet Union in 1984 had an impact on all CEE countries. This reform was in response to demographic developments and labour market problems. The reform primarily sought to improve the quality and quantity of vocational schools and establish closer links with the labour market (Kuebert 1987). Since that reform, initial training was mainly provided in two types of schools in most CEE countries:

- secondary technical schools; which provided qualifications at intermediate level ("technicians") for various sectors of industry, agriculture and services, and for non-academic staff in the health, social and cultural services. The system included vocational schools for management and staff and additionally awarded certificates of general education,
- secondary vocational schools; that offered a wider choice of courses and led to the qualification of 'skilled worker' ("blue collar" workers) (Weilnböck et al. 1997), co-operating with partner companies (school-based apprenticeship).

Unfortunately, in terms of aligning the schools with the labour market, neither the reforms nor the provision of company internships of several weeks duration for vocational school students were wholly successful (BIBB 1997). Companies became increasingly critical of the separation of working and learning and of theory and practice. Graduates from vocational schools had poor occupational skills, as academic knowledge and theoretical subjects dominated curricula. The mismatch of demand and supply of qualifications resulted in serious production problems. Some limited innovations fostering more practice orientation were introduced just before the political upheaval in 1989/90 but were unable to gain momentum (BIBB 1997).

In CEE countries, labour markets were characterised by high participation rates, labour shortages, low productivity and extensive labour hoarding by enterprises. Most of the working population was employed within industry or agriculture while services, especially personal services, trade, communications and producer services were significantly underdeveloped. This situation changed rapidly after the political upheavals in 1989–1990. Technological underdevelopment undermined the development of new markets resulting in falling output, lengthy recession and rising unemployment. Falling demand was reflected in an oversupply of labour, and unemployment, practically unknown under the communist regime, started to accelerate (Nesporova 1997). All CEE countries had to introduce fundamental reforms in vocational education and training in order to meet the identified needs of the economy and labour market. This task was strongly influenced by the need to overcome "systemic imprints" (BIBB 1996, p. 13), i.e. the industrial qualification of skilled workers geared to a planned economy, and thus to redevelop or revitalise craft, commercial and service-oriented training (Eberhardt and Shcherbak 2017).

Many practical problems had to be solved in the first transformation period:

- Most of the companies that previously participated in full-time school-based vocational training as so-called partner companies ceased to do so.
- Self-governing bodies of the industry (competent bodies) and social partners were in a consolidation stage; in most CEE countries their role within IVET was neither substantive nor legally anchored.
- Vocational training continued to be provided according to old training programmes, although to some extent according to independently revised occupational profiles. The old "register of occupations" (nomenklatura) persisted; and modern standards corresponding to the needs of the market economy were missing.
- In IVET schools, teachers struggled with their own responsibility (oftenwithout appropriate support) to re-orientate teaching; curriculum design for new occupations was assigned directly to schools.
- Teaching and learning materials used in IVET schools were outdated, the equipment and premises (workshops, teaching rooms, etc.) at schools were in need of improvement (Eberhardt 1998).

Accordingly, the first pilot projects to enable policy learning started in 1990/91 in CEE countries, funded by foreign donors and reflecting a broad range of IVET systems in western (EU) countries. Alongside various EU programmes and national policy formulations, bilateral and international donor programmes also played an important role as drivers for change in VET policy (Nielsen 2004). One of these programmes was the German Federal Government´s TRANSFORM Advisory Programme. The programme started its work even before the European Training Foundation (ETF) in Turin was established and before European Programmes like PHARE (PHARE 2010) or TACIS (TACIS 1992) came into force. PHARE programme "Poland and Hungary: Assistance for Restructuring their Economies" in 2010 covered 10 countries: Czech Republic, Estonia, Hungary, Latvia, Lithuania, Poland, Slovakia and Slovenia, Bulgaria and Romania, and assisted them in a period of massive economic restructuring and political change. The so-called „Successor states" of the Soviet Union, namely Armenia, Azerbaijan, Belarus, Georgia, Kazakhstan, Kirgizstan, Moldova, Mongolia, the Russian Federation, Turkmenistan, Tadzhikistan, the Ukraine and Uzbekistan were subsumed under the TACIS (Technical Assistance to the Commonwealth of Independent States) programme. TACIS became operational in 1991 to support the EU's relations with the countries of Eastern Europe and Central Asia (EECA) and merged 2007 into the European Neighbourhood and Partnership Instrument (ENPI), the financial instrument of the European Neighbourhood Policy.

## Strengthening the reform processes: The German Federal Government's TRANSFORM Advisory Programme (1992–1998)

On 13 July 1993, the German Federal Cabinet adopted an advisory programme under the name "TRANSFORM," which aimed at combining German activities "*to build democracy and a social market economy in the Central and Eastern European (CEE) countries and the Newly Independent States of the former Soviet Union (NIS)*" (BMWi 1996). In the period from 1993 to 1995, nearly DM 300 million (~150 million €) annually, and for 1996 DM 285 million (~147 million €) was made available for cooperation with Poland, the Czech and Slovak Republics, Hungary, Bulgaria, Estonia, Latvia, Lithuania, as well as with Russia, Ukraine and Belarus. According to the Federal Ministry of Economics, TRANSFORM was "*after the expiration of the other major projects of German economic support for the reforming countries – such as transfer roubles and reintegration assistance in the double-digit billions – practically the only original German measure in the development of a market economy and democracy in Eastern Europe*" (BMWi 1996, p. 3). It was implemented with the involvement of all federal ministries under the leadership of the Federal Foreign Office. The programme emphasised:

- consultation in order to create the framework for a social market economy and to build up small and medium-sized structures,
- assistance for business restructuring, privatisation and deconcentrating,
- the establishment of a tax, customs and budget system as well as a banking, stock exchange and insurance system,

- consulting in the agricultural sector,
- legal consulting with a focus on commercial law,
- assistance in the establishment and reorganization of administrative structures,
- accompanying consulting in the fields of labour market and social policy and environmental protection, and
- training and further training of business specialists and managers (management training, vocational training and continuing education, qualification measures) (cf. BMWi 1996, p. 4).

Until 1995, approximately one-sixth of the total funds available (DM 140 million; ~70 million €) were used for the training of skilled workers and managers (BMWi 1995, p. 29). Corresponding measures were carried out by the Federal Foreign Office, the Federal Ministry of Education and Science and by the Federal Ministries of Agriculture (BML), the Interior (BMI) and Justice (BMJ) and their mandataries. The tasks assigned to BIBB in 1992/1993 by the then Federal Ministry of Education and Science (BMBW) ranged from conceptual considerations, their administrative and technical implementation until appropriate measures and projects to monitor and reflect the work undertaken in TRANSFORM. The range of tasks of the Federal Institute accordingly included the following essentials:

- technical advice on VET-system development in close consultation with partner countries,
- collaborative design of bilateral IVET-projects in pilot schools / pilot areas according to the demands of partner countries,
- tendering and awarding of jointly agreed projects to German contractors,
- implementation, monitoring and evaluation of projects (e.g. in institution building (vocational training institutes) or in the field of vocational training research) (cf. BIBB 1995).

From 1993 to 2000, BIBB funded projects on initial and continuing vocational training in the eleven TRANSFORM countries with a total volume of around DM 44.2 million (~22 million €). Special emphasis was placed "*in terms of the volume of funding used (….) on the Russian Federation, Ukraine and Poland*" (Hoene and Höhns 2001, p. 2). Funding was at its peak in 1995–1997 but was slowly phased out in subsequent years.

All the pilot projects undertaken under the framework of the German TRANSFORM programme emerged as a result of consultation between German and CEE countries representatives. Agreed projects were anchored in local needs and aligned with national VET policies (where they existed); consultancy and support were driven by the demand of the respective CEE country. CEE countries decided in which geographic region, in what occupational field and with whom the co-operation should take place. An effective instrument to achieve sustainable effects has been seen in the promotion of the establishment of small "VET pilot centres" for the training of apprentices and employees. Thirty-three pilot centres in eleven CEE countries were established at IVET schools. Existing premises were expanded, and workshops were equipped according to modern working conditions and health and safety requirements. These pilot centres were meant to become the *"nucleus of system development*" (BIBB 1996). They were supposed to be an exemplary model of vocational education and training reform. The pilot centres were designed to have a regional and supra-regional impact and significantly drive the practical transfer of the results to other schools within a sector or even beyond (Eberhardt and Shcherbak 2017). The prevailing view was that project results could only achieve long-term sustainability if they aligned with the framework of conditions in the host country and national IVET strategies. Therefore, co-operation within the framework of the programme was not geared to simply "export" the German dual system (Eberhardt 1997, p. 45). The Federal Ministry for Economic Cooperation and Development (BMZ) and Kreditanstalt für Wiederaufbau (Credit Institute for Reconstruction), which evaluated twenty-one VET projects funded under the TRANSFORM-programme, supported this position. They came the conclusion that:

> Dual training system [is] currently not transferable. Model projects to introduce dual training based on the German model may make sense in individual cases and under special conditions. Under the given conditions, however, they can still be multiplied too little and can therefore only remain the exception for the time being (BMWI and KfW 1999, p. 5).

According to the evaluation, partner countries particularly appreciated the following features of cooperation: "Orientation towards the needs of their country, the practical relevance, long-term nature and flexibility as well as the result orientation and the effort to achieve sustainability of work results" (BMWI and KfW 1999, p. 2).

## Getting ready for the European Union: Pre-accession to EU-policies (1994–2004) (EU 2021) and first phase of membership of most CEE countries (2004–2010)

Before this chapter moves on to the second phase of Western European involvement within CEE countries, it is important to highlight the motivation of the German activities described in the previous sub section. The main interest was to open new markets and to find cheap suppliers for German companies. Whilst supporting CEE companies to become ready for the market economy, company-based apprenticeship was thus an option for "policy learning". The bilateral activities between Germany and CEE countries were superseded by the activities of the European Union (EU), however. Whilst the EU respects the "principle of subsidiarity" in educational issues, it is nevertheless able to provide "recommendations". The most prominent one from the 1990s was the "Bologna-process" (EHEA 2021), which aimed to unify the structure of higher education (HE) . Almost all member states (and aspirant states) followed Bologna. At that time VET, and especially IVET, was not high on the agenda of EU, but, reflecting the neo-liberal turn in these years, the focus was on the "T" for Training in VET, whilst neglecting the "E" for Education. Thus, a trend to tailor-made qualifications and modularised approaches were part of the EU's strategies. In this period of co-operation, company-based apprenticeship even lost its status as a "suggestion".

Shortly after the fall of Berlin wall, the European Union offered support to CEE countries. In December 1989 at the EU's Strasbourg Summit, the European ministers asked the Council of the European Communities to adopt the necessary measures to establish the European Training Foundation (ETF). This became operational in 1994 (West 2014). Ten days later European Union's (EU) PHARE Programme of co-operation and assistance was adopted to support the transition towards a market economy in CEE countries (Nielsen 1997). Between 1990 and 1993, 431 million ECU (European Currency Units; prior to the Euro; 1 ECU = 1€) were spent on education, training and research. Between 1994 and 1996, this rose to 443.4 million ECUs. The programme addressed the development of curricula for new sectors, the revision of curricula for a range of broad-based occupations, the need for large-scale staff development and the upgrading of school equipment, as well as feasibility studies and policy development. By requiring key players to co-operate, the PHARE programme aimed to change strategy and has helped to build coherent national training policies. In addition, several partnerships with training institutions in EU Member States have been launched (Mawson 1997). At the European Council's meeting in Essen at the end of 1994, the PHARE Programme was mentioned as one of the cornerstones of the pre-accession strategy, particularly for the provision of economic assistance. "Comparative Analysis of the PHARE Countries" was published in 1996 and draw the conclusion that there were "*no definite clear-cut models to be followed, nor can Western solutions be imposed*" (Kuebart 1996). Although considerable effort has been made in the CEE countries, the lack of experience both in identifying new competences and the lack of professional expertise in defining new occupations, qualification standards and curricula have proved to be major obstacles (Weilnböck-Buck et al. 1997). The hope of CEE countries to find "EU-standards" that they could use as a reference faded very quickly: there were no common European qualification standards, only an agreement on fostering transparency and the description of different qualification levels. Hence, CEE countries were confronted with a broad and confusing variety of country-specific definitions of the knowledge and skills necessary for both specific tasks and occupations (Kunzmann et al. 1998).

At the same time as the CEE countries were in the process of joining the EU, but unconnected to this, Germany faced a succession of economic challenges, resulting in the country being dubbed the "sick man of [old] Europe" (Economist 2004). Consequently, the neoliberal turn in EU policy and by implication in VET increased even further. This culminated in the establishment of the European Qualification Framework (EQF 2008), which was inspired by UK VET, and the modularisation of IVET via "the establishment of a European Credit System for Vocational Education and Training", which was strongly criticised in Germany (ECVET 2009). ECVET, however, was largely unsuccessful, and as Germany was one of the countries that suffered less from the economic crisis in 2008/2009, the country's economy and apprenticeship system returned to consideration at EU level.

## European initiatives for apprenticeships (2011-ongoing)

With accession to the EU, CEE countries became eligible to participate in Community initiatives such as LEONARDO DA VINCI (EU support for vocational education and training), PETRA (Action programme for the vocational training of young people and their preparation for adult and working life) or COMENIUS (EU programme for schools, helps foreign language learning and improves intercultural awareness), which were merged in 2007–2013 under the flagship programme LIFELONG LEARNING (Lifelong learning: a new education and training programme to build the Knowledge Society) and continued from 2014 under the ERASMUS+ programme (EU programme for education, training, youth and sport). The Copenhagen Declaration of the Council of Ministers and the Commission of 2002 set the central cornerstones for further Europeanisation of vocational education and training in terms of content and pogramme. The primary impact of these programmes with respect to the European integration process can be seen in the shift towards an outcome orientation and the use of qualifications frameworks. The establishment of qualifications frameworks enabled systemic restructuring of VET systems and the redesign of standards and qualifications in a number of CEE countries. An important aspect of this was the focus on the active involvement of potential stakeholders both in the discussion of reform and IVET design.

In the aftermath of economic crisis of 2008–2009, EU authorities and member states launched work-based learning and apprenticeship initiatives in school-based VET systems in order to address increased youth unemployment. The European Alliance for Apprenticeship, which was launched 2013, mobilised EU member states, European Free Trade Associations and EU candidate countries to improve the supply, quality and image of apprenticeships (EAfA 2020). In the term 2014–2020, the Erasmus+ programme assigned almost 3 billion € to the Erasmus+ Strategic Partnership.

The Council Recommendation "on a European framework for quality and efficient apprenticeship training" (Council of the European Union 2018), has given further impetus to the development of apprenticeships. This recommendation characterises apprenticeship – without prejudice to national terminology – according to four main principles:

a) "it imparts substantial parts of work based learning in companies,
b) it leads to nationally recognised qualifications/standards,
c) it describes rights and obligation of all those involved in training (apprentice, employer, VET institution), and
d) a financial compensation that is offered to the apprentice for the work-based component."

(Council of the European Union 2018).

Meanwhile almost 500 VET projects (many of which had CEE countries participation) worked on questions of apprenticeship schemes and served as experimental spaces for domestic reform initiatives. The topics ranged from training provision, implementation and governance issues. In this respect, the European Social Fund (ESF) is not to be underestimated. It provided funding of nearly 15 billion € during the same period (2014–2020) in order to improve the labour market relevance of education and training systems and to promote lifelong learning. The European initiatives it supported also provided a framework for intense policy learning.

## Policy learning; between innovation and persistency

According to Moyson et al. (2017) "one of the complications in studying policy learning is that it occurs in a policy process" (Moyson et al. 2017). Thus, policy learning does not take place without context. Although CEE countries shared similar social and economic problems, they represented "different strands of socialism" (Kuebart 1996) and therefore had different experiences concerning economic reforms before 1989. Against this background, considerable differences were evident in the priorities for economic restructuring in each country as demonstrated by attitudes towards the privatisation of state-owned enterprises and in the approach to reform in general after 1989. While some countries such as Hungary and Poland began to re-organise their markets and welfare systems very quickly, others, like Bulgaria, proceeded at a slower pace.

The same applied to the IVET reform. Almost all CEE countries faced the problem of having insufficient resources for wholesale IVET reform. The strong educational support structure from former times, notably vocational education and training delivered via methodological centres, pedagogical innovation centres or comparable institutions, was interrupted after 1989. A "*severe antipathy towards vocational education research and development institutes set in*" (Nielsen 2004, p. 42). In contrast, there was a great openness to learn about proven approaches from the West and to receive some support in addressing the challenges:

> All CEECs were inundated with foreign advisers, teams of experts from different international organisations, representatives of foundations, numerous Western universities and the like. Many of these came at the invitation of national authorities and institutions, many spontaneously and at the initiative of various Western bodies (Kalous 1997, p. 4).

Consequently, different approaches were pursued often reflecting conflicting policy and thus IVET policies sometimes varied from year to year, and from country to country. Much effort has been put into the reorganisation of structures and procedures in education and training, and a lot of energy into drafting new legislation. Ministries and other public bodies responsible for implementing restructured IVET, needed support to ensure that reforms such as occupational profiles, new curricula and examinations were universally accepted and that the results of pilot projects were transferred into practice. During this experimental phase, national research institutes ("methodological centres") were needed. In many CEE countries, they had already existed for a quite long time (e.g. Poland, Hungary, Czechoslovakia, and Russia). However, after the political change, they came under pressure. Their staff was reduced, tasks were restricted and their budgets cut; sometimes they were even were dismantled for political reasons. Countries, that were previously part of the Soviet Union, were in a worse situation: they did not run their own research institutions having been completely dependent on Moscow. Latvia and Lithuania started building new (quite small) institutes in the 1990s (BIBB 1998). Many of these centres adopted (in cooperation with the European Training Foundation) the role of "National

Observatories" in order to get more data on IVET transformation, labour market and industry development (Laur-Ernst 2008).

Policy learning in CEE countries has taken place against the backdrop of rapid and frequent change (including frequent changes of government and policy). Innovations and reform projects in IVET still face enormous hurdles and run the risk of being completely abandoned in the event of policy changes. Considering the complexity of IVET systems and their determinants, especially when introducing dual components, it is evident that policy learning designed to transform IVET will not be accomplished quickly. Even more: policy learning always takes place between the poles of "innovation" and "persistence"; it requires creativity and trust in order for appropriate solutions for clearly defined problems to be developed. It is also significant that political declarations of intent and the insight, need or openness of practitioners and potential stakeholders are often far apart. Furthermore, any lessons of policy learning are likely to be applied under entirely different, cultural, social, historical and system-specific conditions. This is especially true when referring to the four above outlined framing pillars of the German dual system: evolutionary institutional development, involvement of companies in training, collective skill formation and holistic vocational principle.

## Evolution or disruption?

The end of the socialist era in CEE countries was not only a political disruption. The Soviet school-based apprenticeship model based on the close cooperation between VET schools and big state owned companies (partner companies) disappeared with the crumbling of the communist economic model and subsequent economic restructuring to facilitate the establishment of the market economy. It led to the establishment of the "market-oriented" school-based VET systems, where in many cases market orientation was only formal and declarative due to the low level of involvement of the economic stakeholders in training. However, the Soviet model (just like any other model) could have been the reference or aim of (re)-developing IVET.

Prior to the re-unification of Germany, The German Democratic Republic (GDR) had been part of the "Eastern Bloc", and as in the other CEE countries, the non-competitive state enterprises had to close. This led to mass-unemployment and an enormous lack of apprenticeship offers in this part of the reunited Germany. It was therefore necessary to establish a school-based IVET system. As in other political spheres, development aims were set (and financed) by Western Germany with the clear vision to return to (West German) company-based apprenticeships when the local economy recovers.

Unlike the GDR, the other CEE countries lacked such close guidance and support:

- in Estonia educational system has undergone several waves of transformations (see the chapter of Loogma in this collection);
- in Lithuania the institutional evolution of social dialogue is marked with abrupt institutional changes and shifts between different patterns of skill formation (see the chapter of Tūtlys et al);
- in Romania skill formation was affected by frequent changes (see the chapter of Vladut);
- in Slovenia skill formation system has seen three turns (see the chapter of Pavlin et al).

In many CEE countries one of the main reasons for the educational reforms was the desire to meet the rules for using the European Union`s cohesion and structural funds (see the chapter of Dvořák and Gal). This argument suggests that CEE countries held a functional or even opportunistic view of IVET.

Examining the CEE chapters alongside this first "German pillar" leads the authors of this chapter to the following conclusion: a coherent long-lasting national aim or vision for the structure of IVET according to national traditions, beliefs and development aims would be of a much higher added value than relying on external recommendations, might those come from Berlin, London or Brussels.

## Involvement of companies

Most of the other country chapters refer implicitly or explicitly to a mismatch between the learning outcomes of school-based IVET and the expectations of employers:

- in Lithuania there is noticed increased employer dissatisfaction with the skills of VET graduate (see the chapter of Tūtlys et al);
- in Poland the involvement of employers, particularly SMEs, in the financing and organization of training for employees is one of the lowest in Europe (the chapter of Dębowski and Stęchły in this collection);
- in Romania employers consider that the state is the only one responsible for skill formation in ensuring the workforce ready for work (the chapter of Vladut);
- or in the Czech Republic the poor reputation of the VET programmes in public VET schools enhance establishment of the private secondary VET schools by the local companies (see the chapter of Dvořák and Gal).

It is not possible to compare the position in the other CEE countries with Germany in this regard, since company-based apprenticeship in most sectors are the only option available to school-leavers wishing to qualify as skilled workers. Companies in German IVET are mentioned as the primary seat of learning in the IVET law (BBiG 2005, § 2). VET laws in most CEE countries, however, include forms of work-based learning (WBL) only as options or alternative pathways to school-based VET. Learning outcomes from the workplace often explicitly need to be recognised formally or assessed again at school. In this regard, more open, encouraging and valuating regulations on WBL could be a promising approach.

## Collective skill formation

The quotation from the Czech Republic in the previous subsection indicates that a successful company in that country would prefer to establish an in-house IVET school rather than collaborate with existing state provision. In other CEE countries the tripartite (state, companies, trade unions) social dialogue is also under-developed. This is due to not only the low expectations and involvement of employers, but also to the social partners, especially the trade unions lacking capacity:

- in Hungary trade unions are not involved in the social dialogue on skills and VET (see the chapter of Laczik and Farkas);
- in Lithuania there are reported low capacities of social partners, especially trade unions in the skill formation (see the chapter of Tūtlys et al);
- in the Czech Republic there is insufficient and uneven involvement of employers and other social partners in VET (see the chapter of Dvořák and Gal);
- in Ukraine trade unions are considered as a weak link in the development of social dialogue on skill formation (the chapter of Melnyk in this collection);
- in Romania the efforts of the employers' associations and trade unions to organize and restructure themselves in the skill formation suffered from relatively low power and representativeness (see the chapter of Vladut);
- in Estonia social partners (employers, unions) were too weak to initiate and support reforms in VET and HE (see the chapter of Loogma).

From the German perspective, two main differences between the German model and practices in most CEE countries are evident. Firstly, there is an unwillingness of the institutions responsible for IVET to delegate competences and responsibility for VET to other stakeholders, and secondly there is the unwillingness of employer`s organisations and trade unions to move other conflicts to the background for the sake of educating and training the next generation.

## Vocational principle – internal flexibility

Holistic approaches and flexible open curricula are based on mutual trust between the colleagues working for the learning venues. Correlated to this internal flexibility is the limited amounted of qualifications on offer, as companies or regions with different core business processes are able offer the same qualification. By contrast, many chapters of this book refer to the fragmentation of the national systems of qualifications:

- in Estonia there is notice over-standardization or inflexibility of the system (see the chapter of Loogma);
- fragmentation of the qualification system with the significant increase of the volume of qualifications is reported in the Czech Republic (see the chapter of Dvořák and Gal);
- in Slovakia over 1,500 occupational standards were developed by the private company in cooperation with newly created 24 sectoral councils and the Alliance of Sectoral Councils financed by ESF projects (see the chapter of Vantuch and Jelínková);
- in Ukraine the newly developed competence-based qualifications co-exist with the multiple outdated former Soviet type occupational standards – qualification characteristics (see the chapter of Melnyk);
- Poland develops alternative pathways to qualifications from the educational sector, like the "market qualifications" (see the chapter of Dębowski and Stęchły).

This difference might be illustrated by the recent findings of a research project in the sector of industrial shoe production (ICSAS 2020): in this sector Germany offers one qualification referenced to European Qualification Framework (EQF) level 3 (leather processing) and another one referenced to level 4 (industrial shoemaker). Romania has nine qualifications on these levels:

- industrial shoemaker (RO, EQF 3);
- cutting operator (EQF 3);
- stitching operator (EQF 3);
- lasting operator (EQF 3);
- soling operator (EQF 3);
- finishing operator (EQF 3);
- technician in textile and leather industry – footwear included (EQF 4);

- technician in footwear industry (EQF 4);
- designer technician in textile and footwear industry (EQF 4).

Although still school-based, the qualification system of Hungary in this regard is more similar to the German model, being based on "vocational principle" than to the former modularised approaches. It is illustrated by the reform of the system of qualifications executed in 2020 when the previous 700 vocational qualifications were replaced with a new register of vocational qualifications containing 174 broad vocational qualifications delivered in the school-based provision (see the chapter of Laczik and Farkas).

## Conclusion

In 2021, vocational education and training and the world of work were still largely disconnected in many CEE countries. Representatives of industry and employers' associations complained about an outdated vocational training system that did not produce the graduates needed within the workplace. The involvement of employers in the design of modern occupational standards and delivering these within the workplace has had a varying degree of success, not least because involvement has been largely confined to large-scale industries. In some countries, the craft sector holds a unique position and has been able to preserve the dual traditions from the past. Vocational training still suffers from a bad reputation in many CEE countries and is seen as an emergency solution for less academically inclined students. Although the legal basis for a modern vocational training system and modern job profiles has been created in many CEE countries during in recent decades, young people prefer to enrol in higher education rather than IVET. In this regard, the CEE countries do not differ from a large number of Western EU member states. The development of apprenticeship schemes is a great challenge for many European countries, especially if there is no apprenticeship tradition upon which to build. According to Cedefop the "lowest common denominator" and the "true nature of apprenticeship" (CEDEFOP 2021) consist of the following basic features:

- legal framework;
- providing a formal and portable qualification;
- alternation between school based and work-based learning (the latter with a meaningful duration);
- contract between learner and company;
- remuneration for the learner (CEDEFOP 2021, summary by the authors).

Policy learning is a multi-directional process. As Peter Grootings stated almost thirty years ago: "For the western countries and international organisations involved in Central and East European VET in transition, there may well be as much to learn as there is to teach" (Grootings 1993). What can German IVET researchers learn from the chapters in this book about the transferability of dual system components?

Looking at the core features of apprenticeship mentioned above, considerable effort has been made in CEE countries to involve employers in the delivery of training. This has met with varying degrees of success and has often been limited to certain sectors or regions. The question of time also deserves special attention here, because reforms seeking to link two different reference systems (the education system and the labour market) clearly cannot be hurried.

In some countries, the political impetus for employers' involvement in social dialogue comes from employers themselves; whilst in others there have been concerted actions to develop social dialogue at sectoral level. The involvement of employers, however, implies that representatives of the education system have to share power, and "common ownership" of the system has yet to be achieved. Against this backdrop, high expectations have been placed on the intermediary organisations with roles as coordinators and "trustees" of IVET. It is, however, perhaps too early to evaluate the effectiveness of these bodies.

Legal foundations have been established in many of the countries considered by this book, which state the core features of apprenticeship. However, these have yet to be fully implemented in many cases and are still fragile, not least, because there is a limited commitment to co-operation in some spheres. Furthermore, there is the potential that reforms that have been introduced could be reversed with changes of government. From a German perspective, it was enlightening to read about the role and relevance that the implementation of National Qualifications Frameworks (NQF) played in most CEE countries. Regardless of their impact in terms of practical implementation, in many countries their development served to link the potential actors in the labour market and the education system, as NQFs play an important role in the governance of skill formation systems and help to position IVET as an important pillar in the countries education systems. In Germany, the development and implementation of the German Qualification Framework (Deutscher Qualifikationsrahmen, DQR) was a rather unenthusiastic and annoying procedure.

Although the collapse of the socialist system demanded policy learning on the macro-level, promising meso-level projects have been described in the previous chapters of this book. Germany provides neither a blueprint nor a silver bullet for IVET but, in common with other countries, does provide examples of apparent good practice. It may be prudent to consider them whilst further developing VET systems.

## References

BBiG (2005). 'Berufsbildungsgesetz (BBiG) § 2 Lernorte der Berufsbildung [Vocational Training Act (BBiG) § 2 Places of Learning in VET]', <https://www.gesetze-im-internet.de/bbig_2005/__2.html>, accessed 6th October 2021.

BIBB (2009). 'In-company vocational training – A worthwhile investment for enterprises', <https://www.bibb.de/en/14060.php>, accessed 6th October 2021.

BIBB (2021). 'Genealogy Datenverarbeitungskaufmann', <https://www.bibb.de/dienst/berufesuche/de/index_berufesuche.php/genealogy/g181>, accessed 6th October 2021.

Bosch, G. (2010). 'Zur Zukunft der dualen Berufsausbildung in Deutschland [On the Future of the Dual Vocational Education and Training in Germany]', In Bosch, G., Krone, S. and D. Langer (eds.), *Das duale Berufsbildungssystem in Deutschland*, pp. 37–61, Wiesbaden: Verlag für Sozialwissenschaften.

Bundesinstitut für Berufsbildung (BIBB) (1995). *Berufsbildung für benachteiligte Jugendliche in Ungarn und Deutschland [Vocational Training for Disadvantaged Young People in Hungary and Germany]*. Berlin: TRANSFORM-Programm.

Bundesinstitut für Berufsbildung (BIBB) (1997). *Berufsbildung in Mittel- und Osteuropa. Grundlagen, Aufgaben, Maßnahmen und Projekte [Vocational Education and Training in Central and Eastern Europe. Basics, Tasks, Measures and Projects]*. Berlin: TRANSFORM-Programm.

Bundesinstitut für Berufsbildung (BIBB) (1998). *Berufsbildungsinstitute in Mittel- und Osteuropa – eine Zusammenstellung von Beiträgen wichtiger wissenschaftlicher Forschungseinrichtungen der Berufsbildung [Vocational Training Institutes in Central and Eastern Europe – a Compilation of Contributions from Important Scientific Research Institutions in Vocational Training]*. Berlin: TRANSFORM-Programm.

Bundesinstitut für Berufsbildung (BIBB) (2021). 'Datenreport 2021', <https://www.bibb.de/datenreport/de/datenreport_2021.php>, accessed 6th October 2021.

Bundesministerium für wirtschaftliche Zusammenarbeit und Entwicklung (BMZ)/ Kreditanstalt für Wiederaufbau (KfW) [Credit Institute for Reconstruction (KfW)] (1999). *TRANSFORM Ergebnisse. Querschnittevaluierung von Projekten im Bereich der Berufsbildung*. Bonn.

Bundesministerium für Wirtschaft in Zusammenarbeit mit der Kreditanstalt für Wiederaufbau (KfW) (1996). 'TRANSFORM. Die Beratung Mittel- und Osteuropas beim Aufbau von Demokratie und sozialer Marktwirtschaft.

Konzept und Beratungsprogramme der Bundesregierung. Fortschreibung 1996 [TRANSFORM. Advising Central and Eastern Europe on Building Democracy and a Social Market Economy. Concept and Advisory Programmes of the Federal Government. Update 1996]', *BMWi Dokumentation*, No. 398, 165.

Busemeyer, M. R. and Thelen, K. (2012). 'Institutional Change in German Vocational Training: From Collectivism towards Segmentalism'. In Busemeyer, M. R. and Trampush, C. (eds.), *The Political Economy of Collective Skill Formation*, pp. 68–100. Oxford: Oxford University Press.

CDG (2021). 'A non-profit association supporting young people in their vocational training to gain work experience in the EU or worldwide', <http://cdg-carlduisberg.com/>, accessed 6th October 2021.

CEDEFOP (2021). 'Apprenticeship: A pill for every ill? Apprenticeship should not just be about bringing people into employment, but about securing their long-term employability', *CEDEFOP Briefing paper March 2021*, <https://www.cedefop.europa.eu/files/9155_en.pdf>, accessed 6th October 2021.

Comenius (2008). 'EU programme for schools, helps foreign language learning and improves intercultural awareness', <https://ec.europa.eu/commission/presscorner/detail/en/IP_08_82>, accessed 6th October 2021.

Council of the European Union (2018). 'European Council Recommendation of 15 March 2018 on a European Framework for Quality and Effective Apprenticeships', *2018/C 153/01*, <https://eur-lex.europa.eu/legal-content/EN/TXT/PDF/?uri=CELEX:32018H0502(01)>, accessed 6th October 2021.

Deissinger, T. (2004). 'Apprenticeship cultures – a comparative view'. In Hemsworth, D. and Roodhouse, S. (eds.), *Apprenticeship: An Historical Re-invention for a Post Industrial World; Proceedings of the Conference held by the University Vocational Awards Council, London, January 2004*, pp. 43–58. Bolton: University Vocational Awards Council.

DQR (2021). 'The German Qualifications Framework for Lifelong Learning', <https://www.dqr.de/dqr/en/home/home_node.html;jsessionid=2F1714B711252A90785807FE2C783DBF.live091>, accessed 6th October 2021.

EAfA (2020). 'The European Alliance for Apprenticeship (EAfA) unites governments and key stakeholders with the aim of strengthening the quality, supply and overall image of apprenticeships across Europe', <https://ec.europa.eu/social/main.jsp?catId=1147&intPageId=5234&langId=en>, accessed 6th October 2021.

Eberhardt, Ch. (1998). *Beratung beim Institutionenaufbau am Beispiel des Methodisch-didaktischen Zentrums in Litauen [Advice on Institutional Development by Following the Example of the Methodological-Didactic Centres in Lithuania]*. Berlin: Bundesinstitut für Berufsbildung, TRANSform-Aufsätze.

Eberhardt, Ch. and Kunzmann, M. (1999). *Transfer und Transformationsprozesse in der Berufsbildung Mittel- und Osteuropas. Möglichkeiten und Bedingungen des Innovationstransfers [Transfer and Transformation Processes in Vocational Education and Training in Central and Eastern Europe. Possibilities and Conditions of Innovation Transfer]*. Berlin: Bundesinstitut für Berufsbildung, TRANSFORM-Programm,

Eberhardt, Ch. and Shcherbak, O. (2017). 'TRANSFORM revisited: Was von bilateralen Bildungskooperationen übrigbleibt und warum. Das Modellvorhaben "kaufmännische Berufsausbildung" in Kiew/Ukraine (1995–1998) [TRANSFORM revisited: What Remains of Bilateral Cooperation in Vocational Education and Why. The Model Project "Commercial Vocational Training" in Kiev/Ukraine (1995–1998)]'. In Geiben, M. (eds.), *Transfer in internationalen Berufsbildungskooperationen*, pp. 93–108. Bonn.

Economist (2004). 'Germany on the Mend', 17.11.2004, <http://www.economist.com/node/3352024>, accessed 10 October 2021.

EHEA (2021). 'European Higher Education Area and Bologna Process', <http://www.ehea.info/>, accessed 10 October 2021.

Erasmus+ (2021). 'EU Programme for Education, Training, Youth and Sport', <https://erasmus-plus.ec.europa.eu/>, accessed 10 October 2021.

ESF (2021). 'The European Social Fund Plus (ESF+) is the European Union (EU)'s main instrument for investing in people', <https://ec.europa.eu/european-social-fund-plus/en>, accessed 10 October 2021.

Euler, D. (2013). *Germany's Dual Vocational Training System: A Model for Other Countries?* Gütersloh: Bertelsmann Stiftung.

European Commission (2006). 'Lifelong Learning: A New Education and Training Programme to Build the Knowledge Society', <https://ec.europa.eu/commission/presscorner/detail/mt/IP_06_1478>, accessed 10 October 2021.

European Commission (2009). 'European Quality Assurance in Vocational Education and Training', <https://ec.europa.eu/social/main.jsp?catId=1536&langId=en>, accessed 10 October 2021.

European Commission (2010). 'EU Support for Vocational Education and Training', <https://ec.europa.eu/commission/presscorner/detail/en/IP_10_1481>, accessed 6 October 2021.

European Commission (2021). 'EU Policies in the Field of Vocational Education and Training', <https://ec.europa.eu/education/policies/eu-policy-in-the-field-of-vocational-education-and-training-vet_en>, accessed 10 October 2021.

European Council (2008). 'Recommendation of the European Parliament and of the Council of 23 April 2008 on the Establishment of the European Qualifications Framework for Lifelong Learning', <https://eur-lex.europa.eu/legal-content/EN/TXT/HTML/?uri=CELEX:32008H0506(01)&from=EN>, accessed 10 October 2021.

European Council (2009). 'Recommendation of the European Parliament and of the Council of 18 June 2009 on the Establishment of a European Credit System for Vocational Education and Training (ECVET)', <https://eur-lex.europa.eu/LexUriServ/LexUriServ.do?uri=OJ:C:2009:155:0011:0018:EN:PDF>, accessed 10 October 2021.

European Training Foundation (ETF) (2000). *Transnational Analysis of Vocational Education and Training Reforms in Central and Eastern Europe.* Torino: ETF.

Fürstenau, B., Pilz, M. and Gonon, P. (2014). 'The Dual System of Vocational Education and Training in Germany – What Can Be Learnt About Education for (Other) Professions'. In S. Billett et al. (eds.), *International Handbook of Research in Professional and Practice-based Learning*, pp. 427–460, Dordrecht: Springer International Handbooks of Education.

Greinert, W.-D. (1995a). *Das duale System der Berufsausbildung in der Bundesrepublik Deutschland [The Dual System of Vocational Education and Training in the German Federal Republic]*. Stuttgart: Holland and Josenhans.

Greinert, W.-D. (1995b). *Das "deutsche System" der Berufsausbildung – Geschichte, Organisation, Perspektiven [The 'German System' of Vocational Education and Training – History, Organisation, Future Prospects]*. Baden-Baden: Nomos Verlagsgesellschaft.

Greinert, W.-D. (2006). 'Geschichte der Berufsausbildung in Deutschland [The History of Vocational Education and Training in Germany]'. In Arnold, R. and Lipsmeier, A (eds.), *Handbuch der Berufsbildung, 2., überarbeitete und aktualisierte Auflage*, pp. 499–505, Wiesbaden: Verlag für Sozialwissenschaften.

Grootings, P. (1993). 'Recent trends in vocational education and training', *European Journal of Education*, 28 (2) 229–240.

ICSAS (2020). 'Sector Qualification Framework (SQF) level 2–4 for Industrial Shoe Production', <http://icsas-project.eu/wp-content/uploads/2020/07/IO6_ComparativeReport_EN.pdf>, accessed 10 October 2021.

IGM (2004). 'IG Metall. Anschluss statt Ausschluss. Zweijährige Berufe helfen benachteiligten Jugendlichen nicht [IG Metall. Inclusion Instead of Exclusion. Two-Year VET Programmes do not Help to Disadvantaged Young People]', <https://wap.igmetall.de/docs_0183607_Anschluss_statt_Ausschluss_f609a40cb4fd0659c932b558be3118aaf6c807b3.pdf>, accessed 10 October 2021.

Kuebart, F. (1987). 'Schulreform, technisch-ökonomische Modernisierung und Berufsausbildung in der Sowjetunion [School Reform, Technical-Economic Modernization and Vocational Education and Training in the Soviet Union]', *BuE*, 40, 1, 35–55.

Kuebart, F. (1996). 'A Comparative Analysis of the Phare Countries. Report on Vocational Education and Training', <URL: https://files.eric.ed.gov/fulltext/ED417283.pdf >, accessed 10 October 2021.

Kunzmann, M., Laur-Ernst, U. and Hoene, B. (1998). *Development of Standards in Vocational Education and Training. Manual, Vol. 1.* Torino: European Training Foundation.

Kunzmann, M. and Wiesner, R. (1988). *Die Berufsbildung ausgewählter sozialistischer Länder Europas, Beiträge zur Berufsbildung [The Vocational Education and Training of Selected Socialist Countries in Europe, Contributions to Vocational Education and Training].* Berlin: Zentralinstitut für Berufsbildung der DDR.

Laur-Ernst, U., Kunzmann, M., and Hoene, B. (1999). *Development of Standards in Vocational Education and Training – Specifications, Experience, Examples, Vol. 2.* Torino: European Training Foundation.

Laur-Ernst, U. (2008). *Transformation of Vocational Education and Training in Central and Eastern Europe: How to Keep the Balance?* Manuscript.

Leontjew, A. N. (1977). *Tätigkeit, Bewußtsein, Persönlichkeit [Activity, Consciousness, Personality].* Stuttgart: E. Klett.

Mawson, T. (1997). 'The opening up of the Leonardo da Vinci programme to the countries of Central and Eastern Europe', *Vocational Training. European Journal*, 11, 75–79.

Moyson, S., Scholten, P. and Weible, C. (2017). 'Policy learning and policy change: Theorizing their relations from different perspectives', *Policy and Society*, 36, 2, 161–177.

Münk, D. (2010). 'Entwicklung der beruflichen Bildung als Geschichte der Arbeitsteilung, Qualifizierung und Entwicklung institutioneller Strukturen [Development of Vocational Education and Training as a History of Division of Labour, Qualification and Development of Institutional Structures]'. In R. Nickolaus, G. Pätzold, H. Reinisch, and T. Tramm (eds.), *Handbuch Berufs- und Wirtschaftspädagogik*, pp. 401–407, Bad Heilbrunn: Klinkhardt.

Nesporova, A. (1997). 'Labour markets and training in Central and Eastern Europe', *Vocational Training. European Journal*, 11, 20–28.

Nielsen, S. (2004). 'VET reforms in Central and Eastern Europe: Achievements and constraints'. In Grootings, P. (ed.), *ETF Yearbook 2004*, pp. 39–54. Torino: European Training Foundation.

Petra (1997). 'Action programme for the vocational training of young people and their preparation for adult and working life', <http://aei.pitt.edu/13120/1/13120.pdf>, accessed 6 October 2021.

PHARE (2010). 'The Phare Programme', <https://web.archive.org/web/20100505090129/http://ec.europa.eu/enlargement/how-does-it-work/financial-assistance/phare/index_en.htm>, accessed 6 October 2021.

Reuling, J. (1998). 'The German 'Berufsprinzip' as a Model for Regulating Training Content and Qualification Standards'. In Nijhof W. J. and Streumer J. N. (eds.), *Key Qualifications in Work and Education*, pp. 63–76. Dordrecht: Springer.

Saniter, A. (2020). 'Arbeitsbasiertes Lernen und Ausbildung von Ausbildern in Spanien, Deutschland, Litauen und Italien [Work-based Learning and Training of Trainers in Spain, Germany, Lithuania and Italy]', *ITB-Forschungsberichte 73*, <https://media.suub.uni-bremen.de/bitstream/elib/4754/4/FB_73.pdf>, accessed 6 October 2021.

SEQUA (2020). 'A development organisation active globally', <https://www.sequa.de/en/sequa/about-us/>, accessed 6 October 2021.

Statistisches Bundesamt (2021). 'Duale Berufsausbildung: Historischer Rückgang der Zahl neuer Ausbildungsverträge im Jahr 2020 [Dual Vocational Education and Training: Historic Decline in the Number of New Training Contracts in 2020]', <https://www.destatis.de/DE/Presse/Pressemitteilungen/2021/08/PD21_379_212.html>, accessed 6 October 2021.

TATICS (1992). 'EC Technical Assistance to the Commonwealth of Independent States and Georgia: The TACIS Programme', <https://ec.europa.eu/commission/presscorner/detail/en/MEMO_92_54>, accessed 6 October 2021.

Weilnböck, I., Baumgartl, B. and Farla, T. (1997). 'Challenges and priorities for vocational training in Central and Eastern European countries', *Vocational Training. European Journal*, 11, 29–42.

# Notes on contributors

*Radostina Angelova* is a senior research manager at Global Metrics Ltd. (Bulgaria) with extensive experience in social, political and marketing research. She has been involved in numerous analytical projects and evaluation assignments in the field of labour markets, social policy and education for the Bulgarian Council of Ministers, Ministry of Labour and Social Policy, and Ministry of Education and Science, among others.

*Branko Bembič* is assistant at the Chair for Organisational and Human Resource Management and Development and researcher at the Centre for Organisational and Human Resources Research, Faculty of Social Sciences, University of Ljubljana, Slovenia. His areas of interest include sociology of work, industrial relations and political and economic history.

*Sandra Bohlinger* is Professor of Adult Education, Continuing VET and comparative education at the Faculty of Education of the Technical University of Dresden, Germany. Her research interest is in vocational education and training, international and comparative education and education policy.

*Nikola Buković* is independent researcher with background in political science, residing in Zagreb (Croatia). He worked as policy expert and manager in nonprofit sector, social development consultant and freelance journalist. His research interests include vocational education and training policy, employment and social policy, civic education, youth participation in policymaking and youth work.

*Ilze Buligina* is researcher at the University of Latvia, Faculty of Business, Management and Economics. Her research interest lies in vocational education and training policy developments, national and sectoral qualifications systems and human resource development.

*Horacy Dębowski* is a researcher at SGH Warsaw School of Economics and vice director of the Central Examination Board in Poland. He is a member of the European Qualifications Framework Advisory Group to the European Commission. His research interests include vocational education and training policies including the design and development of qualifications frameworks.

*Dominik Dvořák* is a senior researcher at the Faculty of Education, Charles University, Prague. His research interests include curriculum and knowledge, education systems, and comparative education. He is an executive editor of the journal Orbis Scholae and has extensive experience as a textbook editor and author.

*Christiane Eberhardt* has been working at the Federal Institute for Vocational Education and Training since 1993 – first in the implementation of bilateral VET projects with countries in Central and Eastern Europe, then in the framework of the European VET programme Leonardo da Vinci. Since 2008, her work has focused on research, consultancy and development on international and European VET policy issues.

*Éva Farkas* is Professor of Education Science and Supervisor at the Doctoral School of Education at the University of Szeged Hungary. Her research areas cover development of adult learning and vocational education and training policies, learning outcomes-based curriculum design, validation of learning outcomes acquired in a non-formal and informal learning context.

*Petr J. Gal* is an upper secondary school teacher and doctoral student at the Faculty of Education, Charles University, Prague. His research interests include structure of secondary schooling, at-risk students and early school leaving.

*Kaloyan Ganev* is an Associate Professor in Economics at Sofia University St. Kliment Ohridski, Bulgaria. His research interests are in macroeconomic modelling (growth and business cycles), applied econometrics, and economic history. He has played a key role in the elaboration of several large-scale policy simulation and forecasting models used by the Bulgarian Council of Ministers, Ministry of Finance, and Ministry of Labour and Social Policy, among others.

*Genutė Gedvilienė* is Professor of Education Science and Researcher at Vytautas Magnus University Institute of Educational Research in Kaunas, Lithuania. Her research addresses VET teacher training, adult education, development of key skills and competencies, informal and non-formal learning policies and practices.

*Dagmar Jelínková* is an analyst at the State Institute of Vocational Education in Bratislava (SIOV). She was a long-term contributor to VET-related reports for the European Training Foundation prior to Slovakia accession to the EU in

2004. Since then, she has been a member of the ReferNet network managed by Cedefop and the SIOV specialist on the European agenda.

*Lina Kaminskienė* is Professor and Chancellor of Education Academy, Vytautas Magnus University. Her research interests involve research on educational and curriculum innovations, personalisation of learning, technology-enhanced learning, self-regulated learning, labour market and social partnership.

*Andrea Laczik* is Head of Research at the Edge Foundation, an Honorary Research Fellow at the University of Oxford, Department of Education. Her areas of research interests include TVET, apprenticeships, work-based learning, employability and skills development, transition from school to work/HE, employer engagement and educational policy. She has a particular interest in comparative and international education, especially in the post-communist East-European countries.

*Krista Loogma* in Professor of Vocational Education at Tallinn University, School of Education, Estonia. Her research is focused on educational changes, vocational education, teachers´ professionalism, skills and competences´ development and work-related learning.

*Jörg Markowitsch* is Senior Partner at 3s Research & Consulting in Vienna, Austria, and policy advisor on national and EU-Level in the area of education and labour markets. His areas of research include comparative research in vocational education and training, European educational policy, skill taxonomies and skills forecasting.

*Teo Matković* is Senior Research Associate at Center for Educational Research and Development, Institute for Social Research in Zagreb, Croatia. His research efforts address access, inequalities and transitions in education and labour market, in the context of implemented policies.

*Sergii Viktorovich Melnyk* is Associate Professor and Head of the Department at the Institute of Educational Analytics of the Ministry of Education and Science of Ukraine, leading researcher at the Institute of Higher Education of the National Academy of Pedagogical Sciences of Ukraine. His research areas cover labour market analysis, skills needs forecasting, development of qualifications and policy of national system of qualifications.

*Samo Pavlin* is Professor of Education and Human Resource Development of Department of Human Resources and Social Management, Faculty of Social Sciences, University of Ljubljana, Slovenia. His research areas cover knowledge management, development of competencies and European developments in higher education and vocational education.

*Andreas Saniter* is a senior researcher and the international research coordinator at the Institute for Technology and Education (ITB), University of Bremen. Educational background in physics and didactics, research interests in expertise development and policy learning.

*Ralitsa Simeonova-Ganeva* is an Associate Professor in Economics at Sofia University St. Kliment Ohridski, Bulgaria. She is an experienced consultant with a demonstrated history in the field of decision analytics, economic modelling and forecasting, and strategic management. Her research addresses economic growth, human capital, labour market forecasting, impact assessment and treatment evaluation of labour market policies, SMEs and entrepreneurship, economic history, etc.

*Klara Skubic Ermenc* is Associate Professor of Comparative Education and Head of the Department of Educational Sciences, Faculty of Arts, University of Ljubljana, Slovenia. Her research areas cover European and global trends in education, particularly in vocational education, as well as in intercultural and inclusive education.

*Biruta Sloka* is professor and senior researcher at University of Latvia, Riga. Her research areas cover social inclusion, development of vocational education and training policies, VET curriculum design, skill formation and qualification systems.

*Eglė Stasiūnaitienė* is Associated Professor of Education Sciences at Vytautas Magnus University in Kaunas, Lithuania. Her field of scientific interests includes inclusive education, career guidance, assessment and recognition of non-formal and informal learning achievements.

*Wojciech Stęchły* is assistant at Warsaw School of Economics and at Educational Research Institute, Poland. His research interests cover institutional economics, skills formation, qualifications systems and public policy of education and learning.

*Vidmantas Tūtlys* is Professor of Education Science and Researcher at Vytautas Magnus University Institute of Educational Research in Kaunas, Lithuania. His research areas cover development of vocational education and training policies, VET curriculum design, skill formation and qualification systems.

*Juraj Vantuch* is an education policy analyst, until 2011 at Comenius University in Bratislava and a freelance since then contributing to reports for Cedefop as the National coordinator within ReferNet and regularly writing reports for the European Commission's DG EAC within its Independent Network of Experts. He co-authored several VET-related comparative, analytical and monitoring studies for the Education ministry.

*Zoica Elena Vladut* is former deputy director of the National Centre for Technical and Vocational Education and Training Development in Romania. She was involved, during 1998–2018, in the development of vocational education and training policies and strategies, VET curriculum design, and qualification system.

*Emma Wallis* is Director of Writepartner. She worked in UK universities for a decade, during which time her research interests focussed on how lifelong learning can be utilised to ameliorate the impact of industrial restructuring. She also has extensive experience of working with UK trade unions.

*Jonathan Winterton* is Professor of Work and Employment and Head of the Department of Work and Employment Relations at Leeds University Business School. His research addresses human capital issues along two axes: one concerned with the quality of work, from high involvement to precarious work, the other with how human capital is developed, deployed, and retained.

# Index

**Baltische Studien zur Erziehungs- und Sozialwissenschaft**

**Baltic Studies in Educational and Social Sciences**

Herausgegeben von Gerd-Bodo von Carlsburg, Natalija Mažeikienė und Airi Liimets

Edited by Gerd-Bodo von Carlsburg, Natalija Mažeikienė and Airi Liimets

| | | |
|---|---|---|
| Band | 1 | Gerd-Bodo Reinert / Irena Musteikienė (Hrsg.): Litauische Gespräche zur Pädagogik. Humanismus - Demokratie - Erziehung. 1999. |
| Band | 2 | Gerd-Bodo Reinert / Irena Musteikienė (Hrsg.): Litauische Gespräche zur Pädagogik II. Staat und Schule. 2000. |
| Band | 3 | Jaan Mikk: Textbook: Research and Writing. 2000. |
| Band | 4 | Gerd-Bodo Reinert / Irena Musteikienė (Hrsg.): Erziehungswandel und moderne pädagogische Verfahren. 2001. |
| Band | 5 | Airi Liimets (Hrsg.): Integration als Problem in der Erziehungswissenschaft. 2001. |
| Band | 6 | Gerd-Bodo Reinert / Irena Musteikienė (Hrsg.): Wissenschaft - Studium - Schule auf neuen Wegen. 2002. |
| Band | 7 | Palmira Jucevičienė / Gediminas Merkys / Gerd-Bodo Reinert: Towards the Learning Society. Educational Issues. 2002. |
| Band | 8 | Gerd-Bodo Reinert / Irena Musteikienė (Hrsg.): Bildung im Zeitalter der Informationsgesellschaft. 2003. |
| Band | 9 | Dalia Ohlinger: Argumentation in der Erst- und Fremdsprache. Pragmalinguistische und grammatikalische Aspekte anhand von Argumentationen deutscher und litauischer Studierender. 2003. |
| Band | 10 | Inga Šukevičiūtė: Interkulturelle Interferenzen im Bereich Wirtschaftskommunikation. Zur Analyse von Geschäftsbriefen im Vergleich Deutschland, Litauen und Russland. 2004. |
| Band | 11 | Gerd-Bodo Reinert von Carlsburg / Irena Musteikienė (Hrsg./eds.): Innovation durch Bildung. Innovation by Education. 2004. |
| Band | 12 | Gerd-Bodo von Carlsburg / Palmira Jucevičienė / Gediminas Merkys (eds.): Learning and Development for Innovation, Networking and Cohesion. 2005. |
| Band | 13 | Gerd-Bodo von Carlsburg / Irena Musteikienė (Hrsg./eds.): Bildungsreform als Lebensreform. Educational Systems Development as Development of Human Being. 2005. |
| Band | 14 | Gerd-Bodo von Carlsburg (Hrsg./ed.): Entwicklung erziehungswissenschaftlicher Paradigmen: Theorie und Praxis. Development of Educational Paradigms: Theory and Practice. 2007. |
| Band | 15 | Gerd-Bodo von Carlsburg (Hrsg./ed.): Bildungs- und Kulturmanagement. The Management of Education and Culture. 2008. |
| Band | 16 | Jaan Mikk / Marika Veisson / Piret Luik (eds.): Reforms and Innovations in Estonian Education. 2008. |

Band 17 Gerd-Bodo von Carlsburg (Hrsg./ed.): Qualität von Bildung und Kultur. Theorie und Praxis. The Quality of Education and Culture. Theoretical and Practical Dimensions. 2009.

Band 18 Airi Liimets (Hrsg.): Denkkulturen. Selbstwerdung des Menschen. Erziehungskulturen. Festschrift für Professor Dr. Dr. h.c. Dr. h.c. Heino Liimets. 2010.

Band 19 Ellu Saar (ed.): Towards a Normal Stratification Order. Actual and Perceived Social Stratification in Post-Socialist Estonia. 2011.

Band 20 Marika Veisson / Eeva Hujala / Peter K. Smith/ Manjula Waniganayake / Eve Kikas (eds.): Global Perspectives in Early Childhood Education. Diversity, Challenges and Possibilities. 2011.

Band 21 Airi Liimets / Marit Mäesalu (eds.): Music Inside and Outside the School. 2011.

Band 22 Gerd-Bodo von Carlsburg (Hrsg./ed.): Enkulturation durch sozialen Kompetenzerwerb. Enculturation by Acquiring of Social Competences. 2011.

Band 23 Reet Liimets: Ich als raumzeitliches Konstrukt. Die Fiktionen vom Leben der estnischen und deutschen Jugendlichen. 2012.

Band 24 Raivo Vetik (ed.): Nation-Building in the Context of Post-Communist Transformation and Globalization. The Case of Estonia. 2012.

Band 25 Airi-Alina Allaste (ed.): Back in the West'. Changing Lifestyles in Transforming Societies. 2013.

Band 26 Gerd-Bodo von Carlsburg (Hrsg./ed.): Bildungswissenschaft auf der Suche nach globaler Identität. Educational Sciences in Search of Global Identity. 2013.

Band 27 Airi Liimets / Marika Veisson (eds): Teachers and Youth in Educational Reality. 2014.

Band 28 Gerd-Bodo von Carlsburg / Thomas Vogel (Hrsg./eds.): Bildungswissenschaften und akademisches Selbstverständnis in einer globalisierten Welt. Education and Academic Self-Concept in the Globalized World. 2014.

Band 29 Marika Veisson / Airi Liimets / Pertti Kansanen / Edgar Krull (eds.): Tradition and Innovation in Education. 2015.

Band 30 Robertas Jucevičius / Jurgita Bruneckienė / Gerd-Bodo von Carlsburg (eds.): International Practices of Smart Development. 2015.

Band 31 Gerd-Bodo von Carlsburg (Hrsg./ed.): Strategien der Lehrerbildung. Zur Steigerung von Lehrkompetenzen und Unterrichtsqualität. Strategies for Teacher Training. Concepts for Improving Skills and Quality of Teaching. 2016.

Band 32 Gerd-Bodo von Carlsburg (Hrsg./ed.): Denk- und Lernkulturen im wissenschaftlichen Diskurs. Cultures of Thinking and Learning in the Scientific Discourse. 2017.

Band 33 Palmira Pečiuliauskienė / Aleksa Valdemaras: Motivation of New Generation Students for Learning Physics and Mathematics. 2018.

Band 34 Gerd-Bodo von Carlsburg (Hrsg. /ed.): Transkulturelle Perspektiven in der Bildung. Transcultural Perspectives in Education. 2019.

Band 35 Giedrė Kvieskienė / Vytautas Kvieska / Gerd-Bodo von Carlsburg: Social Clustering: Paradigm of Trust. 2021.

Band 36 Natalija Mažeikienė (ed.): Learning the Nuclear: Educational Tourism in (Post)Industrial Sites. 2021.

Band 37 Gerd-Bodo von Carlsburg / Annette Miriam Stross (Hrsg./eds.): (Un)pädagogische Visionen für das 21. Jahrhundert. Geistes und sozialwissenschaftliche Entwürfe nach dem Ende der ‹großen› Menschheitsgeschichte. 2022.

Band 38 Jurga Bučaitė-Vilkė (ed.): Social Investment and Territorial Inequalities: Mapping Policies and Services in the Baltic States. 2022.

**Neue Denkansätze in den Bildungs- und Sozialwissenschaften**

**New Approaches in Educational and Social Sciences**

Herausgegeben von Gerd-Bodo von Carlsburg, Natalija Mažeikienė und Airi Liimets

Edited by Gerd-Bodo von Carlsburg, Natalija Mažeikienė and Airi Liimets

Band 39 Gerd-Bodo von Carlsburg / Giedrė Kvieskienė (eds.): Prototype Modelling in Social-Emotional Education. At the Example of a Covid-19 Online Learning Environment. 2022.

Band 40 Vidmantas Tūtlys / Jörg Markowitsch / Jonathan Winterton / Samo Pavlin (eds.): Skill Formation in Central and Eastern Europe. A search for Patterns and Directions of Development. 2022.

www.peterlang.com

www.ingramcontent.com/pod-product-compliance
Ingram Content Group UK Ltd.
Pitfield, Milton Keynes, MK11 3LW, UK
UKHW041822031026
15587UKWH00002B/502

9 783631 810927